Measuring Globalisation

THE ROLE OF MULTINATIONALS IN OECD ECONOMIES

VOLUME I: MANUFACTURING SECTOR

Mesurer la mondialisation

LE POIDS DES MULTINATIONALES DANS LES ÉCONOMIES DE L'OCDE

VOLUME I : SECTEUR MANUFACTURIER

2001

ORGANISATION FOR ECONOMIC CO-OPERATION AND DEVELOPMENT

Pursuant to Article 1 of the Convention signed in Paris on 14th December 1960, and which came into force on 30th September 1961, the Organisation for Economic Co-operation and Development (OECD) shall promote policies designed:

- to achieve the highest sustainable economic growth and employment and a rising standard of living in Member countries, while maintaining financial stability, and thus to contribute to the development of the world economy;
- to contribute to sound economic expansion in Member as well as non-member countries in the process of economic development; and
- to contribute to the expansion of world trade on a multilateral, non-discriminatory basis in accordance with international obligations.

The original Member countries of the OECD are Austria, Belgium, Canada, Denmark, France, Germany, Greece, Iceland, Ireland, Italy, Luxembourg, the Netherlands, Norway, Portugal, Spain, Sweden, Switzerland, Turkey, the United Kingdom and the United States. The following countries became Members subsequently through accession at the dates indicated hereafter: Japan (28th April 1964), Finland (28th January 1969), Australia (7th June 1971), New Zealand (29th May 1973), Mexico (18th May 1994), the Czech Republic (21st December 1995), Hungary (7th May 1996), Poland (22nd November 1996), Korea (12th December 1996) and the Slovak Republic (14th December 2000). The Commission of the European Communities takes part in the work of the OECD (Article 13 of the OECD Convention).

ORGANISATION DE COOPÉRATION ET DE DÉVELOPPEMENT ÉCONOMIQUES

En vertu de l'article 1er de la Convention signée le 14 décembre 1960, à Paris, et entrée en vigueur le 30 septembre 1961, l'Organisation de Coopération et de Développement Économiques (OCDE) a pour objectif de promouvoir des politiques visant :

- à réaliser la plus forte expansion de l'économie et de l'emploi et une progression du niveau de vie dans les pays Membres, tout en maintenant la stabilité financière, et à contribuer ainsi au développement de l'économie mondiale ;
- à contribuer à une saine expansion économique dans les pays Membres, ainsi que les pays non membres, en voie de développement économique ;
- à contribuer à l'expansion du commerce mondial sur une base multilatérale et non discriminatoire conformément aux obligations internationales.

Les pays Membres originaires de l'OCDE sont : l'Allemagne, l'Autriche, la Belgique, le Canada, le Danemark, l'Espagne, les États-Unis, la France, la Grèce, l'Irlande, l'Islande, l'Italie, le Luxembourg, la Norvège, les Pays-Bas, le Portugal, le Royaume-Uni, la Suède, la Suisse et la Turquie. Les pays suivants sont ultérieurement devenus Membres par adhésion aux dates indiquées ci-après : le Japon (28 avril 1964), la Finlande (28 janvier 1969), l'Australie (7 juin 1971), la Nouvelle-Zélande (29 mai 1973), le Mexique (18 mai 1994), la République tchèque (21 décembre 1995), la Hongrie (7 mai 1996), la Pologne (22 novembre 1996), la Corée (12 décembre 1996) et la République slovaque (14 décembre 2000). La Commission des Communautés européennes participe aux travaux de l'OCDE (article 13 de la Convention de l'OCDE).

FOREWORD

This publication presents statistical data on the share of OECD economies controlled by multinationals at a global and sectoral level. It has been prepared by the Economic Analysis and Statistics Division of the OECD Directorate for Science, Technology and Industry, under the auspices of the Working Party on Industrial Statistics of the Committee on Industry and Business Environment (Expert Group on Globalisation). It is designed to supply reliable and relatively detailed information to governments, investors, globalisation researchers and the public at large.

The database used for this publication is regularly updated and serves as a reference for analysis of the economic impact of international direct investment on the economies of OECD countries.

The country tables and accompanying technical notes were revised by national experts. The Secretariat wishes to thank representatives of all national administrations who helped in the preparation of this publication.

This book is published on the responsibility of the Secretary-General of the OECD.

AVANT-PROPOS

Cette publication présente les données statistiques sur la part des économies de l'OCDE contrôlée par les firmes multinationales au niveau global et sectoriel. Elle a été préparée par la Division des analyses économiques et statistiques de la Direction de la science, de la technologie et de l'industrie du Secrétariat de l'OCDE sous les auspices du Groupe de travail sur les statistiques industrielles du Comité de l'industrie et de l'environnement de l'entreprise (Groupe d'experts sur la mondialisation). Elle a comme objectif de fournir des informations fiables et relativement détaillées aux autorités des pays de l'OCDE, aux investisseurs, aux chercheurs qui s'intéressent à la mondialisation ainsi qu'au grand public.

La base de données qui a été mise au point pour cette publication est régulièrement mise à jour et constitue une base de référence pour l'analyse de l'impact économique de l'investissement direct international sur les économies des pays de l'OCDE.

Les tableaux par pays et les notes techniques qui les accompagnent ont été révisés par des experts nationaux. Le Secrétariat tient à remercier les représentants de toutes les administrations nationales qui ont apporté leur concours à la préparation de cette publication.

Cet ouvrage est publié sous la responsabilité du Secrétaire général de l'OCDE.

TABLE OF CONTENTS/TABLE DES MATIÈRES

Part I

Share of foreign affiliates in manufacturing output, employment, labour productivity, R&D, exports, wages and salaries

Partie I

**Part de la production, de l'emploi, de la productivité, de la R-D, des exportations et des salaires
sous contrôle étranger dans l'industrie manufacturière**

Activity of foreign affiliates and share of OECD economies controlled by multinationals (tables and methodological notes)
Activité des filiales étrangères et part des économies de l'OCDE contrôlée par les firmes multinationales (tableaux et notes méthodologiques)

INTRODUCTION

Since the mid-1980s and with the quickening pace of globalisation of the economy, foreign direct investment has become central to worldwide industrial restructuring and one of the most dynamic elements of international transactions.

Until recently, the only internationally available information on foreign investment was on capital stocks and flows, collected for balance of payments statistics. This information is still published by the OECD in its *International Direct Investment Statistics Yearbook*.

The need to assess the role and impact of direct investment, not only in financial terms but also in the context of its impact on jobs, sales and trade, has underlined the importance of having data indicative of the industrial activity of multinational firms.

To meet these new needs in analysing the globalisation process, the OECD Industry Committee requested its Working Party on Statistics as from 1990 to arrange for the regular collection of data on the performance of foreign affiliates in the manufacturing sectors of the OECD countries.

More recently, at the request of the Committee on Industry and Business Environment, Secretariat surveys have been extended to cover the activities of multinational firms abroad (outward investment) in the manufacturing sector, on the one hand, and the activities of multinational firms in the service sector, on the other. The latter type of data are collected using a questionnaire prepared jointly by the OECD and Eurostat. For the first time, these data will be published in a companion volume devoted to services.

The data in this volume relate mainly to the manufacturing industry, inward and outward investments.

Most of the countries that cannot as yet reply to the Secretariat surveys are preparing their own national surveys so as to be able to take part in the exercise as soon as possible.

The 18 variables requested in the OECD questionnaires are covered in a somewhat uneven manner across countries. Data in this volume relate to the years 1994/95 -1998/99 and are classified according to ISIC Revision 3.

The publication gives not only basic data but also the share of an industry that is "controlled" by foreign multinationals in each country. To obtain these percentages, the same surveys were used to collect data on the activity of all firms (domestic and foreign) in each country and for each of the variables available. This has been essential since the data on the "national total" and on multinational firms are not always based on the same statistical unit. While most of the industrial variables correspond to "establishments", data on multinational firms are collected at a higher level, *i.e.* "firms", each of which may include several establishments. This means that the figures for a sector's production or employment, for instance, will differ depending on whether the sectoral data refer to "establishments" or "firms".

For certain variables, in particular exports or imports, it has not been possible to produce data on the activity of multinational firms and on all of the firms in a country on a comparable basis (firms or establishments). Work is under way in the countries concerned to solve this problem.

Also, unlike data on direct investment flows which cover any investment representing more than 10% of a firm's capital, data on the activity of affiliates are based on the concept of controlling interest. This is more difficult to assess, which is why the statistical test for data collection is that of a majority interest (over 50% of shares that carry voting rights on a company's board of management). It is assumed that ownership of more than 50% of the shares in a company gives real control over its management, even though such control may sometimes be exercised with less than 50% of the shares. The United States, for instance, includes in its data firms under minority control (between 10 and 50%), where investors may influence the management of firms without necessarily having a controlling interest.

This volume is in two parts. Part I presents the main findings, a series of commented diagrams showing trends in the different variables (output, employment, productivity, R&D, etc.) displayed by foreign multinationals and domestic firms in total manufacturing industry, leading sectors and a more detailed geographical breakdown as well. Part II provides basic data but also details of the share of each sector controlled by foreign multinationals for all the industrial variables available, and the country of origin or destination of those multinational firms. Technical notes giving details of sources and definitions accompany the data.

INTRODUCTION

Depuis la seconde moitié des années 80 et l'accélération du processus de globalisation de l'économie, l'investissement direct étranger est au coeur de la restructuration industrielle mondiale et un des éléments les plus dynamiques des transactions internationales.

Jusqu'à récemment, les seules informations diffusées au plan international relatives aux investissements étrangers concernaient les flux et les stocks de capitaux recueillis dans le cadre des balances des paiements. Ces données sont toujours publiées par l'OCDE sous le titre *Annuaire des statistiques d'investissement direct international.*

Le besoin d'évaluer le rôle et l'impact des investissements directs non seulement sur le plan financier mais aussi dans le cadre de l'emploi, des ventes et du commerce, a mis en évidence la nécessité de disposer également de données qui caractérisent l'activité industrielle des firmes multinationales.

Pour répondre à ces nouveaux besoins analytiques du processus de globalisation, le Comité de l'industrie de l'OCDE, dès 1990, a demandé à son groupe de travail statistique d'organiser sur une base régulière la collecte de données concernant au départ l'activité des filiales étrangères dans les pays de l'OCDE dans le secteur manufacturier.

Plus récemment, à la demande du Comité de l'industrie et de l'environnement de l'entreprise, les enquêtes du Secrétariat ont été étendues afin de couvrir d'une part les activités des firmes multinationales à l'étranger (investissements sortants) et d'autre part les activités des firmes multinationales dans le secteur des services. La collecte de cette dernière catégorie de données est organisée à partir d'un questionnaire établi conjointement par l'OCDE et Eurostat. Ces données seront publiées pour la première fois dans un second volume consacré aux services.

Les résultats présentés dans ce volume concernent essentiellement l'industrie manufacturière et se réfèrent aux investissements entrants et sortants.

La plupart des pays qui ne sont pas encore en mesure de répondre aux enquêtes du Secrétariat organisent la préparation de telles enquêtes afin de pouvoir y participer dans les meilleurs délais.

Les 18 variables demandées dans les questionnaires de l'OCDE sont couvertes de manière assez inégale de la part des pays. Les données présentées dans ce volume concernent la période 1994/95 -1998/99 et sont classées selon la CITI révision 3.

Avec les données de base, est également présentée pour tous les pays, la part de chaque industrie qui est « contrôlée » par des multinationales étrangères. Pour pouvoir calculer ces pourcentages, il a fallu collecter dans le cadre des mêmes enquêtes des données concernant l'activité de l'ensemble des firmes (nationales et étrangères) dans chaque pays et pour chacune des variables disponibles. Cette collecte s'est avérée indispensable dans la mesure où les données concernant le

« total national » et celles des firmes multinationales ne se réfèrent pas systématiquement à la même unité statistique. Tandis que la plupart des variables industrielles correspondent aux « établissements », les données sur les firmes multinationales sont collectées à un niveau plus élevé, celui des « firmes » dont chacune peut disposer de nombreux établissements. Ainsi la production ou l'emploi par exemple d'un secteur prendront des valeurs différentes selon que le secteur est constitué à partir de données sur les « établissements » ou sur les « firmes ».

Les données concernant l'activité des firmes multinationales et celles de l'ensemble des firmes d'un pays n'ont pu être établies sur une base comparable (firmes ou établissements) pour certaines variables notamment celles des exportations et des importations. Des travaux sont en cours dans les pays concernés pour résoudre cette difficulté.

Par ailleurs, contrairement aux données sur les flux d'investissements directs qui concernent tous les investissements supérieurs à 10 % du capital des firmes, les données sur l'activité des filiales reposent sur la notion de contrôle. Il s'agit d'une notion plus difficile à mesurer, c'est la raison pour laquelle le critère statistique choisi pour la collecte des données est celui du contrôle majoritaire (plus de 50 % des actions d'une société donnant droit de vote au conseil d'administration). On suppose que le fait de posséder plus de 50 % des actions d'une société permet d'exercer un réel contrôle sur sa gestion, même si dans certains cas ce contrôle peut être exercé avec la possession de moins de 50 % des actions. Les États-Unis, par exemple, incluent dans leurs données les firmes sous contrôle minoritaire (entre 10 et 50 %), ce qui correspond aux investisseurs qui exercent une certaine influence sur la gestion des firmes en question mais pas nécessairement un véritable contrôle.

Ce volume comprend deux parties. La partie I présente les principaux résultats, une série de graphiques commentés concernant l'évolution des différentes caractéristiques (production, emploi, productivité, R-D, etc.) des multinationales étrangères et des firmes nationales du total manufacturier et des principaux secteurs, ainsi qu'une distribution géographique plus détaillée. La partie II présente les données de base mais également des données détaillées concernant la part de chaque secteur contrôlée par des multinationales étrangères pour toutes les variables industrielles disponibles, ainsi que les pays d'origine ou d'accueil de ces firmes multinationales. Ces données sont accompagnées de notes techniques qui fournissent des précisions quant aux sources et aux définitions utilisées.

MAIN FINDINGS

- In 1998, the percentage of industrial production generated by firms under foreign control varied from 70% in Ireland and Hungary, to less than 2% in Japan. In most other European countries this was between 25 and 30%, while in the United States, it was18% (Figure 3).

- The United States attracted more than 40% of the direct investments made in the OECD area[1] and almost 48% of the industrial production generated by these investments within this area (Figure 2).

- In some countries, notably Japan, Ireland, France, the United Kingdom and the United States, the great majority of investments, and the related industrial production, were concentrated (between 60 and 80%) in high-technology sectors (Figure 4). In other countries (*e.g.* Norway, Poland) they were concentrated in the medium- and low-technology sectors.

- The compensation per employee of firms under foreign control in all countries was substantially higher than the average for national firms (Figure 8).

- In 1998, the United States attracted to their territory R&D investments worth more than USD 20 billions from foreign firms, that is approximately 55% of the investments of R&D made by these firms in the OECD area (Figure 10).

- Between 1991 and 1998, the United States was the country with the greatest increase in number of people employed by foreign affiliates, with more than 400 000 additional persons (including creations via greenfields and post transferrals via acquisitions). During the same period, the number of people employed by foreign affiliates of Hungary and Poland increased by 350 000 and 220 000, respectively. In other countries, the number of people employed also progressed with the exception of Germany (Figure 6), which lost almost 240 000 jobs in the same period.

- In certain countries, notably the United States, Japan and Finland, the level of production achieved by foreign subsidiaries' of national firms was far greater than total exports for these countries. This phenomenon highlights the importance of direct investment in capturing overseas markets (Figure 13).

---

1.   The United States' GDP represents 30% in the OECD area.

PRINCIPAUX RÉSULTATS

- En 1998, la production manufacturière sous contrôle étranger variait entre 70 % en Irlande et en Hongrie, et moins de 2 % au Japon. Dans la plupart des autres pays européens, ce pourcentage se situait entre 25 et 30 %, et à 18 % environ aux États-Unis (Figure 3).

- Les États-Unis attirent plus de 40 % du total des investissements directs destinés à la zone OCDE[1] et presque 48 % de la production manufacturière engendrée par ces investissements à l'intérieur de cette zone (Figure 2).

- Dans certains pays, notamment au Japon, en Irlande, en France, au Royaume-Uni et aux États-Unis, la grande majorité des investissements, et la production manufacturière des filiales étrangères associée, est concentrée (entre 60 et 80 %) dans des secteurs de haute technologie (Figure 4). D'autres pays (par exemple Norvège, Pologne) sont plus attractifs dans les secteurs de moyenne et faible technologie.

- La rémunération par employé des sociétés sous contrôle étranger était notoirement plus élevée que la moyenne de celle des sociétés nationales (Figure 8).

- En 1998, les États-Unis attiraient sur leur territoire plus de 20 USD milliards d'investissements en matière de R-D en provenance des firmes étrangères, c'est-à-dire environ 55 % des investissements de R-D effectués par ces firmes dans la zone OCDE (Figure 10).

- Entre 1991 et 1998, les États-Unis est le pays ayant bénéficié de la plus forte hausse en nombre d'employés par les filiales étrangères avec plus de 400 000 personnes employées (incluant les créations via les "greenfields" ou les transferts via les acquisitions). Durant la même période, le nombre de personnes employées par les filiales étrangères en Hongrie et en Pologne avait progressé respectivement de 350 000 et 220 000. Dans les autres pays, le nombre de ces emplois a également progressé sauf en Allemagne (Figure 6), qui, au cours de la même période, enregistre une perte de 240 000 emplois.

- Dans certains pays, notamment aux États-Unis, au Japon et en Finlande, la production des filiales des firmes nationales à l'étranger a été largement supérieure aux exportations globales de ces pays. Ce phénomène souligne l'importance de l'investissement direct dans la conquête d'un marché à l'étranger (Figure 13).

---

1.   Le PIB des États-Unis correspond à 30% du total OCDE.

Part I

Share of foreign affiliates in manufacturing output, employment, labour productivity, R&D, exports, wages and salaries

Figure 1. Trend of the manufacturing production (or turnover) under foreign control in selected OECD areas

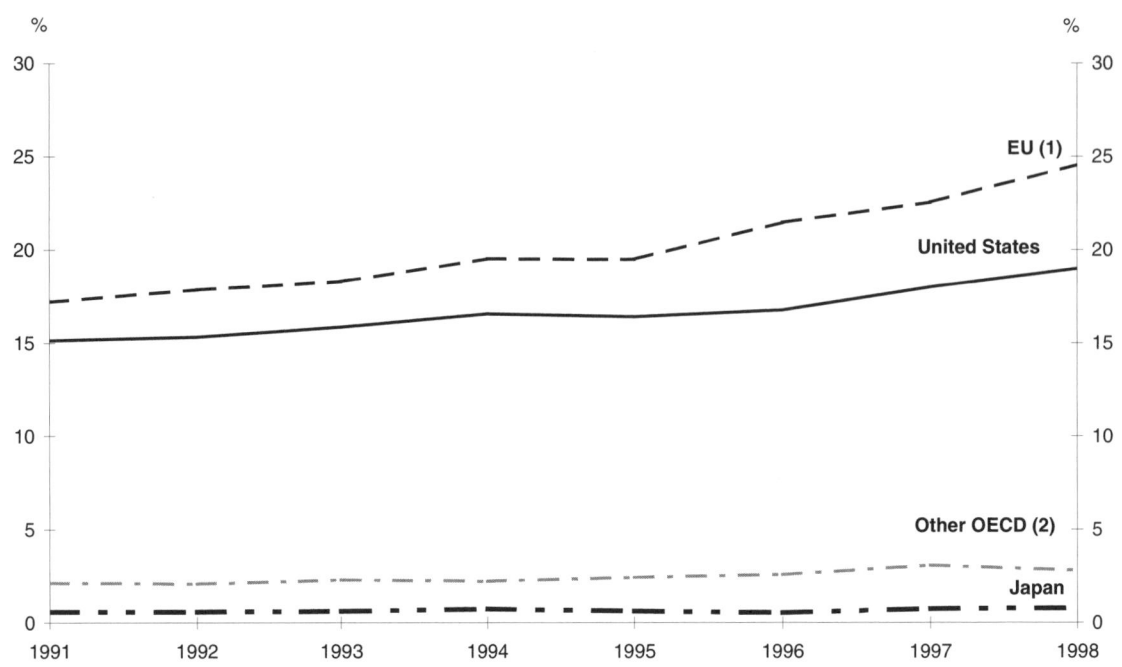

(1) Germany, France, United Kingdom (1997), Italy, Netherlands, Sweden, Ireland, Finland.
(2) Norway, Hungary, Turkey, Canada, Czech Republic.
Source: OECD, Activities of Foreign Affiliates database.

- While progression of firms under foreign control was relatively modest in Japan and other OECD countries, it was stronger in the United States and above all in the European Union where the penetration of these firms under foreign control in manufacturing production was about 25%.

Indicators on the activities of firms under foreign control usefully complement information on foreign direct investment flows and stocks since they provide a means of analysing the performance of these firms and their contribution to the economy of the host country.

Ownership of 10% of a company's voting shares or voting power is the criterion normally used to indicate the existence of a direct investment relationship and influence over the management of the firm in question. In contrast, control implies the ability to shape a company's activities. This entails ownership of a majority of ordinary shares (more than 50%) or voting power on the board of directors. Variables such as turnover or number of employees are attributed in full to the investor that controls the company.

The share of firms under foreign control in an economy depends on a variety of factors, in particular the size and attractiveness of the country and how easy it is, from an institutional point of view, to make such investments. The available data, in the manufacturing sector, on firms under foreign control show that in the 1990s their turnover increased more rapidly than that of firms under national control.

Figure 2. Trend in the share of foreign affiliates in manufacturing production (or turnover) in selected OECD countries

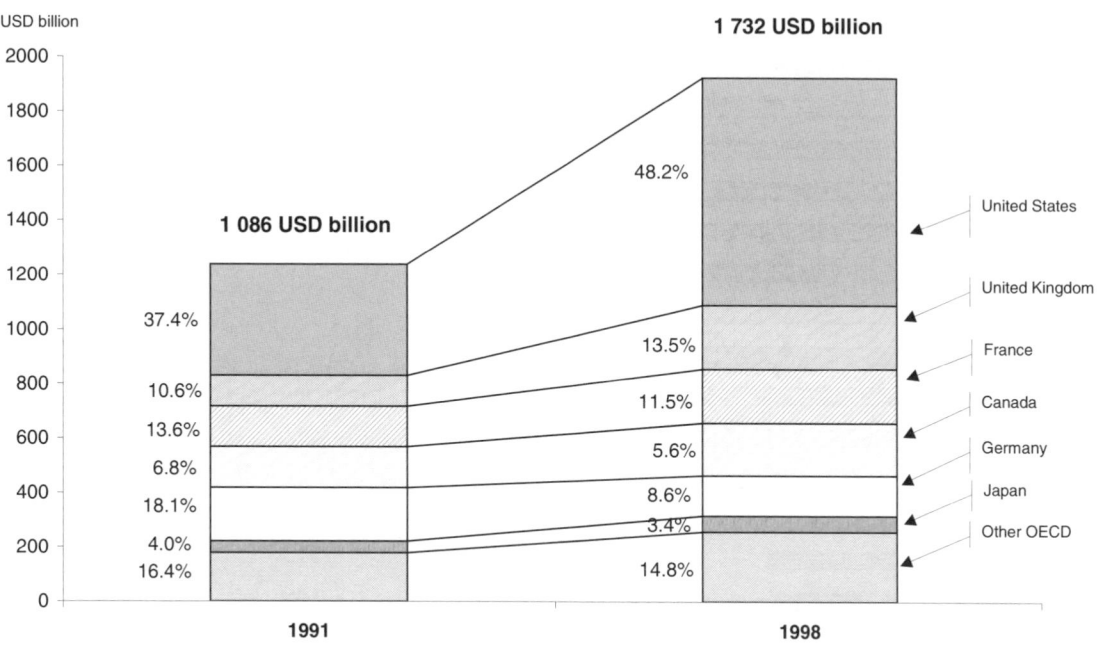

Source: OECD, Activities of Foreign Affiliates database.

- Between 1991 and 1998, the level of production of firms under foreign control (in absolute value) progressed in all the major countries, with the exception of Germany where it marked a decline.

- During the same period, the level of production of foreign firms doubled in the United States which attracted thereafter half of the production of these firms within the OECD area.

- The United States and the United Kingdom are the only major countries in the OECD area where the level of production of firms under foreign control increased both in value and percentage terms.

Figure 3. Share of foreign affiliates in manufacturing production (or turnover)

1998 or latest available year

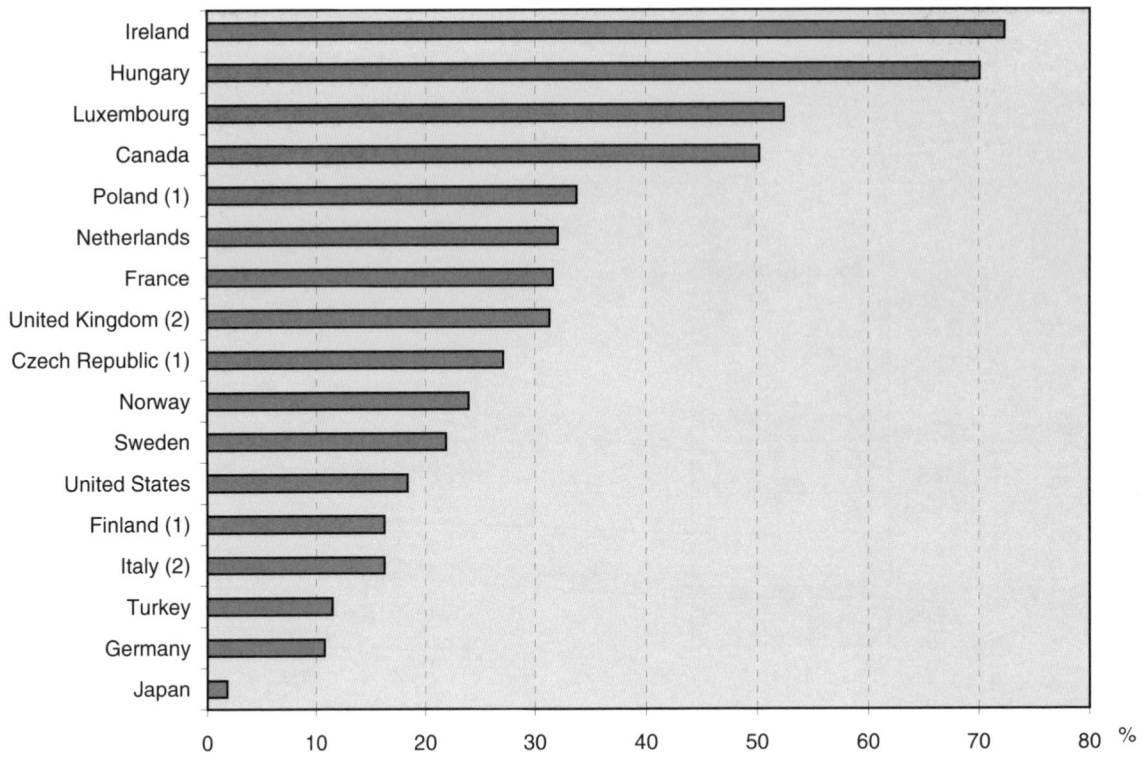

1: 1999, 2: 1997.
Source: OECD, Activities of Foreign Affiliates database.

- The share of firms under foreign control in the total turnover of the manufacturing sector in 1998 varied from 70% in Ireland and Hungary to less than 2% in Japan.

- The share of these firms in the total turnover of the manufacturing industry also exceeded 30% in Canada, France, the United Kingdom, the Netherlands, Luxembourg and Poland.

- In the European Union, the penetration of firms under foreign control was weakest in Germany and, to a lesser extent, Italy, among others.

- In Japan, on the other hand, in spite of a relative progression in the level of production of firms under foreign control during recent years, the penetration remained the weakest inside the OECD area.

Figure 4. Share of production of firms under foreign control belonging to the "High- Medium-high-technology" group of industries, as compared to their share in the manufacturing production of these firms and to the total national production

1998 or latest available year

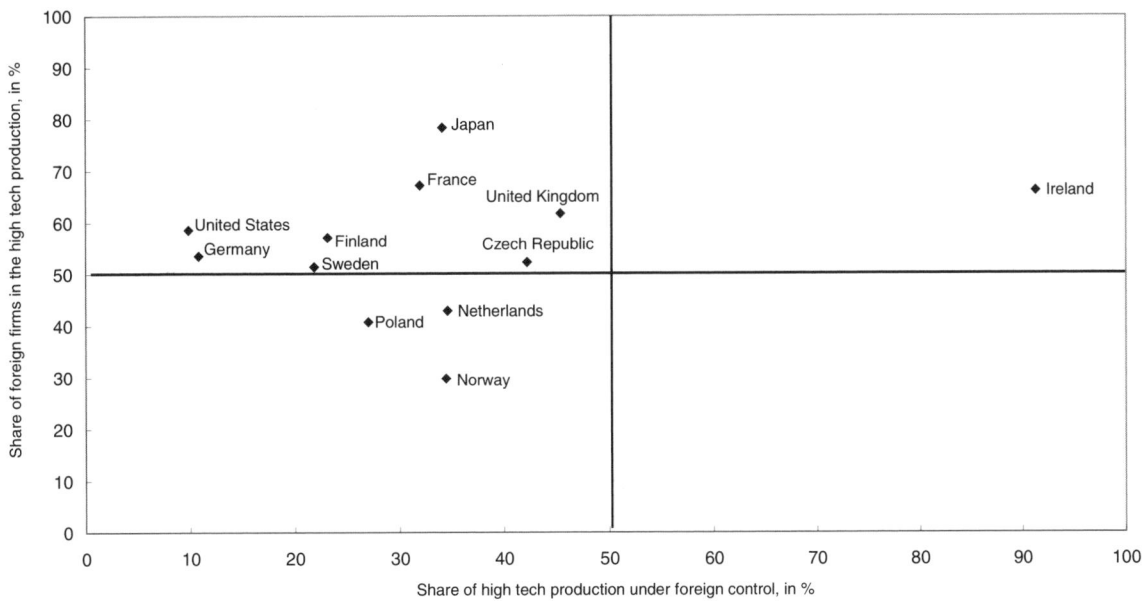

Source: OECD, Activities of Foreign Affiliates database.

- The technological level of direct investments varied from one host country to another. The countries which attracted the most investments from industries in the high- and medium-high-technology (see Appendix) group were Japan, France, the United Kingdom, the United States and Ireland.

- The Netherlands, Norway and Poland attracted the majority of investments from industries that were technologically less intensive.

- In Japan, where firms under foreign control accounted for less than 2% of manufacturing production, those belonging to the technologically-intensive group of industries represented more than 30% of the production of this same group of industries and more than 80% of the production of all the firms under foreign control.

- In Ireland, the high- and medium-high-technology group of industries accounted for more than 65% of the production of foreign firms. These foreign firms represented more than 90% of national production in this group of industries.

Figure 5. Share of foreign affiliates in manufacturing employment

1998 or latest available year

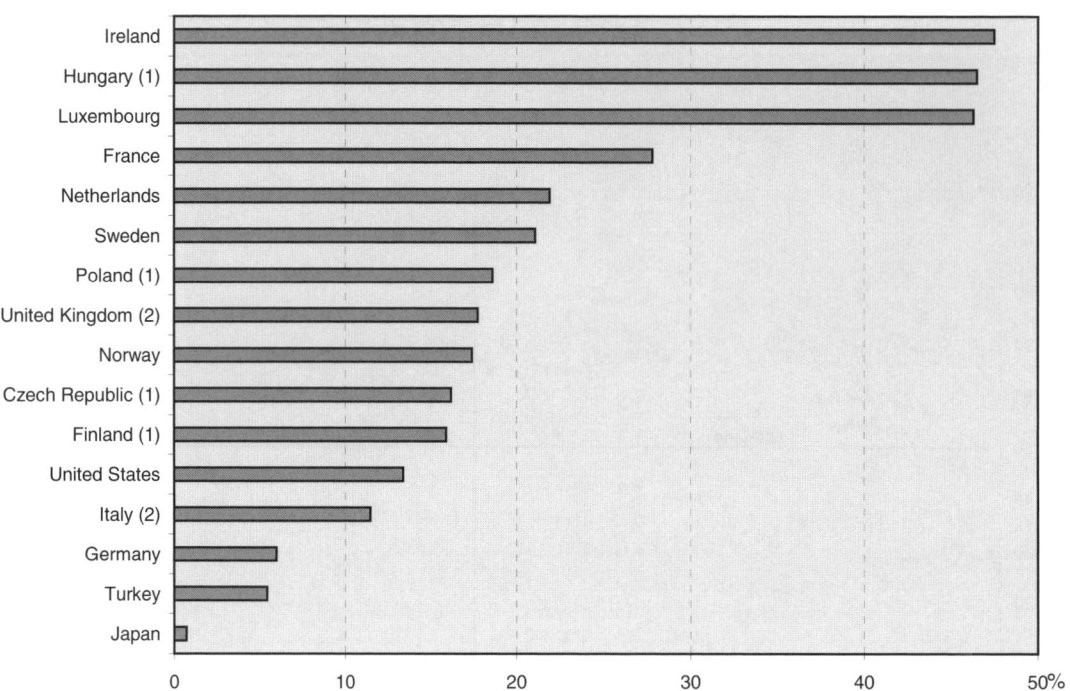

1: 1999, 2: 1997.
Source: OECD, Activities of Foreign Affiliates database.

- Employment under foreign control in OECD countries follows the same pattern as production except in terms of percentage of total employment, which is lower since foreign direct investments are more capital than labour intensive. This may also explain noticeable differences from one country to another, notably between France and the United Kingdom. The share of employment under foreign control is greater in France than in the United Kingdom while production under foreign control is about the same in both countries (Figure 5).

- In absolute terms, between 1990 and 1998, the share of employment held by firms under foreign control increased considerably in all countries except Germany. It is worth noting, however, that in all countries this progress does not necessarily imply new job creations but rather a change of ownership due to the acquisition of existing firms by foreign investors (Figure 6).

- In absolute terms, the United States, during this period, benefited the most, with more than 400 000 posts in total, including both new post creations (via "greenfields") and post transferrals (via acquisitions), followed by Hungary and Poland where the number of people employed by foreign affiliates increased by 350 000 and 220 000 respectively.

Figure 6. Numbers employed by foreign affiliates in the manufacturing sector, change between 1990 and 1998 in thousands

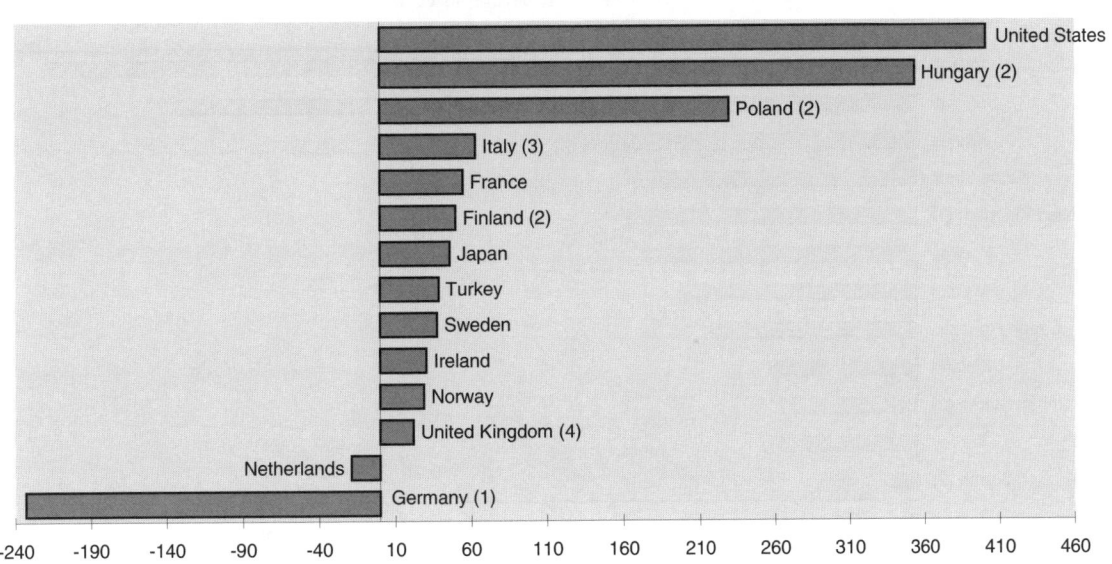

1: 1990-99, 2: 1993-99, 3: 1989-99, 4: 1989-97.
Source: OECD, Activities of Foreign Affiliates database.

Figure 7. Share of value added under foreign control in the manufacturing sector

1998 or latest available year

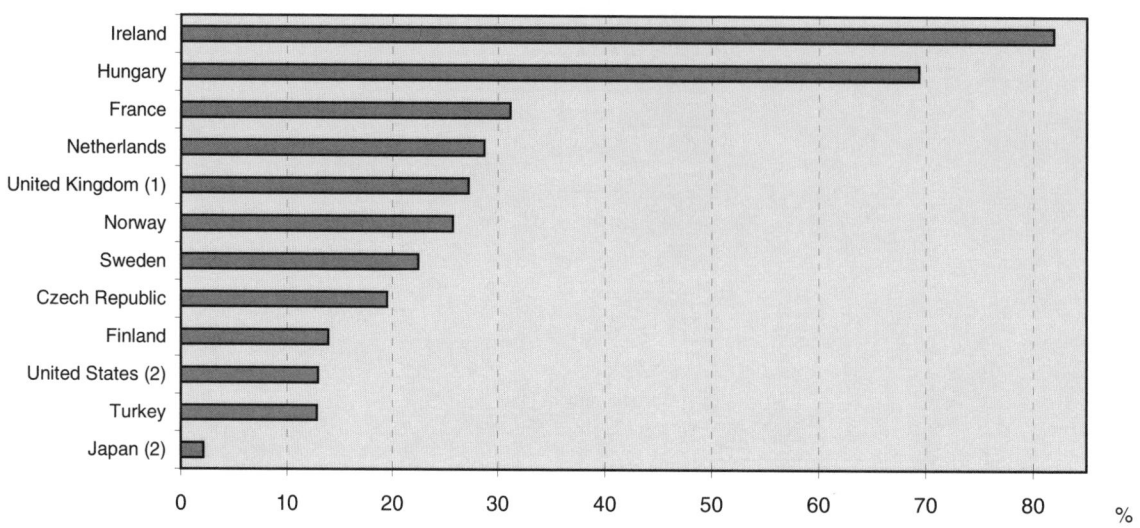

1: 1999, 2: 1997, 3: 1996.
Source: OECD, Activities of Foreign Affiliates database.

Figure 8. Compensation per employee of foreign affiliates in the manufacturing sector

National firms = 100

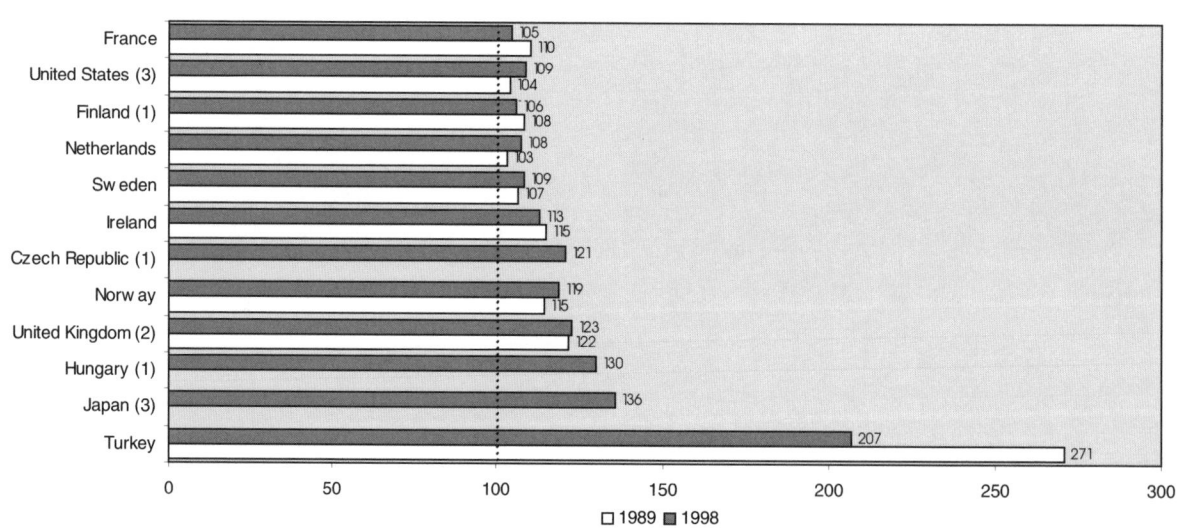

1: 1989-99, 2: 1989-97, 3: 1989-96.
Source: OECD, Activities of Foreign Affiliates database.

- In Ireland and Hungary, between 70 and 80% of value added in the manufacturing sector was generated by firms under foreign control. In France, the United Kingdom, the Netherlands and Norway, their contribution was between 25 and 30%. In other countries, it was lower than 20%.

- Compensation per employee of firms under foreign control in some countries was slightly higher than the average for national firms whereas for others this gap was bigger.

Figure 9. Gross output per employee in the manufacturing sector

National firms = 100

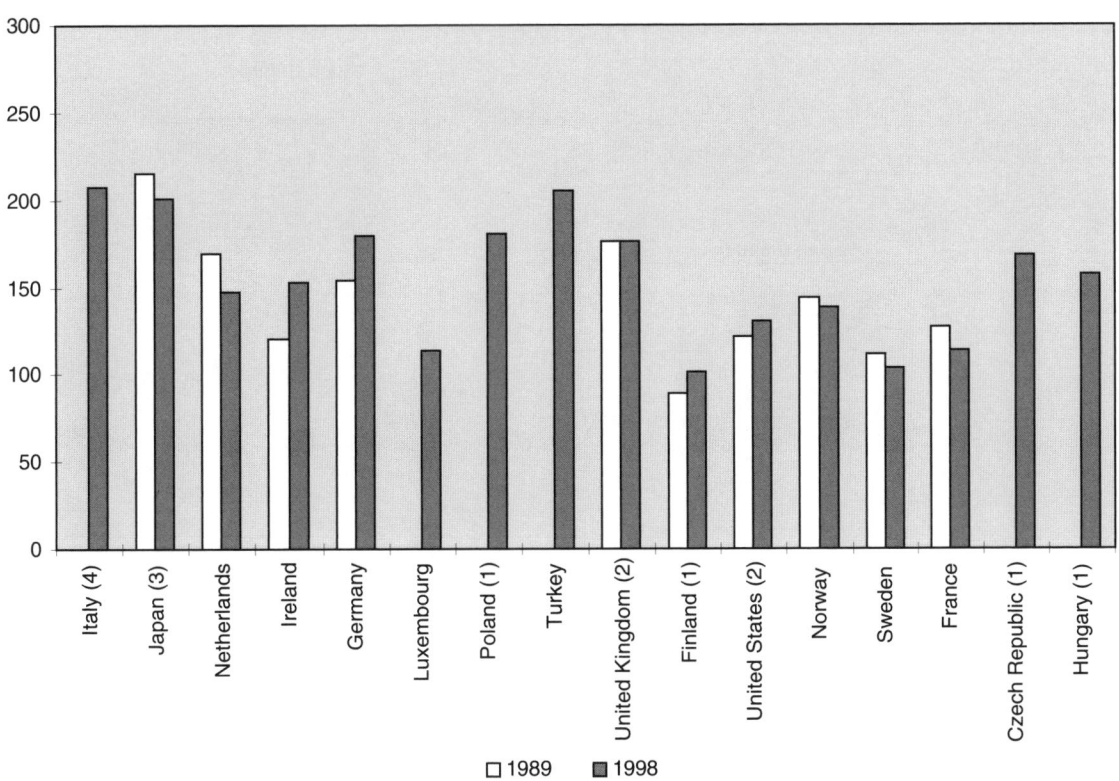

1: 1999, 2: 1997, 3: 1996, 4: 1995.
Source: OECD, Activities of Foreign Affiliates database.

- Gross output per employee in the manufacturing sector in the majority of countries was greater than the average for national firms. This result showed that firms with a strong international dimension had a higher level of productivity than those, which were less internationalised.

- It is worth noting that the national firms referred to above included numerous small and medium-sized companies, which lacked a strong international dimension.

- This result also reflects the sectoral orientation of foreign direct investment, which is more capital-intensive.

Figure 10. Trend in the share of R&D expenditure under foreign control in the manufacturing industry in selected OECD countries

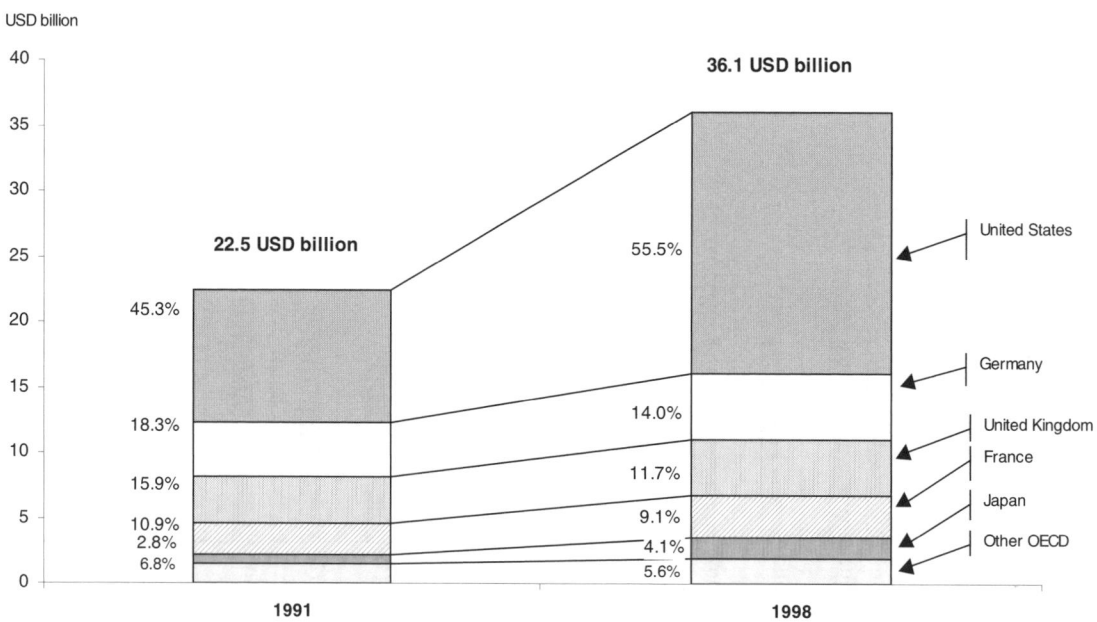

Source: OECD, Activities of Foreign Affiliates database.

Figure 11. Share of foreign affiliates in manufacturing R&D

1998 or latest available year

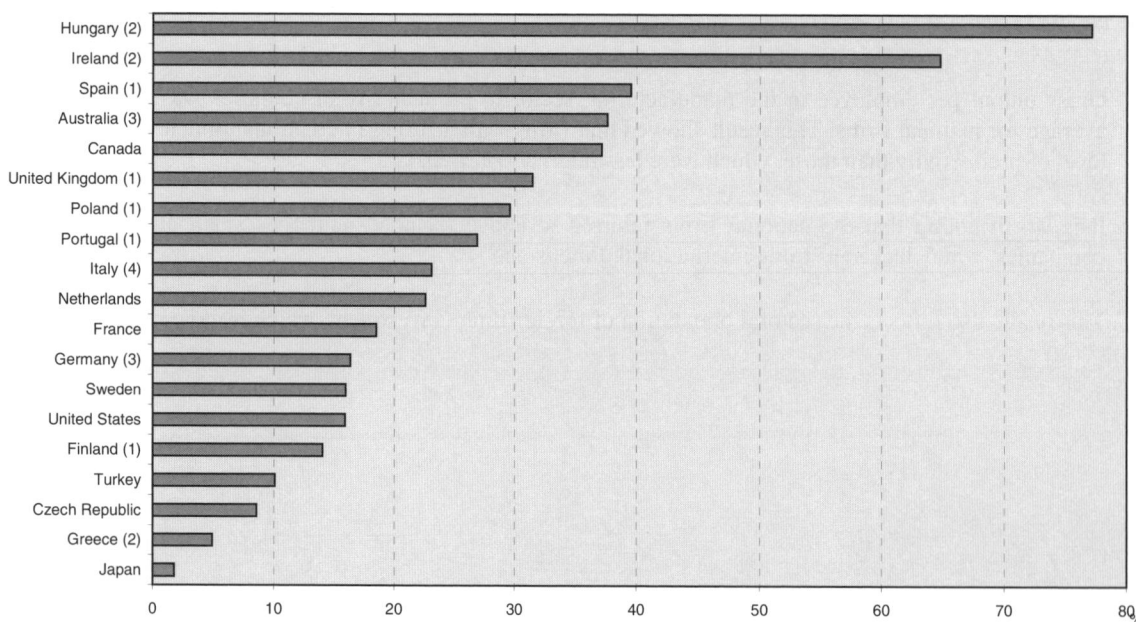

1: 1999, 2: 1997, 3:1995, 4: 1992.
Source: OECD, Activities of Foreign Affiliates database.

26

Figure 12. Share of foreign affiliates' R&D and production (or turnover) in total manufacturing R&D and production (or turnover)

1998 or latest available year

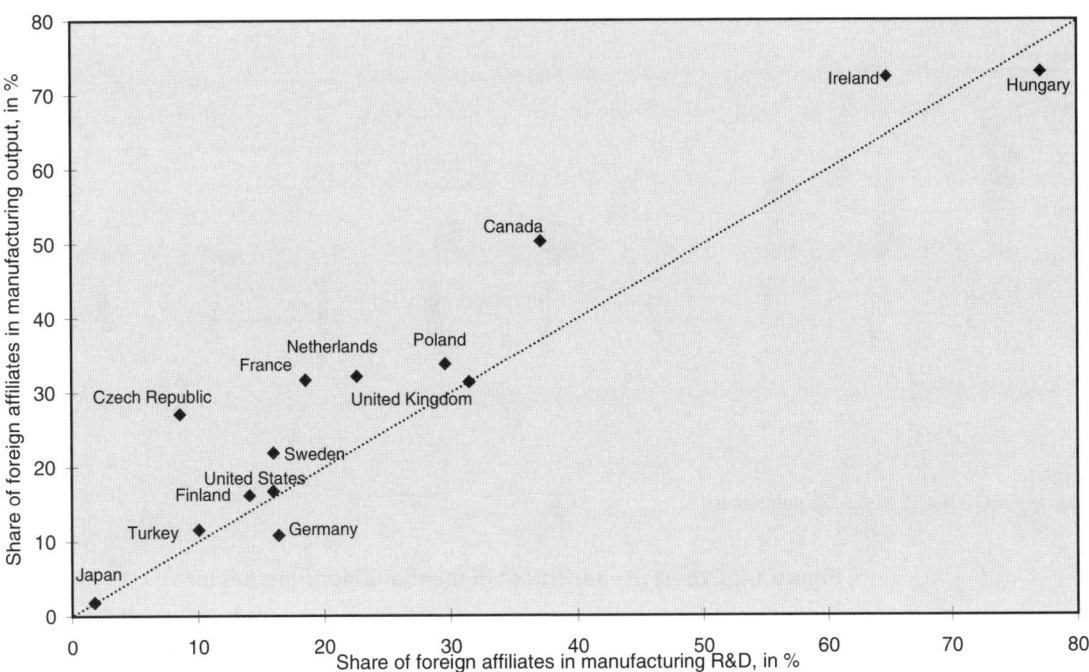

Source: OECD, Activities of Foreign Affiliates database.

- In the United States, foreign firms accounted for more than USD 20 billion of R&D investments, amounting to approximately 55% of the total R&D investments by foreign affiliates in the OECD area (Figure 10).

- R&D investments of foreign firms between 1991 and 1998 rose in value in all the major countries including Germany, where production under foreign control declined. In contrast, their share in total OECD fell in all countries except in the United States.

- In Hungary and Ireland, firms under foreign control performed more than 60 or 70% (respectively) of R&D in the manufacturing sector, whereas in the Czech Republic, Greece and Japan, they performed less than 10% (Figure 11).

- The production and R&D activities of firms under foreign control showed many general similarities. Some of the discrepancies observed between these two activities could be due either to variations in the technological intensity of investing sectors or to a preference for transferring technology from parent companies to subsidiaries rather than making an important effort of R&D effort locally (Figure 12).

27

Figure 13. Turnover of subsidiaries of national firms located abroad compared to national exports

1998 or latest available year

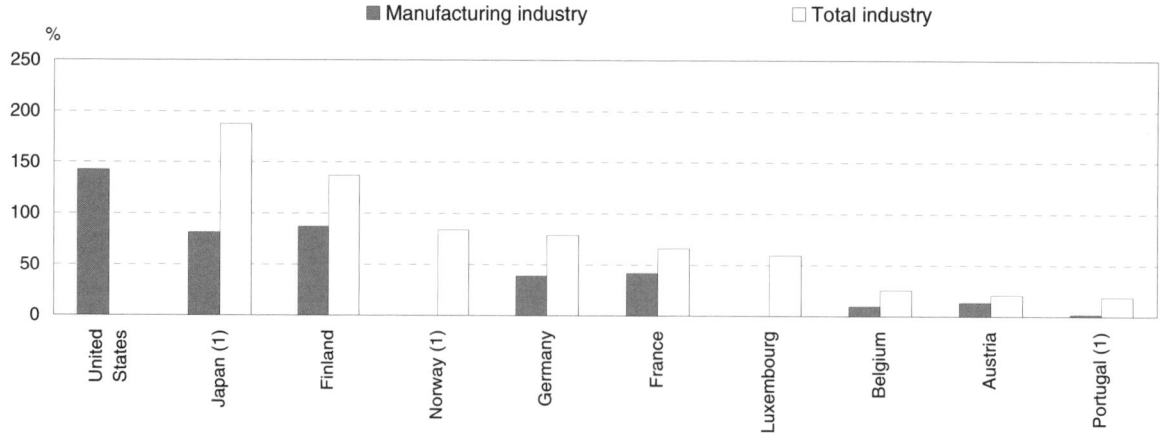

1: 1997.
Source: OECD, FATS and ADB databases.

Figure 14. Export propensities¹ in the manufacturing sector

1998 or latest available year

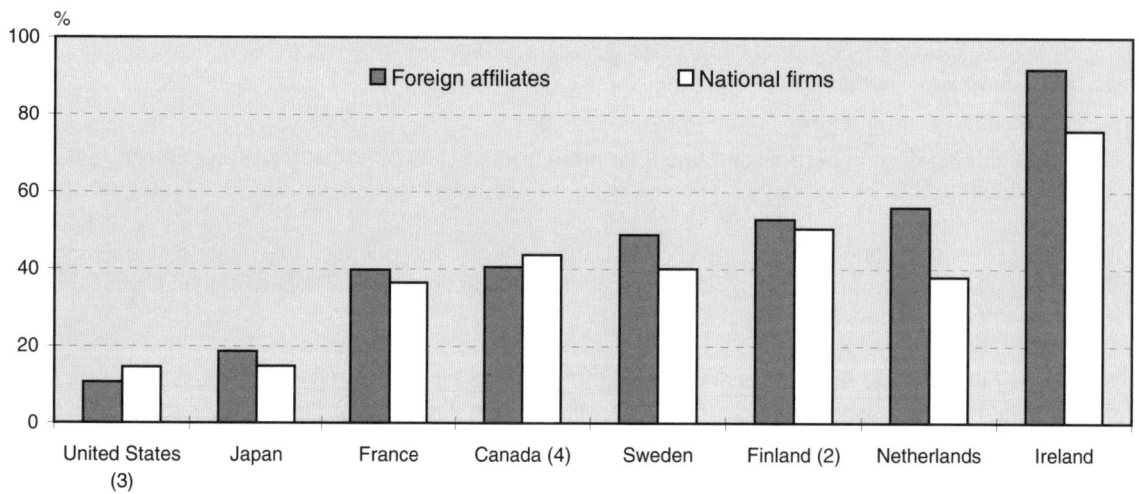

1: Exports/production (or turnover).
2: 1999, 3: 1996, 4:1995.
Source: OECD, Activities of Foreign Affiliates database.

- Figure 13 shows that in several countries, the production (or turnover) of their subsidiaries abroad was far greater than the total exports (of national and foreign firms). This phenomenon, which was clearly the case for the United States, Japan and Finland, highlights the importance of direct investment in capturing overseas market.

- With the exception of the United States and Canada, the export propensities (export/production) of the foreign subsidiaries were generally higher than that of national firms (Figure 14).

Figure 15. Exposure of domestic markets to trade and direct investments

1998 or latest available year

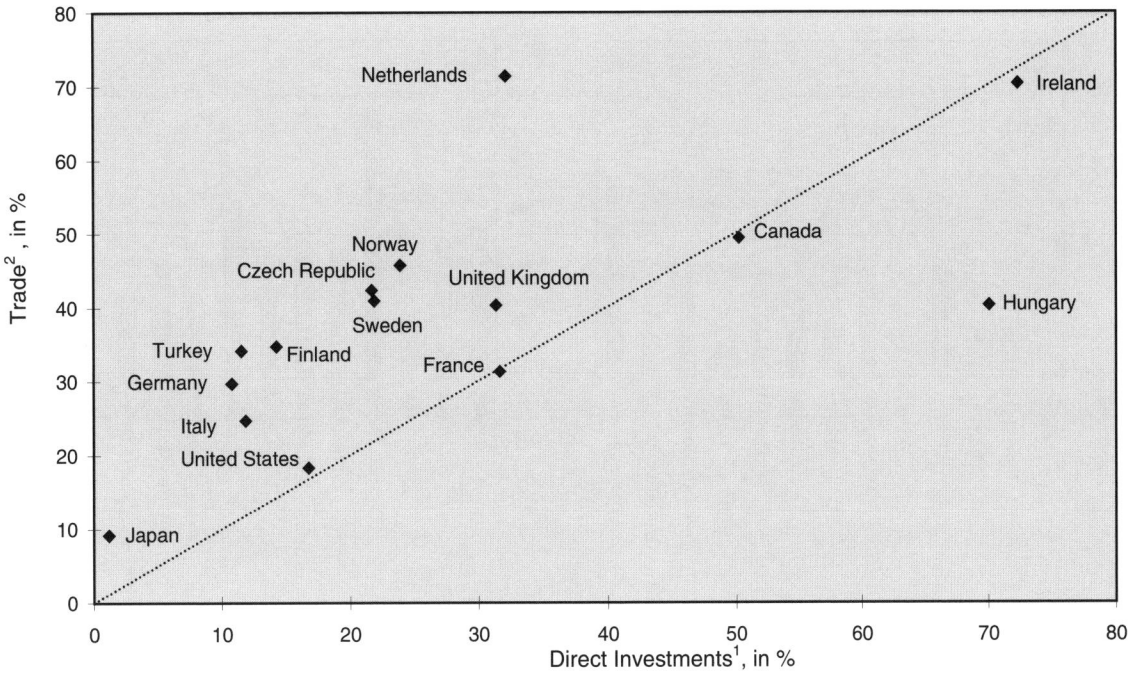

1. Production (or turnover) of foreign affiliates/total production (or turnover).
2. Imports/domestic demand.
Source: OECD, Activities of Foreign Affiliates database.

- Demand on domestic markets depends on the foreign supply, which takes the form of either imports or the production of foreign subsidiaries on their territory. The vast majority of countries depended more on imports than on the production of firms under foreign control.

- However, in certain countries, dependence on these two types of foreign supply was strong but balanced (Ireland and Canada). In others, it was balanced but moderate or weak (France, the United States).

- In Hungary, the domestic demand depended twice as much on the production of foreign firms as on imports, while the opposite effect was observed in the Netherlands.

Figure 16. Share of production (or turnover) of foreign affiliates in selected industrial sectors

1998 or latest available year

Food, beverages and tobacco (ISIC 15/16)

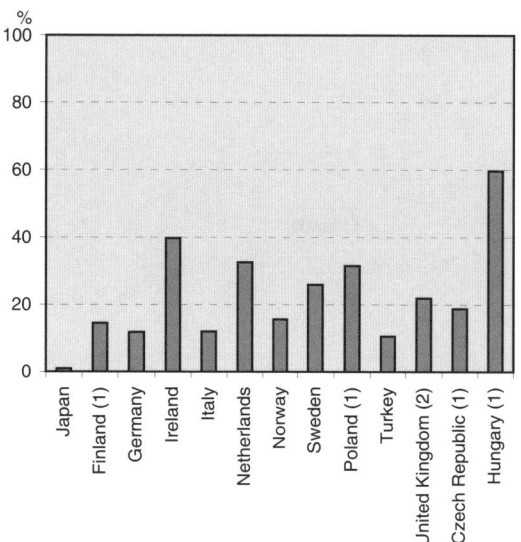

Chemical products (ISIC 24)

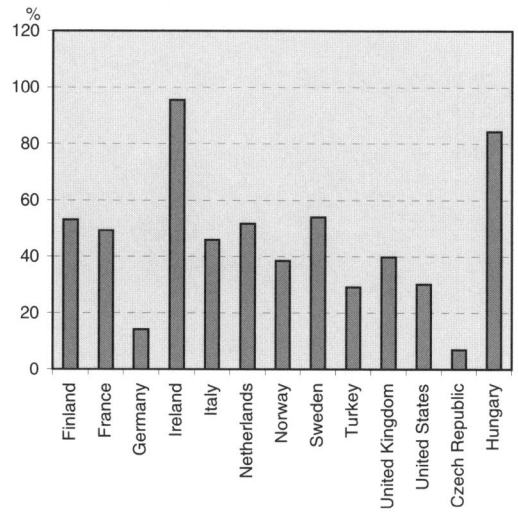

Pharmaceuticals (ISIC 2423)

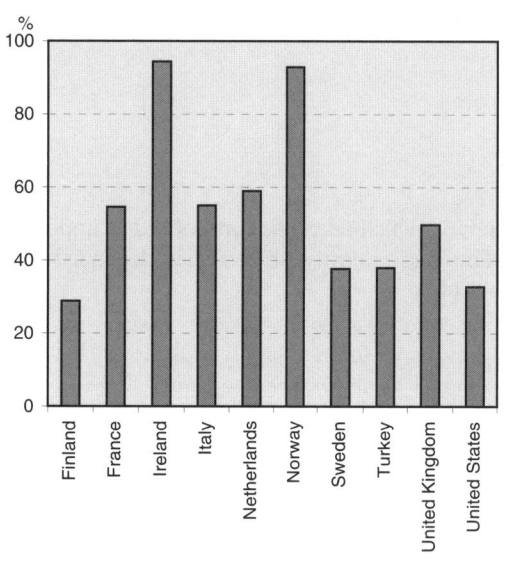

Motor vehicles (CITI 34)

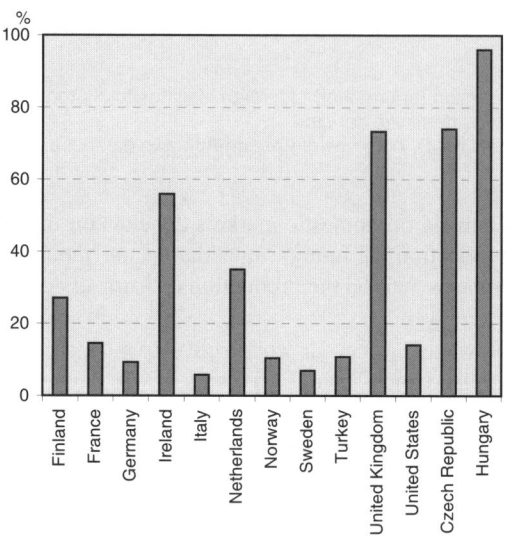

Note: 1999 for Finland, Hungary, Poland and the Czech Republic; 1997 for the United States, Italy and the United Kingdom.
Source: OECD, Activities of Foreign Affiliates database.

Figure 16. Share of production (or turnover) of foreign affiliates in selected industrial sectors

1998 or latest available year *(continued)*

Non-electrical machinery (ISIC 29/30)

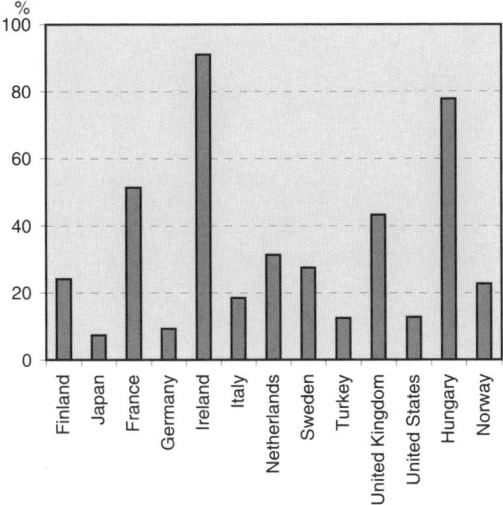

Computers (ISIC 30)

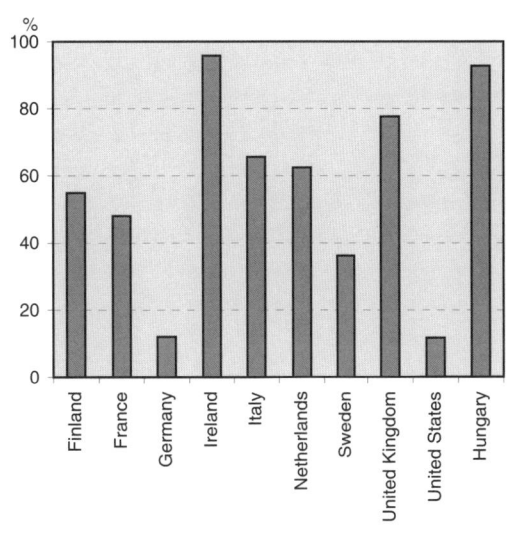

Electronic equipment (ISIC 32)

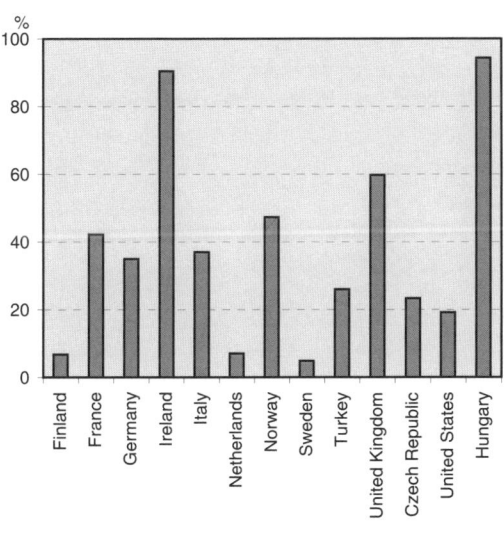

Instruments (ISIC 33)

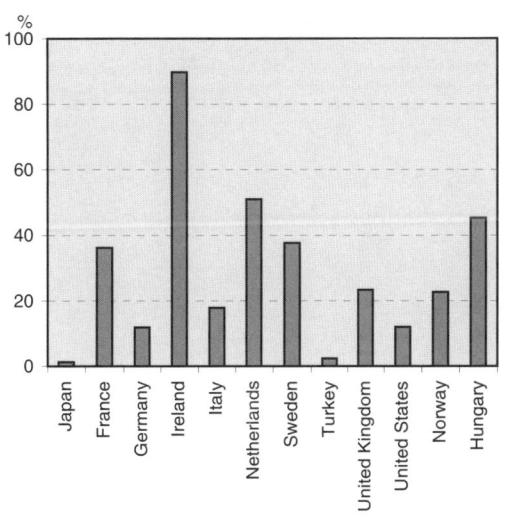

Note: 1999 for Finland, Hungary, Poland and the Czech Republic; 1997 for the United States, Italy and the United Kingdom.
Source: OECD, Activities of Foreign Affiliates database.

Partie I

Part de la production, de l'emploi, de la productivité, de la R-D, des exportations et des salaires sous contrôle étranger dans l'industrie manufacturière

**Figure 1. Évolution de la production manufacturière sous contrôle étranger
dans certaines zones de l'OCDE**

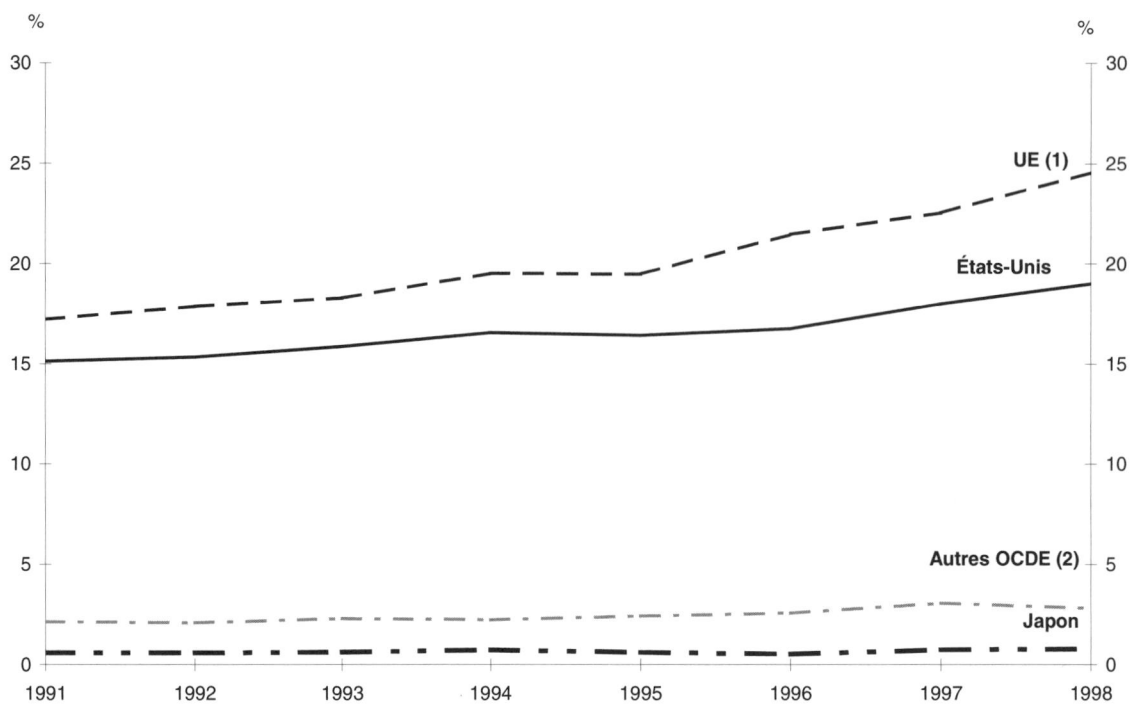

(1) Allemagne, France, Royaume-Uni (1997), Italie, Pays-Bas, Suède, Irlande, Finlande.
(2) Norvège, Hongrie, Turquie, Canada, République tchèque.
S*ource :* OCDE, base de données sur l'activité des filiales étrangères.

- Tandis que la progression des firmes sous contrôle étranger était relativement modeste au Japon et dans les autres pays OCDE, elle était plus vigoureuse aux États-Unis et surtout dans l'Union européenne où la pénétration de ces firmes dans la production manufacturière a été d'environ 25 %.

Les indicateurs sur l'activité des firmes sous contrôle étranger complètent l'information sur les flux et les stocks d'investissements directs étrangers, dans la mesure où ils permettent d'analyser la performance de ces firmes ainsi que leur contribution à l'activité économique des pays d'accueil.

Le critère de possession de 10 % des actions donnant droit de vote est réputé indiquer l'existence d'une relation d'investissement direct et d'une influence sur la gestion de l'entreprise en question. En revanche, le contrôle implique la capacité de façonner les activités d'une société. Cela suppose la possession d'une majorité d'actions ordinaires (plus de 50 %) ou des droits de vote au conseil d'administration. Des variables telles que le chiffre d'affaires ou les effectifs sont alors attribuées intégralement à l'investisseur qui contrôle l'entreprise.

La part des firmes sous contrôle étranger dans une économie dépend de divers facteurs, en particulier de la taille et de l'attractivité du pays ainsi que de la facilité, du point de vue institutionnel, avec laquelle ces investissements peuvent être effectués. Les données disponibles des firmes sous contrôle étranger montrent que, dans les années 90, leur chiffre d'affaires dans le secteur manufacturier a augmenté plus vite que celui des firmes sous contrôle national.

**Figure 2. Évolution de la part de la production manufacturière sous contrôle étranger
dans certains pays de la zone OCDE**

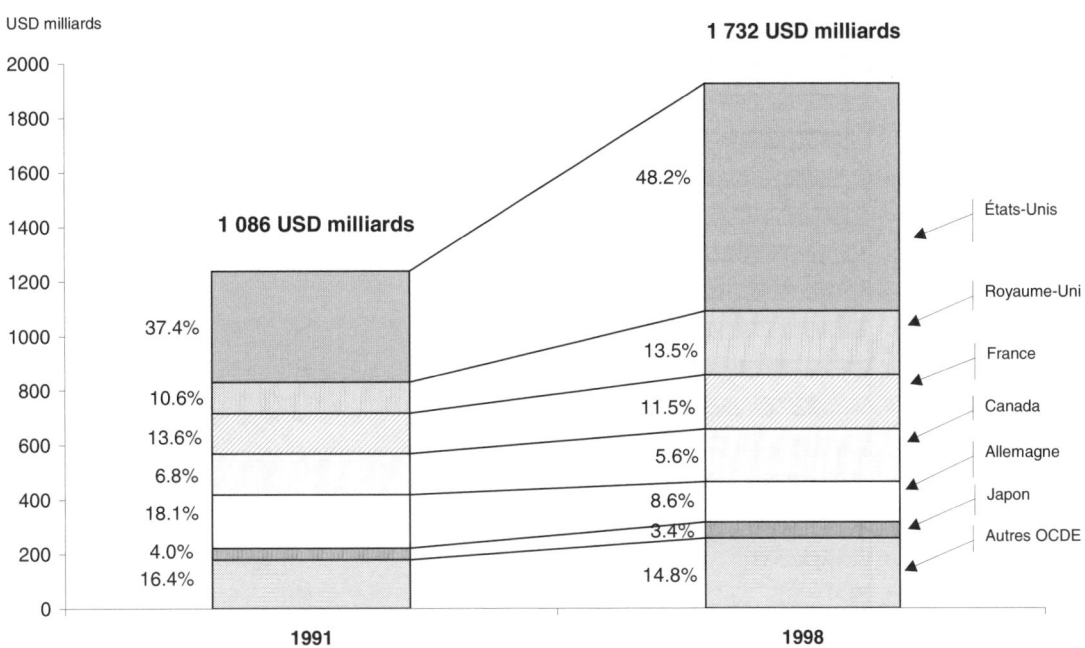

Source : OCDE, base de données sur l'activité des filiales étrangères.

- La production sous contrôle étranger entre 1991 et 1998 (en valeur absolue) a progressé dans tous les grands pays, à l'exception de l'Allemagne où elle a marqué une baisse.

- Au cours de la même période, la production des firmes étrangères a doublé aux États-Unis, qui attirent désormais la moitié de la production de ces sociétés à l'intérieur de la zone OCDE.

- Les États-Unis et le Royaume-Uni sont les seuls grands pays dont la production sous contrôle étranger a progressé à la fois en valeur et en pourcentage dans la zone OCDE.

Figure 3. Part de la production (ou du chiffre d'affaires) sous contrôle étranger du secteur manufacturier

1998 ou dernière année disponible

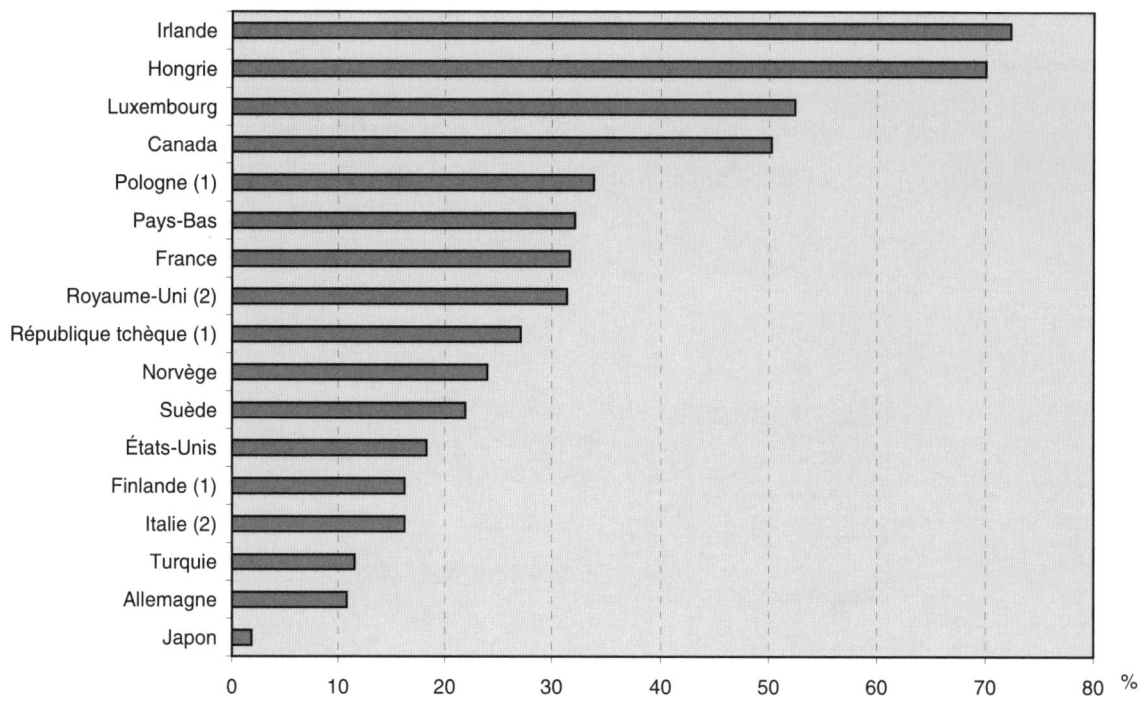

1: 1999, 2: 1997.
S*ource :* OCDE, base de données sur l'activité des filiales étrangères.

- La part du chiffre d'affaires des firmes sous contrôle étranger dans le total du secteur manufacturier en 1998 varie entre 70 % en Irlande et en Hongrie, et moins de 2 % au Japon.

- Le poids de ces firmes dans le chiffre d'affaires du total de l'industrie manufacturière dépassait également 30 % au Canada, en France, au Royaume-Uni, aux Pays-Bas, au Luxembourg et en Pologne.

- Dans l'Union européenne, c'était en Allemagne, et dans une moindre mesure en Italie, que la pénétration des firmes sous contrôle étranger était parmi la plus faible.

- Au Japon en revanche, malgré une relative progression de la production sous contrôle étranger au cours des dernières années, la pénétration reste toujours la plus faible de la zone OCDE.

Figure 4. Part de la production des firmes sous contrôle étranger dans le groupe des industries des technologies "haute - moyenne haute" comparée à leur part dans la production manufacturière de ces firmes et au total de la production nationale

1998 ou dernière année disponible

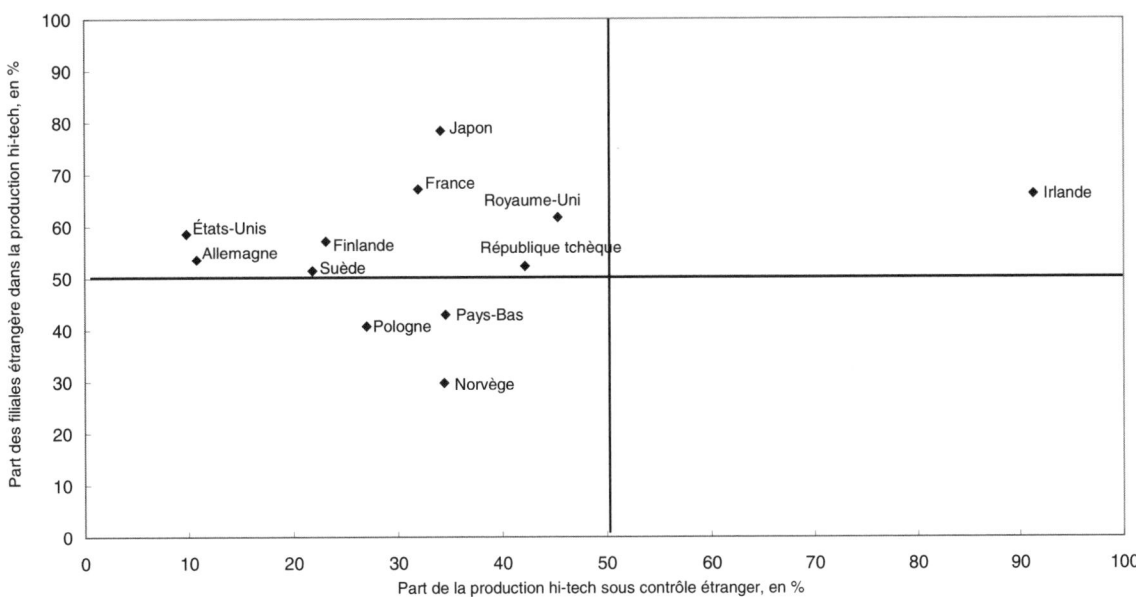

Source : OCDE, base de données sur l'activité des filiales étrangères.

- Le niveau technologique des investissements directs est assez différent selon le pays d'accueil. Les pays qui attirent les investissements dans les industries de haute et moyenne haute technologie (cf. annexe) sont le Japon, la France, le Royaume-Uni, les États-Unis et l'Irlande.

- Les Pays-Bas, la Norvège et la Pologne attirent majoritairement des investissements dans les industries technologiquement moins intensives.

- Au Japon où les firmes sous contrôle étranger représentent moins de 2 % de la production manufacturière, les firmes étrangères appartenant aux secteurs technologiquement intensifs représentent plus de 30 % de la production de ces mêmes secteurs et plus de 80 % de la production de l'ensemble des firmes sous contrôle étranger.

- En Irlande, plus de 65 % de la production des firmes étrangères concerne les secteurs de haute et moyenne haute technologie. Cette production correspond à plus de 90 % de la production nationale de ces industries.

Figure 5. Part de l'emploi sous contrôle étranger dans l'industrie manufacturière

1998 ou dernière année disponible

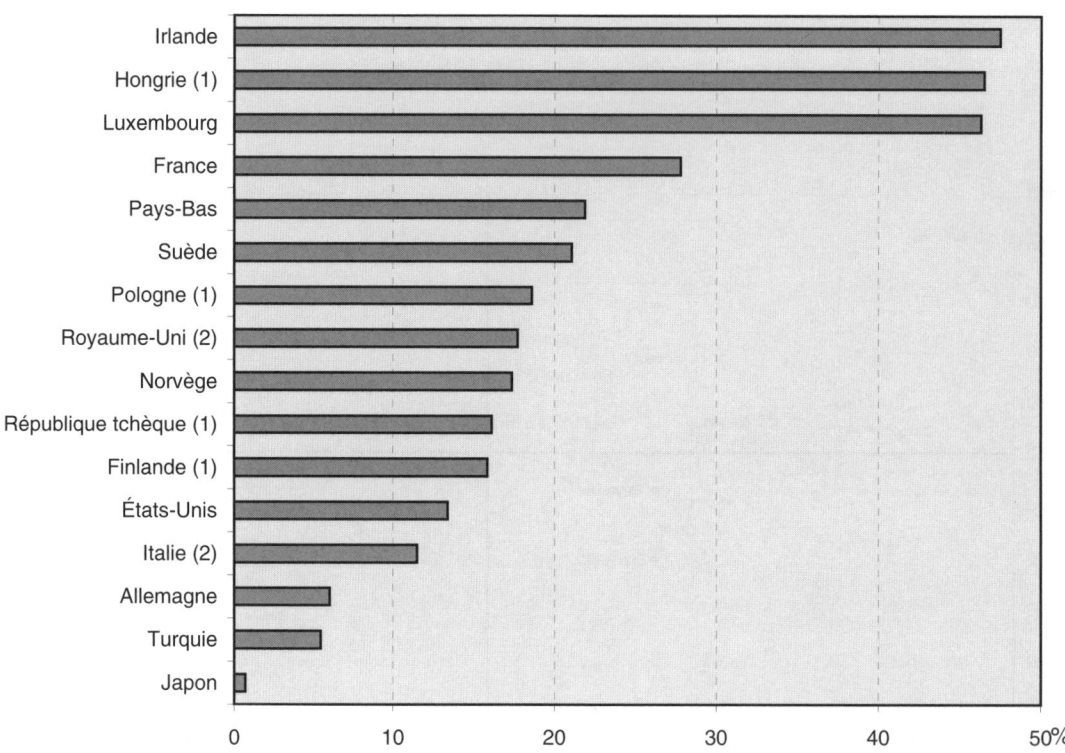

1: 1999, 2: 1997.
Source : OCDE, base de données sur l'activité des filiales étrangères.

- L'emploi sous contrôle étranger dans les pays de l'OCDE suit les mêmes tendances que la production, mais ces pourcentages dans l'emploi total sont inférieurs du fait que les investissements directs étrangers sont plus intensifs en capital qu'en travail. Cela peut expliquer aussi certaines différences constatées entre pays, notamment entre la France et le Royaume-Uni. La part de l'emploi sous contrôle étranger est supérieure en France qu'au Royaume-Uni, bien que la production sous contrôle étranger soit du même ordre dans les deux pays (Figure 5).

- En termes absolus, entre 1990 et 1998, le nombre de personnes employées par les firmes sous contrôle étranger a sensiblement progressé dans tous les pays sauf en Allemagne. Il convient toutefois de rappeler que dans tous les pays, cette progression n'implique pas nécessairement de nouvelles créations d'emplois, mais le plus souvent un changement de propriété dû au passage sous contrôle étranger des firmes existantes (Figure 6).

- Les États-Unis ont bénéficié le plus en termes absolus (plus de 400 000 postes) d'emplois créés (grâce aux "greenfields") ou maintenus (à travers les acquisitions), suivis par la Hongrie et la Pologne dont les emplois passés sous contrôle étranger entre 1990 et 1998 ont progressé de 350 000 et 220 000 respectivement.

Figure 6. Nombre de salariés des firmes sous contrôle étranger dans l'industrie manufacturière, variation entre 1990 et 1998 ou années les plus proches, en milliers

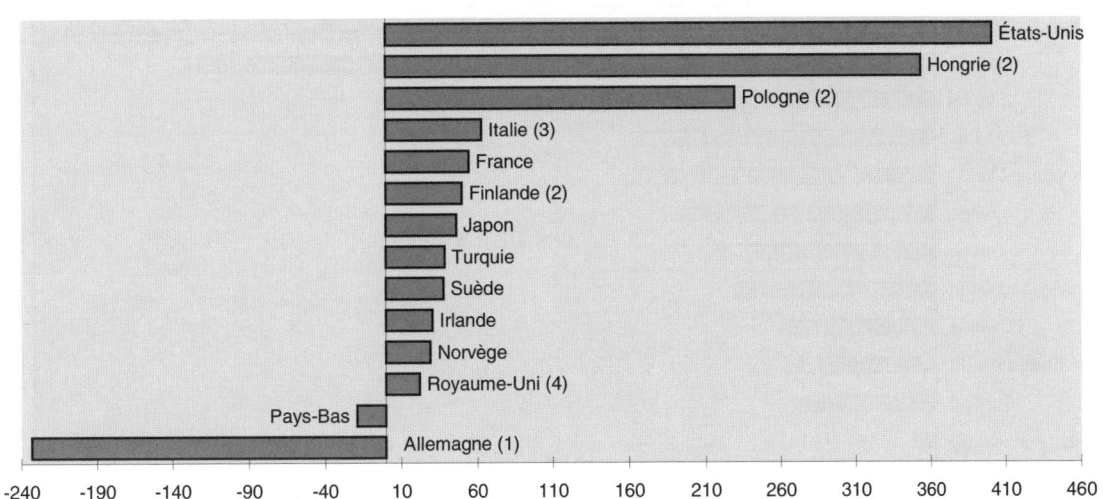

1: 1990-99, 2: 1993-99, 3: 1989-99, 4: 1989-97.
Source : OCDE, base de données sur l'activité des filiales étrangères.

Figure 7. Part de la valeur ajoutée sous contrôle étranger du secteur manufacturier

1998 ou dernière année disponible

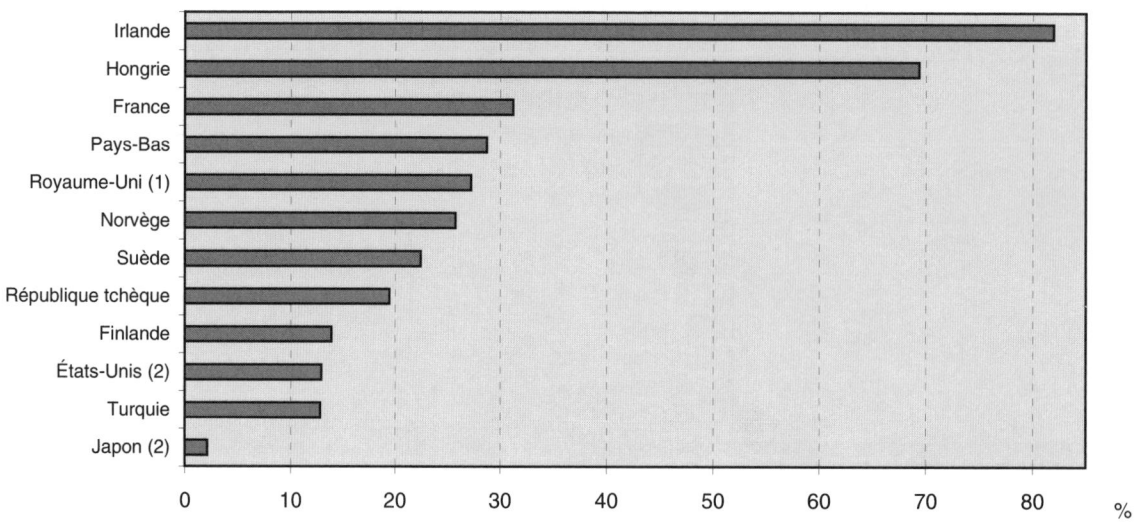

1: 1999, 2: 1997, 3: 1996.
Source : OCDE, base de données sur l'activité des filiales étrangères.

Figure 8. Rémunération par employé des sociétés sous contrôle étranger dans l'industrie manufacturière

Firmes nationales = 100

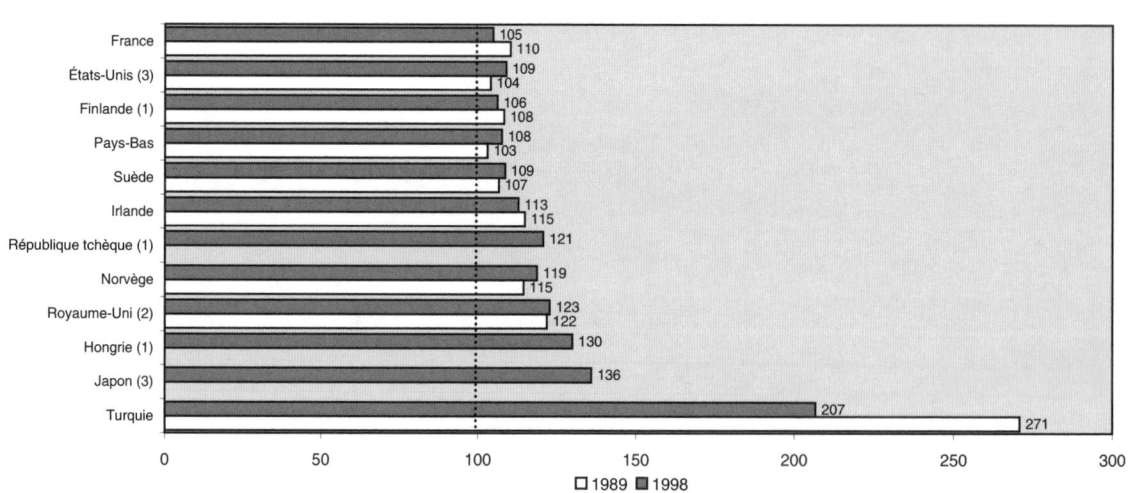

1: 1989-99, 2: 1989-97, 3: 1989-96.
Source : OCDE, base de données sur l'activité des filiales étrangères.

- En Irlande et en Hongrie, entre 70 et 80 % de la valeur ajoutée de l'industrie manufacturière est engendrée par les firmes sous contrôle étranger. En France, au Royaume-Uni, aux Pays-Bas et en Norvège, cette contribution se situe entre 25 et 30 %. Dans les autres pays, elle est inférieure à 20 %.

- Alors que dans certains pays, la rémunération par employé des firmes sous contrôle étranger est légèrement supérieure à celle de la moyenne des firmes nationales, dans d'autres cette différence est plus importante.

Figure 9. Production brute par employé dans l'industrie manufacturière

Firmes nationales = 100

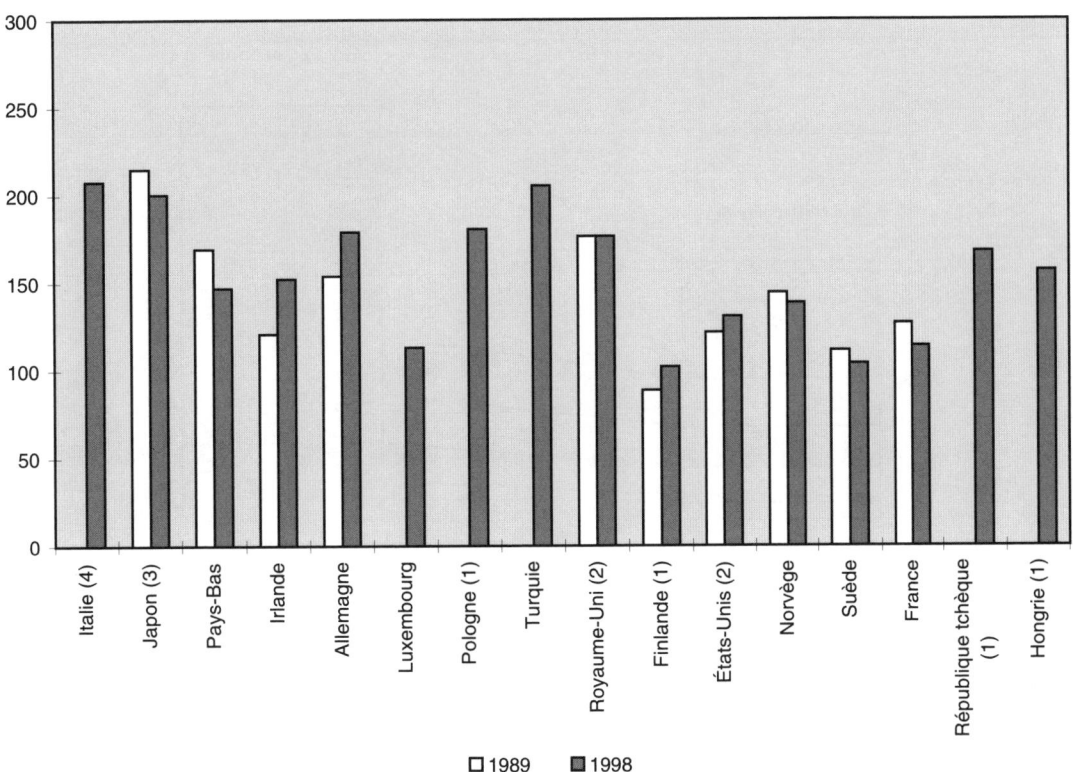

☐ 1989   ■ 1998

1: 1999, 2: 1997, 3: 1996, 4: 1995.
Source : OCDE, base de données sur l'activité des filiales étrangères.

- La production brute par employé dans l'industrie manufacturière dans la majorité des pays est supérieure à la moyenne des firmes nationales. Ce résultat confirme l'hypothèse selon laquelle la productivité des firmes les plus internationales est supérieure à celle des firmes qui le sont sensiblement moins.

- Il convient de rappeler que, parmi les firmes nationales, on compte de nombreuses petites et moyennes entreprises faiblement internationalisées.

- Ce résultat reflète également l'orientation sectorielle des investissements directs, plus intensifs en capital.

Figure 10. Évolution de la part des dépenses de R-D sous contrôle étranger dans l'industrie manufacturière dans certains pays de la zone OCDE

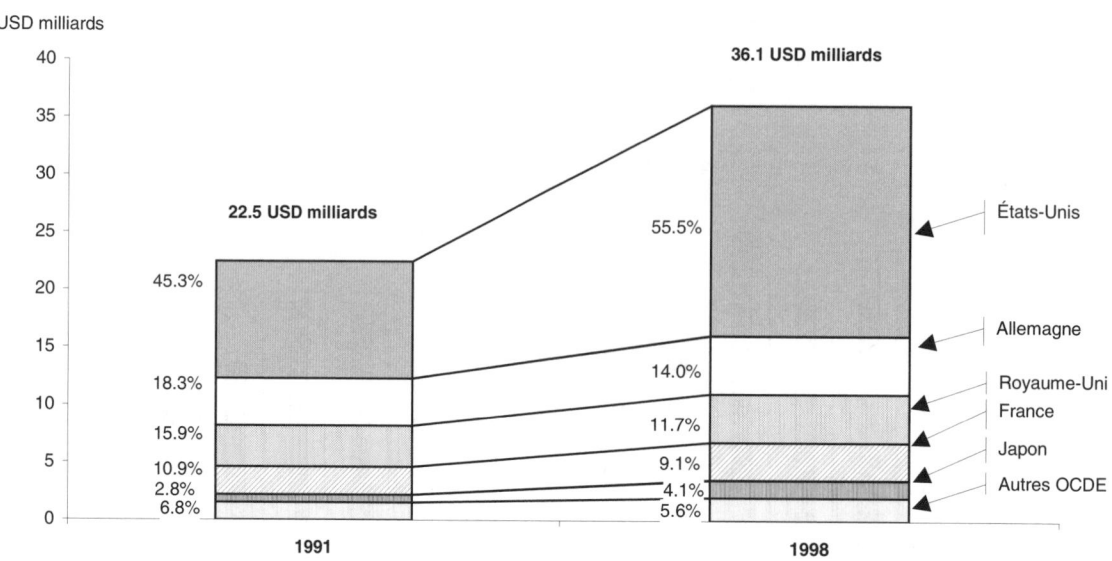

Source : OCDE, base de données sur l'activité des filiales étrangères.

Figure 11. Part des firmes sous contrôle étranger dans la R-D manufacturière

1998 ou dernière année disponible

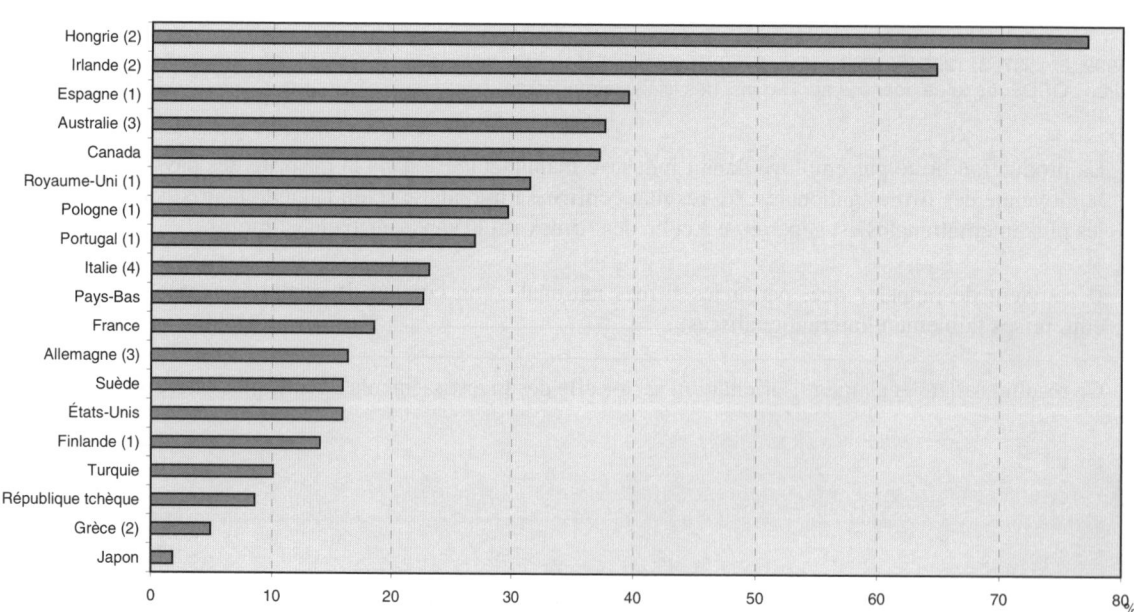

1: 1999, 2: 1997, 3:1995, 4: 1992.
Source : OCDE, base de données sur l'activité des filiales étrangères.

Figure 12. Part de la R-D et de la production (ou du chiffre d'affaires) des filiales étrangères dans la R-D et la production totale de l'industrie manufacturière

1998 ou dernière année disponible

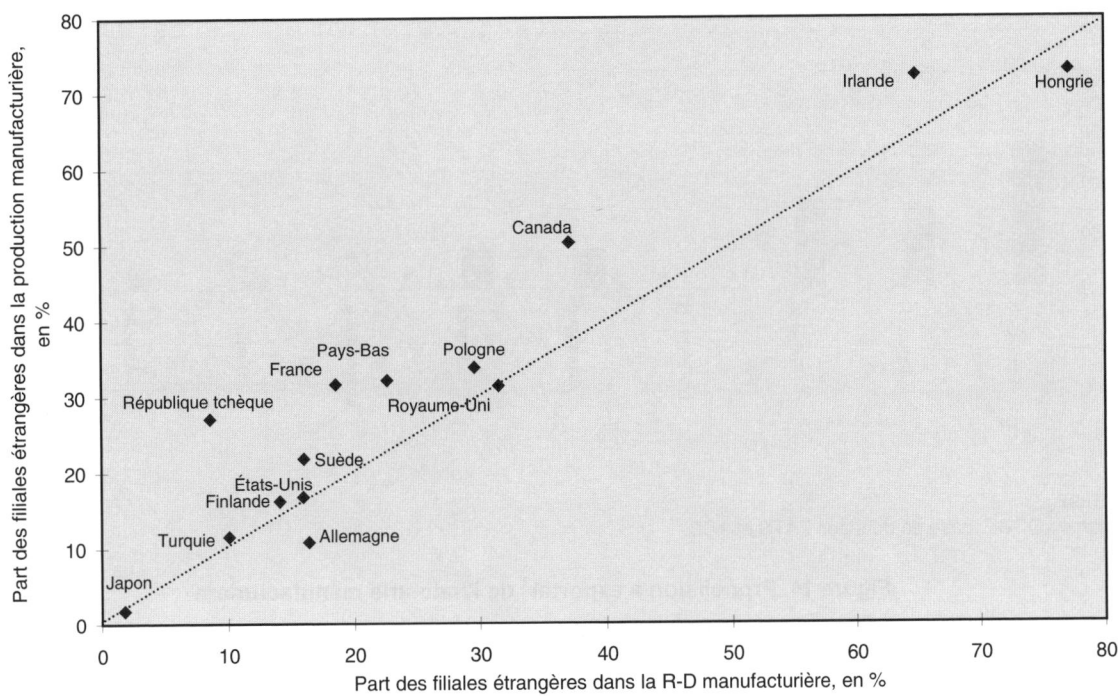

Source : OCDE, base de données sur l'activité des filiales étrangères.

- Les États-Unis attirent sur leur territoire plus de USD 20 milliards d'investissements en matière de R-D en provenance des firmes étrangères, c'est à dire environ 55 % des investissements de R-D de ces firmes dans la zone OCDE (Figure 10).

- Les investissements de R-D des firmes étrangères entre 1991 et 1998 ont progressé en valeur dans tous les grands pays, y compris l'Allemagne où la production sous contrôle étranger au cours de cette période a reculé. En revanche, leur poids dans le total OCDE a baissé dans tous les pays sauf aux États-Unis.

- En Hongrie, et en Irlande les firmes sous contrôle étranger réalisent plus de 60 et 70 % (respectivement) de la R-D du secteur manufacturier, tandis qu'en République tchèque, en Grèce et au Japon elles réalisent moins de 10 % (Figure 11).

- L'activité de production des firmes sous contrôle étranger et l'activité de R-D de ces mêmes firmes sont en général assez liées. Les quelques écarts observés entre ces deux activités pourraient être dûs soit aux secteurs d'investissements plus ou moins techniquement intensifs, soit à la préférence de transférer la technologie des maisons mères vers les filiales plutôt que d'effectuer un effort important de R-D localement (Figure 12).

Figure 13. Chiffre d'affaires des filiales de firmes nationales implantées à l'étranger rapporté aux exportations nationales

1998 ou dernière année disponible

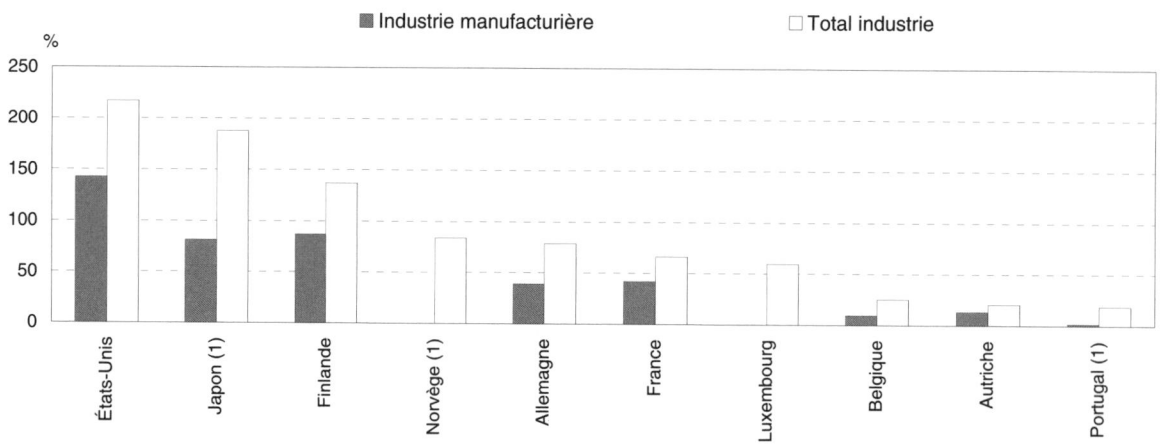

1: 1997.
Source : OCDE, base de données FATS et ADB.

Figure 14. Propension à exporter[1] de l'industrie manufacturière

1998 ou dernière année disponible

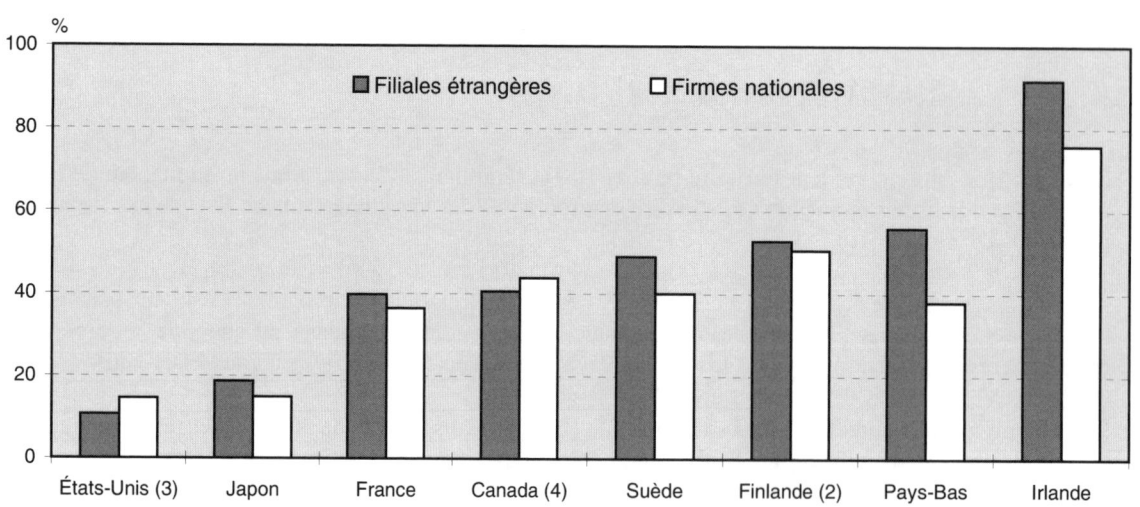

1: Exportations/production (ou chiffre d'affaires).
2: 1999, 3: 1996, 4:1995.
Source : OCDE, base de données sur l'activité des filiales étrangères.

- La figure 13 montre que dans plusieurs pays la production (ou le chiffre d'affaires) de leurs filiales dans les pays où elles sont implantées dépasse largement les exportations totales (des firmes nationales et étrangères). Ce phénomène qui caractérise davantage les États-Unis, le Japon et la Finlande, souligne l'importance de l'investissement direct dans la conquête d'un marché à l'étranger.

- La propension à exporter (exportation/production) des filiales étrangères est en général plus élevée que celle des firmes nationales, sauf aux États-Unis et au Canada (Figure 14).

44

Figure 15. Degré d'exposition des marchés intérieurs au commerce et à l'investissement direct

1998 ou dernière année disponible

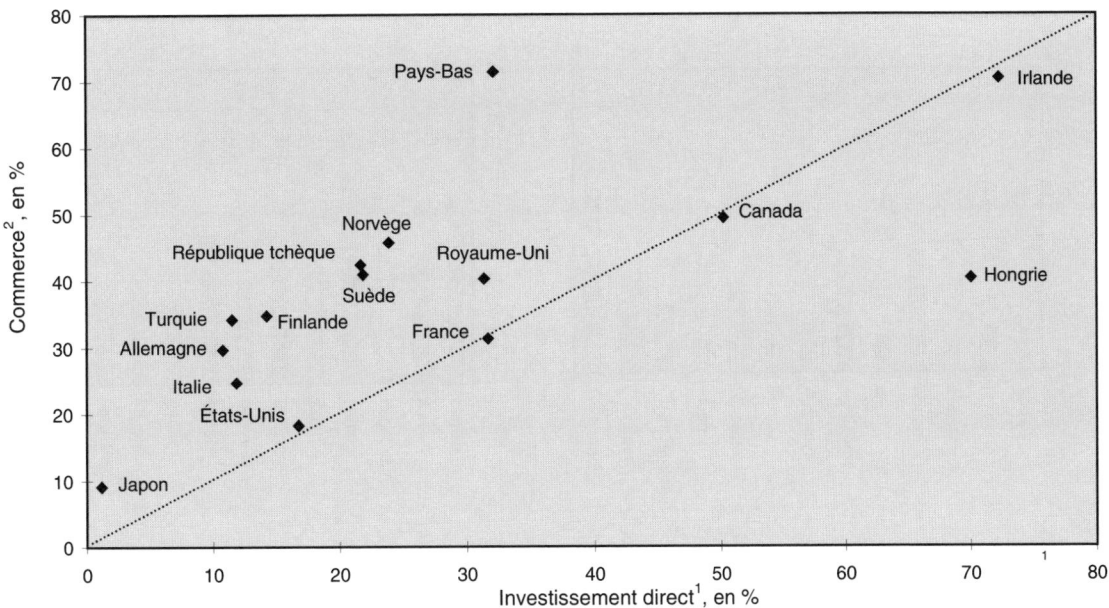

1. Production (ou chiffre d'affaires) des firmes sous contrôle étranger/production (ou chiffre d'affaires) total.
2. Importations/demande intérieure.
Source : OCDE, base de données sur l'activité des filiales étrangères.

- La demande des marchés domestiques dépend de l'offre étrangère qui provient soit des importations soit de la production des filiales étrangères implantées sur leur territoire. Dans la grande majorité des pays, cette dépendance est plus grande vis-à-vis des importations que de la production des firmes sous contrôle étranger.

- Toutefois, dans certains pays, la dépendance envers cette offre étrangère est forte mais assez équilibrée (cas de l'Irlande et du Canada). Dans d'autres, elle est également équilibrée mais assez modérée ou faible (France, États-Unis).

- En revanche, en Hongrie, la demande intérieure dépend deux fois plus de la production des firmes étrangères que des importations, phénomène inverse de ce qui est observé aux Pays-Bas.

Figure 16. Part de la production (ou du chiffre d'affaires) des firmes sous contrôle étranger dans quelques secteurs industriels

1998 ou dernière année disponible

Alimentation, boisson, tabac (CITI 15/16)

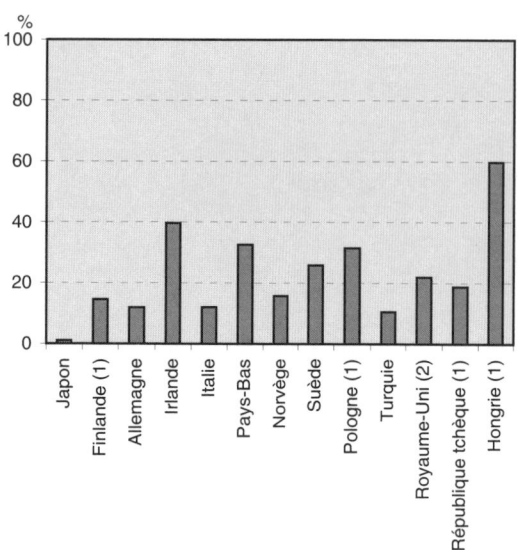

Produits chimiques (CITI 24)

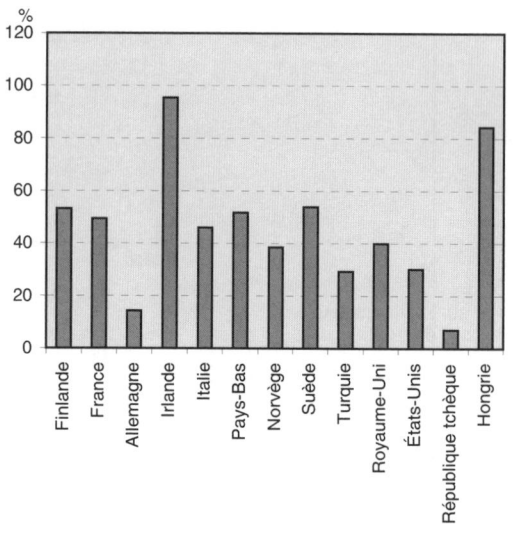

Produits pharmaceutiques (CITI 2423)

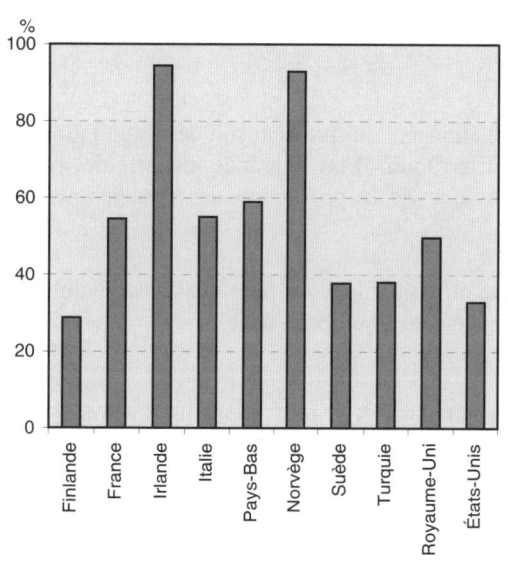

Automobile (CITI 34)

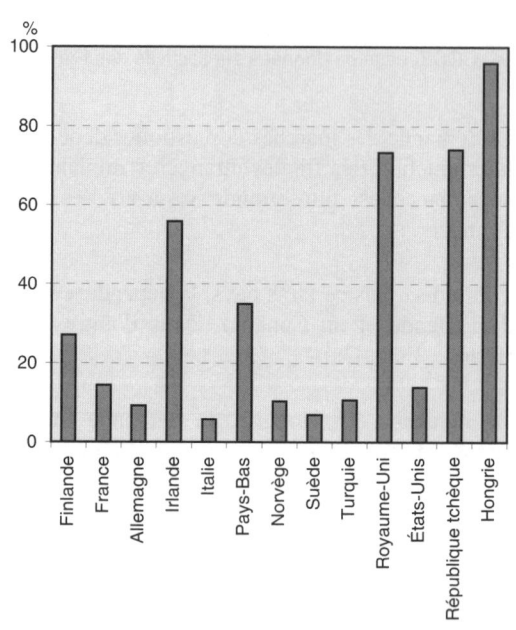

Note : 1999 pour la Finlande, la Hongrie, la Pologne et la République tchèque ; 1997 pour les États-Unis, l'Italie et le Royaume-Uni.
S*ource :* OCDE, base de données sur l'activité des filiales étrangères.

Figure 16. Part de la production (ou du chiffre d'affaires) des firmes sous contrôle étranger dans quelques secteurs industriels *(suite)*

1998 ou dernière année disponible

Machines non électriques (CITI 29/30)

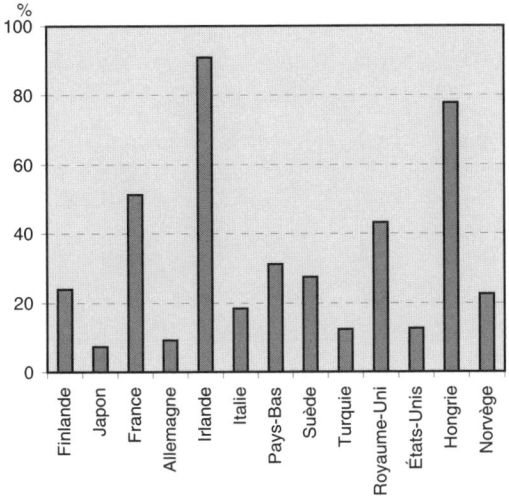

Ordinateurs (CITI 30)

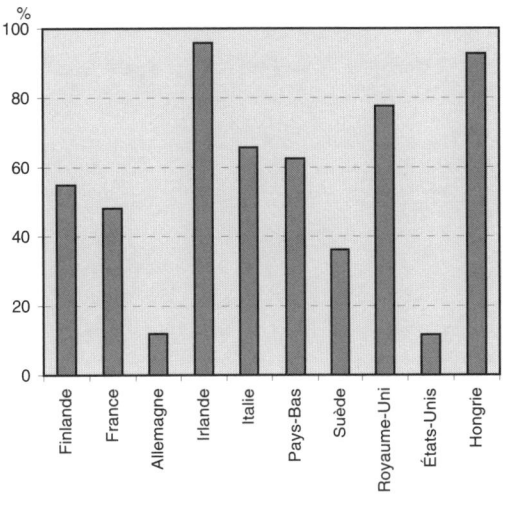

Electronique (CITI 32)

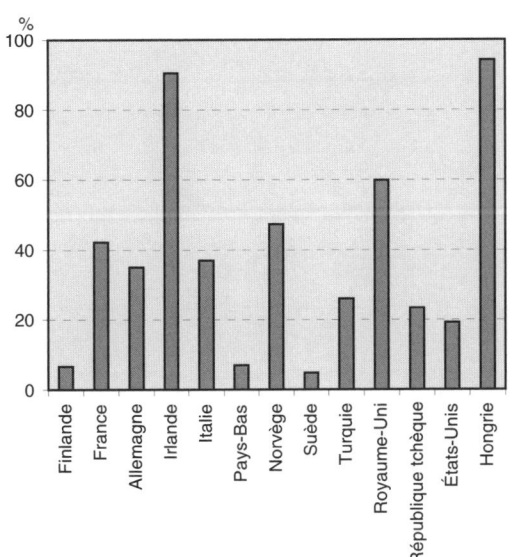

Instruments (CITI 33)

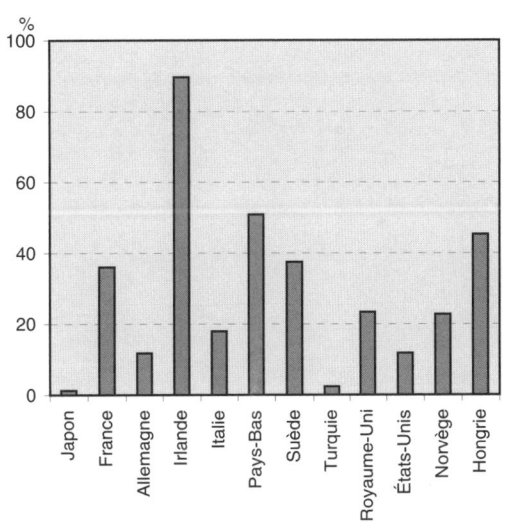

Note : 1999 pour la Finlande, la Hongrie, la Pologne et la République tchèque ; 1997 pour les États-Unis, l'Italie et le Royaume-Uni.
S*ource :* OCDE, base de données sur l'activité des filiales étrangères.

47

Part II - Partie II

Activity of foreign affiliates and share of OECD economies controlled by multinational firms

Activité des filiales étrangères et part des économies de l'OCDE contrôlée par les firmes multinationales

List of variables and availability of data by country

Liste des variables et disponibilité des données par pays

Inward investments/Investissements entrants

	1	2	3	4	5	6	7	8	9	10	11	12	13	14	15	16	17	18
Canada	X		X				X	X		X		X		X				X
Czech Republic / République tchèque	X	X	X	X	X	X	X	X	X									
Finland / Finlande	X	X		X	X	X	X	X	X	X	X			X			X	X
France	X	X	X	X	X	X	X	X	X	X				X				
Germany / Allemagne	X	X		X			X	X							X	X	X	X
Hungary / Hongrie	X	X		X	X	X	X		X	X	X						X	
Ireland / Irlande	X	X	X		X	X	X			X	X							
Italy / Italie	X	X		X														
Japan / Japon	X	X		X	X	X	X	X	X	X	X	X	X	X	X		X	X
Luxembourg	X	X		X													X	
Netherlands / Pays-Bas	X	X	X	X	X	X	X		X	X	X	X	X	X				X
Norway / Norvège	X	X	X	X	X	X			X					X				
Poland / Pologne	X	X		X			X	X	X	X	X							X
Sweden / Suède	X	X	X	X	X	X	X		X	X	X	X		X				X
Turkey / Turquie	X	X	X	X	X	X	X	X	X									
United Kingdom / Royaume-Uni	X	X	X	X	X	X	X		X					X				
United States / Etats-Unis	X	X		X	X	X	X	X	X	X	X	X	X	X	X	X	X	

1. Number of enterprises/establishments
2. Number of employees
3. Production
4. Turnover
5. Value added
6. Compensation of employees
7. R&D expenditure
8. Number of researchers
9. Gross fixed capital formation
10. Total exports
11. Total imports
12. Intra-firm exports
13. Intra-firms imports
14. Gross operating surplus
15. Technological payments
16. Technological receipts
17. Stock of foreign direct investment
18. Capital under foreign influence

1. Nombre d'entreprises/établissements
2. Nombre de salariés
3. Production
4. Chiffre d'affaires
5. Valeur ajoutée
6. Salaires et charges sociales
7. Dépenses de R-D
8. Nombre de chercheurs
9. Formation brute de capital fixe
10. Exportations totales
11. Importations totales
12. Exportations intra-firme
13. Importations intra-firme
14. Excédent brut d'exploitation
15. Paiements technologiques
16. Recettes technologiques
17. Stock d'investissement direct étranger
18. Capital sous influence étrangère

Outward investments/Investissements sortants

	1	2	3	4	5	6	7	8	9	10	11	12	13	14	15	16	17	18
Germany / Allemagne	X	X		X													X	X
Italy / Italie	X	X		X														
Luxembourg	X	X		X													X	
Sweden / Suède		X					X	X										
United States / Etats-Unis	X	X		X	X	X	X			X	X	X	X	X				

1. Number of enterprises/establishments	1. Nombre d'entreprises/établissements
2. Number of employees	2. Nombre de salariés
3. Production	3. Production
4. Turnover	4. Chiffre d'affaires
5. Value added	5. Valeur ajoutée
6. Compensation of employeess	6. Salaires et charges sociales
7. R&D expenditure	7. Dépenses de R-D
8. Number of researchers	8. Nombre de chercheurs
9. Gross fixed capital formation	9. Formation brute de capital fixe
10. Total exports	10. Exportations totales
11. Total imports	11. Importations totales
12. Intra-firm exports	12. Exportations intra-firme
13. Intra-firms imports	13. Importations intra-firme
14. Gross operating surplus	14. Excédent brut d'exploitation
15. Technological payments	15. Paiements technologiques
16. Technological receipts	16. Recettes technologiques
17. Stock of foreign direct investment	17. Stock d'investissement direct étranger
18. Capital under foreign influence	18. Capital sous influence étrangère

CANADA

CANADA

Table 1A - Tableau 1A

NUMBER OF ENTERPRISES / NOMBRE D'ENTREPRISES

| | | Foreign affiliates (Units) | | | | | As a % of national total | | | | |
		Filiales étrangères (Unités)					En % du total national				
By industry (ISIC Rev. 3)		1994	1995	1996	1997	1998	1994	1995	1996	1997	1998
10/14	Mining & quarrying	207	198	178	172	..	..	..	..	..	..
15/37	**TOTAL MANUFACTURING**	**1 894**	**1 946**	**1 816**	**1 788**	..	**25.1**	**25.1**	**26.4**	**29.1**	..
15/16	Food, beverages, tobacco	145	147	144	136	..	..	..	..	..	..
17/19	Textiles, clothing, leather, footwear	74	77	78	72	..	..	..	..	..	..
20/22	Wood and paper products	213	213	211	197	..	..	..	..	..	..
20	Wood products	59	61	59	54	..	..	..	..	..	..
21/22	Paper, printing and publishing	154	152	152	143	..	..	..	..	..	..
23/25	Chemicals, Total	335	332	308	312	..	..	..	..	..	..
23	Refined petroleum, nuclear fuel	85	81	75	74	..	..	..	..	..	..
24/25	Chemicals, rubber & plastics prod.	250	251	233	238	..	..	..	..	..	..
24	Chemical products	149	147	143	140	..	..	..	..	..	..
2423	Pharmaceuticals	..	..	..	..	..	..	..	..	..	..
25	Rubber and plastics products	101	104	90	98	..	..	..	..	..	..
26	Non-metallic mineral products	119	125	117	117	..	..	..	..	..	..
27/28	Basic & fabricated metals	232	233	203	204	..	..	..	..	..	..
27	Basic metals	69	70	64	68	..	..	..	..	..	..
28	Fabricated metal products	163	163	139	136	..	..	..	..	..	..
29/32	Machinery, Total	274	295	266	268	..	..	..	..	..	..
29/30	Non-electrical machinery	156	168	150	151	..	..	..	..	..	..
29	Non-electrical machinery nec	..	..	..	..	..	..	..	..	..	..
30	Office and computing machinery	..	..	..	..	..	..	..	..	..	..
31/32	Electrical & electronic equipment	118	127	116	117	..	..	..	..	..	..
31	Electrical machinery nec	70	69	62	60	..	..	..	..	..	..
32	Radio, TV & communications eq.	48	58	54	57	..	..	..	..	..	..
33	Scientific instruments	51	51	44	52	..	..	..	..	..	..
34/35	Transportation equipment	159	166	157	153	..	..	..	..	..	..
34	Motor vehicles	125	133	124	121	..	..	..	..	..	..
35	Other transport equipment	34	33	33	32	..	..	..	..	..	..
351	Shipbuilding & repairing	..	..	..	..	..	..	..	..	..	..
353	Aircraft and spacecraft	..	..	..	..	..	..	..	..	..	..
36/37	Other manufacturing	292	307	288	277	..	..	..	..	..	..
40/45	Construction, electricity, gas & water	520	536	519	506	..	..	..	..	..	..
50/55	Trade, repair, hotels & restaurants	2 121	2 202	2 102	2 109	..	..	..	..	..	..
65/74	Finance, insurance, business services	2 648	2 766	2 693	2 693	..	..	..	..	..	..
	OTHER ACTIVITIES	146	156	145	233	..	..	..	..	..	..
01/99	**GRAND TOTAL**	**7 536**	**7 804**	**7 453**	**7 501**	..	**19.4**	**19.6**	**20.9**	**24.4**	..

Total manufacturing by investing country	1994	1995	1996	1997	1998	As a % of total manufacturing by foreign affiliates				
						1994	1995	1996	1997	1998
All countries	**1 894**	**1 946**	**1 816**	**1 788**	..	**100.0**	**100.0**	**100.0**	**100.0**	..
United States	985	1 002	888	890	..	52.0	51.5	48.9	49.8	..
Canada	..	..	..	..	..	..	..	..	..	..
Mexico					..					..
Japan	109	113	123	119	..	5.8	5.8	6.8	6.7	..
Europe	692	701	686	658	..	36.5	36.0	37.8	36.8	..
European Union (15)	602	603	587	579	..	31.8	31.0	32.3	32.4	..
Belgium	..	..	..	..	..	..	..	..	..	..
France	91	86	89	84	..	4.8	4.4	4.9	4.7	..
Germany	126	126	123	122	..	6.7	6.5	6.8	6.8	..
Italy	22	22	22	24	..	1.2	1.1	1.2	1.3	..
Netherlands	41	48	47	45	..	2.2	2.5	2.6	2.5	..
Spain	..	..	..	..	..	..	..	..	..	..
Sweden	30	30	27	27	..	1.6	1.5	1.5	1.5	..
United Kingdom	244	245	233	213	..	12.9	12.6	12.8	11.9	..
Switzerland	60	63	63	63	..	3.2	3.2	3.5	3.5	..
Australia and New Zealand	29	32	28	22	..	1.5	1.6	1.5	1.2	..
Asia (non-OECD)	36	44	43	43	..	1.9	2.3	2.4	2.4	..
Latin America	..	..	..	..	..	..	..	..	..	..

Note: Majority foreign-owned firms.
        Firmes sous contrôle étranger majoritaire.

CANADA

Inward investments

Table 2A - Tableau 2A

PRODUCTION BY INDUSTRY

PRODUCTION PAR INDUSTRIE

| | | Foreign affiliates *(Millions of CAD)* | | | | | As a % of national total | | | | |
| | | Filiales étrangères *(Millions de CAD)* | | | | | En % du total national | | | | |
ISIC Revision 3		1994	1995	1996	1997	1998	1994	1995	1996	1997	1998
10/14	Mining & quarrying	16 454	17 443	21 602	23 619	23 310	47.9	49.0	48.9	49.8	53.2
15/37	**TOTAL MANUFACTURING**	**225 273**	**254 467**	**267 806**	**285 553**	**293 678**	**51.2**	**51.2**	**50.9**	**49.6**	**50.3**
15/16	Food, beverages, tobacco	..	..	..	..	..	..	..	..	..	..
17/19	Textiles, clothing, leather, footwear	..	..	..	..	..	..	..	..	..	..
20/22	Wood and paper products	18 306	23 295	20 578	18 921	19 403	27.3	28.7	26.3	22.8	23.8
20	Wood products	10 903	14 006	10 669	9 531	10 493	30.3	31.5	27.7	23.8	26.9
21/22	Paper, printing and publishing	7 403	9 289	9 909	9 390	8 910	23.9	25.3	25.1	21.8	20.9
23/25	Chemicals, Total	46 497	48 460	55 776	60 334	55 886	60.5	61.0	62.8	57.6	58.4
23	Refined petroleum, nuclear fuel	23 189	23 329	29 073	32 046	26 767	50.6	51.0	55.2	49.6	49.3
24/25	Chemicals, rubber & plastics prod.	23 308	25 131	26 703	28 287	29 119	75.0	74.5	73.9	70.5	70.5
24	Chemical products	17 337	18 471	19 664	20 485	20 972	85.3	84.2	84.9	83.8	83.9
2423	Pharmaceuticals	..	..	..	..	..	..	..	..	..	..
25	Rubber and plastics products	5 971	6 660	7 039	7 802	8 147	55.5	56.5	54.3	49.8	49.9
26	Non-metallic mineral products	7 916	8 530	9 672	10 662	10 473	65.2	67.6	68.8	68.8	64.2
27/28	Basic & fabricated metals	11 347	13 240	13 516	12 209	14 050	28.6	29.1	27.9	25.1	27.7
27	Basic metals	4 656	5 824	6 192	5 302	6 780	22.0	24.2	24.7	21.2	26.7
28	Fabricated metal products	6 692	7 416	7 324	6 907	7 270	36.2	34.6	31.4	29.4	28.7
29/32	Machinery, Total	14 605	15 107	24 706	23 756	24 477	49.8	47.7	55.8	47.4	44.4
29/30	Non-electrical machinery	6 153	7 330	7 396	8 163	8 363	53.6	51.5	48.7	45.9	42.0
29	Non-electrical machinery nec	..	..	..	..	..	..	..	..	..	..
30	Office and computing machinery	..	..	..	..	..	..	..	..	..	..
31/32	Electrical & electronic equipment	8 452	7 777	17 310	15 593	16 114	47.3	44.5	59.5	48.2	45.8
31	Electrical machinery nec	5 994	4 582	4 968	4 294	4 883	80.0	75.2	72.6	67.9	69.0
32	Radio, TV & communications eq.	2 458	3 195	12 342	11 299	11 231	23.7	28.1	55.5	43.5	40.0
33	Scientific instruments	1 875	2 146	2 262	2 223	2 420	64.3	63.5	63.8	54.6	55.2
34/35	Transportation equipment	85 348	92 463	94 640	108 020	113 635	82.4	81.7	80.2	80.9	81.3
34	Motor vehicles	81 480	88 329	90 171	103 374	108 043	86.8	86.2	85.2	86.1	85.8
35	Other transport equipment	3 868	4 134	4 469	4 645	5 592	40.0	38.6	36.7	34.3	40.5
351	Shipbuilding & repairing	..	..	..	..	..	..	..	..	..	..
353	Aircraft and spacecraft	..	..	..	..	..	..	..	..	..	..
36/37	Other manufacturing	11 779	23 390	15 882	16 275	18 219	32.1	44.7	32.8	32.0	34.8
40/45	Construction, electricity, gas & water	6 977	9 577	11 980	12 501	17 637	5.5	7.1	8.8	8.1	10.4
50/55	Trade, repair, hotels & restaurants	90 716	101 482	115 678	122 325	137 607	20.1	21.1	22.6	22.3	24.7
65/74	Finance, insurance, business services	51 319	49 490	52 748	54 592	57 507	24.5	22.2	22.6	22.3	23.0
	OTHER ACTIVITIES	10 754	15 154	18 394	21 513	23 555	10.2	13.2	13.5	15.3	16.7
01/99	**GRAND TOTAL**	**401 493**	**447 613**	**488 207**	**520 103**	**553 294**	**29.4**	**30.1**	**30.8**	**30.4**	**31.7**

Note: Majority foreign-owned firms.
Firmes sous contrôle étranger majoritaire.

Table 3A - Tableau 3A

PRODUCTION BY COUNTRY OF ORIGIN IN THE MANUFACTURING SECTOR

PRODUCTION PAR PAYS D'ORIGINE DANS L'INDUSTRIE MANUFACTURIÈRE

Country of origin (UBO)	Production *(Millions of CAD)* / Production *(Millions de CAD)*					As a % of all countries / En % du total des pays				
	1994	1995	1996	1997	1998	1994	1995	1996	1997	1998
All countries	**225 273**	**254 467**	**267 806**	**285 553**	**293 678**	100.0	100.0	100.0	100.0	100.0
Total OECD	..	..	260 737	276 411	286 571	..	..	97.4	96.8	97.6
United States	161 012	186 331	193 552	202 226	213 651	71.5	73.2	72.3	70.8	72.8
Canada	..	..	..	..	..	..	..	..	..	..
Mexico	..	..	..	..	..	..	..	..	..	..
Japan	9 418	10 514	11 035	14 113	15 366	4.2	4.1	4.1	4.9	5.2
Korea	..	..	..	..	..	..	..	..	..	..
Australia	..	..	..	..	659	..	..	..	..	0.2
New Zealand	..	..	..	..	..	..	..	..	..	..
Europe	46 529	47 547	52 362	59 199	57 031	..	..	..	..	..
European Union (15)	42 496	43 334	48 066	55 104	51 368	20.7	18.7	19.6	20.7	19.4
Austria	..	..	..	..	427	18.9	17.0	17.9	19.3	17.5
Belgium	..	..	..	..	..	..	..	..	..	0.1
Denmark	..	..	..	..	301	..	..	..	..	..
Finland	1 259	1 592	1 404	1 502	1 450	..	..	..	..	0.1
France	7 086	7 243	7 734	7 781	8 049	0.6	0.6	0.5	0.5	0.5
Germany	8 164	8 439	9 193	11 514	9 587	3.1	2.8	2.9	2.7	2.7
Greece	..	..	..	..	0	3.6	3.3	3.4	4.0	3.3
Ireland	..	..	..	..	142	..	..	..	..	0.0
Italy	1 369	1 959	2 415	5 260	4 385	..	..	..	..	0.0
Luxembourg	..	..	..	..	..	0.6	0.8	0.9	1.8	1.5
Netherlands	7 020	7 631	8 595	9 178	7 690	..	..	..	..	..
Portugal	..	..	..	..	0	3.1	3.0	3.2	3.2	2.6
Spain	..	..	..	..	..	..	..	..	..	0.0
Sweden	1 733	2 177	2 271	3 067	3 617	..	..	..	..	..
United Kingdom	15 276	13 393	13 848	14 119	13 597	0.8	0.9	0.8	1.1	1.2
Czech Republic	..	..	..	..	0	6.8	5.3	5.2	4.9	4.6
Hungary	..	..	..	..	0	..	..	..	..	0.0
Iceland	..	..	..	..	..	..	..	..	..	0.0
Norway	..	..	..	..	360	..	..	..	..	..
Poland	..	..	..	..	0	..	..	..	..	0.1
Slovak Republic	..	..	..	..	0	..	..	..	..	..
Switzerland	3 842	3 911	4 252	4 407	5 257	..	..	..	..	0.0
Turkey	..	..	..	..	..	1.7	1.5	1.6	1.5	1.8
Non-OECD Europe, of which:	..	..	..	..	..	..	..	..	..	..
Baltic countries	..	..	..	..	0	..	..	..	..	..
Bulgaria	..	..	..	..	0	..	..	..	..	0.0
Croatia	..	..	..	..	0	..	..	..	..	0.0
Romania	..	..	..	..	0	..	..	..	..	0.0
Russian Federation	..	..	..	..	..	..	..	..	..	0.0
Slovenia	..	..	..	..	0	..	..	..	..	0.0
Ukraine	..	..	..	..	0	..	..	..	..	0.0
Yugoslavia	..	..	..	..	..	..	..	..	..	0.0
Non-OECD Asia, of which:	1 807	2 744	2 977	3 157	3 482	0.8	1.1	1.1	1.1	1.2
China	..	..	..	..	..	..	..	..	..	..
Chinese Taipei	..	..	..	..	0	..	..	..	..	0.0
Hong Kong (China)	..	..	1 380	1 459	..	..	..	0.5	0.5	..
India	..	..	..	..	..	..	..	..	..	..
Indonesia	..	..	..	..	..	..	..	..	..	..
Malaysia	..	..	..	..	..	..	..	..	..	..
Philippines	..	..	..	..	0	..	..	..	..	0.0
Singapore	..	..	..	..	..	..	..	..	..	..
Thailand	..	..	..	..	0	..	..	..	..	0.0
Near and Middle East	..	..	..	..	..	..	..	..	..	..
Africa	..	..	..	..	1 230	..	..	..	..	0.4
Latin America, of which:	..	..	427	458	526	..	..	..	..	..
Argentina	..	..	..	..	..	..	..	..	..	0.0
Brazil	..	..	..	..	..	0.0	0.0	0.0	0.0	0.0
Chile	..	..	..	..	0	0.0	0.0	0.0	0.0	0.0

Note: Majority foreign-owned firms.
Firmes sous contrôle étranger majoritaire.

Table 4A - Tableau 4A
R&D EXPENDITURE / DÉPENSES DE R-D

By industry (ISIC Rev. 3)	Foreign affiliates (Millions of CAD) Filiales étrangères (Millions de CAD)					As a % of national total En % du total national				
	1994	1995	1996	1997	1998	1994	1995	1996	1997	1998
10/14 Mining & quarrying	37	35	37	104	60	19.3	17.0	18.4	55.3	48.4
15/37 TOTAL MANUFACTURING	**1 750**	**1 825**	**1 898**	**2 229**	**2 300**	**38.7**	**37.1**	**37.5**	**39.2**	**37.1**
15/16 Food, beverages, tobacco	49	50	45	46	35	47.1	43.5	42.1	47.4	43.2
17/19 Textiles, clothing, leather, footwear	43	46	43	44	43	72.9	70.8	74.1	71.0	70.5
20/22 Wood and paper products	5	6	10	7	15	3.0	3.1	5.7	3.9	9.0
20 Wood products	1	1	..	1	..	2.4	2.4	..	2.5	..
21/22 Paper, printing and publishing	4	5	9	6	..	3.3	3.3	6.5	4.3	..
23/25 Chemicals, Total	..	..	..	..	..	..	..	..	..	..
23 Refined petroleum, nuclear fuel	..	..	..	..	..	..	..	..	..	..
24/25 Chemicals, rubber & plastics prod.	..	..	..	..	..	..	..	..	..	..
24 Chemical products	451	506	517	512	526	79.7	78.4	78.6	77.8	75.9
2423 Pharmaceuticals	326	357	406	397	409	84.9	81.0	81.5	79.2	75.6
25 Rubber and plastics products	..	..	..	..	..	..	..	..	..	..
26 Non-metallic mineral products	4	4	3	3	2	25.0	30.8	25.0	30.0	25.0
27/28 Basic & fabricated metals	16	13	11	13	9	5.8	5.0	4.3	5.0	3.6
27 Basic metals	3	2	3	4	1	1.8	1.3	2.0	2.6	0.7
28 Fabricated metal products	13	11	8	9	8	11.6	10.3	7.8	8.4	7.5
29/32 Machinery, Total	571	601	584	700	821	25.6	24.8	23.2	24.9	24.8
29/30 Non-electrical machinery	256	250	225	263	267	49.5	46.4	43.9	47.6	44.1
29 Non-electrical machinery nec	34	49	38	56	51	18.3	24.4	20.9	28.3	25.8
30 Office and computing machinery	222	201	187	207	216	67.1	59.5	56.7	58.5	53.1
31/32 Electrical & electronic equipment	315	351	359	437	554	18.4	18.6	17.9	19.3	20.5
31 Electrical machinery nec	40	45	39	55	54	48.8	51.1	42.4	50.9	53.5
32 Radio, TV & communications eq.	275	306	320	382	500	16.9	17.0	16.7	17.7	19.2
33 Scientific instruments	17	13	16	21	24	18.3	12.3	15.1	18.6	17.8
34/35 Transportation equipment	503	495	568	779	736	60.8	54.8	60.0	61.3	55.8
34 Motor vehicles	170	120	106	140	131	80.6	65.2	62.4	70.4	68.9
35 Other transport equipment	333	375	462	639	605	54.1	52.2	59.5	59.7	53.5
351 Shipbuilding & repairing	..	..	..	..	..	..	..	..	..	..
353 Aircraft and spacecraft	332	373	461	636	599	54.2	52.2	59.8	60.2	53.6
36/37 Other manufacturing	8	14	16	20	14	14.8	25.0	27.1	28.6	28.0
40/45 Construction, electricity, gas & water	6	6	4	5	6	2.4	2.6	1.5	2.4	2.5
50/55 Trade, repair, hotels & restaurants	188	223	267	346	375	25.6	28.2	36.2	42.0	47.1
65/74 Finance, insurance, business services	251	272	323	309	357	13.9	15.1	18.8	17.7	21.0
OTHER ACTIVITIES	17	16	22	18	20	28.3	25.0	31.4	29.0	33.3
01/99 GRAND TOTAL	**2 249**	**2 377**	**2 551**	**3 011**	**3 118**	**29.7**	**29.7**	**31.7**	**34.6**	**34.2**

Total manufacturing by investing country						As a % of total manufacturing by foreign affiliates				
All countries	**1 750**	**1 825**	**1 898**	**2 229**	**2 300**	**100.0**	**100.0**	**100.0**	**100.0**	**100.0**
United States	1 335	1 377	1 401	1 719	1 753	76.3	75.5	73.8	77.1	76.2
Canada	..	..	..	..	..	..	..	..	..	..
Mexico	..	..	..	..	..	..	..	..	..	..
Japan	12	12	12	20	29	0.7	0.7	0.6	0.9	1.3
Europe	374	409	457	464	497	21.4	22.4	24.1	20.8	21.6
European Union (15)	..	..	..	..	..	..	..	..	..	..
Belgium	..	..	..	..	..	..	..	..	..	..
France	..	..	..	..	..	..	..	..	..	..
Germany	..	..	..	..	..	..	..	..	..	..
Italy	..	..	..	..	..	..	..	..	..	..
Netherlands	..	..	..	..	..	..	..	..	..	..
Spain	..	..	..	..	..	..	..	..	..	..
Sweden	..	..	..	..	..	..	..	..	..	..
United Kingdom	..	..	..	..	..	..	..	..	..	..
Switzerland	..	..	..	..	..	..	..	..	..	..
Australia and New Zealand	..	..	..	..	..	..	..	..	..	..
Asia (non-OECD)	..	..	..	..	..	..	..	..	..	..
Latin America	..	..	..	..	..	..	..	..	..	..

Note: Majority foreign-owned firms.
Firmes sous contrôle étranger majoritaire.

Inward investments

Investissements entrants

Table 5A - Tableau 5A

NUMBER OF RESEARCHERS / NOMBRE DE CHERCHEURS

By industry (ISIC Rev. 3)	Foreign affiliates (FTE) Filiales étrangères (EPT)					As a % of national total En % du total national				
	1994	1995	1996	1997	1998	1994	1995	1996	1997	1998
10/14 Mining & quarrying	96	125	147	147	120	15.0	16.8	21.3	29.7	32.7
15/37 **TOTAL MANUFACTURING**	**7 879**	**7 781**	**7 817**	**8 327**	**8 394**	**30.6**	**29.2**	**28.2**	**27.7**	**28.2**
15/16 Food, beverages, tobacco	241	271	230	266	197	36.1	39.0	33.9	43.8	35.8
17/19 Textiles, clothing, leather, footwear	144	144	148	141	131	60.0	52.0	60.4	56.2	67.9
20/22 Wood and paper products	30	26	46	49	53	3.2	2.9	6.1	7.0	8.6
20 Wood products	14	9	6	9	..	4.3	3.4	2.4	3.9	..
21/22 Paper, printing and publishing	16	17	40	40	..	2.6	2.8	7.9	8.4	..
23/25 Chemicals, Total	..	..	..	..	..	..	..	..	..	..
23 Refined petroleum, nuclear fuel	..	..	..	..	..	..	..	..	..	..
24/25 Chemicals, rubber & plastics prod.	..	..	..	..	..	..	..	..	..	..
24 Chemical products	1 771	1 722	1 661	1 663	1 691	70.0	68.0	69.2	67.8	71.5
2423 Pharmaceuticals	1 183	1 102	1 108	1 142	1 260	83.2	79.3	79.7	76.5	78.9
25 Rubber and plastics products	..	..	..	..	..	..	..	..	..	..
26 Non-metallic mineral products	19	24	18	17	16	13.0	20.5	18.4	18.9	23.9
27/28 Basic & fabricated metals	61	75	58	73	57	4.1	5.0	4.1	5.4	4.7
27 Basic metals	13	16	17	22	14	1.8	2.4	2.7	3.7	2.5
28 Fabricated metal products	48	59	41	51	43	6.2	7.2	5.3	6.7	6.6
29/32 Machinery, Total	3 911	3 711	3 628	3 815	3 905	26.2	23.4	21.4	20.1	20.1
29/30 Non-electrical machinery	1 860	1 686	1 320	1 432	1 288	50.2	45.4	37.3	39.1	35.7
29 Non-electrical machinery nec	143	186	210	264	223	14.3	17.3	18.3	22.2	20.2
30 Office and computing machinery	1 717	1 500	1 110	1 168	1 065	63.4	56.8	46.5	47.2	42.6
31/32 Electrical & electronic equipment	2 051	2 025	2 308	2 383	2 617	18.2	16.7	17.2	15.5	16.6
31 Electrical machinery nec	226	227	213	294	259	39.6	37.5	30.3	39.8	43.4
32 Radio, TV & communications eq.	1 825	1 798	2 095	2 089	2 358	17.1	15.6	16.5	14.3	15.5
33 Scientific instruments	89	80	109	141	134	12.1	9.2	11.9	13.9	12.5
34/35 Transportation equipment	1 318	1 408	1 621	1 898	1 965	42.9	48.4	49.9	52.8	55.3
34 Motor vehicles	248	300	281	372	401	44.8	43.7	41.8	54.2	54.4
35 Other transport equipment	1 070	1 108	1 340	1 526	1 564	42.5	49.8	52.0	52.5	55.5
351 Shipbuilding & repairing	..	..	..	..	..	..	..	..	..	..
353 Aircraft and spacecraft	1 059	1 097	1 332	1 496	1 522	42.7	50.3	53.0	43.3	55.4
36/37 Other manufacturing	68	111	122	126	113	14.9	22.3	25.5	25.0	29.4
40/45 Construction, electricity, gas & water	46	54	43	37	40	4.3	5.3	4.2	4.2	5.3
50/55 Trade, repair, hotels & restaurants	877	1 146	1 255	1 398	1 761	18.3	23.1	27.1	29.1	39.3
65/74 Finance, insurance, business services	1 528	2 028	2 242	2 188	2 164	10.7	13.2	15.3	14.7	16.3
OTHER ACTIVITIES	55	53	41	43	46	15.6	13.8	12.1	13.2	16.8
01/99 **GRAND TOTAL**	**10 481**	**11 187**	**11 545**	**12 140**	**12 525**	**22.4**	**22.8**	**23.5**	**23.6**	**25.6**

Total manufacturing by investing country						As a % of total manufacturing by foreign affiliates				
All countries	**7 879**	**7 781**	**7 817**	**8 327**	**8 394**	**100.0**	**100.0**	**100.0**	**100.0**	**100.0**
United States	5 958	5 868	5 912	6 276	6 303	75.6	75.4	75.6	75.4	75.1
Canada	..	..	..	..	..	..	..	..	..	..
Mexico	..	..	..	..	..	..	..	..	..	..
Japan	79	77	94	168	169	1.0	1.0	1.2	2.0	2.0
Europe	1 730	1 728	1 675	1 746	1 836	22.0	22.2	21.4	21.0	21.9
European Union (15)	..	..	..	..	..	..	..	..	..	..
Belgium	..	..	..	..	..	..	..	..	..	..
France	..	..	..	..	..	..	..	..	..	..
Germany	..	..	..	..	..	..	..	..	..	..
Italy	..	..	..	..	..	..	..	..	..	..
Netherlands	..	..	..	..	..	..	..	..	..	..
Spain	..	..	..	..	..	..	..	..	..	..
Sweden	..	..	..	..	..	..	..	..	..	..
United Kingdom	..	..	..	..	..	..	..	..	..	..
Switzerland	..	..	..	..	..	..	..	..	..	..
Australia and New Zealand	..	..	..	..	..	..	..	..	..	..
Asia (non-OECD)	..	..	..	..	..	..	..	..	..	..
Latin America	..	..	..	..	..	..	..	..	..	..

Note: Majority foreign-owned firms.
Firmes sous contrôle étranger majoritaire.

Inward investments

Investissements entrants

Table 6A - Tableau 6A

GROSS OPERATING SURPLUS / EXCÉDENT BRUT D'EXPLOITATION

By industry (ISIC Rev. 3)		Foreign affiliates (Millions of CAD) Filiales étrangères (Millions de CAD)					As a % of national total En % du total national				
		1994	1995	1996	1997	1998	1994	1995	1996	1997	1998
10/14	Mining & quarrying	2 000	1 621	3 019	2 479	1 444	41.4	39.6	43.6	39.7	53.8
15/37	TOTAL MANUFACTURING	13 544	19 200	17 200	20 566	18 781	50.8	50.2	53.3	53.9	53.0
15/16	Food, beverages, tobacco	..	..	..	..	..	..	..	..	..	..
17/19	Textiles, clothing, leather, footwear	..	..	..	..	..	..	..	..	..	..
20/22	Wood and paper products	1 955	3 977	1 359	912	828	34.1	35.4	26.2	20.1	15.6
20	Wood products	1 518	2 654	938	584	464	35.7	37.1	35.9	35.7	23.1
21/22	Paper, printing and publishing	437	1 323	421	328	364	29.4	32.4	16.4	11.3	11.0
23/25	Chemicals, Total	3 785	4 775	4 814	5 299	3 876	68.5	69.8	70.1	64.8	64.6
23	Refined petroleum, nuclear fuel	1 870	2 079	2 156	2 870	1 887	62.9	60.9	61.8	59.6	59.2
24/25	Chemicals, rubber & plastics prod.	1 915	2 696	2 658	2 429	1 989	75.2	78.8	78.8	72.2	70.8
24	Chemical products	1 555	2 226	2 108	1 839	1 443	85.3	87.1	89.9	90.6	88.9
2423	Pharmaceuticals	..	..	..	..	..	..	..	..	..	..
25	Rubber and plastics products	360	470	550	590	546	49.7	54.1	53.4	44.3	46.1
26	Non-metallic mineral products	509	820	997	1 156	864	48.4	77.4	78.3	79.7	82.5
27/28	Basic & fabricated metals	569	1 130	1 036	844	1 130	23.8	31.4	30.7	22.4	30.3
27	Basic metals	355	795	643	401	719	23.7	31.3	29.9	17.5	33.1
28	Fabricated metal products	214	335	393	443	411	24.1	31.5	31.9	29.9	26.4
29/32	Machinery, Total	559	941	1 661	1 856	1 892	37.8	48.7	64.4	54.0	50.0
29/30	Non-electrical machinery	314	449	424	510	565	53.6	47.9	51.3	52.8	49.0
29	Non-electrical machinery nec	..	..	..	..	..	..	..	..	..	..
30	Office and computing machinery	..	..	..	..	..	..	..	..	..	..
31/32	Electrical & electronic equipment	244	493	1 236	1 346	1 327	27.4	49.5	70.5	54.4	50.4
31	Electrical machinery nec	131	251	242	289	346	76.2	80.2	78.3	80.7	79.4
32	Radio, TV & communications eq.	114	241	994	1 057	981	15.8	35.3	68.9	50.0	44.7
33	Scientific instruments	115	172	129	166	195	72.8	79.6	84.3	73.5	49.4
34/35	Transportation equipment	2 619	3 389	3 204	5 571	5 032	69.1	70.0	63.6	74.2	72.6
34	Motor vehicles	2 438	3 094	2 832	5 083	4 636	74.9	76.8	73.6	81.2	79.4
35	Other transport equipment	180	295	372	488	396	33.6	36.3	31.4	39.0	36.3
351	Shipbuilding & repairing	..	..	..	..	..	..	..	..	..	..
353	Aircraft and spacecraft	..	..	..	..	..	..	..	..	..	..
36/37	Other manufacturing	473	1 018	840	1 180	1 063	19.4	29.0	31.1	32.7	45.1
40/45	Construction, electricity, gas & water	256	147	318	412	362	1.8	1.0	2.2	2.7	2.1
50/55	Trade, repair, hotels & restaurants	2 645	2 841	3 667	5 128	5 578	16.2	16.0	19.6	23.8	22.8
65/74	Finance, insurance, business services	5 773	7 297	8 279	9 349	6 974	23.8	22.2	22.3	22.4	17.1
	OTHER ACTIVITIES	900	63	1 454	2 031	2 175	9.0	0.7	13.0	15.5	19.4
01/99	GRAND TOTAL	25 117	31 170	33 936	39 966	35 314	26.0	26.7	28.1	29.4	26.8

Total manufacturing by investing country	1994	1995	1996	1997	1998	As a % of total manufacturing by foreign affiliates				
						1994	1995	1996	1997	1998
All countries	13 544	19 200	17 200	20 566	18 781	100.0	100.0	100.0	100.0	100.0
United States	9 377	13 303	11 720	13 876	13 586	69.2	69.3	68.1	67.5	72.3
Canada	..	..	..	..	..	..	..	..	..	..
Mexico	..	..	..	..	..	..	..	..	..	..
Japan	363	629	366	628	498	2.7	3.3	2.1	3.1	2.7
Europe	3 019	3 945	4 111	4 765	..	22.3	20.5	23.9	23.2	..
European Union (15)	2 859	3 800	3 921	4 842	3 920	21.1	19.8	22.8	23.5	20.9
Belgium	..	..	..	..	..	..	..	..	..	..
France	327	381	436	591	381	2.4	2.0	2.5	2.9	2.0
Germany	548	741	763	935	719	4.0	3.9	4.4	4.5	3.8
Italy	44	91	92	143	..	0.3	0.5	0.5	0.7	..
Netherlands	625	816	672	1 007	721	4.6	4.3	3.9	4.9	3.8
Spain	..	..	..	..	..	..	..	..	..	..
Sweden	54	224	144	192	..	0.4	1.2	0.8	0.9	..
United Kingdom	1 152	1 349	1 489	1 576	1 439	8.5	7.0	8.7	7.7	7.7
Switzerland	148	104	189	247	184	1.1	0.5	1.1	1.2	1.0
Australia and New Zealand	411	643	228	135	..	3.0	3.3	1.3	0.7	..
Asia (non-OECD)	158	389	426	430	310	1.2	2.0	2.5	2.1	1.7
Latin America	..	..	49	64	76	..	..	0.3	0.3	0.4

Note: Majority foreign-owned firms.
Firmes sous contrôle étranger majoritaire.

Table 7A - Tableau 7A

CAPITAL UNDER FOREIGN INFLUENCE / CAPITAL SOUS INFLUENCE ÉTRANGÈRE

| | | Foreign affiliates *(Millions of CAD)* | | | | | | | | |
| | | Filiales étrangères *(Millions de CAD)* | | | | | | | | |
By industry (ISIC Rev. 3)		1989	1990	1991	1992	1993	1994	1995	1996	1997	1998
10/14	Mining & quarrying	..	..	..	..	30 075	32 933	34 791	38 613	49 580	59 653
15/37	**TOTAL MANUFACTURING**	..	..	..	..	**169 853**	**175 732**	**194 110**	**206 736**	**217 176**	**241 787**
15/16	Food, beverages, tobacco	..	..	..	..	..	..	..	..	..	..
17/19	Textiles, clothing, leather, footwear	..	..	..	..	..	..	..	..	..	..
20/22	Wood and paper products	..	..	..	..	23 411	24 945	29 458	29 690	28 185	29 145
20	Wood products	..	..	..	..	14 321	15 452	19 725	16 477	13 108	15 070
21/22	Paper, printing and publishing	..	..	..	..	9 090	9 493	9 733	13 213	15 077	14 075
23/25	Chemicals, Total	..	..	..	..	48 829	49 377	50 288	52 188	57 287	53 948
23	Refined petroleum, nuclear fuel	..	..	..	..	28 108	28 022	26 643	26 827	31 326	26 162
24/25	Chemicals, rubber & plastics prod.	..	..	..	..	20 721	21 355	23 646	25 361	25 961	27 786
24	Chemical products	..	..	..	..	15 595	16 473	18 098	19 170	20 177	21 050
2423	Pharmaceuticals	..	..	..	..	..	..	..	..	..	..
25	Rubber and plastics products	..	..	..	..	5 126	4 880	5 548	6 191	5 784	6 736
26	Non-metallic mineral products	..	..	..	..	7 431	7 982	8 405	9 240	10 650	11 730
27/28	Basic & fabricated metals	..	..	..	..	10 591	12 483	13 228	14 073	12 335	15 200
27	Basic metals	..	..	..	..	5 949	7 106	7 585	8 541	7 154	9 914
28	Fabricated metal products	..	..	..	..	4 642	5 377	5 643	5 532	5 181	5 286
29/32	Machinery, Total	..	..	..	..	10 431	10 928	11 151	15 123	15 726	18 262
29/30	Non-electrical machinery	..	..	..	..	3 345	4 201	4 567	4 634	4 973	5 426
29	Non-electrical machinery nec	..	..	..	..	..	..	..	..	..	..
30	Office and computing machinery	..	..	..	..	..	..	..	..	..	..
31/32	Electrical & electronic equipment	..	..	..	..	7 086	6 727	6 584	10 489	10 753	12 836
31	Electrical machinery nec	..	..	..	..	4 732	4 642	3 321	3 286	3 097	3 506
32	Radio, TV & communications eq.	..	..	..	..	2 354	2 086	3 262	7 203	7 657	9 330
33	Scientific instruments	..	..	..	..	1 438	1 408	1 603	1 440	1 573	1 677
34/35	Transportation equipment	..	..	..	..	31 295	33 033	37 439	40 629	45 306	49 893
34	Motor vehicles	..	..	..	..	28 205	29 983	34 099	37 084	41 415	45 357
35	Other transport equipment	..	..	..	..	3 090	3 050	3 340	3 546	3 890	4 536
351	Shipbuilding & repairing	..	..	..	..	..	..	..	..	..	..
353	Aircraft and spacecraft	..	..	..	..	..	..	..	..	..	..
36/37	Other manufacturing	..	..	..	..	9 638	7 691	14 189	11 412	11 321	12 682
40/45	Construction, electricity, gas & water	..	..	..	..	9 117	7 925	8 275	9 938	9 529	11 026
50/55	Trade, repair, hotels & restaurants	..	..	..	..	46 625	52 478	57 567	64 150	72 395	85 396
65/74	Finance, insurance, business services	..	..	..	..	229 803	243 399	254 927	292 812	305 199	331 269
	OTHER ACTIVITIES	..	..	..	..	9 680	10 067	17 203	18 332	20 579	24 319
01/99	**GRAND TOTAL**	..	..	..	..	**495 153**	**522 533**	**566 873**	**630 582**	**674 458**	**753 450**

Total manufacturing by investing country

	1989	1990	1991	1992	1993	1994	1995	1996	1997	1998
All countries	..	..	..	..	**169 853**	**175 732**	**194 110**	**206 736**	**217 176**	**241 787**
United States	..	..	..	..	102 025	109 739	125 715	130 942	132 954	157 798
Canada	..	..	..	..	..	..	..	..	..	..
Mexico	..	..	..	..	..	..	..	..	..	..
Japan	..	..	..	..	8 225	8 238	8 477	9 284	10 550	11 296
Europe										
European Union (15)	..	..	..	..	44 972	42 213	43 782	49 246	52 835	54 176
Belgium	..	..	..	..	..	..	..	..	..	..
France	..	..	..	..	8 143	8 494	8 340	8 974	9 000	9 727
Germany	..	..	..	..	5 854	5 937	6 473	6 408	7 871	7 683
Italy	..	..	..	..	..	..	..	..	..	..
Netherlands	..	..	..	..	7 509	7 467	8 053	8 299	8 157	8 501
Spain	..	..	..	..	..	..	..	..	..	..
Sweden	..	..	..	..	..	..	..	..	..	..
United Kingdom	..	..	..	..	16 994	17 100	16 665	17 447	17 454	17 410
Switzerland	..	..	..	..	2 915	3 079	2 892	2 996	3 394	4 223
Australia and New Zealand	..	..	..	..	..	..	..	..	..	..
Asia (non-OECD)	..	..	..	..	3 792	4 383	4 541	4 716	8 708	6 189
Latin America	..	..	..	..	..	..	..	405	431	564

Note: Majority foreign-owned firms.
Firmes sous contrôle étranger majoritaire.

Table 8A - Tableau 8A

TOTAL EXPORTS / EXPORTATIONS TOTALES

By industry (ISIC Rev. 3)	Foreign affiliates *(Millions of CAD)* Filiales étrangères *(Millions de CAD)*					As a % of national total En % du total national				
	1994	1995	1996	1997	1998	1994	1995	1996	1997	1998
10/14 Mining & quarrying	9 223	11 023	..	..	..	..	..	..	..	..
15/37 TOTAL MANUFACTURING	**91 957**	**102 405**	..	..	..	..	..	..	..	..
15/16 Food, beverages, tobacco	2 032	2 075	..	..	..	..	..	..	..	..
17/19 Textiles, clothing, leather, footwear	1 714	1 791	..	..	..	..	..	..	..	..
20/22 Wood and paper products	9 758	12 196	..	..	..	..	..	..	..	..
20 Wood products	7 309	9 454	..	..	..	..	..	..	..	..
21/22 Paper, printing and publishing	2 449	2 743	..	..	..	..	..	..	..	..
23/25 Chemicals, Total	7 367	8 289	..	..	..	..	..	..	..	..
23 Refined petroleum, nuclear fuel	2 595	2 689	..	..	..	..	..	..	..	..
24/25 Chemicals, rubber & plastics prod.	4 773	5 601	..	..	..	..	..	..	..	..
24 Chemical products	2 831	2 666	..	..	..	..	..	..	..	..
2423 Pharmaceuticals	..	..	..	..	..	..	..	..	..	..
25 Rubber and plastics products	1 942	2 935	..	..	..	..	..	..	..	..
26 Non-metallic mineral products	1 498	2 604	..	..	..	..	..	..	..	..
27/28 Basic & fabricated metals	3 728	4 673	..	..	..	..	..	..	..	..
27 Basic metals	754	987	..	..	..	..	..	..	..	..
28 Fabricated metal products	2 974	3 686	..	..	..	..	..	..	..	..
29/32 Machinery, Total	6 434	8 035	..	..	..	..	..	..	..	..
29/30 Non-electrical machinery	4 002	5 342	..	..	..	..	..	..	..	..
29 Non-electrical machinery nec	..	..	..	..	..	..	..	..	..	..
30 Office and computing machinery	..	..	..	..	..	..	..	..	..	..
31/32 Electrical & electronic equipment	2 432	2 693	..	..	..	..	..	..	..	..
31 Electrical machinery nec	1 553	1 693	..	..	..	..	..	..	..	..
32 Radio, TV & communications eq.	879	1 000	..	..	..	..	..	..	..	..
33 Scientific instruments	630	670	..	..	..	..	..	..	..	..
34/35 Transportation equipment	56 269	59 250	..	..	..	..	..	..	..	..
34 Motor vehicles	53 583	56 386	..	..	..	..	..	..	..	..
35 Other transport equipment	2 686	2 864	..	..	..	..	..	..	..	..
351 Shipbuilding & repairing	..	..	..	..	..	..	..	..	..	..
353 Aircraft and spacecraft	..	..	..	..	..	..	..	..	..	..
36/37 Other manufacturing	2 528	2 822	..	..	..	..	..	..	..	..
40/45 Construction, electricity, gas & water	696	645	..	..	..	..	..	..	..	..
50/55 Trade, repair, hotels & restaurants	4 576	6 133	..	..	..	..	..	..	..	..
65/74 Finance, insurance, business services	6 758	8 123	..	..	..	..	..	..	..	..
OTHER ACTIVITIES	1 754	1 985	..	..	..	..	..	..	..	..
01/99 GRAND TOTAL	**114 031**	**130 313**	..	..	..	..	..	..	..	..

Total manufacturing by investing country						As a % of total manufacturing by foreign affiliates				
All countries	**91 957**	**102 405**	..	..	..	**100.0**	**100.0**	..	..	..
United States	75 824	84 096	..	..	..	82.5	82.1	..	..	..
Canada	..	..	..	..	..	..	..	..	..	..
Mexico	..	..	..	..	..	..	..	..	..	..
Japan	4 241	4 629	..	..	..	4.6	4.5	..	..	..
Europe	9 124	10 759	..	..	..	9.9	10.5	..	..	..
European Union (15)	7 608	8 877	..	..	..	8.3	8.7	..	..	..
Belgium	..	..	..	..	..	..	..	..	..	..
France	1 700	1 934	..	..	..	1.8	1.9	..	..	..
Germany	2 172	2 803	..	..	..	2.4	2.7	..	..	..
Italy	807	1 082	..	..	..	0.9	1.1	..	..	..
Netherlands	315	585	..	..	..	0.3	0.6	..	..	..
Spain	..	..	..	..	..	..	..	..	..	..
Sweden	..	..	..	..	..	..	..	..	..	..
United Kingdom	2 558	2 580	..	..	..	2.8	2.5	..	..	..
Switzerland	432	487	..	..	..	0.5	0.5	..	..	..
Australia and New Zealand	1 099	1 463	..	..	..	1.2	1.4	..	..	..
Asia (non-OECD)	442	730	..	..	..	0.5	0.7	..	..	..
Latin America	..	..	..	..	..	..	..	..	..	..

Note: Majority foreign-owned firms.
Firmes sous contrôle étranger majoritaire.

Inward investments   *Investissements entrants*

Table 9A - Tableau 9A

INTRA-FIRM EXPORTS / EXPORTATIONS INTRA-FIRME

| | | Foreign affiliates *(Millions of CAD)* | | | | | | | | | |
| | | Filiales étrangères *(Millions de CAD)* | | | | | | | | | |
By industry (ISIC Rev. 3)		1989	1990	1991	1992	1993	1994	1995	1996	1997	1998
10/14	Mining & quarrying	..	..	1 184	1 464	1 443	2 953	..	..	..	..
15/37	**TOTAL MANUFACTURING**	..	..	**34 636**	**40 264**	**48 081**	**55 773**	..	..	..	..
15/16	Food, beverages, tobacco	..	..	486	564	571	669	..	..	..	..
17/19	Textiles, clothing, leather, footwear	..	..	428	475	643	802	..	..	..	..
20/22	Wood and paper products	..	..	999	984	1 350	1 325	..	..	..	..
20	Wood products	..	..	696	650	824	746	..	..	..	..
21/22	Paper, printing and publishing	..	..	303	334	526	579	..	..	..	..
23/25	Chemicals, Total	..	..	2 631	2 960	3 350	3 736	..	..	..	..
23	Refined petroleum, nuclear fuel	..	..	1 009	1 036	1 166	1 126	..	..	..	..
24/25	Chemicals, rubber & plastics prod.	..	..	1 622	1 925	2 184	2 611	..	..	..	..
24	Chemical products	..	..	996	1 215	1 288	1 519	..	..	..	..
2423	Pharmaceuticals	..	..	..	..	..	..	..	..	..	..
25	Rubber and plastics products	..	..	626	709	896	1 092	..	..	..	..
26	Non-metallic mineral products	..	..	460	471	612	728	..	..	..	..
27/28	Basic & fabricated metals	..	..	917	910	944	1 342	..	..	..	..
27	Basic metals	..	..	102	62	133	182	..	..	..	..
28	Fabricated metal products	..	..	815	848	811	1 160	..	..	..	..
29/32	Machinery, Total	..	..	2 058	2 002	2 290	3 197	..	..	..	..
29/30	Non-electrical machinery	..	..	1 367	1 223	1 472	2 363	..	..	..	..
29	Non-electrical machinery nec	..	..	..	..	..	..	..	..	..	..
30	Office and computing machinery	..	..	..	..	..	..	..	..	..	..
31/32	Electrical & electronic equipment	..	..	691	779	818	835	..	..	..	..
31	Electrical machinery nec	..	..	450	530	580	615	..	..	..	..
32	Radio, TV & communications eq.	..	..	241	249	238	220	..	..	..	..
33	Scientific instruments	..	..	234	315	363	380	..	..	..	..
34/35	Transportation equipment	..	..	26 067	31 181	37 356	42 787	..	..	..	..
34	Motor vehicles	..	..	25 220	30 326	36 620	41 996	..	..	..	..
35	Other transport equipment	..	..	847	855	736	791	..	..	..	..
351	Shipbuilding & repairing	..	..	..	..	..	..	..	..	..	..
353	Aircraft and spacecraft	..	..	..	..	..	..	..	..	..	..
36/37	Other manufacturing	..	..	357	402	604	807	..	..	..	..
40/45	Construction, electricity, gas & water	..	..	..	..	..	..	..	..	..	..
50/55	Trade, repair, hotels & restaurants	..	..	856	1 034	1 203	1 044	..	..	..	..
65/74	Finance, insurance, business services	..	..	..	..	..	..	..	..	..	..
	OTHER ACTIVITIES	..	..	36	63	130	213	..	..	..	..
01/99	**GRAND TOTAL**	..	..	**42 021**	**47 209**	**55 107**	**65 209**	..	..	..	..

Total manufacturing by investing country

	1989	1990	1991	1992	1993	1994	1995	1996	1997	1998
All countries	..	..	**34 636**	**40 264**	**48 081**	**55 773**	..	..	..	..
United States	..	..	31 327	37 049	43 917	50 006	..	..	..	..
Canada	..	..	..	..	..	..	..	..	..	..
Mexico	..	..	..	..	..	..	..	..	..	..
Japan	..	..	959	703	1 300	2 651	..	..	..	..
Europe	..	..	1 959	2 123	2 470	2 771	..	..	..	..
European Union (15)	..	..	1 213	1 416	1 700	1 846	..	..	..	..
Belgium	..	..	..	..	..	..	..	..	..	..
France	..	..	669	832	865	731	..	..	..	..
Germany	..	..	295	355	600	730	..	..	..	..
Italy	..	..	..	..	..	..	..	..	..	..
Netherlands	..	..	..	..	..	..	..	..	..	..
Spain	..	..	..	..	..	..	..	..	..	..
Sweden	..	..	..	..	..	..	..	..	..	..
United Kingdom	..	..	431	359	377	419	..	..	..	..
Switzerland	..	..	142	169	190	176	..	..	..	..
Australia and New Zealand	..	..	152	169	170	229	..	..	..	..
Asia (non-OECD)	..	..	217	191	218	108	..	..	..	..
Latin America	..	..	..	..	..	..	..	..	..	..

Note: Majority foreign-owned firms.
       Firmes sous contrôle étranger majoritaire.

CANADA

Source

For *Number of enterprises*, *Production* and *Gross operating surplus*, the data are prepared by the Industrial Organisation and Finance Division of Statistics Canada.

From reference period 1997, ownership and control information is obtained primarily through ownership returns filed by corporations liable under the Corporations Returns Act (CRA). Additional ownership information is obtained from both Canadian and international publications. The results of this survey are reported in the publication entitled *Corporations Returns Act, Foreign Control in the Canadian Economy* (Catalogue 61-220-XPB).

Financial information for large, non-government business enterprises is provided by Statistics Canada's *Quarterly Financial Survey of Enterprises* (Catalogue 61-008). Financial estimates for smaller firms are based on corporate tax data from Revenue Canada.

For *R&D expenditure* and *Number of researchers*, the data come from the industrial R&D survey carried out by the Science, Innovation and Electronic Information Division of Statistics Canada. The legal entity (firm) is the basic unit. The data are published in the annual report *Industrial Research and Development* (Catalogue 88-202-XIB).

For all variables, the data refer to majority foreign-owned enterprises.

National totals: provided by Statistics Canada and fully compatible with foreign affiliates' data.

Industrial classification

For all variables, the data are classified according to the principal industrial activity of the affiliate.

The industrial classification used for the Canadian tables is the national classification converted to ISIC Revision 3.

Variables

- *Production* is defined as the operating revenue, *i.e.* the revenue derived from the sales of goods and services.

- *R&D expenditure* refer to expenditure by the affiliate itself.

- *Number of researchers* refers to scientists and engineers engaged in research and development as well as senior R&D administrators. It is expressed in full-time equivalent.

- *Gross operating surplus* corresponds to operating profit.

Geographical breakdown

In most cases of foreign control, the country of control classification is the country of residence of the ultimate foreign parent corporation. A company whose voting rights are owned equally by Canadian and foreign-controlled corporations is given to the country of control code of the foreign-controlled owner. If two foreign-controlled corporations jointly own an equal amount of the voting rights of a Canadian resident company, the country of control is assigned according to an order of precedence of the countries of control based on their aggregate level of foreign direct investment in Canada (*i.e.* the United States takes precedence, followed by the United Kingdom, etc.).

CANADA

Source

Pour le *Nombre d'entreprises*, la *Production* et l'*Excédent brut d'exploitation*, les données émanent de la Division de l'Organisation et des Finances de l'Industrie de Statistique Canada.

A compter de l'année de référence 1997, les données sur la propriété et le contrôle proviennent principalement des déclarations de propriété de capital-actions soumises par les personnes morales (sociétés) assujetties à la Loi sur les Déclarations des Personnes Morales (LDPM). Des renseignements complémentaires sur la propriété sont également tirés d'un certain nombre de publications canadiennes et internationales. Les résultats de cette enquête sont rapportés dans la publication *Loi sur les déclarations des personnes morales, contrôle étranger de l'économie canadienne* (61-220-XPB au catalogue).

Les données financières relatives aux grandes entreprises non publiques sont tirées de l'Enquête financière trimestrielle de Statistique Canada (61-008 au catalogue). Les estimations financières relatives aux plus petites sociétés sont fondées sur les données fiscales de Revenu Canada.

Pour les *Dépenses de R-D* et *le Nombre de chercheurs*, les données proviennent de l'enquête sur la R-D industrielle menée par la Division de la Science, de l'Innovation et de l'Information Électronique de Statistique Canada. L'unité de base est l'entité légale (société). Les données sont publiées dans le rapport annuel *Recherche et développement industriels* (88-202-XIB au catalogue).

Pour toutes les variables, les données font référence aux entreprises dans lesquelles la participation étrangère dépasse 50 % des actions avec droit de vote.

Totaux nationaux : fournis par Statistique Canada et entièrement compatibles avec les données relatives aux filiales étrangères.

Classification industrielle

Pour toutes les variables, les données sont classées selon l'activité industrielle principale de l'entreprise affiliée.

La classification industrielle utilisée pour les tableaux canadiens est la classification nationale adaptée pour correspondre à la CITI révision 3.

Variables

- La *Production* est définie par le revenu d'exploitation, c'est-à-dire le revenu provenant de la vente de biens et services.

- Les *Dépenses de R-D* concernent les dépenses effectuées par les filiales pour elles-mêmes.

- Le *Nombre de chercheurs* fait référence aux scientifiques et ingénieurs travaillant dans la recherche-développement, ainsi qu'aux administrateurs seniors de R-D. Il est exprimé en équivalent plein-temps.

- L'*Excédent brut d'exploitation* correspond au bénéfice d'exploitation.

Ventilation géographique

Dans la plupart des cas, le pays d'origine est celui de la société mère étrangère bénéficiaire ultime. Une entreprise pour laquelle les droits de vote sont répartis également entre des sociétés canadiennes et étrangères est classée selon le pays du contrôleur étranger. Si deux sociétés étrangères détiennent des droits de vote équivalents sur une entreprise résidant au Canada, le pays d'origine est attribué selon un ordre de priorité des pays fondé sur leur niveau agrégé d'investissement direct au Canada (*i.e.* les États-Unis ont la priorité, suivis par le Royaume-Uni, etc.).

CZECH REPUBLIC

Sources and Methods

RÉPUBLIQUE TCHÈQUE

Sources et méthodes

Table 1A - Tableau 1A

NUMBER OF ENTERPRISES / NOMBRE D'ENTREPRISES

		Foreign affiliates *(Units)* Filiales étrangères *(Unités)*					As a % of national total En % du total national				
By industry (ISIC Rev. 3)		1995	1996	1997	1998	1999	1995	1996	1997	1998	1999
10/14	Mining & quarrying	..	..	9	14	14	..	..	2.9	5.2	4.7
15/37	**TOTAL MANUFACTURING**	..	..	**1 717**	**1 634**	**2 082**	..	..	**1.2**	**1.3**	**1.5**
15/16	Food, beverages, tobacco	..	..	74	80	133	..	..	1.2	1.2	2.2
17/19	Textiles, clothing, leather, footwear	..	..	175	197	399	..	..	1.0	1.3	2.4
20/22	Wood and paper products	..	..	193	202	200	..	..	0.6	0.7	0.7
20	Wood products	..	..	111	85	106	..	..	0.5	0.4	0.5
21/22	Paper, printing and publishing	..	..	82	117	94	..	..	1.3	1.8	1.4
23/25	Chemicals, Total	..	..	..	..	..	..	..	..	..	..
23	Refined petroleum, nuclear fuel	..	..	..	..	..	..	..	..	..	..
24/25	Chemicals, rubber & plastics prod.	..	..	223	169	206	..	..	4.7	4.3	4.4
24	Chemical products	..	..	44	28	45	..	..	4.1	1.8	3.1
2423	Pharmaceuticals	..	..	..	..	..	..	..	..	..	..
25	Rubber and plastics products	..	..	179	141	161	..	..	4.9	6.0	5.0
26	Non-metallic mineral products	..	..	85	140	84	..	..	1.2	2.2	1.3
27/28	Basic & fabricated metals	..	..	393	298	333	..	..	1.1	1.0	1.0
27	Basic metals	..	..	13	19	22	..	..	2.6	4.5	5.9
28	Fabricated metal products	..	..	380	279	311	..	..	1.0	1.0	1.0
29/32	Machinery, Total	..	..	..	..	..	..	..	..	..	..
29/30	Non-electrical machinery	..	..	..	..	..	..	..	..	..	..
29	Non-electrical machinery nec	..	..	164	213	231	..	..	2.1	3.5	3.8
30	Office and computing machinery	..	..	..	..	..	..	..	..	..	..
31/32	Electrical & electronic equipment	..	..	207	160	203	..	..	1.5	1.1	1.3
31	Electrical machinery nec	..	..	176	110	167	..	..	1.8	0.8	1.2
32	Radio, TV & communications eq.	..	..	31	50	36	..	..	0.7	2.3	1.6
33	Scientific instruments	..	..	50	57	88	..	..	1.1	1.6	2.2
34/35	Transportation equipment	..	..	42	52	63	..	..	5.7	4.9	9.5
34	Motor vehicles	..	..	33	44	55	..	..	9.6	6.4	19.1
35	Other transport equipment	..	..	9	8	8	..	..	2.3	2.1	2.2
351	Shipbuilding & repairing	..	..	..	..	..	..	..	..	..	..
353	Aircraft and spacecraft	..	..	..	..	..	..	..	..	..	..
36/37	Other manufacturing	..	..	103	61	133	..	..	0.7	0.4	0.9
40/45	Construction, electricity, gas & water	..	..	566	220	702	..	..	0.5	0.2	0.6
50/55	Trade, repair, hotels & restaurants	..	..	5 702	7 000	5 489	..	..	2.4	2.6	2.2
65/74	Finance, insurance, business services	..	..	2 545	2 601	3 609	..	..	1.5	1.4	1.8
	OTHER ACTIVITIES	..	..	568	627	581	..	..	0.4	0.4	0.4
01/99	**GRAND TOTAL**	..	..	**11 107**	**12 096**	**12 477**	..	..	**1.4**	**1.4**	**1.4**

Total manufacturing by investing country							*As a % of total manufacturing by foreign affiliates*				
All countries		..	..	1 717	1 634	2 082	..	..	100.0	100.0	100.0
United States		..	..	..	..	..	..	..	..	..	..
Canada		..	..	..	..	..	..	..	..	..	..
Mexico		..	..	..	..	..	..	..	..	..	..
Japan		..	..	..	..	..	..	..	..	..	..
Europe		..	..	..	..	..	..	..	..	..	..
European Union (15)		..	..	..	..	..	..	..	..	..	..
Belgium		..	..	..	..	..	..	..	..	..	..
France		..	..	..	..	..	..	..	..	..	..
Germany		..	..	..	..	..	..	..	..	..	..
Italy		..	..	..	..	..	..	..	..	..	..
Netherlands		..	..	..	..	..	..	..	..	..	..
Spain		..	..	..	..	..	..	..	..	..	..
Sweden		..	..	..	..	..	..	..	..	..	..
United Kingdom		..	..	..	..	..	..	..	..	..	..
Switzerland		..	..	..	..	..	..	..	..	..	..
Australia and New Zealand		..	..	..	..	..	..	..	..	..	..
Asia (non-OECD)		..	..	..	..	..	..	..	..	..	..
Latin America		..	..	..	..	..	..	..	..	..	..

Note: Majority foreign-owned enterprises.
Entreprises sous contrôle étranger majoritaire.

Inward investments

Investissements entrants

Table 2A - Tableau 2A

NUMBER OF EMPLOYEES / NOMBRE DE SALARIÉS

By industry (ISIC Rev. 3)	Foreign affiliates (Units) Filiales étrangères (Unités)					As a % of national total En % du total national				
	1995	1996	1997	1998	1999	1995	1996	1997	1998	1999
10/14 Mining & quarrying	..	..	0	0	0	..	..	0.0	0.0	0.0
15/37 TOTAL MANUFACTURING	..	..	**144 000**	**172 000**	**203 000**	..	..	**10.7**	**13.2**	**16.2**
15/16 Food, beverages, tobacco	..	..	10 000	11 000	17 000	..	..	6.1	7.0	11.4
17/19 Textiles, clothing, leather, footwear	..	..	13 000	16 000	21 000	..	..	8.1	10.5	14.4
20/22 Wood and paper products	..	..	11 000	12 000	14 000	..	..	10.0	11.2	13.9
20 Wood products	..	..	5 000	5 000	6 000	..	..	9.4	9.8	12.8
21/22 Paper, printing and publishing	..	..	6 000	7 000	8 000	..	..	10.5	12.5	14.8
23/25 Chemicals, Total	..	..	..	..	..	..	..	..	..	..
23 Refined petroleum, nuclear fuel	..	..	..	..	..	..	..	..	..	..
24/25 Chemicals, rubber & plastics prod.	..	..	14 000	16 000	16 000	..	..	14.0	16.3	16.3
24 Chemical products	..	..	3 000	4 000	4 000	..	..	6.1	8.5	8.7
2423 Pharmaceuticals	..	..	..	..	..	..	..	..	..	..
25 Rubber and plastics products	..	..	11 000	12 000	12 000	..	..	21.6	23.5	23.1
26 Non-metallic mineral products	..	..	7 000	8 000	9 000	..	..	8.3	9.8	11.3
27/28 Basic & fabricated metals	..	..	17 000	21 000	20 000	..	..	7.3	9.0	9.2
27 Basic metals	..	..	2 000	4 000	3 000	..	..	2.0	4.4	3.6
28 Fabricated metal products	..	..	15 000	17 000	17 000	..	..	11.3	11.8	12.6
29/32 Machinery, Total	..	..	..	..	..	..	..	..	..	..
29/30 Non-electrical machinery	..	..	..	..	..	..	..	..	..	..
29 Non-electrical machinery nec	..	..	11 000	12 000	17 000	..	..	6.1	7.4	10.9
30 Office and computing machinery	..	..	..	..	..	..	..	..	..	..
31/32 Electrical & electronic equipment	..	..	21 000	29 000	34 000	..	..	20.2	27.6	32.4
31 Electrical machinery nec	..	..	17 000	22 000	25 000	..	..	21.3	27.8	31.3
32 Radio, TV & communications eq.	..	..	4 000	7 000	9 000	..	..	16.7	26.9	36.0
33 Scientific instruments	..	..	4 000	5 000	5 000	..	..	13.8	17.2	18.5
34/35 Transportation equipment	..	..	28 000	34 000	39 000	..	..	28.9	35.8	41.1
34 Motor vehicles	..	..	27 000	33 000	38 000	..	..	43.5	49.3	55.1
35 Other transport equipment	..	..	1 000	1 000	1 000	..	..	2.9	3.6	3.8
351 Shipbuilding & repairing	..	..	..	..	..	..	..	..	..	..
353 Aircraft and spacecraft	..	..	..	..	..	..	..	..	..	..
36/37 Other manufacturing	..	..	7 000	7 000	10 000	..	..	8.9	9.2	13.5
40/45 Construction, electricity, gas & water	..	..	6 000	5 000	11 000	..	..	1.3	1.2	2.9
50/55 Trade, repair, hotels & restaurants	..	..	66 000	85 000	90 000	..	..	10.4	13.9	14.8
65/74 Finance, insurance, business services	..	..	29 000	33 000	39 000	..	..	8.6	9.9	12.0
OTHER ACTIVITIES	..	..	8 000	9 000	13 000	..	..	1.2	1.4	2.1
01/99 GRAND TOTAL	..	..	**253 000**	**304 000**	**356 000**	..	..	**7.2**	**9.0**	**11.0**

Total manufacturing by investing country						As a % of total manufacturing by foreign affiliates				
All countries	..	..	**144 000**	**172 000**	**203 000**	..	..	**100.0**	**100.0**	**100.0**
United States	..	..	..	..	..	..	..	..	..	..
Canada	..	..	..	..	..	..	..	..	..	..
Mexico	..	..	..	..	..	..	..	..	..	..
Japan	..	..	..	..	..	..	..	..	..	..
Europe	..	..	..	..	..	..	..	..	..	..
European Union (15)	..	..	..	..	..	..	..	..	..	..
Belgium	..	..	..	..	..	..	..	..	..	..
France	..	..	..	..	..	..	..	..	..	..
Germany	..	..	..	..	..	..	..	..	..	..
Italy	..	..	..	..	..	..	..	..	..	..
Netherlands	..	..	..	..	..	..	..	..	..	..
Spain	..	..	..	..	..	..	..	..	..	..
Sweden	..	..	..	..	..	..	..	..	..	..
United Kingdom	..	..	..	..	..	..	..	..	..	..
Switzerland	..	..	..	..	..	..	..	..	..	..
Australia and New Zealand	..	..	..	..	..	..	..	..	..	..
Asia (non-OECD)	..	..	..	..	..	..	..	..	..	..
Latin America	..	..	..	..	..	..	..	..	..	..

Note: Majority foreign-owned enterprises.
Entreprises sous contrôle étranger majoritaire.

Table 3A - Tableau 3A

PRODUCTION

By industry (ISIC Rev. 3)	Foreign affiliates (Millions of CZK) Filiales étrangères (Millions de CZK)					As a % of national total En % du total national				
	1995	1996	1997	1998	1999	1995	1996	1997	1998	1999
10/14 Mining & quarrying	..	..	619	712	1 021	..	..	1.0	1.2	1.8
15/37 **TOTAL MANUFACTURING**	..	..	**271 566**	**352 150**	**438 637**	..	..	**17.9**	**21.8**	**27.6**
15/16 Food, beverages, tobacco	..	..	34 870	37 818	51 489	..	..	13.0	13.9	19.8
17/19 Textiles, clothing, leather, footwear	..	..	7 829	10 585	15 538	..	..	9.6	12.8	18.6
20/22 Wood and paper products	..	..	18 950	20 177	27 917	..	..	15.5	15.0	21.0
20 Wood products	..	..	5 211	5 235	11 359	..	..	11.8	11.0	23.2
21/22 Paper, printing and publishing	..	..	13 739	14 942	16 558	..	..	17.6	17.2	19.7
23/25 Chemicals, Total	..	..	..	..	..	..	..	..	..	..
23 Refined petroleum, nuclear fuel	..	..	..	..	..	..	..	..	..	..
24/25 Chemicals, rubber & plastics prod.	..	..	25 718	32 292	33 701	..	..	16.5	19.5	19.8
24 Chemical products	..	..	6 507	7 177	6 311	..	..	6.7	7.1	6.3
2423 Pharmaceuticals	..	..	..	..	..	..	..	..	..	..
25 Rubber and plastics products	..	..	19 211	25 115	27 390	..	..	32.7	38.7	39.2
26 Non-metallic mineral products	..	..	11 985	14 222	19 956	..	..	13.9	15.8	20.8
27/28 Basic & fabricated metals	..	..	25 790	41 439	39 639	..	..	9.4	14.1	15.5
27 Basic metals	..	..	5 029	8 361	10 527	..	..	3.4	5.4	8.5
28 Fabricated metal products	..	..	20 761	33 078	29 112	..	..	16.4	23.6	22.1
29/32 Machinery, Total	..	..	..	..	..	..	..	..	..	..
29/30 Non-electrical machinery	..	..	..	..	..	..	..	..	..	..
29 Non-electrical machinery nec	..	..	13 774	17 225	22 932	..	..	9.8	11.0	17.5
30 Office and computing machinery	..	..	..	..	..	..	..	..	..	..
31/32 Electrical & electronic equipment	..	..	17 940	28 865	41 850	..	..	19.4	27.3	37.3
31 Electrical machinery nec	..	..	15 499	23 001	29 520	..	..	21.4	28.1	35.1
32 Radio, TV & communications eq.	..	..	2 441	5 864	12 330	..	..	12.4	24.8	44.0
33 Scientific instruments	..	..	3 707	6 320	8 690	..	..	17.1	24.0	33.3
34/35 Transportation equipment	..	..	98 631	127 504	157 253	..	..	59.5	68.2	75.1
34 Motor vehicles	..	..	98 005	126 855	156 551	..	..	69.3	75.3	82.4
35 Other transport equipment	..	..	626	649	702	..	..	2.6	3.5	3.6
351 Shipbuilding & repairing	..	..	..	..	..	..	..	..	..	..
353 Aircraft and spacecraft	..	..	..	..	..	..	..	..	..	..
36/37 Other manufacturing	..	..	12 219	13 781	16 452	..	..	20.0	22.4	25.1
40/45 Construction, electricity, gas & water	..	..	8 409	9 791	24 523	..	..	1.3	1.5	3.8
50/55 Trade, repair, hotels & restaurants	..	..	89 062	110 640	123 126	..	..	20.3	23.8	26.7
65/74 Finance, insurance, business services	..	..	63 316	63 479	78 453	..	..	17.0	15.0	18.9
OTHER ACTIVITIES	..	..	19 873	28 113	26 276	..	..	4.1	5.3	4.7
01/99 **GRAND TOTAL**	..	..	**452 845**	**564 885**	**692 036**	..	..	**12.9**	**15.1**	**18.5**

Total manufacturing by investing country						As a % of total manufacturing by foreign affiliates				
All countries	..	..	271 566	352 150	438 637	..	..	100.0	100.0	100.0
United States	..	..	..	..	..	..	..	..	..	..
Canada	..	..	..	..	..	..	..	..	..	..
Mexico	..	..	..	..	..	..	..	..	..	..
Japan	..	..	..	..	..	..	..	..	..	..
Europe	..	..	..	..	..	..	..	..	..	..
European Union (15)	..	..	..	..	..	..	..	..	..	..
Belgium	..	..	..	..	..	..	..	..	..	..
France	..	..	..	..	..	..	..	..	..	..
Germany	..	..	..	..	..	..	..	..	..	..
Italy	..	..	..	..	..	..	..	..	..	..
Netherlands	..	..	..	..	..	..	..	..	..	..
Spain	..	..	..	..	..	..	..	..	..	..
Sweden	..	..	..	..	..	..	..	..	..	..
United Kingdom	..	..	..	..	..	..	..	..	..	..
Switzerland	..	..	..	..	..	..	..	..	..	..
Australia and New Zealand	..	..	..	..	..	..	..	..	..	..
Asia (non-OECD)	..	..	..	..	..	..	..	..	..	..
Latin America	..	..	..	..	..	..	..	..	..	..

Note: Majority foreign-owned enterprises.
Entreprises sous contrôle étranger majoritaire.

Inward investments

Investissements entrants

Table 4A - Tableau 4A

TURNOVER / CHIFFRE D'AFFAIRES

| | | Foreign affiliates *(Millions of CZK)* | | | | | As a % of national total | | | | |
| | | Filiales étrangères *(Millions de CZK)* | | | | | En % du total national | | | | |
By industry (ISIC Rev. 3)		1995	1996	1997	1998	1999	1995	1996	1997	1998	1999
10/14	Mining & quarrying	..	..	612	706	1 028	..	..	0.9	1.1	1.6
15/37	**TOTAL MANUFACTURING**	..	..	**289 136**	**367 083**	**463 084**	..	..	**17.8**	**21.7**	**27.1**
15/16	Food, beverages, tobacco	..	..	35 628	41 996	55 797	..	..	11.4	13.6	18.7
17/19	Textiles, clothing, leather, footwear	..	..	7 879	10 765	16 059	..	..	9.3	12.7	18.3
20/22	Wood and paper products	..	..	20 932	21 289	29 695	..	..	16.3	15.1	21.5
20	Wood products	..	..	5 347	5 329	11 998	..	..	11.8	10.8	23.2
21/22	Paper, printing and publishing	..	..	15 585	15 960	17 697	..	..	18.8	17.5	20.4
23/25	Chemicals, Total	..	..	..	..	..	..	..	..	..	..
23	Refined petroleum, nuclear fuel	..	..				..	..			
24/25	Chemicals, rubber & plastics prod.	..	..	28 344	36 130	37 061	..	..	17.3	20.5	20.3
24	Chemical products	..	..	6 554	7 458	7 169	..	..	6.5	7.0	6.6
2423	Pharmaceuticals	..	..				..	..			
25	Rubber and plastics products	..	..	21 790	28 672	29 892	..	..	34.3	40.7	40.1
26	Non-metallic mineral products	..	..	13 562	15 096	21 313	..	..	15.4	16.6	21.5
27/28	Basic & fabricated metals	..	..	26 746	41 832	47 398	..	..	9.7	14.4	17.4
27	Basic metals	..	..	4 987	8 597	10 764	..	..	3.5	5.9	8.5
28	Fabricated metal products	..	..	21 759	33 235	36 634	..	..	16.0	23.0	25.2
29/32	Machinery, Total	..	..	..	..	..	..	..	..	..	..
29/30	Non-electrical machinery	..	..				..	..			
29	Non-electrical machinery nec	..	..	14 228	18 316	24 506	..	..	8.9	11.1	15.8
30	Office and computing machinery	..	..	..	..	..	..	..	..	..	..
31/32	Electrical & electronic equipment	..	..	19 530	30 708	43 762	..	..	19.7	27.4	37.5
31	Electrical machinery nec	..	..	17 081	24 485	31 500	..	..	22.3	28.7	36.1
32	Radio, TV & communications eq.	..	..	2 449	6 223	12 262	..	..	10.9	23.4	41.8
33	Scientific instruments	..	..	3 786	6 706	9 119	..	..	15.9	23.9	32.4
34/35	Transportation equipment	..	..	106 350	128 316	158 387	..	..	62.1	67.1	73.4
34	Motor vehicles	..	..	105 651	127 680	157 649	..	..	70.5	74.0	81.3
35	Other transport equipment	..	..	699	636	738	..	..	3.3	3.4	3.4
351	Shipbuilding & repairing	..	..				..	..			
353	Aircraft and spacecraft	..	..	..	..	..	..	..	..	..	..
36/37	Other manufacturing	..	..	11 989	13 930	16 669	..	..	18.6	21.7	24.4
40/45	Construction, electricity, gas & water	..	..	9 240	10 205	27 008	..	..	1.4	1.6	4.1
50/55	Trade, repair, hotels & restaurants	..	..	301 751	447 315	475 756	..	..	16.3	22.2	24.1
65/74	Finance, insurance, business services	..	..	53 997	48 763	65 034	..	..	17.7	15.2	19.3
	OTHER ACTIVITIES	..	..	21 010	28 301	26 703	..	..	3.8	4.8	4.3
01/99	**GRAND TOTAL**	..	..	**675 746**	**902 373**	**1058 613**	..	..	**13.4**	**16.9**	**19.7**

Total manufacturing by investing country							As a % of total manufacturing by foreign affiliates				
All countries		..	..	289 136	367 083	463 084	..	..	100.0	100.0	100.0
United States		..	..	..	..	..	..	..	..	..	..
Canada		..	..	..	..	..	..	..	..	..	..
Mexico		..	..	..	..	..	..	..	..	..	..
Japan		..	..	..	..	..	..	..	..	..	..
Europe		..	..	..	..	..	..	..	..	..	..
European Union (15)		..	..	..	..	..	..	..	..	..	..
Belgium		..	..	..	..	..	..	..	..	..	..
France		..	..	..	..	..	..	..	..	..	..
Germany		..	..	..	..	..	..	..	..	..	..
Italy		..	..	..	..	..	..	..	..	..	..
Netherlands		..	..	..	..	..	..	..	..	..	..
Spain		..	..	..	..	..	..	..	..	..	..
Sweden		..	..	..	..	..	..	..	..	..	..
United Kingdom		..	..	..	..	..	..	..	..	..	..
Switzerland		..	..	..	..	..	..	..	..	..	..
Australia and New Zealand		..	..	..	..	..	..	..	..	..	..
Asia (non-OECD)		..	..	..	..	..	..	..	..	..	..
Latin America		..	..	..	..	..	..	..	..	..	..

Note: Majority foreign-owned enterprises.
Entreprises sous contrôle étranger majoritaire.

Inward investments *Investissements entrants*

Table 5A - Tableau 5A
VALUE ADDED / VALEUR AJOUTÉE

By industry (ISIC Rev. 3)	Foreign affiliates (Millions of CZK) / Filiales étrangères (Millions de CZK)					As a % of national total / En % du total national				
	1995	1996	1997	1998	1999	1995	1996	1997	1998	1999
10/14 Mining & quarrying	..	..	281	272	320	..	..	0.9	0.9	1.1
15/37 **TOTAL MANUFACTURING**	..	..	**67 314**	**81 208**	**108 114**	..	..	**16.8**	**19.5**	**25.5**
15/16 Food, beverages, tobacco	..	..	9 268	9 402	14 940	..	..	16.8	17.2	25.4
17/19 Textiles, clothing, leather, footwear	..	..	2 659	3 329	4 609	..	..	10.2	12.5	16.6
20/22 Wood and paper products	..	..	4 994	4 390	6 768	..	..	15.6	12.9	19.8
20 Wood products	..	..	1 308	1 137	2 998	..	..	11.4	9.7	24.3
21/22 Paper, printing and publishing	..	..	3 686	3 253	3 770	..	..	17.9	14.6	17.3
23/25 Chemicals, Total	..	..	..	..	..	..	..	..	..	..
23 Refined petroleum, nuclear fuel	..	..	..	..	..	..	..	..	..	..
24/25 Chemicals, rubber & plastics prod.	..	..	8 012	9 155	10 917	..	..	18.5	20.3	23.1
24 Chemical products	..	..	2 053	2 244	1 978	..	..	7.9	8.4	7.5
2423 Pharmaceuticals	..	..	..	..	..	..	..	..	..	..
25 Rubber and plastics products	..	..	5 959	6 911	8 939	..	..	34.7	37.6	43.1
26 Non-metallic mineral products	..	..	4 185	4 969	6 882	..	..	12.7	14.4	19.3
27/28 Basic & fabricated metals	..	..	5 900	9 124	10 100	..	..	8.8	12.5	15.6
27 Basic metals	..	..	897	1 755	1 948	..	..	2.9	5.4	8.4
28 Fabricated metal products	..	..	5 003	7 369	8 152	..	..	13.9	18.3	19.5
29/32 Machinery, Total	..	..	..	..	..	..	..	..	..	..
29/30 Non-electrical machinery	..	..	..	..	..	..	..	..	..	..
29 Non-electrical machinery nec	..	..	4 065	4 681	6 533	..	..	8.9	10.0	14.8
30 Office and computing machinery	..	..	..	..	..	..	..	..	..	..
31/32 Electrical & electronic equipment	..	..	5 466	8 496	11 385	..	..	19.2	27.3	33.9
31 Electrical machinery nec	..	..	4 697	6 981	8 794	..	..	20.9	28.8	33.1
32 Radio, TV & communications eq.	..	..	769	1 515	2 591	..	..	12.9	22.2	36.9
33 Scientific instruments	..	..	1 054	1 724	2 789	..	..	13.4	18.6	28.7
34/35 Transportation equipment	..	..	19 340	23 329	29 626	..	..	49.1	58.7	67.0
34 Motor vehicles	..	..	19 149	23 146	29 434	..	..	62.6	67.7	77.3
35 Other transport equipment	..	..	191	183	192	..	..	2.2	3.3	3.1
351 Shipbuilding & repairing	..	..	..	..	..	..	..	..	..	..
353 Aircraft and spacecraft	..	..	..	..	..	..	..	..	..	..
36/37 Other manufacturing	..	..	2 270	2 479	3 230	..	..	13.6	15.2	18.0
40/45 Construction, electricity, gas & water	..	..	2 050	2 372	5 441	..	..	1.3	1.5	3.4
50/55 Trade, repair, hotels & restaurants	..	..	33 812	46 750	49 021	..	..	20.9	25.4	27.3
65/74 Finance, insurance, business services	..	..	22 051	27 472	30 482	..	..	15.3	14.4	18.0
OTHER ACTIVITIES	..	..	5 074	6 891	5 185	..	..	3.0	3.5	2.5
01/99 **GRAND TOTAL**	..	..	**130 582**	**164 965**	**198 563**	..	..	**12.3**	**14.0**	**17.0**

Total manufacturing by investing country						As a % of total manufacturing by foreign affiliates				
All countries	..	..	67 314	81 208	108 114	..	..	100.0	100.0	100.0
United States	..	..	..	..	..	..	..	..	..	..
Canada	..	..	..	..	..	..	..	..	..	..
Mexico	..	..	..	..	..	..	..	..	..	..
Japan	..	..	..	..	..	..	..	..	..	..
Europe	..	..	..	..	..	..	..	..	..	..
European Union (15)	..	..	..	..	..	..	..	..	..	..
Belgium	..	..	..	..	..	..	..	..	..	..
France	..	..	..	..	..	..	..	..	..	..
Germany	..	..	..	..	..	..	..	..	..	..
Italy	..	..	..	..	..	..	..	..	..	..
Netherlands	..	..	..	..	..	..	..	..	..	..
Spain	..	..	..	..	..	..	..	..	..	..
Sweden	..	..	..	..	..	..	..	..	..	..
United Kingdom	..	..	..	..	..	..	..	..	..	..
Switzerland	..	..	..	..	..	..	..	..	..	..
Australia and New Zealand	..	..	..	..	..	..	..	..	..	..
Asia (non-OECD)	..	..	..	..	..	..	..	..	..	..
Latin America	..	..	..	..	..	..	..	..	..	..

Note: Majority foreign-owned enterprises.
Entreprises sous contrôle étranger majoritaire.

Inward investments   *Investissements entrants*

Table 6A - Tableau 6A

COMPENSATION OF EMPLOYEES / SALAIRES ET CHARGES SOCIALES

By industry (ISIC Rev. 3)		Foreign affiliates (Millions of CZK) Filiales étrangères (Millions de CZK)					As a % of national total En % du total national				
		1995	1996	1997	1998	1999	1995	1996	1997	1998	1999
10/14	Mining & quarrying	..	..	94	96	137	..	..	0.8	0.8	1.1
15/37	**TOTAL MANUFACTURING**	..	..	**21 396**	**27 585**	**35 015**	..	..	**13.0**	**15.6**	**19.6**
15/16	Food, beverages, tobacco	..	..	1 845	2 386	3 660	..	..	9.5	11.9	17.9
17/19	Textiles, clothing, leather, footwear	..	..	1 272	1 663	2 256	..	..	9.2	11.4	15.5
20/22	Wood and paper products	..	..	1 612	2 028	2 437	..	..	12.2	14.3	17.1
20	Wood products	..	..	585	640	912	..	..	11.2	11.9	16.7
21/22	Paper, printing and publishing	..	..	1 027	1 388	1 525	..	..	12.9	15.8	17.4
23/25	Chemicals, Total	..	..	..	..	..	..	..	..	..	..
23	Refined petroleum, nuclear fuel	..	..	..	..	..	..	..	..	..	..
24/25	Chemicals, rubber & plastics prod.	..	..	2 104	2 703	2 876	..	..	15.3	18.1	18.1
24	Chemical products	..	..	468	580	638	..	..	6.4	7.5	7.7
2423	Pharmaceuticals	..	..	..	..	..	..	..	..	..	..
25	Rubber and plastics products	..	..	1 636	2 123	2 238	..	..	25.4	29.3	29.2
26	Non-metallic mineral products	..	..	1 071	1 373	1 739	..	..	9.9	11.6	14.5
27/28	Basic & fabricated metals	..	..	2 729	3 538	3 674	..	..	8.8	10.3	11.3
27	Basic metals	..	..	361	628	615	..	..	2.5	4.3	4.4
28	Fabricated metal products	..	..	2 368	2 910	3 059	..	..	14.2	14.7	16.3
29/32	Machinery, Total	..	..	..	..	..	..	..	..	..	..
29/30	Non-electrical machinery	..	..	..	..	..	..	..	..	..	..
29	Non-electrical machinery nec	..	..	1 661	2 042	2 963	..	..	7.1	8.7	12.5
30	Office and computing machinery	..	..	..	..	..	..	..	..	..	..
31/32	Electrical & electronic equipment	..	..	2 788	3 772	4 929	..	..	21.2	26.2	32.1
31	Electrical machinery nec	..	..	2 289	2 941	3 800	..	..	22.4	27.0	31.8
32	Radio, TV & communications eq.	..	..	499	831	1 129	..	..	17.3	23.8	33.3
33	Scientific instruments	..	..	486	717	894	..	..	13.6	18.3	22.6
34/35	Transportation equipment	..	..	4 890	6 329	8 173	..	..	35.9	42.2	49.0
34	Motor vehicles	..	..	4 781	6 236	8 079	..	..	52.0	56.3	63.7
35	Other transport equipment	..	..	109	93	94	..	..	2.5	2.4	2.3
351	Shipbuilding & repairing	..	..	..	..	..	..	..	..	..	..
353	Aircraft and spacecraft	..	..	..	..	..	..	..	..	..	..
36/37	Other manufacturing	..	..	880	947	1 220	..	..	11.3	11.3	14.4
40/45	Construction, electricity, gas & water	..	..	1 068	1 014	2 266	..	..	1.8	1.7	3.9
50/55	Trade, repair, hotels & restaurants	..	..	13 265	18 074	18 677	..	..	18.8	24.3	24.5
65/74	Finance, insurance, business services	..	..	6 813	8 825	11 815	..	..	12.6	14.9	19.0
	OTHER ACTIVITIES	..	..	1 553	2 171	2 352	..	..	2.0	2.7	2.8
01/99	**GRAND TOTAL**	..	..	**44 189**	**57 765**	**70 262**	..	..	**10.1**	**12.5**	**14.9**

Total manufacturing by investing country						As a % of total manufacturing by foreign affiliates				
All countries	..	..	**21 396**	**27 585**	**35 015**	..	..	**100.0**	**100.0**	**100.0**
United States	..	..	..	..	..	..	..	..	..	..
Canada	..	..	..	..	..	..	..	..	..	..
Mexico	..	..	..	..	..	..	..	..	..	..
Japan	..	..	..	..	..	..	..	..	..	..
Europe	..	..	..	..	..	..	..	..	..	..
European Union (15)	..	..	..	..	..	..	..	..	..	..
Belgium	..	..	..	..	..	..	..	..	..	..
France	..	..	..	..	..	..	..	..	..	..
Germany	..	..	..	..	..	..	..	..	..	..
Italy	..	..	..	..	..	..	..	..	..	..
Netherlands	..	..	..	..	..	..	..	..	..	..
Spain	..	..	..	..	..	..	..	..	..	..
Sweden	..	..	..	..	..	..	..	..	..	..
United Kingdom	..	..	..	..	..	..	..	..	..	..
Switzerland	..	..	..	..	..	..	..	..	..	..
Australia and New Zealand	..	..	..	..	..	..	..	..	..	..
Asia (non-OECD)	..	..	..	..	..	..	..	..	..	..
Latin America	..	..	..	..	..	..	..	..	..	..

Note: Majority foreign-owned enterprises.
Entreprises sous contrôle étranger majoritaire.

Inward investments   *Investissements entrants*

Table 7A - Tableau 7A
R&D EXPENDITURE / DÉPENSES DE R-D

By industry (ISIC Rev. 3)	Foreign affiliates (Millions of CZK) / Filiales étrangères (Millions de CZK)					As a % of national total / En % du total national				
	1995	1996	1997	1998	1999	1995	1996	1997	1998	1999
10/14 Mining & quarrying	..	..	0	0	0	..	..	0.0	0.0	0.0
15/37 **TOTAL MANUFACTURING**	..	..	114	304	899	..	..	1.2	2.7	8.6
15/16 Food, beverages, tobacco	..	..	0	0	14	..	..	0.0	0.0	22.0
17/19 Textiles, clothing, leather, footwear	..	..	0	0	0	..	..	0.0	0.0	0.0
20/22 Wood and paper products	..	..	0	0	0	..	..	0.0	0.0	0.0
20 Wood products	..	..	0	0	0	..	..	0.0	0.0	0.0
21/22 Paper, printing and publishing	..	..	0	0	0	..	..	0.0	0.0	0.0
23/25 Chemicals, Total	..	..	2	3	14	..	..	0.2	0.2	1.1
23 Refined petroleum, nuclear fuel	..	..	0	0	0	..	..	0.0	0.0	0.0
24/25 Chemicals, rubber & plastics prod.	..	..	2	3	14	..	..	0.2	0.2	1.1
24 Chemical products	..	..	2	3	7	..	..	0.3	0.3	0.7
2423 Pharmaceuticals	..	..	0	0	0	..	..	0.0	0.0	0.0
25 Rubber and plastics products	..	..	0	0	8	..	..	0.0	0.0	3.0
26 Non-metallic mineral products	..	..	0	0	2	..	..	0.0	0.0	0.9
27/28 Basic & fabricated metals	..	..	0	37	23	..	..	0.0	4.4	2.7
27 Basic metals	..	..	0	34	20	..	..	0.0	5.6	4.5
28 Fabricated metal products	..	..	0	3	3	..	..	0.0	1.4	0.7
29/32 Machinery, Total	..	..	41	71	147	..	..	2.2	3.3	7.6
29/30 Non-electrical machinery	..	..	41	0	7	..	..	3.0	0.0	0.5
29 Non-electrical machinery nec	..	..	41	0	7	..	..	3.0	0.0	0.5
30 Office and computing machinery	..	..	0	0	0	..	..	0.0	0.0	0.0
31/32 Electrical & electronic equipment	..	..	0	71	140	..	..	0.0	9.4	20.6
31 Electrical machinery nec	..	..	0	48	58	..	..	0.0	12.8	15.9
32 Radio, TV & communications eq.	..	..	0	23	82	..	..	0.0	6.0	26.0
33 Scientific instruments	..	..	0	2	14	..	..	0.0	1.5	4.9
34/35 Transportation equipment	..	..	71	191	685	..	..	1.5	3.3	12.6
34 Motor vehicles	..	..	70	190	685	..	..	2.4	4.6	17.0
35 Other transport equipment	..	..	1	1	0	..	..	0.0	0.1	0.0
351 Shipbuilding & repairing	..	..	0	0	0	..	..	..	..	..
353 Aircraft and spacecraft	..	..	1	0	0	..	..	0.0	0.0	0.0
36/37 Other manufacturing	..	..	0	0	0	..	..	0.0	0.0	0.0
40/45 Construction, electricity, gas & water	..	..	0	0	0	..	..	0.0	0.0	0.0
50/55 Trade, repair, hotels & restaurants	..	..	0	0	0	..	..	0.0	0.0	0.0
65/74 Finance, insurance, business services	..	..	41	88	58	..	..	1.6	3.0	1.8
OTHER ACTIVITIES	..	..	0	0	0	..	..	0.0	0.0	0.0
01/99 **GRAND TOTAL**	..	..	155	391	957	..	..	1.3	2.7	6.4

Total manufacturing by investing country						As a % of total manufacturing by foreign affiliates				
All countries	..	..	114	304	899	..	..	100.0	100.0	100.0
United States	..	..	..	..	..	..	..	..	..	..
Canada	..	..	..	..	..	..	..	..	..	..
Mexico	..	..	..	..	..	..	..	..	..	..
Japan	..	..	..	..	..	..	..	..	..	..
Europe	..	..	..	..	..	..	..	..	..	..
European Union (15)	..	..	..	..	..	..	..	..	..	..
Belgium	..	..	..	..	..	..	..	..	..	..
France	..	..	..	..	..	..	..	..	..	..
Germany	..	..	..	..	..	..	..	..	..	..
Italy	..	..	..	..	..	..	..	..	..	..
Netherlands	..	..	..	..	..	..	..	..	..	..
Spain	..	..	..	..	..	..	..	..	..	..
Sweden	..	..	..	..	..	..	..	..	..	..
United Kingdom	..	..	..	..	..	..	..	..	..	..
Switzerland	..	..	..	..	..	..	..	..	..	..
Australia and New Zealand	..	..	..	..	..	..	..	..	..	..
Asia (non-OECD)	..	..	..	..	..	..	..	..	..	..
Latin America	..	..	..	..	..	..	..	..	..	..

Note: Majority foreign-owned enterprises.
          Entreprises sous contrôle étranger majoritaire.

Inward investments

Investissements entrants

Table 8A - Tableau 8A

NUMBER OF RESEARCHERS / NOMBRE DE CHERCHEURS

		Foreign affiliates (FTE) Filiales étrangères (EPT)					As a % of national total En % du total national				
By industry (ISIC Rev. 3)		1995	1996	1997	1998	1999	1995	1996	1997	1998	1999
10/14	Mining & quarrying	..	..	0	0	0	..	..	0.0	0.0	0.0
15/37	**TOTAL MANUFACTURING**	..	..	5	44	114	..	..	0.1	1.3	3.1
15/16	Food, beverages, tobacco	..	..	0	0	10	..	..	0.0	0.0	30.3
17/19	Textiles, clothing, leather, footwear	..	..	0	0	0	..	..	0.0	0.0	0.0
20/22	Wood and paper products	..	..	0	0	0	..	..	0.0	0.0	0.0
20	Wood products	..	..	0	0	0	..	..	0.0	0.0	0.0
21/22	Paper, printing and publishing	..	..	0	0	0	..	..	0.0	0.0	0.0
23/25	Chemicals, Total	..	..	0	0	5	..	..	0.0	0.0	0.9
23	Refined petroleum, nuclear fuel	..	..	0	0	0	..	..	0.0	0.0	0.0
24/25	Chemicals, rubber & plastics prod.	..	..	0	0	5	..	..	0.0	0.0	0.9
24	Chemical products	..	..	0	0	5	..	..	0.0	0.0	1.1
2423	Pharmaceuticals	..	..	0	0	0	..	..	0.0	0.0	0.0
25	Rubber and plastics products	..	..	0	0	0	..	..	0.0	0.0	0.0
26	Non-metallic mineral products	..	..	0	0	0	..	..	0.0	0.0	0.0
27/28	Basic & fabricated metals	..	..	0	32	9	..	..	0.0	12.2	2.8
27	Basic metals	..	..	0	30	3	..	..	0.0	18.3	2.4
28	Fabricated metal products	..	..	0	2	6	..	..	0.0	2.0	3.2
29/32	Machinery, Total	..	..	5	7	50	..	..	0.5	0.7	4.5
29/30	Non-electrical machinery	..	..	5	0	4	..	..	0.6	0.0	0.5
29	Non-electrical machinery nec	..	..	5	0	4	..	..	0.7	0.0	0.5
30	Office and computing machinery	..	..	0	0	0	..	..	0.0	0.0	0.0
31/32	Electrical & electronic equipment	..	..	0	7	46	..	..	0.0	2.2	12.9
31	Electrical machinery nec	..	..	0	0	6	..	..	0.0	0.0	4.1
32	Radio, TV & communications eq.	..	..	0	7	40	..	..	0.0	4.4	19.0
33	Scientific instruments	..	..	0	5	6	..	..	0.0	4.4	2.8
34/35	Transportation equipment	..	..	0	0	34	..	..	0.0	0.0	2.8
34	Motor vehicles	..	..	0	0	34	..	..	0.0	0.0	3.9
35	Other transport equipment	..	..	0	0	0	..	..	0.0	0.0	0.0
351	Shipbuilding & repairing	..	..	0	0	0	..	..	0.0	0.0	0.0
353	Aircraft and spacecraft	..	..	0	0	0	..	..	0.0	0.0	0.0
36/37	Other manufacturing	..	..	0	0	0	..	..	0.0	0.0	0.0
40/45	Construction, electricity, gas & water	..	..	0	0	0	..	..	0.0	0.0	0.0
50/55	Trade, repair, hotels & restaurants	..	..	0	0	0	..	..	0.0	0.0	0.0
65/74	Finance, insurance, business services	..	..	9	14	40	..	..	0.6	1.0	2.2
	OTHER ACTIVITIES	..	..	0	0	0	..	..	0.0	0.0	0.0
01/99	**GRAND TOTAL**	..	..	14	58	154	..	..	0.3	1.1	2.7

Total manufacturing by investing country							As a % of total manufacturing by foreign affiliates				
All countries		..	..	5	44	114	..	..	100.0	100.0	100.0
United States		..	..	..	..	..	..	..	..	..	..
Canada		..	..	..	..	..	..	..	..	..	..
Mexico		..	..	..	..	..	..	..	..	..	..
Japan		..	..	..	..	..	..	..	..	..	..
Europe		..	..	..	..	..	..	..	..	..	..
European Union (15)		..	..	..	..	..	..	..	..	..	..
Belgium		..	..	..	..	..	..	..	..	..	..
France		..	..	..	..	..	..	..	..	..	..
Germany		..	..	..	..	..	..	..	..	..	..
Italy		..	..	..	..	..	..	..	..	..	..
Netherlands		..	..	..	..	..	..	..	..	..	..
Spain		..	..	..	..	..	..	..	..	..	..
Sweden		..	..	..	..	..	..	..	..	..	..
United Kingdom		..	..	..	..	..	..	..	..	..	..
Switzerland		..	..	..	..	..	..	..	..	..	..
Australia and New Zealand		..	..	..	..	..	..	..	..	..	..
Asia (non-OECD)		..	..	..	..	..	..	..	..	..	..
Latin America		..	..	..	..	..	..	..	..	..	..

Note: Majority foreign-owned enterprises.
Entreprises sous contrôle étranger majoritaire.

Inward investments *Investissements entrants*

Table 9A - Tableau 9A

GROSS FIXED CAPITAL FORMATION / FORMATION BRUTE DE CAPITAL FIXE

		Foreign affiliates *(Millions of CZK)* Filiales étrangères *(Millions de CZK)*					As a % of national total *En % du total national*				
By industry (ISIC Rev. 3)		1995	1996	1997	1998	1999	1995	1996	1997	1998	1999
10/14	Mining & quarrying	..	..	89	43	41	..	..	1.1	0.5	0.6
15/37	**TOTAL MANUFACTURING**	..	..	**29 584**	**38 921**	**48 852**	..	..	**21.9**	**31.2**	**35.9**
15/16	Food, beverages, tobacco	..	..	2 002	2 960	3 672	..	..	10.8	18.6	29.0
17/19	Textiles, clothing, leather, footwear	..	..	1 405	1 636	2 112	..	..	22.4	24.9	31.9
20/22	Wood and paper products	..	..	1 638	3 445	3 115	..	..	13.9	29.5	31.7
20	Wood products	..	..	595	495	2 029	..	..	14.2	17.7	51.2
21/22	Paper, printing and publishing	..	..	1 043	2 950	1 086	..	..	13.8	33.3	18.5
23/25	Chemicals, Total	..	..	..	..	..	..	..	..	..	..
23	Refined petroleum, nuclear fuel	..	..	..	..	..	..	..	..	..	..
24/25	Chemicals, rubber & plastics prod.	..	..	3 447	4 181	5 102	..	..	21.5	22.5	30.6
24	Chemical products	..	..	614	741	1 137	..	..	6.0	6.1	12.4
2423	Pharmaceuticals	..	..	..	..	..	..	..	..	..	..
25	Rubber and plastics products	..	..	2 833	3 440	3 965	..	..	49.4	52.7	53.0
26	Non-metallic mineral products	..	..	2 409	2 107	2 504	..	..	19.2	15.9	20.4
27/28	Basic & fabricated metals	..	..	2 687	4 425	3 754	..	..	9.9	24.1	13.9
27	Basic metals	..	..	335	627	904	..	..	2.2	8.0	5.0
28	Fabricated metal products	..	..	2 352	3 798	2 850	..	..	20.4	36.1	32.2
29/32	Machinery, Total	..	..	..	..	..	..	..	..	..	..
29/30	Non-electrical machinery	..	..	..	..	..	..	..	..	..	..
29	Non-electrical machinery nec	..	..	1 897	1 374	2 037	..	..	15.8	17.7	26.9
30	Office and computing machinery	..	..	..	..	..	..	..	..	..	..
31/32	Electrical & electronic equipment	..	..	3 021	5 987	6 991	..	..	36.3	53.9	64.2
31	Electrical machinery nec	..	..	2 304	5 092	4 099	..	..	36.1	58.5	59.8
32	Radio, TV & communications eq.	..	..	717	895	2 892	..	..	37.1	37.3	71.6
33	Scientific instruments	..	..	381	533	1 317	..	..	26.9	36.9	57.5
34/35	Transportation equipment	..	..	10 202	11 330	17 305	..	..	67.8	73.6	80.0
34	Motor vehicles	..	..	10 158	11 303	17 279	..	..	76.1	79.1	83.4
35	Other transport equipment	..	..	44	27	26	..	..	2.6	2.4	2.8
351	Shipbuilding & repairing	..	..	..	..	..	..	..	..	..	..
353	Aircraft and spacecraft	..	..	..	..	..	..	..	..	..	..
36/37	Other manufacturing	..	..	459	780	719	..	..	11.1	26.5	20.7
40/45	Construction, electricity, gas & water	..	..	327	1 223	3 284	..	..	0.5	1.8	4.0
50/55	Trade, repair, hotels & restaurants	..	..	18 672	20 660	22 739	..	..	27.5	35.7	40.4
65/74	Finance, insurance, business services	..	..	2 317	8 641	15 796	..	..	2.2	7.0	15.0
	OTHER ACTIVITIES	..	..	2 260	1 591	1 873	..	..	2.0	1.6	2.2
01/99	**GRAND TOTAL**	..	..	**53 249**	**71 079**	**92 585**	..	..	**10.7**	**14.6**	**19.5**

Total manufacturing by investing country							As a % of total manufacturing by foreign affiliates				
All countries		..	..	29 584	38 921	48 852	..	..	100.0	100.0	100.0
United States		..	..	..	..	..	..	..	..	..	..
Canada		..	..	..	..	..	..	..	..	..	..
Mexico		..	..	..	..	..	..	..	..	..	..
Japan		..	..	..	..	..	..	..	..	..	..
Europe		..	..	..	..	..	..	..	..	..	..
European Union (15)		..	..	..	..	..	..	..	..	..	..
Belgium		..	..	..	..	..	..	..	..	..	..
France		..	..	..	..	..	..	..	..	..	..
Germany		..	..	..	..	..	..	..	..	..	..
Italy		..	..	..	..	..	..	..	..	..	..
Netherlands		..	..	..	..	..	..	..	..	..	..
Spain		..	..	..	..	..	..	..	..	..	..
Sweden		..	..	..	..	..	..	..	..	..	..
United Kingdom		..	..	..	..	..	..	..	..	..	..
Switzerland		..	..	..	..	..	..	..	..	..	..
Australia and New Zealand		..	..	..	..	..	..	..	..	..	..
Asia (non-OECD)		..	..	..	..	..	..	..	..	..	..
Latin America		..	..	..	..	..	..	..	..	..	..

Note: Majority foreign-owned enterprises.
Entreprises sous contrôle étranger majoritaire.

CZECH REPUBLIC

Source

The data are prepared by the Czech Statistical Office. For all variables except *R&D expenditure* and *Number of researchers*, they are extracted from the annual structural survey. No special survey on enterprises with foreign participation is conducted, they are identified in the Business Register. The information on the share of foreign participation is updated by the Czech National Bank. Data are available separately for majority foreign-owned firms, minority foreign-owned firms and national firms. The data in this publication refer to majority foreign-owned enterprises, which have a foreign capital share of more than 50%.

Data on *R&D expenditure* and *Number of researchers* come from the annual survey on R&D and licences carried out by the Science and Information unit of the Czech Statistical Office. In 1997 and 1998, it covered units employing at least 20 employees; from 1999, all units are covered.

National totals: data come from the Czech Statistical Office and are fully compatible with foreign affiliates' data.

Industrial classification

For all variables, the data are classified according to the principal industrial activity of the affiliate.

The data are converted from the national industrial classification (OKEC) based on NACE Revision 1 to ISIC Revision 3.

Variables

- *Number of enterprises* is the average number of enterprises which were active for at least a part of the year.

- *Number of employees* is not expressed on a full-time equivalent basis. It encompasses all categories of permanent, temporary and seasonal employees, except for persons on maternity leave and apprentices.

- *Production* (gross output) is the sum of market and non-market outputs produced by domestic producers over a given period. It is equal to the sum of revenues from sales of own products, goods, works and services provided to the other establishments within the enterprise and includes also changes in stocks of own production and work in progress. Costs incurred on sold goods and VAT are excluded. The valuation is in producer prices, excluding VAT.

- *Value added* is obtained by subtracting the value of inputs (the cost of materials, fuel and other supplies) from the value of gross output.

- *Compensation of employees* is defined as the amount paid during the year to employees before deduction of taxes and pension contributions. It includes overtime cash payments, bonuses, holiday and sick leave payments, etc.

- *R&D expenditure* is intramural expenditure on R&D performed by foreign affiliates, whatever the source of funds.

- *Number of researchers* is in fact the total number of employees working directly on R&D, as well as those providing direct services such as R&D managers, administrators and clerical staff. It is expressed on a full-time equivalent basis.

- *Gross fixed capital formation* is expenditure on the purchase of tangible assets (by either purchase or own activity), plus the overall value of tangible assets acquired free of charge.

RÉPUBLIQUE TCHÈQUE

Source

Les données émanent de l'Office tchèque de la statistique. Pour toutes les variables à l'exception des *Dépenses de R-D* et du *Nombre de chercheurs*, elles proviennent de l'enquête structurelle annuelle. Aucune enquête spécifique relative aux entreprises à participation étrangère n'est réalisée. Celles-ci sont identifiées dans le registre du commerce. Les informations relatives au degré de participation étrangère sont mises à jour par la Banque Nationale tchèque. Des données sont disponibles séparément pour les entreprises à participation étrangère majoritaire, minoritaire, ainsi que pour les entreprises nationales. Les données de cette publication font référence aux entreprises sous contrôle étranger majoritaire, où la part du capital en mains étrangères est de plus de 50 %.

Pour les *Dépenses de R-D* et le *Nombre de chercheurs*, les données proviennent de l'enquête annuelle sur la R-D et les licences menée par l'unité de la Science et de l'Information de l'Office tchèque de la statistique. En 1997 et 1998, cette enquête couvrait les unités employant au moins 20 salariés ; à partir de 1999 toutes les unités sont couvertes.

Totaux nationaux : les données sont fournies par l'Office tchèque de la statistique et sont entièrement compatibles avec les données relatives aux filiales étrangères.

Classification industrielle

Pour toutes les variables, les données sont classées selon l'activité industrielle principale de l'entreprise affiliée.

Les données sont converties de la classification industrielle nationale (OKEC) fondée sur la NACE révision 1 vers la CITI révision 3.

Variables

- Le *Nombre d'entreprises* est le nombre moyen d'entreprises qui étaient en activité pendant une partie de l'année au moins.

- Le *Nombre de salariés* n'est pas exprimé en équivalent plein-temps. Il comprend toutes les catégories de personnel (permanent, temporaire, saisonnier), à l'exception des personnes en congé de maternité et des apprentis.

- La *Production* (production brute) est la somme des biens et services marchands et non marchands élaborés par des producteurs sur le territoire national sur une période donnée. Elle est égale à la somme des revenus tirés des ventes des produits de l'entreprise, des biens, travaux et services fournis à d'autres établissements de l'entreprise et inclut les variations de stocks de sa propre production et des travaux en cours. Les frais encourus sur les produits vendus et la TVA sont exclus. L'évaluation se fait au prix départ-usine, non compris la TVA.

- La *Valeur ajoutée* est obtenue en soustrayant la valeur des consommations intermédiaires (coût des matières premières, combustible et autres fournitures) de la valeur de la production brute.

- Les *Salaires et charges sociales* sont définis comme les sommes versées pendant l'année aux salariés avant déduction des impôts et des cotisations de sécurité sociale. Ils incluent les paiements en espèces pour les heures supplémentaires, les primes, les congés payés et congés de maladie, etc.

- Les *Dépenses de R-D* sont les dépenses intra-muros de R-D exécutées par les filiales étrangères, quelle que soit la source de financement.

- Le *Nombre de chercheurs* est en fait le nombre total de salariés travaillant directement à la R-D, ainsi que les salariés apportant un soutien direct tels que les gestionnaires et administrateurs de R-D et le personnel de bureau. Il est exprimé en équivalent plein-temps.

- La *Formation brute de capital fixe* est donnée par la valeur des acquisitions d'actifs tangibles (y compris les biens fabriqués par le personnel de l'unité pour l'usage de ce dernier), plus la valeur totale des actifs tangibles acquis gratuitement.

FINLAND

FINLANDE

Table 1A - Tableau 1A

NUMBER OF ENTERPRISES / NOMBRE D'ENTREPRISES

| | | Foreign affiliates *(Units)* | | | | | As a % of national total | | | | |
| | | Filiales étrangères *(Unités)* | | | | | En % du total national | | | | |
By industry (ISIC Rev. 3)		1995	1996	1997	1998	1999	1995	1996	1997	1998	1999
10/14	Mining & quarrying	5	7	10	7	8	0.4	0.5	0.8	0.6	0.6
15/37	**TOTAL MANUFACTURING**	257	288	321	341	367	1.1	1.1	1.2	1.3	1.4
15/16	Food, beverages, tobacco	19	13	18	14	23	1.1	0.7	0.9	0.7	1.1
17/19	Textiles, clothing, leather, footwear	8	9	11	13	14	0.3	0.3	0.4	0.4	0.5
20/22	Wood and paper products	25	28	35	34	42	0.5	0.5	0.6	0.5	0.7
20	Wood products	..	..	..	12	13	..	..	..	0.4	0.4
21/22	Paper, printing and publishing	..	..	..	22	29	..	..	..	0.7	1.0
23/25	Chemicals, Total	46	53	63	70	73	5.3	5.7	6.5	6.9	7.2
23	Refined petroleum, nuclear fuel	2	2	2	1	1	25.0	25.0	22.2	10.0	11.1
24/25	Chemicals, rubber & plastics prod.	44	51	61	69	72	5.1	5.5	6.3	6.8	7.2
24	Chemical products	32	36	44	43	49	12.5	12.7	14.4	13.6	15.5
2423	Pharmaceuticals	2	3	6	3	3	14.3	13.6	27.3	14.3	15.0
25	Rubber and plastics products	12	15	17	26	23	2.0	2.3	2.6	3.8	3.4
26	Non-metallic mineral products	20	28	22	25	27	2.3	3.1	2.3	2.5	2.8
27/28	Basic & fabricated metals	29	37	41	46	44	0.7	0.9	0.9	1.0	1.0
27	Basic metals	8	7	10	10	6	6.5	5.2	7.0	6.2	4.2
28	Fabricated metal products	21	30	31	36	38	0.5	0.7	0.7	0.8	0.9
29/32	Machinery, Total	81	92	94	99	99	2.0	2.1	2.1	2.2	2.2
29/30	Non-electrical machinery	54	61	59	60	58	1.6	1.7	1.6	1.6	1.6
29	Non-electrical machinery nec	50	57	55	58	54	1.5	1.6	1.6	1.6	1.5
30	Office and computing machinery	4	4	4	2	4	7.4	7.0	6.7	3.1	6.3
31/32	Electrical & electronic equipment	27	31	35	39	41	3.6	3.9	4.2	4.7	5.0
31	Electrical machinery nec	19	22	24	25	30	4.1	4.4	4.8	5.1	6.2
32	Radio, TV & communications eq.	8	9	11	14	11	2.9	2.9	3.4	4.1	3.3
33	Scientific instruments	12	12	13	13	19	1.6	1.5	1.6	1.6	2.2
34/35	Transportation equipment	9	9	14	11	11	1.2	1.1	1.6	1.2	1.3
34	Motor vehicles	4	3	6	2	2	1.5	1.1	2.2	0.7	0.7
35	Other transport equipment	5	6	8	9	9	1.0	1.1	1.4	1.4	1.6
351	Shipbuilding & repairing	4	5	7	8	8	0.9	1.0	1.3	1.4	1.5
353	Aircraft and spacecraft	0	0	0	0	0	0.0	0.0	0.0	0.0	0.0
36/37	Other manufacturing	8	7	10	16	15	0.3	0.3	0.4	0.6	0.5
40/45	Construction, electricity, gas & water	38	52	63	57	76	0.2	0.2	0.2	0.2	0.3
50/55	Trade, repair, hotels & restaurants	781	843	957	718	722	1.4	1.4	1.6	1.1	1.2
65/74	Finance, insurance, business services	256	264	342	263	319	0.8	0.7	0.9	0.6	0.7
	OTHER ACTIVITIES	139	148	195	105	131	0.3	0.3	0.3	0.2	0.2
01/99	**GRAND TOTAL**	1 476	1 602	1 888	1 491	1 623	0.8	0.8	0.9	0.7	0.7

Total manufacturing by investing country						*As a % of total manufacturing by foreign affiliates*				
All countries	257	288	321	341	367	100.0	100.0	100.0	100.0	100.0
United States	34	51	62	61	64	13.2	17.7	19.3	17.9	17.4
Canada	..	4	4	..	..	..	1.4	1.2	..	..
Mexico	0	0	0	0	..	0.0	0.0	0.0	0.0	..
Japan	6	2	7	6	6	2.3	0.7	2.2	1.8	1.6
Europe	..	229	245	..	..	..	79.5	76.3	..	..
European Union (15)	168	183	194	208	234	65.4	63.5	60.4	61.0	63.8
Belgium	..	0	1	..	..	..	0.0	0.3	..	..
France	..	8	11	16	14	..	2.8	3.4	4.7	3.8
Germany	..	16	23	16	19	..	5.6	7.2	4.7	5.2
Italy	..	2	3	..	..	..	0.7	0.9	..	..
Netherlands	..	22	22	20	31	..	7.6	6.9	5.9	8.4
Spain	0	0	0	0	..	0.0	0.0	0.0	0.0	..
Sweden	..	88	83	..	..	..	30.6	25.9	..	..
United Kingdom	..	22	22	25	28	..	7.6	6.9	7.3	7.6
Switzerland	..	24	25	26	24	..	8.3	7.8	7.6	6.5
Australia and New Zealand	0	0	0	0	..	0.0	0.0	0.0	0.0	..
Asia (non-OECD)	..	1	2	2	3	..	0.3	0.6	0.6	0.8
Latin America	0	0	1	1	0	0.0	0.0	0.3	0.3	0.0

Note: Majority foreign-owned enterprises. From 1998, branch offices of foreign enterprises are excluded from the survey.
Entreprises sous contrôle étranger majoritaire. A partir de 1998, les succursales des entreprises étrangères sont exclues de l'enquête.

Inward investments   *Investissements entrants*

Table 2A - Tableau 2A

NUMBER OF EMPLOYEES BY INDUSTRY

NOMBRE DE SALARIÉS PAR INDUSTRIE

| | | Foreign affiliates *(Units)* | | | | | As a % of national total | | | | |
| | | Filiales étrangères *(Unités)* | | | | | En % du total national | | | | |
ISIC Revision 3		1995	1996	1997	1998	1999	1995	1996	1997	1998	1999
10/14	Mining & quarrying	..	853	897	398	504	..	17.6	16.7	10.1	14.8
15/37	**TOTAL MANUFACTURING**	**37 892**	**44 838**	**50 627**	**57 559**	**66 755**	**9.7**	**11.3**	**12.4**	**13.8**	**15.9**
15/16	Food, beverages, tobacco	2 796	2 238	2 895	2 196	5 372	6.1	4.9	6.4	5.0	12.7
17/19	Textiles, clothing, leather, footwear	349	420	682	1 106	1 087	1.9	2.4	3.9	6.6	6.9
20/22	Wood and paper products	1 448	1 438	1 701	2 687	3 872	1.5	1.5	1.7	2.7	3.9
20	Wood products	..	..	..	883	1 030	..	..	..	3.2	3.7
21/22	Paper, printing and publishing	..	..	..	1 804	2 842	..	..	..	2.5	4.0
23/25	Chemicals, Total	..	..	..	..	..	..	..	..	..	..
23	Refined petroleum, nuclear fuel	..	..	..	..	..	..	..	..	..	..
24/25	Chemicals, rubber & plastics prod.	3 441	5 465	7 066	7 651	9 388	11.0	17.5	22.2	22.7	27.3
24	Chemical products	2 288	4 069	5 488	5 711	7 413	12.3	22.1	30.5	31.0	40.4
2423	Pharmaceuticals	..	..	..	1 608	1 592	..	..	..	27.1	28.9
25	Rubber and plastics products	1 153	1 396	1 578	1 940	1 974	9.1	10.8	11.5	12.7	12.3
26	Non-metallic mineral products	3 482	4 487	3 267	4 060	4 229	25.6	36.2	24.3	27.9	27.0
27/28	Basic & fabricated metals	3 610	4 931	5 471	5 780	5 685	8.3	10.6	10.7	11.2	11.1
27	Basic metals	1 194	..	284	462	272	7.1	..	1.6	2.5	1.6
28	Fabricated metal products	2 416	..	5 187	5 318	5 413	9.0	..	15.5	16.0	16.0
29/32	Machinery, Total	..	..	..	..	25 323	..	..	..	..	22.9
29/30	Non-electrical machinery	..	..	..	..	11 293	..	..	..	..	19.0
29	Non-electrical machinery nec	6 037	7 414	8 562	9 957	10 526	11.4	13.5	15.3	17.1	18.4
30	Office and computing machinery	..	..	..	..	767	..	..	..	..	36.8
31/32	Electrical & electronic equipment	7 673	10 381	10 967	12 283	14 030	21.4	25.5	25.0	25.9	27.3
31	Electrical machinery nec	6 055	9 062	8 704	8 336	9 058	41.2	54.4	51.6	50.7	56.5
32	Radio, TV & communications eq.	1 618	1 319	2 263	3 947	4 972	7.6	5.5	8.4	12.7	14.0
33	Scientific instruments	1 386	1 451	1 694	1 873	2 401	16.1	15.5	17.7	18.6	21.3
34/35	Transportation equipment	..	..	..	..	..	..	..	..	..	..
34	Motor vehicles	..	..	..	..	..	..	..	..	..	..
35	Other transport equipment	..	..	..	6 702	6 976	..	..	..	60.6	61.1
351	Shipbuilding & repairing	..	..	..	6 638	6 431	..	..	..	68.5	67.3
353	Aircraft and spacecraft	0	0	0	0	0	0.0	0.0	0.0	0.0	0.0
36/37	Other manufacturing	729	650	1 189	1 673	1 348	5.0	4.4	7.5	10.5	8.3
40/45	Construction, electricity, gas & water	4 819	6 098	6 365	9 646	10 950	5.3	6.2	5.9	8.3	9.0
50/55	Trade, repair, hotels & restaurants	23 113	24 081	27 340	35 317	35 389	9.9	9.9	10.9	14.1	13.7
65/74	Finance, insurance, business services	8 208	11 241	14 676	16 876	19 663	4.9	6.7	8.3	10.3	10.6
	OTHER ACTIVITIES	..	5 694	6 915	7 745	10 655	..	2.6	3.1	3.9	5.2
01/99	**GRAND TOTAL**	**79 682**	**92 805**	**106 820**	**127 542**	**143 915**	**7.4**	**8.2**	**9.1**	**11.1**	**12.1**

Note: Majority foreign-owned firms.
Firmes sous contrôle étranger majoritaire.

Inward investments

Investissements entrants

Table 3A - Tableau 3A

NUMBER OF EMPLOYEES BY COUNTRY OF ORIGIN IN THE MANUFACTURING SECTOR

NOMBRE DE SALARIÉS PAR PAYS D'ORIGINE DANS L'INDUSTRIE MANUFACTURIÈRE

Country of origin (UBO)	Number of employees (Units) Nombre de salariés (Unités)					As a % of all countries En % du total des pays				
	1995	1996	1997	1998	1999	1995	1996	1997	1998	1999
All countries	37 892	44 838	50 627	57 559	66 755	100.0	100.0	100.0	100.0	100.0
Total OECD	..	..	..	56 415	65 749	..	..	..	98.0	98.5
United States	4 224	7 115	9 113	9 739	10 256	11.1	15.9	18.0	16.9	15.4
Canada	..	..	..	418	509	..	..	..	0.7	0.8
Mexico	0	0	0	0	0	0.0	0.0	0.0	0.0	0.0
Japan	..	..	..	1 055	1 125	..	..	..	1.8	1.7
Korea	0	..	0	0	0	0.0	..	0.0	0.0	0.0
Australia	..	..	..	0	0	..	..	..	0.0	0.0
New Zealand	..	..	..	0	0	..	..	..	0.0	0.0
Europe	..	36 728	38 894	45 203	53 858	..	81.9	76.8	78.5	80.7
European Union (15)	17 524	20 993	22 989	26 784	34 156	46.2	46.8	45.4	46.5	51.2
Austria	..	..	..	..	830	..	..	..	..	1.2
Belgium	..	..	..	..	0	..	..	..	..	0.0
Denmark	..	..	..	2 265	3 998	..	..	..	3.9	6.0
Finland	..	..	..	..	..	..	..	..	..	..
France	..	631	1 029	1 697	1 257	..	1.4	2.0	2.9	1.9
Germany	690	2 602	2 716	2 059	2 727	1.8	5.8	5.4	3.6	4.1
Greece	..	..	..	0	0	..	..	..	0.0	0.0
Ireland	0	..	0	0	722	0.0	..	0.0	0.0	1.1
Italy	..	..	..	699	480	..	..	..	1.2	0.7
Luxembourg	..	..	..	0	578	..	..	..	0.0	0.9
Netherlands	3 714	3 685	4 231	3 328	6 672	9.8	8.2	8.4	5.8	10.0
Portugal	0	..	0	0	..	0.0	..	0.0	0.0	..
Spain	0	0	0	0	..	0.0	0.0	0.0	0.0	..
Sweden	8 038	8 483	8 849	11 923	11 220	21.2	18.9	17.5	20.7	16.8
United Kingdom	2 957	3 701	3 199	4 563	5 087	7.8	8.3	6.3	7.9	7.6
Czech Republic	..	..	..	0	0	..	..	..	0.0	0.0
Hungary	..	..	..	0	0	..	..	..	0.0	0.0
Iceland	..	..	..	0	0	..	..	..	0.0	0.0
Norway	..	..	..	8 991	11 068	..	..	..	15.6	16.6
Poland	..	..	..	0	0	..	..	..	0.0	0.0
Slovak Republic	..	..	..	0	0	..	..	..	0.0	0.0
Switzerland	7 924	8 682	8 643	9 427	8 634	20.9	19.4	17.1	16.4	12.9
Turkey	..	..	..	0	0	..	..	..	0.0	0.0
Non-OECD Europe, of which:	..	..	..	0	0	..	..	..	0.0	0.0
Baltic countries	..	..	..	0	0	..	..	..	0.0	0.0
Bulgaria	..	..	..	0	0	..	..	..	0.0	0.0
Croatia	..	..	..	0	0	..	..	..	0.0	0.0
Romania	..	..	..	0	0	..	..	..	0.0	0.0
Russian Federation	..	..	..	0	0	..	..	..	0.0	0.0
Slovenia	..	..	..	0	0	..	..	..	0.0	0.0
Ukraine	..	..	..	0	0	..	..	..	0.0	0.0
Yugoslavia	..	..	..	0	0	..	..	..	0.0	0.0
Non-OECD Asia, of which:	..	..	..	..	1 006	..	..	..	..	1.5
China	..	..	..	0	0	..	..	..	0.0	0.0
Chinese Taipei	0	..	0	0	0	0.0	..	0.0	0.0	0.0
Hong Kong (China)	0	..	0	0	..	0.0	..	0.0	0.0	..
India	..	..	..	0	0	..	..	..	0.0	0.0
Indonesia	..	..	..	0	..	..	..	..	0.0	..
Malaysia	..	..	..	0	..	..	..	..	0.0	..
Philippines	..	..	..	0	0	..	..	..	0.0	0.0
Singapore	0	..	..	..	0	0.0	..	..	..	0.0
Thailand	..	..	..	0	0	..	..	..	0.0	0.0
Near and Middle East	..	..	..	0	0	..	..	..	0.0	0.0
Africa	..	..	..	0	0	..	..	..	0.0	0.0
Latin America, of which:	0	0	..	..	0	0.0	0.0	..	..	0.0
Argentina	..	..	..	0	0	..	..	..	0.0	0.0
Brazil	0	..	0	0	0	0.0	..	0.0	0.0	0.0
Chile	..	..	..	0	0	..	..	..	0.0	0.0

Note: Majority foreign-owned firms.
Firmes sous contrôle étranger majoritaire.

Inward investments 　　　　　　　　　　　　　　　　　　　　　　　*Investissements entrants*

Table 4A - Tableau 4A

TURNOVER BY INDUSTRY

CHIFFRE D'AFFAIRES PAR INDUSTRIE

		Foreign affiliates *(Millions of FIM)* **Filiales étrangères** *(Millions de FIM)*					*As a % of national total* *En % du total national*				
ISIC Revision 3		1995	1996	1997	1998	1999	1995	1996	1997	1998	1999
10/14	Mining & quarrying	..	1 045	1 305	627	747	..	22.8	25.3	14.8	20.3
15/37	**TOTAL MANUFACTURING**	**38 427**	**50 366**	**61 646**	**67 536**	**81 685**	**10.1**	**12.7**	**13.7**	**14.3**	**16.2**
15/16	Food, beverages, tobacco	3 109	2 831	3 724	2 557	6 831	6.7	6.0	7.7	5.3	14.5
17/19	Textiles, clothing, leather, footwear	303	352	564	925	919	3.6	4.3	6.4	10.0	10.2
20/22	Wood and paper products	2 378	2 509	3 114	3 889	4 987	2.2	2.3	2.4	2.9	3.7
20	Wood products	..	..	..	1 111	1 183	..	..	..	4.0	4.0
21/22	Paper, printing and publishing	..	..	..	2 778	3 804	..	..	..	2.6	3.6
23/25	Chemicals, Total	..	..	..	..	..	..	..	..	..	..
23	Refined petroleum, nuclear fuel	..	..	..	..	..	..	..	..	..	..
24/25	Chemicals, rubber & plastics prod.	5 122	8 075	11 661	12 203	16 406	15.8	24.9	30.0	32.1	41.5
24	Chemical products	4 187	6 894	10 346	10 489	14 652	18.2	30.3	39.3	39.5	53.1
2423	Pharmaceuticals	..	..	..	1 399	1 332	..	..	..	29.9	28.8
25	Rubber and plastics products	935	1 181	1 315	1 714	1 753	9.9	12.1	10.4	14.9	14.6
26	Non-metallic mineral products	2 526	3 829	3 485	4 637	5 025	29.1	44.9	34.2	38.8	37.2
27/28	Basic & fabricated metals	2 968	4 718	5 235	5 523	5 395	7.8	11.7	11.5	11.9	11.7
27	Basic metals	1 163	..	290	511	210	5.1	..	1.2	2.1	0.9
28	Fabricated metal products	1 805	..	4 945	5 012	5 185	11.6	..	23.8	23.0	23.0
29/32	Machinery, Total	..	..	..	..	29 876	..	..	..	..	18.7
29/30	Non-electrical machinery	..	..	..	..	14 376	..	..	..	..	24.0
29	Non-electrical machinery nec	5 471	6 831	8 288	10 060	10 625	13.1	14.7	16.8	18.8	20.0
30	Office and computing machinery	..	..	..	..	3 751	..	..	..	..	54.9
31/32	Electrical & electronic equipment	7 738	10 666	13 061	13 690	15 500	21.7	23.9	23.4	18.4	15.6
31	Electrical machinery nec	5 946	9 159	9 662	9 099	9 826	50.9	62.1	62.0	59.4	66.1
32	Radio, TV & communications eq.	1 792	1 507	3 399	4 591	5 674	7.5	5.1	8.4	7.8	6.7
33	Scientific instruments	771	1 024	1 387	1 379	2 171	13.6	15.7	19.0	17.0	23.6
34/35	Transportation equipment	..	..	..	..	..	..	..	..	..	..
34	Motor vehicles	..	..	..	..	..	..	..	..	..	..
35	Other transport equipment	..	..	..	7 152	7 766	..	..	..	67.6	74.5
351	Shipbuilding & repairing	..	..	..	6 901	7 485	..	..	..	72.1	79.5
353	Aircraft and spacecraft	0	0	0	0	0	0.0	0.0	0.0	0.0	0.0
36/37	Other manufacturing	308	307	616	1 015	1 018	4.3	4.0	7.0	10.5	9.4
40/45	Construction, electricity, gas & water	4 905	6 062	7 212	10 986	13 748	6.4	7.0	7.7	9.7	11.6
50/55	Trade, repair, hotels & restaurants	48 980	60 987	75 872	82 495	91 624	13.6	15.6	17.7	18.3	19.3
65/74	Finance, insurance, business services	5 249	6 989	6 723	10 240	11 627	8.9	11.3	9.8	12.8	12.4
	OTHER ACTIVITIES	..	7 473	8 764	9 619	13 461	..	6.5	6.7	6.4	8.4
01/99	**GRAND TOTAL**	**103 079**	**132 922**	**161 520**	**181 502**	**212 891**	**10.6**	**12.6**	**13.7**	**14.3**	**15.7**

Note: Majority foreign-owned firms.
Firmes sous contrôle étranger majoritaire.

Inward investments

Table 5A - Tableau 5A

TURNOVER BY COUNTRY OF ORIGIN IN THE MANUFACTURING SECTOR

CHIFFRE D'AFFAIRES PAR PAYS D'ORIGINE DANS L'INDUSTRIE MANUFACTURIÈRE

Country of origin (UBO)	Turnover (Millions of FIM) Chiffre d'affaires (Millions de FIM)					As a % of all countries En % du total des pays				
	1995	1996	1997	1998	1999	1995	1996	1997	1998	1999
All countries	38 427	50 366	61 646	67 536	81 685	100.0	100.0	100.0	100.0	100.0
Total OECD	..	..	..	66 253	80 781	..	..	..	98.1	98.9
United States	5 002	8 764	12 248	13 029	14 895	13.0	17.4	19.9	19.3	18.2
Canada	..	..	..	455	662	..	..	..	0.7	0.8
Mexico	0	0	0	0	0	0.0	0.0	0.0	0.0	0.0
Japan	..	..	..	3 808	4 162	..	..	..	5.6	5.1
Korea	0	..	0	0	0	0.0	..	0.0	0.0	0.0
Australia	..	..	..	0	0	..	..	..	0.0	0.0
New Zealand	..	..	..	0	0	..	..	..	0.0	0.0
Europe	..	39 050	43 996	48 961	61 062	..	77.5	71.4	72.5	74.8
European Union (15)	16 824	21 849	26 743	29 186	38 274	43.8	43.4	43.4	43.2	46.9
Austria	..	..	..	..	975	..	..	..	..	1.2
Belgium	..	..	..	..	0	..	..	..	..	0.0
Denmark	..	..	..	2 308	6 637	..	..	..	3.4	8.1
Finland	..	..	..	..	..	..	..	..	..	..
France	..	558	1 094	1 726	1 346	..	1.1	1.8	2.6	1.6
Germany	531	2 493	2 980	2 118	2 768	1.4	4.9	4.8	3.1	3.4
Greece	..	..	..	0	0	..	..	..	0.0	0.0
Ireland	0	..	0	0	1 476	0.0	..	0.0	0.0	1.8
Italy	..	..	..	455	258	..	..	..	0.7	0.3
Luxembourg	..	..	..	0	475	..	..	..	0.0	0.6
Netherlands	4 869	5 880	7 106	4 882	7 231	12.7	11.7	11.5	7.2	8.9
Portugal	0	..	0	0	..	0.0	..	0.0	0.0	..
Spain	0	0	0	0	..	0.0	0.0	0.0	0.0	..
Sweden	7 511	7 885	9 255	12 852	11 092	19.5	15.7	15.0	19.0	13.6
United Kingdom	2 265	3 508	3 367	4 585	5 686	5.9	7.0	5.5	6.8	7.0
Czech Republic	..	..	..	0	0	..	..	..	0.0	0.0
Hungary	..	..	..	0	0	..	..	..	0.0	0.0
Iceland	..	..	..	0	0	..	..	..	0.0	0.0
Norway	..	..	..	9 486	13 862	..	..	..	14.0	17.0
Poland	..	..	..	0	0	..	..	..	0.0	0.0
Slovak Republic	..	..	..	0	0	..	..	..	0.0	0.0
Switzerland	7 937	8 276	8 997	10 289	8 926	20.7	16.4	14.6	15.2	10.9
Turkey	..	..	..	0	0	..	..	..	0.0	0.0
Non-OECD Europe, of which:	..	..	..	0	0	..	..	..	0.0	0.0
Baltic countries	..	..	..	0	0	..	..	..	0.0	0.0
Bulgaria	..	..	..	0	0	..	..	..	0.0	0.0
Croatia	..	..	..	0	0	..	..	..	0.0	0.0
Romania	..	..	..	0	0	..	..	..	0.0	0.0
Russian Federation	..	..	..	0	0	..	..	..	0.0	0.0
Slovenia	..	..	..	0	0	..	..	..	0.0	0.0
Ukraine	..	..	..	0	0	..	..	..	0.0	0.0
Yugoslavia	..	..	..	0	0	..	..	..	0.0	0.0
Non-OECD Asia, of which:	..	..	..	..	904	..	..	..	..	1.1
China	..	..	..	0	0	..	..	..	0.0	0.0
Chinese Taipei	0	..	0	0	0	0.0	..	0.0	0.0	0.0
Hong Kong (China)	0	..	0	0	..	0.0	..	0.0	0.0	..
India	..	..	..	0	0	..	..	..	0.0	0.0
Indonesia	..	..	..	0	..	..	..	..	0.0	..
Malaysia	..	..	..	0	..	..	..	..	0.0	..
Philippines	..	..	..	0	0	..	..	..	0.0	0.0
Singapore	0	..	..	..	0	0.0	..	..	..	0.0
Thailand	..	..	..	0	0	..	..	..	0.0	0.0
Near and Middle East	..	..	..	0	0	..	..	..	0.0	0.0
Africa	..	..	..	0	0	..	..	..	0.0	0.0
Latin America, of which:	0	0	..	..	0	0.0	0.0	..	..	0.0
Argentina	..	..	..	0	0	..	..	..	0.0	0.0
Brazil	0	..	0	0	0	0.0	..	0.0	0.0	0.0
Chile	..	..	..	0	0	..	..	..	0.0	0.0

Note: Majority foreign-owned firms.
Firmes sous contrôle étranger majoritaire.

Table 6A - Tableau 6A

VALUE ADDED / VALEUR AJOUTÉE

| | | Foreign affiliates (Millions of FIM) | | | | | As a % of national total | | | | |
| | | Filiales étrangères (Millions de FIM) | | | | | En % du total national | | | | |
By industry (ISIC Rev. 3)		1995	1996	1997	1998	1999	1995	1996	1997	1998	1999
10/14	Mining & quarrying	..	315	403	191	233	..	18.6	20.9	12.5	17.9
15/37	**TOTAL MANUFACTURING**	12 100	15 653	19 387	21 013	24 767	9.7	12.6	13.8	14.0	16.0
15/16	Food, beverages, tobacco	816	722	1 056	778	2 017	6.8	6.1	8.6	6.5	17.3
17/19	Textiles, clothing, leather, footwear	107	135	184	296	281	3.3	4.1	5.5	8.4	8.2
20/22	Wood and paper products	541	571	716	910	1 414	1.3	1.6	1.7	2.2	3.4
20	Wood products	..	..	..	211	241	..	..	..	2.9	3.3
21/22	Paper, printing and publishing	..	..	..	699	1 173	..	..	..	2.0	3.4
23/25	Chemicals, Total										
23	Refined petroleum, nuclear fuel	..	..	..	..	..	..	..	..	..	..
24/25	Chemicals, rubber & plastics prod.	1 603	2 455	3 626	3 643	5 084	14.1	21.5	28.7	27.1	35.1
24	Chemical products	1 270	2 019	3 138	3 040	4 439	16.0	26.2	36.9	34.9	47.3
2423	Pharmaceuticals	..	..	..	612	609	..	..	..	29.5	28.2
25	Rubber and plastics products	333	436	488	603	645	9.6	11.8	11.8	12.7	12.7
26	Non-metallic mineral products	996	1 449	1 297	1 665	1 745	28.3	42.8	31.7	34.6	33.0
27/28	Basic & fabricated metals	1 043	1 441	1 696	1 806	1 803	7.2	10.3	10.8	11.3	11.6
27	Basic metals	413	..	97	148	83	5.0	..	1.3	2.1	1.3
28	Fabricated metal products	630	..	1 599	1 658	1 720	10.1	..	19.5	18.3	18.9
29/32	Machinery, Total	..	..	..	..	9 307	..	..	..	..	19.2
29/30	Non-electrical machinery	..	..	..	..	3 790	..	..	..	..	23.2
29	Non-electrical machinery nec	1 769	2 266	2 932	3 358	3 600	11.6	13.7	17.2	19.0	22.3
30	Office and computing machinery	..	..	..	..	190	..	..	..	..	92.7
31/32	Electrical & electronic equipment	2 468	3 845	4 680	5 224	5 517	20.7	26.7	23.9	19.7	17.1
31	Electrical machinery nec	1 950	3 040	3 163	3 047	3 165	48.8	61.1	59.5	58.3	64.6
32	Radio, TV & communications eq.	518	805	1 517	2 177	2 352	6.6	8.5	10.6	10.2	8.6
33	Scientific instruments	349	440	617	602	848	13.9	15.3	18.9	17.7	22.0
34/35	Transportation equipment	..	..	..	..	..	..	..	..	..	..
34	Motor vehicles	..	..	..	..	..	..	..	..	..	..
35	Other transport equipment	..	..	..	1 924	1 547	..	..	..	63.3	58.0
351	Shipbuilding & repairing	..	..	..	1 904	1 466	..	..	..	70.9	66.1
353	Aircraft and spacecraft	0	0	0	0	0	0.0	0.0	0.0	0.0	0.0
36/37	Other manufacturing	144	161	269	337	323	5.1	5.5	8.4	9.4	8.6
40/45	Construction, electricity, gas & water	1 261	1 614	1 566	2 528	2 987	5.0	5.9	5.3	6.6	7.7
50/55	Trade, repair, hotels & restaurants	8 106	8 761	9 738	12 178	12 851	14.5	15.3	16.1	18.6	19.3
65/74	Finance, insurance, business services	2 192	2 995	3 212	4 153	4 921	8.3	9.4	9.6	9.8	11.1
	OTHER ACTIVITIES	..	1 558	1 649	1 954	2 893	..	2.8	2.8	3.0	4.5
01/99	**GRAND TOTAL**	25 240	30 896	35 955	42 017	48 651	9.0	10.4	11.1	11.6	13.1

Total manufacturing by investing country							As a % of total manufacturing by foreign affiliates				
All countries		12 100	15 653	19 387	21 013	24 767	100.0	100.0	100.0	100.0	100.0
United States		..	2 952	4 467	4 558	5 211	..	18.9	23.0	21.7	21.0
Canada		..	..	..	..	..	..	..	..	..	..
Mexico		0	0	0	0	..	0.0	0.0	0.0	0.0	..
Japan		..	..	..	327	320	..	..	..	1.6	1.3
Europe		..	12 273	14 201	..	..	..	78.4	73.3	..	..
European Union (15)		5 213	7 170	8 684	9 794	12 574	43.1	45.8	44.8	46.6	50.8
Belgium		..	..	..	..	..	..	..	..	..	..
France		..	208	426	658	514	..	1.3	2.2	3.1	2.1
Germany		..	844	944	831	1 127	..	5.4	4.9	4.0	4.6
Italy		..	..	..	..	..	..	..	..	..	..
Netherlands		..	1 515	1 952	1 525	2 361	..	9.7	10.1	7.3	9.5
Spain		0	0	0	0	..	0.0	0.0	0.0	0.0	..
Sweden		..	2 784	3 352	..	..	..	17.8	17.3	..	..
United Kingdom		..	1 253	1 006	1 596	1 934	..	8.0	5.2	7.6	7.8
Switzerland		..	2 885	3 146	3 424	3 089	..	18.4	16.2	16.3	12.5
Australia and New Zealand		0	0	0	0	..	0.0	0.0	0.0	0.0	..
Asia (non-OECD)		..	..	..	..	126	..	..	..	..	0.5
Latin America		0	0	..	..	0	0.0	0.0	..	..	0.0

Note: Majority foreign-owned enterprises.
Entreprises sous contrôle étranger majoritaire.

Inward investments
Investissements entrants

Table 7A - Tableau 7A

COMPENSATION OF EMPLOYEES / SALAIRES ET CHARGES SOCIALES

By industry (ISIC Rev. 3)	Foreign affiliates (Millions of FIM) Filiales étrangères (Millions de FIM)					As a % of national total En % du total national				
	1995	1996	1997	1998	1999	1995	1996	1997	1998	1999
10/14 Mining & quarrying	..	177	191	87	108	..	22.5	21.5	11.8	17.5
15/37 TOTAL MANUFACTURING	**7 580**	**9 175**	**10 607**	**12 106**	**14 370**	**10.8**	**12.7**	**14.0**	**14.7**	**16.9**
15/16 Food, beverages, tobacco	530	456	603	431	1 058	7.0	6.1	8.0	5.5	13.8
17/19 Textiles, clothing, leather, footwear	72	79	117	189	185	3.2	3.6	5.3	8.0	8.1
20/22 Wood and paper products	312	316	365	563	843	1.6	1.6	1.8	2.6	3.9
20 Wood products	..	..	..	152	173	..	..	..	3.3	3.7
21/22 Paper, printing and publishing	..	..	..	411	670	..	..	..	2.5	4.0
23/25 Chemicals, Total	..	..	..	..	..	..	..	..	..	..
23 Refined petroleum, nuclear fuel	..	..	..	..	..	..	..	..	..	..
24/25 Chemicals, rubber & plastics prod.	711	1 122	1 490	1 598	2 228	12.2	19.1	24.1	23.6	31.3
24 Chemical products	507	869	1 207	1 244	1 837	13.9	23.7	32.0	31.3	44.1
2423 Pharmaceuticals	..	..	..	289	335	..	..	..	26.4	31.3
25 Rubber and plastics products	204	253	283	354	391	9.4	11.5	11.7	12.6	13.3
26 Non-metallic mineral products	623	900	659	879	955	27.3	42.4	27.8	32.8	31.9
27/28 Basic & fabricated metals	698	998	1 109	1 187	1 162	8.7	11.9	12.2	12.0	11.9
27 Basic metals	240	..	56	88	50	6.6	..	1.5	2.2	1.3
28 Fabricated metal products	458	..	1 053	1 099	1 112	10.6	..	19.7	18.5	18.7
29/32 Machinery, Total	..	..	..	..	5 500	..	..	..	..	23.1
29/30 Non-electrical machinery	..	..	..	..	2 627	..	..	..	..	20.6
29 Non-electrical machinery nec	1 229	1 576	1 875	2 232	2 441	12.0	14.6	16.8	18.0	19.8
30 Office and computing machinery	..	..	..	..	186	..	..	..	..	41.2
31/32 Electrical & electronic equipment	1 579	2 184	2 393	2 599	2 873	25.1	29.8	29.7	27.2	25.9
31 Electrical machinery nec	1 258	1 921	1 909	1 802	1 956	47.0	60.4	59.5	56.5	61.8
32 Radio, TV & communications eq.	321	263	484	797	917	8.9	6.3	10.0	12.5	11.6
33 Scientific instruments	284	301	379	403	559	17.4	17.8	19.6	20.2	23.6
34/35 Transportation equipment	..	..	..	..	..	..	..	..	..	..
34 Motor vehicles	..	..	..	..	..	..	..	..	..	..
35 Other transport equipment	..	..	..	1 411	1 414	..	..	..	63.0	63.2
351 Shipbuilding & repairing	..	..	..	1 394	1 340	..	..	..	70.9	70.7
353 Aircraft and spacecraft	0	0	0	0	0	0.0	0.0	0.0	0.0	0.0
36/37 Other manufacturing	94	102	188	257	230	4.7	5.1	8.7	10.5	9.2
40/45 Construction, electricity, gas & water	1 013	1 213	1 226	1 768	2 114	7.1	8.0	7.3	8.4	9.8
50/55 Trade, repair, hotels & restaurants	5 087	5 534	6 209	7 812	8 088	15.1	15.9	16.9	19.1	19.9
65/74 Finance, insurance, business services	1 627	2 204	2 276	3 068	3 562	9.0	11.3	10.9	13.0	13.8
OTHER ACTIVITIES	..	997	1 173	1 475	2 127	..	3.3	3.8	4.3	6.2
01/99 GRAND TOTAL	**16 301**	**19 300**	**21 683**	**26 316**	**30 368**	**10.0**	**11.2**	**11.9**	**13.0**	**14.6**

Total manufacturing by investing country						As a % of total manufacturing by foreign affiliates				
All countries	7 580	9 175	10 607	12 106	14 370	100.0	100.0	100.0	100.0	100.0
United States	..	1 560	2 020	2 182	2 313	..	17.0	19.0	18.0	16.1
Canada	..	..	..	..	..	..	..	..	..	..
Mexico	0	0	0	0	..	0.0	0.0	0.0	0.0	..
Japan	..	..	..	219	264	..	..	..	1.8	1.8
Europe	..	7 447	8 048	..	..	..	81.2	75.9	..	..
European Union (15)	..	4 229	4 688	5 482	7 146	..	46.1	44.2	45.3	49.7
Belgium	..	..	..	..	..	..	..	..	..	..
France	..	116	209	349	263	..	1.3	2.0	2.9	1.8
Germany	..	545	589	409	585	..	5.9	5.6	3.4	4.1
Italy	..	..	..	..	..	..	..	..	..	..
Netherlands	..	840	934	748	1 355	..	9.2	8.8	6.2	9.4
Spain	0	0	0	0	..	0.0	0.0	0.0	0.0	..
Sweden	..	1 657	1 804	..	..	..	18.1	17.0	..	..
United Kingdom	..	762	600	941	1 100	..	8.3	5.7	7.8	7.7
Switzerland	..	1 826	1 903	2 071	1 981	..	19.9	17.9	17.1	13.8
Australia and New Zealand	0	0	0	0	..	0.0	0.0	0.0	0.0	..
Asia (non-OECD)	..	..	..	..	183	..	..	..	..	1.3
Latin America	0	0	..	..	0	0.0	0.0	..	..	0.0

Note: Majority foreign-owned enterprises.
Entreprises sous contrôle étranger majoritaire.

Inward investments *Investissements entrants*

Table 8A - Tableau 8A

R&D EXPENDITURE / DÉPENSES DE R-D

By industry (ISIC Rev. 3)	Foreign affiliates (Millions of FIM) / Filiales étrangères (Millions de FIM)					As a % of national total / En % du total national				
	1995	1996	1997	1998	1999	1995	1996	1997	1998	1999
10/14 Mining & quarrying	..	..	10	6	0	..	..	32.3	12.2	0.0
15/37 TOTAL MANUFACTURING	815	..	1 054	1 242	1 815	12.1	..	11.5	11.3	14.1
15/16 Food, beverages, tobacco	12	..	7	14	71	4.6	..	2.4	4.1	22.2
17/19 Textiles, clothing, leather, footwear	..	..	..	11	6	..	..	..	15.1	8.0
20/22 Wood and paper products	3	..	..	4	9	0.7	..	..	0.8	1.9
20 Wood products	..	..	..	0	0	..	..	..	0.0	0.0
21/22 Paper, printing and publishing	..	..	..	4	9	..	..	..	0.9	2.1
23/25 Chemicals, Total	..	..	..	217	412	..	..	..	16.5	31.1
23 Refined petroleum, nuclear fuel	..	..	..	0	0	..	..	..	..	..
24/25 Chemicals, rubber & plastics prod.	..	..	..	217	412	..	..	..	..	..
24 Chemical products	48	..	195	214	404	5.6	..	23.0	22.9	38.2
2423 Pharmaceuticals	..	..	..	147	156	..	..	..	..	..
25 Rubber and plastics products	..	..	..	3	8	..	..	..	..	..
26 Non-metallic mineral products	23	..	26	25	28	29.1	..	34.7	31.3	26.4
27/28 Basic & fabricated metals	..	..	..	70	76	..	..	..	19.3	20.1
27 Basic metals	..	..	..	0	0	..	..	..	0.0	0.0
28 Fabricated metal products	4	..	53	70	76	2.4	..	38.4	44.0	46.6
29/32 Machinery, Total	..	..	..	..	939	..	..	..	..	10.3
29/30 Non-electrical machinery	..	..	..	..	255	..	..	..	..	..
29 Non-electrical machinery nec	61	..	86	154	228	7.6	..	7.7	11.1	15.4
30 Office and computing machinery	..	..	..	..	27	..	..	..	..	..
31/32 Electrical & electronic equipment	402	..	497	552	684	14.4	..	..	..	..
31 Electrical machinery nec	267	..	293	291	288	69.2	..	..	..	..
32 Radio, TV & communications eq.	135	..	204	261	396	5.6	..	..	..	..
33 Scientific instruments	27	..	104	110	213	6.0	..	16.9	15.8	25.0
34/35 Transportation equipment	..	..	..	..	..	..	..	..	..	..
34 Motor vehicles	..	..	..	..	..	..	..	..	..	..
35 Other transport equipment	..	..	..	44	39	..	..	..	53.7	45.9
351 Shipbuilding & repairing	..	..	..	39	39	..	..	..	..	..
353 Aircraft and spacecraft	..	..	..	0	0	..	..	..	..	..
36/37 Other manufacturing	..	..	..	5	2	..	..	..	8.5	2.5
40/45 Construction, electricity, gas & water	..	..	22	20	16	..	..	8.0	7.0	5.1
50/55 Trade, repair, hotels & restaurants	..	..	42	133	103	..	..	27.3	65.5	41.2
65/74 Finance, insurance, business services	..	..	379	362	406	..	..	..	..	..
OTHER ACTIVITIES	..	..	3	3	5	..	..	..	..	..
01/99 GRAND TOTAL	..	..	1 510	1 767	2 345	..	..	13.3	13.2	14.9

Total manufacturing by investing country						As a % of total manufacturing by foreign affiliates				
All countries	815	..	1 054	1 242	1 815	100.0	..	100.0	100.0	100.0
United States	..	..	380	439	577	..	..	36.1	35.3	31.8
Canada	..	..	..	..	..	..	..	..	..	..
Mexico	..	..	..	0	..	..	..	..	0.0	..
Japan	..	..	..	48	50	..	..	..	3.9	2.8
Europe	..	..	..	..	..	..	..	..	..	..
European Union (15)	..	..	338	395	684	..	..	32.1	31.8	37.7
Belgium	..	..	..	..	..	..	..	..	..	..
France	..	..	..	13	5	..	..	..	1.0	0.3
Germany	..	..	..	149	152	..	..	..	12.0	8.4
Italy	..	..	..	..	..	..	..	..	..	..
Netherlands	..	..	..	42	85	..	..	..	3.4	4.7
Spain	..	..	..	0	..	..	..	..	0.0	..
Sweden	..	..	..	..	..	..	..	..	..	..
United Kingdom	..	..	..	68	116	..	..	..	5.5	6.4
Switzerland	..	..	..	292	264	..	..	..	23.5	14.5
Australia and New Zealand	..	..	..	0	..	..	..	..	0.0	..
Asia (non-OECD)	..	..	..	..	34	..	..	..	..	1.9
Latin America	..	..	..	0	0	..	..	..	0.0	0.0

Note: Majority foreign-owned enterprises.
Entreprises sous contrôle étranger majoritaire.

Inward investments   *Investissements entrants*

Table 9A - Tableau 9A
NUMBER OF RESEARCHERS / NOMBRE DE CHERCHEURS

By industry (ISIC Rev. 3)	Foreign affiliates (Units) Filiales étrangères (Unités)					As a % of national total En % du total national				
	1995	1996	1997	1998	1999	1995	1996	1997	1998	1999
10/14 Mining & quarrying	..	..	34	20	0	..	..	44.2	24.1	0.0
15/37 TOTAL MANUFACTURING	**2 076**	..	**2 934**	**3 100**	**3 266**	**11.0**	..	**13.3**	**12.5**	**14.6**
15/16 Food, beverages, tobacco	31	..	25	36	149	4.2	..	3.3	4.3	24.5
17/19 Textiles, clothing, leather, footwear	..	..	..	28	13	..	..	..	11.8	7.7
20/22 Wood and paper products	23	..	..	11	20	1.6	..	..	0.8	2.0
20 Wood products	..	..	..	2	1	..	..	..	1.1	1.2
21/22 Paper, printing and publishing	..	..	..	9	19	..	..	..	0.8	2.1
23/25 Chemicals, Total	..	..	..	592	751	..	..	..	..	26.2
23 Refined petroleum, nuclear fuel	..	..	..	0	0	..	..	..	..	..
24/25 Chemicals, rubber & plastics prod.	..	..	..	592	751	..	..	..	..	..
24 Chemical products	121	..	504	574	735	5.2	..	21.9	22.7	33.3
2423 Pharmaceuticals	..	..	..	377	389	..	..	..	..	..
25 Rubber and plastics products	..	..	..	18	15	..	..	..	..	..
26 Non-metallic mineral products	82	..	116	91	51	32.5	..	47.2	35.4	28.8
27/28 Basic & fabricated metals	..	..	..	167	139	..	..	..	15.6	18.9
27 Basic metals	..	..	..	0	0	..	..	..	0.0	0.0
28 Fabricated metal products	26	..	144	167	139	4.0	..	27.7	31.6	44.0
29/32 Machinery, Total	..	..	..	..	1 575	..	..	..	..	10.9
29/30 Non-electrical machinery	..	..	..	..	449	..	..	..	..	..
29 Non-electrical machinery nec	186	..	248	397	391	8.9	..	8.4	12.3	17.3
30 Office and computing machinery	..	..	..	..	58	..	..	..	..	..
31/32 Electrical & electronic equipment	888	..	1 280	1 187	1 126	12.0	..	..	..	..
31 Electrical machinery nec	564	..	759	647	608	58.8	..	..	..	..
32 Radio, TV & communications eq.	324	..	521	540	518	5.0	..	..	..	..
33 Scientific instruments	103	..	296	302	486	8.5	..	18.6	17.0	27.2
34/35 Transportation equipment	..	..	..	..	..	..	..	..	..	..
34 Motor vehicles	..	..	..	..	..	..	..	..	..	..
35 Other transport equipment	..	..	..	175	63	..	..	..	54.2	35.8
351 Shipbuilding & repairing	..	..	..	152	63	..	..	..	..	..
353 Aircraft and spacecraft	..	..	..	0	0	..	..	..	..	..
36/37 Other manufacturing	..	..	..	13	7	..	..	..	5.7	3.1
40/45 Construction, electricity, gas & water	..	..	135	119	23	..	..	13.7	11.6	5.3
50/55 Trade, repair, hotels & restaurants	..	..	80	292	174	..	..	13.4	47.9	43.5
65/74 Finance, insurance, business services	..	..	823	738	701	..	..	..	..	..
OTHER ACTIVITIES	..	..	10	11	8	..	..	..	..	..
01/99 GRAND TOTAL	..	..	**4 016**	**4 280**	**4 172**	..	..	**13.8**	**13.2**	**15.0**

Total manufacturing by investing country						As a % of total manufacturing by foreign affiliates				
All countries	2 076	..	2 934	3 100	3 266	100.0	..	100.0	100.0	100.0
United States	..	..	923	977	925	..	..	31.5	31.5	28.3
Canada	..	..	..	..	..	..	..	..	..	..
Mexico	..	..	..	0	..	..	..	..	0.0	..
Japan	..	..	..	125	108	..	..	..	4.0	3.3
Europe	..	..	..	..	..	..	..	..	..	..
European Union (15)	..	..	1 067	1 115	1 307	..	..	36.4	36.0	40.0
Belgium	..	..	..	..	..	..	..	..	..	..
France	..	..	..	56	14	..	..	..	1.8	0.4
Germany	..	..	..	369	372	..	..	..	11.9	11.4
Italy	..	..	..	..	..	..	..	..	..	..
Netherlands	..	..	..	169	191	..	..	..	5.5	5.8
Spain	..	..	..	0	..	..	..	..	0.0	..
Sweden	..	..	..	..	..	..	..	..	..	..
United Kingdom	..	..	..	167	204	..	..	..	5.4	6.2
Switzerland	..	..	..	637	520	..	..	..	20.5	15.9
Australia and New Zealand	..	..	..	0	..	..	..	..	0.0	..
Asia (non-OECD)	..	..	..	..	54	..	..	..	..	1.7
Latin America	..	..	..	0	0	..	..	..	0.0	0.0

Note: Majority foreign-owned enterprises. Total R&D personnel rather than researchers.
Entreprises sous contrôle étranger majoritaire. Ensemble du personnel de R-D plutôt que chercheurs.

Inward investments

Investissements entrants

Table 10A - Tableau 10A
GROSS FIXED CAPITAL FORMATION / FORMATION BRUTE DE CAPITAL FIXE

| | | Foreign affiliates *(Millions of FIM)* | | | | | As a % of national total | | | | |
| | | Filiales étrangères *(Millions de FIM)* | | | | | En % du total national | | | | |
By industry (ISIC Rev. 3)		1995	1996	1997	1998	1999	1995	1996	1997	1998	1999
10/14	Mining & quarrying	..	57	86	45	51	..	13.8	18.0	10.8	12.6
15/37	**TOTAL MANUFACTURING**	**1 844**	**1 599**	**2 131**	**3 112**	**2 941**	**8.2**	**6.5**	**7.8**	**14.4**	**15.4**
15/16	Food, beverages, tobacco	87	170	123	209	652	3.0	7.4	5.7	11.9	37.0
17/19	Textiles, clothing, leather, footwear	14	4	26	12	6	3.8	1.5	6.7	3.7	2.7
20/22	Wood and paper products	91	126	105	233	173	1.2	1.1	1.0	3.3	2.9
20	Wood products	..	..	..	38	33	..	..	..	2.4	2.2
21/22	Paper, printing and publishing	..	..	..	196	140	..	..	..	3.5	3.1
23/25	Chemicals, Total	..	..	..	..	..	..	..	..	..	..
23	Refined petroleum, nuclear fuel	..	..	..	..	..	..	..	..	..	..
24/25	Chemicals, rubber & plastics prod.	634	352	731	1 165	923	32.4	17.8	24.7	37.8	40.4
24	Chemical products	595	291	684	1 068	849	42.1	20.7	29.9	50.5	60.1
2423	Pharmaceuticals	..	..	..	32	95	..	..	..	16.2	46.1
25	Rubber and plastics products	39	61	47	98	74	7.2	10.6	6.9	10.1	8.5
26	Non-metallic mineral products	105	163	151	267	340	18.9	34.9	16.8	39.9	38.0
27/28	Basic & fabricated metals	214	152	188	272	150	6.8	5.1	4.6	8.7	6.1
27	Basic metals	143	..	9	17	37	6.2	..	0.3	1.0	2.9
28	Fabricated metal products	71	..	179	255	113	8.3	..	15.6	17.9	9.6
29/32	Machinery, Total	..	..	..	..	389	..	..	..	..	8.8
29/30	Non-electrical machinery	..	..	..	..	153	..	..	..	..	10.1
29	Non-electrical machinery nec	161	150	210	138	158	9.1	7.3	12.5	9.3	10.5
30	Office and computing machinery	..	..	..	..	- 5	..	..	..	..	..
31/32	Electrical & electronic equipment	305	342	420	382	236	10.7	22.5	20.0	15.2	8.1
31	Electrical machinery nec	202	275	268	141	64	44.2	55.4	44.4	25.5	22.7
32	Radio, TV & communications eq.	103	67	152	241	172	4.3	6.5	10.1	12.3	6.5
33	Scientific instruments	23	30	39	139	152	13.6	16.2	12.0	37.1	56.5
34/35	Transportation equipment	..	..	..	..	..	..	..	..	..	..
34	Motor vehicles	..	..	..	..	..	..	..	..	..	..
35	Other transport equipment	..	..	..	220	107	..	..	..	76.7	92.2
351	Shipbuilding & repairing	..	..	..	219	58	..	..	..	83.9	55.2
353	Aircraft and spacecraft	0	0	0	0	0	0.0	0.0	0.0	0.0	0.0
36/37	Other manufacturing	9	5	22	46	12	3.0	1.7	5.1	12.1	3.6
40/45	Construction, electricity, gas & water	82	153	555	301	84	1.1	3.2	4.6	4.9	1.5
50/55	Trade, repair, hotels & restaurants	879	1 239	1 676	1 014	872	13.7	15.9	20.1	20.3	12.7
65/74	Finance, insurance, business services	972	1 125	499	537	475	10.9	22.4	9.5	18.9	9.1
	OTHER ACTIVITIES	..	155	257	303	370	..	1.2	2.1	2.6	2.7
01/99	**GRAND TOTAL**	**4 024**	**4 329**	**5 205**	**5 311**	**4 792**	**7.2**	**7.8**	**7.9**	**11.2**	**9.4**

Total manufacturing by investing country							As a % of total manufacturing by foreign affiliates				
All countries		**1 844**	**1 599**	**2 131**	**3 112**	**2 941**	**100.0**	**100.0**	**100.0**	**100.0**	**100.0**
United States		..	364	503	688	647	..	22.8	23.6	22.1	22.0
Canada		..	..	..	..	..	..	..	..	..	..
Mexico		0	0	0	0	..	0.0	0.0	0.0	0.0	..
Japan		..	..	..	33	8	..	..	..	1.1	0.3
Europe		..	1 201	1 532	..	..	..	75.1	71.9	..	..
European Union (15)		..	801	1 184	1 598	1 973	..	50.1	55.6	51.3	67.1
Belgium		..	..	..	..	..	..	..	..	..	..
France		..	33	189	108	45	..	2.1	8.9	3.5	1.5
Germany		..	86	135	116	139	..	5.4	6.3	3.7	4.7
Italy		..	..	..	..	..	..	..	..	..	..
Netherlands		..	163	240	536	745	..	10.2	11.3	17.2	25.3
Spain		0	0	0	0	..	0.0	0.0	0.0	0.0	..
Sweden		..	299	371	..	..	..	18.7	17.4	..	..
United Kingdom		..	176	136	175	145	..	11.0	6.4	5.6	4.9
Switzerland		..	238	186	250	- 55	..	14.9	8.7	8.0	-1.9
Australia and New Zealand		0	0	0	0	..	0.0	0.0	0.0	0.0	..
Asia (non-OECD)		..	..	..	..	21	..	..	..	..	0.7
Latin America		0	0	..	..	0	0.0	0.0	..	..	0.0

Note: Majority foreign-owned enterprises. New definition from 1998. See country notes.
Entreprises sous contrôle étranger majoritaire. Changement de définition à partir de 1998. Voir les notes par pays.

FINLAND

FINLANDE

Inward investments

Investissements entrants

Table 11A - Tableau 11A

TOTAL EXPORTS BY INDUSTRY

EXPORTATIONS TOTALES PAR INDUSTRIE

ISIC Revision 3		Foreign affiliates (Millions of FIM) Filiales étrangères (Millions de FIM)					As a % of national total En % du total national				
		1995	1996	1997	1998	1999	1995	1996	1997	1998	1999
10/14	Mining & quarrying	..	..	..	..	331	..	..	..	..	44.2
15/37	**TOTAL MANUFACTURING**	**20 593**	**31 301**	**34 799**	**37 742**	**43 216**	..	..	..	**15.6**	**16.9**
15/16	Food, beverages, tobacco	..	..	..	395	602	..	..	..	6.4	10.4
17/19	Textiles, clothing, leather, footwear	..	..	..	369	379	..	..	..	10.6	12.1
20/22	Wood and paper products	..	..	..	1 208	2 214	..	..	..	1.6	3.1
20	Wood products	..	..	..	453	520	..	..	..	3.0	3.4
21/22	Paper, printing and publishing	..	..	..	755	1 694	..	..	..	1.3	3.0
23/25	Chemicals, Total	..	..	..	..	..	..	..	..	..	..
23	Refined petroleum, nuclear fuel	..	..	..	..	..	..	..	..	..	..
24/25	Chemicals, rubber & plastics prod.	..	..	..	5 701	8 566	..	..	..	33.3	47.9
24	Chemical products	..	..	..	5 242	7 964	..	..	..	41.9	59.5
2423	Pharmaceuticals	..	..	..	833	864	..	..	..	37.7	37.4
25	Rubber and plastics products	..	..	..	459	601	..	..	..	10.0	13.3
26	Non-metallic mineral products	..	..	..	1 457	1 477	..	..	..	47.5	47.0
27/28	Basic & fabricated metals	..	..	..	3 052	2 664	..	..	..	14.5	13.2
27	Basic metals	..	..	..	133	78	..	..	..	0.9	0.5
28	Fabricated metal products	..	..	..	2 919	2 586	..	..	..	49.4	49.0
29/32	Machinery, Total	..	..	..	..	18 595	..	..	..	..	17.0
29/30	Non-electrical machinery	..	..	..	..	8 617	..	..	..	..	26.3
29	Non-electrical machinery nec	..	..	..	6 396	7 146	..	..	..	20.8	23.6
30	Office and computing machinery	..	..	..	..	1 471	..	..	..	..	59.4
31/32	Electrical & electronic equipment	..	..	..	9 201	9 978	..	..	..	15.4	13.0
31	Electrical machinery nec	..	..	..	5 601	6 209	..	..	..	66.3	77.1
32	Radio, TV & communications eq.	..	..	..	3 600	3 769	..	..	..	7.0	5.5
33	Scientific instruments	..	..	..	1 041	1 458	..	..	..	22.2	26.3
34/35	Transportation equipment	..	..	..	..	..	..	..	..	..	..
34	Motor vehicles	..	..	..	..	..	..	..	..	..	..
35	Other transport equipment	..	..	..	6 042	6 223	..	..	..	86.9	89.8
351	Shipbuilding & repairing	..	..	..	6 027	6 176	..	..	..	89.7	93.0
353	Aircraft and spacecraft	..	..	..	0	0	..	..	..	0.0	0.0
36/37	Other manufacturing	..	..	..	310	224	..	..	..	12.1	10.2
40/45	Construction, electricity, gas & water	..	..	..	..	1 085	..	..	..	..	25.1
50/55	Trade, repair, hotels & restaurants	..	..	..	..	..	..	..	..	..	..
65/74	Finance, insurance, business services	..	..	..	..	..	..	..	..	..	..
	OTHER ACTIVITIES	..	..	..	..	..	..	..	..	..	..
01/99	**GRAND TOTAL**	..	..	..	..	..	..	..	..	..	..

Note: Majority foreign-owned firms.
Firmes sous contrôle étranger majoritaire.

93

Table 12A - Tableau 12A

TOTAL EXPORTS BY COUNTRY OF ORIGIN IN THE MANUFACTURING SECTOR

EXPORTATIONS TOTALES PAR PAYS D'ORIGINE DANS L'INDUSTRIE MANUFACTURIÈRE

Country of origin (UBO)	Total exports (Millions of FIM) Exportations totales (Millions de FIM)					As a % of all countries En % du total des pays				
	1995	1996	1997	1998	1999	1995	1996	1997	1998	1999
All countries	20 593	31 301	34 799	37 742	43 216	100.0	100.0	100.0	100.0	100.0
Total OECD	..	..	..	36 768	42 556	..	..	..	97.4	98.5
United States	..	..	..	9 049	9 096	..	..	..	24.0	21.0
Canada	..	..	..	302	442	..	..	..	0.8	1.0
Mexico	..	..	..	0	0	..	..	..	0.0	0.0
Japan	..	..	..	2 193	1 923	..	..	..	5.8	4.4
Korea	..	..	..	0	0	..	..	..	0.0	0.0
Australia	..	..	..	0	0	..	..	..	0.0	0.0
New Zealand	..	..	..	0	0	..	..	..	0.0	0.0
Europe	..	..	..	25 224	31 095	..	..	..	66.8	72.0
European Union (15)	..	..	..	12 617	16 401	..	..	..	33.4	38.0
Austria	..	..	..	..	702	..	..	..	..	1.6
Belgium	..	..	..	..	0	..	..	..	..	0.0
Denmark	..	..	..	565	1 586	..	..	..	1.5	3.7
Finland	..	..	..	..	..	..	..	..	..	..
France	..	..	..	680	518	..	..	..	1.8	1.2
Germany	..	..	..	1 003	1 127	..	..	..	2.7	2.6
Greece	..	..	..	0	0	..	..	..	0.0	0.0
Ireland	..	..	..	0	13	..	..	..	0.0	0.0
Italy	..	..	..	282	99	..	..	..	0.7	0.2
Luxembourg	..	..	..	0	302	..	..	..	0.0	0.7
Netherlands	..	..	..	1 688	2 466	..	..	..	4.5	5.7
Portugal	..	..	..	0	..	..	..	..	0.0	..
Spain	..	..	..	0	..	..	..	..	0.0	..
Sweden	..	..	..	5 512	5 879	..	..	..	14.6	13.6
United Kingdom	..	..	..	2 790	3 624	..	..	..	7.4	8.4
Czech Republic	..	..	..	0	0	..	..	..	0.0	0.0
Hungary	..	..	..	0	0	..	..	..	0.0	0.0
Iceland	..	..	..	0	0	..	..	..	0.0	0.0
Norway	..	..	..	7 246	9 903	..	..	..	19.2	22.9
Poland	..	..	..	0	0	..	..	..	0.0	0.0
Slovak Republic	..	..	..	0	0	..	..	..	0.0	0.0
Switzerland	..	..	..	5 361	4 791	..	..	..	14.2	11.1
Turkey	..	..	..	0	0	..	..	..	0.0	0.0
Non-OECD Europe, of which:	..	..	..	0	0	..	..	..	0.0	0.0
Baltic countries	..	..	..	0	0	..	..	..	0.0	0.0
Bulgaria	..	..	..	0	0	..	..	..	0.0	0.0
Croatia	..	..	..	0	0	..	..	..	0.0	0.0
Romania	..	..	..	0	0	..	..	..	0.0	0.0
Russian Federation	..	..	..	0	0	..	..	..	0.0	0.0
Slovenia	..	..	..	0	0	..	..	..	0.0	0.0
Ukraine	..	..	..	0	0	..	..	..	0.0	0.0
Yugoslavia	..	..	..	0	0	..	..	..	0.0	0.0
Non-OECD Asia, of which:	..	..	..	..	660	..	..	..	..	1.5
China	..	..	..	0	0	..	..	..	0.0	0.0
Chinese Taipei	..	..	..	0	0	..	..	..	0.0	0.0
Hong Kong (China)	..	..	..	0	..	..	..	..	0.0	..
India	..	..	..	0	0	..	..	..	0.0	0.0
Indonesia	..	..	..	0	..	..	..	..	0.0	..
Malaysia	..	..	..	0	..	..	..	..	0.0	..
Philippines	..	..	..	0	0	..	..	..	0.0	0.0
Singapore	..	..	..	..	0	..	..	..	..	0.0
Thailand	..	..	..	0	0	..	..	..	0.0	0.0
Near and Middle East	..	..	..	0	0	..	..	..	0.0	0.0
Africa	..	..	..	0	0	..	..	..	0.0	0.0
Latin America, of which:	..	..	..	..	0	..	..	..	..	0.0
Argentina	..	..	..	0	0	..	..	..	0.0	0.0
Brazil	..	..	..	0	0	..	..	..	0.0	0.0
Chile	..	..	..	0	0	..	..	..	0.0	0.0

Note: Majority foreign-owned firms.
Firmes sous contrôle étranger majoritaire.

Inward investments

Investissements entrants

Table 13A - Tableau 13A

TOTAL IMPORTS BY INDUSTRY

IMPORTATIONS TOTALES PAR INDUSTRIE

| | | Foreign affiliates (Millions of FIM) | | | | | As a % of national total | | | | |
| | | Filiales étrangères (Millions de FIM) | | | | | En % du total national | | | | |
ISIC Revision 3		1995	1996	1997	1998	1999	1995	1996	1997	1998	1999
10/14	Mining & quarrying	..	..	..	..	..	..	..	..	..	..
15/37	**TOTAL MANUFACTURING**	**8 272**	**11 574**	**12 768**	**14 046**	..	..	..	..	**22.0**	..
15/16	Food, beverages, tobacco	..	..	..	634	..	..	..	..	12.7	..
17/19	Textiles, clothing, leather, footwear	..	..	..	283	..	..	..	..	15.6	..
20/22	Wood and paper products	..	..	..	406	..	..	..	..	5.3	..
20	Wood products	..	..	..	72	..	..	..	..	15.1	..
21/22	Paper, printing and publishing	..	..	..	334	..	..	..	..	4.7	..
23/25	Chemicals, Total	..	..	..	..	..	..	..	..	..	..
23	Refined petroleum, nuclear fuel	..	..	..	..	..	..	..	..	..	..
24/25	Chemicals, rubber & plastics prod.	..	..	..	2 345	..	..	..	..	30.1	..
24	Chemical products	..	..	..	1 961	..	..	..	..	34.1	..
2423	Pharmaceuticals	..	..	..	196	..	..	..	..	23.7	..
25	Rubber and plastics products	..	..	..	384	..	..	..	..	18.8	..
26	Non-metallic mineral products	..	..	..	732	..	..	..	..	64.3	..
27/28	Basic & fabricated metals	..	..	..	717	..	..	..	..	8.4	..
27	Basic metals	..	..	..	203	..	..	..	..	2.7	..
28	Fabricated metal products	..	..	..	514	..	..	..	..	50.0	..
29/32	Machinery, Total	..	..	..	..	..	..	..	..	..	..
29/30	Non-electrical machinery	..	..	..	..	..	..	..	..	..	..
29	Non-electrical machinery nec	..	..	..	1 614	..	..	..	..	21.5	..
30	Office and computing machinery	..	..	..	..	..	..	..	..	..	..
31/32	Electrical & electronic equipment	..	..	..	2 764	..	..	..	..	26.7	..
31	Electrical machinery nec	..	..	..	2 012	..	..	..	..	68.8	..
32	Radio, TV & communications eq.	..	..	..	752	..	..	..	..	10.1	..
33	Scientific instruments	..	..	..	223	..	..	..	..	21.2	..
34/35	Transportation equipment	..	..	..	..	..	..	..	..	..	..
34	Motor vehicles	..	..	..	..	..	..	..	..	..	..
35	Other transport equipment	..	..	..	1 507	..	..	..	..	86.0	..
351	Shipbuilding & repairing	..	..	..	1 353	..	..	..	..	90.9	..
353	Aircraft and spacecraft	..	..	..	0	..	..	..	..	0.0	..
36/37	Other manufacturing	..	..	..	166	..	..	..	..	23.5	..
40/45	Construction, electricity, gas & water	..	..	..	..	..	..	..	..	..	..
50/55	Trade, repair, hotels & restaurants	..	..	..	..	..	..	..	..	..	..
65/74	Finance, insurance, business services	..	..	..	..	..	..	..	..	..	..
	OTHER ACTIVITIES	..	..	..	..	..	..	..	..	..	..
01/99	**GRAND TOTAL**	..	..	..	..	..	..	..	..	..	..

Note: Majority foreign-owned firms.
Firmes sous contrôle étranger majoritaire.

Table 14A - Tableau 14A

TOTAL IMPORTS BY COUNTRY OF ORIGIN IN THE MANUFACTURING SECTOR

IMPORTATIONS TOTALES PAR PAYS D'ORIGINE DANS L'INDUSTRIE MANUFACTURIÈRE

Country of origin (UBO)	Total imports *(Millions of FIM)* Importations totales *(Millions de FIM)*					As a % of all countries En % du total des pays				
	1995	1996	1997	1998	1999	1995	1996	1997	1998	1999
All countries	8 272	11 574	12 768	14 046	..	100.0	100.0	100.0	100.0	..
Total OECD	..	..	..	13 311	..	..	..	..	94.8	..
United States	..	..	..	1 280	..	..	..	..	9.1	..
Canada	..	..	..	225	..	..	..	..	1.6	..
Mexico	..	..	..	0	..	..	..	..	0.0	..
Japan	..	..	..	2 350	..	..	..	..	16.7	..
Korea	..	..	..	0	..	..	..	..	0.0	..
Australia	..	..	..	0	..	..	..	..	0.0	..
New Zealand	..	..	..	0	..	..	..	..	0.0	..
Europe	..	..	..	9 457	..	..	..	..	67.3	..
European Union (15)	..	..	..	5 363	..	..	..	..	38.2	..
Austria	..	..	..	..	..	..	..	..	..	..
Belgium	..	..	..	..	..	..	..	..	..	..
Denmark	..	..	..	369	..	..	..	..	2.6	..
Finland	..	..	..	..	..	..	..	..	..	..
France	..	..	..	364	..	..	..	..	2.6	..
Germany	..	..	..	406	..	..	..	..	2.9	..
Greece	..	..	..	0	..	..	..	..	0.0	..
Ireland	..	..	..	0	..	..	..	..	0.0	..
Italy	..	..	..	107	..	..	..	..	0.8	..
Luxembourg	..	..	..	0	..	..	..	..	0.0	..
Netherlands	..	..	..	803	..	..	..	..	5.7	..
Portugal	..	..	..	0	..	..	..	..	0.0	..
Spain	..	..	..	0	..	..	..	..	0.0	..
Sweden	..	..	..	2 150	..	..	..	..	15.3	..
United Kingdom	..	..	..	1 090	..	..	..	..	7.8	..
Czech Republic	..	..	..	0	..	..	..	..	0.0	..
Hungary	..	..	..	0	..	..	..	..	0.0	..
Iceland	..	..	..	0	..	..	..	..	0.0	..
Norway	..	..	..	1 805	..	..	..	..	12.9	..
Poland	..	..	..	0	..	..	..	..	0.0	..
Slovak Republic	..	..	..	0	..	..	..	..	0.0	..
Switzerland	..	..	..	2 289	..	..	..	..	16.3	..
Turkey	..	..	..	0	..	..	..	..	0.0	..
Non-OECD Europe, of which:	..	..	..	0	..	..	..	..	0.0	..
Baltic countries	..	..	..	0	..	..	..	..	0.0	..
Bulgaria	..	..	..	0	..	..	..	..	0.0	..
Croatia	..	..	..	0	..	..	..	..	0.0	..
Romania	..	..	..	0	..	..	..	..	0.0	..
Russian Federation	..	..	..	0	..	..	..	..	0.0	..
Slovenia	..	..	..	0	..	..	..	..	0.0	..
Ukraine	..	..	..	0	..	..	..	..	0.0	..
Yugoslavia	..	..	..	0	..	..	..	..	0.0	..
Non-OECD Asia, of which:	..	..	..	..	..	..	..	..	..	..
China	..	..	..	0	..	..	..	..	0.0	..
Chinese Taipei	..	..	..	0	..	..	..	..	0.0	..
Hong Kong (China)	..	..	..	0	..	..	..	..	0.0	..
India	..	..	..	0	..	..	..	..	0.0	..
Indonesia	..	..	..	0	..	..	..	..	0.0	..
Malaysia	..	..	..	0	..	..	..	..	0.0	..
Philippines	..	..	..	0	..	..	..	..	0.0	..
Singapore	..	..	..	..	..	..	..	..	..	..
Thailand	..	..	..	0	..	..	..	..	0.0	..
Near and Middle East	..	..	..	0	..	..	..	..	0.0	..
Africa	..	..	..	0	..	..	..	..	0.0	..
Latin America, of which:	..	..	..	..	..	..	..	..	..	..
Argentina	..	..	..	0	..	..	..	..	0.0	..
Brazil	..	..	..	0	..	..	..	..	0.0	..
Chile	..	..	..	0	..	..	..	..	0.0	..

Note: Majority foreign-owned firms.
Firmes sous contrôle étranger majoritaire.

Inward investments

Investissements entrants

Table 15A - Tableau 15A

GROSS OPERATING SURPLUS / EXCÉDENT BRUT D'EXPLOITATION

		Foreign affiliates *(Millions of FIM)* Filiales étrangères *(Millions de FIM)*					As a % of national total En % du total national				
By industry (ISIC Rev. 3)		1995	1996	1997	1998	1999	1995	1996	1997	1998	1999
10/14	Mining & quarrying	..	138	212	103	125	..	15.2	20.3	13.1	18.2
15/37	**TOTAL MANUFACTURING**	4 520	6 478	8 780	8 919	10 397	8.2	12.6	13.5	13.3	14.8
15/16	Food, beverages, tobacco	287	266	453	343	959	6.4	5.9	9.6	8.3	24.0
17/19	Textiles, clothing, leather, footwear	35	56	67	106	97	3.4	5.2	6.0	9.2	8.7
20/22	Wood and paper products	230	255	351	354	570	1.1	1.5	1.6	1.7	2.8
20	Wood products	..	..	..	59	68	..	..	..	2.1	2.6
21/22	Paper, printing and publishing	..	..	..	295	502	..	..	..	1.7	2.8
23/25	Chemicals, Total	..	..	..	..	..	..	..	..	..	..
23	Refined petroleum, nuclear fuel	..	..	..	..	..	..	..	..	..	..
24/25	Chemicals, rubber & plastics prod.	890	1 334	2 136	2 025	2 856	16.0	24.0	33.0	30.3	38.8
24	Chemical products	762	1 151	1 931	1 779	2 602	17.9	28.5	40.8	37.6	49.9
2423	Pharmaceuticals	..	..	..	304	273	..	..	..	30.5	25.0
25	Rubber and plastics products	128	183	205	246	254	9.8	12.1	11.8	12.6	11.8
26	Non-metallic mineral products	373	550	639	787	790	30.1	43.7	37.1	37.3	34.6
27/28	Basic & fabricated metals	345	444	586	619	641	5.3	7.9	8.8	10.2	11.0
27	Basic metals	174	..	40	61	33	3.8	..	1.0	2.0	1.2
28	Fabricated metal products	171	..	546	558	608	8.9	..	19.3	18.2	19.2
29/32	Machinery, Total	..	..	..	..	3 807	..	..	..	..	15.4
29/30	Non-electrical machinery	..	..	..	..	1 163	..	..	..	..	32.6
29	Non-electrical machinery nec	540	689	1 057	1 129	1 159	10.9	11.9	18.0	21.6	30.4
30	Office and computing machinery	..	..	..	..	4	..	..	..	..	..
31/32	Electrical & electronic equipment	889	1 661	2 287	2 650	2 644	15.9	23.4	19.9	15.9	12.5
31	Electrical machinery nec	692	1 119	1 254	1 235	1 209	52.3	62.2	59.6	61.2	69.7
32	Radio, TV & communications eq.	197	542	1 033	1 415	1 435	4.6	10.2	11.0	9.6	7.4
33	Scientific instruments	64	139	238	194	289	7.2	11.7	17.9	14.7	19.6
34/35	Transportation equipment	..	..	..	..	..	..	..	..	..	..
34	Motor vehicles	..	..	..	..	..	..	..	..	..	..
35	Other transport equipment	..	..	..	520	133	..	..	..	64.8	31.1
351	Shipbuilding & repairing	..	..	..	517	126	..	..	..	71.7	39.1
353	Aircraft and spacecraft	0	0	0	0	0	0.0	0.0	0.0	0.0	0.0
36/37	Other manufacturing	51	59	81	75	93	6.2	6.3	7.9	6.7	7.5
40/45	Construction, electricity, gas & water	248	400	339	680	873	2.3	3.3	2.7	4.0	5.0
50/55	Trade, repair, hotels & restaurants	3 019	3 227	3 529	4 338	4 762	13.7	14.3	14.9	17.6	18.5
65/74	Finance, insurance, business services	565	792	936	1 092	1 359	6.8	6.4	7.5	5.8	7.4
	OTHER ACTIVITIES	..	562	476	468	767	..	2.3	1.7	1.6	2.5
01/99	**GRAND TOTAL**	8 940	11 596	14 272	15 599	18 283	7.6	9.3	10.0	9.9	11.3

Total manufacturing by investing country							As a % of total manufacturing by foreign affiliates				
	All countries	4 520	6 478	8 780	8 919	10 397	100.0	100.0	100.0	100.0	100.0
	United States	..	1 392	2 448	2 385	2 898	..	21.5	27.9	26.7	27.9
	Canada	..	..	..	..	..	..	..	..	..	..
	Mexico	0	0	0	0	..	0.0	0.0	0.0	0.0	..
	Japan	..	..	..	102	57	..	..	..	1.1	0.5
	Europe	..	4 826	6 153	..	..	..	74.5	70.1	..	..
	European Union (15)	..	2 941	3 996	4 301	5 428	..	45.4	45.5	48.2	52.2
	Belgium	..	..	..	..	..	..	..	..	..	..
	France	..	93	218	315	251	..	1.4	2.5	3.5	2.4
	Germany	..	299	355	417	542	..	4.6	4.0	4.7	5.2
	Italy	..	..	..	..	..	..	..	..	..	..
	Netherlands	..	676	1 018	778	1 006	..	10.4	11.6	8.7	9.7
	Spain	0	0	0	0	..	0.0	0.0	0.0	0.0	..
	Sweden	..	1 128	1 548	..	..	..	17.4	17.6	..	..
	United Kingdom	..	490	406	657	833	..	7.6	4.6	7.4	8.0
	Switzerland	..	1 059	1 243	1 345	1 108	..	16.3	14.2	15.1	10.7
	Australia and New Zealand	0	0	0	0	..	0.0	0.0	0.0	0.0	..
	Asia (non-OECD)	..	..	..	..	- 57	..	..	..	..	-0.5
	Latin America	0	0	..	..	0	0.0	0.0	..	..	0.0

Note: Majority foreign-owned enterprises.
Entreprises sous contrôle étranger majoritaire.

Inward investments

Investissements entrants

Table 16A - Tableau 16A

STOCK OF FOREIGN DIRECT INVESTMENT / STOCK D'INVESTISSEMENT DIRECT ÉTRANGER

| | | Foreign affiliates *(Millions of FIM)* | | | | | | | | | |
| | | Filiales étrangères *(Millions de FIM)* | | | | | | | | | |
By industry (ISIC Rev. 3)		1990	1991	1992	1993	1994	1995	1996	1997	1998	1999
10/14	Mining & quarrying	..	..	..	..	..	..	..	..	..	..
15/37	**TOTAL MANUFACTURING**	..	..	8 915	12 122	17 460	..	..	..	..	..
15/16	Food, beverages, tobacco	..	..	691	765	770	..	..	..	..	..
17/19	Textiles, clothing, leather, footwear	..	..	242	241	..	..	..	..	..	..
20/22	Wood and paper products	..	..	414	337	447	..	..	..	..	..
20	Wood products	..	..	..	..	95	..	..	..	..	..
21/22	Paper, printing and publishing	..	..	..	..	352	..	..	..	..	..
23/25	Chemicals, Total	..	..	996	1 664	..	..	..	..	..	..
23	Refined petroleum, nuclear fuel	..	..	0	0	..	..	..	..	..	..
24/25	Chemicals, rubber & plastics prod.	..	..	996	1 664	5 315	..	..	..	..	..
24	Chemical products	..	..	..	..	5 048	..	..	..	..	..
2423	Pharmaceuticals	..	..	..	..	..	..	..	..	..	..
25	Rubber and plastics products	..	..	..	..	267	..	..	..	..	..
26	Non-metallic mineral products	..	..	..	..	..	..	..	..	..	..
27/28	Basic & fabricated metals	..	..	..	..	1 552	..	..	..	..	..
27	Basic metals	..	..	..	..	745	..	..	..	..	..
28	Fabricated metal products	..	..	599	565	807	..	..	..	..	..
29/32	Machinery, Total	..	..	..	..	..	..	..	..	..	..
29/30	Non-electrical machinery	..	..	..	..	..	..	..	..	..	..
29	Non-electrical machinery nec	..	..	..	..	1 056	..	..	..	..	..
30	Office and computing machinery	..	..	..	..	..	..	..	..	..	..
31/32	Electrical & electronic equipment	..	..	3 906	4 848	4 911	..	..	..	..	..
31	Electrical machinery nec	..	..	..	..	..	..	..	..	..	..
32	Radio, TV & communications eq.	..	..	..	..	..	..	..	..	..	..
33	Scientific instruments	..	..	..	..	..	..	..	..	..	..
34/35	Transportation equipment	..	..	..	..	..	..	..	..	..	..
34	Motor vehicles	..	..	..	..	..	..	..	..	..	..
35	Other transport equipment	..	..	..	..	..	..	..	..	..	..
351	Shipbuilding & repairing	..	..	..	..	..	..	..	..	..	..
353	Aircraft and spacecraft	..	..	..	..	..	..	..	..	..	..
36/37	Other manufacturing	..	..	..	244	221	..	..	..	..	..
40/45	Construction, electricity, gas & water	..	..	..	..	..	..	..	..	..	..
50/55	Trade, repair, hotels & restaurants	..	..	5 911	6 769	8 192	..	..	..	..	..
65/74	Finance, insurance, business services	..	..	1 359	2 220	2 090	..	..	..	..	..
	OTHER ACTIVITIES	..	..	..	905	644	..	..	..	..	..
01/99	**GRAND TOTAL**	..	..	16 440	22 128	28 667	..	..	..	..	..

Total manufacturing by investing country

	1990	1991	1992	1993	1994	1995	1996	1997	1998	1999
All countries	..	..	8 915	12 122	17 460	..	..	..	..	..
United States	..	..	..	1 023	1 600	..	..	..	..	..
Canada	..	..	..	0	0	..	..	..	..	..
Mexico	..	..	..	0	0	..	..	..	..	..
Japan	..	..	..	..	..	..	..	..	..	..
Europe	..	..	..	11 154	15 809	..	..	..	..	..
European Union (15)	..	..	..	6 236	11 154	..	..	..	..	..
Belgium	..	..	..	..	..	..	..	..	..	..
France	..	..	..	372	..	..	..	..	..	..
Germany	..	..	..	341	798	..	..	..	..	..
Italy	..	..	..	..	..	..	..	..	..	..
Netherlands	..	..	..	..	..	..	..	..	..	..
Spain	..	..	..	..	0	..	..	..	..	..
Sweden	..	..	..	2 645	3 386	..	..	..	..	..
United Kingdom	..	..	..	106	75	..	..	..	..	..
Switzerland	..	..	..	..	..	..	..	..	..	..
Australia and New Zealand	..	..	..	0	0	..	..	..	..	..
Asia (non-OECD)	..	..	..	0	7	..	..	..	..	..
Latin America	..	..	..	0	0	..	..	..	..	..

Note: Majority foreign-owned firms. Based on Bank of Finland's **direct investment statistics**. *Office and computing machinery* (ISIC 30) and *Scientific instruments* (33) are included in *Electrical and electronic equipment* (31/32).
Firmes sous contrôle étranger majoritaire. Données fondées sur les **statistiques d'investissement direct** de la Banque de Finlande. Les *Machines de bureau et ordinateurs* (CITI 30) et les *Instruments* (33) sont compris dans le *Matériel électrique et électronique* (31/32).

Table 17A - Tableau 17A

CAPITAL UNDER FOREIGN INFLUENCE / CAPITAL SOUS INFLUENCE ÉTRANGÈRE

By industry (ISIC Rev. 3)	Foreign affiliates (Millions of FIM) Filiales étrangères (Millions de FIM)									
	1990	1991	1992	1993	1994	1995	1996	1997	1998	1999
10/14 Mining & quarrying	..	..	..	..	..	..	..	..	..	..
15/37 TOTAL MANUFACTURING	..	..	21 252	29 194	38 880	..	..	..	..	..
15/16 Food, beverages, tobacco	..	..	1 264	1 460	1 457	..	..	..	..	..
17/19 Textiles, clothing, leather, footwear	..	..	518	400	..	..	..	..	..	..
20/22 Wood and paper products	..	..	1 052	1 035	1 274	..	..	..	..	..
20 Wood products	..	..	..	..	260	..	..	..	..	..
21/22 Paper, printing and publishing	..	..	..	..	1 014	..	..	..	..	..
23/25 Chemicals, Total	..	..	1 981	3 296	..	..	..	..	..	..
23 Refined petroleum, nuclear fuel	..	..	0	0	..	..	..	..	..	..
24/25 Chemicals, rubber & plastics prod.	..	..	1 981	3 296	8 258	..	..	..	..	..
24 Chemical products	..	..	..	..	7 746	..	..	..	..	..
2423 Pharmaceuticals	..	..	..	..	..	..	..	..	..	..
25 Rubber and plastics products	..	..	..	..	512	..	..	..	..	..
26 Non-metallic mineral products	..	..	..	..	..	..	..	..	..	..
27/28 Basic & fabricated metals	..	..	..	..	2 467	..	..	..	..	..
27 Basic metals	..	..	..	..	1 008	..	..	..	..	..
28 Fabricated metal products	..	..	1 007	1 020	1 459	..	..	..	..	..
29/32 Machinery, Total	..	..	..	..	..	..	..	..	..	..
29/30 Non-electrical machinery	..	..	..	..	..	..	..	..	..	..
29 Non-electrical machinery nec	..	..	..	..	2 863	..	..	..	..	..
30 Office and computing machinery	..	..	..	..	..	..	..	..	..	..
31/32 Electrical & electronic equipment	..	..	9 723	11 577	13 289	..	..	..	..	..
31 Electrical machinery nec	..	..	..	..	..	..	..	..	..	..
32 Radio, TV & communications eq.	..	..	..	..	..	..	..	..	..	..
33 Scientific instruments	..	..	..	..	..	..	..	..	..	..
34/35 Transportation equipment	..	..	..	..	..	..	..	..	..	..
34 Motor vehicles	..	..	..	..	..	..	..	..	..	..
35 Other transport equipment	..	..	..	..	..	..	..	..	..	..
351 Shipbuilding & repairing	..	..	..	..	..	..	..	..	..	..
353 Aircraft and spacecraft	..	..	..	..	..	..	..	..	..	..
36/37 Other manufacturing	..	..	..	439	365	..	..	..	..	..
40/45 Construction, electricity, gas & water	..	..	..	..	..	..	..	..	..	..
50/55 Trade, repair, hotels & restaurants	..	..	15 259	14 464	18 923	..	..	..	..	..
65/74 Finance, insurance, business services	..	..	10 402	9 918	16 566	..	..	..	..	..
OTHER ACTIVITIES	..	..	..	2 805	3 179	..	..	..	..	..
01/99 GRAND TOTAL	..	..	48 147	56 669	78 656	..	..	..	..	..

Total manufacturing by investing country

	1990	1991	1992	1993	1994	1995	1996	1997	1998	1999
All countries	..	..	21 252	29 194	38 880	..	..	..	..	..
United States	..	..	..	1 765	2 660	..	..	..	..	..
Canada	..	..	..	0	0	..	..	..	..	..
Mexico	..	..	..	0	0	..	..	..	..	..
Japan	..	..	..	..	..	..	..	..	..	..
Europe	..	..	..	27 102	35 967	..	..	..	..	..
European Union (15)	..	..	..	14 869	21 831	..	..	..	..	..
Belgium	..	..	..	..	..	..	..	..	..	..
France	..	..	..	487	..	..	..	..	..	..
Germany	..	..	..	936	1 407	..	..	..	..	..
Italy	..	..	..	..	..	..	..	..	..	..
Netherlands	..	..	..	..	..	..	..	..	..	..
Spain	..	..	..	..	0	..	..	..	..	..
Sweden	..	..	..	6 142	7 182	..	..	..	..	..
United Kingdom	..	..	..	464	334	..	..	..	..	..
Switzerland	..	..	..	..	..	..	..	..	..	..
Australia and New Zealand	..	..	..	0	0	..	..	..	..	..
Asia (non-OECD)	..	..	..	0	12	..	..	..	..	..
Latin America	..	..	..	0	0	..	..	..	..	..

Note: Majority foreign-owned firms. Based on Bank of Finland's **direct investment statistics**. *Office and computing machinery* (ISIC 30) and *Scientific instruments* (33) are included in *Electrical and electronic equipment* (31/32).
Firmes sous contrôle étranger majoritaire. Données fondées sur les **statistiques d'investissement direct** de la Banque de Finlande. Les *Machines de bureau et ordinateurs* (CITI 30) et les *Instruments* (33) sont compris dans le *Matériel électrique et électronique* (31/32).

FINLAND

Source

The data are prepared by Statistics Finland, which provides data on majority foreign-owned firms from three sources:

- The Structural Business Statistics database is used for production of most of the economic indicators required. It is compiled using a direct data collection, administrative data and the Business Register. The direct inquiry provides financial statements data for all the largest enterprises in Finland. Administrative data from the National Board of Taxes provides financial statements data for all the remaining enterprises. The Business Register is used as a frame and provides information on principal activity and number of personnel for enterprises not surveyed by direct inquiry.

- The FDI survey data from the Bank of Finland provides information on direct foreign owners. This information is obtained by a universe inquiry run at five year intervals. It is supplemented every year with a limited survey. Other sources are also used to update this information (annual reports of enterprises, information on corporate acquisistions).

- The Enterprise Group Register is used to identify indirectly foreign-owned enterprises. It provides information on ownership relations between enterprises belonging to a group. The size threshold is approximately 60 persons employed in a group.

The data are not published regularly. Latest publication: *Foreign-owned Enterprises in Finland, 1998.*

For *R&D expenditure* and *Number of researchers*, data come from the biennial R&D survey (annual from 1997 onwards) conducted by Statistics Finland. The survey is a census for enterprises with at least 100 employees, enterprises having conducted R&D in the previous year, and enterprises receiving government support for R&D. There is a stratified random sampling for remaining enterprises with 10-99 employees.

National totals: provided by Statistics Finland and fully compatible with foreign affiliates' data. Data are published separately in *Financial Statements Statistics*.

Industrial classification

For all variables, the data are classified according to the principal industrial activity of the affiliate.

The industrial classification used for the Finnish tables is ISIC Revision 3.

Variables *Turnover*, *Value added*, *Compensation of employees*, *Gross fixed capital formation* and *Gross operating surplus* are not available for *Financial intermediation* (ISIC 65/67).

Variables

- *Number of employees* is an annual average and is not expressed on a full-time equivalent basis.

- *R&D expenditure* refers to expenditure by the affiliate itself.

- *Number of researchers* refers to all employees engaged in research and development. From 1999 onwards, it is expressed in full-time equivalent.

- Prior to 1998, *Gross fixed capital formation* refers to "gross tangible investment" as disposals of fixed assets are not deducted.

Geographical breakdown

The country of origin is that of the "ultimate beneficial owner".

FINLANDE

Source

Les données émanent de l'Office finlandais de statistiques, qui fournit des données sur les entreprises à participation étrangère majoritaire provenant de trois sources :

- La base de données des Statistiques Structurelles d'Entreprises est utilisée pour produire la plupart des indicateurs économiques requis. Elle est mise à jour à partir d'une collecte directe de données, de données administratives et du registre du commerce. L'enquête directe fournit des données financières pour les entreprises finlandaises les plus importantes. L'administration fiscale (*National Board of Taxes*) fournit des données financières pour les entreprises restantes. Le registre du commerce sert de cadre, et fournit également des informations sur l'activité principale et le personnel des entreprises qui ne sont pas directement enquêtées.

- L'enquête sur les investissements directs de la Banque de Finlande fournit des informations sur les propriétaires étrangers directs. Cette information est obtenue grâce à une enquête exhaustive réalisée tous les cinq ans. Elle est complétée chaque année par une enquête plus restreinte. D'autres sources sont également utilisées pour mettre à jour ces informations (rapports annuels d'entreprises, informations sur les acquisitions de sociétés).

- Le Registre des Groupes d'Entreprises sert à identifier les entreprises détenues indirectement par l'étranger. Il contient des informations sur les relations de propriété entre entreprises appartenant au même groupe. Le seuil de taille pour les groupes est d'environ 60 salariés.

Les données ne sont pas publiées régulièrement. Dernière publication : *Foreign-owned Enterprises in Finland, 1998*.

Pour les *Dépenses de R-D* et le *Nombre de chercheurs*, les données sont issues de l'enquête biennale sur la R-D (annuelle à compter de 1997) de l'Office finlandais de statistiques. L'enquête est exhaustive pour les entreprises de plus de 100 salariés, pour celles qui ont effectué des dépenses de recherche l'année précédente et pour celles qui reçoivent des subventions de R-D de la part de l'État. Un échantillonnage stratifié aléatoire est utilisé pour le reste des entreprises de 10 à 99 salariés.

Totaux nationaux : fournis par l'Office finlandais de statistiques et entièrement compatibles avec les données relatives aux filiales étrangères. Les données sont publiées dans *Financial Statements Statistics*.

Classification industrielle

Pour toutes les variables, les données sont classées selon l'activité industrielle principale de l'entreprise affiliée.

La classification industrielle utilisée pour les tableaux de la Finlande est la CITI révision 3.

Les variables *Chiffre d'affaires*, *Valeur ajoutée*, *Salaires*, *Formation brute de capital fixe* et *Excédent brut d'exploitation* ne sont pas disponibles pour le secteur *Intermédiation financière* (CITI 65/67).

Variables

- Le *Nombre de salariés* est une moyenne annuelle et n'est pas exprimé en équivalent plein-temps.

- Les *Dépenses de R-D* concernent les dépenses effectuées par les filiales pour elles-mêmes.

- Le *Nombre de chercheurs* fait référence à l'ensemble des salariés travaillant dans la recherche-développement. A partir de 1999, il est exprimé en équivalent plein-temps.

- Avant 1998, la *Formation brute de capital fixe* correspond à l'"investissement brut en actif corporel" puisque les cessions d'actifs immobilisés sont incluses.

Ventilation géographique

Le pays d'origine est celui du "bénéficiaire ultime de l'investissement".

FRANCE

Sources and Methods

FRANCE

Inward investments

Investissements entrants

Table 1A - Tableau 1A
NUMBER OF ENTERPRISES / NOMBRE D'ENTREPRISES

| | | Foreign affiliates *(Units)* | | | | As a % of national total | | | | |
| | | Filiales étrangères *(Unités)* | | | | En % du total national | | | | |
By industry (ISIC Rev. 3)		1994	1995	1996	1997	1998	1994	1995	1996	1997	1998
10/14	Mining & quarrying	45	54	49	42	38	12.8	15.0	15.0	13.5	12.3
15/37	**TOTAL MANUFACTURING**	**2 446**	**2 730**	**2 787**	**2 971**	**2 964**	**10.8**	**12.2**	**12.6**	**13.5**	**13.4**
15/16	Food, beverages, tobacco	..	..	..	..	..	..	..	..	..	..
17/19	Textiles, clothing, leather, footwear	173	195	203	208	197	4.5	5.3	5.7	6.2	6.2
20/22	Wood and paper products	263	328	333	354	370	7.9	9.8	10.1	11.1	11.7
20	Wood products	..	..	..	44	47	..	..	..	6.8	7.2
21/22	Paper, printing and publishing	..	..	..	310	323	..	..	..	12.2	12.8
23/25	Chemicals, Total	627	658	652	689	675	24.1	25.2	25.0	26.1	25.1
23	Refined petroleum, nuclear fuel	..	..	..	..	..	..	..	..	..	..
24/25	Chemicals, rubber & plastics prod.	627	658	652	689	675	24.1	25.2	25.0	26.1	25.1
24	Chemical products	420	409	389	414	404	34.3	34.2	32.9	34.8	33.0
2423	Pharmaceuticals	109	106	101	101	103	35.9	37.7	37.7	37.3	36.8
25	Rubber and plastics products	207	249	263	275	271	15.0	17.6	18.5	19.0	18.5
26	Non-metallic mineral products	118	134	152	154	143	12.0	14.3	16.6	16.8	15.4
27/28	Basic & fabricated metals	281	312	329	376	408	5.8	6.4	6.7	7.4	8.1
27	Basic metals	72	82	84	92	102	14.9	16.8	17.5	19.4	22.0
28	Fabricated metal products	209	230	245	284	306	4.8	5.2	5.5	6.2	6.7
29/32	Machinery, Total	579	653	673	734	713	16.3	18.4	18.9	20.5	19.8
29/30	Non-electrical machinery	391	460	461	501	492	17.2	20.6	20.3	21.7	21.3
29	Non-electrical machinery nec	375	438	438	477	470	17.1	20.4	19.9	21.3	21.0
30	Office and computing machinery	16	22	23	24	22	19.8	25.0	31.5	31.6	29.3
31/32	Electrical & electronic equipment	188	193	212	233	221	14.8	14.7	16.5	18.3	17.1
31	Electrical machinery nec	130	131	143	155	144	17.1	17.3	19.5	21.4	19.4
32	Radio, TV & communications eq.	58	62	69	78	77	11.4	11.2	12.6	14.1	13.9
33	Scientific instruments	131	147	143	147	153	14.0	15.9	15.6	16.1	16.8
34/35	Transportation equipment	145	162	154	164	162	17.3	19.5	19.4	20.0	19.7
34	Motor vehicles	112	124	122	128	127	20.6	22.9	23.4	24.1	23.7
35	Other transport equipment	33	38	32	36	35	11.3	13.1	11.7	12.5	12.2
351	Shipbuilding & repairing	10	11	5	4	..	9.9	11.3	5.7	4.5	..
353	Aircraft and spacecraft	4	7	7	11	11	4.3	7.2	7.7	11.1	11.0
36/37	Other manufacturing	84	87	99	103	105	6.7	7.2	8.3	8.8	7.6
40/45	Construction, electricity, gas & water	..	..	..	..	..	..	..	..	..	..
50/55	Trade, repair, hotels & restaurants	..	..	..	..	..	..	..	..	..	..
65/74	Finance, insurance, business services	..	..	..	..	..	..	..	..	..	..
	OTHER ACTIVITIES	..	..	..	..	..	..	..	..	..	..
01/99	**GRAND TOTAL**	..	..	..	..	..	..	..	..	..	..

Total manufacturing by investing country	1994	1995	1996	1997	1998	As a % of total manufacturing by foreign affiliates				
						1994	1995	1996	1997	1998
All countries	**2 446**	**2 730**	**2 787**	**2 971**	**2 964**	**100.0**	**100.0**	**100.0**	**100.0**	**100.0**
United States	491	561	589	642	..	20.1	20.5	21.1	21.6	..
Canada	..	..	..	..	..	..	..	..	..	..
Mexico	..	..	..	..	..	..	..	..	..	..
Japan	73	78	78	81	80	3.0	2.9	2.8	2.7	2.7
Europe	..	..	..	..	..	..	..	..	..	..
European Union (15)	1 471	1 676	1 717	1 823	1 820	60.1	61.4	61.6	61.4	61.4
Belgium	..	..	..	..	..	..	..	..	..	..
France	..	..	..	..	..	..	..	..	..	..
Germany	506	576	569	573	578	20.7	21.1	20.4	19.3	19.5
Italy	..	..	..	..	..	..	..	..	..	..
Netherlands	146	168	160	145	161	6.0	6.2	5.7	4.9	5.4
Spain	..	..	..	..	..	..	..	..	..	..
Sweden	..	..	..	..	..	..	..	..	..	..
United Kingdom	328	353	388	430	409	13.4	12.9	13.9	14.5	13.8
Switzerland	275	300	281	260	..	11.2	11.0	10.1	8.8	..
Australia and New Zealand	..	..	..	..	..	..	..	..	..	..
Asia (non-OECD)	17	20	29	9	6	0.7	0.7	1.0	0.3	0.2
Latin America	2	2	5	4	5	0.1	0.1	0.2	0.1	0.2

Note: Majority foreign-owned firms. Food (ISIC 15/16), energy industries (ISIC 10, 11, 23) and *Recycling* (37) are excluded. *Total Manufacturing* includes *Mining & quarrying except energy producing materials* (ISIC 13/14).
Firmes sous contrôle étranger majoritaire. L'industrie agro-alimentaire (CITI 15/16), l'énergie (CITI 10, 11, 23) et la *Récupération* (37) ne sont pas couvertes. Le *Total manufacturier* comprend l'*Extraction de produits non énergétiques* (CITI 13/14).

Table 2A - Tableau 2A

NUMBER OF EMPLOYEES BY INDUSTRY

NOMBRE DE SALARIÉS PAR INDUSTRIE

| | | Foreign affiliates *(Units)* | | | | | As a % of national total | | | | |
| | | Filiales étrangères *(Unités)* | | | | | En % du total national | | | | |
ISIC Revision 3		1994	1995	1996	1997	1998	1994	1995	1996	1997	1998
10/14	Mining & quarrying	6 205	6 756	6 513	8 216	5 818	24.9	27.2	27.1	34.5	25.5
15/37	**TOTAL MANUFACTURING**	**659 420**	**715 932**	**742 663**	**789 204**	**816 192**	**23.1**	**25.1**	**25.8**	**27.4**	**27.8**
15/16	Food, beverages, tobacco	..	..	..	..	..	..	..	..	..	..
17/19	Textiles, clothing, leather, footwear	31 832	35 582	36 496	34 862	35 846	10.9	12.6	13.5	13.4	14.2
20/22	Wood and paper products	58 544	66 699	65 582	70 382	72 161	20.5	23.4	23.1	24.9	25.4
20	Wood products	..	..	..	7 210	7 716	..	..	..	16.8	17.7
21/22	Paper, printing and publishing	..	..	..	63 172	64 445	..	..	..	26.4	26.8
23/25	Chemicals, Total	171 535	179 475	185 165	185 856	191 891	36.9	38.5	38.9	38.5	38.2
23	Refined petroleum, nuclear fuel	..	..	..	..	..	..	..	..	..	..
24/25	Chemicals, rubber & plastics prod.	171 535	179 475	185 165	185 856	191 891	36.9	38.5	38.9	38.5	38.2
24	Chemical products	121 332	123 938	124 125	124 880	128 371	43.6	44.9	44.3	44.1	44.7
2423	Pharmaceuticals	45 916	47 500	49 964	50 250	52 673	51.1	54.0	55.8	53.1	54.4
25	Rubber and plastics products	50 203	55 537	61 040	60 976	63 520	26.9	29.1	31.3	30.5	29.4
26	Non-metallic mineral products	33 364	37 250	40 283	38 912	37 749	25.3	28.4	30.5	29.9	28.9
27/28	Basic & fabricated metals	48 391	52 280	59 910	76 176	86 770	11.3	12.0	13.3	16.6	18.6
27	Basic metals	17 951	19 570	20 276	23 936	28 038	13.7	14.7	15.4	18.4	21.4
28	Fabricated metal products	30 440	32 710	39 634	52 240	58 732	10.2	10.7	12.5	15.9	17.6
29/32	Machinery, Total	193 945	210 847	222 289	243 561	244 068	34.5	36.5	37.3	40.4	38.9
29/30	Non-electrical machinery	125 505	132 698	137 232	145 915	137 786	42.1	44.3	44.8	47.4	43.0
29	Non-electrical machinery nec	99 274	107 759	112 578	118 072	123 761	38.9	41.8	42.2	44.3	45.3
30	Office and computing machinery	26 231	24 939	24 654	27 843	14 025	60.7	59.9	62.2	68.1	29.8
31/32	Electrical & electronic equipment	68 440	78 149	85 057	97 646	106 282	26.0	28.2	29.3	33.0	34.5
31	Electrical machinery nec	42 592	45 699	49 863	58 905	59 092	27.5	29.3	31.5	36.8	35.7
32	Radio, TV & communications eq.	25 848	32 450	35 194	38 741	47 190	23.7	26.8	26.6	28.5	33.2
33	Scientific instruments	27 774	31 086	30 938	30 992	33 739	23.2	27.4	27.8	28.0	29.9
34/35	Transportation equipment	70 651	77 617	75 142	78 316	84 085	16.8	18.3	18.1	19.2	20.6
34	Motor vehicles	61 446	68 195	66 568	65 534	70 208	20.8	22.6	22.6	22.9	24.4
35	Other transport equipment	9 205	9 422	8 574	12 782	13 877	7.3	7.7	7.1	10.6	11.4
351	Shipbuilding & repairing	..	1 286	347	352	..	..	8.7	2.3	2.4	..
353	Aircraft and spacecraft	..	1 624	1 720	5 610	6 506	..	2.0	2.1	6.9	8.0
36/37	Other manufacturing	17 179	18 340	20 345	21 931	24 065	14.7	16.1	17.3	19.2	18.7
40/45	Construction, electricity, gas & water	..	..	..	..	..	..	..	..	..	..
50/55	Trade, repair, hotels & restaurants	..	..	..	..	..	..	..	..	..	..
65/74	Finance, insurance, business services	..	..	..	..	..	..	..	..	..	..
	OTHER ACTIVITIES	..	..	..	..	..	..	..	..	..	..
01/99	**GRAND TOTAL**	..	..	..	..	..	..	..	..	..	..

Note: Majority foreign-owned firms. Food (ISIC 15/16), energy industries (ISIC 10, 11, 23) and *Recycling* (37) are excluded. *Total Manufacturing* includes *Mining & quarrying except energy producing materials* (ISIC 13/14).
Firmes sous contrôle étranger majoritaire. L'industrie agro-alimentaire (CITI 15/16), l'énergie (CITI 10, 11, 23) et la *Récupération* (37) ne sont pas couvertes. Le *Total manufacturier* comprend l'*Extraction de produits non énergétiques* (CITI 13/14).

Table 3A - Tableau 3A

NUMBER OF EMPLOYEES BY COUNTRY OF ORIGIN IN THE MANUFACTURING SECTOR

NOMBRE DE SALARIÉS PAR PAYS D'ORIGINE DANS L'INDUSTRIE MANUFACTURIÈRE

Country of origin (UBO)	Number of employees (Units) Nombre de salariés (Unités)					As a % of all countries En % du total des pays				
	1994	1995	1996	1997	1998	1994	1995	1996	1997	1998
All countries	**659 420**	**715 932**	**742 663**	**789 204**	**816 192**	**100.0**	**100.0**	**100.0**	**100.0**	**100.0**
Total OECD	**650 129**	**704 769**	**732 826**	**773 144**	**806 044**	**98.6**	**98.4**	**98.7**	**98.0**	**98.8**
United States	208 606	224 113	235 421	241 364	242 122	31.6	31.3	31.7	30.6	29.7
Canada	9 160	11 128	11 860	14 274	16 540	1.4	1.6	1.6	1.8	2.0
Mexico	..	..	..	307	206	..	..	..	0.0	0.0
Japan	21 212	22 496	23 873	24 147	28 034	3.2	3.1	3.2	3.1	3.4
Korea	..	..	1 274	1 349	1 370	..	..	0.2	0.2	0.2
Australia	..	..	..	2 395	1 076	..	..	..	0.3	0.1
New Zealand	..	..	..	0	872	..	..	..	0.0	0.1
Europe	**411 036**	**446 218**	**460 729**	**427 817**	**522 096**	**62.3**	**62.3**	**62.0**	**54.2**	**64.0**
European Union (15)	**350 621**	**382 409**	**398 326**	**417 272**	**433 205**	**53.2**	**53.4**	**53.6**	**52.9**	**53.1**
Austria	..	..	..	..	..	..	..	..	..	..
Belgium	32 297	32 681	32 142	41 622	42 882	4.9	4.6	4.3	5.3	5.3
Denmark	..	..	..	7 672	7 544	..	..	..	1.0	0.9
Finland	9 802	11 971	12 036	12 917	12 745	1.5	1.7	1.6	1.6	1.6
France	..	..	..	..	..	..	..	..	..	..
Germany	116 284	128 502	135 172	137 946	150 694	17.6	17.9	18.2	17.5	18.5
Greece	..	..	..	0	0	..	..	..	0.0	0.0
Ireland	6 960	6 954	7 221	7 159	6 264	1.1	1.0	1.0	0.9	0.8
Italy	39 497	43 582	40 555	38 849	37 680	6.0	6.1	5.5	4.9	4.6
Luxembourg	..	..	..	..	..	..	..	..	..	..
Netherlands	39 438	46 470	44 711	43 357	47 021	6.0	6.5	6.0	5.5	5.8
Portugal	0	0	0	..	..	0.0	0.0	0.0	..	..
Spain	3 021	3 330	2 289	3 532	5 262	0.5	0.5	0.3	0.4	0.6
Sweden	20 817	22 837	27 497	30 492	32 278	3.2	3.2	3.7	3.9	4.0
United Kingdom	76 504	77 989	87 371	91 594	88 463	11.6	10.9	11.8	11.6	10.8
Czech Republic	..	..	..	0	0	..	..	..	0.0	0.0
Hungary	..	..	..	0	0	..	..	..	0.0	0.0
Iceland	..	..	..	0	0	..	..	..	0.0	0.0
Norway	..	..	..	2 682	2 994	..	..	..	0.3	0.4
Poland	..	..	..	0		..	..	..	..	0.0
Slovak Republic	..	..	..	..	0	..	..	..	0.0	..
Switzerland	57 159	61 102	59 805	69 278	79 556	8.7	8.5	8.1	8.8	9.7
Turkey	..	..	..	0	0	..	..	..	0.0	0.0
Non-OECD Europe, of which:	..	..	..	..	6 272	..	..	..	..	0.8
Baltic countries	..	..	..	..	0	..	..	..	..	0.0
Bulgaria	..	..	..	..	0	..	..	..	..	0.0
Croatia	..	..	..	..	0	..	..	..	..	0.0
Romania	..	..	..	..	0	..	..	..	..	0.0
Russian Federation	..	..	..	..	0	..	..	..	..	0.0
Slovenia	..	..	..	..	0	..	..	..	..	0.0
Ukraine	..	..	..	..	0	..	..	..	..	0.0
Yugoslavia	..	..	..	..	0	..	..	..	..	0.0
Non-OECD Asia, of which:	**2 127**	**3 301**	**4 952**	**1 491**	**758**	**0.3**	**0.5**	**0.7**	**0.2**	**0.1**
China	..	..	..	0	0	..	..	..	0.0	0.0
Chinese Taipei	399	0	0	0	0	0.1	0.0	0.0	0.0	0.0
Hong Kong (China)	906	1 162	1 767	..	0	0.1	0.2	0.2	..	0.0
India	..	..	..	0	0	..	..	..	0.0	0.0
Indonesia	..	..	..	0	0	..	..	..	0.0	0.0
Malaysia	..	..	..	0	0	..	..	..	0.0	0.0
Philippines	..	..	..	0	0	..	..	..	0.0	0.0
Singapore	0	0	0	..	0	0.0	0.0	0.0	..	0.0
Thailand	..	..	..	0	0	..	..	..	0.0	0.0
Near and Middle East	..	..	..	**2 677**	**2 182**	..	..	..	**0.3**	**0.3**
Africa	..	..	..	**1 182**	**688**	..	..	..	**0.1**	**0.1**
Latin America, of which:	**98**	..	**273**	**241**	**248**	**0.0**	..	**0.0**	**0.0**	**0.0**
Argentina	..	..	..	0	0	..	..	..	0.0	0.0
Brazil	..	..	..	..	..	..	..	..	..	..
Chile	..	..	..	0	0	..	..	..	0.0	0.0

Note: Majority foreign-owned firms. Up to 1996, data for non-OECD Asia include those for Korea. From 1997, data for Belgium include those for Luxembourg.
Firmes sous contrôle étranger majoritaire. Jusqu'en 1996, les chiffres pour l'Asie hors OCDE comprennent ceux de la Corée. A partir de 1997, les données de la Belgique comprennent celles du Luxembourg.

Table 4A - Tableau 4A
PRODUCTION

By industry (ISIC Rev. 3)	Foreign affiliates (Millions of FRF) Filiales étrangères (Millions de FRF)					As a % of national total En % du total national				
	1994	1995	1996	1997	1998	1994	1995	1996	1997	1998
10/14 Mining & quarrying	6 765	7 417	6 952	8 800	6 192	38.4	34.6	35.0	42.6	30.7
15/37 TOTAL MANUFACTURING	**682 212**	**789 484**	**803 822**	**892 112**	**934 640**	**31.5**	**28.6**	**28.8**	**29.9**	**29.2**
15/16 Food, beverages, tobacco	..	..	..	..	..	..	..	..	..	..
17/19 Textiles, clothing, leather, footwear	20 246	23 766	25 259	26 685	28 548	14.5	13.6	14.7	15.5	16.1
20/22 Wood and paper products	75 873	96 626	91 073	95 742	99 448	36.6	34.0	32.8	33.9	33.9
20 Wood products	..	..	..	6 921	8 155	..	..	..	20.6	22.6
21/22 Paper, printing and publishing	..	..	..	88 821	91 293	..	..	..	35.6	35.5
23/25 Chemicals, Total	229 327	255 862	254 278	278 925	286 188	53.1	43.5	42.5	42.8	42.3
23 Refined petroleum, nuclear fuel	..	..	..	..	..	..	..	..	..	..
24/25 Chemicals, rubber & plastics prod.	229 327	255 862	254 278	278 925	286 188	53.1	43.5	42.5	42.8	42.3
24 Chemical products	192 168	212 961	208 219	230 772	234 051	57.6	47.2	45.2	46.2	46.1
2423 Pharmaceuticals	68 104	72 919	75 386	81 622	88 812	76.4	50.6	52.2	49.8	51.6
25 Rubber and plastics products	37 159	42 901	46 060	48 153	52 137	38.0	31.3	33.4	31.7	30.9
26 Non-metallic mineral products	30 087	34 179	34 306	34 802	36 101	36.2	32.1	32.8	32.3	32.3
27/28 Basic & fabricated metals	42 733	50 368	57 443	71 929	81 988	14.6	13.9	15.8	18.4	20.2
27 Basic metals	21 543	26 478	27 843	33 060	36 130	14.6	16.0	16.9	18.4	19.3
28 Fabricated metal products	21 191	23 890	29 600	38 870	45 858	14.6	12.2	15.0	18.5	21.0
29/32 Machinery, Total	185 717	214 761	226 844	257 403	261 411	48.8	40.6	41.4	44.6	41.1
29/30 Non-electrical machinery	127 930	144 853	149 652	163 190	149 802	56.9	51.1	52.0	55.2	47.3
29 Non-electrical machinery nec	81 411	96 098	99 518	109 911	119 524	48.5	45.5	45.7	49.1	49.9
30 Office and computing machinery	46 519	48 755	50 135	53 279	30 278	81.7	67.6	71.5	74.2	39.0
31/32 Electrical & electronic equipment	57 787	69 908	77 191	94 213	111 609	37.1	28.5	29.6	33.4	34.9
31 Electrical machinery nec	31 958	36 682	39 348	48 540	50 593	38.1	28.2	30.1	35.8	34.5
32 Radio, TV & communications eq.	25 829	33 227	37 843	45 673	61 016	35.9	28.7	29.1	31.3	35.3
33 Scientific instruments	19 887	22 553	26 719	27 657	31 177	25.1	25.8	28.0	29.0	32.9
34/35 Transportation equipment	60 372	70 987	66 389	74 523	83 508	12.7	13.4	12.4	12.2	12.2
34 Motor vehicles	53 280	64 048	60 234	64 748	71 030	14.5	15.2	14.2	13.6	13.2
35 Other transport equipment	7 092	6 939	6 155	9 775	12 478	6.4	6.3	5.5	7.3	8.5
351 Shipbuilding & repairing	..	1 119	271	294	..	..	9.5	2.9	2.8	..
353 Aircraft and spacecraft	..	1 185	1 259	4 250	5 853	..	1.5	1.5	4.2	5.2
36/37 Other manufacturing	11 206	12 964	14 560	15 646	20 079	20.8	17.5	19.4	20.5	20.6
40/45 Construction, electricity, gas & water	..	..	..	..	..	..	..	..	..	..
50/55 Trade, repair, hotels & restaurants	..	..	..	..	..	..	..	..	..	..
65/74 Finance, insurance, business services	..	..	..	..	..	..	..	..	..	..
OTHER ACTIVITIES	..	..	..	..	..	..	..	..	..	..
01/99 GRAND TOTAL	..	..	..	..	..	..	..	..	..	..

Total manufacturing by investing country						As a % of total manufacturing by foreign affiliates				
All countries	**682 212**	**789 484**	**803 822**	**892 112**	**934 640**	**100.0**	**100.0**	**100.0**	**100.0**	**100.0**
United States	238 817	264 852	271 513	296 692	..	35.0	33.5	33.8	33.3	..
Canada	..	..	..	..	..	..	..	..	..	..
Mexico	..	..	..	..	..	..	..	..	..	..
Japan	20 976	24 580	26 553	29 741	33 659	3.1	3.1	3.3	3.3	3.6
Europe	..	..	..	..	..	..	..	..	..	..
European Union (15)	346 129	406 321	414 478	452 748	497 234	50.7	51.5	51.6	50.8	53.2
Belgium	..	..	..	..	..	..	..	..	..	..
France	..	..	..	..	..	..	..	..	..	..
Germany	108 704	125 147	135 926	146 652	163 072	15.9	15.9	16.9	16.4	17.4
Italy	..	..	..	..	..	..	..	..	..	..
Netherlands	42 657	52 737	49 359	50 982	65 078	6.3	6.7	6.1	5.7	7.0
Spain	..	..	..	..	..	..	..	..	..	..
Sweden	..	..	..	..	..	..	..	..	..	..
United Kingdom	75 389	79 198	90 056	94 847	98 070	11.1	10.0	11.2	10.6	10.5
Switzerland	56 735	63 039	60 938	68 489	..	8.3	8.0	7.6	7.7	..
Australia and New Zealand	..	..	..	..	..	..	..	..	..	..
Asia (non-OECD)	1 666	2 694	3 827	1 067	525	0.2	0.3	0.5	0.1	0.1
Latin America	..	..	..	379	456	..	..	..	0.0	0.0

Note: Majority foreign-owned firms. Food (ISIC 15/16), energy industries (ISIC 10, 11, 23) and *Recycling* (37) are excluded. *Total Manufacturing* includes *Mining & quarrying except energy producing materials* (ISIC 13/14).

Firmes sous contrôle étranger majoritaire. L'industrie agro-alimentaire (CITI 15/16), l'énergie (CITI 10, 11, 23) et la *Récupération* (37) ne sont pas couvertes. Le *Total manufacturier* comprend l'*Extraction de produits non énergétiques* (CITI 13/14).

Table 5A - Tableau 5A

TURNOVER BY INDUSTRY

CHIFFRE D'AFFAIRES PAR INDUSTRIE

| | | Foreign affiliates *(Millions of FRF)* | | | | | As a % of national total | | | | |
| | | Filiales étrangères *(Millions de FRF)* | | | | | En % du total national | | | | |
ISIC Revision 3		1994	1995	1996	1997	1998	1994	1995	1996	1997	1998
10/14	Mining & quarrying	7 260	7 820	7 459	9 243	6 575	32.8	34.7	35.6	42.8	31.2
15/37	**TOTAL MANUFACTURING**	**826 880**	**952 329**	**965 840**	**1 059 512**	**1 116 985**	**28.7**	**31.0**	**31.2**	**32.0**	**31.7**
15/16	Food, beverages, tobacco	..	..	..	..	..	..	..	..	..	..
17/19	Textiles, clothing, leather, footwear	22 677	25 629	27 354	29 434	31 491	12.2	13.5	14.9	15.8	16.6
20/22	Wood and paper products	82 953	102 440	96 113	102 645	107 258	29.6	34.0	32.8	34.3	34.4
20	Wood products	..	..	..	7 396	8 575	..	..	..	21.0	22.5
21/22	Paper, printing and publishing	..	..	..	95 249	98 683	..	..	..	36.1	36.1
23/25	Chemicals, Total	277 175	313 327	305 866	340 849	351 116	44.5	46.1	44.9	45.4	45.4
23	Refined petroleum, nuclear fuel	..	..	..	..	..	..	..	..	..	..
24/25	Chemicals, rubber & plastics prod.	277 175	313 327	305 866	340 849	351 116	44.5	46.1	44.9	45.4	45.4
24	Chemical products	234 627	264 627	254 135	284 979	290 830	48.5	49.9	48.0	48.7	49.2
2423	Pharmaceuticals	77 350	86 265	92 516	100 487	110 698	51.7	53.3	55.2	53.8	54.6
25	Rubber and plastics products	42 548	48 700	51 732	55 869	60 286	30.6	32.7	34.2	33.9	33.1
26	Non-metallic mineral products	35 526	39 697	40 206	41 942	43 532	30.4	33.5	34.5	34.7	34.5
27/28	Basic & fabricated metals	48 122	55 038	62 257	77 685	87 859	13.7	14.2	16.2	18.8	20.6
27	Basic metals	24 126	28 152	29 400	34 811	38 070	15.5	15.7	16.8	18.2	19.3
28	Fabricated metal products	23 997	26 886	32 857	42 875	49 789	12.2	12.9	15.7	19.3	21.7
29/32	Machinery, Total	227 644	266 337	283 257	316 977	329 705	42.2	44.9	45.6	48.5	45.8
29/30	Non-electrical machinery	153 267	177 096	182 915	195 708	188 643	51.8	54.9	55.4	57.9	51.4
29	Non-electrical machinery nec	97 709	117 023	119 991	131 931	144 610	43.9	48.9	48.6	51.7	52.4
30	Office and computing machinery	55 558	60 073	62 924	63 778	44 033	75.8	72.0	75.7	77.3	48.1
31/32	Electrical & electronic equipment	74 377	89 242	100 342	121 269	141 062	30.5	33.0	34.5	38.3	40.0
31	Electrical machinery nec	37 367	42 180	47 029	57 565	58 684	28.7	30.4	33.2	39.1	37.3
32	Radio, TV & communications eq.	37 010	47 061	53 313	63 703	82 378	32.6	35.9	35.7	37.7	42.1
33	Scientific instruments	27 237	30 975	32 636	34 179	37 678	28.5	31.0	31.4	32.6	36.1
34/35	Transportation equipment	85 916	96 855	94 585	89 208	99 693	14.6	16.2	15.6	13.2	13.3
34	Motor vehicles	78 430	89 689	87 962	78 771	86 503	16.7	18.4	17.8	14.5	14.4
35	Other transport equipment	7 486	7 166	6 623	10 437	13 190	6.3	6.4	5.8	7.8	8.9
351	Shipbuilding & repairing	..	1 187	271	295	..	..	9.9	2.9	2.8	..
353	Aircraft and spacecraft	..	1 166	1 271	4 287	5 911	..	1.4	1.5	4.2	5.3
36/37	Other manufacturing	12 369	14 211	16 107	17 350	22 079	15.5	17.7	19.5	20.8	20.9
40/45	Construction, electricity, gas & water	..	..	..	..	..	..	..	..	..	..
50/55	Trade, repair, hotels & restaurants	..	..	..	..	..	..	..	..	..	..
65/74	Finance, insurance, business services	..	..	..	..	..	..	..	..	..	..
	OTHER ACTIVITIES	..	..	..	..	..	..	..	..	..	..
01/99	**GRAND TOTAL**	..	..	..	..	..	..	..	..	..	..

Note: Majority foreign-owned firms. Food (ISIC 15/16), energy industries (ISIC 10, 11, 23) and *Recycling* (37) are excluded. *Total Manufacturing* includes *Mining & quarrying except energy producing materials* (ISIC 13/14).
Firmes sous contrôle étranger majoritaire. L'industrie agro-alimentaire (CITI 15/16), l'énergie (CITI 10, 11, 23) et la *Récupération* (37) ne sont pas couvertes. Le *Total manufacturier* comprend l'*Extraction de produits non énergétiques* (CITI 13/14).

Inward investments

Investissements entrants

Table 6A - Tableau 6A

TURNOVER BY COUNTRY OF ORIGIN IN THE MANUFACTURING SECTOR

CHIFFRE D'AFFAIRES PAR PAYS D'ORIGINE DANS L'INDUSTRIE MANUFACTURIÈRE

Country of origin (UBO)	Turnover (Millions of FRF) Chiffre d'affaires (Millions de FRF)					As a % of all countries En % du total des pays				
	1994	1995	1996	1997	1998	1994	1995	1996	1997	1998
All countries	**826 880**	**952 329**	**965 840**	**1059 512**	**1116 985**	100.0	100.0	100.0	100.0	100.0
Total OECD	**817 685**	**937 926**	**954 101**	**1041 981**	**1108 003**	98.9	98.5	98.8	98.3	99.2
United States	302 234	336 213	343 469	360 961	356 889	36.6	35.3	35.6	34.1	32.0
Canada	7 991	12 446	14 411	18 687	20 110	1.0	1.3	1.5	1.8	1.8
Mexico	..	..	..	277	234	..	..	..	0.0	0.0
Japan	27 873	32 563	36 646	41 803	47 720	3.4	3.4	3.8	3.9	4.3
Korea	..	..	1 490	1 954	2 094	..	..	0.2	0.2	0.2
Australia	..	..	..	3 172	1 060	..	..	..	0.3	0.1
New Zealand	..	..	..	0	1 706	..	..	..	0.0	0.2
Europe	479 759	555 954	558 714	538 446	683 465	58.0	58.4	57.8	50.8	61.2
European Union (15)	406 863	474 852	479 954	527 269	579 215	49.2	49.9	49.7	49.8	51.9
Austria	..	..	..	..	..	..	..	..	..	..
Belgium	37 332	40 956	37 188	47 816	50 656	4.5	4.3	3.9	4.5	4.5
Denmark	..	..	..	10 873	11 289	..	..	..	1.0	1.0
Finland	10 394	14 464	14 415	17 515	16 700	1.3	1.5	1.5	1.7	1.5
France	..	..	..	..	..	..	..	..	..	..
Germany	127 037	147 490	155 914	167 657	186 017	15.4	15.5	16.1	15.8	16.7
Greece	..	..	..	0	0	..	..	..	0.0	0.0
Ireland	7 488	9 669	8 471	8 869	6 918	0.9	1.0	0.9	0.8	0.6
Italy	44 562	53 552	44 928	46 699	49 474	5.4	5.6	4.7	4.4	4.4
Luxembourg	..	..	..	..	..	..	..	..	..	..
Netherlands	55 485	68 070	61 357	68 244	86 075	6.7	7.1	6.4	6.4	7.7
Portugal	0	0	0	..	..	0.0	0.0	0.0	..	..
Spain	2 652	2 728	2 006	3 122	6 061	0.3	0.3	0.2	0.3	0.5
Sweden	26 638	35 193	39 178	44 503	50 278	3.2	3.7	4.1	4.2	4.5
United Kingdom	88 023	92 789	104 024	109 905	113 248	10.6	9.7	10.8	10.4	10.1
Czech Republic	..	..	..	0	0	..	..	..	0.0	0.0
Hungary	..	..	..	0	0	..	..	..	0.0	0.0
Iceland	..	..	..	0	0	..	..	..	0.0	0.0
Norway	..	..	..	6 495	6 677	..	..	..	0.6	0.6
Poland	..	..	..	0	..	..	..	..	..	0.0
Slovak Republic	..	..	..	..	0	..	..	..	0.0	..
Switzerland	67 151	74 483	72 355	81 333	92 271	8.1	7.8	7.5	7.7	8.3
Turkey	..	..	..	0	0	..	..	..	0.0	0.0
Non-OECD Europe, of which:	..	..	..	..	5 275	..	..	..	..	0.5
Baltic countries	..	..	..	..	0	..	..	..	..	0.0
Bulgaria	..	..	..	..	0	..	..	..	..	0.0
Croatia	..	..	..	..	0	..	..	..	..	0.0
Romania	..	..	..	..	0	..	..	..	..	0.0
Russian Federation	..	..	..	..	0	..	..	..	..	0.0
Slovenia	..	..	..	..	0	..	..	..	..	0.0
Ukraine	..	..	..	..	0	..	..	..	..	0.0
Yugoslavia	..	..	..	..	0	..	..	..	..	0.0
Non-OECD Asia, of which:	2 105	2 786	4 187	1 154	528	0.3	0.3	0.4	0.1	0.0
China	..	..	..	0	0	..	..	..	0.0	0.0
Chinese Taipei	570	0	0	0	0	0.1	0.0	0.0	0.0	0.0
Hong Kong (China)	695	719	952	..	0	0.1	0.1	0.1	..	0.0
India	..	..	..	0	0	..	..	..	0.0	0.0
Indonesia	..	..	..	0	0	..	..	..	0.0	0.0
Malaysia	..	..	..	0	0	..	..	..	0.0	0.0
Philippines	..	..	..	0	0	..	..	..	0.0	0.0
Singapore	0	0	0	..	0	0.0	0.0	0.0	..	0.0
Thailand	..	..	..	0	0	..	..	..	0.0	0.0
Near and Middle East	..	..	..	2 506	2 147	..	..	..	0.2	0.2
Africa	..	..	..	2 335	571	..	..	..	0.2	0.1
Latin America, of which:	43	..	472	390	461	0.0	..	0.0	0.0	0.0
Argentina	..	..	..	0	0	..	..	..	0.0	0.0
Brazil	..	..	..	..	..	..	..	..	..	..
Chile	..	..	..	0	0	..	..	..	0.0	0.0

Note: Majority foreign-owned firms. Up to 1996, data for non-OECD Asia include those for Korea. From 1997, data for Belgium include those for Luxembourg.

Firmes sous contrôle étranger majoritaire. Jusqu'en 1996, les chiffres pour l'Asie hors OCDE comprennent ceux de la Corée. A partir de 1997, les données de la Belgique comprennent celles du Luxembourg.

Table 7A - Tableau 7A

VALUE ADDED / VALEUR AJOUTÉE

		Foreign affiliates (Millions of FRF)					As a % of national total				
		Filiales étrangères (Millions de FRF)					En % du total national				
By industry (ISIC Rev. 3)		1994	1995	1996	1997	1998	1994	1995	1996	1997	1998
10/14	Mining & quarrying	2 591	2 821	2 609	3 429	2 621	29.1	30.9	31.1	40.8	31.8
15/37	**TOTAL MANUFACTURING**	**251 265**	**288 216**	**286 970**	**312 565**	**322 022**	**27.2**	**30.0**	**30.4**	**31.6**	**31.2**
15/16	Food, beverages, tobacco	..	..	..	..	..	..	..	..	..	..
17/19	Textiles, clothing, leather, footwear	7 494	8 272	8 444	8 733	9 281	11.9	13.6	14.7	15.1	16.2
20/22	Wood and paper products	24 843	30 905	28 736	31 066	32 244	25.9	30.7	29.3	30.8	31.3
20	Wood products	..	..	..	1 915	2 160	..	..	..	17.8	19.3
21/22	Paper, printing and publishing	..	..	..	29 151	30 083	..	..	..	32.3	32.8
23/25	Chemicals, Total	81 597	93 968	93 559	99 239	101 448	42.1	44.8	45.1	45.0	44.9
23	Refined petroleum, nuclear fuel	..	..	..	..	..	..	..	..	..	..
24/25	Chemicals, rubber & plastics prod.	81 597	93 968	93 559	99 239	101 448	42.1	44.8	45.1	45.0	44.9
24	Chemical products	65 744	76 741	74 888	79 220	80 925	46.8	49.4	49.2	48.5	49.7
2423	Pharmaceuticals	26 656	30 346	32 208	33 357	35 016	55.2	57.1	58.6	56.1	56.6
25	Rubber and plastics products	15 853	17 227	18 671	20 020	20 523	29.8	31.7	33.7	34.9	32.4
26	Non-metallic mineral products	13 262	15 278	14 578	14 360	15 195	28.5	32.1	31.9	31.1	31.5
27/28	Basic & fabricated metals	14 592	15 948	18 032	23 850	26 004	12.1	12.2	14.5	17.7	19.2
27	Basic metals	5 882	6 717	6 693	8 421	9 141	13.9	13.8	15.3	17.9	19.4
28	Fabricated metal products	8 709	9 231	11 340	15 429	16 863	11.0	11.3	14.0	17.5	19.1
29/32	Machinery, Total	70 261	80 624	80 237	88 841	88 231	37.7	41.0	40.5	43.6	41.1
29/30	Non-electrical machinery	48 114	54 108	53 370	56 272	51 259	47.6	51.7	51.2	53.3	46.0
29	Non-electrical machinery nec	31 864	35 630	36 622	40 031	42 829	41.0	44.6	45.3	48.2	49.9
30	Office and computing machinery	16 250	18 478	16 749	16 241	8 430	69.6	74.5	71.4	72.1	32.8
31/32	Electrical & electronic equipment	22 147	26 516	26 867	32 569	36 972	25.9	28.9	28.7	33.2	35.8
31	Electrical machinery nec	13 137	14 680	15 619	18 865	18 717	27.0	29.5	31.8	37.0	36.1
32	Radio, TV & communications eq.	9 010	11 836	11 247	13 704	18 255	24.5	28.2	25.2	29.1	35.5
33	Scientific instruments	9 541	10 687	10 893	11 270	11 445	24.7	28.3	28.7	29.1	30.1
34/35	Transportation equipment	22 557	24 912	24 606	26 010	29 120	16.0	17.9	17.9	17.3	17.3
34	Motor vehicles	20 494	22 478	22 357	22 103	24 187	20.8	22.8	23.2	21.4	20.9
35	Other transport equipment	2 062	2 434	2 249	3 907	4 933	4.8	6.0	5.5	8.2	9.4
351	Shipbuilding & repairing	..	336	78	100	..	..	9.4	2.5	3.1	..
353	Aircraft and spacecraft	..	523	562	2 061	2 935	..	1.8	1.8	5.6	7.1
36/37	Other manufacturing	4 529	4 801	5 276	5 766	6 433	15.5	16.8	18.5	20.3	20.0
40/45	Construction, electricity, gas & water	..	..	..	..	..	..	..	..	..	..
50/55	Trade, repair, hotels & restaurants	..	..	..	..	..	..	..	..	..	..
65/74	Finance, insurance, business services	..	..	..	..	..	..	..	..	..	..
	OTHER ACTIVITIES	..	..	..	..	..	..	..	..	..	..
01/99	**GRAND TOTAL**	..	..	..	..	..	..	..	..	..	..

Total manufacturing by investing country						As a % of total manufacturing by foreign affiliates				
All countries	251 265	288 216	286 970	312 565	322 022	100.0	100.0	100.0	100.0	100.0
United States	90 185	101 960	101 086	105 440	..	35.9	35.4	35.2	33.7	..
Canada	..	..	..	..	..	..	..	..	..	..
Mexico	..	..	..	..	..	..	..	..	..	..
Japan	7 134	8 427	9 287	10 264	11 066	2.8	2.9	3.2	3.3	3.4
Europe	..	..	..	..	..	..	..	..	..	..
European Union (15)	125 806	144 205	145 519	157 590	169 753	50.1	50.0	50.7	50.4	52.7
Belgium	..	..	..	..	..	..	..	..	..	..
France	..	..	..	..	..	..	..	..	..	..
Germany	41 398	46 966	49 303	52 450	57 089	16.5	16.3	17.2	16.8	17.7
Italy	..	..	..	..	..	..	..	..	..	..
Netherlands	14 674	16 964	15 513	16 716	19 759	5.8	5.9	5.4	5.3	6.1
Spain	..	..	..	..	..	..	..	..	..	..
Sweden	..	..	..	..	..	..	..	..	..	..
United Kingdom	27 971	29 170	31 821	33 173	34 382	11.1	10.1	11.1	10.6	10.7
Switzerland	22 121	23 462	22 949	26 945	..	8.8	8.1	8.0	8.6	..
Australia and New Zealand	..	..	..	..	..	..	..	..	..	..
Asia (non-OECD)	464	857	936	340	82	0.2	0.3	0.3	0.1	0.0
Latin America	..	..	..	68	115	..	..	..	0.0	0.0

Note: Majority foreign-owned firms. Food (ISIC 15/16), energy industries (ISIC 10, 11, 23) and Recycling (37) are excluded. *Total Manufacturing* includes *Mining & quarrying except energy producing materials* (ISIC 13/14).
Firmes sous contrôle étranger majoritaire. L'industrie agro-alimentaire (CITI 15/16), l'énergie (CITI 10, 11, 23) et la *Récupération* (37) ne sont pas couvertes. Le *Total manufacturier* comprend l'*Extraction de produits non énergétiques* (CITI 13/14).

Table 8A - Tableau 8A

COMPENSATION OF EMPLOYEES / SALAIRES ET CHARGES SOCIALES

By industry (ISIC Rev. 3)	Foreign affiliates (Millions of FRF) Filiales étrangères (Millions de FRF)					As a % of national total En % du total national				
	1994	1995	1996	1997	1998	1994	1995	1996	1997	1998
10/14 Mining & quarrying	1 395	1 531	1 512	1 955	1 490	25.0	27.0	27.3	34.7	27.8
15/37 TOTAL MANUFACTURING	**161 180**	**176 095**	**181 996**	**193 742**	**198 868**	**25.2**	**27.1**	**27.7**	**29.1**	**29.1**
15/16 Food, beverages, tobacco	..	..	..	..	..	..	..	..	..	..
17/19 Textiles, clothing, leather, footwear	5 667	6 321	6 419	6 204	6 565	12.3	13.9	15.0	15.0	15.8
20/22 Wood and paper products	14 815	16 928	17 153	18 306	18 394	22.2	25.1	25.5	26.9	26.8
20 Wood products	..	..	..	1 274	1 418	..	..	..	17.5	19.1
21/22 Paper, printing and publishing	..	..	..	17 032	16 975	..	..	..	28.0	27.7
23/25 Chemicals, Total	47 098	50 583	50 992	52 487	54 658	40.5	42.3	42.2	41.5	41.7
23 Refined petroleum, nuclear fuel	..	..	..	..	..	..	..	..	..	..
24/25 Chemicals, rubber & plastics prod.	47 098	50 583	50 992	52 487	54 658	40.5	42.3	42.2	41.5	41.7
24 Chemical products	36 910	39 167	38 654	39 760	41 575	46.1	47.6	46.7	45.9	46.8
2423 Pharmaceuticals	14 730	15 802	16 355	16 954	18 245	55.3	57.5	59.9	55.6	56.4
25 Rubber and plastics products	10 188	11 417	12 338	12 726	13 084	28.2	30.5	32.5	31.9	30.9
26 Non-metallic mineral products	7 857	8 791	9 155	9 401	9 235	27.5	30.4	31.5	32.0	31.3
27/28 Basic & fabricated metals	10 094	10 903	12 743	15 817	17 797	11.2	11.7	13.6	16.4	18.3
27 Basic metals	4 046	4 372	4 751	5 470	6 126	13.0	13.7	15.0	17.2	19.5
28 Fabricated metal products	6 048	6 531	7 993	10 347	11 671	10.3	10.7	12.8	16.0	17.8
29/32 Machinery, Total	48 886	53 066	55 814	59 466	58 536	36.2	37.9	38.4	40.5	37.8
29/30 Non-electrical machinery	33 863	35 320	36 337	37 986	33 907	46.0	47.9	48.6	50.6	42.7
29 Non-electrical machinery nec	22 859	25 389	26 558	28 042	29 525	40.5	43.8	44.4	46.4	47.5
30 Office and computing machinery	11 005	9 931	9 778	9 944	4 382	64.0	63.4	65.3	67.8	25.5
31/32 Electrical & electronic equipment	15 022	17 746	19 478	21 480	24 629	24.4	26.8	27.7	30.0	32.6
31 Electrical machinery nec	8 906	9 866	10 964	12 870	12 876	26.1	28.2	30.7	35.2	34.0
32 Radio, TV & communications eq.	6 117	7 880	8 513	8 610	11 753	22.4	25.3	24.6	24.5	31.2
33 Scientific instruments	7 428	8 300	8 487	8 767	9 402	23.6	27.4	28.3	29.3	30.8
34/35 Transportation equipment	14 615	16 031	15 675	17 085	18 209	14.7	16.1	15.6	16.9	18.0
34 Motor vehicles	12 833	14 096	13 904	14 091	14 765	19.9	21.6	21.1	21.5	22.5
35 Other transport equipment	1 782	1 935	1 771	2 994	3 444	5.1	5.6	5.1	8.4	9.7
351 Shipbuilding & repairing	..	244	81	80	..	..	8.4	2.8	2.8	..
353 Aircraft and spacecraft	315	402	425	1 559	1 910	1.2	1.5	1.6	5.8	7.1
36/37 Other manufacturing	3 325	3 642	4 045	4 256	4 582	16.0	17.6	19.4	20.5	19.9
40/45 Construction, electricity, gas & water	..	..	..	..	..	..	..	..	..	..
50/55 Trade, repair, hotels & restaurants	..	..	..	..	..	..	..	..	..	..
65/74 Finance, insurance, business services	..	..	..	..	..	..	..	..	..	..
OTHER ACTIVITIES	..	..	..	..	..	..	..	..	..	..
01/99 GRAND TOTAL	..	..	..	..	..	..	..	..	..	..

Total manufacturing by investing country						As a % of total manufacturing by foreign affiliates				
All countries	161 180	176 095	181 996	193 742	198 868	100.0	100.0	100.0	100.0	100.0
United States	56 789	59 804	62 304	64 405	..	35.2	34.0	34.2	33.2	..
Canada	..	..	..	..	..	..	..	..	..	..
Mexico	..	..	..	..	..	..	..	..	..	..
Japan	4 623	4 960	5 295	5 561	6 258	2.9	2.8	2.9	2.9	3.1
Europe	..	..	..	..	..	..	..	..	..	..
European Union (15)	81 077	89 762	93 586	98 080	103 462	50.3	51.0	51.4	50.6	52.0
Belgium	..	..	..	..	..	..	..	..	..	..
France	..	..	..	..	..	..	..	..	..	..
Germany	27 328	30 659	32 503	33 725	36 520	17.0	17.4	17.9	17.4	18.4
Italy	..	..	..	..	..	..	..	..	..	..
Netherlands	9 677	11 576	10 525	10 317	12 410	6.0	6.6	5.8	5.3	6.2
Spain	..	..	..	..	..	..	..	..	..	..
Sweden	..	..	..	..	..	..	..	..	..	..
United Kingdom	17 630	18 217	20 798	21 524	21 208	10.9	10.3	11.4	11.1	10.7
Switzerland	14 059	15 218	14 925	17 219	..	8.7	8.6	8.2	8.9	..
Australia and New Zealand	..	..	..	..	..	..	..	..	..	..
Asia (non-OECD)	377	647	879	296	107	0.2	0.4	0.5	0.2	0.1
Latin America	..	..	..	46	52	..	..	..	0.0	0.0

Note: Majority foreign-owned firms. Food (ISIC 15/16), energy industries (ISIC 10, 11, 23) and Recycling (37) are excluded. *Total Manufacturing* includes *Mining & quarrying except energy producing materials* (ISIC 13/14).
Firmes sous contrôle étranger majoritaire. L'industrie agro-alimentaire (CITI 15/16), l'énergie (CITI 10, 11, 23) et la *Récupération* (37) ne sont pas couvertes. Le *Total manufacturier* comprend l'*Extraction de produits non énergétiques* (CITI 13/14).

Inward investments

Investissements entrants

Table 9A - Tableau 9A
R&D EXPENDITURE / DÉPENSES DE R-D

By industry (ISIC Rev. 3)		Foreign affiliates *(Millions of FRF)* Filiales étrangères *(Millions de FRF)*					As a % of national total En % du total national				
		1994	1995	1996	1997	1998	1994	1995	1996	1997	1998
10/14	Mining & quarrying	8	3	10	..	9	4.7	1.7	7.2	..	1.6
15/37	**TOTAL MANUFACTURING**	13 121	16 027	15 900	..	18 367	15.7	19.4	18.6	..	18.5
15/16	Food, beverages, tobacco	284	265	320	..	341	22.9	20.9	24.1	..	15.8
17/19	Textiles, clothing, leather, footwear	152	161	241	..	142	24.6	25.2	37.7	..	20.7
20/22	Wood and paper products	218	199	199	..	160	69.9	64.4	71.6	..	36.4
20	Wood products	..	..	..	..	8	..	..	..	..	9.3
21/22	Paper, printing and publishing	..	..	..	..	152	..	..	..	..	43.1
23/25	Chemicals, Total	5 875	6 576	6 343	..	5 520	38.7	42.3	34.4	..	20.5
23	Refined petroleum, nuclear fuel	83	82	83	..	210	14.1	13.7	13.9	..	12.1
24/25	Chemicals, rubber & plastics prod.	5 792	6 494	6 260	..	5 309	39.7	43.5	35.1	..	21.0
24	Chemical products	5 536	6 171	5 940	..	5 101	44.0	48.4	39.4	..	23.1
2423	Pharmaceuticals	3 800	4 289	4 220	..	3 269	55.7	63.5	47.8	..	22.1
25	Rubber and plastics products	257	323	320	..	208	12.8	14.8	11.6	..	6.5
26	Non-metallic mineral products	78	142	191	..	253	10.8	18.0	22.7	..	17.7
27/28	Basic & fabricated metals	220	224	254	..	171	9.5	9.2	10.8	..	5.5
27	Basic metals	78	70	74	..	46	6.9	6.1	6.4	..	2.4
28	Fabricated metal products	142	154	180	..	125	12.1	11.9	15.2	..	10.5
29/32	Machinery, Total	4 142	5 954	..	..	9 473	17.7	26.2	..	..	34.9
29/30	Non-electrical machinery	2 162	2 259	..	..	3 149	26.1	29.2	..	..	39.1
29	Non-electrical machinery nec	1 082	1 178	1 256	..	2 023	20.8	24.4	26.4	..	38.1
30	Office and computing machinery	1 080	1 081	..	..	1 125	35.0	37.3	..	..	41.1
31/32	Electrical & electronic equipment	1 980	3 695	3 352	..	6 324	13.1	24.6	22.0	..	33.1
31	Electrical machinery nec	681	827	1 184	..	938	18.0	20.0	30.7	..	22.2
32	Radio, TV & communications eq.	1 299	2 868	2 168	..	5 386	11.4	26.4	19.0	..	36.2
33	Scientific instruments	1 225	1 263	1 253	..	1 044	10.6	11.5	11.9	..	12.7
34/35	Transportation equipment	862	1 166	1 206	..	1 223	3.1	4.2	4.3	..	4.4
34	Motor vehicles	748	1 014	1 068	..	1 057	5.7	7.6	8.5	..	7.6
35	Other transport equipment	114	152	138	..	166	0.8	1.0	0.9	..	1.2
351	Shipbuilding & repairing	..	..	..	..	0	..	..	..	..	0.0
353	Aircraft and spacecraft	..	83	88	..	129	..	0.6	0.6	..	1.0
36/37	Other manufacturing	65	77	61	..	42	19.6	22.3	18.3	..	5.1
40/45	Construction, electricity, gas & water	24	20	19	..	98	0.9	0.7	0.5	..	2.3
50/55	Trade, repair, hotels & restaurants	311	337	429	..	0	35.3	41.9	50.6	..	0.0
65/74	Finance, insurance, business services	1 881	2 225	2 353	..	297	10.6	11.7	13.1	..	5.7
	OTHER ACTIVITIES	55	42	54	..	174	1.5	1.1	1.4	..	2.6
01/99	**GRAND TOTAL**	15 400	18 663	18 765	..	18 945	14.2	17.1	16.7	..	16.4

Total manufacturing by investing country						As a % of total manufacturing by foreign affiliates				
All countries	13 121	16 027	15 900	..	18 367	100.0	100.0	100.0	..	100.0
United States	..	..	..	..	6 015	..	..	..	..	32.7
Canada	..	..	..	..	904	..	..	..	..	4.9
Mexico	..	..	..	..	..	..	..	..	..	..
Japan	..	..	..	..	172	..	..	..	..	0.9
Europe	..	..	..	..	..	..	..	..	..	..
European Union (15)	..	..	..	..	10 007	..	..	..	..	54.5
Belgium	..	..	..	..	..	..	..	..	..	..
France	..	..	..	..	..	..	..	..	..	..
Germany	..	..	..	..	2 768	..	..	..	..	15.1
Italy	..	..	..	..	..	..	..	..	..	..
Netherlands	..	..	1 428	..	3 977	..	..	9.0	..	21.7
Spain	..	..	..	..	..	..	..	..	..	..
Sweden	..	..	..	..	..	..	..	..	..	..
United Kingdom	..	..	..	..	1 976	..	..	..	..	10.8
Switzerland	..	..	..	..	1 201	..	..	..	..	6.5
Australia and New Zealand	..	..	..	..	..	..	..	..	..	..
Asia (non-OECD)	..	..	..	..	13	..	..	..	..	0.1
Latin America	..	..	..	..	0	..	..	..	..	0.0

Note: Majority foreign-owned firms.
Firmes sous contrôle étranger majoritaire.

Table 10A - Tableau 10A

NUMBER OF RESEARCHERS / NOMBRE DE CHERCHEURS

		Foreign affiliates *(FTE)* Filiales étrangères *(EPT)*					As a % of national total En % du total national				
By industry (ISIC Rev. 3)		1994	1995	1996	1997	1998	1994	1995	1996	1997	1998
10/14	Mining & quarrying	5	..	5	..	6	7.5	..	8.2	..	2.7
15/37	**TOTAL MANUFACTURING**	..	..	..	..	**11 636**	..	..	..	..	**19.8**
15/16	Food, beverages, tobacco	215	200	219	..	169	23.9	22.5	23.1	..	11.3
17/19	Textiles, clothing, leather, footwear	..	..	..	..	100	..	..	..	..	20.3
20/22	Wood and paper products	..	..	..	..	92	..	..	..	..	26.7
20	Wood products	..	..	..	..	4	..	..	..	..	5.7
21/22	Paper, printing and publishing	..	..	..	..	88	..	..	..	..	32.1
23/25	Chemicals, Total	..	..	..	..	2 463	..	..	..	..	19.8
23	Refined petroleum, nuclear fuel	39	36	35	..	98	13.4	12.1	12.6	..	10.4
24/25	Chemicals, rubber & plastics prod.	..	..	..	..	2 365	..	..	..	..	20.6
24	Chemical products	..	..	..	..	2 258	..	..	..	..	22.1
2423	Pharmaceuticals	..	..	..	..	1 359	..	..	..	..	21.6
25	Rubber and plastics products	..	..	..	..	106	..	..	..	..	8.5
26	Non-metallic mineral products	..	..	..	..	168	..	..	..	..	21.4
27/28	Basic & fabricated metals	..	..	..	..	98	..	..	..	..	4.6
27	Basic metals	..	..	..	..	25	..	..	..	..	2.4
28	Fabricated metal products	..	..	..	..	72	..	..	..	..	6.8
29/32	Machinery, Total	..	..	..	..	6 875	..	..	..	..	33.9
29/30	Non-electrical machinery	..	..	..	..	1 818	..	..	..	..	29.0
29	Non-electrical machinery nec	..	..	..	..	887	..	..	..	..	25.5
30	Office and computing machinery	..	..	..	..	931	..	..	..	..	33.3
31/32	Electrical & electronic equipment	..	..	..	..	5 057	..	..	..	..	36.1
31	Electrical machinery nec	..	..	..	..	664	..	..	..	..	23.1
32	Radio, TV & communications eq.	..	..	..	..	4 393	..	..	..	..	39.5
33	Scientific instruments	..	..	..	..	910	..	..	..	..	12.2
34/35	Transportation equipment	..	..	..	..	735	..	..	..	..	5.6
34	Motor vehicles	664	516	648	..	602	16.1	11.3	13.1	..	9.1
35	Other transport equipment	..	..	..	..	133	..	..	..	..	2.0
351	Shipbuilding & repairing	..	..	..	..	0	..	..	..	..	0.0
353	Aircraft and spacecraft	..	..	..	..	105	..	..	..	..	1.7
36/37	Other manufacturing	..	..	..	..	26	..	..	..	..	7.3
40/45	Construction, electricity, gas & water	13	8	9	..	36	0.8	0.5	0.4	..	1.4
50/55	Trade, repair, hotels & restaurants	233	231	290	..	0	29.5	33.5	42.2	..	0.0
65/74	Finance, insurance, business services	1 143	1 290	1 392	..	332	8.6	9.4	10.6	..	5.1
	OTHER ACTIVITIES	27	23	20	..	60	1.0	0.8	0.7	..	1.3
01/99	**GRAND TOTAL**	..	..	..	..	**12 069**	..	..	..	..	**16.6**

Total manufacturing by investing country						As a % of total manufacturing by foreign affiliates				
All countries	..	..	..	..	**11 636**	..	..	..	..	**100.0**
United States	..	..	..	..	3 945	..	..	..	..	33.9
Canada	..	..	..	..	1 112	..	..	..	..	9.6
Mexico	..	..	..	..	..	..	..	..	..	..
Japan	..	..	..	..	112	..	..	..	..	1.0
Europe	..	..	..	..	..	..	..	..	..	..
European Union (15)	..	..	..	..	5 638	..	..	..	..	48.5
Belgium	..	..	..	..	..	..	..	..	..	..
France	..	..	..	..	..	..	..	..	..	..
Germany	..	..	..	..	1 154	..	..	..	..	9.9
Italy	..	..	..	..	..	..	..	..	..	..
Netherlands	..	..	..	..	2 517	..	..	..	..	21.6
Spain	..	..	..	..	..	..	..	..	..	..
Sweden	..	..	..	..	..	..	..	..	..	..
United Kingdom	..	..	..	..	975	..	..	..	..	8.4
Switzerland	..	..	..	..	760	..	..	..	..	6.5
Australia and New Zealand	..	..	..	..	..	..	..	..	..	..
Asia (non-OECD)	..	..	..	..	3	..	..	..	..	0.0
Latin America	..	..	..	..	0	..	..	..	..	0.0

Note: Majority foreign-owned firms.
Firmes sous contrôle étranger majoritaire.

Inward investments

Investissements entrants

Table 11A - Tableau 11A

GROSS FIXED CAPITAL FORMATION / FORMATION BRUTE DE CAPITAL FIXE

By industry (ISIC Rev. 3)		Foreign affiliates (Millions of FRF) Filiales étrangères (Millions de FRF)					As a % of national total En % du total national				
		1994	1995	1996	1997	1998	1994	1995	1996	1997	1998
10/14	Mining & quarrying	718	884	683	600	622	40.3	43.1	36.2	40.6	38.1
15/37	**TOTAL MANUFACTURING**	**28 465**	**36 676**	**37 882**	**38 125**	**45 081**	**28.3**	**32.1**	**30.8**	**31.7**	**34.9**
15/16	Food, beverages, tobacco	..	..	..	..	..	..	..	..	..	..
17/19	Textiles, clothing, leather, footwear	623	846	949	772	817	13.4	15.8	18.9	15.1	15.2
20/22	Wood and paper products	2 923	3 691	3 936	3 929	5 406	32.2	36.8	34.9	37.7	42.4
20	Wood products	..	..	..	251	474	..	..	..	20.5	29.4
21/22	Paper, printing and publishing	..	..	..	3 678	4 932	..	..	..	40.0	44.3
23/25	Chemicals, Total	9 739	10 994	12 077	12 491	15 199	44.6	44.0	42.7	43.6	46.9
23	Refined petroleum, nuclear fuel	..	..	..	..	..	..	..	..	..	..
24/25	Chemicals, rubber & plastics prod.	9 739	10 994	12 077	12 491	15 199	44.6	44.0	42.7	43.6	46.9
24	Chemical products	7 828	8 320	9 083	9 398	11 119	48.2	46.5	44.3	46.9	50.0
2423	Pharmaceuticals	2 813	2 650	3 169	3 737	3 895	57.3	55.0	56.4	58.6	58.1
25	Rubber and plastics products	1 911	2 673	2 994	3 093	4 079	33.9	37.7	38.6	35.9	40.1
26	Non-metallic mineral products	1 300	2 061	2 232	1 857	2 156	26.1	33.6	34.7	31.4	33.0
27/28	Basic & fabricated metals	1 587	1 849	2 144	2 977	3 925	14.7	14.9	15.4	19.6	23.4
27	Basic metals	607	793	845	988	1 412	13.5	15.2	13.2	13.9	19.4
28	Fabricated metal products	980	1 056	1 299	1 989	2 513	15.5	14.7	17.2	24.6	26.5
29/32	Machinery, Total	7 494	11 215	10 450	9 757	10 950	41.1	52.7	46.0	45.6	47.4
29/30	Non-electrical machinery	4 687	5 717	5 845	5 065	4 643	60.0	62.3	59.9	59.6	48.5
29	Non-electrical machinery nec	2 271	3 476	3 378	3 436	3 879	44.9	52.8	48.3	52.3	52.7
30	Office and computing machinery	2 416	2 240	2 467	1 629	764	87.7	86.2	89.4	84.5	34.7
31/32	Electrical & electronic equipment	2 807	5 498	4 605	4 691	6 307	26.9	45.4	35.5	36.4	46.6
31	Electrical machinery nec	1 374	1 524	1 929	2 219	2 198	30.6	31.0	35.0	42.3	35.5
32	Radio, TV & communications eq.	1 433	3 974	2 676	2 472	4 109	24.1	55.3	35.8	32.3	55.9
33	Scientific instruments	874	973	1 050	1 015	1 188	32.1	38.0	39.7	40.7	42.1
34/35	Transportation equipment	2 875	3 785	3 928	4 265	4 154	11.9	14.0	14.0	15.9	17.2
34	Motor vehicles	2 719	3 576	3 611	3 933	3 727	12.8	15.0	14.7	17.1	19.1
35	Other transport equipment	155	209	316	332	427	5.4	6.5	8.8	8.6	9.1
351	Shipbuilding & repairing	..	23	10	8	..	..	7.9	2.2	2.2	..
353	Aircraft and spacecraft	..	31	50	149	246	..	1.3	2.0	5.1	6.5
36/37	Other manufacturing	332	379	434	461	664	14.9	15.3	16.6	17.2	18.2
40/45	Construction, electricity, gas & water	..	..	..	..	..	..	..	..	..	..
50/55	Trade, repair, hotels & restaurants	..	..	..	..	..	..	..	..	..	..
65/74	Finance, insurance, business services	..	..	..	..	..	..	..	..	..	..
	OTHER ACTIVITIES	..	..	..	..	..	..	..	..	..	..
01/99	**GRAND TOTAL**	..	..	..	..	..	..	..	..	..	..

Total manufacturing by investing country	1994	1995	1996	1997	1998	As a % of total manufacturing by foreign affiliates				
All countries	**28 465**	**36 676**	**37 882**	**38 125**	**45 081**	**100.0**	**100.0**	**100.0**	**100.0**	**100.0**
United States	10 412	11 637	13 436	12 910	..	36.6	31.7	35.5	33.9	..
Canada	..	..	..	..	..	..	..	..	..	..
Mexico	..	..	..	..	..	..	..	..	..	..
Japan	993	1 308	1 298	1 642	2 656	3.5	3.6	3.4	4.3	5.9
Europe	..	..	..	..	..	..	..	..	..	..
European Union (15)	13 561	18 307	18 772	18 658	24 092	47.6	49.9	49.6	48.9	53.4
Belgium	..	..	..	..	..	..	..	..	..	..
France	..	..	..	..	..	..	..	..	..	..
Germany	4 502	5 492	6 469	6 211	7 344	15.8	15.0	17.1	16.3	16.3
Italy	..	..	..	..	..	..	..	..	..	..
Netherlands	1 980	2 564	2 202	1 914	4 698	7.0	7.0	5.8	5.0	10.4
Spain	..	..	..	..	..	..	..	..	..	..
Sweden	..	..	..	..	..	..	..	..	..	..
United Kingdom	2 964	3 332	3 620	3 842	4 121	10.4	9.1	9.6	10.1	9.1
Switzerland	2 451	2 789	2 884	2 721	..	8.6	7.6	7.6	7.1	..
Australia and New Zealand	..	..	..	..	..	..	..	..	..	..
Asia (non-OECD)	91	200	218	36	9	0.3	0.5	0.6	0.1	0.0
Latin America	..	..	..	3	6	..	..	..	0.0	0.0

Note: Majority foreign-owned firms. Food (ISIC 15/16), energy industries (ISIC 10, 11, 23) and *Recycling* (37) are excluded. *Total Manufacturing* includes *Mining & quarrying except energy producing materials* (ISIC 13/14).
Firmes sous contrôle étranger majoritaire. L'industrie agro-alimentaire (CITI 15/16), l'énergie (CITI 10, 11, 23) et la *Récupération* (37) ne sont pas couvertes. Le *Total manufacturier* comprend l'*Extraction de produits non énergétiques* (CITI 13/14).

Table 12A - Tableau 12A

TOTAL EXPORTS BY INDUSTRY

EXPORTATIONS TOTALES PAR INDUSTRIE

| | | Foreign affiliates (Millions of FRF) | | | | | As a % of national total | | | | |
| | | Filiales étrangères (Millions de FRF) | | | | | En % du total national | | | | |
ISIC Revision 3		1994	1995	1996	1997	1998	1994	1995	1996	1997	1998
10/14	Mining & quarrying	1 208	1 402	1 207	1 393	1 185	47.5	50.5	46.9	53.9	46.4
15/37	**TOTAL MANUFACTURING**	**280 017**	**346 789**	**362 801**	**415 275**	**444 127**	**31.0**	**35.3**	**35.2**	**35.5**	**34.6**
15/16	Food, beverages, tobacco	..	..	..	..	..	..	..	..	..	..
17/19	Textiles, clothing, leather, footwear	8 137	9 109	10 056	11 483	13 387	16.0	16.9	18.7	20.3	22.0
20/22	Wood and paper products	21 720	29 441	27 070	31 205	31 486	51.6	60.4	58.9	61.6	57.8
20	Wood products	..	..	..	2 599	2 492	..	..	..	43.3	34.7
21/22	Paper, printing and publishing	..	..	..	28 607	28 994	..	..	..	64.1	61.3
23/25	Chemicals, Total	84 384	100 402	104 401	122 005	123 333	43.9	47.4	47.3	48.4	47.3
23	Refined petroleum, nuclear fuel	..	..	..	..	..	..	..	..	..	..
24/25	Chemicals, rubber & plastics prod.	84 384	100 402	104 401	122 005	123 333	43.9	47.4	47.3	48.4	47.3
24	Chemical products	72 488	86 851	88 438	103 842	103 264	46.4	50.2	49.4	50.6	50.0
2423	Pharmaceuticals	15 962	18 390	20 925	23 023	26 921	55.7	57.3	58.6	54.2	55.4
25	Rubber and plastics products	11 896	13 551	15 963	18 163	20 069	33.1	34.9	38.2	39.1	37.1
26	Non-metallic mineral products	6 998	8 994	8 969	10 533	10 972	29.8	35.6	34.7	37.1	37.6
27/28	Basic & fabricated metals	16 777	18 866	20 317	25 888	27 962	15.6	16.2	17.8	20.2	21.0
27	Basic metals	9 490	11 780	12 215	15 022	15 749	14.0	14.6	15.7	17.1	17.6
28	Fabricated metal products	7 287	7 087	8 102	10 866	12 213	18.3	19.8	22.1	27.3	27.9
29/32	Machinery, Total	96 213	123 666	135 094	151 679	166 349	47.6	53.7	53.7	54.5	52.4
29/30	Non-electrical machinery	67 843	84 386	88 821	94 310	96 366	57.2	63.1	63.8	66.0	60.9
29	Non-electrical machinery nec	44 220	54 877	56 633	62 051	69 233	49.0	55.7	55.6	59.1	59.1
30	Office and computing machinery	23 623	29 509	32 188	32 259	27 133	83.2	84.0	85.8	85.1	66.2
31/32	Electrical & electronic equipment	28 370	39 280	46 273	57 368	69 983	34.0	40.7	41.3	42.3	44.0
31	Electrical machinery nec	12 465	15 525	18 111	22 859	22 728	30.3	33.2	35.9	40.6	36.7
32	Radio, TV & communications eq.	15 905	23 755	28 162	34 510	47 255	37.7	47.7	45.6	43.5	48.7
33	Scientific instruments	11 764	13 561	14 509	16 241	17 708	36.7	40.2	36.7	36.7	42.5
34/35	Transportation equipment	29 760	37 834	37 205	40 400	45 120	12.8	15.6	14.5	13.1	12.6
34	Motor vehicles	27 288	35 051	34 483	35 272	38 840	15.4	18.5	17.2	15.0	14.3
35	Other transport equipment	2 471	2 783	2 721	5 128	6 280	4.4	5.3	4.9	7.1	7.3
351	Shipbuilding & repairing	..	554	125	189	..	..	8.0	2.7	2.8	..
353	Aircraft and spacecraft	..	546	622	2 614	3 474	..	1.4	1.4	4.6	5.0
36/37	Other manufacturing	3 057	3 513	3 971	4 448	6 622	17.3	18.7	20.1	21.2	25.0
40/45	Construction, electricity, gas & water	..	..	..	..	..	..	..	..	..	..
50/55	Trade, repair, hotels & restaurants	..	..	..	..	..	..	..	..	..	..
65/74	Finance, insurance, business services	..	..	..	..	..	..	..	..	..	..
	OTHER ACTIVITIES	..	..	..	..	..	..	..	..	..	..
01/99	**GRAND TOTAL**	..	..	..	..	..	..	..	..	..	..

Note: Majority foreign-owned firms. Food (ISIC 15/16), energy industries (ISIC 10, 11, 23) and *Recycling* (37) are excluded. *Total Manufacturing* includes *Mining & quarrying except energy producing materials* (ISIC 13/14).

Firmes sous contrôle étranger majoritaire. L'industrie agro-alimentaire (CITI 15/16), l'énergie (CITI 10, 11, 23) et la *Récupération* (37) ne sont pas couvertes. Le *Total manufacturier* comprend l'*Extraction de produits non énergétiques* (CITI 13/14).

Table 13A - Tableau 13A

TOTAL EXPORTS BY COUNTRY OF ORIGIN IN THE MANUFACTURING SECTOR
EXPORTATIONS TOTALES PAR PAYS D'ORIGINE DANS L'INDUSTRIE MANUFACTURIÈRE

Country of origin (UBO)	Total exports (Millions of FRF) Exportations totales (Millions de FRF)					As a % of all countries En % du total des pays				
	1994	1995	1996	1997	1998	1994	1995	1996	1997	1998
All countries	**280 017**	**346 789**	**362 801**	**415 275**	**444 127**	**100.0**	**100.0**	**100.0**	**100.0**	**100.0**
Total OECD	**276 659**	**338 820**	**356 261**	**406 634**	**440 120**	**98.8**	**97.7**	**98.2**	**97.9**	**99.1**
United States	117 910	141 292	148 172	164 158	164 704	42.1	40.7	40.8	39.5	37.1
Canada	1 948	3 861	5 467	7 857	7 579	0.7	1.1	1.5	1.9	1.7
Mexico	..	..	..	99	129	..	..	..	0.0	0.0
Japan	11 677	13 632	17 685	20 687	22 526	4.2	3.9	4.9	5.0	5.1
Korea	..	..	1 153	109	283	..	..	0.3	0.0	0.1
Australia	..	..	..	1 001	317	..	..	..	0.2	0.1
New Zealand	..	..	..	0	423	..	..	..	0.0	0.1
Europe	**145 688**	**179 925**	**184 727**	**187 255**	**246 120**	**52.0**	**51.9**	**50.9**	**45.1**	**55.4**
European Union (15)	**120 585**	**151 733**	**157 746**	**182 409**	**209 154**	**43.1**	**43.8**	**43.5**	**43.9**	**47.1**
Austria	..	..	..	..	..	..	..	..	..	..
Belgium	11 530	13 206	13 017	16 345	16 212	4.1	3.8	3.6	3.9	3.7
Denmark	..	..	..	3 337	3 664	..	..	..	0.8	0.8
Finland	3 694	6 123	6 224	8 615	8 037	1.3	1.8	1.7	2.1	1.8
France	..	..	..	..	..	..	..	..	..	..
Germany	38 492	47 738	54 523	58 631	66 196	13.7	13.8	15.0	14.1	14.9
Greece	..	..	..	0	0	..	..	..	0.0	0.0
Ireland	1 769	2 662	2 530	2 881	1 513	0.6	0.8	0.7	0.7	0.3
Italy	9 909	14 530	11 009	13 326	13 802	3.5	4.2	3.0	3.2	3.1
Luxembourg	..	..	..	..	..	..	..	..	..	..
Netherlands	17 641	20 048	20 693	25 685	39 000	6.3	5.8	5.7	6.2	8.8
Portugal	0	0	0	..	..	0.0	0.0	0.0	..	..
Spain	744	789	708	837	2 333	0.3	0.2	0.2	0.2	0.5
Sweden	8 374	13 735	14 557	16 707	19 882	3.0	4.0	4.0	4.0	4.5
United Kingdom	25 822	29 621	30 695	35 426	37 534	9.2	8.5	8.5	8.5	8.5
Czech Republic	..	..	..	0	0	..	..	..	0.0	0.0
Hungary	..	..	..	0	0	..	..	..	0.0	0.0
Iceland	..	..	..	0	0	..	..	..	0.0	0.0
Norway	..	..	..	1 433	1 278	..	..	..	0.3	0.3
Poland	..	..	..	0	..	..	..	..	..	0.0
Slovak Republic	..	..	..	..	0	..	..	..	0.0	..
Switzerland	23 342	26 746	25 606	28 882	33 726	8.3	7.7	7.1	7.0	7.6
Turkey	..	..	..	0	0	..	..	..	0.0	0.0
Non-OECD Europe, of which:	..	..	..	..	1 961	..	..	..	..	0.4
Baltic countries	..	..	..	..	0	..	..	..	..	0.0
Bulgaria	..	..	..	..	0	..	..	..	..	0.0
Croatia	..	..	..	..	0	..	..	..	..	0.0
Romania	..	..	..	..	0	..	..	..	..	0.0
Russian Federation	..	..	..	..	0	..	..	..	..	0.0
Slovenia	..	..	..	..	0	..	..	..	..	0.0
Ukraine	..	..	..	..	0	..	..	..	..	0.0
Yugoslavia	..	..	..	..	0	..	..	..	..	0.0
Non-OECD Asia, of which:	972	1 431	2 602	810	422	0.3	0.4	0.7	0.2	0.1
China	..	..	..	0	0	..	..	..	0.0	0.0
Chinese Taipei	9	0	0	0	0	0.0	0.0	0.0	0.0	0.0
Hong Kong (China)	505	591	660	..	0	0.2	0.2	0.2	..	0.0
India	..	..	..	0	0	..	..	..	0.0	0.0
Indonesia	..	..	..	0	0	..	..	..	0.0	0.0
Malaysia	..	..	..	0	0	..	..	..	0.0	0.0
Philippines	..	..	..	0	0	..	..	..	0.0	0.0
Singapore	0	0	0	..	0	0.0	0.0	0.0	..	0.0
Thailand	..	..	..	0	0	..	..	..	0.0	0.0
Near and Middle East	..	..	..	1 037	1 034	..	..	..	0.2	0.2
Africa	..	..	..	1 750	371	..	..	..	0.4	0.1
Latin America, of which:	4	..	238	199	219	0.0	..	0.1	0.0	0.0
Argentina	..	..	..	0	0	..	..	..	0.0	0.0
Brazil	..	..	..	..	..	..	..	..	..	..
Chile	..	..	..	0	0	..	..	..	0.0	0.0

Note: Majority foreign-owned firms. Up to 1996, data for non-OECD Asia include those for Korea. From 1997, data for Belgium include those for Luxembourg.
Firmes sous contrôle étranger majoritaire. Jusqu'en 1996, les chiffres pour l'Asie hors OCDE comprennent ceux de la Corée. A partir de 1997, les données de la Belgique comprennent celles du Luxembourg.

Table 14A - Tableau 14A

GROSS OPERATING SURPLUS / EXCÉDENT BRUT D'EXPLOITATION

By industry (ISIC Rev. 3)	Foreign affiliates (Millions of FRF) Filiales étrangères (Millions de FRF)					As a % of national total En % du total national				
	1994	1995	1996	1997	1998	1994	1995	1996	1997	1998
10/14 Mining & quarrying	1 027	1 098	902	1 254	960	37.4	38.3	39.6	58.0	42.3
15/37 **TOTAL MANUFACTURING**	75 575	94 624	86 533	99 078	101 495	32.3	37.4	37.7	37.7	35.9
15/16 Food, beverages, tobacco	..	..	..	..	..	..	..	..	..	..
17/19 Textiles, clothing, leather, footwear	1 407	1 471	1 506	1 993	2 142	10.3	12.2	13.0	15.1	16.8
20/22 Wood and paper products	8 659	12 139	9 765	10 830	11 611	34.9	42.9	37.6	39.4	40.8
20 Wood products	..	..	..	488	567	..	..	..	17.4	18.5
21/22 Paper, printing and publishing	..	..	..	10 342	11 045	..	..	..	41.9	43.5
23/25 Chemicals, Total	29 487	37 226	36 101	40 183	39 324	44.6	48.5	49.4	50.5	49.8
23 Refined petroleum, nuclear fuel	..	..	..	..	..	..	..	..	..	..
24/25 Chemicals, rubber & plastics prod.	29 487	37 226	36 101	40 183	39 324	44.6	48.5	49.4	50.5	49.8
24 Chemical products	24 749	32 490	31 015	34 180	33 245	47.6	51.5	52.5	52.0	53.7
2423 Pharmaceuticals	10 136	12 176	13 216	13 889	13 535	54.5	55.8	56.2	56.3	55.8
25 Rubber and plastics products	4 738	4 736	5 087	6 003	6 080	33.5	34.7	36.3	43.4	35.7
26 Non-metallic mineral products	4 616	5 520	4 418	3 913	4 903	30.4	34.9	32.3	28.4	31.5
27/28 Basic & fabricated metals	3 611	4 011	4 106	6 442	6 448	15.0	13.6	17.9	21.5	21.8
27 Basic metals	1 445	1 882	1 425	2 327	2 329	17.1	14.3	16.1	19.7	19.0
28 Fabricated metal products	2 166	2 129	2 681	4 115	4 119	13.8	13.1	19.1	22.6	23.7
29/32 Machinery, Total	17 590	23 143	19 766	24 177	24 342	41.7	50.2	47.7	53.9	52.2
29/30 Non-electrical machinery	11 686	15 906	13 969	15 002	14 360	51.7	62.5	59.2	61.7	56.5
29 Non-electrical machinery nec	7 219	8 176	7 858	9 588	10 692	42.4	47.2	48.6	54.4	58.3
30 Office and computing machinery	4 467	7 730	6 111	5 414	3 668	80.6	95.1	82.2	81.0	51.9
31/32 Electrical & electronic equipment	5 904	7 237	5 797	9 174	9 982	30.1	35.1	32.5	44.6	47.0
31 Electrical machinery nec	3 491	3 948	3 672	4 846	4 656	29.3	33.3	35.1	42.9	43.4
32 Radio, TV & communications eq.	2 414	3 289	2 125	4 329	5 326	31.4	37.5	28.8	46.8	50.7
33 Scientific instruments	1 567	1 740	1 700	1 747	1 237	32.2	32.7	30.2	27.0	24.2
34/35 Transportation equipment	6 655	7 413	7 364	7 381	9 085	20.0	24.6	27.4	18.8	16.2
34 Motor vehicles	6 520	7 072	7 039	6 672	7 902	23.1	26.5	30.0	22.1	18.5
35 Other transport equipment	134	341	325	709	1 183	2.7	9.8	9.5	7.8	8.8
351 Shipbuilding & repairing	..	78	- 10	19	..	..	15.2	-34.5	10.1	..
353 Aircraft and spacecraft	..	79	94	366	859	..	5.4	4.4	4.7	7.3
36/37 Other manufacturing	956	864	905	1 157	1 443	14.0	13.6	15.1	19.2	20.1
40/45 Construction, electricity, gas & water	..	..	..	..	..	..	..	..	..	..
50/55 Trade, repair, hotels & restaurants	..	..	..	..	..	..	..	..	..	..
65/74 Finance, insurance, business services	..	..	..	..	..	..	..	..	..	..
OTHER ACTIVITIES	..	..	..	..	..	..	..	..	..	..
01/99 **GRAND TOTAL**	..	..	..	..	..	..	..	..	..	..

Total manufacturing by investing country						As a % of total manufacturing by foreign affiliates				
All countries	75 575	94 624	86 533	99 078	101 495	100.0	100.0	100.0	100.0	100.0
United States	28 443	36 352	32 569	34 576	..	37.6	38.4	37.6	34.9	..
Canada	..	..	..	..	..	..	..	..	..	..
Mexico	..	..	..	..	..	..	..	..	..	..
Japan	2 060	2 990	3 392	4 058	4 138	2.7	3.2	3.9	4.1	4.1
Europe	..	..	..	..	..	..	..	..	..	..
European Union (15)	37 298	45 394	42 330	49 425	54 530	49.4	48.0	48.9	49.9	53.7
Belgium	..	..	..	..	..	..	..	..	..	..
France	..	..	..	..	..	..	..	..	..	..
Germany	11 639	13 307	13 476	15 248	16 612	15.4	14.1	15.6	15.4	16.4
Italy	..	..	..	..	..	..	..	..	..	..
Netherlands	4 195	4 325	4 015	5 408	5 993	5.6	4.6	4.6	5.5	5.9
Spain	..	..	..	..	..	..	..	..	..	..
Sweden	..	..	..	..	..	..	..	..	..	..
United Kingdom	8 703	9 142	8 806	9 528	10 613	11.5	9.7	10.2	9.6	10.5
Switzerland	6 741	6 706	6 539	7 976	..	8.9	7.1	7.6	8.1	..
Australia and New Zealand	..	..	..	..	..	..	..	..	..	..
Asia (non-OECD)	68	171	15	36	- 16	0.1	0.2	0.0	0.0	0.0
Latin America	..	..	..	16	54	..	..	..	0.0	0.1

Note: Majority foreign-owned firms. Food (ISIC 15/16), energy industries (ISIC 10, 11, 23) and *Recycling* (37) are excluded. *Total Manufacturing* includes *Mining & quarrying except energy producing materials* (ISIC 13/14).

Firmes sous contrôle étranger majoritaire. L'industrie agro-alimentaire (CITI 15/16), l'énergie (CITI 10, 11, 23) et la *Récupération* (37) ne sont pas couvertes. Le *Total manufacturier* comprend l'*Extraction de produits non énergétiques* (CITI 13/14).

FRANCE

Source

The data are prepared by the *Service des Statistiques Industrielles* (SESSI), Ministry of Industry, for all variables except *R&D expenditure* and *Number of researchers*. They are derived from the register containing declarations of foreign participation at the *Direction du Trésor*. This file is complemented with results from the Institut National de la Statistique et des Études Économiques (INSEE) survey on financial ties. Only the manufacturing sector and mining and quarrying are covered, except food and energy industries. The data refer to majority foreign-owned firms (foreign participating interests of 50% at the latest) and include indirect investments. The results are published annually in *L'implantation étrangère dans l'industrie française*.

Data on *R&D expenditure* and *Number of researchers* come from the annual survey on the resources devoted to R&D in the business sector conducted by the Ministry of higher education, research and technology.

National totals: come from the annual business survey conducted by the SESSI, which covers all firms with 20 or more employees.

Industrial classification

For all variables, the data are classified according to the principal industrial activity of the affiliate.

The industrial classification used for the French tables is the national classification converted to ISIC Revision 3.

The following notes concern all variables except *R&D expenditure* and *Number of researchers*. Energy industries – *i.e. Coke and refined petroleum products* (23) and *Crude petroleum, natural gas production* and *Coal mining* (10 to 12) –, *Food, beverages and tobacco* (15/16) and *Recycling* (37) are not covered. *Total manufacturing* includes *Mining and quarrying except energy producing materials* (13 to 14).

Variables

- *Number of employees* is not expressed on a full-time equivalent basis.

- *Value added* is valued in market prices.

Geographical breakdown

The country of origin is that of the "ultimate beneficial owner".

The detail by country is available when a country controls at least three firms in a given sector.

Up to and including 1996, data for the Asia (non-OECD) area include those for Korea. From 1997, the figures for Belgium include those for Luxembourg.

FRANCE

Source

Les données émanent du Service des Statistiques Industrielles (SESSI) du Ministère de l'Industrie pour toutes les variables, sauf les *Dépenses de R-D* et le *Nombre de chercheurs*. Elles proviennent du fichier des déclarations de prises de participations étrangères de la Direction du Trésor, auquel s'ajoutent les résultats de l'enquête de l'Institut National de la Statistique et des Études Économiques (INSEE) sur les liaisons financières. Seules les industries manufacturières et extractives sont couvertes, hors agro-alimentaire et énergie. Les données sont relatives aux entreprises sous contrôle étranger majoritaire (participation supérieure ou égale à 50 %) et comprennent les investissements indirects. Les résultats sont publiés chaque année dans *L'implantation étrangère dans l'industrie française*.

Les données sur les *Dépenses de R-D* et le *Nombre de chercheurs* proviennent de l'enquête annuelle sur les moyens consacrés à la R-D dans les entreprises menée par le Ministère de l'Éducation Nationale, de la Recherche et de la Technologie.

Totaux nationaux : les données proviennent de l'enquête annuelle d'entreprise du SESSI, qui s'adresse à toutes les entreprises employant au moins 20 salariés.

Classification industrielle

Pour toutes les variables, les données sont classées selon l'activité industrielle principale de l'entreprise affiliée.

La classification industrielle utilisée pour les tableaux français est la classification nationale adaptée pour correspondre à la CITI révision 3.

Les notes suivantes concernent toutes les variables sauf les *Dépenses de R-D* et le *Nombre de chercheurs*. L'énergie – *i.e. Produits pétroliers raffinés et coke* (23) et *Extraction de pétrole, de gaz naturel et de charbon* (10 à 12) –, les *Produits alimentaires, boissons et tabac* (15/16) et les produits issus de *Recyclage* (37) ne sont pas couverts. Le *Total manufacturier* comprend l'*Extraction de produits non énergétiques* (13 à 14).

Variables

- Le *Nombre de salariés* n'est pas exprimé en équivalent plein-temps.

- La *Valeur ajoutée* est évaluée aux prix du marché.

Ventilation géographique

Le pays d'origine est celui du "bénéficiaire ultime de l'investissement".

Le détail par pays est disponible quand un pays contrôle au moins trois entreprises dans un secteur donné.

Jusqu'en 1996 inclus, les données pour l'Asie hors OCDE comprennent celles de la Corée. A partir de 1997, les chiffres pour la Belgique incluent ceux du Luxembourg.

GERMANY

A. Inward investments

B. Outward investments

Sources and Methods

ALLEMAGNE

A. Investissements entrants

B. Investissements sortants

Sources et méthodes

Inward investments   *Investissements entrants*

Table 1A - Tableau 1A
NUMBER OF ENTERPRISES / NOMBRE D'ENTREPRISES

| | | Foreign affiliates (Units) | | | | | As a % of national total | | | | |
| | | Filiales étrangères (Unités) | | | | | En % du total national | | | | |
By industry (ISIC Rev. 3)		1995	1996	1997	1998	1999	1995	1996	1997	1998	1999
10/14	Mining & quarrying	20	18	22	22	24	4.0	3.6	4.5	4.7	..
15/37	**TOTAL MANUFACTURING**	1 516	1 499	1 509	1 526	1 514	4.1	4.1	4.0	4.1	..
15/16	Food, beverages, tobacco	94	91	85	82	83	2.2	2.2	1.7	1.7	..
17/19	Textiles, clothing, leather, footwear	68	71	72	74	71	2.7	3.1	3.4	3.7	..
20/22	Wood and paper products	124	121	115	121	124	2.5	2.5	2.4	2.5	..
20	Wood products	17	22	21	23	22	1.2	1.6	..	1.6	..
21/22	Paper, printing and publishing	107	99	94	98	102	3.0	2.8	..	2.9	..
23/25	Chemicals, Total	291	279	267	265	268	7.6	7.3	6.9	6.9	..
23	Refined petroleum, nuclear fuel	7	7	6	6	5	12.5	13.5	13.3	13.6	..
24/25	Chemicals, rubber & plastics prod.	284	272	261	259	263	7.5	7.2	6.9	6.8	..
24	Chemical products	179	172	161	160	159	14.1	13.6	12.9	12.8	..
2423	Pharmaceuticals	..	..	..	..	..	..	..	..	..	..
25	Rubber and plastics products	105	100	100	99	104	4.2	4.0	3.9	3.9	..
26	Non-metallic mineral products	64	58	56	48	48	3.0	2.7	2.7	2.4	..
27/28	Basic & fabricated metals	180	180	172	170	169	2.8	2.8	2.6	2.5	..
27	Basic metals	43	49	42	44	43	4.6	5.4	4.7	4.9	..
28	Fabricated metal products	137	131	130	126	126	2.5	2.4	2.2	2.1	..
29/32	Machinery, Total	513	510	535	535	505	6.3	6.4	6.6	6.5	..
29/30	Non-electrical machinery	358	354	366	364	347	6.1	6.2	6.2	6.2	..
29	Non-electrical machinery nec	330	326	337	338	324	5.8	5.8	5.9	5.9	..
30	Office and computing machinery	28	28	29	26	23	18.4	17.9	17.6	16.5	..
31/32	Electrical & electronic equipment	155	156	169	171	158	6.9	7.1	7.5	7.5	..
31	Electrical machinery nec	124	109	112	115	105	6.9	6.2	6.2	6.3	..
32	Radio, TV & communications eq.	31	47	57	56	53	6.8	10.5	13.0	12.1	..
33	Scientific instruments	92	98	100	116	125	5.3	5.8	5.1	6.2	..
34/35	Transportation equipment	44	46	58	64	68	4.1	4.4	5.3	5.7	..
34	Motor vehicles	29	28	36	41	44	3.6	3.6	4.4	4.9	..
35	Other transport equipment	15	18	22	23	24	5.3	6.8	8.1	8.2	..
351	Shipbuilding & repairing	..	..	..	..	..	..	..	..	..	..
353	Aircraft and spacecraft	..	..	..	..	..	..	..	..	..	..
36/37	Other manufacturing	46	45	49	51	53	2.0	2.1	2.3	2.5	..
40/45	Construction, electricity, gas & water	176	173	166	174	168	0.7	0.7	0.7	..	..
50/55	Trade, repair, hotels & restaurants	3 761	3 746	3 743	3 683	3 626	..	..	..	..	..
65/74	Finance, insurance, business services	2 212	2 287	2 357	2 558	2 611	..	..	..	..	..
	OTHER ACTIVITIES	357	367	378	380	415	..	..	..	..	..
01/99	**GRAND TOTAL**	8 042	8 090	8 175	8 343	8 358	..	..	..	..	..

Total manufacturing by investing country						As a % of total manufacturing by foreign affiliates				
All countries	1 516	1 499	1 509	1 526	1 514	100.0	100.0	100.0	100.0	100.0
United States	311	310	304	298	281	20.5	20.7	20.1	19.5	18.6
Canada	17	..	..	..	..	1.1	..	..	..	..
Mexico	..	..	..	..	..	..	..	..	..	..
Japan	59	56	58	62	64	3.9	3.7	3.8	4.1	4.2
Europe	1 137	0	..	..	..	75.0	0.0	..	..	..
European Union (15)	771	795	806	825	841	50.9	53.0	53.4	54.1	55.5
Belgium	59	0	..	..	..	3.9	0.0	..	..	..
France	127	126	124	133	127	8.4	8.4	8.2	8.7	8.4
Germany	..	..	..	..	..	..	..	..	..	..
Italy	50	..	..	..	..	3.3	..	..	..	..
Netherlands	214	220	236	243	251	14.1	14.7	15.6	15.9	16.6
Spain	10	..	..	..	..	0.7	..	..	..	..
Sweden	37	..	..	..	..	2.4	..	..	..	..
United Kingdom	104	110	111	101	108	6.9	7.3	7.4	6.6	7.1
Switzerland	357	316	314	308	301	23.5	21.1	20.8	20.2	19.9
Australia and New Zealand	4	..	..	..	..	0.3	..	..	..	..
Asia (non-OECD)	10	10	15	19	19	0.7	0.7	1.0	1.2	1.3
Latin America	28	25	24	19	13	1.8	1.7	1.6	1.2	0.9

Note: Majority foreign-owned firms. Data by country of origin may not add because of double countings for multinational enterprises.
Firmes sous contrôle étranger majoritaire. Les données par pays investisseur peuvent ne pas s'additionner en raison de doubles comptages pour les entreprises multinationales.

Inward investments

Investissements entrants

Table 2A - Tableau 2A

NUMBER OF EMPLOYEES BY INDUSTRY
NOMBRE DE SALARIÉS PAR INDUSTRIE

		Foreign affiliates (Units) Filiales étrangères (Unités)					As a % of national total En % du total national				
ISIC Revision 3		1995	1996	1997	1998	1999	1995	1996	1997	1998	1999
10/14	Mining & quarrying	4 000	4 000	4 000	3 000	3 000	2.2	2.4	2.8	2.3	..
15/37	**TOTAL MANUFACTURING**	**494 000**	**455 000**	**436 000**	**392 000**	**386 000**	**7.2**	**7.0**	**6.7**	**6.0**	**..**
15/16	Food, beverages, tobacco	35 000	30 000	30 000	28 000	27 000	6.3	5.4	5.0	4.8	..
17/19	Textiles, clothing, leather, footwear	9 000	11 000	9 000	8 000	9 000	3.1	4.3	3.7	3.4	..
20/22	Wood and paper products	18 000	14 000	12 000	17 000	18 000	2.7	2.1	1.9	2.7	..
20	Wood products	2 000	2 000	2 000	3 000	5 000	..	..	..	2.7	..
21/22	Paper, printing and publishing	16 000	12 000	10 000	13 000	14 000	..	..	..	2.5	..
23/25	Chemicals, Total	98 000	80 000	77 000	73 000	79 000	10.4	8.8	8.7	8.4	..
23	Refined petroleum, nuclear fuel	6 000	6 000	5 000	5 000	4 000	24.3	26.2	23.9	23.9	..
24/25	Chemicals, rubber & plastics prod.	92 000	75 000	72 000	68 000	75 000	10.0	8.5	8.3	8.0	..
24	Chemical products	70 000	56 000	56 000	51 000	51 000	12.7	10.4	11.0	10.3	..
2423	Pharmaceuticals	..	..	..	..	..	..	..	..	..	..
25	Rubber and plastics products	22 000	19 000	16 000	17 000	23 000	6.0	5.4	4.5	4.7	..
26	Non-metallic mineral products	12 000	12 000	11 000	10 000	10 000	4.2	4.5	4.3	4.0	..
27/28	Basic & fabricated metals	38 000	37 000	34 000	36 000	34 000	4.2	4.3	4.0	4.2	..
27	Basic metals	14 000	14 000	12 000	17 000	15 000	4.7	5.0	4.4	6.2	..
28	Fabricated metal products	24 000	23 000	22 000	19 000	19 000	4.0	4.0	3.8	3.2	..
29/32	Machinery, Total	152 000	138 000	132 000	128 000	114 000	8.4	8.0	7.9	7.6	..
29/30	Non-electrical machinery	86 000	82 000	74 000	72 000	62 000	7.7	7.7	7.1	6.9	..
29	Non-electrical machinery nec	73 000	69 000	67 000	66 000	57 000	7.0	6.8	6.8	6.6	..
30	Office and computing machinery	13 000	13 000	7 000	6 000	5 000	19.5	23.1	11.9	11.5	..
31/32	Electrical & electronic equipment	67 000	56 000	58 000	56 000	52 000	9.5	8.5	9.2	8.8	..
31	Electrical machinery nec	28 000	27 000	27 000	28 000	26 000	5.2	5.3	5.5	5.7	..
32	Radio, TV & communications eq.	39 000	30 000	31 000	28 000	26 000	23.6	20.0	22.3	20.0	..
33	Scientific instruments	19 000	17 000	15 000	17 000	15 000	8.8	8.1	6.9	7.9	..
34/35	Transportation equipment	107 000	110 000	110 000	68 000	75 000	11.9	12.5	12.3	7.3	..
34	Motor vehicles	102 000	102 000	101 000	58 000	61 000	13.5	13.7	13.1	7.2	..
35	Other transport equipment	5 000	9 000	9 000	10 000	14 000	3.6	6.7	7.1	8.0	..
351	Shipbuilding & repairing	..	..	..	..	..	..	..	..	..	..
353	Aircraft and spacecraft	..	..	..	..	..	..	..	..	..	..
36/37	Other manufacturing	6 000	5 000	6 000	6 000	5 000	2.4	2.1	2.5	2.5	..
40/45	Construction, electricity, gas & water	18 000	17 000	17 000	16 000	15 000	1.0	1.0	1.1	..	..
50/55	Trade, repair, hotels & restaurants	177 000	178 000	189 000	171 000	196 000	..	..	..	..	..
65/74	Finance, insurance, business services	65 000	67 000	68 000	73 000	73 000	..	..	..	..	..
	OTHER ACTIVITIES	39 000	38 000	38 000	46 000	54 000	..	..	..	..	..
01/99	**GRAND TOTAL**	**796 000**	**758 000**	**752 000**	**701 000**	**727 000**	**..**	**..**	**..**	**..**	**..**

Note: Majority foreign-owned firms.
Firmes sous contrôle étranger majoritaire.

Table 3A - Tableau 3A

NUMBER OF EMPLOYEES BY COUNTRY OF ORIGIN IN THE MANUFACTURING SECTOR

NOMBRE DE SALARIÉS PAR PAYS D'ORIGINE DANS L'INDUSTRIE MANUFACTURIÈRE

Country of origin (immediate controller)	Number of employees (Units) Nombre de salariés (Unités)					As a % of all countries En % du total des pays				
	1995	1996	1997	1998	1999	1995	1996	1997	1998	1999
All countries	**494 000**	**455 000**	**436 000**	**392 000**	**386 000**	**100.0**	**100.0**	**100.0**	**100.0**	**100.0**
Total OECD	..	..	..	**385 000**	**380 000**	..	..	..	**98.2**	**98.4**
United States	211 000	207 000	193 000	139 000	132 000	42.7	45.5	44.3	35.5	34.2
Canada	7 000	..	..	7 000	8 000	1.4	..	..	1.8	2.1
Mexico	..	..	..	..	..	..	..	..	..	..
Japan	16 000	15 000	16 000	17 000	16 000	3.2	3.3	3.7	4.3	4.1
Korea	1 000	..	..	2 000	2 000	0.2	..	..	0.5	0.5
Australia	..	..	..	..	..	..	..	..	..	..
New Zealand	..	..	..	0	0	..	..	..	0.0	0.0
Europe	**276 000**	..	..	**240 000**	**244 000**	**55.9**	..	..	**61.2**	**63.2**
European Union (15)	**205 000**	**188 000**	**175 000**	**178 000**	**184 000**	**41.5**	**41.3**	**40.1**	**45.4**	**47.7**
Austria	..	..	..	15 000	16 000	..	..	..	3.8	4.1
Belgium	8 000	..	..	10 000	11 000	1.6	..	..	2.6	2.8
Denmark	..	..	..	9 000	10 000	..	..	..	2.3	2.6
Finland	3 000	..	..	3 000	3 000	0.6	..	..	0.8	0.8
France	36 000	34 000	32 000	37 000	34 000	7.3	7.5	7.3	9.4	8.8
Germany	..	..	..	..	..	..	..	..	..	..
Greece	..	..	..	0	0	..	..	..	0.0	0.0
Ireland	..	..	..	0	0	..	..	..	0.0	0.0
Italy	12 000	..	..	10 000	10 000	2.4	..	..	2.6	2.6
Luxembourg	..	..	..	11 000	10 000	..	..	..	2.8	2.6
Netherlands	102 000	89 000	78 000	70 000	68 000	20.6	19.6	17.9	17.9	17.6
Portugal	..	..	..	..	0	..	..	..	..	0.0
Spain	2 000	..	..	4 000	14 000	0.4	..	..	1.0	3.6
Sweden	11 000	..	..	11 000	10 000	2.2	..	..	2.8	2.6
United Kingdom	19 000	20 000	20 000	20 000	22 000	3.8	4.4	4.6	5.1	5.7
Czech Republic	..	..	..	..	..	..	..	..	..	..
Hungary	..	..	..	0	0	..	..	..	0.0	0.0
Iceland	..	..	..	0	0	..	..	..	0.0	0.0
Norway	..	..	..	1 000	2 000	..	..	..	0.3	0.5
Poland	..	..	..	0	0	..	..	..	..	..
Slovak Republic	..	..	..	0	0	..	..	..	0.0	0.0
Switzerland	76 000	62 000	68 000	66 000	68 000	15.4	13.6	15.6	16.8	17.6
Turkey	..	..	..	0	0	..	..	..	0.0	0.0
Non-OECD Europe, of which:	..	..	..	**6 000**	**5 000**	..	..	..	**1.5**	**1.3**
Baltic countries	..	..	..	0	0	..	..	..	0.0	0.0
Bulgaria	..	..	..	0	0	..	..	..	0.0	0.0
Croatia	..	..	..	..	..	..	..	..	..	..
Romania	..	..	..	0	0	..	..	..	0.0	0.0
Russian Federation	..	..	..	..	..	..	..	..	..	..
Slovenia	..	..	..	..	..	..	..	..	..	..
Ukraine	..	..	..	0	0	..	..	..	0.0	0.0
Yugoslavia	..	..	..	0	0	..	..	..	0.0	0.0
Non-OECD Asia, of which:	**3 000**	**0**	**1 000**	**1 000**	**1 000**	**0.6**	**0.0**	**0.2**	**0.3**	**0.3**
China	..	..	..	0	..	..	..	..	0.0	..
Chinese Taipei	0	..	..	..	..	0.0	..	..	..	..
Hong Kong (China)	..	..	..	0	0	..	..	..	0.0	0.0
India	..	..	..	..	..	..	..	..	..	..
Indonesia	..	..	..	..	0	..	..	..	..	0.0
Malaysia	..	..	..	0	0	..	..	..	0.0	0.0
Philippines	..	..	..	0	0	..	..	..	0.0	0.0
Singapore	..	..	..	..	..	..	..	..	..	..
Thailand	..	..	..	0	0	..	..	..	0.0	0.0
Near and Middle East	..	..	..	**1 000**	**1 000**	..	..	..	**0.3**	**0.3**
Africa	..	..	..	**0**	**1 000**	..	..	..	**0.0**	**0.3**
Latin America, of which:	**8 000**	**5 000**	**4 000**	**4 000**	**10 000**	**1.6**	**1.1**	**0.9**	**1.0**	**2.6**
Argentina	..	..	..	0	..	..	..	..	0.0	..
Brazil	1 000	..	..	1 000	..	0.2	..	..	0.3	..
Chile	..	..	..	0	0	..	..	..	0.0	0.0

Note: Majority foreign-owned firms. Data may not add because of double countings for multinational enterprises. Data for non-OECD Europe include those for Czech Republic, Hungary, Poland, Slovak Republic and Turkey.
Firmes sous contrôle étranger majoritaire. Les données peuvent ne pas s'additionner en raison de doubles comptages pour les entreprises multinationales. Les données pour l'Europe hors OCDE comprennent celles de la République tchèque, de la Hongrie, de la Pologne, de la République slovaque et de la Turquie.

Table 4A - Tableau 4A

TURNOVER BY INDUSTRY

CHIFFRE D'AFFAIRES PAR INDUSTRIE

| | | Foreign affiliates *(Millions of DEM)* | | | | | As a % of national total | | | | |
| | | Filiales étrangères *(Millions de DEM)* | | | | | En % du total national | | | | |
ISIC Revision 3		1995	1996	1997	1998	1999	1995	1996	1997	1998	1999
10/14	Mining & quarrying	800	1 100	1 100	800	1 200	2.0	3.8	4.2	3.3	..
15/37	**TOTAL MANUFACTURING**	**272 400**	**270 000**	**276 400**	**249 300**	**232 700**	**13.1**	**12.8**	**12.5**	**10.8**	..
15/16	Food, beverages, tobacco	33 200	31 700	31 200	30 600	29 500	13.3	12.6	11.9	11.8	..
17/19	Textiles, clothing, leather, footwear	2 400	2 400	2 100	2 100	2 300	3.9	4.0	3.5	3.5	..
20/22	Wood and paper products	7 500	6 000	5 800	8 100	8 500	4.9	3.9	3.6	5.0	..
20	Wood products	700	700	800	1 200	1 500	2.3	2.4	..	3.8	..
21/22	Paper, printing and publishing	6 800	5 300	5 000	6 900	6 900	5.6	4.2	..	5.2	..
23/25	Chemicals, Total	85 300	83 000	90 700	82 700	70 300	19.8	19.2	20.7	18.9	..
23	Refined petroleum, nuclear fuel	40 900	45 500	48 900	43 800	28 900	35.2	37.5	44.0	40.3	..
24/25	Chemicals, rubber & plastics prod.	44 400	37 600	41 900	38 900	41 400	14.1	12.1	12.8	11.8	..
24	Chemical products	38 400	32 000	36 600	33 100	33 700	17.0	14.3	15.6	14.2	..
2423	Pharmaceuticals	..	..	..	..	..	..	..	..	..	..
25	Rubber and plastics products	6 000	5 600	5 200	5 700	7 700	6.8	6.4	5.6	6.0	..
26	Non-metallic mineral products	3 700	3 600	3 900	3 700	3 400	5.0	5.1	5.6	5.3	..
27/28	Basic & fabricated metals	12 000	12 000	12 100	12 800	12 100	5.1	5.4	5.2	5.2	..
27	Basic metals	6 400	6 300	6 400	7 900	7 100	6.0	6.5	6.2	7.4	..
28	Fabricated metal products	5 500	5 700	5 700	4 900	5 000	4.3	4.5	4.3	3.5	..
29/32	Machinery, Total	61 800	59 900	55 100	57 600	51 000	13.1	12.6	11.1	10.9	..
29/30	Non-electrical machinery	35 700	35 100	27 700	29 300	24 900	12.7	12.2	9.3	9.3	..
29	Non-electrical machinery nec	23 000	23 000	24 200	25 500	21 600	9.1	8.9	9.1	9.0	..
30	Office and computing machinery	12 700	12 100	3 500	3 800	3 300	41.8	41.6	11.4	12.0	..
31/32	Electrical & electronic equipment	26 100	24 800	27 400	28 300	26 100	13.8	13.2	13.7	13.4	..
31	Electrical machinery nec	8 200	8 200	9 300	10 100	8 400	5.9	5.9	6.2	6.3	..
32	Radio, TV & communications eq.	17 800	16 600	18 100	18 200	17 700	36.2	34.2	36.4	35.0	..
33	Scientific instruments	6 000	5 700	5 400	5 900	5 000	14.1	13.0	11.4	11.8	..
34/35	Transportation equipment	58 800	64 200	68 200	44 000	48 900	18.7	18.7	17.9	10.0	..
34	Motor vehicles	56 400	60 300	64 000	36 900	40 100	20.1	19.7	18.8	9.2	..
35	Other transport equipment	2 500	3 800	4 200	7 100	8 700	7.5	10.1	10.5	17.3	..
351	Shipbuilding & repairing	..	..	..	..	..	..	..	..	..	..
353	Aircraft and spacecraft	..	..	..	..	..	..	..	..	..	..
36/37	Other manufacturing	1 700	1 600	1 800	1 800	1 700	3.2	3.0	3.3	3.1	..
40/45	Construction, electricity, gas & water	4 000	4 600	4 700	4 300	3 500	0.8	1.0	1.0	..	..
50/55	Trade, repair, hotels & restaurants	197 300	203 200	214 100	215 300	219 000	..	..	..	..	..
65/74	Finance, insurance, business services	35 200	37 000	37 600	39 900	40 700	..	..	..	..	..
	OTHER ACTIVITIES	11 700	11 000	13 700	13 700	15 900	..	..	..	..	..
01/99	**GRAND TOTAL**	**521 400**	**526 900**	**547 600**	**523 400**	**513 000**	..	..	..	..	..

Note: Majority foreign-owned firms.
Firmes sous contrôle étranger majoritaire.

Table 5A - Tableau 5A

TURNOVER BY COUNTRY OF ORIGIN IN THE MANUFACTURING INDUSTRY

CHIFFRE D'AFFAIRES PAR PAYS D'ORIGINE DANS L'INDUSTRIE MANUFACTURIÈRE

Country of origin (immediate controller)	Turnover (Millions of DEM) Chiffre d'affaires (Millions de DEM)					As a % of all countries En % du total des pays				
	1995	1996	1997	1998	1999	1995	1996	1997	1998	1999
All countries	**272 400**	**270 000**	**276 400**	**249 300**	**232 700**	**100.0**	**100.0**	**100.0**	**100.0**	**100.0**
Total OECD	..	..	..	245 900	..	..	..	..	98.6	..
United States	141 700	148 200	144 300	99 700	83 300	52.0	54.9	52.2	40.0	35.8
Canada	3 800	..	..	2 100	..	1.4	..	..	0.8	..
Mexico	..	..	..	..	..	..	..	..	..	..
Japan	7 100	7 400	7 300	9 000	7 600	2.6	2.7	2.6	3.6	3.3
Korea	..	..	..	600	..	..	..	..	0.2	..
Australia	..	..	..	..	..	..	..	..	..	..
New Zealand	..	..	..	0	..	..	..	..	0.0	..
Europe	135 300	..	..	145 500	..	49.7	..	..	58.4	..
European Union (15)	108 800	106 300	103 900	108 800	109 200	39.9	39.4	37.6	43.6	46.9
Austria	..	..	..	6 700	..	..	..	..	2.7	..
Belgium	3 200	..	..	4 800	..	1.2	..	..	1.9	..
Denmark	..	..	..	3 000	..	..	..	..	1.2	..
Finland	..	..	..	2 000	..	..	..	..	0.8	..
France	12 300	10 800	10 900	13 800	12 100	4.5	4.0	3.9	5.5	5.2
Germany	..	..	..	..	..	..	..	..	..	..
Greece	..	..	..	0	..	..	..	..	0.0	..
Ireland	..	..	..	200	..	..	..	..	0.1	..
Italy	6 300	..	..	10 100	..	2.3	..	..	4.1	..
Luxembourg	..	..	..	5 700	..	..	..	..	2.3	..
Netherlands	68 300	67 400	63 000	59 900	57 500	25.1	25.0	22.8	24.0	24.7
Portugal	..	..	..	..	.	..	..	..	..	..
Spain	1 400	..	..	4 800	..	0.5	..	..	1.9	..
Sweden	4 600	..	..	5 700	..	1.7	..	..	2.3	..
United Kingdom	28 600	32 100	32 800	33 400	36 800	10.5	11.9	11.9	13.4	15.8
Czech Republic	..	..	..	..	..	..	..	..	..	..
Hungary	..	..	..	0	..	..	..	..	0.0	..
Iceland	..	..	..	0	..	..	..	..	0.0	..
Norway	..	..	..	300	..	..	..	..	0.1	..
Poland	..	..	..	0	..	..	..	..	..	..
Slovak Republic	..	..	..	0	..	..	..	..	0.0	..
Switzerland	28 800	24 200	28 800	39 300	38 500	10.6	9.0	10.4	15.8	16.5
Turkey	..	..	..	100	..	..	..	..	0.0	..
Non-OECD Europe, of which:	..	..	..	3 400	..	..	..	..	1.4	..
Baltic countries	..	..	..	0	..	..	..	..	0.0	..
Bulgaria	..	..	..	0	..	..	..	..	0.0	..
Croatia	..	..	..	..	..	..	..	..	..	..
Romania	..	..	..	0	..	..	..	..	0.0	..
Russian Federation	..	..	..	..	..	..	..	..	..	..
Slovenia	..	..	..	..	..	..	..	..	..	..
Ukraine	..	..	..	0	..	..	..	..	0.0	..
Yugoslavia	..	..	..	0	..	..	..	..	0.0	..
Non-OECD Asia, of which:	700	100	300	400	400	0.3	0.0	0.1	0.2	0.2
China	..	..	..	0	..	..	..	..	0.0	..
Chinese Taipei	..	..	..	..	..	..	..	..	..	..
Hong Kong (China)	..	..	..	0	..	..	..	..	0.0	..
India	..	..	..	..	..	..	..	..	..	..
Indonesia	..	..	..	..	..	..	..	..	..	..
Malaysia	..	..	..	100	..	..	..	..	0.0	..
Philippines	..	..	..	0	..	..	..	..	0.0	..
Singapore	..	..	..	..	..	..	..	..	..	..
Thailand	..	..	..	0	..	..	..	..	0.0	..
Near and Middle East	..	..	..	200	..	..	..	..	0.1	..
Africa	..	..	..	100	..	..	..	..	0.0	..
Latin America, of which:	4 000	1 700	1 700	1 600	2 700	1.5	0.6	0.6	0.6	1.2
Argentina	..	..	..	0	..	..	..	..	0.0	..
Brazil	..	..	..	200	..	..	..	..	0.1	..
Chile	..	..	..	0	..	..	..	..	0.0	..

Note: Majority foreign-owned firms. Data may not add because of double countings for multinational enterprises. Data for non-OECD Europe include those for Czech Republic, Hungary, Poland, Slovak Republic and Turkey.

Firmes sous contrôle étranger majoritaire. Les données peuvent ne pas s'additionner en raison de doubles comptages pour les entreprises multinationales. Les données pour l'Europe hors OCDE comprennent celles de la République tchèque, de la Hongrie, de la Pologne, de la République slovaque et de la Turquie.

Inward investments   *Investissements entrants*

Table 6A - Tableau 6A

R&D EXPENDITURE / DÉPENSES DE R-D

By industry (ISIC Rev. 3)	Foreign affiliates (Millions of DEM) Filiales étrangères (Millions de DEM)					As a % of national total En % du total national				
	1994	1995	1996	1997	1998	1994	1995	1996	1997	1998
10/14 Mining & quarrying	..	..	..	..	..	..	..	..	..	..
15/37 **TOTAL MANUFACTURING**	..	**6 778**	..	**8 124**	..	..	**16.4**	..	..	..
15/16 Food, beverages, tobacco	..	..	..	..	..	..	..	..	..	..
17/19 Textiles, clothing, leather, footwear	..	..	..	..	..	..	..	..	..	..
20/22 Wood and paper products	..	..	..	..	..	..	..	..	..	..
20 Wood products	..	..	..	..	..	..	..	..	..	..
21/22 Paper, printing and publishing	..	..	..	..	..	..	..	..	..	..
23/25 Chemicals, Total	..	537	..	..	..	..	6.1	..	..	..
23 Refined petroleum, nuclear fuel	..	..	..	..	..	..	..	..	..	..
24/25 Chemicals, rubber & plastics prod.	..	..	..	..	..	..	..	..	..	..
24 Chemical products	..	..	..	..	..	..	..	..	..	..
2423 Pharmaceuticals	..	..	..	..	..	..	..	..	..	..
25 Rubber and plastics products	..	..	..	..	..	..	..	..	..	..
26 Non-metallic mineral products	..	..	..	..	..	..	..	..	..	..
27/28 Basic & fabricated metals	..	..	..	..	..	..	..	..	..	..
27 Basic metals	..	..	..	..	..	..	..	..	..	..
28 Fabricated metal products	..	..	..	..	..	..	..	..	..	..
29/32 Machinery, Total	..	..	..	..	..	..	..	..	..	..
29/30 Non-electrical machinery	..	..	..	..	..	..	..	..	..	..
29 Non-electrical machinery nec	..	474	..	..	..	..	17.6	..	..	..
30 Office and computing machinery	..	..	..	..	..	..	..	..	..	..
31/32 Electrical & electronic equipment	..	2 410	..	..	..	..	23.1	..	..	..
31 Electrical machinery nec	..	..	..	..	..	..	..	..	..	..
32 Radio, TV & communications eq.	..	..	..	..	..	..	..	..	..	..
33 Scientific instruments	..	..	..	..	..	..	..	..	..	..
34/35 Transportation equipment	..	..	..	..	..	..	..	..	..	..
34 Motor vehicles	..	2 071	..	..	..	..	19.3	..	..	..
35 Other transport equipment	..	..	..	..	..	..	..	..	..	..
351 Shipbuilding & repairing	..	..	..	..	..	..	..	..	..	..
353 Aircraft and spacecraft	..	..	..	..	..	..	..	..	..	..
36/37 Other manufacturing	..	..	..	..	..	..	..	..	..	..
40/45 Construction, electricity, gas & water	..	..	..	..	..	..	..	..	..	..
50/55 Trade, repair, hotels & restaurants	..	..	..	..	..	..	..	..	..	..
65/74 Finance, insurance, business services	..	..	..	..	..	..	..	..	..	..
OTHER ACTIVITIES	..	..	..	..	..	..	..	..	..	..
01/99 **GRAND TOTAL**	..	**6 811**	..	..	..	..	**16.1**	..	..	..

Total manufacturing by investing country						As a % of total manufacturing by foreign affiliates				
All countries	..	**6 778**	..	**8 124**	..	..	**100.0**	..	**100.0**	..
United States	..	3 473	..	..	..	..	51.2	..	..	..
Canada	..	..	..	..	..	..	..	..	..	..
Mexico	..	..	..	..	..	..	..	..	..	..
Japan	..	..	..	..	..	..	..	..	..	..
Europe	..	3 219	..	..	..	..	47.5	..	..	..
European Union (15)	..	2 090	..	..	..	..	30.8	..	..	..
Belgium	..	..	..	..	..	..	..	..	..	..
France	..	1 197	..	..	..	..	17.7	..	..	..
Germany	..	..	..	..	..	..	..	..	..	..
Italy	..	..	..	..	..	..	..	..	..	..
Netherlands	..	573	..	..	..	..	8.5	..	..	..
Spain	..	..	..	..	..	..	..	..	..	..
Sweden	..	..	..	..	..	..	..	..	..	..
United Kingdom	..	..	..	..	..	..	..	..	..	..
Switzerland	..	1 040	..	..	..	..	15.3	..	..	..
Australia and New Zealand	..	..	..	..	..	..	..	..	..	..
Asia (non-OECD)	..	..	..	..	..	..	..	..	..	..
Latin America	..	..	..	..	..	..	..	..	..	..

Note: Sample of 500 R&D-intensive companies. Majority foreign-owned firms.
         Échantillon de 500 sociétés à forte intensité de R-D. Firmes sous contrôle étranger majoritaire.

Inward investments

Investissements entrants

Table 7A - Tableau 7A

NUMBER OF RESEARCHERS / NOMBRE DE CHERCHEURS

By industry (ISIC Rev. 3)	Foreign affiliates (FTE) Filiales étrangères (EPT)					As a % of national total En % du total national				
	1994	1995	1996	1997	1998	1994	1995	1996	1997	1998
10/14 Mining & quarrying	..	..	..	..	..	..	..	..	..	..
15/37 **TOTAL MANUFACTURING**	..	32 314	..	37 394	..	..	15.9	..	..	..
15/16 Food, beverages, tobacco	..	..	..	..	..	..	..	..	..	..
17/19 Textiles, clothing, leather, footwear	..	..	..	..	..	..	..	..	..	..
20/22 Wood and paper products	..	..	..	..	..	..	..	..	..	..
20 Wood products	..	..	..	..	..	..	..	..	..	..
21/22 Paper, printing and publishing	..	..	..	..	..	..	..	..	..	..
23/25 Chemicals, Total	..	3 027	..	..	..	..	7.0	..	..	..
23 Refined petroleum, nuclear fuel	..	..	..	..	..	..	..	..	..	..
24/25 Chemicals, rubber & plastics prod.	..	..	..	..	..	..	..	..	..	..
24 Chemical products	..	..	..	..	..	..	..	..	..	..
2423 Pharmaceuticals	..	..	..	..	..	..	..	..	..	..
25 Rubber and plastics products	..	..	..	..	..	..	..	..	..	..
26 Non-metallic mineral products	..	..	..	..	..	..	..	..	..	..
27/28 Basic & fabricated metals	..	..	..	..	..	..	..	..	..	..
27 Basic metals	..	..	..	..	..	..	..	..	..	..
28 Fabricated metal products	..	..	..	..	..	..	..	..	..	..
29/32 Machinery, Total	..	..	..	..	..	..	..	..	..	..
29/30 Non-electrical machinery	..	..	..	..	..	..	..	..	..	..
29 Non-electrical machinery nec	..	2 460	..	..	..	..	16.1	..	..	..
30 Office and computing machinery	..	..	..	..	..	..	..	..	..	..
31/32 Electrical & electronic equipment	..	11 862	..	..	..	..	20.1	..	..	..
31 Electrical machinery nec	..	..	..	..	..	..	..	..	..	..
32 Radio, TV & communications eq.	..	..	..	..	..	..	..	..	..	..
33 Scientific instruments	..	..	..	..	..	..	..	..	..	..
34/35 Transportation equipment	..	..	..	..	..	..	..	..	..	..
34 Motor vehicles	..	9 237	..	..	..	..	19.1	..	..	..
35 Other transport equipment	..	..	..	..	..	..	..	..	..	..
351 Shipbuilding & repairing	..	..	..	..	..	..	..	..	..	..
353 Aircraft and spacecraft	..	..	..	..	..	..	..	..	..	..
36/37 Other manufacturing	..	..	..	..	..	..	..	..	..	..
40/45 Construction, electricity, gas & water	..	..	..	..	..	..	..	..	..	..
50/55 Trade, repair, hotels & restaurants	..	..	..	..	..	..	..	..	..	..
65/74 Finance, insurance, business services	..	..	..	..	..	..	..	..	..	..
OTHER ACTIVITIES	..	..	..	..	..	..	..	..	..	..
01/99 **GRAND TOTAL**	..	32 442	..	..	..	..	15.5	..	..	..

Total manufacturing by investing country						As a % of total manufacturing by foreign affiliates				
All countries	..	32 314	..	37 394	..	..	100.0	..	100.0	..
United States	..	15 607	..	..	..	..	48.3	..	..	..
Canada	..	..	..	..	..	..	..	..	..	..
Mexico	..	..	..	..	..	..	..	..	..	..
Japan	..	..	..	..	..	..	..	..	..	..
Europe	..	16 067	..	..	..	..	49.7	..	..	..
European Union (15)	..	10 051	..	..	..	..	31.1	..	..	..
Belgium	..	..	..	..	..	..	..	..	..	..
France	..	5 075	..	..	..	..	15.7	..	..	..
Germany	..	..	..	..	..	..	..	..	..	..
Italy	..	..	..	..	..	..	..	..	..	..
Netherlands	..	5 135	..	..	..	..	15.9	..	..	..
Spain	..	..	..	..	..	..	..	..	..	..
Sweden	..	..	..	..	..	..	..	..	..	..
United Kingdom	..	..	..	..	..	..	..	..	..	..
Switzerland	..	5 500	..	..	..	..	17.0	..	..	..
Australia and New Zealand	..	..	..	..	..	..	..	..	..	..
Asia (non-OECD)	..	..	..	..	..	..	..	..	..	..
Latin America	..	..	..	..	..	..	..	..	..	..

Note: Sample of 500 R&D-intensive companies. Majority foreign-owned firms. Total R&D personnel rather than researchers.
Échantillon de 500 sociétés à forte intensité de R-D. Firmes sous contrôle étranger majoritaire. Ensemble du personnel de R-D plutôt que chercheurs.

Inward investments

Investissements entrants

Table 8A - Tableau 8A

TECHNOLOGICAL PAYMENTS / PAIEMENTS TECHNOLOGIQUES

By industry (ISIC Rev. 3)		Foreign affiliates (Millions of DEM) / Filiales étrangères (Millions de DEM)					As a % of national total / En % du total national				
		1995	1996	1997	1998	1999	1995	1996	1997	1998	1999
10/14	Mining & quarrying	..	2	2	..	..	..	..	..	..	..
15/37	**TOTAL MANUFACTURING**	3 226	1 897	1 400	1 633	..	..	54.2	46.7	48.8	..
15/16	Food, beverages, tobacco	351	324	249	246	..	..	94.2	94.0	97.2	..
17/19	Textiles, clothing, leather, footwear	10	4	3	6	..	..	..	..	..	..
20/22	Wood and paper products	..	..	..	..	..	..	..	..	..	..
20	Wood products	..	..	..	..	..	..	..	..	..	..
21/22	Paper, printing and publishing	..	..	..	..	..	..	..	..	..	..
23/25	Chemicals, Total	679	605	..	..	..	..	..	..	..	..
23	Refined petroleum, nuclear fuel	2	2	..	..	..	..	..	..	..	..
24/25	Chemicals, rubber & plastics prod.	677	603	350	458	..	..	..	..	..	..
24	Chemical products	624	570	311	418	..	..	36.8	30.4	33.1	..
2423	Pharmaceuticals	..	..	..	..	..	..	..	..	..	..
25	Rubber and plastics products	53	33	39	39	..	..	..	..	..	..
26	Non-metallic mineral products	28	27	28	25	..	..	..	..	..	..
27/28	Basic & fabricated metals	83	..	82	55	..	..	..	..	..	..
27	Basic metals	14	..	25	7	..	..	..	..	..	..
28	Fabricated metal products	69	54	57	48	..	..	..	..	..	..
29/32	Machinery, Total	2 013	780	591	665	..	..	63.1	45.0	50.5	..
29/30	Non-electrical machinery	1 617	407	135	195	..	..	..	..	..	..
29	Non-electrical machinery nec	48	46	104	143	..	..	26.3	48.8	59.8	..
30	Office and computing machinery	1 569	361	31	52	..	..	..	..	..	..
31/32	Electrical & electronic equipment	396	373	456	470	..	..	..	..	..	..
31	Electrical machinery nec	320	58	84	69	..	..	..	..	..	..
32	Radio, TV & communications eq.	76	315	372	401	..	..	..	..	..	..
33	Scientific instruments	24	26	28	54	..	..	..	..	..	..
34/35	Transportation equipment	..	38	32	54	..	..	61.3	38.1	50.0	..
34	Motor vehicles	27	37	24	51	..	..	..	..	..	..
35	Other transport equipment	..	1	8	3	..	..	..	..	..	..
351	Shipbuilding & repairing	..	..	..	..	..	..	..	..	..	..
353	Aircraft and spacecraft	..	..	..	..	..	..	..	..	..	..
36/37	Other manufacturing	6	24	17	12	..	..	..	..	..	..
40/45	Construction, electricity, gas & water	13	4	3	..	..	..	..	..	..	..
50/55	Trade, repair, hotels & restaurants	343	258	194	179	..	..	65.2	74.6	69.4	..
65/74	Finance, insurance, business services	229	1 343	1 578	1 671	..	..	90.1	92.3	83.6	..
	OTHER ACTIVITIES	..	15	7	12	..	..	..	..	..	..
01/99	**GRAND TOTAL**	3 828	3 520	3 191	3 498	..	66.6	64.8	63.3	62.0	..

Total manufacturing by investing country	1995	1996	1997	1998	1999	As a % of total manufacturing by foreign affiliates				
All countries	3 226	1 897	1 400	1 633	..	100.0	100.0	100.0	100.0	..
United States	..	..	..	..	..	..	..	..	..	..
Canada	..	..	..	..	..	..	..	..	..	..
Mexico	..	..	..	..	..	..	..	..	..	..
Japan	..	..	..	..	..	..	..	..	..	..
Europe	..	..	..	..	..	..	..	..	..	..
European Union (15)	..	..	..	..	..	..	..	..	..	..
Belgium	..	..	..	..	..	..	..	..	..	..
France	..	..	..	..	..	..	..	..	..	..
Germany	..	..	..	..	..	..	..	..	..	..
Italy	..	..	..	..	..	..	..	..	..	..
Netherlands	..	..	..	..	..	..	..	..	..	..
Spain	..	..	..	..	..	..	..	..	..	..
Sweden	..	..	..	..	..	..	..	..	..	..
United Kingdom	..	..	..	..	..	..	..	..	..	..
Switzerland	..	..	..	..	..	..	..	..	..	..
Australia and New Zealand	..	..	..	..	..	..	..	..	..	..
Asia (non-OECD)	..	..	..	..	..	..	..	..	..	..
Latin America	..	..	..	..	..	..	..	..	..	..

Note: **All foreign-owned firms** with foreign participating interests of more than 20%. Up to 1994, ISIC 28 includes 33 and ISIC 36/37 includes 26. See country notes.
Toutes les firmes sous contrôle étranger pour lesquelles la participation étrangère dépasse 20%. Jusqu'en 1994, la CITI 28 comprend 33 et la CITI 36/37 comprend 26. Voir les notes par pays.

Inward investments   *Investissements entrants*

Table 9A - Tableau 9A

TECHNOLOGICAL RECEIPTS / RECETTES TECHNOLOGIQUES

By industry (ISIC Rev. 3)	Foreign affiliates (Millions of DEM) Filiales étrangères (Millions de DEM)					As a % of national total En % du total national				
	1995	1996	1997	1998	1999	1995	1996	1997	1998	1999
10/14 Mining & quarrying	..	0	0	..	..	..	..	..	..	..
15/37 TOTAL MANUFACTURING	**751**	**688**	**799**	**1 122**	..	..	**22.4**	**22.7**	**27.4**	..
15/16 Food, beverages, tobacco	2	1	7	3	..	..	3.8	22.6	10.7	..
17/19 Textiles, clothing, leather, footwear	138	1	0	0	..	..	..	..	..	..
20/22 Wood and paper products	..	..	..	..	..	..	..	..	..	..
20 Wood products	..	..	..	..	..	..	..	..	..	..
21/22 Paper, printing and publishing	..	..	..	..	..	..	..	..	..	..
23/25 Chemicals, Total	216	272	..	..	..	..	..	..	..	..
23 Refined petroleum, nuclear fuel	0	0	..	..	..	..	..	..	..	..
24/25 Chemicals, rubber & plastics prod.	216	272	220	512	..	..	..	..	..	..
24 Chemical products	214	272	215	509	..	..	16.6	13.0	23.9	..
2423 Pharmaceuticals	..	..	..	..	..	..	..	..	..	..
25 Rubber and plastics products	2	0	5	4	..	..	..	..	..	..
26 Non-metallic mineral products	1	3	3	2	..	..	..	..	..	..
27/28 Basic & fabricated metals	4	..	6	5	..	..	..	..	..	..
27 Basic metals	0	..	0	0	..	..	..	..	..	..
28 Fabricated metal products	4	3	6	5	..	..	..	..	..	..
29/32 Machinery, Total	85	80	66	65	..	..	9.5	6.4	6.7	..
29/30 Non-electrical machinery	44	37	20	21	..	..	..	..	..	..
29 Non-electrical machinery nec	11	6	18	18	..	..	2.8	9.2	7.7	..
30 Office and computing machinery	33	31	2	3	..	..	..	..	..	..
31/32 Electrical & electronic equipment	41	43	46	44	..	..	..	..	..	..
31 Electrical machinery nec	38	24	24	21	..	..	..	..	..	..
32 Radio, TV & communications eq.	3	19	22	23	..	..	..	..	..	..
33 Scientific instruments	0	4	9	6	..	..	..	..	..	..
34/35 Transportation equipment	..	319	470	499	..	..	67.3	69.8	62.1	..
34 Motor vehicles	300	319	463	494	..	..	..	..	..	..
35 Other transport equipment	..	0	7	5	..	..	..	..	..	..
351 Shipbuilding & repairing	..	..	..	..	..	..	..	..	..	..
353 Aircraft and spacecraft	..	..	..	..	..	..	..	..	..	..
36/37 Other manufacturing	0	0	0	0	..	..	..	..	..	..
40/45 Construction, electricity, gas & water	0	0	0	..	..	..	..	..	..	..
50/55 Trade, repair, hotels & restaurants	110	192	31	64	..	..	91.9	72.1	78.0	..
65/74 Finance, insurance, business services	23	102	57	78	..	..	27.1	16.4	20.1	..
OTHER ACTIVITIES	..	0	0	2	..	..	..	..	..	..
01/99 GRAND TOTAL	**884**	**983**	**888**	**1 267**	..	**27.6**	**26.6**	**22.1**	**27.3**	..

Total manufacturing by investing country						As a % of total manufacturing by foreign affiliates				
All countries	751	688	799	1 122	..	100.0	100.0	100.0	100.0	..
United States	..	..	..	..	..	..	..	..	..	..
Canada	..	..	..	..	..	..	..	..	..	..
Mexico	..	..	..	..	..	..	..	..	..	..
Japan	..	..	..	..	..	..	..	..	..	..
Europe	..	..	..	..	..	..	..	..	..	..
European Union (15)	..	..	..	..	..	..	..	..	..	..
Belgium	..	..	..	..	..	..	..	..	..	..
France	..	..	..	..	..	..	..	..	..	..
Germany	..	..	..	..	..	..	..	..	..	..
Italy	..	..	..	..	..	..	..	..	..	..
Netherlands	..	..	..	..	..	..	..	..	..	..
Spain	..	..	..	..	..	..	..	..	..	..
Sweden	..	..	..	..	..	..	..	..	..	..
United Kingdom	..	..	..	..	..	..	..	..	..	..
Switzerland	..	..	..	..	..	..	..	..	..	..
Australia and New Zealand	..	..	..	..	..	..	..	..	..	..
Asia (non-OECD)	..	..	..	..	..	..	..	..	..	..
Latin America	..	..	..	..	..	..	..	..	..	..

Note: **All foreign-owned firms** with foreign participating interests of more than 20%. Up to 1994, ISIC 28 includes 33 and ISIC 36/37 includes 26. See country notes.
Toutes les firmes sous contrôle étranger pour lesquelles la participation étrangère dépasse 20%. Jusqu'en 1994, la CITI 28 comprend 33 et la CITI 36/37 comprend 26. Voir les notes par pays.

Inward investments — Investissements entrants

Table 10A - Tableau 10A

STOCK OF FOREIGN DIRECT INVESTMENT / STOCK D'INVESTISSEMENT DIRECT ÉTRANGER

| | Foreign affiliates (Millions of DEM) | | | | | | | | |
| | Filiales étrangères (Millions de DEM) | | | | | | | | |
By industry (ISIC Rev. 3)	1990	1991	1992	1993	1994	1995	1996	1997	1998	1999
10/14 Mining & quarrying	- 26	..	23	21	888	1 249	1 231	1 259	1 054	930
15/37 TOTAL MANUFACTURING	**38 821**	**39 891**	**58 774**	**51 260**	**50 541**	**54 762**	**49 361**	**57 177**	**63 784**	**70 284**
15/16 Food, beverages, tobacco	3 357	..	5 306	5 870	5 789	5 928	4 312	4 370	5 357	5 714
17/19 Textiles, clothing, leather, footwear	414	..	943	595	589	537	629	537	684	763
20/22 Wood and paper products	960	..	1 598	1 731	1 731	1 580	1 415	1 449	2 923	3 191
20 Wood products	..	..	..	..	..	75	76	84	649	746
21/22 Paper, printing and publishing	..	..	..	..	..	1 505	1 339	1 365	2 274	2 445
23/25 Chemicals, Total	13 080	..	21 384	..	16 909	18 914	16 059	22 440	23 688	24 668
23 Refined petroleum, nuclear fuel	4 785	..	7 349	4 665	4 377	4 984	3 194	4 704	4 848	3 543
24/25 Chemicals, rubber & plastics prod.	8 295	..	14 035	13 301	12 532	13 930	12 865	17 736	18 840	21 125
24 Chemical products	6 910	..	10 974	11 446	10 707	12 432	11 417	16 262	16 866	18 776
2423 Pharmaceuticals	..	..	..	..	..	..	..	..	..	..
25 Rubber and plastics products	1 385	..	3 061	1 855	1 824	1 498	1 448	1 474	1 974	2 349
26 Non-metallic mineral products	593	..	808	984	1 245	1 443	1 556	1 629	2 133	1 933
27/28 Basic & fabricated metals	2 422	..	3 297	..	3 518	3 676	3 701	3 915	4 004	4 011
27 Basic metals	1 083	..	1 456	1 990	2 144	2 200	2 036	2 269	2 438	2 299
28 Fabricated metal products	1 339	..	1 841	1 789	1 374	1 476	1 665	1 646	1 566	1 713
29/32 Machinery, Total	11 660	..	16 072	..	12 442	13 006	12 629	13 918	14 753	19 341
29/30 Non-electrical machinery	7 301	..	7 883	..	6 953	8 156	7 145	7 266	7 517	6 894
29 Non-electrical machinery nec	3 029	..	4 204	3 995	4 517	5 168	5 145	6 377	6 669	6 066
30 Office and computing machinery	4 272	..	3 679	2 137	2 436	2 988	2 000	889	844	829
31/32 Electrical & electronic equipment	4 359	..	8 189	6 942	5 489	4 850	5 484	6 651	7 240	12 446
31 Electrical machinery nec	4 359	..	8 189	6 942	5 489	1 966	2 256	2 627	2 859	2 719
32 Radio, TV & communications eq.	..	..	..	..	0	2 884	3 228	4 024	4 381	9 727
33 Scientific instruments	1 055	..	1 093	1 121	1 021	1 809	1 538	1 533	1 873	1 793
34/35 Transportation equipment	5 133	..	8 045	..	7 107	7 439	7 193	6 884	7 873	8 420
34 Motor vehicles	5 108	..	7 437	5 232	6 367	6 815	5 754	5 579	6 053	6 307
35 Other transport equipment	25	..	608	673	740	624	1 439	1 305	1 820	2 113
351 Shipbuilding & repairing	..	..	..	..	..	..	..	..	..	..
353 Aircraft and spacecraft	22	..	604	670	739	..	..	..	..	..
36/37 Other manufacturing	147	..	227	233	189	431	329	503	497	449
40/45 Construction, electricity, gas & water	137	..	590	630	1 375	1 015	1 141	1 204	1 078	1 182
50/55 Trade, repair, hotels & restaurants	8 993	..	35 020	35 903	38 177	36 932	37 012	39 891	40 152	43 297
65/74 Finance, insurance, business services	46 468	..	89 970	109 428	129 513	150 091	175 917	200 814	262 768	328 665
OTHER ACTIVITIES	265	..	1 537	1 381	1 594	2 182	2 238	2 899	3 068	4 009
01/99 GRAND TOTAL	**94 658**	..	**185 914**	**198 623**	**222 088**	**246 231**	**266 901**	**303 244**	**371 904**	**448 365**

Total manufacturing by investing country

	1990	1991	1992	1993	1994	1995	1996	1997	1998	1999
All countries	**38 821**	**39 891**	**58 774**	**51 260**	**50 541**	**54 762**	**49 361**	**57 177**	**63 784**	**70 284**
United States	18 313	..	23 589	19 113	20 042	22 790	20 679	21 702	20 495	18 524
Canada	..	..	651	..	..	675	..	..	..	..
Mexico	..	..	..	..	..	..	..	..	..	..
Japan	1 007	..	1 824	1 645	1 531	1 726	1 808	1 933	2 426	2 513
Europe	..	..	20 170	..	0	28 669	..	..	..	..
European Union (15)	14 000	..	24 960	22 636	21 580	23 492	21 478	26 153	31 237	39 418
Belgium	..	..	338	..	..	975	..	..	..	..
France	1 642	..	3 351	2 784	2 735	3 620	3 237	3 181	3 710	3 787
Germany	..	..	..	..	..	..	..	..	..	..
Italy	..	..	993	..	..	1 043	..	..	..	..
Netherlands	7 563	..	11 730	11 994	10 446	11 180	9 548	12 852	14 314	20 845
Spain	..	..	70	..	..	181	..	..	..	..
Sweden	..	..	635	..	..	564	..	..	..	..
United Kingdom	2 393	..	4 246	2 059	1 857	1 808	1 838	2 238	2 551	3 040
Switzerland	4 116	..	6 273	5 548	5 353	4 731	3 922	6 053	7 020	7 202
Australia and New Zealand	..	..	37	..	..	21	..	..	..	..
Asia (non-OECD)	5	..	..	167	1	532	20	51	85	84
Latin America	603	..	434	603	424	342	253	176	120	116

Note: Majority foreign-owned firms. Data by country of origin may not add because of double countings for multinational enterprises. New definition from 1992. See country notes.
Firmes sous contrôle étranger majoritaire. Les données par pays investisseur peuvent ne pas s'additionner en raison de doubles comptages pour les entreprises multinationales. Changement de définition à partir de 1992. Voir les notes par pays.

Inward investments — *Investissements entrants*

Table 11A - Tableau 11A
CAPITAL UNDER FOREIGN INFLUENCE / CAPITAL SOUS INFLUENCE ÉTRANGÈRE

| | | Foreign affiliates *(Millions of DEM)* | | | | | | | | | |
| | | Filiales étrangères *(Millions de DEM)* | | | | | | | | | |
By industry (ISIC Rev. 3)		1990	1991	1992	1993	1994	1995	1996	1997	1998	1999
10/14	Mining & quarrying	- 26	..	- 38	- 45	834	1 145	1 017	1 031	827	864
15/37	**TOTAL MANUFACTURING**	**37 611**	**38 216**	**34 349**	**30 431**	**32 055**	**32 992**	**29 993**	**36 810**	**40 159**	**41 781**
15/16	Food, beverages, tobacco	3 203	..	2 941	3 362	3 865	4 017	3 037	2 951	3 396	3 335
17/19	Textiles, clothing, leather, footwear	371	..	551	355	342	349	422	314	437	513
20/22	Wood and paper products	911	..	749	850	1 232	1 004	862	910	1 764	1 931
20	Wood products	..	..	..	..	..	50	40	38	158	216
21/22	Paper, printing and publishing	..	..	..	..	..	955	823	872	1 606	1 715
23/25	Chemicals, Total	12 823	..	13 067	..	11 878	11 752	9 885	15 145	15 119	13 283
23	Refined petroleum, nuclear fuel	4 761	..	4 555	3 271	3 634	3 815	2 189	3 785	4 219	2 459
24/25	Chemicals, rubber & plastics prod.	8 062	..	8 512	8 205	8 244	7 937	7 697	11 360	10 900	10 823
24	Chemical products	6 696	..	7 016	7 247	7 036	7 013	6 789	10 430	9 607	9 307
2423	Pharmaceuticals	..	..	..	..	..	..	..	..	..	..
25	Rubber and plastics products	1 366	..	1 496	958	1 208	924	908	930	1 293	1 517
26	Non-metallic mineral products	556	..	609	748	955	1 168	1 116	1 142	1 555	1 428
27/28	Basic & fabricated metals	2 239	..	2 235	..	1 888	1 650	1 913	2 093	2 363	2 416
27	Basic metals	1 066	..	1 143	1 328	1 178	939	980	995	1 357	1 331
28	Fabricated metal products	1 173	..	1 092	1 021	710	711	933	1 098	1 006	1 084
29/32	Machinery, Total	11 219	..	8 895	..	6 576	6 770	6 896	8 225	8 922	12 815
29/30	Non-electrical machinery	7 032	..	4 408	..	3 660	3 722	3 915	4 425	4 856	4 215
29	Non-electrical machinery nec	2 762	..	2 286	2 370	2 853	2 910	3 028	3 954	4 380	3 702
30	Office and computing machinery	4 270	..	2 122	714	807	811	887	471	476	513
31/32	Electrical & electronic equipment	4 187	..	4 487	3 983	2 916	3 048	2 981	3 800	4 066	8 600
31	Electrical machinery nec	4 187	..	4 487	3 983	2 916	1 017	1 281	1 493	1 533	1 184
32	Radio, TV & communications eq.	..	..	..	..	..	2 031	1 701	2 308	2 533	7 416
33	Scientific instruments	1 033	..	558	554	495	1 103	930	911	1 119	887
34/35	Transportation equipment	5 122	..	4 604	..	4 708	4 911	4 771	4 839	5 186	4 943
34	Motor vehicles	5 100	..	4 248	3 162	4 354	4 660	3 806	3 794	4 198	3 746
35	Other transport equipment	22	..	356	356	354	252	964	1 045	988	1 196
351	Shipbuilding & repairing	..	..	..	..	..	..	..	..	..	..
353	Aircraft and spacecraft	19	..	353	354	353	..	..	..	..	..
36/37	Other manufacturing	134	..	141	153	115	268	162	280	298	231
40/45	Construction, electricity, gas & water	33	..	124	44	700	415	440	585	486	488
50/55	Trade, repair, hotels & restaurants	8 803	..	10 671	10 808	11 800	12 105	12 032	12 606	12 815	14 538
65/74	Finance, insurance, business services	44 280	..	52 852	61 978	70 404	81 753	99 099	111 296	144 034	166 853
	OTHER ACTIVITIES	249	..	284	163	203	- 264	- 97	- 27	546	755
01/99	**GRAND TOTAL**	**90 950**	..	**98 241**	**103 379**	**115 997**	**128 147**	**142 484**	**162 301**	**198 866**	**225 279**

Total manufacturing by investing country

All countries	37 611	38 216	34 349	30 431	32 055	32 992	29 993	36 810	40 159	41 781
United States	18 048	..	13 758	11 361	13 308	14 024	13 015	14 565	13 735	10 430
Canada	..	..	351	297	..	331	..	..	..	..
Mexico	..	..	..	..	..	..	..	..	..	..
Japan	902	..	1 005	834	787	976	1 062	1 166	1 453	1 492
Europe	..	..	18 847	17 254	..	17 120	..	..	..	..
European Union (15)	13 533	..	14 823	13 509	13 124	14 072	12 762	16 557	19 727	24 982
Belgium	..	..	273	344	..	739	..	..	..	..
France	1 586	..	2 141	1 868	1 795	2 053	2 065	2 092	2 696	2 272
Germany	..	..	..	..	..	..	..	..	..	..
Italy	..	..	803	375	..	668	..	..	..	..
Netherlands	7 325	..	7 392	7 425	6 430	6 875	5 876	8 648	9 571	14 067
Spain	..	..	66	95	..	108	..	..	..	..
Sweden	..	..	312	360	..	327	..	..	..	..
United Kingdom	2 351	..	2 070	1 183	1 156	1 147	1 015	1 431	1 564	1 758
Switzerland	3 764	..	3 743	3 448	3 437	2 893	2 139	3 707	3 589	3 275
Australia and New Zealand	..	..	21	19	..	20	..	..	..	..
Asia (non-OECD)	5	..	248	158	- 1	405	10	23	50	41
Latin America	588	..	99	270	275	113	143	110	63	57

Note: Majority foreign-owned firms. Data by country of origin may not add because of double countings for multinational enterprises.
Firmes sous contrôle étranger majoritaire. Les données par pays investisseur peuvent ne pas s'additionner en raison de doubles comptages pour les entreprises multinationales.

Outward investments   *Investissements sortants*

Table 1B - Tableau 1B

NUMBER OF ENTERPRISES / NOMBRE D'ENTREPRISES

By industry (ISIC Rev. 3)	Foreign affiliates (Units) / Filiales étrangères (Unités)					As a % of national total / En % du total national				
	1995	1996	1997	1998	1999	1995	1996	1997	1998	1999
10/14 Mining & quarrying	89	..	83	108	156	17.8	..	17.1	23.3	..
15/37 TOTAL MANUFACTURING	4 415	..	5 335	5 609	5 679	11.8	..	14.0	14.9	..
15/16 Food, beverages, tobacco	182	..	206	220	223	4.3	..	4.1	4.5	..
17/19 Textiles, clothing, leather, footwear	306	..	317	318	331	12.1	..	14.8	15.8	..
20/22 Wood and paper products	264	..	309	336	357	5.3	..	6.3	7.0	..
20 Wood products	60	..	68	65	68	4.1	..	..	4.6	..
21/22 Paper, printing and publishing	204	..	241	271	289	5.8	..	..	8.0	..
23/25 Chemicals, Total	1 166	..	1 382	1 390	1 342	30.4	..	35.8	36.0	..
23 Refined petroleum, nuclear fuel	12	..	50	49	51	21.4	..	111.1	111.4	..
24/25 Chemicals, rubber & plastics prod.	1 154	..	1 332	1 341	1 291	30.6	..	35.0	35.1	..
24 Chemical products	828	..	922	918	819	65.3	..	73.9	73.4	..
2423 Pharmaceuticals	..	..	..	..	..	..	..	..	..	..
25 Rubber and plastics products	326	..	410	424	472	13.0	..	16.0	16.5	..
26 Non-metallic mineral products	203	..	376	330	312	9.4	..	18.0	16.2	..
27/28 Basic & fabricated metals	533	..	593	664	678	8.2	..	8.8	9.8	..
27 Basic metals	94	..	99	112	115	10.0	..	11.1	12.5	..
28 Fabricated metal products	439	..	494	552	563	7.9	..	8.5	9.4	..
29/32 Machinery, Total	1 158	..	1 393	1 512	1 542	14.3	..	17.1	18.5	..
29/30 Non-electrical machinery	760	..	900	966	951	13.0	..	15.3	16.4	..
29 Non-electrical machinery nec	750	..	889	955	945	13.2	..	15.5	16.6	..
30 Office and computing machinery	10	..	11	11	6	6.6	..	6.7	7.0	..
31/32 Electrical & electronic equipment	398	..	494	546	591	17.7	..	22.0	23.8	..
31 Electrical machinery nec	354	..	381	403	435	19.7	..	21.1	22.0	..
32 Radio, TV & communications eq.	44	..	113	143	156	9.7	..	25.7	31.0	..
33 Scientific instruments	193	..	223	234	255	11.2	..	11.4	12.5	..
34/35 Transportation equipment	304	..	406	461	476	28.1	..	37.3	41.3	..
34 Motor vehicles	261	..	351	402	418	32.5	..	42.9	48.0	..
35 Other transport equipment	43	..	55	59	58	15.3	..	20.4	21.1	..
351 Shipbuilding & repairing	..	..	..	..	..	..	..	..	..	..
353 Aircraft and spacecraft	..	..	..	..	..	..	..	..	..	..
36/37 Other manufacturing	107	..	132	146	164	4.7	..	6.2	7.1	..
40/45 Construction, electricity, gas & water	222	..	277	312	376	0.9	..	1.2	..	..
50/55 Trade, repair, hotels & restaurants	6 529	..	7 416	7 931	8 161	..	..	..	..	..
65/74 Finance, insurance, business services	3 108	..	3 652	3 948	4 311	..	..	..	..	..
OTHER ACTIVITIES	812	..	968	1 038	1 052	..	..	..	..	..
01/99 GRAND TOTAL	15 174	..	17 730	18 946	19 734	..	..	..	..	..

Total manufacturing by country of location						As a % of total manufacturing by foreign affiliates				
All countries	4 415	..	5 335	5 609	5 679	100.0	..	100.0	100.0	100.0
United States	512	..	555	548	481	11.6	..	10.4	9.8	8.5
Canada	..	..	..	..	..	..	..	..	..	..
Mexico	..	..	..	..	..	..	..	..	..	..
Japan	40	..	41	46	51	0.9	..	0.8	0.8	0.9
Europe	..	..	..	..	..	..	..	..	..	..
European Union (15)	1 982	..	2 257	2 220	2 205	44.9	..	42.3	39.6	38.8
Belgium	..	..	..	..	..	..	..	..	..	..
France	455	..	518	490	483	10.3	..	9.7	8.7	8.5
Germany	..	..	..	..	..	..	..	..	..	..
Italy	..	..	..	..	..	..	..	..	..	..
Netherlands	..	..	..	..	..	..	..	..	..	..
Spain	..	..	..	..	..	..	..	..	..	..
Sweden	..	..	..	..	..	..	..	..	..	..
United Kingdom	246	..	294	289	294	5.6	..	5.5	5.2	5.2
Switzerland	..	..	..	..	..	..	..	..	..	..
Australia and New Zealand	..	..	..	..	..	..	..	..	..	..
Asia (non-OECD)	296	..	478	578	615	6.7	..	9.0	10.3	10.8
Latin America	333	..	372	396	408	7.5	..	7.0	7.1	7.2

Note: Foreign affiliates majority-owned by national firms. Data for Latin America include those for Mexico.
Filiales étrangères détenues majoritairement par des firmes nationales. Les données pour l'Amérique Latine comprennent celles du Mexique.

Outward investments   *Investissements sortants*

Table 2B - Tableau 2B

NUMBER OF EMPLOYEES / NOMBRE DE SALARIÉS

| | | Foreign affiliates *(Units)* | | | | | As a % of national total | | | | |
| | | Filiales étrangères *(Unités)* | | | | | En % du total national | | | | |
By industry (ISIC Rev. 3)		1995	1996	1997	1998	1999	1995	1996	1997	1998	1999
10/14	Mining & quarrying	6 000	..	7 000	6 000	14 000	3.3	..	4.9	4.5	..
15/37	**TOTAL MANUFACTURING**	**982 000**	..	**1 116 000**	**1 302 000**	**1 204 000**	**14.4**	..	**17.2**	**20.0**	..
15/16	Food, beverages, tobacco	30 000	..	42 000	45 000	44 000	5.4	..	7.0	7.7	..
17/19	Textiles, clothing, leather, footwear	70 000	..	71 000	70 000	80 000	24.4	..	29.2	30.1	..
20/22	Wood and paper products	28 000	..	36 000	35 000	38 000	4.2	..	5.6	5.5	..
20	Wood products	7 000	..	10 000	9 000	11 000	..	..	..	8.0	..
21/22	Paper, printing and publishing	21 000	..	26 000	26 000	27 000	..	..	..	4.9	..
23/25	Chemicals, Total	265 000	..	270 000	261 000	246 000	28.1	..	30.5	29.9	..
23	Refined petroleum, nuclear fuel	1 000	..	6 000	6 000	6 000	4.1	..	28.7	28.7	..
24/25	Chemicals, rubber & plastics prod.	264 000	..	264 000	255 000	241 000	28.8	..	30.6	29.9	..
24	Chemical products	220 000	..	210 000	196 000	177 000	39.8	..	41.2	39.6	..
2423	Pharmaceuticals	..	..	..	..	..	..	..	..	..	..
25	Rubber and plastics products	44 000	..	54 000	59 000	63 000	12.1	..	15.3	16.5	..
26	Non-metallic mineral products	37 000	..	62 000	71 000	67 000	13.1	..	24.3	28.4	..
27/28	Basic & fabricated metals	76 000	..	82 000	89 000	87 000	8.5	..	9.7	10.3	..
27	Basic metals	23 000	..	23 000	25 000	24 000	7.7	..	8.4	9.2	..
28	Fabricated metal products	53 000	..	59 000	64 000	63 000	8.8	..	10.3	10.8	..
29/32	Machinery, Total	256 000	..	296 000	338 000	320 000	14.1	..	17.7	20.1	..
29/30	Non-electrical machinery	130 000	..	148 000	158 000	143 000	11.7	..	14.2	15.1	..
29	Non-electrical machinery nec	125 000	..	141 000	150 000	143 000	11.9	..	14.4	15.1	..
30	Office and computing machinery	6 000	..	7 000	8 000	0	9.0	..	11.9	15.3	..
31/32	Electrical & electronic equipment	125 000	..	147 000	181 000	177 000	17.7	..	23.2	28.5	..
31	Electrical machinery nec	113 000	..	124 000	150 000	145 000	21.0	..	25.1	30.3	..
32	Radio, TV & communications eq.	13 000	..	23 000	31 000	32 000	7.9	..	16.6	22.1	..
33	Scientific instruments	33 000	..	28 000	36 000	39 000	15.2	..	12.9	16.7	..
34/35	Transportation equipment	159 000	..	202 000	327 000	250 000	17.8	..	22.5	35.1	..
34	Motor vehicles	152 000	..	192 000	317 000	235 000	20.1	..	24.9	39.3	..
35	Other transport equipment	7 000	..	10 000	11 000	15 000	5.0	..	7.9	8.8	..
351	Shipbuilding & repairing	..	..	..	..	..	..	..	..	..	..
353	Aircraft and spacecraft	..	..	..	..	..	..	..	..	..	..
36/37	Other manufacturing	28 000	..	28 000	29 000	32 000	11.0	..	11.6	12.2	..
40/45	Construction, electricity, gas & water	39 000	..	43 000	39 000	45 000	2.1	..	2.7	..	..
50/55	Trade, repair, hotels & restaurants	343 000	..	393 000	435 000	472 000	..	..	..	..	..
65/74	Finance, insurance, business services	76 000	..	99 000	112 000	137 000	..	..	..	..	..
	OTHER ACTIVITIES	63 000	..	98 000	108 000	110 000	..	..	..	..	..
01/99	**GRAND TOTAL**	**1 509 000**	..	**1 755 000**	**2 002 000**	**1 982 000**	..	..	..	..	..

Total manufacturing by country of location						As a % of total manufacturing by foreign affiliates				
All countries	982 000	..	1 116 000	1 302 000	1 204 000	100.0	..	100.0	100.0	100.0
United States	133 000	..	128 000	217 000	120 000	13.5	..	11.5	16.7	10.0
Canada	..	..	..	..	..	..	..	..	..	..
Mexico	..	..	..	..	..	..	..	..	..	..
Japan	10 000	..	11 000	8 000	18 000	1.0	..	1.0	0.6	1.5
Europe	..	..	..	..	..	..	..	..	..	..
European Union (15)	358 000	..	395 000	412 000	396 000	36.5	..	35.4	31.6	32.9
Belgium	..	..	..	..	..	..	..	..	..	..
France	75 000	..	85 000	84 000	80 000	7.6	..	7.6	6.5	6.6
Germany	..	..	..	..	..	..	..	..	..	..
Italy	..	..	..	..	..	..	..	..	..	..
Netherlands	..	..	..	..	..	..	..	..	..	..
Spain	..	..	..	..	..	..	..	..	..	..
Sweden	..	..	..	..	..	..	..	..	..	..
United Kingdom	30 000	..	33 000	34 000	37 000	3.1	..	3.0	2.6	3.1
Switzerland	..	..	..	..	..	..	..	..	..	..
Australia and New Zealand	..	..	..	..	..	..	..	..	..	..
Asia (non-OECD)	92 000	..	106 000	128 000	121 000	9.4	..	9.5	9.8	10.0
Latin America	127 000	..	121 000	127 000	117 000	12.9	..	10.8	9.8	9.7

Note: Foreign affiliates majority-owned by national firms. Data for Latin America include those for Mexico.
Filiales étrangères détenues majoritairement par des firmes nationales. Les données pour l'Amérique Latine comprennent celles du Mexique.

Outward investments *Investissements sortants*

Table 3B - Tableau 3B
TURNOVER / CHIFFRE D'AFFAIRES

| | Foreign affiliates (Millions of DEM) | | | | | As a % of national total | | | | |
| | Filiales étrangères (Millions de DEM) | | | | | En % du total national | | | | |
By industry (ISIC Rev. 3)	1995	1996	1997	1998	1999	1995	1996	1997	1998	1999
10/14 Mining & quarrying	4 900	..	6 500	4 900	9 500	12.3	..	24.8	20.4	..
15/37 TOTAL MANUFACTURING	**248 000**	**288 200**	**332 400**	**455 900**	**371 200**	**11.9**	**13.7**	**15.1**	**19.7**	**..**
15/16 Food, beverages, tobacco	6 800	..	10 400	10 700	10 600	2.7	..	4.0	4.1	..
17/19 Textiles, clothing, leather, footwear	5 800	..	5 900	6 000	6 500	9.3	..	9.8	9.9	..
20/22 Wood and paper products	7 500	..	10 700	11 500	12 000	4.9	..	6.7	7.1	..
20 Wood products	700	..	800	700	800	2.3	..	..	2.2	..
21/22 Paper, printing and publishing	6 900	..	9 900	10 800	11 300	5.7	..	..	8.2	..
23/25 Chemicals, Total	96 100	..	120 800	110 100	105 300	22.3	..	27.6	25.2	..
23 Refined petroleum, nuclear fuel	300	..	4 200	4 300	4 400	0.3	..	3.8	4.0	..
24/25 Chemicals, rubber & plastics prod.	95 800	..	116 600	105 800	100 900	30.5	..	35.7	32.2	..
24 Chemical products	85 200	..	102 000	90 600	82 900	37.8	..	43.5	38.8	..
2423 Pharmaceuticals	..	..	..	..	..	..	..	..	..	..
25 Rubber and plastics products	10 700	..	14 600	15 200	18 100	12.0	..	15.8	16.0	..
26 Non-metallic mineral products	6 400	..	12 600	14 100	13 100	8.6	..	17.9	20.2	..
27/28 Basic & fabricated metals	16 300	..	21 300	21 300	20 400	7.0	..	9.1	8.6	..
27 Basic metals	5 900	..	6 500	7 200	6 200	5.6	..	6.3	6.7	..
28 Fabricated metal products	10 400	..	14 900	14 100	14 300	8.1	..	11.4	10.1	..
29/32 Machinery, Total	50 400	..	68 700	83 300	82 100	10.7	..	13.8	15.8	..
29/30 Non-electrical machinery	28 700	..	38 100	41 300	39 500	10.2	..	12.8	13.1	..
29 Non-electrical machinery nec	26 100	..	34 400	36 800	39 000	10.4	..	12.9	13.0	..
30 Office and computing machinery	2 600	..	3 700	4 400	500	8.6	..	12.1	13.8	..
31/32 Electrical & electronic equipment	21 700	..	30 600	42 000	42 600	11.5	..	15.3	19.9	..
31 Electrical machinery nec	18 300	..	23 000	32 800	32 800	13.1	..	15.3	20.6	..
32 Radio, TV & communications eq.	3 400	..	7 600	9 200	9 900	6.9	..	15.3	17.7	..
33 Scientific instruments	4 800	..	5 200	6 900	10 100	11.3	..	11.0	13.7	..
34/35 Transportation equipment	50 800	..	72 700	187 600	105 900	16.2	..	19.1	42.6	..
34 Motor vehicles	48 200	..	69 600	184 500	101 100	17.2	..	20.4	46.1	..
35 Other transport equipment	2 600	..	3 100	3 100	4 800	7.8	..	7.7	7.6	..
351 Shipbuilding & repairing	..	..	..	..	..	..	..	..	..	..
353 Aircraft and spacecraft	..	..	..	..	..	..	..	..	..	..
36/37 Other manufacturing	3 100	..	3 900	4 500	5 000	5.8	..	7.1	7.8	..
40/45 Construction, electricity, gas & water	7 600	..	10 000	8 400	13 700	1.6	..	2.1	..	..
50/55 Trade, repair, hotels & restaurants	210 400	..	277 600	318 900	348 500	..	..	..	..	..
65/74 Finance, insurance, business services	29 200	..	38 200	46 000	55 600	..	..	..	..	..
OTHER ACTIVITIES	19 400	..	34 600	36 100	44 200	..	..	..	..	..
01/99 GRAND TOTAL	**519 400**	**..**	**699 200**	**870 200**	**842 900**	**..**	**..**	**..**	**..**	**..**

Total manufacturing by country of location						As a % of total manufacturing by foreign affiliates				
All countries	248 000	288 200	332 400	455 900	371 200	100.0	100.0	100.0	100.0	100.0
United States	50 700	..	67 600	166 300	63 300	20.4	..	20.3	36.5	17.1
Canada	..	..	..	..	..	..	..	..	..	..
Mexico	..	..	..	..	..	..	..	..	..	..
Japan	7 600	..	8 100	4 700	10 000	3.1	..	2.4	1.0	2.7
Europe	..	..	..	..	..	..	..	..	..	..
European Union (15)	123 100	..	152 200	161 400	169 400	49.6	..	45.8	35.4	45.6
Belgium	..	..	..	..	..	..	..	..	..	..
France	25 800	..	32 400	28 600	27 300	10.4	..	9.7	6.3	7.4
Germany	..	..	..	..	..	..	..	..	..	..
Italy	..	..	..	..	..	..	..	..	..	..
Netherlands	..	..	..	..	..	..	..	..	..	..
Spain	..	..	..	..	..	..	..	..	..	..
Sweden	..	..	..	..	..	..	..	..	..	..
United Kingdom	9 100	..	11 500	11 700	13 600	3.7	..	3.5	2.6	3.7
Switzerland	..	..	..	..	..	..	..	..	..	..
Australia and New Zealand	..	..	..	..	..	..	..	..	..	..
Asia (non-OECD)	8 700	..	13 000	14 900	12 700	3.5	..	3.9	3.3	3.4
Latin America	21 000	..	31 400	34 900	35 400	8.5	..	9.4	7.7	9.5

Note: Foreign affiliates majority-owned by national firms. Data for Latin America include those for Mexico.
Filiales étrangères détenues majoritairement par des firmes nationales. Les données pour l'Amérique Latine comprennent celles du Mexique.

Outward investments   *Investissements sortants*

Table 4B - Tableau 4B

STOCK OF FOREIGN DIRECT INVESTMENT / STOCK D'INVESTISSEMENT DIRECT ÉTRANGER

| | Foreign affiliates (Millions of DEM) | | | | | | | | | |
| | Filiales étrangères (Millions de DEM) | | | | | | | | | |
By industry (ISIC Rev. 3)	1990	1991	1992	1993	1994	1995	1996	1997	1998	1999
10/14 Mining & quarrying	1 193	..	3 502	3 347	..	3 587	..	3 752	4 153	5 461
15/37 **TOTAL MANUFACTURING**	47 256	54 276	69 928	74 512	75 061	84 029	96 151	115 836	150 984	155 331
15/16 Food, beverages, tobacco	976	..	1 408	1 911	..	2 652	..	3 821	3 606	4 318
17/19 Textiles, clothing, leather, footwear	1 171	..	1 867	1 917	..	2 317	..	2 812	2 667	3 288
20/22 Wood and paper products	1 410	..	1 235	1 118	..	2 691	..	4 208	4 554	4 880
20 Wood products	..	..	..	..	..	226	..	313	220	255
21/22 Paper, printing and publishing	..	..	..	..	..	2 465	..	3 895	4 335	4 625
23/25 Chemicals, Total	18 358	..	30 090	32 917	..	35 912	..	44 058	44 966	53 540
23 Refined petroleum, nuclear fuel	50	..	55	60	..	81	..	1 190	1 126	991
24/25 Chemicals, rubber & plastics prod.	18 308	..	30 035	32 857	..	35 830	..	42 868	43 840	52 549
24 Chemical products	16 141	..	27 421	29 899	..	32 945	..	38 385	39 102	45 930
2423 Pharmaceuticals	..	..	..	..	..	..	..	..	..	..
25 Rubber and plastics products	2 167	..	2 614	2 958	..	2 885	..	4 482	4 738	6 619
26 Non-metallic mineral products	1 464	..	1 876	2 247	..	3 346	..	6 772	7 612	10 500
27/28 Basic & fabricated metals	3 081	..	4 931	4 975	..	5 820	..	7 887	8 237	8 614
27 Basic metals	1 000	..	1 381	1 253	..	2 249	..	2 605	2 900	2 932
28 Fabricated metal products	2 081	..	3 550	3 722	..	3 571	..	5 282	5 337	5 682
29/32 Machinery, Total	11 840	..	17 551	18 893	..	17 198	..	25 165	29 112	38 207
29/30 Non-electrical machinery	4 529	..	7 295	7 644	..	10 369	..	14 916	15 675	15 891
29 Non-electrical machinery nec	4 361	..	7 165	7 562	..	9 514	..	13 508	14 428	15 845
30 Office and computing machinery	168	..	130	82	..	855	..	1 409	1 247	46
31/32 Electrical & electronic equipment	7 311	..	10 256	11 249	..	6 829	..	10 249	13 437	22 315
31 Electrical machinery nec	7 311	..	10 256	11 249	..	5 968	..	8 028	10 804	19 561
32 Radio, TV & communications eq.	..	..	..	..	..	861	..	2 221	2 633	2 754
33 Scientific instruments	540	..	957	1 137	..	2 142	..	2 111	2 598	3 735
34/35 Transportation equipment	7 735	..	9 425	8 709	..	11 077	..	17 696	46 227	26 657
34 Motor vehicles	7 610	..	9 185	8 521	..	10 667	..	17 067	45 474	24 392
35 Other transport equipment	125	..	240	188	..	410	..	629	753	2 265
351 Shipbuilding & repairing	..	..	3	4	..	..	..	..	..	..
353 Aircraft and spacecraft	7	..	72	68	..	..	..	..	..	..
36/37 Other manufacturing	681	..	587	689	..	874	..	1 306	1 404	1 593
40/45 Construction, electricity, gas & water	388	..	764	826	..	987	..	1 263	1 635	2 125
50/55 Trade, repair, hotels & restaurants	19 299	..	38 379	38 497	..	41 654	..	55 473	61 836	68 256
65/74 Finance, insurance, business services	86 687	..	113 854	129 231	..	155 763	..	211 636	234 117	372 434
OTHER ACTIVITIES	1 225	..	2 657	2 776	..	3 283	..	8 756	10 501	11 368
01/99 **GRAND TOTAL**	156 048	..	229 085	249 189	..	289 303	..	396 717	463 227	614 974

Total manufacturing by country of location

	1990	1991	1992	1993	1994	1995	1996	1997	1998	1999
All countries	47 256	54 276	69 928	74 512	75 061	84 029	96 151	115 836	150 984	155 331
United States	11 256	..	18 821	22 230	..	18 533	..	22 278	47 616	29 992
Canada	..	..	..	..	..	..	..	..	..	..
Mexico	..	..	..	..	..	..	..	..	..	..
Japan	967	..	1 380	1 542	..	2 299	..	2 647	2 396	4 426
Europe	..	..	..	..	..	..	..	..	..	..
European Union (15)	23 901	..	31 637	30 361	..	34 850	..	47 746	52 024	66 873
Belgium	..	..	..	..	..	..	..	..	..	..
France	4 318	..	6 396	6 057	..	7 974	..	9 933	9 547	7 327
Germany	..	..	..	..	..	..	..	..	..	..
Italy	..	..	..	..	..	..	..	..	..	..
Netherlands	..	..	..	..	..	..	..	..	..	..
Spain	..	..	..	..	..	..	..	..	..	..
Sweden	..	..	..	..	..	..	..	..	..	..
United Kingdom	2 134	..	2 350	2 791	..	2 931	..	4 545	4 346	6 150
Switzerland	..	..	..	..	..	..	..	..	..	..
Australia and New Zealand	..	..	..	..	..	..	..	..	..	..
Asia (non-OECD)	1 115	..	1 816	1 932	..	3 395	..	6 104	7 059	7 516
Latin America	5 840	..	8 205	8 074	..	9 011	..	14 360	13 986	15 360

Note: Foreign affiliates majority-owned by national firms. Data for Latin America include those for Mexico.

Filiales étrangères détenues majoritairement par des firmes nationales. Les données pour l'Amérique Latine comprennent celles du Mexique.

Outward investments   *Investissements sortants*

Table 5B - Tableau 5B

CAPITAL UNDER FOREIGN INFLUENCE / CAPITAL SOUS INFLUENCE ÉTRANGÈRE

| | | Foreign affiliates *(Millions of DEM)* | | | | | | | | | |
| | | Filiales étrangères *(Millions de DEM)* | | | | | | | | | |
By industry (ISIC Rev. 3)		1990	1991	1992	1993	1994	1995	1996	1997	1998	1999
10/14	Mining & quarrying	1 224	..	1 460	1 558	..	2 276	..	2 614	3 011	4 139
15/37	**TOTAL MANUFACTURING**	**43 108**	**49 305**	**55 266**	**56 641**	**68 901**	**67 084**	**76 497**	**88 872**	**118 452**	**116 586**
15/16	Food, beverages, tobacco	914	..	1 220	1 614	..	2 188	..	3 113	2 882	3 126
17/19	Textiles, clothing, leather, footwear	1 028	..	1 469	1 397	..	1 690	..	1 909	1 775	2 294
20/22	Wood and paper products	1 131	..	1 105	889	..	2 110	..	3 382	3 644	3 780
20	Wood products	..	..	..	..	..	110	..	136	93	91
21/22	Paper, printing and publishing	..	..	..	..	..	2 000	..	3 246	3 551	3 689
23/25	Chemicals, Total	17 204	..	24 585	26 045	..	29 475	..	34 422	32 833	40 208
23	Refined petroleum, nuclear fuel	50	..	48	51	..	65	..	1 098	1 024	853
24/25	Chemicals, rubber & plastics prod.	17 154	..	24 537	25 994	..	29 410	..	33 324	31 809	39 355
24	Chemical products	15 126	..	22 288	23 465	..	27 109	..	29 863	27 892	34 255
2423	Pharmaceuticals	..	..	..	..	..	..	..	..	..	..
25	Rubber and plastics products	2 028	..	2 250	2 529	..	2 301	..	3 462	3 917	5 100
26	Non-metallic mineral products	1 393	..	1 339	1 579	..	2 773	..	5 548	6 434	9 453
27/28	Basic & fabricated metals	2 781	..	4 146	4 117	..	4 811	..	6 647	6 925	7 128
27	Basic metals	908	..	1 240	1 088	..	1 998	..	2 275	2 526	2 551
28	Fabricated metal products	1 873	..	2 906	3 029	..	2 813	..	4 373	4 399	4 577
29/32	Machinery, Total	10 577	..	12 493	13 286	..	12 756	..	18 255	20 159	25 800
29/30	Non-electrical machinery	4 074	..	5 397	5 787	..	7 637	..	11 093	11 452	12 041
29	Non-electrical machinery nec	3 940	..	5 362	5 726	..	7 288	..	10 707	11 079	11 999
30	Office and computing machinery	134	..	35	61	..	349	..	385	373	42
31/32	Electrical & electronic equipment	6 503	..	7 096	7 499	..	5 119	..	7 163	8 707	13 759
31	Electrical machinery nec	6 503	..	7 096	7 499	..	4 576	..	5 904	7 091	12 015
32	Radio, TV & communications eq.	..	..	..	..	..	543	..	1 258	1 616	1 744
33	Scientific instruments	530	..	787	916	..	1 633	..	1 454	1 954	2 941
34/35	Transportation equipment	6 899	..	7 614	6 206	..	8 961	..	13 124	40 820	20 680
34	Motor vehicles	6 813	..	7 568	6 116	..	8 615	..	12 600	40 207	19 273
35	Other transport equipment	86	..	46	90	..	346	..	523	613	1 407
351	Shipbuilding & repairing	..	..	3	3	..	..	..	..	..	..
353	Aircraft and spacecraft	6	..	- 4	45	..	..	..	..	..	..
36/37	Other manufacturing	651	..	506	593	..	688	..	1 017	1 026	1 176
40/45	Construction, electricity, gas & water	322	..	454	598	..	702	..	819	1 101	1 402
50/55	Trade, repair, hotels & restaurants	17 555	..	22 424	21 647	..	24 564	..	32 656	37 366	42 135
65/74	Finance, insurance, business services	81 304	..	102 596	118 078	..	138 260	..	190 463	208 906	336 692
	OTHER ACTIVITIES	1 177	..	2 091	2 264	..	2 481	..	6 598	8 015	8 273
01/99	**GRAND TOTAL**	**144 690**	**..**	**184 290**	**200 785**	**..**	**235 367**	**..**	**322 022**	**376 851**	**509 227**

Total manufacturing by country of location

	1990	1991	1992	1993	1994	1995	1996	1997	1998	1999
All countries	**43 108**	**49 305**	**55 266**	**56 641**	**68 901**	**67 084**	**76 497**	**88 872**	**118 452**	**116 586**
United States	11 009	..	14 523	16 169	..	14 569	..	17 549	41 327	20 739
Canada	..	..	..	..	..	..	..	..	..	..
Mexico	..	..	..	..	..	..	..	..	..	..
Japan	690	..	1 015	1 229	..	1 819	..	2 365	2 009	3 887
Europe	..	..	..	..	..	..	..	..	..	..
European Union (15)	21 881	..	24 892	22 884	..	28 629	..	37 906	40 580	51 749
Belgium	..	..	..	..	..	..	..	..	..	..
France	4 018	..	5 275	4 931	..	6 817	..	6 561	6 071	5 812
Germany	..	..	..	..	..	..	..	..	..	..
Italy	..	..	..	..	..	..	..	..	..	..
Netherlands	..	..	..	..	..	..	..	..	..	..
Spain	..	..	..	..	..	..	..	..	..	..
Sweden	..	..	..	..	..	..	..	..	..	..
United Kingdom	2 049	..	1 493	1 839	..	2 114	..	3 604	3 446	4 425
Switzerland	..	..	..	..	..	..	..	..	..	..
Australia and New Zealand	..	..	..	..	..	..	..	..	..	..
Asia (non-OECD)	889	..	1 202	1 277	..	2 126	..	3 489	4 419	5 544
Latin America	4 933	..	7 135	6 945	..	7 694	..	11 026	10 770	11 706

Note: Foreign affiliates majority-owned by national firms. Data for Latin America include those for Mexico.
Filiales étrangères détenues majoritairement par des firmes nationales. Les données pour l'Amérique Latine comprennent celles du Mexique.

GERMANY

A. Inward investments

Source

For all variables except *R&D expenditure* and *Number of researchers*, the data are prepared by the Deutsche Bundesbank. The data are based on annual stock surveys of direct investment (non-residents' assets in the economic territory), which cover all enterprises in Germany directly owned by foreigners. From 1999, the submission of reports is required of every German enterprise with a balance sheet total of more than DEM 1 million in which a non-resident (or several economically linked non-residents) holds 50% or more of the shares or voting rights of the German enterprise; reports are also required of German enterprises with a balance sheet total of more than DEM 10 million in which a non-resident (or several economically linked non-residents) hold at least 10% but less than 50% of the shares or voting rights in the German enterprise concerned. Prior to 1999, the enterprises covered were those with foreign participating interests of more than 20% and with a balance sheet total exceeding DEM 1 million. The results are published in Statistical Special Publication *International capital links*. The data on technological receipts and payments come from the balance of payments statistics and are published every two years in *Technological Services in the Balance of Payments*.

The data refer to firms with a foreign majority participating interest for *Number of enterprises, Number of employees, Turnover, Stock of foreign direct investment* and *Capital under foreign influence*. The data refer to firms with a foreign participating interest of at least 20% for *Technological payments* and *receipts*. For all foreign-owned firms, the figures are affected in full and not prorata of the level of ownership.

For *R&D expenditure* and *Number of researchers*, data come from a survey on the R&D activities of foreign affiliates operating in Germany conducted by SV-Wissenschaftsstatistik. This survey analyses the performance of 500 R&D-intensive companies according to their nationality (majority-owned). In 1995, these firms accounted for 83% of the total R&D carried out in Germany and employed 75% of all R&D personnel.

National totals:

- *Number of enterprises*, *Number of employees* and *Turnover:* the results come from a survey conducted by the Federal Statistical Office, which covers enterprises in the mining and manufacturing industry with 20 or more employees.

- All other variables: same source as foreign affiliates' data.

Industrial classification

For all variables, the data are classified according to the principal industrial activity of the affiliate.

The industrial classification used for the German tables is ISIC Revision 3.

Variables

- *Number of employees* is based on the figures provided by enterprises on a voluntary basis. It is partly estimated for each economic sector. No distinction is made between full-time and part-time employees.

- *Number of researchers* is in fact the total number of employees working on R&D expressed in full-time equivalent.

- *Technological payments* and *receipts* correspond to expenditures on and receipts from patents, inventions and processes by enterprises in which foreigners hold participating interests of more than 20%.

- Up to 1991, *Stock of foreign direct investment* is defined as the capital stock and is based on the current balance sheets of the affiliates, taking account of the capital share of the investor. From 1992, it is defined as the primary foreign investment capital and the lending by foreign shareholders and by other affiliated enterprises abroad.

- *Capital under foreign influence* is defined as the primary foreign investment capital excluding lending.

Geographical breakdown

The investor's country is the country of the immediate controller.

The data are processed separately for each individual investing country. Therefore, double countings are not eliminated in all tables for reasons of consistency, *i.e.* in the case of majority interests involving several countries, the variables are assigned in full to each country.

B. Outward investments

Source

For all variables, the data are prepared by the Deutsche Bundesbank. The data are based on annual stock surveys of direct investment (residents' assets in foreign economic territories), which cover all enterprises abroad directly owned by German investors with a balance sheet total exceeding DEM 1 million. The results are published in Statistical Special Publication *International Capital Links*.

The data refer to foreign affiliates majority-owned by national firms.

National totals: the results come from a survey conducted by the Federal Statistical Office, which covers enterprises in the mining and manufacturing industry with 20 or more employees.

Industrial classification

For all variables, the data are classified according to the principal industrial activity of the affiliate.

The industrial classification used for the German tables is the national industrial classification, converted to Revision 3 up to 1994. From 1995, data have been directly processed using ISIC Revision 3.

The following notes refer to data up to 1994:

- *Mining and quarrying* (10/14) excludes *Quarrying* and includes *Coke oven products* (231).

- *Wood and paper products* (20/22) excludes *Publishing* (221) and *Reproduction of recorded media* (223).

- *Refined petroleum and coal products manufacturing* (23) excludes *Processing of nuclear fuel* (233) and *Coke oven products* (231).

- *Chemical products* (24) includes *Processing of nuclear fuel* (233).

- *Pharmaceuticals* (2423) is not available separately.

- *Non-metallic mineral products* (26) includes *Quarrying*.

- *Fabricated metal products* (28) includes *Manufacturing of weapons and ammunition* (2927).

- *Non-electrical machinery n.e.c.* (29) excludes *Manufacturing of weapons and ammunition* (2927) and *Manufacturing of domestic appliances n.e.c.* (293).

- *Electrical machinery* (31) includes *Electronic equipment* (32), *Reproduction of recorded media* (223) and *Manufacturing of domestic appliances n.e.c.* (293).

- *Motor vehicles* (34) includes *Transport equipment n.e.c.* (359).

- *Other transport equipment* (35) excludes *Transport equipment n.e.c.* (359).

- *Finance, insurance, real estate and business services* (65/74) includes *Publishing* (221) and *Property administration* (75).

Variables

- *Number of employees* is based on the figures provided by enterprises on a voluntary basis. It is partly estimated for each economic sector. No distinction is made between full-time and part-time employees.

Geographical breakdown

The country of location is the country of the immediate controller.

ALLEMAGNE

A. Investissements entrants

Source

Pour l'ensemble des variables à l'exception des *Dépenses de R-D* et du *Nombre de chercheurs*, les données émanent de la Deustche Bundesbank. Elles sont basées sur les enquêtes annuelles de stocks d'investissement direct (actifs des non résidents sur le territoire économique) qui couvrent toutes les entreprises d'Allemagne détenues directement par l'étranger. A partir de 1999, toute entreprise d'Allemagne dont le total du bilan dépasse DEM 1 million et dans laquelle un non résident (ou plusieurs non résidents avec un lien économique) détient au moins 50 % des actions ou des droits de vote a une obligation de déclaration ; les déclarations sont également nécessaires pour les entreprises d'Allemagne dont le total du bilan dépasse DEM 10 millions et dans lesquelles un non résident (ou plusieurs non résidents avec un lien économique) détient au moins 10 % mais moins de 50 % des actions ou des droits de vote. Avant 1999, les entreprises couvertes étaient celles dans lesquelles la participation étrangère était de plus de 20 % et dont le total du bilan de l'entreprise bénéficiaire de l'investissement dépassait DEM 1 million. Les résultats paraissent dans la publication statistique spéciale *Kapitalverflechtung mit dem Ausland* (Participations croisées internationales). Les données sur les recettes et paiements technologiques proviennent des statistiques de la balance des paiements et sont publiées tous les deux ans dans *Technologische Dienstleistungen in der Zahlungsbilanz* (Services technologiques dans la balance des paiements).

Les données se rapportent aux entreprises dans lesquelles l'étranger détient une participation majoritaire et concernent les variables suivantes : *Nombre d'entreprises, Nombre de salariés, Chiffre d'affaires, Stock d'investissement direct étranger* et *Capital sous influence étrangère*. Pour les *Paiements* et *Recettes technologiques*, les données se rapportent aux entreprises à participation étrangère d'au moins 20 %. Pour toutes les entreprises sous contrôle étranger, les chiffres sont affectés en totalité et non au prorata du niveau de participation au capital.

Pour les *Dépenses de R-D* et le *Nombre de chercheurs*, les données proviennent d'une enquête sur les activités de R-D des filiales étrangères opérant en Allemagne menée par SV-Wissenschaftsstatistik. Elle analyse les résultats de 500 sociétés à forte intensité de R-D en tenant compte de leur nationalité (contrôle majoritaire). En 1995, ces firmes représentaient 83 % de la R-D totale effectuée en Allemagne et 75 % du personnel de R-D.

Totaux nationaux :

- *Nombre d'entreprises, Nombre de salariés* et *Chiffre d'affaires :* les résultats proviennent d'une enquête menée par l'office statistique fédéral, qui couvre les entreprises de l'industrie extractive et manufacturière employant au moins 20 salariés.

- Autres variables : même source que les données relatives aux filiales étrangères.

Classification industrielle

Pour toutes les variables, les données sont classées selon l'activité industrielle principale de l'entreprise affiliée.

La classification industrielle utilisée pour les tableaux allemands est la CITI révision 3.

Variables

- Le *Nombre de salariés* est fondé sur les chiffres fournis par les entreprises sur la base du volontariat. Il est partiellement estimé pour chaque secteur économique. Il n'est fait aucune distinction entre les salariés à temps plein et à temps partiel.

- Le *Nombre de chercheurs* est en fait le nombre total de salariés travaillant dans le domaine de la R-D exprimé en équivalent plein-temps.

- Les *Paiements* et *Recettes technologiques* correspondent aux montants dépensés pour et encaissés sur brevets, inventions et procédés par les entreprises dans lesquelles des étrangers détiennent des participations de plus de 20 %.

- Jusqu'en 1991, le *Stock d'investissement direct étranger* est défini comme le stock de capital et s'appuie sur les bilans actuels des filiales, compte tenu de la participation en capital de l'investisseur. A partir de 1992, il est défini comme l'investissement direct primaire en capital plus les prêts accordés par les actionnaires étrangers et par les autres firmes affiliées à l'étranger.

- Le *Capital sous influence étrangère* est défini l'investissement direct primaire en capital, à l'exclusion des prêts.

Ventilation géographique

Le pays de l'investisseur est le pays où s'exerce le contrôle immédiat.

Les données sont traitées séparément pour chaque pays investisseur. C'est pourquoi les doubles comptages ne sont pas éliminés dans tous les tableaux pour des raisons de cohérence, c'est-à-dire que dans le cas d'intérêts majoritaires impliquant plusieurs pays, les variables sont attribuées pleinement à chacun.

B. Investissements sortants

Source

Pour l'ensemble des variables, les données émanent de la Deustche Bundesbank. Elles sont basées sur les enquêtes annuelles de stocks d'investissement direct (actifs des résidents dans les territoires économiques étrangers) qui couvrent toutes les entreprises étrangères détenues directement par des investisseurs allemands dont le total du bilan dépasse DEM 1 million. Les résultats paraissent dans la publication statistique spéciale *Kapitalverflechtung mit dem Ausland* (Participations croisées internationales).

Les données font référence aux filiales étrangères dans lesquelles l'investisseur allemand détient une participation majoritaire.

Totaux nationaux : les résultats proviennent d'une enquête menée par l'office statistique fédéral, qui couvre les entreprises de l'industrie extractive et manufacturière employant au moins 20 salariés.

Classification industrielle

Pour toutes les variables, les données sont classées selon l'activité industrielle principale de l'entreprise affiliée.

La classification industrielle utilisée pour les tableaux allemands est la classification industrielle nationale adaptée pour correspondre à la CITI révision 3 jusqu'en 1994. A partir de 1995, les données ont été compilées directement en CITI révision 3.

Les notes suivantes se rapportent aux données jusqu'en 1994 :

- *Industries extractives* (10/14) à l'exclusion des *Carrières* et y compris la *Cokéfaction* (231).

- *Production de bois et papier* (20/22) à l'exclusion de l'*Édition* (221) et de la *Reproduction de supports enregistrés* (223).

- *Fabrication de produits pétroliers raffinés et de produits du charbon* (23) à l'exclusion du *Traitement de combustibles nucléaires* (233) et de la *Cokéfaction* (231).

- *Produits chimiques* (24), y compris le *Traitement de combustibles nucléaires* (233).

- *Produits pharmaceutiques* (2423) non disponible séparément.

- *Produits minéraux non métalliques* (26) y compris les *Carrières*.

- *Ouvrages en métaux* (28) y compris la *Fabrication d'armes et de munitions* (2927).

- *Machines et matériel n.c.a.* (29) à l'exclusion de la *Fabrication d'armes et de munitions* (2927) et de la *Fabrication d'appareils domestiques n.c.a.* (293).

- *Machines et appareils électriques* (31) y compris *Équipement électronique* (32), *Reproduction de supports enregistrés* (223) et *Fabrication d'appareils domestiques n.c.a.* (293).

- *Véhicules automobiles* (34) y compris les *Matériels de transport n.c.a.* (359).

- *Autres matériels de transport* (35) à l'exclusion des *Matériels de transport n.c.a.* (359).

- *Finance, assurance, immobilier et services aux entreprises* (65/74) y compris l'*Édition* (221) et l'*Administration publique* (75).

Variables

- Le *Nombre de salariés* est fondé sur les chiffres fournis par les entreprises sur la base du volontariat. Il est partiellement estimé pour chaque secteur économique. Il n'est fait aucune distinction entre les salariés à temps plein et à temps partiel.

Ventilation géographique

Le pays d'implantation est le pays où s'exerce le contrôle immédiat.

HUNGARY

Sources and Methods

HONGRIE

Sources et méthodes

Inward investments

Investissements entrants

Table 1A - Tableau 1A

NUMBER OF ENTERPRISES / NOMBRE D'ENTREPRISES

| | | Foreign affiliates *(Units)* | | | | | As a % of national total | | | | |
| | | Filiales étrangères *(Unités)* | | | | | En % du total national | | | | |
By industry (ISIC Rev. 3)		1995	1996	1997	1998	1999	1995	1996	1997	1998	1999
10/14	Mining & quarrying	69	77	82	78	74	27.6	26.6	25.9	23.9	20.0
15/37	**TOTAL MANUFACTURING**	**4 195**	**4 312**	**4 245**	**4 065**	**4 113**	**13.9**	**12.8**	**12.1**	**11.9**	**11.4**
15/16	Food, beverages, tobacco	577	544	517	484	467	15.6	14.0	13.1	13.1	12.3
17/19	Textiles, clothing, leather, footwear	559	601	591	598	610	15.6	15.2	14.4	14.2	13.7
20/22	Wood and paper products	751	744	743	660	678	11.8	10.1	9.2	8.1	7.8
20	Wood products	..	231	..	220	219	..	..	..	10.0	9.1
21/22	Paper, printing and publishing	..	513	..	440	459	..	..	..	7.4	7.3
23/25	Chemicals, Total	393	402	408	393	415	18.8	18.0	17.5	17.4	17.6
23	Refined petroleum, nuclear fuel	..	4	..	3	3	..	..	..	25.0	25.0
24/25	Chemicals, rubber & plastics prod.	..	398	..	390	412	..	..	..	17.4	17.6
24	Chemical products	..	162	..	151	152	..	..	..	22.2	21.6
2423	Pharmaceuticals	..	31	..	..	..	..	..	..	..	..
25	Rubber and plastics products	..	236	..	239	260	..	..	..	15.3	15.8
26	Non-metallic mineral products	170	178	188	175	176	18.4	17.0	17.1	15.4	14.5
27/28	Basic & fabricated metals	479	518	514	518	537	11.9	11.6	11.3	11.0	10.5
27	Basic metals	..	52	..	51	51	..	..	..	16.2	15.5
28	Fabricated metal products	..	466	..	467	486	..	..	..	10.6	10.2
29/32	Machinery, Total	..	841	..	749	748	..	..	..	12.8	12.7
29/30	Non-electrical machinery	..	544	..	462	444	..	..	..	12.7	12.2
29	Non-electrical machinery nec	..	509	..	429	410	..	..	..	12.7	12.2
30	Office and computing machinery	..	35	..	33	34	..	..	..	12.6	12.1
31/32	Electrical & electronic equipment	..	297	..	287	304	..	..	..	12.9	13.5
31	Electrical machinery nec	..	153	..	171	181	..	..	..	13.2	13.9
32	Radio, TV & communications eq.	..	144	..	116	123	..	..	..	12.5	13.1
33	Scientific instruments	..	171	..	161	140	..	..	..	11.2	9.3
34/35	Transportation equipment	..	108	..	119	119	..	..	..	22.7	21.1
34	Motor vehicles	..	73	..	89	91	..	..	..	28.9	27.7
35	Other transport equipment	..	35	..	30	28	..	..	..	13.8	12.0
351	Shipbuilding & repairing	..	15	..	..	..	..	..	..	..	..
353	Aircraft and spacecraft	..	..	..	..	..	..	..	..	..	..
36/37	Other manufacturing	199	204	188	208	223	12.0	10.7	9.5	9.3	9.0
40/45	Construction, electricity, gas & water	1 254	1 261	1 174	1 134	1 181	7.7	6.9	6.0	5.4	5.2
50/55	Trade, repair, hotels & restaurants	13 347	13 897	13 587	13 520	13 082	18.5	17.2	16.4	15.5	14.4
65/74	Finance, insurance, business services	3 734	4 041	4 188	4 866	5 407	8.6	7.6	7.9	7.7	7.7
	OTHER ACTIVITIES	2 497	2 542	2 462	2 609	2 576	8.4	7.0	6.5	6.2	5.5
01/99	**GRAND TOTAL**	**25 096**	**26 130**	**25 738**	**26 272**	**26 433**	**13.1**	**11.8**	**11.3**	**10.6**	**9.9**

Grand total by investing country							As a % of grand total by foreign affiliates				
All countries	25 096	26 130	25 738	26 272	26 433		100.0	100.0	100.0	100.0	100.0
United States	..	..	..	..	..		..	..	..	..	..
Canada	..	..	..	..	..		..	..	..	..	..
Mexico	..	..	..	..	..		..	..	..	..	..
Japan	..	..	..	..	..		..	..	..	..	..
Europe	..	..	..	..	..		..	..	..	..	..
European Union (15)	..	..	..	..	..		..	..	..	..	..
Belgium	..	..	..	..	..		..	..	..	..	..
France	..	..	..	..	..		..	..	..	..	..
Germany	..	..	..	..	..		..	..	..	..	..
Italy	..	..	..	..	..		..	..	..	..	..
Netherlands	..	..	..	..	..		..	..	..	..	..
Spain	..	..	..	..	..		..	..	..	..	..
Sweden	..	..	..	..	..		..	..	..	..	..
United Kingdom	..	..	..	..	..		..	..	..	..	..
Switzerland	..	..	..	..	..		..	..	..	..	..
Australia and New Zealand	..	..	..	..	..		..	..	..	..	..
Asia (non-OECD)	..	..	..	..	..		..	..	..	..	..
Latin America	..	..	..	..	..		..	..	..	..	..

Note: All foreign-owned firms (more than 10% of capital share).
Toutes les firmes sous contrôle étranger (plus de 10% du capital détenu par l'étranger).

Inward investments

Investissements entrants

Table 2A - Tableau 2A
NUMBER OF EMPLOYEES / NOMBRE DE SALARIÉS

| | | Foreign affiliates (Units) | | | | | As a % of national total | | | | |
| | | Filiales étrangères (Unités) | | | | | En % du total national | | | | |
By industry (ISIC Rev. 3)		1995	1996	1997	1998	1999	1995	1996	1997	1998	1999
10/14	Mining & quarrying	2 483	5 589	5 168	3 104	2 184	14.0	33.8	38.6	29.7	23.9
15/37	**TOTAL MANUFACTURING**	**288 294**	**297 448**	**324 086**	**356 269**	**367 187**	**37.4**	**35.6**	**41.2**	**45.0**	**46.5**
15/16	Food, beverages, tobacco	60 927	52 198	52 178	56 635	54 376	40.8	34.7	37.9	41.0	41.7
17/19	Textiles, clothing, leather, footwear	43 031	43 694	47 226	51 479	53 627	32.6	30.3	33.5	37.4	39.5
20/22	Wood and paper products	18 029	17 950	19 039	17 693	16 339	26.7	27.2	28.8	28.1	25.5
20	Wood products	..	..	..	5 334	5 001	..	..	..	23.3	21.3
21/22	Paper, printing and publishing	..	..	..	12 359	11 338	..	..	..	30.9	27.9
23/25	Chemicals, Total	49 986	57 385	56 751	57 723	59 601	55.1	63.5	63.8	65.7	68.0
23	Refined petroleum, nuclear fuel	..	..	..	15 072	14 644	..	..	..	99.9	99.6
24/25	Chemicals, rubber & plastics prod.	..	..	..	42 651	44 957	..	..	..	58.6	61.6
24	Chemical products	..	..	..	29 420	28 332	..	..	..	72.3	73.7
2423	Pharmaceuticals	..	..	..	..	..	..	..	..	..	..
25	Rubber and plastics products	..	..	..	13 231	16 625	..	..	..	41.2	48.1
26	Non-metallic mineral products	16 609	14 983	15 938	17 514	16 363	46.7	42.8	46.3	50.5	49.1
27/28	Basic & fabricated metals	18 959	20 157	22 631	26 478	23 988	21.2	22.7	26.3	32.5	29.4
27	Basic metals	..	..	..	8 277	8 272	..	..	..	36.6	39.2
28	Fabricated metal products	..	..	..	18 201	15 716	..	..	..	30.9	25.9
29/32	Machinery, Total	..	..	..	84 638	103 010	..	..	..	52.9	60.1
29/30	Non-electrical machinery	..	..	..	32 725	32 663	..	..	..	44.9	43.3
29	Non-electrical machinery nec	..	..	..	28 567	27 374	..	..	..	42.3	43.1
30	Office and computing machinery	..	..	..	4 158	5 289	..	..	..	77.3	44.3
31/32	Electrical & electronic equipment	..	..	..	51 913	70 347	..	..	..	59.6	73.3
31	Electrical machinery nec	..	..	..	37 339	45 834	..	..	..	67.0	72.8
32	Radio, TV & communications eq.	..	..	..	14 574	24 513	..	..	..	46.4	74.2
33	Scientific instruments	..	..	..	6 151	5 967	..	..	..	35.1	39.0
34/35	Transportation equipment	..	..	..	30 638	26 723	..	..	..	71.1	64.4
34	Motor vehicles	..	..	..	27 760	24 455	..	..	..	79.1	74.1
35	Other transport equipment	..	..	..	2 878	2 268	..	..	..	36.0	26.7
351	Shipbuilding & repairing	..	..	..	..	..	..	..	..	..	..
353	Aircraft and spacecraft	..	..	..	..	..	..	..	..	..	..
36/37	Other manufacturing	6 194	6 116	5 688	7 320	7 193	22.9	21.3	21.0	26.2	25.1
40/45	Construction, electricity, gas & water	56 364	52 360	51 717	48 133	41 639	22.8	22.7	23.1	21.4	18.5
50/55	Trade, repair, hotels & restaurants	88 249	86 647	87 221	96 907	96 983	22.1	20.5	21.4	22.3	22.0
65/74	Finance, insurance, business services	21 513	28 129	29 172	32 836	35 356	14.0	15.1	16.5	15.9	16.5
	OTHER ACTIVITIES	44 910	45 958	45 657	43 452	40 710	8.9	9.3	9.5	9.2	8.9
01/99	**GRAND TOTAL**	**501 813**	**516 131**	**543 021**	**580 701**	**584 059**	**24.0**	**23.6**	**26.0**	**27.2**	**27.4**

Grand total by investing country							As a % of grand total by foreign affiliates				
All countries		501 813	516 131	543 021	580 701	584 059	100.0	100.0	100.0	100.0	100.0
United States		..	..	..	..	..	..	..	..	..	..
Canada		..	..	..	..	..	..	..	..	..	..
Mexico		..	..	..	..	..	..	..	..	..	..
Japan		..	..	..	..	..	..	..	..	..	..
Europe		..	..	..	..	..	..	..	..	..	..
European Union (15)		..	..	..	..	..	..	..	..	..	..
Belgium		..	..	..	..	..	..	..	..	..	..
France		..	..	..	..	..	..	..	..	..	..
Germany		..	..	..	..	..	..	..	..	..	..
Italy		..	..	..	..	..	..	..	..	..	..
Netherlands		..	..	..	..	..	..	..	..	..	..
Spain		..	..	..	..	..	..	..	..	..	..
Sweden		..	..	..	..	..	..	..	..	..	..
United Kingdom		..	..	..	..	..	..	..	..	..	..
Switzerland		..	..	..	..	..	..	..	..	..	..
Australia and New Zealand		..	..	..	..	..	..	..	..	..	..
Asia (non-OECD)		..	..	..	..	..	..	..	..	..	..
Latin America		..	..	..	..	..	..	..	..	..	..

Note: All foreign-owned firms (more than 10% of capital share).

Toutes les firmes sous contrôle étranger (plus de 10% du capital détenu par l'étranger).

Table 3A - Tableau 3A

TURNOVER / CHIFFRE D'AFFAIRES

| | | Foreign affiliates *(Billions of HUF)* | | | | | As a % of national total | | | | |
| | | Filiales étrangères *(Milliards de HUF)* | | | | | En % du total national | | | | |
By industry (ISIC Rev. 3)		1995	1996	1997	1998	1999	1995	1996	1997	1998	1999
10/14	Mining & quarrying	14	28	41	35	29	27.2	43.5	54.1	46.4	37.9
15/37	**TOTAL MANUFACTURING**	2 244	3 142	4 436	5 686	6 950	56.6	62.4	66.1	70.1	73.0
15/16	Food, beverages, tobacco	537	641	740	912	986	52.9	51.4	51.5	57.0	59.7
17/19	Textiles, clothing, leather, footwear	89	108	133	180	230	45.1	45.3	45.2	51.0	56.1
20/22	Wood and paper products	159	258	249	298	301	48.2	65.9	51.8	53.3	47.5
20	Wood products	..	..	..	53	63	..	..	..	45.7	44.8
21/22	Paper, printing and publishing	..	..	..	245	238	..	..	..	55.3	48.2
23/25	Chemicals, Total	633	935	1 211	1 237	1 392	71.3	83.6	84.9	84.1	85.5
23	Refined petroleum, nuclear fuel	..	..	..	583	673	..	..	..	100.0	99.9
24/25	Chemicals, rubber & plastics prod.	..	..	..	654	719	..	..	..	73.7	75.3
24	Chemical products	..	..	..	509	539	..	..	..	83.7	84.3
2423	Pharmaceuticals	..	..	..	..	..	..	..	..	..	..
25	Rubber and plastics products	..	..	..	145	180	..	..	..	51.9	57.0
26	Non-metallic mineral products	82	102	139	174	203	58.2	65.0	68.9	70.2	71.1
27/28	Basic & fabricated metals	145	162	226	305	324	32.4	34.7	36.0	43.4	42.5
27	Basic metals	..	..	..	170	177	..	..	..	47.7	49.7
28	Fabricated metal products	..	..	..	135	147	..	..	..	39.1	36.2
29/32	Machinery, Total	..	..	..	1 415	2 106	..	..	..	78.6	84.3
29/30	Non-electrical machinery	..	..	..	725	936	..	..	..	75.9	77.7
29	Non-electrical machinery nec	..	..	..	233	264	..	..	..	52.7	55.0
30	Office and computing machinery	..	..	..	493	672	..	..	..	95.8	92.7
31/32	Electrical & electronic equipment	..	..	..	690	1 170	..	..	..	81.5	90.4
31	Electrical machinery nec	..	..	..	294	483	..	..	..	79.9	85.4
32	Radio, TV & communications eq.	..	..	..	396	688	..	..	..	82.8	94.2
33	Scientific instruments	..	..	..	42	49	..	..	..	40.7	45.2
34/35	Transportation equipment	..	..	..	1 078	1 303	..	..	..	94.7	93.8
34	Motor vehicles	..	..	..	1 053	1 281	..	..	..	96.8	96.0
35	Other transport equipment	..	..	..	25	22	..	..	..	48.6	40.6
351	Shipbuilding & repairing	..	..	..	..	..	..	..	..	..	..
353	Aircraft and spacecraft	..	..	..	..	..	..	..	..	..	..
36/37	Other manufacturing	22	26	28	45	57	34.3	33.0	28.8	32.8	36.3
40/45	Construction, electricity, gas & water	487	680	970	1 073	1 107	37.0	40.6	44.5	40.3	36.8
50/55	Trade, repair, hotels & restaurants	1 447	1 933	2 256	3 242	3 944	35.2	37.2	36.2	39.8	42.2
65/74	Finance, insurance, business services	197	266	478	494	584	26.3	26.8	34.4	29.8	30.0
	OTHER ACTIVITIES	367	523	658	795	939	24.4	27.1	27.3	28.2	29.4
01/99	**GRAND TOTAL**	4 756	6 573	8 838	11 324	13 553	40.7	44.1	46.5	48.2	50.0

Grand total by investing country							As a % of grand total by foreign affiliates				
All countries		4 756	6 573	8 838	11 324	13 553	100.0	100.0	100.0	100.0	100.0
United States		..	..	..	..	..	..	..	..	..	..
Canada		..	..	..	..	..	..	..	..	..	..
Mexico		..	..	..	..	..	..	..	..	..	..
Japan		..	..	..	..	..	..	..	..	..	..
Europe		..	..	..	..	..	..	..	..	..	..
European Union (15)		..	..	..	..	..	..	..	..	..	..
Belgium		..	..	..	..	..	..	..	..	..	..
France		..	..	..	..	..	..	..	..	..	..
Germany		..	..	..	..	..	..	..	..	..	..
Italy		..	..	..	..	..	..	..	..	..	..
Netherlands		..	..	..	..	..	..	..	..	..	..
Spain		..	..	..	..	..	..	..	..	..	..
Sweden		..	..	..	..	..	..	..	..	..	..
United Kingdom		..	..	..	..	..	..	..	..	..	..
Switzerland		..	..	..	..	..	..	..	..	..	..
Australia and New Zealand		..	..	..	..	..	..	..	..	..	..
Asia (non-OECD)		..	..	..	..	..	..	..	..	..	..
Latin America		..	..	..	..	..	..	..	..	..	..

Note: All foreign-owned firms (more than 10% of capital share).
Toutes les firmes sous contrôle étranger (plus de 10% du capital détenu par l'étranger).

Inward investments

Investissements entrants

Table 4A - Tableau 4A

VALUE ADDED / VALEUR AJOUTÉE

		Foreign affiliates *(Billions of HUF)* Filiales étrangères *(Milliards de HUF)*					As a % of national total En % du total national				
By industry (ISIC Rev. 3)		1995	1996	1997	1998	1999	1995	1996	1997	1998	1999
10/14	Mining & quarrying	..	9	16	11	10	..	..	51.6	38.4	33.7
15/37	**TOTAL MANUFACTURING**	..	**790**	**1 140**	**1 390**	**1 543**	..	..	**68.3**	**69.3**	**70.4**
15/16	Food, beverages, tobacco	..	122	154	177	187	..	..	58.8	58.9	61.9
17/19	Textiles, clothing, leather, footwear	..	42	58	70	84	..	..	50.4	52.2	56.6
20/22	Wood and paper products	..	46	67	73	69	..	..	52.8	52.0	45.7
20	Wood products	..	..	..	14	15	..	..	..	46.3	44.1
21/22	Paper, printing and publishing	..	..	..	59	54	..	..	..	53.5	46.2
23/25	Chemicals, Total	..	287	351	395	426	..	..	87.3	87.4	88.0
23	Refined petroleum, nuclear fuel	..	..	..	169	197	..	..	..	100.0	99.9
24/25	Chemicals, rubber & plastics prod.	..	..	..	226	229	..	..	..	79.8	79.7
24	Chemical products	..	..	..	183	177	..	..	..	89.0	88.4
2423	Pharmaceuticals	..	..	..	..	..	..	..	..	..	..
25	Rubber and plastics products	..	..	..	43	52	..	..	..	55.3	59.9
26	Non-metallic mineral products	..	38	51	64	72	..	..	69.9	71.4	72.5
27/28	Basic & fabricated metals	..	35	54	69	67	..	..	39.1	42.5	39.6
27	Basic metals	..	..	..	26	24	..	..	..	45.3	48.6
28	Fabricated metal products	..	..	..	42	42	..	..	..	40.9	35.8
29/32	Machinery, Total	..	..	..	303	356	..	..	..	71.4	73.2
29/30	Non-electrical machinery	..	..	..	152	133	..	..	..	67.8	59.4
29	Non-electrical machinery nec	..	..	..	66	69	..	..	..	48.8	48.9
30	Office and computing machinery	..	..	..	86	64	..	..	..	96.6	77.5
31/32	Electrical & electronic equipment	..	..	..	151	224	..	..	..	75.5	84.9
31	Electrical machinery nec	..	..	..	102	142	..	..	..	80.8	84.7
32	Radio, TV & communications eq.	..	..	..	49	82	..	..	..	66.4	85.3
33	Scientific instruments	..	..	..	16	18	..	..	..	44.2	47.6
34/35	Transportation equipment	..	..	..	211	250	..	..	..	91.3	90.4
34	Motor vehicles	..	..	..	206	245	..	..	..	95.1	94.4
35	Other transport equipment	..	..	..	6	6	..	..	..	38.1	31.3
351	Shipbuilding & repairing	..	..	..	..	..	..	..	..	..	..
353	Aircraft and spacecraft	..	..	..	..	..	..	..	..	..	..
36/37	Other manufacturing	..	7	10	12	14	..	..	38.5	34.4	36.6
40/45	Construction, electricity, gas & water	..	121	207	237	244	..	..	42.7	40.3	36.5
50/55	Trade, repair, hotels & restaurants	..	190	270	318	350	..	..	40.7	38.9	39.8
65/74	Finance, insurance, business services	..	65	108	156	196	..	..	26.5	30.1	31.1
	OTHER ACTIVITIES	..	180	269	324	392	..	..	32.3	32.4	34.6
01/99	**GRAND TOTAL**	**999**	**1 354**	**1 950**	**2 436**	**2 735**	**38.6**	**42.7**	**47.7**	**49.1**	**49.4**

Grand total by investing country						As a % of grand total by foreign affiliates				
All countries	999	1 354	1 950	2 436	2 735	100.0	100.0	100.0	100.0	100.0
United States	..	..	..	..	..	..	..	..	..	..
Canada	..	..	..	..	..	..	..	..	..	..
Mexico	..	..	..	..	..	..	..	..	..	..
Japan	..	..	..	..	..	..	..	..	..	..
Europe	..	..	..	..	..	..	..	..	..	..
European Union (15)	..	..	..	..	..	..	..	..	..	..
Belgium	..	..	..	..	..	..	..	..	..	..
France	..	..	..	..	..	..	..	..	..	..
Germany	..	..	..	..	..	..	..	..	..	..
Italy	..	..	..	..	..	..	..	..	..	..
Netherlands	..	..	..	..	..	..	..	..	..	..
Spain	..	..	..	..	..	..	..	..	..	..
Sweden	..	..	..	..	..	..	..	..	..	..
United Kingdom	..	..	..	..	..	..	..	..	..	..
Switzerland	..	..	..	..	..	..	..	..	..	..
Australia and New Zealand	..	..	..	..	..	..	..	..	..	..
Asia (non-OECD)	..	..	..	..	..	..	..	..	..	..
Latin America	..	..	..	..	..	..	..	..	..	..

Note: All foreign-owned firms (more than 10% of capital share).
Toutes les firmes sous contrôle étranger (plus de 10% du capital détenu par l'étranger).

Inward investments   *Investissements entrants*

Table 5A - Tableau 5A

COMPENSATION OF EMPLOYEES / SALAIRES ET CHARGES SOCIALES

By industry (ISIC Rev. 3)	Foreign affiliates (Billions of HUF) Filiales étrangères (Milliards de HUF)					As a % of national total En % du total national				
	1995	1996	1997	1998	1999	1995	1996	1997	1998	1999
10/14 Mining & quarrying	1 618	6 037	5 968	4 054	3 779	12.4	38.0	41.6	32.8	26.6
15/37 TOTAL MANUFACTURING	**184 191**	**235 536**	**317 579**	**412 981**	**497 254**	**46.8**	**50.8**	**55.3**	**58.3**	**60.5**
15/16 Food, beverages, tobacco	37 826	43 243	50 039	65 928	76 656	50.4	49.3	51.6	54.5	57.2
17/19 Textiles, clothing, leather, footwear	16 145	20 677	26 421	34 699	42 206	38.8	41.1	43.1	47.1	50.5
20/22 Wood and paper products	15 055	17 757	22 419	24 516	24 542	40.1	42.7	46.2	46.3	41.1
20 Wood products	..	..	..	4 580	5 112	..	..	..	37.5	35.5
21/22 Paper, printing and publishing	..	..	..	19 936	19 430	..	..	..	49.0	42.9
23/25 Chemicals, Total	44 143	55 252	77 632	93 856	111 734	66.2	75.6	78.3	78.2	81.3
23 Refined petroleum, nuclear fuel	..	..	..	30 069	34 960	..	..	..	100.0	99.8
24/25 Chemicals, rubber & plastics prod.	..	..	..	63 787	76 773	..	..	..	71.0	74.9
24 Chemical products	..	..	..	49 897	56 467	..	..	..	82.1	83.6
2423 Pharmaceuticals	..	..	..	..	..	..	..	..	..	..
25 Rubber and plastics products	..	..	..	13 890	20 306	..	..	..	47.7	58.1
26 Non-metallic mineral products	9 940	11 993	15 582	20 311	23 570	54.4	54.9	59.7	62.2	63.8
27/28 Basic & fabricated metals	12 171	15 451	21 323	29 734	32 114	25.9	30.0	33.5	41.1	38.3
27 Basic metals	..	..	..	11 421	13 245	..	..	..	42.7	46.3
28 Fabricated metal products	..	..	..	18 313	18 869	..	..	..	40.2	34.1
29/32 Machinery, Total	..	..	..	91 305	130 188	..	..	..	60.7	67.7
29/30 Non-electrical machinery	..	..	..	34 455	42 608	..	..	..	50.2	50.6
29 Non-electrical machinery nec	..	..	..	29 361	33 758	..	..	..	46.9	48.7
30 Office and computing machinery	..	..	..	5 094	8 850	..	..	..	84.0	59.1
31/32 Electrical & electronic equipment	..	..	..	56 851	87 579	..	..	..	69.6	81.0
31 Electrical machinery nec	..	..	..	39 552	56 380	..	..	..	76.1	80.6
32 Radio, TV & communications eq.	..	..	..	17 298	31 199	..	..	..	58.3	81.7
33 Scientific instruments	..	..	..	6 451	7 442	..	..	..	39.6	43.2
34/35 Transportation equipment	..	..	..	40 327	41 208	..	..	..	78.2	72.8
34 Motor vehicles	..	..	..	36 931	37 863	..	..	..	86.4	82.3
35 Other transport equipment	..	..	..	3 396	3 345	..	..	..	38.5	31.5
351 Shipbuilding & repairing	..	..	..	..	..	..	..	..	..	..
353 Aircraft and spacecraft	..	..	..	..	..	..	..	..	..	..
36/37 Other manufacturing	2 841	3 475	3 749	5 854	7 595	30.1	30.8	29.5	34.2	38.7
40/45 Construction, electricity, gas & water	42 981	51 771	59 058	68 969	71 012	31.0	33.1	33.9	32.3	29.0
50/55 Trade, repair, hotels & restaurants	58 070	74 237	89 664	121 514	146 752	32.8	34.7	36.1	39.5	41.1
65/74 Finance, insurance, business services	18 576	24 491	35 372	50 240	66 931	21.5	22.5	26.4	27.6	30.6
OTHER ACTIVITIES	38 839	50 741	62 636	70 194	82 855	15.7	17.6	18.2	17.4	18.0
01/99 GRAND TOTAL	**344 273**	**442 813**	**570 278**	**727 952**	**868 582**	**32.6**	**35.5**	**38.3**	**39.8**	**41.0**

Grand total by investing country						As a % of grand total by foreign affiliates				
All countries	344 273	442 813	570 278	727 952	868 582	100.0	100.0	100.0	100.0	100.0
United States	..	..	..	..	..	..	..	..	..	..
Canada	..	..	..	..	..	..	..	..	..	..
Mexico	..	..	..	..	..	..	..	..	..	..
Japan	..	..	..	..	..	..	..	..	..	..
Europe	..	..	..	..	..	..	..	..	..	..
European Union (15)	..	..	..	..	..	..	..	..	..	..
Belgium	..	..	..	..	..	..	..	..	..	..
France	..	..	..	..	..	..	..	..	..	..
Germany	..	..	..	..	..	..	..	..	..	..
Italy	..	..	..	..	..	..	..	..	..	..
Netherlands	..	..	..	..	..	..	..	..	..	..
Spain	..	..	..	..	..	..	..	..	..	..
Sweden	..	..	..	..	..	..	..	..	..	..
United Kingdom	..	..	..	..	..	..	..	..	..	..
Switzerland	..	..	..	..	..	..	..	..	..	..
Australia and New Zealand	..	..	..	..	..	..	..	..	..	..
Asia (non-OECD)	..	..	..	..	..	..	..	..	..	..
Latin America	..	..	..	..	..	..	..	..	..	..

Note: All foreign-owned firms (more than 10% of capital share).
Toutes les firmes sous contrôle étranger (plus de 10% du capital détenu par l'étranger).

Table 6A - Tableau 6A
R&D EXPENDITURE / DÉPENSES DE R-D

		Foreign affiliates (Billions of HUF) Filiales étrangères (Milliards de HUF)					As a % of national total En % du total national				
By industry (ISIC Rev. 3)		1995	1996	1997	1998	1999	1995	1996	1997	1998	1999
10/14	Mining & quarrying	..	..	0.0	..	..	..	..	0.0	..	..
15/37	TOTAL MANUFACTURING	..	..	15.4	..	..	..	..	77.2	..	..
15/16	Food, beverages, tobacco	..	..	0.2	..	..	..	..	26.5	..	..
17/19	Textiles, clothing, leather, footwear	..	..	0.0	..	..	..	..	60.0	..	..
20/22	Wood and paper products	..	..	0.0	..	..	..	..	10.0	..	..
20	Wood products	..	..	..	..	..	..	..	..	..	..
21/22	Paper, printing and publishing	..	..	..	..	..	..	..	..	..	..
23/25	Chemicals, Total	..	..	11.9	..	..	..	..	85.5	..	..
23	Refined petroleum, nuclear fuel	..	..	..	..	..	..	..	..	..	..
24/25	Chemicals, rubber & plastics prod.	..	..	..	..	..	..	..	..	..	..
24	Chemical products	..	..	..	..	..	..	..	..	..	..
2423	Pharmaceuticals	..	..	..	..	..	..	..	..	..	..
25	Rubber and plastics products	..	..	..	..	..	..	..	..	..	..
26	Non-metallic mineral products	..	..	0.0	..	..	..	..	14.3	..	..
27/28	Basic & fabricated metals	..	..	0.1	..	..	..	..	33.3	..	..
27	Basic metals	..	..	..	..	..	..	..	..	..	..
28	Fabricated metal products	..	..	..	..	..	..	..	..	..	..
29/32	Machinery, Total	..	..	..	..	..	..	..	..	..	..
29/30	Non-electrical machinery	..	..	..	..	..	..	..	..	..	..
29	Non-electrical machinery nec	..	..	..	..	..	..	..	..	..	..
30	Office and computing machinery	..	..	..	..	..	..	..	..	..	..
31/32	Electrical & electronic equipment	..	..	..	..	..	..	..	..	..	..
31	Electrical machinery nec	..	..	..	..	..	..	..	..	..	..
32	Radio, TV & communications eq.	..	..	..	..	..	..	..	..	..	..
33	Scientific instruments	..	..	..	..	..	..	..	..	..	..
34/35	Transportation equipment	..	..	..	..	..	..	..	..	..	..
34	Motor vehicles	..	..	..	..	..	..	..	..	..	..
35	Other transport equipment	..	..	..	..	..	..	..	..	..	..
351	Shipbuilding & repairing	..	..	..	..	..	..	..	..	..	..
353	Aircraft and spacecraft	..	..	..	..	..	..	..	..	..	..
36/37	Other manufacturing	..	..	0.0	..	..	..	..	0.0	..	..
40/45	Construction, electricity, gas & water	..	..	0.1	..	..	..	..	6.4	..	..
50/55	Trade, repair, hotels & restaurants	..	..	0.1	..	..	..	..	70.6	..	..
65/74	Finance, insurance, business services	..	..	0.4	..	..	..	..	32.7	..	..
	OTHER ACTIVITIES	..	..	0.8	..	..	..	..	21.9	..	..
01/99	GRAND TOTAL	3.9	8.6	16.7	20.7	..	21.8	44.4	65.3	78.5	..

Grand total by investing country							As a % of grand total by foreign affiliates				
All countries	3.9	8.6	16.7	20.7	..	100.0	100.0	100.0	100.0	..
United States	..	..	..	..	..	..	..	..	..	..
Canada	..	..	..	..	..	..	..	..	..	..
Mexico	..	..	..	..	..	..	..	..	..	..
Japan	..	..	..	..	..	..	..	..	..	..
Europe	..	..	..	..	..	..	..	..	..	..
European Union (15)	..	..	..	..	..	..	..	..	..	..
Belgium	..	..	..	..	..	..	..	..	..	..
France	..	..	..	..	..	..	..	..	..	..
Germany	..	..	..	..	..	..	..	..	..	..
Italy	..	..	..	..	..	..	..	..	..	..
Netherlands	..	..	..	..	..	..	..	..	..	..
Spain	..	..	..	..	..	..	..	..	..	..
Sweden	..	..	..	..	..	..	..	..	..	..
United Kingdom	..	..	..	..	..	..	..	..	..	..
Switzerland	..	..	..	..	..	..	..	..	..	..
Australia and New Zealand	..	..	..	..	..	..	..	..	..	..
Asia (non-OECD)	..	..	..	..	..	..	..	..	..	..
Latin America	..	..	..	..	..	..	..	..	..	..

Note: All foreign-owned firms (more than 10% of capital share).
Toutes les firmes sous contrôle étranger (plus de 10% du capital détenu par l'étranger).

Inward investments

Investissements entrants

Table 7A - Tableau 7A

GROSS FIXED CAPITAL FORMATION / FORMATION BRUTE DE CAPITAL FIXE

By industry (ISIC Rev. 3)		Foreign affiliates *(Billions of HUF)* Filiales étrangères *(Milliards de HUF)*					As a % of national total En % du total national				
		1995	1996	1997	1998	1999	1995	1996	1997	1998	1999
10/14	Mining & quarrying	2	2	3	4	5	..	..	..	..	..
15/37	**TOTAL MANUFACTURING**	173	215	295	420	562	..	..	..	..	..
15/16	Food, beverages, tobacco	42	30	42	48	56	..	..	..	..	..
17/19	Textiles, clothing, leather, footwear	4	4	15	15	15	..	..	..	..	..
20/22	Wood and paper products	6	8	13	22	16	..	..	..	..	..
20	Wood products	..	..	..	4	4	..	..	..	..	..
21/22	Paper, printing and publishing	..	..	..	19	12	..	..	..	..	..
23/25	Chemicals, Total	61	67	96	149	181	..	..	..	..	..
23	Refined petroleum, nuclear fuel	..	..	..	65	72	..	..	..	..	..
24/25	Chemicals, rubber & plastics prod.	..	..	..	84	109	..	..	..	..	..
24	Chemical products	..	..	..	66	90	..	..	..	..	..
2423	Pharmaceuticals	..	..	..	0	..	..	..	..	..	..
25	Rubber and plastics products	..	..	..	18	19	..	..	..	..	..
26	Non-metallic mineral products	9	10	17	20	20	..	..	..	..	..
27/28	Basic & fabricated metals	8	18	19	20	21	..	..	..	..	..
27	Basic metals	..	..	..	11	12	..	..	..	..	..
28	Fabricated metal products	..	..	..	9	9	..	..	..	..	..
29/32	Machinery, Total	..	..	..	77	132	..	..	..	..	..
29/30	Non-electrical machinery	..	..	..	29	34	..	..	..	..	..
29	Non-electrical machinery nec	..	..	..	15	26	..	..	..	..	..
30	Office and computing machinery	..	..	..	14	8	..	..	..	..	..
31/32	Electrical & electronic equipment	..	..	..	49	97	..	..	..	..	..
31	Electrical machinery nec	..	..	..	29	48	..	..	..	..	..
32	Radio, TV & communications eq.	..	..	..	20	49	..	..	..	..	..
33	Scientific instruments	..	..	..	4	4	..	..	..	..	..
34/35	Transportation equipment	..	..	..	61	116	..	..	..	..	..
34	Motor vehicles	..	..	..	60	115	..	..	..	..	..
35	Other transport equipment	..	..	..	1	1	..	..	..	..	..
351	Shipbuilding & repairing	..	..	..	..	..	..	..	..	..	..
353	Aircraft and spacecraft	..	..	..	..	..	..	..	..	..	..
36/37	Other manufacturing	1	1	1	4	2	..	..	..	..	..
40/45	Construction, electricity, gas & water	60	61	69	105	103	..	..	..	..	..
50/55	Trade, repair, hotels & restaurants	25	57	41	73	88	..	..	..	..	..
65/74	Finance, insurance, business services	14	12	7	54	37	..	..	..	..	..
	OTHER ACTIVITIES	100	109	142	161	158	..	..	..	..	..
01/99	**GRAND TOTAL**	374	456	557	818	952	55.4	51.5	49.8	57.2	56.9

Grand total by investing country	1995	1996	1997	1998	1999	As a % of grand total by foreign affiliates				
All countries	374	456	557	818	952	100.0	100.0	100.0	100.0	100.0
United States	..	..	..	..	..	..	..	..	..	..
Canada	..	..	..	..	..	..	..	..	..	..
Mexico	..	..	..	..	..	..	..	..	..	..
Japan	..	..	..	..	..	..	..	..	..	..
Europe	..	..	..	..	..	..	..	..	..	..
European Union (15)	..	..	..	..	..	..	..	..	..	..
Belgium	..	..	..	..	..	..	..	..	..	..
France	..	..	..	..	..	..	..	..	..	..
Germany	..	..	..	..	..	..	..	..	..	..
Italy	..	..	..	..	..	..	..	..	..	..
Netherlands	..	..	..	..	..	..	..	..	..	..
Spain	..	..	..	..	..	..	..	..	..	..
Sweden	..	..	..	..	..	..	..	..	..	..
United Kingdom	..	..	..	..	..	..	..	..	..	..
Switzerland	..	..	..	..	..	..	..	..	..	..
Australia and New Zealand	..	..	..	..	..	..	..	..	..	..
Asia (non-OECD)	..	..	..	..	..	..	..	..	..	..
Latin America	..	..	..	..	..	..	..	..	..	..

Note: All foreign-owned firms (more than 10% of capital share).
Toutes les firmes sous contrôle étranger (plus de 10% du capital détenu par l'étranger).

Table 8A - Tableau 8A

TOTAL EXPORTS BY COUNTRY OF ORIGIN IN THE TOTAL INDUSTRY

EXPORTATIONS TOTALES PAR PAYS D'ORIGINE DANS L'ENSEMBLE DE L'INDUSTRIE

Country of origin (immediate controller)	Total exports (Billions of HUF) Exportations totales (Milliards de HUF)					As a % of all countries En % du total des pays				
	1995	1996	1997	1998	1999	1995	1996	1997	1998	1999
All countries	937	1 639	2 649	3 806	4 749	100.0	100.0	100.0	100.0	100.0
Total OECD	..	..	2 224	3 262	4 275	..	..	83.9	85.7	90.0
United States	29	46	88	194	282	3.1	2.8	3.3	5.1	5.9
Canada	..	..	6	11	5	..	..	0.2	0.3	0.1
Mexico	..	..	1	10	15	..	..	0.0	0.3	0.3
Japan	..	..	10	13	14	..	..	0.4	0.3	0.3
Korea	..	..	5	3	7	..	..	0.2	0.1	0.1
Australia	..	..	3	3	4	..	..	0.1	0.1	0.1
New Zealand	..	..	0	0	0	..	..	0.0	0.0	0.0
Europe	..	..	..	..	..	..	..	..	..	..
European Union (15)	603	1 183	1 948	2 817	3 660	64.4	72.2	73.5	74.0	77.1
Austria	98	177	298	374	400	10.4	10.8	11.3	9.8	8.4
Belgium	..	..	57	109	161	..	..	2.2	2.9	3.4
Denmark	..	..	10	18	22	..	..	0.4	0.5	0.5
Finland	..	..	14	18	16	..	..	0.5	0.5	0.3
France	40	65	100	138	213	4.2	4.0	3.8	3.6	4.5
Germany	272	566	1 063	1 432	1 851	29.0	34.5	40.1	37.6	39.0
Greece	..	..	10	9	12	..	..	0.4	0.2	0.2
Ireland	..	..	12	53	58	..	..	0.4	1.4	1.2
Italy	78	111	140	196	258	8.4	6.7	5.3	5.2	5.4
Luxembourg	..	..	1	1	1	..	..	0.0	0.0	0.0
Netherlands	28	48	76	203	275	3.0	2.9	2.9	5.3	5.8
Portugal	..	..	3	13	28	..	..	0.1	0.3	0.6
Spain	..	..	45	69	81	..	..	1.7	1.8	1.7
Sweden	..	..	19	33	45	..	..	0.7	0.9	0.9
United Kingdom	..	..	99	151	239	..	..	3.8	4.0	5.0
Czech Republic	..	..	46	63	70	..	..	1.7	1.7	1.5
Hungary	..	..	..	..	..	..	..	..	..	..
Iceland	..	..	0	0	0	..	..	0.0	0.0	0.0
Norway	..	..	5	5	5	..	..	0.2	0.1	0.1
Poland	..	..	71	84	95	..	..	5.2	3.1	1.6
Slovak Republic	..	..	32	50	47	..	..	2.7	2.2	2.0
Switzerland	14	21	31	44	56	1.5	1.3	1.2	1.2	1.2
Turkey	..	..	10	14	14	..	..	0.4	0.4	0.3
Non-OECD Europe, of which:	..	..	..	..	..	..	..	..	..	..
Baltic countries	..	..	11	14	15	..	..	0.4	0.4	0.3
Bulgaria	..	..	6	7	10	..	..	0.2	0.2	0.2
Croatia	..	..	25	28	27	..	..	0.9	0.7	0.6
Romania	..	..	37	75	72	..	..	1.4	2.0	1.5
Russian Federation	..	..	137	119	74	..	..	1.2	1.3	1.0
Slovenia	..	..	35	32	44	..	..	1.3	0.8	0.9
Ukraine	..	..	30	30	21	..	..	1.1	0.8	0.4
Yugoslavia	..	..	20	21	15	..	..	0.7	0.5	0.3
Non-OECD Asia, of which:	..	..	..	..	..	..	..	..	..	..
China	..	..	2	3	16	..	..	0.1	0.1	0.3
Chinese Taipei	..	..	3	..	0	..	..	0.1	..	0.0
Hong Kong (China)	..	..	2	2	4	..	..	0.1	0.1	0.1
India	..	..	2	2	3	..	..	0.1	0.0	0.1
Indonesia	..	..	2	1	1	..	..	0.1	0.0	0.0
Malaysia	..	..	..	..	5	..	..	..	..	0.1
Philippines	..	..	0	0	0	..	..	0.0	0.0	0.0
Singapore	..	..	3	29	48	..	..	0.1	0.8	1.0
Thailand	..	..	1	1	2	..	..	0.0	0.0	0.0
Near and Middle East	..	..	..	..	..	..	..	..	..	..
Africa	..	..	..	..	..	..	..	..	..	..
Latin America, of which:	..	..	..	..	..	..	..	..	..	..
Argentina	..	..	2	4	2	..	..	0.1	0.1	0.0
Brazil	..	..	6	16	8	..	..	0.2	0.4	0.2
Chile	..	..	1	1	1	..	..	0.0	0.0	0.0

Note: All foreign-owned firms (more than 10% of capital share).
Toutes les firmes sous contrôle étranger (plus de 10% du capital détenu par l'étranger).

Table 9A - Tableau 9A

TOTAL IMPORTS BY COUNTRY OF ORIGIN IN THE TOTAL INDUSTRY

IMPORTATIONS TOTALES PAR PAYS D'ORIGINE DANS L'ENSEMBLE DE L'INDUSTRIE

Country of origin (immediate controller)	Total imports (Billions of HUF) Importations totales (Milliards de HUF)					As a % of all countries En % du total des pays				
	1995	1996	1997	1998	1999	1995	1996	1997	1998	1999
All countries	1 217	1 941	2 881	4 088	5 083	100.0	100.0	100.0	100.0	100.0
Total OECD	..	..	2 241	3 266	4 138	..	..	77.8	79.9	81.4
United States	38	60	110	159	169	3.1	3.1	3.8	3.9	3.3
Canada	..	..	12	18	11	..	..	0.4	0.4	0.2
Mexico	..	..	12	26	39	..	..	0.4	0.6	0.8
Japan	..	..	103	168	224	..	..	3.6	4.1	4.4
Korea	..	..	25	50	72	..	..	0.9	1.2	1.4
Australia	..	..	2	4	3	..	..	0.1	0.1	0.1
New Zealand	..	..	0	1	1	..	..	0.0	0.0	0.0
Europe	..	..	..	..	..	..	..	..	..	..
European Union (15)	759	1 206	1 822	2 619	3 278	62.3	62.2	63.2	64.1	64.5
Austria	125	223	329	428	480	10.3	11.5	11.4	10.5	9.4
Belgium	..	..	50	80	115	..	..	1.7	2.0	2.3
Denmark	..	..	15	21	25	..	..	0.5	0.5	0.5
Finland	..	..	33	47	64	..	..	1.1	1.2	1.3
France	55	82	133	190	223	4.5	4.2	4.6	4.6	4.4
Germany	292	519	802	1 200	1 532	24.0	26.7	27.8	29.4	30.1
Greece	..	..	7	8	9	..	..	0.2	0.2	0.2
Ireland	..	..	9	15	32	..	..	0.3	0.4	0.6
Italy	95	129	183	261	348	7.8	6.6	6.4	6.4	6.8
Luxembourg	..	..	1	2	4	..	..	0.0	0.1	0.1
Netherlands	37	46	70	95	124	3.0	2.4	2.4	2.3	2.4
Portugal	..	..	12	15	21	..	..	0.4	0.4	0.4
Spain	..	..	39	68	89	..	..	1.3	1.7	1.8
Sweden	..	..	39	50	61	..	..	1.4	1.2	1.2
United Kingdom	..	..	100	140	151	..	..	3.5	3.4	3.0
Czech Republic	..	..	52	73	85	..	..	1.8	1.8	1.7
Hungary	..	..	..	..	..	..	..	..	..	..
Iceland	..	..	0	0	0	..	..	0.0	0.0	0.0
Norway	..	..	2	4	8	..	..	0.1	0.1	0.1
Poland	..	..	41	64	85	..	..	10.9	7.8	6.6
Slovak Republic	..	..	32	51	70	..	..	1.4	1.6	1.7
Switzerland	29	36	49	67	76	2.4	1.9	1.7	1.6	1.5
Turkey	..	..	10	12	19	..	..	0.4	0.3	0.4
Non-OECD Europe, of which:	..	..	..	..	..	..	..	..	..	..
Baltic countries	..	..	1	1	2	..	..	0.0	0.0	0.0
Bulgaria	..	..	3	4	5	..	..	0.1	0.1	0.1
Croatia	..	..	5	9	7	..	..	0.2	0.2	0.1
Romania	..	..	14	20	31	..	..	0.5	0.5	0.6
Russian Federation	..	..	315	318	337	..	..	1.1	1.3	1.4
Slovenia	..	..	11	18	26	..	..	0.4	0.4	0.5
Ukraine	..	..	33	26	28	..	..	1.1	0.6	0.6
Yugoslavia	..	..	7	7	3	..	..	0.2	0.2	0.1
Non-OECD Asia, of which:	..	..	..	..	..	..	..	..	..	..
China	..	..	37	65	113	..	..	1.3	1.6	2.2
Chinese Taipei	..	..	19	..	0	..	..	0.7	..	0.0
Hong Kong (China)	..	..	6	12	19	..	..	0.2	0.3	0.4
India	..	..	6	10	10	..	..	0.2	0.2	0.2
Indonesia	..	..	7	12	17	..	..	0.2	0.3	0.3
Malaysia	..	..	..	..	45	..	..	..	..	0.9
Philippines	..	..	4	12	18	..	..	0.1	0.3	0.4
Singapore	..	..	40	74	90	..	..	1.4	1.8	1.8
Thailand	..	..	25	25	30	..	..	0.9	0.6	0.6
Near and Middle East	..	..	..	..	..	..	..	..	..	..
Africa	..	..	..	..	..	..	..	..	..	..
Latin America, of which:	..	..	..	..	..	..	..	..	..	..
Argentina	..	..	3	10	2	..	..	0.1	0.2	0.0
Brazil	..	..	23	37	41	..	..	0.8	0.9	0.8
Chile	..	..	0	0	0	..	..	0.0	0.0	0.0

Note: All foreign-owned firms (more than 10% of capital share).
Toutes les firmes sous contrôle étranger (plus de 10% du capital détenu par l'étranger).

Inward investments   *Investissements entrants*

Table 10A - Tableau 10A

STOCK OF FOREIGN DIRECT INVESTMENT / STOCK D'INVESTISSEMENT DIRECT ÉTRANGER

By industry (ISIC Rev. 3)		Foreign affiliates *(Billions of HUF)* Filiales étrangères *(Milliards de HUF)*								
		1990	1991	1992	1993	1994	1995	1996	1997	1998	1999
10/14	Mining & quarrying	..	..	7	9	9	11	20	23	12	11
15/37	**TOTAL MANUFACTURING**	..	..	**218**	**331**	**405**	**555**	**640**	**805**	**907**	**981**
15/16	Food, beverages, tobacco	..	..	78	112	132	157	147	212	231	230
17/19	Textiles, clothing, leather, footwear	..	..	10	14	17	26	32	37	41	43
20/22	Wood and paper products	..	..	15	22	26	38	43	51	51	53
20	Wood products	..	..	..	..	..	..	11	..	11	11
21/22	Paper, printing and publishing	..	..	..	..	..	..	32	..	41	43
23/25	Chemicals, Total	..	..	29	37	54	109	140	170	174	191
23	Refined petroleum, nuclear fuel	..	..	..	..	..	..	31	..	55	51
24/25	Chemicals, rubber & plastics prod.	..	..	..	..	..	..	109	..	119	141
24	Chemical products	..	..	..	..	..	..	80	..	87	96
2423	Pharmaceuticals	..	..	..	..	..	..	34	..	0	..
25	Rubber and plastics products	..	..	..	..	..	..	28	..	33	45
26	Non-metallic mineral products	..	..	19	28	33	41	45	51	60	67
27/28	Basic & fabricated metals	..	..	15	23	26	34	40	60	75	77
27	Basic metals	..	..	..	..	..	..	23	..	29	31
28	Fabricated metal products	..	..	..	..	..	..	18	..	46	46
29/32	Machinery, Total	..	..	..	..	..	..	121	..	152	192
29/30	Non-electrical machinery	..	..	..	..	..	..	34	..	46	52
29	Non-electrical machinery nec	..	..	..	..	..	..	32	..	40	45
30	Office and computing machinery	..	..	..	..	..	..	2	..	6	7
31/32	Electrical & electronic equipment	..	..	..	..	..	..	87	..	106	140
31	Electrical machinery nec	..	..	..	..	..	..	71	..	75	87
32	Radio, TV & communications eq.	..	..	..	..	..	..	16	..	31	53
33	Scientific instruments	..	..	..	..	..	..	8	..	12	7
34/35	Transportation equipment	..	..	..	..	..	..	56	..	103	111
34	Motor vehicles	..	..	..	..	..	..	54	..	99	107
35	Other transport equipment	..	..	..	..	..	..	2	..	4	4
351	Shipbuilding & repairing	..	..	..	..	..	..	0	..	0	..
353	Aircraft and spacecraft	..	..	..	..	..	..	..	..	..	..
36/37	Other manufacturing	..	..	3	5	6	6	7	9	9	11
40/45	Construction, electricity, gas & water	..	..	19	31	43	218	289	332	394	332
50/55	Trade, repair, hotels & restaurants	..	..	70	116	157	189	231	309	333	369
65/74	Finance, insurance, business services	..	..	74	104	146	189	263	385	491	627
	OTHER ACTIVITIES	..	..	14	72	74	143	160	192	228	305
01/99	**GRAND TOTAL**	**93**	**215**	**402**	**663**	**834**	**1 305**	**1 603**	**2 046**	**2 364**	**2 625**

Grand total by investing country

	1990	1991	1992	1993	1994	1995	1996	1997	1998	1999
All countries	**93**	**215**	**402**	**663**	**834**	**1 305**	**1 603**	**2 046**	**2 364**	**2 625**
United States	..	..	46	135	118	209	265	312	285	231
Canada	..	..	2	4	7	8	6	22	6	7
Mexico	..	..	..	..	..	..	..	..	..	..
Japan	..	..	10	17	16	17	25	31	43	51
Europe	..	..	281	452	641	995	1 145	1 577	..	..
European Union (15)	..	..	166	332	435	735	862	1 266	..	..
Belgium	..	..	11	28	32	55	58	88	61	57
France	..	..	19	31	43	106	121	118	142	163
Germany	..	..	69	183	184	322	368	507	648	716
Italy	..	..	12	25	39	49	59	69	71	71
Netherlands	..	..	33	36	92	137	148	298	376	589
Spain	..	..	0	1	1	2	2	2	3	10
Sweden	..	..	4	5	9	9	10	18	17	18
United Kingdom	..	..	18	25	37	50	90	156	151	50
Switzerland	..	..	16	13	32	38	35	54	73	65
Australia and New Zealand	..	..	..	..	..	..	..	..	..	..
Asia (non-OECD)	..	..	4	3	3	26	38	26	..	..
Latin America	..	..	0	..	..	6	5	3	..	..

Note: All foreign-owned firms (more than 10% of capital share).
Toutes les firmes sous contrôle étranger (plus de 10% du capital détenu par l'étranger).

HUNGARY

Source

The data are prepared by the Financial Statistical Department of the Hungarian Central Statistical Office (HCSO). The annual corporation-tax declarations, the annual investment survey and the external trade data collection of FDI are the most important data sources. In Hungary, all enterprises with legal entity and unincorporated enterprises with turnover greater than USD 500 000 are required to submit a detailed corporation-tax declaration. This includes the value of the stock of foreign direct investment and its distribution by industrial sector, but does not provide any information on the country of origin. Therefore, since 1992 the HCSO has organised an annual survey on FDI. In 1997, the sample included 5 000 enterprises selected on the corporation-tax declarations, covering 88% of the total stocks of FDI. From 1999 onwards, the data of country of origin of inward foreign direct investment position is based on information collected by the National Bank of Hungary. This sample survey covers 1 500 enterprises operating by significant FDI amounting to 83% of total FDI calculated from the tax files. The results are published in *Foreign Direct Investment in Hungary.*

National totals:

- *Number of enterprises*, *Number of employees*, *Turnover*, *Value added*, *Compensation of employees* and *Gross fixed capital formation:* provided by the HCSO and compatible with foreign affiliates' data.

- *R&D expenditure:* data are extracted from the OECD R&D database.

Industrial classification

For all variables, the data are classified according to the principal industrial activity of the affiliate.

The industrial classification used is the national classification (TEÁOR 92) converted to ISIC Revision 3.

For *Number of employees Turnover, Value added, Compensation of employees* and *Gross fixed capital formation, Financial intermediation* (ISIC 65/67) is excluded from *Finance, insurance and business services* (65/74).

Variables

- *Number of enterprises* refers to incorporated or unincorporated enterprises with more than 10% foreign capital share which submitted a corporation-tax declaration.

- *Number of employees:* the number of persons in a legal work relationship exceeding five working days.

- *Gross fixed capital formation* consists of the value of outlays which change or extend the stock of fixed assets. Non-deductible VAT is included.

Geographical breakdown

The breakdown by country of origin is only available for the variables *Total exports* and *imports*. The breakdown is for the *Grand total* (all activities) and not for *Total manufacturing* as is the case for other countries. The investor's country is the country of the immediate controller.

HONGRIE

Source

Les données émanent du Département des statistiques financières de l'office central des statistiques hongrois (HCSO). Les déclarations fiscales annuelles des entreprises, l'enquête annuelle sur les investissements et la collecte des données du commerce extérieur sont les principales sources de données. En Hongrie, toutes les entreprises ayant un statut légal ainsi que les entreprises individuelles présentant un chiffre d'affaires annuel supérieur à USD 500 000 sont tenues d'établir des déclarations fiscales détaillées. Celles-ci comprennent la valeur du capital et sa répartition par secteur industriel, mais ne fournissent aucune information relative au pays d'origine. En conséquence, depuis 1992 le HCSO menait une enquête annuelle auprès des entreprises concernées par l'investissement direct. En 1997, l'échantillon comprenait 5 000 entreprises sélectionnées sur la base des déclarations fiscales, couvrant plus de 88 % du total de l'encours de l'IDE. A partir de 1999, les données relatives au pays d'origine de l'encours d'IDE sont basées sur les informations collectées par la Banque Nationale de Hongrie. Cette enquête par échantillon couvre 1 500 entreprises réalisant des IDE significatifs qui totalisent 83 % des IDE calculés à partir des fichiers fiscaux. Les résultats sont publiés dans *Foreign Direct Investment in Hungary*.

Totaux nationaux :

- *Nombre d'entreprises, Nombre de salariés, Chiffre d'affaires, Valeur ajoutée, Salaires* et *Formation brute de capital fixe* : fournis par le HCSO et compatibles avec les données relatives aux filiales étrangères.

- *Dépenses de R-D* : les données sont extraites de la base de données R-D de l'OCDE.

Classification industrielle

Pour toutes les variables, les données sont classées selon l'activité industrielle principale de l'entreprise affiliée.

La classification industrielle utilisée est la classification nationale (TEÁOR 92) adaptée pour correspondre à la CITI révision 3.

Pour les variables *Nombre de salariés, Chiffre d'affaires, Valeur ajoutée, Salaires* et *Formation brute de capital fixe*, les *Activités financières* (CITI 65/67) ne sont pas comprises dans *Finance, assurance et services aux entreprises* (65/74).

Variables

- Le *Nombre d'entreprises* fait référence aux sociétés et entreprises individuelles dont plus de 10 % du capital est détenu par l'étranger et ayant rempli une déclaration fiscale.

- Le *Nombre de salariés* est le nombre de personnes ayant un contrat de travail légal de plus de cinq jours avec l'employeur. Il est exprimé en équivalent plein-temps.

- La *Formation brute de capital fixe* consiste dans la valeur des dépenses effectuées pour modifier ou acquérir le stock d'actifs fixes. La TVA non déductible est incluse.

Ventilation géographique

La ventilation par pays d'origine est seulement disponible pour les variables *Exportations* et *Importations totales*. La ventilation concerne le *Total général* (toutes activités) et non le *Total manufacturier* comme pour les autres pays. Le pays investisseur est celui où se situe le contrôle immédiat.

IRELAND

IRLANDE

Inward investments

Investissements entrants

Table 1A - Tableau 1A

NUMBER OF ESTABLISHMENTS / NOMBRE D'ÉTABLISSEMENTS

		Foreign affiliates *(Units)* Filiales étrangères *(Unités)*					As a % of national total En % du total national				
By industry (ISIC Rev. 3)		1994	1995	1996	1997	1998	1994	1995	1996	1997	1998
10/14	Mining & quarrying	..	..	..	..	..	..	..	..	..	..
15/37	**TOTAL MANUFACTURING**	726	725	728	735	725	15.8	15.7	15.8	15.5	15.4
15/16	Food, beverages, tobacco	89	86	85	86	81	11.1	10.3	10.2	10.2	10.0
17/19	Textiles, clothing, leather, footwear	71	64	62	56	44	15.9	15.2	15.5	13.9	11.8
20/22	Wood and paper products	45	54	52	56	51	5.9	7.2	6.9	7.0	6.3
20	Wood products	7	7	7	10	8	3.3	3.4	3.3	4.4	3.5
21/22	Paper, printing and publishing	38	47	45	46	43	7.0	8.6	8.3	8.0	7.4
23/25	Chemicals, Total	161	159	160	170	173	33.3	33.5	33.5	33.2	33.6
23	Refined petroleum, nuclear fuel	..	..	..	..	..	..	..	..	..	..
24/25	Chemicals, rubber & plastics prod.	161	159	160	170	173	33.3	33.5	33.5	33.2	33.6
24	Chemical products	107	110	112	120	120	43.7	45.3	47.3	48.0	49.6
2423	Pharmaceuticals	43	43	41	40	41	67.2	68.3	65.1	60.6	64.1
25	Rubber and plastics products	54	49	48	50	53	22.7	21.2	19.9	19.1	19.4
26	Non-metallic mineral products	14	16	16	17	19	4.8	5.7	5.7	5.9	6.6
27/28	Basic & fabricated metals	53	49	46	45	47	9.5	9.1	8.6	8.4	8.8
27	Basic metals	..	..	..	..	..	..	..	..	..	..
28	Fabricated metal products	..	..	..	..	..	..	..	..	..	..
29/32	Machinery, Total	179	182	187	184	187	29.5	29.5	29.2	27.2	27.5
29/30	Non-electrical machinery	100	98	103	96	96	24.6	24.0	24.4	21.7	21.4
29	Non-electrical machinery nec	64	64	68	65	64	19.1	19.0	19.3	17.4	17.3
30	Office and computing machinery	36	34	35	31	32	50.7	47.9	50.0	44.3	41.0
31/32	Electrical & electronic equipment	79	84	84	88	91	39.3	40.4	38.4	37.6	39.1
31	Electrical machinery nec	52	58	58	60	62	35.1	37.4	34.9	33.5	34.3
32	Radio, TV & communications eq.	27	26	26	28	29	50.9	49.1	49.1	50.9	55.8
33	Scientific instruments	68	69	70	71	73	51.9	51.1	50.4	51.1	51.0
34/35	Transportation equipment	19	18	21	21	21	13.7	12.2	14.7	16.2	16.8
34	Motor vehicles	9	9	11	..	..	9.8	9.1	11.6	..	..
35	Other transport equipment	10	9	10	..	..	21.3	18.8	20.8	..	..
351	Shipbuilding & repairing	..	..	..	..	..	..	..	..	..	..
353	Aircraft and spacecraft	..	..	..	..	..	..	..	..	..	..
36/37	Other manufacturing	27	28	29	29	29	7.0	7.0	7.3	7.0	6.8
40/45	Construction, electricity, gas & water	..	..	..	..	..	..	..	..	..	..
50/55	Trade, repair, hotels & restaurants	..	..	..	..	..	..	..	..	..	..
65/74	Finance, insurance, business services	..	..	..	..	..	..	..	..	..	..
	OTHER ACTIVITIES	..	..	..	..	..	..	..	..	..	..
01/99	**GRAND TOTAL**	..	..	..	..	..	..	..	..	..	..

Total manufacturing by investing country						As a % of total manufacturing by foreign affiliates				
All countries	726	725	728	735	725	100.0	100.0	100.0	100.0	100.0
United States	285	289	286	284	295	39.3	39.9	39.3	38.6	40.7
Canada	13	13	17	12	12	1.8	1.8	2.3	1.6	1.7
Mexico	..	..	..	..	..	..	..	..	..	..
Japan	19	21	23	26	23	2.6	2.9	3.2	3.5	3.2
Europe	..	..	..	..	..	..	..	..	..	..
European Union (15)	328	346	344	355	345	45.2	47.7	47.3	48.3	47.6
Belgium	10	11	11	9	8	1.4	1.5	1.5	1.2	1.1
France	35	36	33	38	35	4.8	5.0	4.5	5.2	4.8
Germany	97	99	98	99	100	13.4	13.7	13.5	13.5	13.8
Italy	..	..	..	..	..	..	..	..	..	..
Netherlands	41	41	42	41	37	5.6	5.7	5.8	5.6	5.1
Spain	..	..	..	..	..	..	..	..	..	..
Sweden	13	13	14	12	11	1.8	1.8	1.9	1.6	1.5
United Kingdom	124	117	117	123	122	17.1	16.1	16.1	16.7	16.8
Switzerland	29	29	31	29	24	4.0	4.0	4.3	3.9	3.3
Australia and New Zealand	..	..	..	..	..	..	..	..	..	..
Asia (non-OECD)	..	..	..	..	..	..	..	..	..	..
Latin America	..	..	..	..	..	..	..	..	..	..

Note: Majority foreign-owned establishments. ISIC 23/25 excludes *Refined petroleum products* (232) which is included in ISIC 36/37.
Etablissements sous contrôle étranger majoritaire. La CITI 23/25 exclut les *Produits pétroliers raffinés* (232), qui sont compris dans la CITI 36/37.

Inward investments   *Investissements entrants*

Table 2A - Tableau 2A
NUMBER OF EMPLOYEES / NOMBRE DE SALARIÉS

By industry (ISIC Rev. 3)	Foreign affiliates (Units) Filiales étrangères (Unités)					As a % of national total En % du total national				
	1994	1995	1996	1997	1998	1994	1995	1996	1997	1998
10/14 Mining & quarrying	..	..	..	..	..	..	..	..	..	..
15/37 TOTAL MANUFACTURING	**95 715**	**103 864**	**106 410**	**114 956**	**115 243**	**46.6**	**47.1**	**47.0**	**47.8**	**47.5**
15/16 Food, beverages, tobacco	12 806	12 535	12 673	12 356	11 903	28.9	27.5	27.3	26.7	25.7
17/19 Textiles, clothing, leather, footwear	9 753	9 257	8 472	7 164	5 855	46.6	45.2	44.7	40.1	37.5
20/22 Wood and paper products	4 878	6 136	6 754	7 959	7 624	21.1	24.9	26.7	28.6	26.8
20 Wood products	574	615	617	1 086	1 032	14.0	13.7	13.4	21.0	20.3
21/22 Paper, printing and publishing	4 304	5 521	6 137	6 873	6 592	22.6	27.5	29.6	30.3	28.3
23/25 Chemicals, Total	18 485	19 269	20 635	21 126	21 788	70.3	69.6	69.2	68.0	68.2
23 Refined petroleum, nuclear fuel	..	..	..	..	..	..	..	..	..	..
24/25 Chemicals, rubber & plastics prod.	18 485	19 269	20 635	21 126	21 788	70.3	69.6	69.2	68.0	68.2
24 Chemical products	13 793	14 391	15 560	16 506	17 123	79.0	79.3	80.0	78.6	79.9
2423 Pharmaceuticals	4 534	4 801	5 345	5 520	5 758	82.8	82.3	82.4	80.1	79.6
25 Rubber and plastics products	4 692	4 878	5 075	4 620	4 665	53.0	51.1	49.0	45.9	44.4
26 Non-metallic mineral products	979	1 406	1 457	1 540	1 623	10.6	14.9	15.2	15.2	16.3
27/28 Basic & fabricated metals	3 322	3 252	3 356	3 734	3 946	26.6	25.4	24.3	26.3	26.4
27 Basic metals	..	..	..	..	..	..	..	..	..	..
28 Fabricated metal products	..	..	..	..	..	..	..	..	..	..
29/32 Machinery, Total	29 231	34 897	35 414	40 548	41 349	71.1	72.3	71.0	70.6	70.8
29/30 Non-electrical machinery	15 838	19 709	20 381	19 622	19 629	66.5	68.8	68.9	64.9	64.6
29 Non-electrical machinery nec	7 238	7 331	7 104	7 060	6 602	53.3	51.6	49.6	46.9	46.0
30 Office and computing machinery	8 600	12 378	13 277	12 562	13 027	84.0	85.8	87.1	82.8	81.2
31/32 Electrical & electronic equipment	13 393	15 188	15 033	20 926	21 720	77.5	77.4	74.1	76.8	77.6
31 Electrical machinery nec	7 055	9 031	8 306	9 157	10 098	69.8	72.9	69.1	66.8	69.1
32 Radio, TV & communications eq.	6 338	6 157	6 727	11 769	11 622	88.2	85.2	81.4	87.1	86.8
33 Scientific instruments	9 439	10 544	11 133	12 686	13 630	88.9	89.2	86.3	87.2	86.3
34/35 Transportation equipment	2 811	2 291	2 453	3 638	3 462	36.6	23.9	25.8	38.6	37.3
34 Motor vehicles	1 568	1 582	1 615	..	..	42.7	35.7	37.0	..	..
35 Other transport equipment	1 243	709	838	..	..	31.0	13.7	16.3	..	..
351 Shipbuilding & repairing	..	..	..	..	..	..	..	..	..	..
353 Aircraft and spacecraft	..	..	..	..	..	..	..	..	..	..
36/37 Other manufacturing	4 011	4 277	4 063	4 205	4 063	41.9	42.0	38.6	36.2	33.4
40/45 Construction, electricity, gas & water	..	..	..	..	..	..	..	..	..	..
50/55 Trade, repair, hotels & restaurants	..	..	..	..	..	..	..	..	..	..
65/74 Finance, insurance, business services	..	..	..	..	..	..	..	..	..	..
OTHER ACTIVITIES	..	..	..	..	..	..	..	..	..	..
01/99 GRAND TOTAL	..	..	..	..	..	..	..	..	..	..

Total manufacturing by investing country						As a % of total manufacturing by foreign affiliates				
All countries	95 715	103 864	106 410	114 956	115 243	100.0	100.0	100.0	100.0	100.0
United States	47 040	54 624	54 167	60 672	66 018	49.1	52.6	50.9	52.8	57.3
Canada	2 051	2 067	2 392	2 259	2 582	2.1	2.0	2.2	2.0	2.2
Mexico	..	..	..	..	..	..	..	..	..	..
Japan	3 227	3 691	3 893	4 218	3 574	3.4	3.6	3.7	3.7	3.1
Europe	..	..	..	..	..	..	..	..	..	..
European Union (15)	34 399	36 043	37 114	38 393	36 668	35.9	34.7	34.9	33.4	31.8
Belgium	966	1 252	1 229	1 050	915	1.0	1.2	1.2	0.9	0.8
France	4 313	4 515	4 525	4 544	4 675	4.5	4.3	4.3	4.0	4.1
Germany	10 987	11 483	10 684	11 082	10 400	11.5	11.1	10.0	9.6	9.0
Italy	..	..	..	..	..	..	..	..	..	..
Netherlands	3 528	3 008	4 327	5 198	4 566	3.7	2.9	4.1	4.5	4.0
Spain	..	..	..	..	..	..	..	..	..	..
Sweden	1 410	1 252	1 288	1 050	833	1.5	1.2	1.2	0.9	0.7
United Kingdom	12 779	11 765	12 283	12 015	11 824	13.4	11.3	11.5	10.5	10.3
Switzerland	3 745	4 121	4 412	4 136	3 505	3.9	4.0	4.1	3.6	3.0
Australia and New Zealand	..	..	..	..	..	..	..	..	..	..
Asia (non-OECD)	..	..	..	..	..	..	..	..	..	..
Latin America	..	..	..	..	..	..	..	..	..	..

Note: Majority foreign-owned establishments. ISIC 23/25 excludes *Refined petroleum products* (232) which is included in ISIC 36/37.
Etablissements sous contrôle étranger majoritaire. La CITI 23/25 exclut les *Produits pétroliers raffinés* (232), qui sont compris dans la CITI 36/37.

Inward investments

Investissements entrants

Table 3A - Tableau 3A
PRODUCTION

By industry (ISIC Rev. 3)	Foreign affiliates (Millions of IEP) / Filiales étrangères (Millions de IEP)					As a % of national total / En % du total national				
	1994	1995	1996	1997	1998	1994	1995	1996	1997	1998
10/14 Mining & quarrying	..	..	..	..	..	..	..	..	..	..
15/37 **TOTAL MANUFACTURING**	17 123	21 896	24 108	28 636	35 024	61.6	65.2	66.4	69.2	72.3
15/16 Food, beverages, tobacco	3 201	3 538	3 786	3 933	4 116	35.8	36.1	38.1	39.0	39.6
17/19 Textiles, clothing, leather, footwear	445	452	447	377	375	52.2	52.5	54.0	47.4	48.3
20/22 Wood and paper products	1 680	2 097	2 635	3 117	3 876	58.2	62.4	66.8	68.3	70.6
20 Wood products	77	93	92	134	158	27.3	28.8	26.8	31.6	33.7
21/22 Paper, printing and publishing	1 603	2 005	2 543	2 983	3 718	61.6	65.9	70.6	72.1	74.1
23/25 Chemicals, Total	4 505	5 345	6 097	7 897	11 607	85.9	86.5	85.9	89.2	92.2
23 Refined petroleum, nuclear fuel	..	..	..	..	..	..	..	..	..	..
24/25 Chemicals, rubber & plastics prod.	4 505	5 345	6 097	7 897	11 607	85.9	86.5	85.9	89.2	92.2
24 Chemical products	4 141	4 925	5 696	7 515	11 181	89.7	90.4	90.0	93.1	95.3
2423 Pharmaceuticals	1 026	1 242	1 257	1 487	1 913	94.5	95.1	94.5	94.4	94.4
25 Rubber and plastics products	364	421	401	381	426	58.0	57.3	51.8	49.1	49.8
26 Non-metallic mineral products	72	112	116	133	166	11.0	15.7	15.3	15.4	18.1
27/28 Basic & fabricated metals	383	397	413	497	564	42.4	39.9	37.8	42.3	43.4
27 Basic metals	..	..	..	..	..	..	..	..	..	..
28 Fabricated metal products	..	..	..	..	..	..	..	..	..	..
29/32 Machinery, Total	5 496	8 495	8 955	10 723	12 146	89.5	92.1	90.7	90.1	89.8
29/30 Non-electrical machinery	4 031	6 556	6 935	7 450	8 832	88.9	92.8	91.8	90.7	91.0
29 Non-electrical machinery nec	589	708	663	654	677	63.8	66.0	59.9	57.1	56.6
30 Office and computing machinery	3 443	5 848	6 272	6 795	8 154	96.7	97.6	97.2	96.1	95.8
31/32 Electrical & electronic equipment	1 465	1 939	2 019	3 273	3 314	88.4	89.7	87.3	89.0	86.9
31 Electrical machinery nec	524	831	910	977	1 049	77.1	82.3	82.5	78.2	80.1
32 Radio, TV & communications eq.	941	1 108	1 109	2 296	2 266	96.2	96.3	91.7	94.6	90.5
33 Scientific instruments	835	930	1 085	1 173	1 350	92.4	92.6	91.5	89.8	89.6
34/35 Transportation equipment	186	200	211	384	433	41.1	38.1	36.5	58.1	57.8
34 Motor vehicles	132	153	161	..	..	56.9	54.7	55.9	..	..
35 Other transport equipment	55	47	49	..	..	24.9	19.2	16.9	..	..
351 Shipbuilding & repairing	..	..	..	..	..	..	..	..	..	..
353 Aircraft and spacecraft	..	..	..	..	..	..	..	..	..	..
36/37 Other manufacturing	319	330	363	402	391	39.0	36.4	36.2	33.2	32.4
40/45 Construction, electricity, gas & water	..	..	..	..	..	..	..	..	..	..
50/55 Trade, repair, hotels & restaurants	..	..	..	..	..	..	..	..	..	..
65/74 Finance, insurance, business services	..	..	..	..	..	..	..	..	..	..
OTHER ACTIVITIES	..	..	..	..	..	..	..	..	..	..
01/99 **GRAND TOTAL**	..	..	..	..	..	..	..	..	..	..

Total manufacturing by investing country						As a % of total manufacturing by foreign affiliates				
All countries	17 123	21 896	24 108	28 636	35 024	100.0	100.0	100.0	100.0	100.0
United States	10 599	14 620	15 814	19 314	26 208	61.9	66.8	65.6	67.4	74.8
Canada	417	463	658	655	769	2.4	2.1	2.7	2.3	2.2
Mexico	..	..	..	..	..	..	..	..	..	..
Japan	708	980	720	681	684	4.1	4.5	3.0	2.4	2.0
Europe	..	..	..	..	..	..	..	..	..	..
European Union (15)	3 964	4 242	4 765	5 267	5 511	23.2	19.4	19.8	18.4	15.7
Belgium	102	137	143	118	91	0.6	0.6	0.6	0.4	0.3
France	587	613	645	680	775	3.4	2.8	2.7	2.4	2.2
Germany	757	890	855	927	1 005	4.4	4.1	3.5	3.2	2.9
Italy	..	..	..	..	..	..	..	..	..	..
Netherlands	631	461	751	931	933	3.7	2.1	3.1	3.3	2.7
Spain	..	..	..	..	..	..	..	..	..	..
Sweden	106	110	119	92	75	0.6	0.5	0.5	0.3	0.2
United Kingdom	1 680	1 726	1 960	2 149	2 228	9.8	7.9	8.1	7.5	6.4
Switzerland	934	1 091	1 394	1 877	1 133	5.5	5.0	5.8	6.6	3.2
Australia and New Zealand	..	..	..	..	..	..	..	..	..	..
Asia (non-OECD)	..	..	..	..	..	..	..	..	..	..
Latin America	..	..	..	..	..	..	..	..	..	..

Note: Majority foreign-owned establishments. ISIC 23/25 excludes *Refined petroleum products* (232) which is included in ISIC 36/37.
Etablissements sous contrôle étranger majoritaire. La CITI 23/25 exclut les *Produits pétroliers raffinés* (232), qui sont compris dans la CITI 36/37.

Table 4A - Tableau 4A

VALUE ADDED / VALEUR AJOUTÉE

By industry (ISIC Rev. 3)	Foreign affiliates *(Millions of IEP)* Filiales étrangères *(Millions de IEP)*					As a % of national total En % du total national				
	1994	1995	1996	1997	1998	1994	1995	1996	1997	1998
10/14 Mining & quarrying	..	..	..	..	..	..	..	..	..	..
15/37 TOTAL MANUFACTURING	**9 818**	**12 490**	**13 975**	**16 793**	**21 712**	**73.7**	**76.9**	**77.1**	**79.2**	**81.9**
15/16 Food, beverages, tobacco	2 269	2 484	2 654	2 823	2 965	65.0	65.6	65.5	67.2	66.2
17/19 Textiles, clothing, leather, footwear	199	189	187	152	196	52.4	50.4	51.1	42.9	51.3
20/22 Wood and paper products	1 260	1 649	2 137	2 547	3 276	66.4	71.8	75.6	76.2	79.0
20 Wood products	33	36	33	56	66	30.6	31.0	26.2	34.6	38.2
21/22 Paper, printing and publishing	1 227	1 613	2 104	2 491	3 209	68.5	73.9	78.0	78.3	80.7
23/25 Chemicals, Total	3 268	3 881	4 459	6 042	9 469	91.4	92.3	91.5	93.8	95.7
23 Refined petroleum, nuclear fuel	..	..	..	..	..	..	..	..	..	..
24/25 Chemicals, rubber & plastics prod.	3 268	3 881	4 459	6 042	9 469	91.4	92.3	91.5	93.8	95.7
24 Chemical products	3 068	3 666	4 258	5 841	9 249	94.3	95.0	94.5	96.3	97.5
2423 Pharmaceuticals	685	849	871	1 016	1 377	95.4	95.9	95.1	94.6	95.1
25 Rubber and plastics products	199	215	201	201	219	61.6	61.8	55.1	53.5	53.8
26 Non-metallic mineral products	42	56	57	64	84	11.1	13.8	13.5	13.3	16.8
27/28 Basic & fabricated metals	134	146	145	183	228	38.6	37.6	34.1	37.8	40.6
27 Basic metals	..	..	..	..	..	..	..	..	..	..
28 Fabricated metal products	..	..	..	..	..	..	..	..	..	..
29/32 Machinery, Total	1 827	3 231	3 387	3 918	4 346	86.0	91.1	89.5	89.6	89.4
29/30 Non-electrical machinery	1 243	2 465	2 410	2 247	2 783	85.3	91.9	89.8	88.1	89.1
29 Non-electrical machinery nec	295	354	331	319	323	64.6	68.3	61.6	58.3	57.1
30 Office and computing machinery	948	2 111	2 079	1 928	2 461	94.7	97.6	96.9	96.3	96.3
31/32 Electrical & electronic equipment	583	766	977	1 672	1 563	87.4	88.6	88.7	91.7	89.8
31 Electrical machinery nec	290	448	532	563	544	81.7	85.6	86.5	84.4	82.7
32 Radio, TV & communications eq.	293	318	446	1 109	1 018	93.9	93.2	91.4	95.8	93.9
33 Scientific instruments	532	578	655	697	774	93.0	93.5	90.8	89.9	89.7
34/35 Transportation equipment	88	93	82	148	172	41.7	37.4	31.7	51.6	53.3
34 Motor vehicles	59	62	51	..	..	61.5	53.1	48.6	..	..
35 Other transport equipment	29	32	31	..	..	25.2	23.8	20.0	..	..
351 Shipbuilding & repairing	..	..	..	..	..	..	..	..	..	..
353 Aircraft and spacecraft	..	..	..	..	..	..	..	..	..	..
36/37 Other manufacturing	199	184	212	219	202	57.8	50.4	52.2	46.8	41.3
40/45 Construction, electricity, gas & water	..	..	..	..	..	..	..	..	..	..
50/55 Trade, repair, hotels & restaurants	..	..	..	..	..	..	..	..	..	..
65/74 Finance, insurance, business services	..	..	..	..	..	..	..	..	..	..
OTHER ACTIVITIES	..	..	..	..	..	..	..	..	..	..
01/99 GRAND TOTAL	..	..	..	..	..	..	..	..	..	..

Total manufacturing by investing country						As a % of total manufacturing by foreign affiliates				
All countries	**9 818**	**12 490**	**13 975**	**16 793**	**21 712**	**100.0**	**100.0**	**100.0**	**100.0**	**100.0**
United States	6 294	8 615	9 636	11 625	17 062	64.1	69.0	69.0	69.2	78.6
Canada	186	245	359	344	268	1.9	2.0	2.6	2.0	1.2
Mexico	..	..	..	..	..	..	..	..	..	..
Japan	243	306	230	237	265	2.5	2.4	1.6	1.4	1.2
Europe	..	..	..	..	..	..	..	..	..	..
European Union (15)	2 176	2 264	2 422	2 774	2 959	22.2	18.1	17.3	16.5	13.6
Belgium	46	63	54	51	38	0.5	0.5	0.4	0.3	0.2
France	310	301	336	356	388	3.2	2.4	2.4	2.1	1.8
Germany	392	453	383	414	451	4.0	3.6	2.7	2.5	2.1
Italy	..	..	..	..	..	..	..	..	..	..
Netherlands	310	247	368	451	487	3.2	2.0	2.6	2.7	2.2
Spain	..	..	..	..	..	..	..	..	..	..
Sweden	56	52	57	42	36	0.6	0.4	0.4	0.3	0.2
United Kingdom	1 003	992	1 074	1 270	1 343	10.2	7.9	7.7	7.6	6.2
Switzerland	692	834	1 149	1 593	937	7.0	6.7	8.2	9.5	4.3
Australia and New Zealand	..	..	..	..	..	..	..	..	..	..
Asia (non-OECD)	..	..	..	..	..	..	..	..	..	..
Latin America	..	..	..	..	..	..	..	..	..	..

Note: Majority foreign-owned establishments. ISIC 23/25 excludes *Refined petroleum products* (232) which is included in ISIC 36/37.
Etablissements sous contrôle étranger majoritaire. La CITI 23/25 exclut les *Produits pétroliers raffinés* (232), qui sont compris dans la CITI 36/37.

Inward investments

Investissements entrants

Table 5A - Tableau 5A

COMPENSATION OF EMPLOYEES / SALAIRES ET CHARGES SOCIALES

By industry (ISIC Rev. 3)	Foreign affiliates *(Millions of IEP)* Filiales étrangères *(Millions de IEP)*					As a % of national total En % du total national				
	1994	1995	1996	1997	1998	1994	1995	1996	1997	1998
10/14 Mining & quarrying	..	..	..	..	..	..	..	..	..	..
15/37 TOTAL MANUFACTURING	**1 590**	**1 757**	**1 868**	**2 091**	**2 282**	**52.1**	**52.6**	**52.0**	**53.3**	**53.7**
15/16 Food, beverages, tobacco	265	275	279	277	272	39.0	38.2	37.2	36.6	34.8
17/19 Textiles, clothing, leather, footwear	110	110	101	86	78	52.1	51.3	49.5	43.7	42.2
20/22 Wood and paper products	87	110	124	150	153	22.9	26.7	28.1	30.0	28.8
20 Wood products	10	11	11	17	22	22.7	21.5	20.4	26.2	31.0
21/22 Paper, printing and publishing	77	99	113	133	131	22.9	27.4	29.1	30.6	28.5
23/25 Chemicals, Total	351	386	413	444	489	75.5	75.9	74.7	73.5	74.7
23 Refined petroleum, nuclear fuel	..	..	..	..	..	..	..	..	..	..
24/25 Chemicals, rubber & plastics prod.	351	386	413	444	489	75.5	75.9	74.7	73.5	74.7
24 Chemical products	276	304	328	366	408	81.4	82.4	82.0	81.2	82.9
2423 Pharmaceuticals	86	97	106	113	128	86.9	87.4	86.9	84.3	83.7
25 Rubber and plastics products	75	82	84	78	81	59.5	58.7	54.9	51.3	49.7
26 Non-metallic mineral products	17	25	27	29	35	11.3	16.5	16.6	16.3	18.1
27/28 Basic & fabricated metals	57	59	62	73	79	33.7	33.2	31.3	34.0	33.5
27 Basic metals	..	..	..	..	..	..	..	..	..	..
28 Fabricated metal products	..	..	..	..	..	..	..	..	..	..
29/32 Machinery, Total	464	545	594	701	807	76.3	77.1	76.2	76.4	76.8
29/30 Non-electrical machinery	267	308	343	331	384	73.2	73.8	73.8	69.7	70.6
29 Non-electrical machinery nec	115	123	121	123	116	60.5	59.7	55.8	53.9	50.7
30 Office and computing machinery	152	185	221	209	267	86.9	87.6	89.1	84.3	84.5
31/32 Electrical & electronic equipment	197	237	251	370	423	81.1	81.8	79.7	83.5	83.4
31 Electrical machinery nec	103	137	137	149	175	74.1	76.9	77.0	73.4	75.1
32 Radio, TV & communications eq.	94	100	114	220	248	90.4	89.7	83.2	92.1	90.5
33 Scientific instruments	141	155	169	204	231	91.0	90.2	88.0	88.7	86.8
34/35 Transportation equipment	41	34	40	63	66	34.7	22.3	23.3	37.5	37.7
34 Motor vehicles	20	21	26	..	..	42.6	35.7	40.0	..	..
35 Other transport equipment	21	12	14	..	..	29.6	13.6	13.0	..	..
351 Shipbuilding & repairing	..	..	..	..	..	..	..	..	..	..
353 Aircraft and spacecraft	..	..	..	..	..	..	..	..	..	..
36/37 Other manufacturing	57	59	59	64	72	48.3	47.1	43.1	40.3	40.0
40/45 Construction, electricity, gas & water	..	..	..	..	..	..	..	..	..	..
50/55 Trade, repair, hotels & restaurants	..	..	..	..	..	..	..	..	..	..
65/74 Finance, insurance, business services	..	..	..	..	..	..	..	..	..	..
OTHER ACTIVITIES	..	..	..	..	..	..	..	..	..	..
01/99 GRAND TOTAL	..	..	..	..	..	..	..	..	..	..

Total manufacturing by investing country						As a % of total manufacturing by foreign affiliates				
All countries	**1 590**	**1 757**	**1 868**	**2 091**	**2 282**	**100.0**	**100.0**	**100.0**	**100.0**	**100.0**
United States	791	906	946	1 104	1 304	49.7	51.6	50.6	52.8	57.2
Canada	37	40	46	51	58	2.3	2.3	2.5	2.4	2.6
Mexico	..	..	..	..	..	..	..	..	..	..
Japan	46	63	65	70	74	2.9	3.6	3.5	3.3	3.2
Europe	..	..	..	..	..	..	..	..	..	..
European Union (15)	566	610	658	692	700	35.6	34.8	35.2	33.1	30.7
Belgium	16	21	21	18	15	1.0	1.2	1.1	0.9	0.7
France	69	73	79	83	85	4.3	4.2	4.2	4.0	3.7
Germany	158	167	168	178	180	9.9	9.5	9.0	8.5	7.9
Italy	..	..	..	..	..	..	..	..	..	..
Netherlands	56	53	80	93	96	3.5	3.0	4.3	4.4	4.2
Spain	..	..	..	..	..	..	..	..	..	..
Sweden	20	20	21	16	13	1.3	1.1	1.1	0.8	0.6
United Kingdom	233	230	242	242	246	14.7	13.1	13.0	11.6	10.8
Switzerland	68	82	92	94	78	4.3	4.7	4.9	4.5	3.4
Australia and New Zealand	..	..	..	..	..	..	..	..	..	..
Asia (non-OECD)	..	..	..	..	..	..	..	..	..	..
Latin America	..	..	..	..	..	..	..	..	..	..

Note: Majority foreign-owned establishments. ISIC 23/25 excludes *Refined petroleum products* (232) which is included in ISIC 36/37.
Etablissements sous contrôle étranger majoritaire. La CITI 23/25 exclut les *Produits pétroliers raffinés* (232), qui sont compris dans la CITI 36/37.

Inward investments   *Investissements entrants*

Table 6A - Tableau 6A

R&D EXPENDITURE BY INDUSTRY

DÉPENSES DE R-D PAR INDUSTRIE

| | | Foreign affiliates *(Millions of IEP)* | | | | | As a % of national total | | | | |
| | | Filiales étrangères *(Millions de IEP)* | | | | | En % du total national | | | | |
ISIC Revision 3		1995	1996	1997	1998	1999	1995	1996	1997	1998	1999
10/14	Mining & quarrying	0.7	..	0.8	..	..	90.2	..	65.3	..	..
15/37	**TOTAL MANUFACTURING**	**201.5**	**..**	**273.0**	**..**	**..**	**63.0**	**..**	**64.8**	**..**	**..**
15/16	Food, beverages, tobacco	12.4	..	17.3	..	..	23.4	..	27.4	..	..
17/19	Textiles, clothing, leather, footwear	5.2	..	3.9	..	..	40.1	..	30.1	..	..
20/22	Wood and paper products	1.6	..	3.7	..	..	19.2	..	29.8	..	..
20	Wood products	0.2	..	2.3	..	..	10.9	..	40.9	..	..
21/22	Paper, printing and publishing	1.3	..	1.5	..	..	21.9	..	20.9	..	..
23/25	Chemicals, Total	68.2	..	82.5	..	..	86.8	..	85.0	..	..
23	Refined petroleum, nuclear fuel	0.0	..	0.0	..	..	0.0	..	..	..	..
24/25	Chemicals, rubber & plastics prod.	68.2	..	82.5	..	..	87.1	..	85.0	..	..
24	Chemical products	65.1	..	79.3	..	..	93.1	..	91.6	..	..
2423	Pharmaceuticals	51.7	..	66.4	..	..	97.0	..	96.0	..	..
25	Rubber and plastics products	3.0	..	3.2	..	..	36.4	..	30.6	..	..
26	Non-metallic mineral products	1.3	..	1.9	..	..	18.9	..	20.2	..	..
27/28	Basic & fabricated metals	2.6	..	7.1	..	..	22.4	..	41.0	..	..
27	Basic metals	0.0	..	0.0	..	..	0.0	..	0.0	..	..
28	Fabricated metal products	2.6	..	7.1	..	..	22.9	..	41.6	..	..
29/32	Machinery, Total	81.0	..	123.6	..	..	75.2	..	76.5	..	..
29/30	Non-electrical machinery	20.1	..	33.0	..	..	58.9	..	62.9	..	..
29	Non-electrical machinery nec	7.0	..	8.5	..	..	42.7	..	44.7	..	..
30	Office and computing machinery	13.1	..	24.5	..	..	73.7	..	73.2	..	..
31/32	Electrical & electronic equipment	61.0	..	90.6	..	..	82.7	..	83.0	..	..
31	Electrical machinery nec	26.4	..	31.4	..	..	76.8	..	74.8	..	..
32	Radio, TV & communications eq.	34.6	..	59.2	..	..	87.8	..	88.2	..	..
33	Scientific instruments	21.3	..	23.6	..	..	84.9	..	83.9	..	..
34/35	Transportation equipment	6.5	..	7.3	..	..	77.1	..	74.4	..	..
34	Motor vehicles	6.3	..	6.1	..	..	78.3	..	76.0	..	..
35	Other transport equipment	0.2	..	1.2	..	..	54.8	..	67.0	..	..
351	Shipbuilding & repairing	..	..	..	..	..	..	..	..	..	..
353	Aircraft and spacecraft	..	..	..	..	..	..	..	..	..	..
36/37	Other manufacturing	0.2	..	0.9	..	..	5.4	..	16.7	..	..
40/45	Construction, electricity, gas & water	0.0	..	0.0	..	..	0.0	..	0.0	..	..
50/55	Trade, repair, hotels & restaurants	0.0	..	0.0	..	..	0.0	..	0.0	..	..
65/74	Finance, insurance, business services	52.6	..	76.1	..	..	76.2	..	73.0	..	..
	OTHER ACTIVITIES	1.3	..	1.3	..	..	38.3	..	18.5	..	..
01/99	**GRAND TOTAL**	**254.9**	**..**	**349.9**	**..**	**..**	**64.6**	**..**	**65.6**	**..**	**..**

Note: Majority foreign-owned firms.
Firmes sous contrôle étranger majoritaire.

Table 7A - Tableau 7A

R&D EXPENDITURE BY COUNTRY OF ORIGIN IN THE MANUFACTURING SECTOR

DÉPENSES DE R-D PAR PAYS D'ORIGINE DANS L'INDUSTRIE MANUFACTURIÈRE

Country of origin (immediate controller)	R&D expenditure (Millions of IEP) Dépenses de R-D (Millions de IEP)					As a % of all countries En % du total des pays				
	1995	1996	1997	1998	1999	1995	1996	1997	1998	1999
All countries	201.5	..	273.0	..	..	100.0	..	100.0	..	..
Total OECD	157.9	..	215.4	..	..	78.3	..	78.9	..	..
United States	141.0	..	197.2	..	..	69.9	..	72.2	..	..
Canada	9.3	..	9.6	..	..	4.6	..	3.5	..	..
Mexico	0.0	..	0.0	..	..	0.0	..	0.0	..	..
Japan	3.2	..	3.9	..	..	1.6	..	1.4	..	..
Korea	0.1	..	0.1	..	..	0.0	..	0.0	..	..
Australia	0.2	..	0.4	..	..	0.1	..	0.2	..	..
New Zealand	0.0	..	0.0	..	..	0.0	..	0.0	..	..
Europe	47.7	..	61.7	..	..	23.7	..	22.6	..	..
European Union (15)	43.7	..	57.5	..	..	21.7	..	21.1	..	..
Austria	0.4	..	0.4	..	..	0.2	..	0.1	..	..
Belgium	0.9	..	0.7	..	..	0.4	..	0.3	..	..
Denmark	0.3	..	0.3	..	..	0.1	..	0.1	..	..
Finland	1.4	..	1.5	..	..	0.7	..	0.5	..	..
France	3.2	..	3.2	..	..	1.6	..	1.2	..	..
Germany	12.8	..	18.2	..	..	6.4	..	6.6	..	..
Greece	0.0	..	0.0	..	..	0.0	..	0.0	..	..
Ireland	..	..	..	..	..	..	..	..	..	..
Italy	0.3	..	0.2	..	..	0.1	..	0.1	..	..
Luxembourg	..	..	..	..	..	..	..	..	..	..
Netherlands	3.9	..	4.1	..	..	1.9	..	1.5	..	..
Portugal	0.0	..	0.0	..	..	0.0	..	0.0	..	..
Spain	0.0	..	1.5	..	..	0.0	..	0.5	..	..
Sweden	2.4	..	3.0	..	..	1.2	..	1.1	..	..
United Kingdom	18.1	..	24.5	..	..	9.0	..	9.0	..	..
Czech Republic	0.0	..	0.0	..	..	0.0	..	0.0	..	..
Hungary	0.0	..	0.0	..	..	0.0	..	0.0	..	..
Iceland	0.0	..	0.0	..	..	0.0	..	0.0	..	..
Norway	0.3	..	0.2	..	..	0.1	..	0.1	..	..
Poland	0.0	..	0.0	..	..	0.0	..	0.0	..	..
Slovak Republic	0.0	..	0.0	..	..	0.0	..	0.0	..	..
Switzerland	3.9	..	4.0	..	..	1.9	..	1.5	..	..
Turkey	0.0	..	0.0	..	..	0.0	..	0.0	..	..
Non-OECD Europe, of which:	0.0	..	0.0	..	..	0.0	..	0.0	..	..
Baltic countries	0.0	..	0.0	..	..	0.0	..	0.0	..	..
Bulgaria	0.0	..	0.0	..	..	0.0	..	0.0	..	..
Croatia	0.0	..	0.0	..	..	0.0	..	0.0	..	..
Romania	0.0	..	0.0	..	..	0.0	..	0.0	..	..
Russian Federation	0.0	..	0.0	..	..	0.0	..	0.0	..	..
Slovenia	0.0	..	0.0	..	..	0.0	..	0.0	..	..
Ukraine	0.0	..	0.0	..	..	0.0	..	0.0	..	..
Yugoslavia	0.0	..	0.0	..	..	0.0	..	0.0	..	..
Non-OECD Asia, of which:	0.0	..	0.0	..	..	0.0	..	0.0	..	..
China	0.0	..	0.0	..	..	0.0	..	0.0	..	..
Chinese Taipei	0.0	..	0.0	..	..	0.0	..	0.0	..	..
Hong Kong (China)	0.0	..	0.0	..	..	0.0	..	0.0	..	..
India	0.0	..	0.0	..	..	0.0	..	0.0	..	..
Indonesia	0.0	..	0.0	..	..	0.0	..	0.0	..	..
Malaysia	0.0	..	0.0	..	..	0.0	..	0.0	..	..
Philippines	0.0	..	0.0	..	..	0.0	..	0.0	..	..
Singapore	0.0	..	0.0	..	..	0.0	..	0.0	..	..
Thailand	0.0	..	0.0	..	..	0.0	..	0.0	..	..
Near and Middle East	0.0	..	0.0	..	..	0.0	..	0.0	..	..
Africa	0.0	..	0.0	..	..	0.0	..	0.0	..	..
Latin America, of which:	0.1	..	0.1	..	..	0.0	..	0.0	..	..
Argentina	0.0	..	0.0	..	..	0.0	..	0.0	..	..
Brazil	0.0	..	0.0	..	..	0.0	..	0.0	..	..
Chile	0.0	..	0.0	..	..	0.0	..	0.0	..	..

Note: Majority foreign-owned firms.
Firmes sous contrôle étranger majoritaire.

Inward investments   *Investissements entrants*

Table 8A - Tableau 8A
TOTAL EXPORTS / EXPORTATIONS TOTALES

| | | Foreign affiliates *(Millions of IEP)* | | | | As a % of national total | | | | |
| | | Filiales étrangères *(Millions de IEP)* | | | | En % du total national | | | | |
By industry (ISIC Rev. 3)		1994	1995	1996	1997	1998	1994	1995	1996	1997	1998
10/14	Mining & quarrying	..	..	..	..	..	..	..	..	..	..
15/37	**TOTAL MANUFACTURING**	14 969	19 478	21 531	25 786	32 168	80.0	82.3	83.9	85.5	87.6
15/16	Food, beverages, tobacco	2 062	2 442	2 565	2 717	2 799	47.8	48.9	53.8	53.5	54.5
17/19	Textiles, clothing, leather, footwear	401	401	381	329	..	72.9	71.2	71.1	63.9	..
20/22	Wood and paper products	1 545	1 892	2 415	..	3 583	87.8	90.9	92.3	..	94.3
20	Wood products	50	64	63	..	113	62.5	64.6	58.9	..	76.4
21/22	Paper, printing and publishing	1 495	1 828	2 352	..	3 470	89.0	92.2	93.7	..	95.0
23/25	Chemicals, Total	4 284	5 118	5 865	..	11 357	95.3	95.3	94.7	..	97.2
23	Refined petroleum, nuclear fuel	..	..	..	..	..	..	..	..	..	..
24/25	Chemicals, rubber & plastics prod.	4 284	5 118	5 865	..	11 357	95.3	95.3	94.7	..	97.2
24	Chemical products	3 993	4 781	5 545	7 177	11 033	96.9	96.9	96.5	97.8	98.3
2423	Pharmaceuticals	..	..	..	..	..	..	..	..	..	..
25	Rubber and plastics products	291	337	320	..	324	78.0	77.1	71.9	..	70.6
26	Non-metallic mineral products	56	82	82	89	93	33.5	45.3	39.4	38.9	44.7
27/28	Basic & fabricated metals	336	347	368	433	499	66.0	62.4	62.2	69.2	71.8
27	Basic metals	..	..	..	..	..	..	..	..	..	..
28	Fabricated metal products	..	..	..	..	..	..	..	..	..	..
29/32	Machinery, Total	5 797	8 667	9 303	11 134	..	94.4	95.8	95.1	94.7	..
29/30	Non-electrical machinery	..	..	..	..	..	..	..	..	..	..
29	Non-electrical machinery nec	556	678	619	616	640	79.9	82.5	75.0	73.8	74.3
30	Office and computing machinery	..	..	..	..	..	..	..	..	..	..
31/32	Electrical & electronic equipment	..	..	..	..	..	..	..	..	..	..
31	Electrical machinery nec	..	..	..	..	..	..	..	..	..	..
32	Radio, TV & communications eq.	..	..	..	..	..	..	..	..	..	..
33	Scientific instruments	..	..	..	..	..	..	..	..	..	..
34/35	Transportation equipment	178	197	202	363	..	64.7	58.6	51.7	78.6	..
34	Motor vehicles	..	..	..	..	..	..	..	..	..	..
35	Other transport equipment	..	..	..	..	..	..	..	..	..	..
351	Shipbuilding & repairing	..	..	..	..	..	..	..	..	..	..
353	Aircraft and spacecraft	..	..	..	..	..	..	..	..	..	..
36/37	Other manufacturing	310	332	350	..	..	61.0	60.6	60.8	..	..
40/45	Construction, electricity, gas & water	..	..	..	..	..	..	..	..	..	..
50/55	Trade, repair, hotels & restaurants	..	..	..	..	..	..	..	..	..	..
65/74	Finance, insurance, business services	..	..	..	..	..	..	..	..	..	..
	OTHER ACTIVITIES	..	..	..	..	..	..	..	..	..	..
01/99	**GRAND TOTAL**	..	..	..	..	..	..	..	..	..	..

Total manufacturing by investing country						As a % of total manufacturing by foreign affiliates				
All countries	14 969	19 478	21 531	25 786	32 168	100.0	100.0	100.0	100.0	100.0
United States	10 075	13 873	15 067	18 396	25 321	67.3	71.2	70.0	71.3	78.7
Canada	..	..	..	1 273	744	..	..	..	4.9	2.3
Mexico	..	..	..	..	..	..	..	..	..	..
Japan	..	..	..	607	..	..	..	..	2.4	..
Europe	..	..	..	..	..	..	..	..	..	..
European Union (15)	2 610	2 929	3 359	3 733	3 815	17.4	15.0	15.6	14.5	11.9
Belgium	..	..	..	43	32	..	..	..	0.2	0.1
France	430	448	479	523	603	2.9	2.3	2.2	2.0	1.9
Germany	711	842	798	851	916	4.7	4.3	3.7	3.3	2.8
Italy	..	..	..	..	..	..	..	..	..	..
Netherlands	537	..	..	798	773	3.6	..	..	3.1	2.4
Spain	..	..	..	..	..	..	..	..	..	..
Sweden	90	81	89	67	51	0.6	0.4	0.4	0.3	0.2
United Kingdom	726	879	1 048	1 178	1 142	4.9	4.5	4.9	4.6	3.6
Switzerland	892	1 005	1 290	1 776	1 051	6.0	5.2	6.0	6.9	3.3
Australia and New Zealand	..	..	..	..	..	..	..	..	..	..
Asia (non-OECD)	..	..	..	..	..	..	..	..	..	..
Latin America	..	..	..	..	..	..	..	..	..	..

Note: Majority foreign-owned establishments. ISIC 29/32 includes *Scientific instruments* (33). ISIC 36/37 includes *Leather and footwear* (19) and *Refined petroleum products* (232).
Etablissements sous contrôle étranger majoritaire. La CITI 29/32 comprend *Instruments* (33). La CITI 36/37 comprend *Cuir et chaussures* (19) et *Produits pétroliers raffinés* (232).

Inward investments　　　　　　　　　　　　　　　　　　　　*Investissements entrants*

Table 9A - Tableau 9A
TOTAL IMPORTS / IMPORTATIONS TOTALES

		Foreign affiliates *(Millions of IEP)* Filiales étrangères *(Millions de IEP)*					As a % of national total En % du total national				
By industry (ISIC Rev. 3)		1994	1995	1996	1997	1998	1994	1995	1996	1997	1998
10/14	Mining & quarrying	..	..	..	..	..	..	..	..	..	..
15/37	**TOTAL MANUFACTURING**	**4 299**	**5 683**	**5 622**	**6 343**	**6 960**	**74.1**	**77.8**	**75.4**	**76.0**	**76.3**
15/16	Food, beverages, tobacco	343	343	342	363	379	47.2	47.4	47.3	47.5	47.7
17/19	Textiles, clothing, leather, footwear	154	166	162	147	..	55.6	55.7	54.5	51.0	..
20/22	Wood and paper products	136	128	172	..	153	38.4	35.5	42.2	..	37.7
20	Wood products	20	20	27	..	28	38.5	39.2	40.9	..	35.9
21/22	Paper, printing and publishing	116	108	145	..	126	38.3	34.8	42.4	..	38.4
23/25	Chemicals, Total	841	1 062	1 140	..	1 636	77.4	80.0	78.2	..	84.5
23	Refined petroleum, nuclear fuel	..	..	..	..	..	..	..	..	..	..
24/25	Chemicals, rubber & plastics prod.	841	1 062	1 140	..	1 636	77.4	80.0	78.2	..	84.5
24	Chemical products	723	908	1 002	1 229	1 481	81.1	84.2	83.3	86.6	89.5
2423	Pharmaceuticals	..	..	..	..	..	..	..	..	..	..
25	Rubber and plastics products	118	154	138	..	155	60.8	61.4	54.5	..	55.0
26	Non-metallic mineral products	16	36	40	44	53	22.2	37.1	36.7	37.0	40.8
27/28	Basic & fabricated metals	136	138	126	141	159	53.8	48.3	43.0	45.8	48.8
27	Basic metals	..	..	..	..	..	..	..	..	..	..
28	Fabricated metal products	..	..	..	..	..	..	..	..	..	..
29/32	Machinery, Total	2 511	3 611	3 428	3 828	..	92.7	94.1	92.0	89.2	..
29/30	Non-electrical machinery	..	..	..	..	..	..	..	..	..	..
29	Non-electrical machinery nec	202	253	235	232	242	74.0	76.7	69.1	68.2	66.7
30	Office and computing machinery	..	..	..	..	..	..	..	..	..	..
31/32	Electrical & electronic equipment	..	..	..	..	..	..	..	..	..	..
31	Electrical machinery nec	..	..	..	..	..	..	..	..	..	..
32	Radio, TV & communications eq.	..	..	..	..	..	..	..	..	..	..
33	Scientific instruments	..	..	..	..	..	..	..	..	..	..
34/35	Transportation equipment	83	92	110	195	..	51.2	52.0	51.6	76.5	..
34	Motor vehicles	..	..	..	..	..	..	..	..	..	..
35	Other transport equipment	..	..	..	..	..	..	..	..	..	..
351	Shipbuilding & repairing	..	..	..	..	..	..	..	..	..	..
353	Aircraft and spacecraft	..	..	..	..	..	..	..	..	..	..
36/37	Other manufacturing	79	107	102	..	..	49.4	52.5	44.7	..	..
40/45	Construction, electricity, gas & water	..	..	..	..	..	..	..	..	..	..
50/55	Trade, repair, hotels & restaurants	..	..	..	..	..	..	..	..	..	..
65/74	Finance, insurance, business services	..	..	..	..	..	..	..	..	..	..
	OTHER ACTIVITIES	..	..	..	..	..	..	..	..	..	..
01/99	**GRAND TOTAL**	..	..	..	..	..	..	..	..	..	..

Total manufacturing by investing country						As a % of total manufacturing by foreign affiliates				
All countries	**4 299**	**5 683**	**5 622**	**6 343**	**6 960**	**100.0**	**100.0**	**100.0**	**100.0**	**100.0**
United States	2 354	3 407	3 090	3 696	4 230	54.8	60.0	55.0	58.3	60.8
Canada	..	..	..	873	320	..	..	..	13.8	4.6
Mexico	..	..	..	..	..	..	..	..	..	..
Japan	..	..	..	91	..	..	..	..	1.4	..
Europe	..	..	..	..	..	..	..	..	..	..
European Union (15)	1 054	1 154	1 377	1 518	1 537	24.5	20.3	24.5	23.9	22.1
Belgium	..	..	..	54	45	..	..	..	0.9	0.6
France	148	186	173	193	251	3.4	3.3	3.1	3.0	3.6
Germany	285	346	347	404	419	6.6	6.1	6.2	6.4	6.0
Italy	..	..	..	..	..	..	..	..	..	..
Netherlands	245	..	..	330	299	5.7	..	..	5.2	4.3
Spain	..	..	..	..	..	..	..	..	..	..
Sweden	40	43	45	35	26	0.9	0.8	0.8	0.6	0.4
United Kingdom	267	297	413	390	388	6.2	5.2	7.3	6.1	5.6
Switzerland	162	159	156	177	98	3.8	2.8	2.8	2.8	1.4
Australia and New Zealand	..	..	..	..	..	..	..	..	..	..
Asia (non-OECD)	..	..	..	..	..	..	..	..	..	..
Latin America	..	..	..	..	..	..	..	..	..	..

Note: Majority foreign-owned establishments. ISIC 29/32 includes *Scientific instruments* (33). ISIC 36/37 includes *Leather and footwear* (19) and *Refined petroleum products* (232).
Etablissements sous contrôle étranger majoritaire. La CITI 29/32 comprend *Instruments* (33). La CITI 36/37 comprend *Cuir et chaussures* (19) et *Produits pétroliers raffinés* (232).

IRELAND

Source

The data are prepared by the Irish Central Statistics Office (CSO) for all variables except *R&D expenditure*. The CSO conducts an annual survey on industrial production which covers separately companies which employ at least three persons and where 50% or more of the share capital is held by non-Irish residents. The *local unit* is the basic unit used in this survey. The data are published in *Census of Industrial Production*.

R&D data come from the biennial R&D survey conducted by the Policy and Advisory Board for Industrial Development (FORFAS). The *enterprise* is the basic unit used in this survey.

National totals: provided by CSO and FORFAS and fully compatible with foreign affiliates' data.

Industrial classification

The data are classified according to the principal industrial activity of the affiliate.

The industrial classification is NACE Revision 1.

For all variables except *R&D expenditure,* data are available only for manufacturing industries, and *Chemicals, Total* (23/25) excludes *Refined petroleum products* (232), which is included in *Other manufacturing* (36/37).

For *Total exports* and *imports, Other manufacturing* (36/37) includes *Leather and footwear* (19) and *Machinery and equipment, total* (29/32) includes *Scientific instruments* (33).

Variables

- *Number of establishments* refers to the number of local units. A local unit is defined as an enterprise or part thereof situated in a geographically identified place. The number includes all the separate industrial local units of multi-location enterprises.

- *Number of employees* consists of the total number of persons who are paid a fixed wage or salary (including part-time workers). Outside piece-workers are excluded.

- *Production* (gross output) represents the net selling value of all goods manufactured in the year, whether sold or not, including work done. From 1991, the value of capital work done on own account is included. Operating subsidies related to the production or sales of output are included in the value of gross output; excise duty and VAT are excluded.

- *Value added* is defined as net output, *i.e.* as the difference between gross output and industrial input. Industrial input consists of the industrial materials, industrial services, fuel and power used in the production of the output. Valuation is exclusive of deductible VAT.

- *Compensation of employees* is defined as the gross amount paid to employees before deduction of income tax, employees' contributions to social security, etc. Payments to outside piece-workers are included.

- *Total exports* represents the value of output which was exported.

- *Total imports* is defined as the value of purchased materials which were imported.

Geographical breakdown

For all variables except *R&D expenditure*, the investor's country is that of the "ultimate beneficial owner". Prior to 1995, the European Union totals include only the former 12 member states.

For *R&D expenditure*, the country of origin is the country of the immediate controller.

IRLANDE

Source

Les données sont fournies par l'Office central des statistiques d'Irlande (CSO) pour toutes les variables, sauf les *Dépenses de R-D*. Le CSO mène une enquête annuelle sur la production industrielle qui distingue les sociétés employant au moins trois personnes et où 50 % ou plus du capital est détenu par des résidents non irlandais. L'unité de base utilisée dans cette enquête est l'*unité locale*. Les données sont publiées dans *Census of Industrial Production*.

Les données de R-D proviennent de l'enquête biennale sur la R-D menée par le Conseil politique et consultatif pour le développement industriel (FORFAS). Dans cette enquête, l'*entreprise* est l'unité de base.

Totaux nationaux : fournis par le CSO et FORFAS et entièrement compatibles avec les données relatives aux filiales étrangères.

Classification industrielle

Les données sont classées selon l'activité industrielle principale de l'entreprise affiliée.

La classification industrielle est la NACE révision 1.

Pour toutes les variables à l'exception des *Dépenses de R-D*, seules les données de l'industrie manufacturière sont disponibles, et *Produits chimiques, total* (23/25) exclut *Produits pétroliers raffinés* (232), qui est compris dans *Autres industries manufacturières* (36/37).

Pour les *Exportations* et *Importations totales*, *Autres industries manufacturières* (36/37) comprend *Cuir et chaussures* (19) et *Machines et matériel, total* (29/32) comprend les *Instruments scientifiques* (33).

Variables

- Le *Nombre d'établissements* correspond au nombre d'unités locales. L'unité locale est définie comme une entreprise ou une partie d'entreprise située à un endroit géographiquement déterminé. Les établissements dénombrés comprennent toutes les unités locales distinctes des entreprises implantées sur plusieurs sites de production.

- Le *Nombre de salariés* correspond à l'ensemble des personnes qui reçoivent un salaire ou un traitement fixe (y compris les employés à temps partiel). Les travailleurs extérieurs rémunérés à la pièce ne sont pas pris en compte.

- La *Production* (production brute) représente la valeur marchande nette de tous les biens fabriqués au cours de l'année, qu'ils soient ou non vendus, et la valeur du travail exécuté. Depuis 1991, la valeur des travaux d'équipement effectués pour compte propre est incluse. Les subventions d'exploitation relatives à la production ou à la vente de la production sont comprises dans la valeur de la production brute ; les droits prélevés par la régie et la TVA en sont exclus.

- La *Valeur ajoutée* se définit en tant que production nette, c'est-à-dire comme différence entre la production brute et la consommation intermédiaire de l'industrie. Celle-ci comprend les matériaux industriels, les services industriels ainsi que le combustible et l'énergie utilisés dans la production. L'évaluation ne tient pas compte de la TVA déductible.

- Les *Salaires* sont définis comme le montant brut payé aux employés avant déduction des impôts sur le revenu, des cotisation de sécurité sociale dues par les salariés, etc.. La rémunération des travailleurs à domicile est comprise.

- Les *Exportations totales* représentent la valeur de la production qui est exportée.

- Les *Importations totales* sont définies comme la valeur des matériaux qui sont importés.

Ventilation géographique

Pour toutes les variables à l'exception des *Dépenses de R-D*, le pays de l'investisseur est le pays du "bénéficiaire ultime de l'investissement". Avant 1995, les données de l'Union européenne ne comprennent que les 12 anciens États membres.

Pour les *Dépenses de R-D*, le pays d'origine est celui du contrôleur immédiat.

ITALY

A. Inward investments

B. Outward investments

Sources and Methods

ITALIE

A. Investissements entrants

Tableau 1A.   Nombre d'entreprises
Tableau 2A.   Nombre de salariés par industrie
Tableau 3A.   Nombre de salariés par pays d'origine dans l'industrie manufacturière
Tableau 4A.   Chiffre d'affaires par industrie
Tableau 5A.   Chiffre d'affaires par pays d'origine dans l'industrie manufacturière

B. Investissements sortants

Tableau 1B.   Nombre d'entreprises
Tableau 2B.   Nombre de salariés par industrie
Tableau 3B.   Nombre de salariés par pays d'implantation dans l'industrie manufacturière
Tableau 4B.   Chiffre d'affaires par industrie
Tableau 5B.   Chiffre d'affaires par pays d'implantation dans l'industrie manufacturière

Sources et méthodes

Table 1A - Tableau 1A

NUMBER OF ENTERPRISES / NOMBRE D'ENTREPRISES

By industry (ISIC Rev. 3)		Foreign affiliates (Units) Filiales étrangères (Unités)					As a % of national total En % du total national				
		1995	1996	1997	1998	1999	1995	1996	1997	1998	1999
10/14	Mining & quarrying	8	..	11	..	11	..	..	..	..	..
15/37	**TOTAL MANUFACTURING**	1 388	..	1 528	..	1 585	..	..	..	..	..
15/16	Food, beverages, tobacco	113	..	98	..	98	..	..	..	..	..
17/19	Textiles, clothing, leather, footwear	58	..	57	..	59	..	..	..	..	..
20/22	Wood and paper products	73	..	89	..	85	..	..	..	..	..
20	Wood products	..	..	0	..	0	..	..	..	..	..
21/22	Paper, printing and publishing	..	..	89	..	85	..	..	..	..	..
23/25	Chemicals, Total	413	..	436	..	453	..	..	..	..	..
23	Refined petroleum, nuclear fuel	14	..	14	..	15	..	..	..	..	..
24/25	Chemicals, rubber & plastics prod.	399	..	422	..	438	..	..	..	..	..
24	Chemical products	295	..	298	..	304	..	..	..	..	..
2423	Pharmaceuticals	96	..	84	..	90	..	..	..	..	..
25	Rubber and plastics products	104	..	124	..	134	..	..	..	..	..
26	Non-metallic mineral products	66	..	74	..	79	..	..	..	..	..
27/28	Basic & fabricated metals	136	..	154	..	166	..	..	..	..	..
27	Basic metals	37	..	46	..	54	..	..	..	..	..
28	Fabricated metal products	99	..	108	..	112	..	..	..	..	..
29/32	Machinery, Total	380	..	425	..	434	..	..	..	..	..
29/30	Non-electrical machinery	240	..	276	..	278	..	..	..	..	..
29	Non-electrical machinery nec	232	..	266	..	268	..	..	..	..	..
30	Office and computing machinery	8	..	10	..	10	..	..	..	..	..
31/32	Electrical & electronic equipment	140	..	149	..	156	..	..	..	..	..
31	Electrical machinery nec	108	..	111	..	116	..	..	..	..	..
32	Radio, TV & communications eq.	32	..	38	..	40	..	..	..	..	..
33	Scientific instruments	71	..	76	..	78	..	..	..	..	..
34/35	Transportation equipment	63	..	86	..	97	..	..	..	..	..
34	Motor vehicles	52	..	71	..	76	..	..	..	..	..
35	Other transport equipment	11	..	15	..	21	..	..	..	..	..
351	Shipbuilding & repairing	2	..	1	..	7	..	..	..	..	..
353	Aircraft and spacecraft	0	..	0	..	0	..	..	..	..	..
36/37	Other manufacturing	30	..	33	..	36	..	..	..	..	..
40/45	Construction, electricity, gas & water	..	..	..	..	..	..	..	..	..	..
50/55	Trade, repair, hotels & restaurants	..	..	..	..	..	..	..	..	..	..
65/74	Finance, insurance, business services	..	..	..	..	..	..	..	..	..	..
	OTHER ACTIVITIES	..	..	..	..	..	..	..	..	..	..
01/99	**GRAND TOTAL**	..	..	..	..	..	..	..	..	..	..

Total manufacturing by investing country	1995	1996	1997	1998	1999	As a % of total manufacturing by foreign affiliates				
						1995	1996	1997	1998	1999
All countries	1 388	..	1 528	..	1 585	100.0	..	100.0	..	100.0
United States	346	..	395	..	415	24.9	..	25.9	..	26.2
Canada	..	..	..	..	..	..	..	..	..	..
Mexico	0	..	0	..	..	0.0	..	0.0	..	..
Japan	38	..	43	..	46	2.7	..	2.8	..	2.9
Europe	..	..	..	..	..	..	..	..	..	..
European Union (15)	847	..	917	..	952	61.0	..	60.0	..	60.1
Belgium	..	..	..	..	..	..	..	..	..	..
France	225	..	221	..	236	16.2	..	14.5	..	14.9
Germany	229	..	263	..	281	16.5	..	17.2	..	17.7
Italy	..	..	..	..	..	..	..	..	..	..
Netherlands	73	..	76	..	70	5.3	..	5.0	..	4.4
Spain	..	..	..	..	..	..	..	..	..	..
Sweden	..	..	..	..	..	..	..	..	..	..
United Kingdom	153	..	169	..	188	11.0	..	11.1	..	11.9
Switzerland	126	..	121	..	117	9.1	..	7.9	..	7.4
Australia and New Zealand	..	..	..	..	..	..	..	..	..	..
Asia (non-OECD)	9	..	10	..	10	0.6	..	0.7	..	0.6
Latin America	3	..	4	..	7	0.2	..	0.3	..	0.4

Note: Majority foreign-owned firms.
Firmes sous contrôle étranger majoritaire.

Inward investments　　　　　　　　　　　　　　　　　　　　*Investissements entrants*

Table 2A - Tableau 2A

NUMBER OF EMPLOYEES BY INDUSTRY

NOMBRE DE SALARIÉS PAR INDUSTRIE

		Foreign affiliates *(FTE)* Filiales étrangères *(EPT)*					As a % of national total En % du total national				
ISIC Revision 3		1995	1996	1997	1998	1999	1995	1996	1997	1998	1999
10/14	Mining & quarrying	905	..	819	..	1 672	..	..	..	..	..
15/37	**TOTAL MANUFACTURING**	**421 024**	..	**457 608**	..	**471 991**	..	..	..	..	..
15/16	Food, beverages, tobacco	38 379	..	40 051	..	36 825	..	..	..	..	..
17/19	Textiles, clothing, leather, footwear	11 603	..	10 645	..	10 673	..	..	..	..	..
20/22	Wood and paper products	14 963	..	15 525	..	15 652	..	..	..	..	..
20	Wood products	..	..	0	..	0	..	..	..	..	..
21/22	Paper, printing and publishing	..	..	15 525	..	15 652	..	..	..	..	..
23/25	Chemicals, Total	116 504	..	122 680	..	122 084	..	..	..	..	..
23	Refined petroleum, nuclear fuel	4 701	..	4 621	..	4 327	..	..	..	..	..
24/25	Chemicals, rubber & plastics prod.	111 803	..	118 059	..	117 757	..	..	..	..	..
24	Chemical products	87 347	..	89 349	..	85 810	..	..	..	..	..
2423	Pharmaceuticals	35 766	..	35 758	..	37 354	..	..	..	..	..
25	Rubber and plastics products	24 456	..	28 710	..	31 947	..	..	..	..	..
26	Non-metallic mineral products	19 089	..	21 147	..	20 728	..	..	..	..	..
27/28	Basic & fabricated metals	25 015	..	33 745	..	37 684	..	..	..	..	..
27	Basic metals	11 575	..	18 238	..	20 432	..	..	..	..	..
28	Fabricated metal products	13 440	..	15 507	..	17 252	..	..	..	..	..
29/32	Machinery, Total	162 081	..	170 570	..	175 285	..	..	..	..	..
29/30	Non-electrical machinery	89 290	..	97 977	..	97 260	..	..	..	..	..
29	Non-electrical machinery nec	74 893	..	83 319	..	84 189	..	..	..	..	..
30	Office and computing machinery	14 397	..	14 658	..	13 071	..	..	..	..	..
31/32	Electrical & electronic equipment	72 791	..	72 593	..	78 025	..	..	..	..	..
31	Electrical machinery nec	43 142	..	45 624	..	44 316	..	..	..	..	..
32	Radio, TV & communications eq.	29 649	..	26 969	..	33 709	..	..	..	..	..
33	Scientific instruments	11 436	..	12 018	..	12 732	..	..	..	..	..
34/35	Transportation equipment	18 521	..	24 995	..	33 711	..	..	..	..	..
34	Motor vehicles	15 633	..	21 341	..	29 458	..	..	..	..	..
35	Other transport equipment	2 888	..	3 654	..	4 253	..	..	..	..	..
351	Shipbuilding & repairing	183	..	115	..	649	..	..	..	..	..
353	Aircraft and spacecraft	0	..	0	..	0	..	..	..	..	..
36/37	Other manufacturing	5 999	..	6 232	..	6 617	..	..	..	..	..
40/45	Construction, electricity, gas & water	..	..	..	..	..	..	..	..	..	..
50/55	Trade, repair, hotels & restaurants	..	..	..	..	..	..	..	..	..	..
65/74	Finance, insurance, business services	..	..	..	..	..	..	..	..	..	..
	OTHER ACTIVITIES	..	..	..	..	..	..	..	..	..	..
01/99	**GRAND TOTAL**	..	..	..	..	..	..	..	..	..	..

Note: Majority foreign-owned firms.
Firmes sous contrôle étranger majoritaire.

Inward investments

Table 3A - Tableau 3A

NUMBER OF EMPLOYEES BY COUNTRY OF ORIGIN IN THE MANUFACTURING SECTOR
NOMBRE DE SALARIÉS PAR PAYS D'ORIGINE DANS L'INDUSTRIE MANUFACTURIÈRE

Country of origin (UBO)	Number of employees (FTE) Nombre de salariés (EPT)					As a % of all countries En % du total des pays				
	1995	1996	1997	1998	1999	1995	1996	1997	1998	1999
All countries	**421 024**	..	**457 608**	..	**471 991**	**100.0**	..	**100.0**	..	**100.0**
Total OECD	**414 104**	..	**447 898**	..	**462 047**	**98.4**	..	**97.9**	..	**97.9**
United States	124 736	..	145 712	..	145 000	29.6	..	31.8	..	30.7
Canada	3 545	..	3 196	..	3 427	0.8	..	0.7	..	0.7
Mexico	0	..	0	..	0	0.0	..	0.0	..	0.0
Japan	7 583	..	10 346	..	13 650	1.8	..	2.3	..	2.9
Korea	195	..	0	..	47	0.0	..	0.0	..	0.0
Australia	78	..	466	..	513	0.0	..	0.1	..	0.1
New Zealand	0	..	0	..	0	0.0	..	0.0	..	0.0
Europe	**278 605**	..	**288 713**	..	**299 905**	**66.2**	..	**63.1**	..	**63.5**
European Union (15)	**246 042**	..	**252 834**	..	**267 420**	**58.4**	..	**55.3**	..	**56.7**
Austria	2 461	..	2 392	..	3 143	0.6	..	0.5	..	0.7
Belgium	4 522	..	4 054	..	3 498	1.1	..	0.9	..	0.7
Denmark	262	..	1 364	..	1 688	0.1	..	0.3	..	0.4
Finland	5 247	..	5 370	..	7 105	1.2	..	1.2	..	1.5
France	70 611	..	65 189	..	67 089	16.8	..	14.2	..	14.2
Germany	56 403	..	62 521	..	76 156	13.4	..	13.7	..	16.1
Greece	101	..	121	..	141	0.0	..	0.0	..	0.0
Ireland	1 566	..	1 490	..	1 367	0.4	..	0.3	..	0.3
Italy	..	..	..	..	..	..	..	..	..	..
Luxembourg	80	..	282	..	311	0.0	..	0.1	..	0.1
Netherlands	19 669	..	22 110	..	19 977	4.7	..	4.8	..	4.2
Portugal	0	..	0	..	0	0.0	..	0.0	..	0.0
Spain	1 519	..	1 506	..	1 484	0.4	..	0.3	..	0.3
Sweden	48 434	..	46 414	..	40 618	11.5	..	10.1	..	8.6
United Kingdom	35 167	..	40 021	..	44 843	8.4	..	8.7	..	9.5
Czech Republic	0	..	0	..	0	0.0	..	0.0	..	0.0
Hungary	0	..	0	..	0	0.0	..	0.0	..	0.0
Iceland	0	..	0	..	0	0.0	..	0.0	..	0.0
Norway	994	..	2 260	..	1 847	0.2	..	0.5	..	0.4
Poland	0	..	0	..	0	0.0	..	0.0	..	0.0
Slovak Republic	0	..	0	..	0	0.0	..	0.0	..	0.0
Switzerland	30 931	..	33 084	..	30 143	7.3	..	7.2	..	6.4
Turkey	0	..	0	..	0	0.0	..	0.0	..	0.0
Non-OECD Europe, of which:	**638**	..	**535**	..	**495**	**0.2**	..	**0.1**	..	**0.1**
Baltic countries	0	..	0	..	0	0.0	..	0.0	..	0.0
Bulgaria	32	..	33	..	39	0.0	..	0.0	..	0.0
Croatia	0	..	0	..	0	0.0	..	0.0	..	0.0
Romania	0	..	0	..	0	0.0	..	0.0	..	0.0
Russian Federation	39	..	26	..	24	0.0	..	0.0	..	0.0
Slovenia	58	..	14	..	12	0.0	..	0.0	..	0.0
Ukraine	0	..	0	..	0	0.0	..	0.0	..	0.0
Yugoslavia	0	..	0	..	0	0.0	..	0.0	..	0.0
Non-OECD Asia, of which:	**1 885**	..	**1 916**	..	**1 820**	**0.4**	..	**0.4**	..	**0.4**
China	0	..	0	..	0	0.0	..	0.0	..	0.0
Chinese Taipei	0	..	0	..	0	0.0	..	0.0	..	0.0
Hong Kong (China)	1 182	..	1 208	..	391	0.3	..	0.3	..	0.1
India	293	..	353	..	1 409	0.1	..	0.1	..	0.3
Indonesia	410	..	334	..	0	0.1	..	0.1	..	0.0
Malaysia	0	..	0	..	0	0.0	..	0.0	..	0.0
Philippines	0	..	0	..	0	0.0	..	0.0	..	0.0
Singapore	0	..	0	..	0	0.0	..	0.0	..	0.0
Thailand	0	..	21	..	20	0.0	..	0.0	..	0.0
Near and Middle East	**890**	..	**326**	..	**331**	**0.2**	..	**0.1**	..	**0.1**
Africa	**937**	..	**744**	..	**409**	**0.2**	..	**0.2**	..	**0.1**
Latin America, of which:	**2 570**	..	**6 189**	..	**6 889**	**0.6**	..	**1.4**	..	**1.5**
Argentina	594	..	3 981	..	4 441	0.1	..	0.9	..	0.9
Brazil	1 976	..	2 208	..	2 064	0.5	..	0.5	..	0.4
Chile	0	..	0	..	0	0.0	..	0.0	..	0.0

Note: Majority foreign-owned firms.
Firmes sous contrôle étranger majoritaire.

Inward investments

Investissements entrants

Table 4A - Tableau 4A

TURNOVER BY INDUSTRY

CHIFFRE D'AFFAIRES PAR INDUSTRIE

		Foreign affiliates *(Billions of ITL)* Filiales étrangères *(Milliards de ITL)*					As a % of national total *En % du total national*				
ISIC Revision 3		1995	1996	1997	1998	1999	1995	1996	1997	1998	1999
10/14	Mining & quarrying	862	..	1 008	..	840	..	..	..	..	..
15/37	**TOTAL MANUFACTURING**	**186 010**	..	**214 709**	..	**240 098**	..	..	..	..	..
15/16	Food, beverages, tobacco	20 315	..	21 463	..	24 238	..	..	..	..	..
17/19	Textiles, clothing, leather, footwear	3 551	..	3 366	..	4 158	..	..	..	..	..
20/22	Wood and paper products	7 374	..	8 045	..	8 836	..	..	..	..	..
20	Wood products	..	..	0	..	0	..	..	..	..	..
21/22	Paper, printing and publishing	..	..	8 045	..	8 836	..	..	..	..	..
23/25	Chemicals, Total	70 483	..	79 369	..	84 663	..	..	..	..	..
23	Refined petroleum, nuclear fuel	11 947	..	10 527	..	10 948	..	..	..	..	..
24/25	Chemicals, rubber & plastics prod.	58 537	..	68 842	..	73 715	..	..	..	..	..
24	Chemical products	51 233	..	59 227	..	62 505	..	..	..	..	..
2423	Pharmaceuticals	16 249	..	18 558	..	21 880	..	..	..	..	..
25	Rubber and plastics products	7 303	..	9 615	..	11 209	..	..	..	..	..
26	Non-metallic mineral products	5 329	..	7 036	..	7 282	..	..	..	..	..
27/28	Basic & fabricated metals	11 023	..	14 624	..	16 063	..	..	..	..	..
27	Basic metals	6 695	..	8 935	..	9 744	..	..	..	..	..
28	Fabricated metal products	4 328	..	5 688	..	6 318	..	..	..	..	..
29/32	Machinery, Total	56 905	..	64 345	..	72 797	..	..	..	..	..
29/30	Non-electrical machinery	34 860	..	40 605	..	42 399	..	..	..	..	..
29	Non-electrical machinery nec	22 801	..	29 248	..	31 709	..	..	..	..	..
30	Office and computing machinery	12 059	..	11 357	..	10 690	..	..	..	..	..
31/32	Electrical & electronic equipment	22 045	..	23 739	..	30 398	..	..	..	..	..
31	Electrical machinery nec	13 070	..	14 674	..	14 641	..	..	..	..	..
32	Radio, TV & communications eq.	8 975	..	9 065	..	15 757	..	..	..	..	..
33	Scientific instruments	3 643	..	4 300	..	4 980	..	..	..	..	..
34/35	Transportation equipment	5 145	..	9 450	..	14 156	..	..	..	..	..
34	Motor vehicles	3 844	..	7 116	..	10 769	..	..	..	..	..
35	Other transport equipment	1 301	..	2 334	..	3 386	..	..	..	..	..
351	Shipbuilding & repairing	40	..	14	..	394	..	..	..	..	..
353	Aircraft and spacecraft	0	..	0	..	0	..	..	..	..	..
36/37	Other manufacturing	2 669	..	2 711	..	2 926	..	..	..	..	..
40/45	Construction, electricity, gas & water	..	..	..	..	..	..	..	..	..	..
50/55	Trade, repair, hotels & restaurants	..	..	..	..	..	..	..	..	..	..
65/74	Finance, insurance, business services	..	..	..	..	..	..	..	..	..	..
	OTHER ACTIVITIES	..	..	..	..	..	..	..	..	..	..
01/99	**GRAND TOTAL**	..	..	..	..	..	..	..	..	..	..

Note: Majority foreign-owned firms.
Firmes sous contrôle étranger majoritaire.

Inward investments

Investissements entrants

Table 5A - Tableau 5A

TURNOVER BY COUNTRY OF ORIGIN IN THE MANUFACTURING SECTOR

CHIFFRE D'AFFAIRES PAR PAYS D'ORIGINE DANS L'INDUSTRIE MANUFACTURIÈRE

Country of origin (UBO)	Turnover (Billions of ITL) Chiffre d'affaires (Milliards de ITL)					As a % of all countries En % du total des pays				
	1995	1996	1997	1998	1999	1995	1996	1997	1998	1999
All countries	**186 010**	..	**214 709**	..	**240 098**	**100.0**	..	**100.0**	..	**100.0**
Total OECD	**183 705**	..	**211 288**	..	**236 849**	**98.8**	..	**98.4**	..	**98.6**
United States	66 635	..	76 949	..	79 966	35.8	..	35.8	..	33.3
Canada	1 484	..	1 481	..	1 816	0.8	..	0.7	..	0.8
Mexico	0	..	0	..	0	0.0	..	0.0	..	0.0
Japan	3 685	..	5 521	..	7 361	2.0	..	2.6	..	3.1
Korea	25	..	0	..	41	0.0	..	0.0	..	0.0
Australia	12	..	175	..	214	0.0	..	0.1	..	0.1
New Zealand	0	..	0	..	0	0.0	..	0.0	..	0.0
Europe	**112 045**	..	**127 335**	..	**147 600**	**60.2**	..	**59.3**	..	**61.5**
European Union (15)	**98 369**	..	**110 099**	..	**130 318**	**52.9**	..	**51.3**	..	**54.3**
Austria	949	..	928	..	1 230	0.5	..	0.4	..	0.5
Belgium	2 658	..	2 207	..	1 723	1.4	..	1.0	..	0.7
Denmark	123	..	593	..	784	0.1	..	0.3	..	0.3
Finland	1 336	..	1 601	..	2 185	0.7	..	0.7	..	0.9
France	25 411	..	27 090	..	29 915	13.7	..	12.6	..	12.5
Germany	24 302	..	28 058	..	38 175	13.1	..	13.1	..	15.9
Greece	40	..	49	..	56	0.0	..	0.0	..	0.0
Ireland	544	..	404	..	428	0.3	..	0.2	..	0.2
Italy	..	..	..	..	..	..	..	..	..	..
Luxembourg	35	..	276	..	268	0.0	..	0.1	..	0.1
Netherlands	13 681	..	17 029	..	17 913	7.4	..	7.9	..	7.5
Portugal	0	..	0	..	0	0.0	..	0.0	..	0.0
Spain	1 094	..	1 103	..	1 074	0.6	..	0.5	..	0.4
Sweden	15 536	..	15 680	..	18 033	8.4	..	7.3	..	7.5
United Kingdom	12 660	..	15 081	..	18 534	6.8	..	7.0	..	7.7
Czech Republic	0	..	0	..	0	0.0	..	0.0	..	0.0
Hungary	0	..	0	..	0	0.0	..	0.0	..	0.0
Iceland	0	..	0	..	0	0.0	..	0.0	..	0.0
Norway	403	..	1 489	..	1 475	0.2	..	0.7	..	0.6
Poland	0	..	0	..	0	0.0	..	0.0	..	0.0
Slovak Republic	0	..	0	..	0	0.0	..	0.0	..	0.0
Switzerland	13 092	..	15 574	..	15 657	7.0	..	7.3	..	6.5
Turkey	0	..	0	..	0	0.0	..	0.0	..	0.0
Non-OECD Europe, of which:	**181**	..	**173**	..	**149**	**0.1**	..	**0.1**	..	**0.1**
Baltic countries	0	..	0	..	0	0.0	..	0.0	..	0.0
Bulgaria	11	..	11	..	11	0.0	..	0.0	..	0.0
Croatia	0	..	0	..	0	0.0	..	0.0	..	0.0
Romania	0	..	0	..	0	0.0	..	0.0	..	0.0
Russian Federation	21	..	38	..	17	0.0	..	0.0	..	0.0
Slovenia	45	..	15	..	16	0.0	..	0.0	..	0.0
Ukraine	0	..	0	..	0	0.0	..	0.0	..	0.0
Yugoslavia	0	..	0	..	0	0.0	..	0.0	..	0.0
Non-OECD Asia, of which:	**447**	..	**625**	..	**418**	**0.2**	..	**0.3**	..	**0.2**
China	0	..	0	..	0	0.0	..	0.0	..	0.0
Chinese Taipei	0	..	0	..	0	0.0	..	0.0	..	0.0
Hong Kong (China)	251	..	337	..	93	0.1	..	0.2	..	0.0
India	127	..	175	..	293	0.1	..	0.1	..	0.1
Indonesia	69	..	74	..	0	0.0	..	0.0	..	0.0
Malaysia	0	..	0	..	0	0.0	..	0.0	..	0.0
Philippines	0	..	0	..	0	0.0	..	0.0	..	0.0
Singapore	0	..	0	..	0	0.0	..	0.0	..	0.0
Thailand	0	..	39	..	31	0.0	..	0.0	..	0.0
Near and Middle East	**539**	..	**192**	..	**214**	**0.3**	..	**0.1**	..	**0.1**
Africa	**455**	..	**426**	..	**158**	**0.2**	..	**0.2**	..	**0.1**
Latin America, of which:	**683**	..	**2 005**	..	**2 311**	**0.4**	..	**0.9**	..	**1.0**
Argentina	263	..	1 525	..	1 566	0.1	..	0.7	..	0.7
Brazil	420	..	480	..	546	0.2	..	0.2	..	0.2
Chile	0	..	0	..	0	0.0	..	0.0	..	0.0

Note: Majority foreign-owned firms.
    Firmes sous contrôle étranger majoritaire.

Outward investments

Investissements sortants

Table 1B - Tableau 1B
NUMBER OF ENTERPRISES / NOMBRE D'ENTREPRISES

| | | Foreign affiliates *(Units)* | | | | | As a % of national total | | | | |
| | | Filiales étrangères *(Unités)* | | | | | En % du total national | | | | |
By industry (ISIC Rev. 3)		1995	1996	1997	1998	1999	1995	1996	1997	1998	1999
10/14	Mining & quarrying	..	..	26	..	26	..	..	..	..	..
15/37	**TOTAL MANUFACTURING**	**1 428**	..	**1 602**	..	**1 849**	..	..	..	..	..
15/16	Food, beverages, tobacco	..	..	229	..	289	..	..	..	..	..
17/19	Textiles, clothing, leather, footwear	..	..	223	..	252	..	..	..	..	..
20/22	Wood and paper products	..	..	142	..	149	..	..	..	..	..
20	Wood products	..	..	0	..	0	..	..	..	..	..
21/22	Paper, printing and publishing	..	..	142	..	149	..	..	..	..	..
23/25	Chemicals, Total	..	..	214	..	245	..	..	..	..	..
23	Refined petroleum, nuclear fuel	..	..	6	..	6	..	..	..	..	..
24/25	Chemicals, rubber & plastics prod.	..	..	208	..	239	..	..	..	..	..
24	Chemical products	..	..	105	..	127	..	..	..	..	..
2423	Pharmaceuticals	..	..	36	..	45	..	..	..	..	..
25	Rubber and plastics products	..	..	103	..	112	..	..	..	..	..
26	Non-metallic mineral products	..	..	89	..	101	..	..	..	..	..
27/28	Basic & fabricated metals	..	..	143	..	172	..	..	..	..	..
27	Basic metals	..	..	65	..	77	..	..	..	..	..
28	Fabricated metal products	..	..	78	..	95	..	..	..	..	..
29/32	Machinery, Total	..	..	376	..	449	..	..	..	..	..
29/30	Non-electrical machinery	..	..	254	..	290	..	..	..	..	..
29	Non-electrical machinery nec	..	..	243	..	282	..	..	..	..	..
30	Office and computing machinery	..	..	11	..	8	..	..	..	..	..
31/32	Electrical & electronic equipment	..	..	122	..	159	..	..	..	..	..
31	Electrical machinery nec	..	..	103	..	134	..	..	..	..	..
32	Radio, TV & communications eq.	..	..	19	..	25	..	..	..	..	..
33	Scientific instruments	..	..	50	..	46	..	..	..	..	..
34/35	Transportation equipment	..	..	92	..	95	..	..	..	..	..
34	Motor vehicles	..	..	84	..	89	..	..	..	..	..
35	Other transport equipment	..	..	8	..	6	..	..	..	..	..
351	Shipbuilding & repairing	..	..	0	..	0	..	..	..	..	..
353	Aircraft and spacecraft	..	..	1	..	0	..	..	..	..	..
36/37	Other manufacturing	..	..	44	..	51	..	..	..	..	..
40/45	Construction, electricity, gas & water	..	..	..	..	..	..	..	..	..	..
50/55	Trade, repair, hotels & restaurants	..	..	..	..	..	..	..	..	..	..
65/74	Finance, insurance, business services	..	..	..	..	..	..	..	..	..	..
	OTHER ACTIVITIES	..	..	..	..	..	..	..	..	..	..
01/99	**GRAND TOTAL**	..	..	..	..	..	..	..	..	..	..

Total manufacturing by country of location							As a % of total manufacturing by foreign affiliates				
	All countries	**1 428**	..	**1 602**	..	**1 849**	**100.0**	..	**100.0**	..	**100.0**
	United States	..	..	144	..	169	..	..	9.0	..	9.1
	Canada	..	..	..	..	..	..	..	..	..	..
	Mexico	..	..	..	..	..	..	..	..	..	..
	Japan	..	..	3	..	1	..	..	0.2	..	0.1
	Europe	..	..	..	..	..	..	..	..	..	..
	European Union (15)	..	..	729	..	818	..	..	45.5	..	44.2
	Belgium	..	..	..	..	..	..	..	..	..	..
	France	..	..	258	..	279	..	..	16.1	..	15.1
	Germany	..	..	105	..	126	..	..	6.6	..	6.8
	Italy	..	..	..	..	..	..	..	..	..	..
	Netherlands	..	..	..	..	..	..	..	..	..	..
	Spain	..	..	..	..	..	..	..	..	..	..
	Sweden	..	..	..	..	..	..	..	..	..	..
	United Kingdom	..	..	70	..	85	..	..	4.4	..	4.6
	Switzerland	..	..	..	..	..	..	..	..	..	..
	Australia and New Zealand	..	..	..	..	..	..	..	..	..	..
	Asia (non-OECD)	..	..	141	..	173	..	..	8.8	..	9.4
	Latin America	..	..	144	..	172	..	..	9.0	..	9.3

Note: Foreign affiliates majority-owned by national firms.
Filiales étrangères détenues majoritairement par des firmes nationales.

Outward investments   *Investissements sortants*

Table 2B - Tableau 2B

NUMBER OF EMPLOYEES BY INDUSTRY

NOMBRE DE SALARIÉS PAR INDUSTRIE

| | | Foreign affiliates *(FTE)* | | | | | As a % of national total | | | | |
| | | Filiales étrangères *(EPT)* | | | | | En % du total national | | | | |
ISIC Revision 3		1995	1996	1997	1998	1999	1995	1996	1997	1998	1999
10/14	Mining & quarrying	..	..	8 190	..	7 349	..	..	..	..	..
15/37	**TOTAL MANUFACTURING**	**388 841**	..	**427 663**	..	**445 920**	..	..	..	..	..
15/16	Food, beverages, tobacco	..	..	63 021	..	86 003	..	..	..	..	..
17/19	Textiles, clothing, leather, footwear	..	..	41 311	..	46 743	..	..	..	..	..
20/22	Wood and paper products	..	..	35 117	..	32 405	..	..	..	..	..
20	Wood products	..	..	0	..	0	..	..	..	..	..
21/22	Paper, printing and publishing	..	..	35 117	..	32 405	..	..	..	..	..
23/25	Chemicals, Total	..	..	45 244	..	45 115	..	..	..	..	..
23	Refined petroleum, nuclear fuel	..	..	557	..	453	..	..	..	..	..
24/25	Chemicals, rubber & plastics prod.	..	..	44 687	..	44 662	..	..	..	..	..
24	Chemical products	..	..	18 625	..	17 408	..	..	..	..	..
2423	Pharmaceuticals	..	..	6 721	..	8 059	..	..	..	..	..
25	Rubber and plastics products	..	..	26 062	..	27 254	..	..	..	..	..
26	Non-metallic mineral products	..	..	23 552	..	24 867	..	..	..	..	..
27/28	Basic & fabricated metals	..	..	32 472	..	39 871	..	..	..	..	..
27	Basic metals	..	..	26 303	..	32 541	..	..	..	..	..
28	Fabricated metal products	..	..	6 169	..	7 330	..	..	..	..	..
29/32	Machinery, Total	..	..	82 094	..	103 819	..	..	..	..	..
29/30	Non-electrical machinery	..	..	51 192	..	70 098	..	..	..	..	..
29	Non-electrical machinery nec	..	..	46 667	..	67 413	..	..	..	..	..
30	Office and computing machinery	..	..	4 525	..	2 685	..	..	..	..	..
31/32	Electrical & electronic equipment	..	..	30 902	..	33 721	..	..	..	..	..
31	Electrical machinery nec	..	..	29 026	..	31 608	..	..	..	..	..
32	Radio, TV & communications eq.	..	..	1 876	..	2 113	..	..	..	..	..
33	Scientific instruments	..	..	15 733	..	6 769	..	..	..	..	..
34/35	Transportation equipment	..	..	83 812	..	54 423	..	..	..	..	..
34	Motor vehicles	..	..	81 175	..	53 556	..	..	..	..	..
35	Other transport equipment	..	..	2 637	..	867	..	..	..	..	..
351	Shipbuilding & repairing	..	..	0	..	0	..	..	..	..	..
353	Aircraft and spacecraft	..	..	1 153	..	0	..	..	..	..	..
36/37	Other manufacturing	..	..	5 307	..	5 905	..	..	..	..	..
40/45	Construction, electricity, gas & water	..	..	..	..	..	..	..	..	..	..
50/55	Trade, repair, hotels & restaurants	..	..	..	..	..	..	..	..	..	..
65/74	Finance, insurance, business services	..	..	..	..	..	..	..	..	..	..
	OTHER ACTIVITIES	..	..	..	..	..	..	..	..	..	..
01/99	**GRAND TOTAL**	..	..	..	..	..	..	..	..	..	..

Note: Foreign affiliates majority-owned by national firms.
Filiales étrangères détenues majoritairement par des firmes nationales.

Outward investments

Investissements sortants

Table 3B - Tableau 3B

NUMBER OF EMPLOYEES BY COUNTRY OF LOCATION IN THE MANUFACTURING SECTOR
NOMBRE DE SALARIÉS PAR PAYS D'IMPLANTATION DANS L'INDUSTRIE MANUFACTURIÈRE

Country of location (UBO)	Number of employees (FTE) Nombre de salariés (EPT)					As a % of all countries En % du total des pays				
	1995	1996	1997	1998	1999	1995	1996	1997	1998	1999
All countries	**388 841**	..	**427 663**	..	**445 920**	**100.0**	..	**100.0**	..	**100.0**
Total OECD	**268 810**	..	**277 505**	..	**303 373**	**69.1**	..	**64.9**	..	**68.0**
United States	31 918	..	39 921	..	43 698	8.2	..	9.3	..	9.8
Canada	3 626	..	8 348	..	10 124	0.9	..	2.0	..	2.3
Mexico	2 801	..	3 654	..	4 772	0.7	..	0.9	..	1.1
Japan	77	..	78	..	17	0.0	..	0.0	..	0.0
Korea	224	..	128	..	177	0.1	..	0.0	..	0.0
Australia	1 490	..	1 562	..	7 141	0.4	..	0.4	..	1.6
New Zealand	0	..	0	..	5	0.0	..	0.0	..	0.0
Europe	**252 690**	..	**252 419**	..	**272 309**	**65.0**	..	**59.0**	..	**61.1**
European Union (15)	**177 471**	..	**172 809**	..	**180 349**	**45.6**	..	**40.4**	..	**40.4**
Austria	3 016	..	2 563	..	2 622	0.8	..	0.6	..	0.6
Belgium	8 072	..	8 981	..	8 086	2.1	..	2.1	..	1.8
Denmark	1 486	..	1 696	..	1 234	0.4	..	0.4	..	0.3
Finland	499	..	366	..	550	0.1	..	0.1	..	0.1
France	65 933	..	59 534	..	66 313	17.0	..	13.9	..	14.9
Germany	33 571	..	37 416	..	35 372	8.6	..	8.7	..	7.9
Greece	4 938	..	5 424	..	4 844	1.3	..	1.3	..	1.1
Ireland	472	..	1 420	..	1 609	0.1	..	0.3	..	0.4
Italy	..	..	..	..	..	..	..	..	..	..
Luxembourg	322	..	328	..	328	0.1	..	0.1	..	0.1
Netherlands	2 316	..	2 151	..	2 674	0.6	..	0.5	..	0.6
Portugal	3 619	..	3 939	..	5 179	0.9	..	0.9	..	1.2
Spain	29 324	..	25 638	..	27 385	7.5	..	6.0	..	6.1
Sweden	1 843	..	651	..	1 154	0.5	..	0.2	..	0.3
United Kingdom	22 060	..	22 702	..	22 999	5.7	..	5.3	..	5.2
Czech Republic	6 262	..	2 767	..	3 258	1.6	..	0.6	..	0.7
Hungary	11 359	..	11 399	..	11 672	2.9	..	2.7	..	2.6
Iceland	0	..	0	..	0	0.0	..	0.0	..	0.0
Norway	140	..	140	..	3 019	0.0	..	0.0	..	0.7
Poland	23 513	..	25 355	..	26 422	0.7	..	0.6	..	0.6
Slovak Republic	2 422	..	2 771	..	3 133	6.0	..	5.9	..	5.9
Switzerland	2 857	..	3 147	..	3 399	0.7	..	0.7	..	0.8
Turkey	4 650	..	5 426	..	6 187	1.2	..	1.3	..	1.4
Non-OECD Europe, of which:	**24 016**	..	**28 605**	..	**34 870**	**6.2**	..	**6.7**	..	**7.8**
Baltic countries	0	..	25	..	40	0.0	..	0.0	..	0.0
Bulgaria	1 936	..	2 301	..	4 594	0.5	..	0.5	..	1.0
Croatia	241	..	368	..	434	0.1	..	0.1	..	0.1
Romania	12 294	..	14 904	..	17 661	3.2	..	3.5	..	4.0
Russian Federation	2 720	..	2 447	..	2 692	0.6	..	0.6	..	0.7
Slovenia	1 746	..	2 584	..	2 522	0.4	..	0.6	..	0.6
Ukraine	837	..	1 036	..	1 986	0.2	..	0.2	..	0.4
Yugoslavia	0	..	0	..	0	0.0	..	0.0	..	0.0
Non-OECD Asia, of which:	**9 697**	..	**13 354**	..	**20 487**	**2.5**	..	**3.1**	..	**4.6**
China	5 396	..	8 495	..	8 498	1.4	..	2.0	..	1.9
Chinese Taipei	60	..	260	..	252	0.0	..	0.1	..	0.1
Hong Kong (China)	50	..	70	..	293	0.0	..	0.0	..	0.1
India	2 147	..	1 817	..	4 703	0.6	..	0.4	..	1.1
Indonesia	67	..	331	..	331	0.0	..	0.1	..	0.1
Malaysia	275	..	345	..	426	0.1	..	0.1	..	0.1
Philippines	378	..	260	..	3 177	0.1	..	0.1	..	0.7
Singapore	255	..	297	..	384	0.1	..	0.1	..	0.1
Thailand	811	..	824	..	1 324	0.2	..	0.2	..	0.3
Near and Middle East	**235**	..	**95**	..	**60**	**0.1**	..	**0.0**	..	**0.0**
Africa	**10 165**	..	**10 123**	..	**15 509**	**2.6**	..	**2.4**	..	**3.5**
Latin America, of which:	**75 918**	..	**97 981**	..	**71 621**	**19.5**	..	**22.9**	..	**16.1**
Argentina	8 257	..	11 009	..	11 162	2.1	..	2.6	..	2.5
Brazil	58 587	..	78 137	..	49 587	15.1	..	18.3	..	11.1
Chile	494	..	1 031	..	1 485	0.1	..	0.2	..	0.3

Note: Foreign affiliates majority-owned by national firms.
Filiales étrangères détenues majoritairement par des firmes nationales.

Outward investments   *Investissements sortants*

Table 4B - Tableau 4B

TURNOVER BY INDUSTRY

CHIFFRE D'AFFAIRES PAR INDUSTRIE

ISIC Revision 3		Foreign affiliates (Billions of ITL) Filiales étrangères (Milliards de ITL)					As a % of national total En % du total national				
		1995	1996	1997	1998	1999	1995	1996	1997	1998	1999
10/14	Mining & quarrying	..	..	6 553	..	7 174	..	..	..	..	..
15/37	**TOTAL MANUFACTURING**	**119 679**	..	**142 280**	..	**156 001**	..	..	..	..	..
15/16	Food, beverages, tobacco	..	..	32 325	..	39 024	..	..	..	..	..
17/19	Textiles, clothing, leather, footwear	..	..	4 415	..	6 462	..	..	..	..	..
20/22	Wood and paper products	..	..	14 786	..	13 968	..	..	..	..	..
20	Wood products	..	..	0	..	0	..	..	..	..	..
21/22	Paper, printing and publishing	..	..	14 786	..	13 968	..	..	..	..	..
23/25	Chemicals, Total	..	..	14 265	..	14 895	..	..	..	..	..
23	Refined petroleum, nuclear fuel	..	..	753	..	698	..	..	..	..	..
24/25	Chemicals, rubber & plastics prod.	..	..	13 512	..	14 197	..	..	..	..	..
24	Chemical products	..	..	6 991	..	7 386	..	..	..	..	..
2423	Pharmaceuticals	..	..	1 829	..	2 175	..	..	..	..	..
25	Rubber and plastics products	..	..	6 521	..	6 812	..	..	..	..	..
26	Non-metallic mineral products	..	..	7 907	..	8 126	..	..	..	..	..
27/28	Basic & fabricated metals	..	..	9 494	..	11 076	..	..	..	..	..
27	Basic metals	..	..	8 066	..	9 078	..	..	..	..	..
28	Fabricated metal products	..	..	1 428	..	1 998	..	..	..	..	..
29/32	Machinery, Total	..	..	26 529	..	35 005	..	..	..	..	..
29/30	Non-electrical machinery	..	..	17 911	..	24 853	..	..	..	..	..
29	Non-electrical machinery nec	..	..	17 054	..	24 488	..	..	..	..	..
30	Office and computing machinery	..	..	857	..	365	..	..	..	..	..
31/32	Electrical & electronic equipment	..	..	8 618	..	10 152	..	..	..	..	..
31	Electrical machinery nec	..	..	8 246	..	9 745	..	..	..	..	..
32	Radio, TV & communications eq.	..	..	372	..	408	..	..	..	..	..
33	Scientific instruments	..	..	3 258	..	1 237	..	..	..	..	..
34/35	Transportation equipment	..	..	27 945	..	24 302	..	..	..	..	..
34	Motor vehicles	..	..	27 477	..	24 051	..	..	..	..	..
35	Other transport equipment	..	..	468	..	252	..	..	..	..	..
351	Shipbuilding & repairing	..	..	0	..	0	..	..	..	..	..
353	Aircraft and spacecraft	..	..	157	..	0	..	..	..	..	..
36/37	Other manufacturing	..	..	1 356	..	1 907	..	..	..	..	..
40/45	Construction, electricity, gas & water	..	..	..	..	..	..	..	..	..	..
50/55	Trade, repair, hotels & restaurants	..	..	..	..	..	..	..	..	..	..
65/74	Finance, insurance, business services	..	..	..	..	..	..	..	..	..	..
	OTHER ACTIVITIES	..	..	..	..	..	..	..	..	..	..
01/99	**GRAND TOTAL**	..	..	..	..	..	..	..	..	..	..

Note: Foreign affiliates majority-owned by national firms.
Filiales étrangères détenues majoritairement par des firmes nationales.

Table 5B - Tableau 5B

TURNOVER BY COUNTRY OF LOCATION IN THE MANUFACTURING SECTOR

CHIFFRE D'AFFAIRES PAR PAYS D'IMPLANTATION DANS L'INDUSTRIE MANUFACTURIÈRE

Country of location (UBO)	Turnover (Billions of ITL) Chiffre d'affaires (Milliards de ITL)					As a % of all countries En % du total des pays				
	1995	1996	1997	1998	1999	1995	1996	1997	1998	1999
All countries	**119 679**	..	**142 280**	..	**156 001**	**100.0**	..	**100.0**	..	**100.0**
Total OECD	**98 984**	..	**113 067**	..	**131 494**	**82.7**	..	**79.5**	..	**84.3**
United States	14 093	..	21 202	..	21 959	11.8	..	14.9	..	14.1
Canada	2 118	..	3 545	..	3 695	1.8	..	2.5	..	2.4
Mexico	229	..	355	..	493	0.2	..	0.2	..	0.3
Japan	12	..	13	..	5	0.0	..	0.0	..	0.0
Korea	33	..	32	..	50	0.0	..	0.0	..	0.0
Australia	357	..	415	..	2 684	0.3	..	0.3	..	1.7
New Zealand	0	..	0	..	1	0.0	..	0.0	..	0.0
Europe	**82 997**	..	**88 631**	..	**104 147**	**69.3**	..	**62.3**	..	**66.8**
European Union (15)	**74 310**	..	**77 841**	..	**89 430**	**62.1**	..	**54.7**	..	**57.3**
Austria	839	..	884	..	1 292	0.7	..	0.6	..	0.8
Belgium	3 919	..	4 560	..	4 636	3.3	..	3.2	..	3.0
Denmark	659	..	569	..	511	0.6	..	0.4	..	0.3
Finland	83	..	67	..	103	0.1	..	0.0	..	0.1
France	27 098	..	26 094	..	32 941	22.6	..	18.3	..	21.1
Germany	17 151	..	16 962	..	19 322	14.3	..	11.9	..	12.4
Greece	1 069	..	1 808	..	1 563	0.9	..	1.3	..	1.0
Ireland	67	..	314	..	589	0.1	..	0.2	..	0.4
Italy	..	..	..	..	..	..	..	..	..	..
Luxembourg	233	..	191	..	195	0.2	..	0.1	..	0.1
Netherlands	1 100	..	1 430	..	1 586	0.9	..	1.0	..	1.0
Portugal	1 093	..	1 175	..	1 411	0.9	..	0.8	..	0.9
Spain	12 329	..	13 383	..	13 612	10.3	..	9.4	..	8.7
Sweden	363	..	255	..	385	0.3	..	0.2	..	0.2
United Kingdom	8 309	..	10 149	..	11 284	6.9	..	7.1	..	7.2
Czech Republic	403	..	191	..	363	0.3	..	0.1	..	0.2
Hungary	1 382	..	1 387	..	1 760	1.2	..	1.0	..	1.1
Iceland	0	..	0	..	0	0.0	..	0.0	..	0.0
Norway	50	..	50	..	1 710	0.0	..	0.0	..	1.1
Poland	3 316	..	4 995	..	5 990	0.2	..	0.1	..	0.1
Slovak Republic	47	..	64	..	135	2.8	..	3.5	..	3.8
Switzerland	1 730	..	1 810	..	2 016	1.4	..	1.3	..	1.3
Turkey	903	..	1 165	..	1 203	0.8	..	0.8	..	0.8
Non-OECD Europe, of which:	**854**	..	**1 126**	..	**1 539**	**0.7**	..	**0.8**	..	**1.0**
Baltic countries	0	..	1	..	2	0.0	..	0.0	..	0.0
Bulgaria	36	..	40	..	217	0.0	..	0.0	..	0.1
Croatia	11	..	32	..	42	0.0	..	0.0	..	0.0
Romania	191	..	260	..	464	0.2	..	0.2	..	0.3
Russian Federation	222	..	178	..	229	0.0	..	0.0	..	0.1
Slovenia	245	..	409	..	320	0.2	..	0.3	..	0.2
Ukraine	56	..	87	..	136	0.0	..	0.1	..	0.1
Yugoslavia	0	..	0	..	0	0.0	..	0.0	..	0.0
Non-OECD Asia, of which:	**374**	..	**834**	..	**1 805**	**0.3**	..	**0.6**	..	**1.2**
China	66	..	396	..	480	0.1	..	0.3	..	0.3
Chinese Taipei	2	..	3	..	32	0.0	..	0.0	..	0.0
Hong Kong (China)	10	..	12	..	46	0.0	..	0.0	..	0.0
India	112	..	142	..	604	0.1	..	0.1	..	0.4
Indonesia	10	..	51	..	75	0.0	..	0.0	..	0.0
Malaysia	6	..	10	..	32	0.0	..	0.0	..	0.0
Philippines	29	..	10	..	262	0.0	..	0.0	..	0.2
Singapore	68	..	130	..	139	0.1	..	0.1	..	0.1
Thailand	65	..	66	..	117	0.1	..	0.0	..	0.1
Near and Middle East	**26**	..	**11**	..	**3**	**0.0**	..	**0.0**	..	**0.0**
Africa	**1 470**	..	**870**	..	**2 329**	**1.2**	..	**0.6**	..	**1.5**
Latin America, of which:	**17 971**	..	**26 372**	..	**18 831**	**15.0**	..	**18.5**	..	**12.1**
Argentina	1 951	..	4 647	..	3 666	1.6	..	3.3	..	2.3
Brazil	15 068	..	20 200	..	13 743	12.6	..	14.2	..	8.8
Chile	87	..	215	..	190	0.1	..	0.2	..	0.1

Note: Foreign affiliates majority-owned by national firms.
Filiales étrangères détenues majoritairement par des firmes nationales.

ITALY

A. Inward investments

Source

The data are extracted from the Reprint database, developed at the Department of Economics and Production of the "Politecnico de Milano" with the support of the Italian National Council for Economy and Labour (CNEL). They are based on a survey (Italia Multinazionale) which covers all Italian enterprises in mining and manufacturing industries in which a foreign person owned or controlled a direct or indirect interest of 50% or more at the end of the fiscal year. The surveys are conducted every two years.

Industrial classification

For all variables, the data are classified according to the principal industrial activity of the affiliate.

The data are converted from the national industry classification to ISIC Revision 3.

Variables

- *Number of enterprises*: all enterprises in the mining and manufacturing industries in which a foreign person owned or controlled a direct or indirect interest of 50% or more at the end of the fiscal year.

- *Number of employees* is the number of full-time equivalent employees on the payroll at the end of the year.

Geographical breakdown

The country of origin is the country of the "ultimate beneficial owner".

B. Outward investments

Source

The data are extracted from the Reprint database, developed at the Department of Economics and Production of the "Politecnico de Milano" with the support of the Italian National Council for Economy and Labour (CNEL). They are based on a survey (Italia Multinazionale) which covers all enterprises in mining and manufacturing industries in which an Italian person owned or controlled a direct or indirect interest of 50% or more at the end of the fiscal year. The surveys are conducted every two years.

Industrial classification

For all variables, the data are classified according to the principal industrial activity of the affiliate.

The data are converted from the national industry classification to ISIC Revision 3.

Variables

- *Number of enterprises*: all enterprises in the mining and manufacturing industries in which an Italian person owned or controlled a direct or indirect interest of 50% or more at the end of the fiscal year.

- *Number of employees* is the number of full-time equivalent employees on the payroll at the end of the year.

Geographical breakdown

The country of destination is the country of the "ultimate beneficial owner".

ITALIE

A. Investissements entrants

Source

Les données sont extraites de la base de données Reprint établie par le Département d'économie et de production du "Politecnico di Milano" avec le soutien du Conseil national italien de l'économie et de la main d'oeuvre (CNEL). Elles s'appuient sur une enquête (Italia Multinazionale) qui couvre toutes les entreprises italiennes de l'industrie minière et manufacturière dans lesquelles des intérêts étrangers possèdent ou contrôlent directement ou indirectement 50 % ou plus du capital à la fin de l'exercice budgétaire. Les enquêtes sont effectuées tous les deux ans.

Classification industrielle

Pour toutes les variables, les données sont classées selon l'activité industrielle principale de l'entreprise affiliée.

Les données de la classification industrielle nationale sont adaptées à la CITI révision 3.

Variables

- *Nombre d'entreprises* : toutes les entreprises des industries minières et manufacturières dans lesquelles des intérêts étrangers possèdent ou contrôlent directement ou indirectement 50 % ou plus du capital à la fin de l'exercice budgétaire.

- *Nombre de salariés* : nombre de personnes employées en équivalent plein-temps à la fin de l'année.

Ventilation géographique

Le pays d'origine est le pays du "bénéficiaire ultime de l'investissement".

B. Investissements sortants

Source

Les données sont extraites de la base de données Reprint établie par le Département d'économie et de production du "Politecnico di Milano" avec le soutien du Conseil national italien de l'économie et de la main d'oeuvre (CNEL). Elles s'appuient sur une enquête (Italia Multinazionale) qui couvre toutes les entreprises de l'industrie minière et manufacturière dans lesquelles des intérêts italiens possèdent ou contrôlent directement ou indirectement 50 % ou plus du capital à la fin de l'exercice budgétaire. Les enquêtes sont effectuées tous les deux ans.

Classification industrielle

Pour toutes les variables, les données sont classées selon l'activité industrielle principale de l'entreprise affiliée.

Les données de la classification industrielle nationale sont adaptées à la CITI révision 3.

Variables

- *Nombre d'entreprises* : toutes les entreprises des industries minières et manufacturières dans lesquelles des intérêts italiens possèdent ou contrôlent directement ou indirectement 50 % ou plus du capital à la fin de l'exercice budgétaire.

- *Nombre de salariés* : nombre de personnes employées en équivalent plein-temps à la fin de l'année.

Ventilation géographique

Le pays de destination est le pays du "bénéficiaire ultime de l'investissement".

JAPAN

Sources and Methods

JAPON

Sources et méthodes

Table 1A - Tableau 1A
NUMBER OF ENTERPRISES / NOMBRE D'ENTREPRISES

| | | Foreign affiliates (Units) | | | | | As a % of national total | | | | |
| | | Filiales étrangères (Unités) | | | | | En % du total national | | | | |
By industry (ISIC Rev. 3)		1994	1995	1996	1997	1998	1994	1995	1996	1997	1998
10/14	Mining & quarrying	0	0	1	1	0	0.0	0.0	0.0	..	..
15/37	**TOTAL MANUFACTURING**	341	275	285	304	286	0.1	0.1	0.1	..	..
15/16	Food, beverages, tobacco	15	8	6	8	8	0.0	0.0	0.0	..	..
17/19	Textiles, clothing, leather, footwear	9	10	9	8	7	0.0	0.0	0.0	..	..
20/22	Wood and paper products	11	14	20	19	17	0.0	0.0	0.0	..	..
20	Wood products	..	..	..	1	1	..	..	..	..	..
21/22	Paper, printing and publishing	..	..	..	18	16	..	..	..	..	..
23/25	Chemicals, Total	97	82	81	83	85	0.7	0.6	0.6	..	..
23	Refined petroleum, nuclear fuel	10	4	4	5	5	1.1	0.4	0.4	..	..
24/25	Chemicals, rubber & plastics prod.	87	78	77	78	80	0.7	0.6	0.7	..	..
24	Chemical products	78	69	64	65	69	..	..	..	..	..
2423	Pharmaceuticals	33	21	19	20	24	..	..	..	..	..
25	Rubber and plastics products	9	9	13	13	11	..	..	..	..	..
26	Non-metallic mineral products	5	3	2	5	6	0.0	0.0	0.0	..	..
27/28	Basic & fabricated metals	16	14	14	19	16	0.0	0.0	0.0	..	..
27	Basic metals	10	8	10	11	8	0.1	0.1	0.1	..	..
28	Fabricated metal products	6	6	4	8	8	0.0	0.0	0.0	..	..
29/32	Machinery, Total	119	79	87	97	91	0.1	0.1	0.1	..	..
29/30	Non-electrical machinery	54	42	48	52	50	0.1	0.1	0.1	..	..
29	Non-electrical machinery nec	54	33	36	45	44	..	..	..	..	..
30	Office and computing machinery	0	9	12	7	6	..	..	..	..	..
31/32	Electrical & electronic equipment	65	37	39	45	41	0.2	0.1	0.1	..	..
31	Electrical machinery nec	20	12	12	18	16	..	..	..	..	..
32	Radio, TV & communications eq.	45	25	27	27	25	..	..	..	..	..
33	Scientific instruments	36	31	31	35	30	0.3	0.3	0.3	..	..
34/35	Transportation equipment	16	15	14	17	15	0.1	0.1	0.1	..	..
34	Motor vehicles	11	11	10	12	10	..	..	..	..	..
35	Other transport equipment	5	4	4	5	5	..	..	..	..	..
351	Shipbuilding & repairing	0	0	0	0	..	0.0	0.0	0.0	..	..
353	Aircraft and spacecraft	2	1	1	1	1	..	..	..	..	..
36/37	Other manufacturing	17	19	21	13	11	0.0	0.0	0.0	..	..
40/45	Construction, electricity, gas & water	2	4	4	4	3	0.0	0.0	0.0	..	..
50/55	Trade, repair, hotels & restaurants	479	587	602	635	603	0.1	0.1	0.1	..	..
65/74	Finance, insurance, business services	88	88	109	119	122	0.0	0.1	0.1	..	..
	OTHER ACTIVITIES	46	67	79	79	68	0.0	0.0	0.0	..	..
01/99	**GRAND TOTAL**	956	1 021	1 080	1 142	1 082	0.0	0.0	0.0	..	..

| Total manufacturing by investing country | 1994 | 1995 | 1996 | 1997 | 1998 | As a % of total manufacturing by foreign affiliates | | | | |
						1994	1995	1996	1997	1998
All countries	341	275	285	304	286	100.0	100.0	100.0	100.0	100.0
United States	160	127	132	129	120	46.9	46.2	46.3	42.4	42.0
Canada	..	..	..	..	..	..	..	..	..	..
Mexico	..	..	..	..	..	..	..	..	..	..
Japan	..	..	..	..	..	..	..	..	..	..
Europe	..	..	..	..	..	..	..	..	..	..
European Union (15)	120	89	91	114	108	35.2	32.4	31.9	37.5	37.8
Belgium	..	..	..	..	..	..	..	..	..	..
France	17	8	6	10	7	5.0	2.9	2.1	3.3	2.4
Germany	36	27	30	37	41	10.6	9.8	10.5	12.2	14.3
Italy	..	..	..	..	..	..	..	..	..	..
Netherlands	20	18	18	24	24	5.9	6.5	6.3	7.9	8.4
Spain	..	..	..	..	..	..	..	..	..	..
Sweden	..	..	..	..	..	..	..	..	..	..
United Kingdom	17	13	17	20	17	5.0	4.7	6.0	6.6	5.9
Switzerland	23	21	23	25	23	6.7	7.6	8.1	8.2	8.0
Australia and New Zealand	..	..	..	..	..	..	..	..	..	..
Asia (non-OECD)	23	23	21	12	16	6.7	8.4	7.4	3.9	5.6
Latin America	2	2	1	1	3	0.6	0.7	0.4	0.3	1.0

Note: Majority foreign-owned firms.
Firmes sous contrôle étranger majoritaire.

Inward investments   *Investissements entrants*

Table 2A - Tableau 2A

NUMBER OF EMPLOYEES BY INDUSTRY

NOMBRE DE SALARIÉS PAR INDUSTRIE

ISIC Revision 3		Foreign affiliates (Units) Filiales étrangères (Unités)					As a % of national total En % du total national				
		1994	1995	1996	1997	1998	1994	1995	1996	1997	1998
10/14	Mining & quarrying	..	..	0	..	0	..	..	0.0	..	..
15/37	**TOTAL MANUFACTURING**	**96 220**	**86 703**	**86 469**	**95 384**	**110 366**	**0.8**	**0.7**	**0.8**	**..**	**..**
15/16	Food, beverages, tobacco	1 436	1 497	1 422	1 690	1 856	0.1	0.1	0.1	..	..
17/19	Textiles, clothing, leather, footwear	1 796	1 782	..	1 839	1 935	0.2	0.2	..	..	..
20/22	Wood and paper products	921	578	757	567	707	0.1	0.0	0.1	..	..
20	Wood products	..	..	..	..	..	..	..	..	..	..
21/22	Paper, printing and publishing	..	..	..	..	..	..	..	..	..	..
23/25	Chemicals, Total	37 284	31 165	32 536	33 104	37 844	4.7	4.2	4.3	..	..
23	Refined petroleum, nuclear fuel	1 554	186	219	1 458	1 471	2.9	0.4	0.4	..	..
24/25	Chemicals, rubber & plastics prod.	35 730	30 979	32 317	31 646	36 373	4.8	4.4	4.6	..	..
24	Chemical products	33 605	30 066	29 782	29 084	33 717	..	..	..	..	..
2423	Pharmaceuticals	20 503	14 509	16 490	16 052	22 632	..	..	..	..	..
25	Rubber and plastics products	2 125	913	2 535	2 562	2 656	..	..	..	..	..
26	Non-metallic mineral products	1 044	129	..	935	755	0.2	0.0	..	..	..
27/28	Basic & fabricated metals	1 404	5 806	5 256	5 723	1 322	0.1	0.4	0.4	..	..
27	Basic metals	1 113	5 337	4 772	4 964	952	0.2	1.0	0.9	..	..
28	Fabricated metal products	291	469	484	759	370	0.0	0.0	0.1	..	..
29/32	Machinery, Total	45 621	38 973	38 872	45 736	43 725	1.4	1.2	1.4	..	..
29/30	Non-electrical machinery	6 610	30 660	29 868	31 505	31 553	0.6	3.1	3.2	..	..
29	Non-electrical machinery nec	6 610	5 785	5 081	31 053	31 230	..	..	..	..	..
30	Office and computing machinery	0	24 875	24 787	452	323	..	..	..	..	..
31/32	Electrical & electronic equipment	39 011	8 313	9 004	14 231	12 172	1.8	0.4	0.5	..	..
31	Electrical machinery nec	1 316	780	1 018	3 184	1 573	..	..	..	..	..
32	Radio, TV & communications eq.	37 695	7 533	7 986	11 047	10 599	..	..	..	..	..
33	Scientific instruments	3 201	2 606	3 349	4 487	3 894	0.9	0.8	1.1	..	..
34/35	Transportation equipment	1 630	1 517	666	809	17 680	0.1	0.1	0.1	..	..
34	Motor vehicles	1 394	1 316	462	591	17 506	..	..	..	..	..
35	Other transport equipment	236	201	204	218	174	..	..	..	..	..
351	Shipbuilding & repairing	0	0	0	0	..	0.0	0.0	0.0	..	..
353	Aircraft and spacecraft	..	..	..	..	..	..	..	..	..	..
36/37	Other manufacturing	1 883	2 650	1 784	494	648	0.1	0.2	0.2	..	..
40/45	Construction, electricity, gas & water	..	..	..	..	859	..	..	..	..	..
50/55	Trade, repair, hotels & restaurants	27 909	37 972	35 088	44 389	42 700	0.3	0.4	0.3	..	..
65/74	Finance, insurance, business services	6 205	3 908	3 843	4 462	5 583	0.2	0.1	0.1	..	..
	OTHER ACTIVITIES	3 266	4 060	4 746	4 350	3 915	0.0	0.1	0.1	..	..
01/99	**GRAND TOTAL**	**133 619**	**132 751**	**130 171**	**149 432**	**163 423**	**0.3**	**0.4**	**0.4**	**..**	**..**

Note: Majority foreign-owned firms.
Firmes sous contrôle étranger majoritaire.

Table 3A - Tableau 3A

NUMBER OF EMPLOYEES BY COUNTRY OF ORIGIN IN THE MANUFACTURING SECTOR

NOMBRE DE SALARIÉS PAR PAYS D'ORIGINE DANS L'INDUSTRIE MANUFACTURIÈRE

Country of origin (immediate controller)	Number of employees (Units) Nombre de salariés (Unités)					As a % of all countries En % du total des pays				
	1994	1995	1996	1997	1998	1994	1995	1996	1997	1998
All countries	96 220	86 703	86 469	95 384	110 366	100.0	100.0	100.0	100.0	100.0
Total OECD	..	..	83 320	92 580	107 217	..	..	96.4	97.1	97.1
United States	69 849	56 556	56 057	60 994	76 594	72.6	65.2	64.8	63.9	69.4
Canada	..	..	4 794	4 793	854	..	..	5.5	5.0	0.8
Mexico	..	..	..	0	0	..	..	..	0.0	0.0
Japan	..	..	..	..	..	..	..	..	..	..
Korea	..	..	90	74	..	..	..	0.1	0.1	..
Australia	..	..	..	160	..	..	..	..	0.2	..
New Zealand	..	..	..	0	0	..	..	..	0.0	0.0
Europe	..	..	23 835	28 441	31 603	..	..	27.6	29.8	28.6
European Union (15)	17 183	16 544	16 193	21 525	23 982	17.9	19.1	18.7	22.6	21.7
Austria	..	..	..	0	0	..	..	..	0.0	0.0
Belgium	..	..	132	159	..	..	..	0.2	0.2	..
Denmark	..	..	..	108	189	..	..	..	0.1	0.2
Finland	..	..	..	..	..	..	..	..	..	..
France	1 083	636	85	395	126	1.1	0.7	0.1	0.4	0.1
Germany	8 278	5 278	6 093	5 981	8 405	8.6	6.1	7.0	6.3	7.6
Greece	..	..	..	..	..	..	..	..	..	..
Ireland	..	..	19	2 935	..	..	..	0.0	3.1	..
Italy	..	..	22	22	24	..	..	0.0	0.0	0.0
Luxembourg	..	..	..	0	0	..	..	..	0.0	0.0
Netherlands	1 599	5 041	5 498	5 131	6 153	1.7	5.8	6.4	5.4	5.6
Portugal	..	..	..	0	0	..	..	..	0.0	0.0
Spain	..	..	..	0	0	..	..	..	0.0	0.0
Sweden	..	..	701	3 172	2 807	..	..	0.8	3.3	2.5
United Kingdom	3 978	1 738	3 415	3 615	3 532	4.1	2.0	3.9	3.8	3.2
Czech Republic	..	..	..	0	0	..	..	..	0.0	0.0
Hungary	..	..	..	0	0	..	..	..	0.0	0.0
Iceland	..	..	..	0	0	..	..	..	0.0	0.0
Norway	..	..	..	..	0	..	..	..	..	0.0
Poland	..	..	..	0	0	..	..	..	0.0	0.0
Slovak Republic	..	..	..	0	0	..	..	..	0.0	0.0
Switzerland	4 680	4 663	5 770	4 993	5 734	4.9	5.4	6.7	5.2	5.2
Turkey	..	..	..	..	0	..	..	..	..	0.0
Non-OECD Europe, of which:	..	..	..	1 882	1 887	..	..	..	2.0	1.7
Baltic countries	..	..	..	0	0	..	..	..	0.0	0.0
Bulgaria	..	..	..	0	0	..	..	..	0.0	0.0
Croatia	..	..	..	0	0	..	..	..	0.0	0.0
Romania	..	..	..	..	..	..	..	..	..	..
Russian Federation	..	..	..	0	0	..	..	..	0.0	0.0
Slovenia	..	..	..	0	0	..	..	..	0.0	0.0
Ukraine	..	..	..	0	0	..	..	..	0.0	0.0
Yugoslavia	..	..	..	0	0	..	..	..	0.0	0.0
Non-OECD Asia, of which:	397	420	394	180	233	0.4	0.5	0.5	0.2	0.2
China	..	..	..	7	8	..	..	..	0.0	0.0
Chinese Taipei	..	..	24	12	115	..	..	0.0	0.0	0.1
Hong Kong (China)	..	..	..	..	..	..	..	..	..	..
India	..	..	..	..	..	..	..	..	..	..
Indonesia	..	..	..	0	0	..	..	..	0.0	0.0
Malaysia	..	..	..	..	0	..	..	..	..	0.0
Philippines	..	..	..	0	0	..	..	..	0.0	0.0
Singapore	..	..	148	150	..	..	..	0.2	0.2	..
Thailand	..	..	..	0	..	..	..	..	0.0	..
Near and Middle East	..	..	..	110	90	..	..	..	0.1	0.1
Africa	..	..	..	..	0	..	..	..	..	0.0
Latin America, of which:	..	..	..	..	..	..	..	..	..	..
Argentina	..	..	..	0	0	..	..	..	0.0	0.0
Brazil	..	..	..	0	0	..	..	..	0.0	0.0
Chile	..	..	..	0	0	..	..	..	0.0	0.0

Note: Majority foreign-owned firms.
Firmes sous contrôle étranger majoritaire.

Inward investments   *Investissements entrants*

Table 4A - Tableau 4A

TURNOVER BY INDUSTRY

CHIFFRE D'AFFAIRES PAR INDUSTRIE

| | | Foreign affiliates *(Billions of JPY)* | | | | | As a % of national total | | | | |
| | | Filiales étrangères *(Milliards de JPY)* | | | | | En % du total national | | | | |
ISIC Revision 3		1994	1995	1996	1997	1998	1994	1995	1996	1997	1998
10/14	Mining & quarrying	..	..	0	..	0	..	..	0.0	..	..
15/37	**TOTAL MANUFACTURING**	**5 489**	**5 183**	**4 990**	**6 773**	**6 808**	**1.4**	**1.3**	**1.2**	**1.6**	**1.8**
15/16	Food, beverages, tobacco	320	337	370	431	442	0.7	0.7	0.9	0.9	1.0
17/19	Textiles, clothing, leather, footwear	67	36	..	43	42	0.3	0.2	..	..	..
20/22	Wood and paper products	17	23	30	25	36	0.0	0.1	0.1	..	..
20	Wood products	..	..	..	..	..	..	..	..	..	..
21/22	Paper, printing and publishing	..	..	..	..	..	..	..	..	..	..
23/25	Chemicals, Total	2 346	1 741	1 429	2 456	2 333	5.1	3.9	2.9	5.0	5.2
23	Refined petroleum, nuclear fuel	577	210	18	574	389	4.8	1.8	0.1	4.3	3.9
24/25	Chemicals, rubber & plastics prod.	1 769	1 531	1 411	1 882	1 944	5.2	4.6	3.9	5.3	5.6
24	Chemical products	1 684	1 495	1 290	1 751	1 821	..	..	..	..	..
2423	Pharmaceuticals	944	723	720	821	1 108	..	..	..	..	..
25	Rubber and plastics products	85	36	122	131	123	..	..	..	..	..
26	Non-metallic mineral products	33	8	..	42	37	0.2	0.1	..	..	..
27/28	Basic & fabricated metals	68	312	349	369	71	0.2	0.6	0.7	..	..
27	Basic metals	53	306	334	344	57	0.2	1.2	1.4	..	..
28	Fabricated metal products	16	6	15	25	14	0.1	0.0	0.1	..	..
29/32	Machinery, Total	2 270	2 385	2 454	3 107	2 686	2.3	2.3	2.3	2.8	2.5
29/30	Non-electrical machinery	244	1 956	1 954	2 256	1 952	0.9	7.1	6.9	7.3	7.3
29	Non-electrical machinery nec	244	372	179	2 221	1 943	..	..	..	..	..
30	Office and computing machinery	0	1 584	1 775	35	9	..	..	..	..	..
31/32	Electrical & electronic equipment	2 026	428	500	851	734	2.9	0.6	0.6	1.1	0.9
31	Electrical machinery nec	68	60	96	102	22	..	..	..	..	..
32	Radio, TV & communications eq.	1 958	368	403	749	712	..	..	..	..	..
33	Scientific instruments	149	84	124	206	161	1.7	0.9	1.3	..	..
34/35	Transportation equipment	84	63	51	56	977	0.2	0.1	0.1	..	..
34	Motor vehicles	78	58	45	50	972	..	..	..	..	..
35	Other transport equipment	5	5	6	7	5	..	..	..	..	..
351	Shipbuilding & repairing	0	0	0	0	..	0.0	0.0	0.0	..	..
353	Aircraft and spacecraft	..	..	..	..	..	..	..	..	..	..
36/37	Other manufacturing	135	196	139	38	22	0.4	0.6	0.4	..	..
40/45	Construction, electricity, gas & water	..	..	..	..	29	..	..	..	..	..
50/55	Trade, repair, hotels & restaurants	4 568	4 903	4 974	5 447	5 083	0.7	0.8	0.8	..	..
65/74	Finance, insurance, business services	294	184	208	220	245	0.3	0.3	0.3	..	..
	OTHER ACTIVITIES	81	375	302	269	239	0.1	0.2	0.2	..	..
01/99	**GRAND TOTAL**	**10 434**	**10 650**	**10 474**	**12 734**	**12 404**	**0.7**	**0.7**	**0.7**	**0.9**	**0.9**

Note: Majority foreign-owned firms.
Firmes sous contrôle étranger majoritaire.

Inward investments

Investissements entrants

Table 5A - Tableau 5A

TURNOVER BY COUNTRY OF ORIGIN IN THE MANUFACTURING SECTOR

CHIFFRE D'AFFAIRES PAR PAYS D'ORIGINE DANS L'INDUSTRIE MANUFACTURIÈRE

Country of origin (immediate controller)	Turnover (Billions of JPY) Chiffre d'affaires (Milliards de JPY)					As a % of all countries En % du total des pays				
	1994	1995	1996	1997	1998	1994	1995	1996	1997	1998
All countries	5 489	5 183	4 990	6 773	6 808	100.0	100.0	100.0	100.0	100.0
Total OECD	..	..	4 893	6 687	6 720	..	..	98.1	98.7	98.7
United States	3 902	3 463	3 438	4 834	5 165	71.1	66.8	68.9	71.4	75.9
Canada	..	..	338	354	80	..	..	6.8	5.2	1.2
Mexico	..	..	..	0	0	..	..	..	0.0	0.0
Japan	..	..	..	..	..	..	..	..	..	..
Korea	..	..	38	32	..	..	..	0.8	0.5	..
Australia	..	..	..	28	..	..	..	..	0.4	..
New Zealand	..	..	..	0	0	..	..	..	0.0	0.0
Europe	..	..	1 101	1 481	1 512	..	..	22.1	21.9	22.2
European Union (15)	1 205	823	815	1 230	1 199	22.0	15.9	16.3	18.2	17.6
Austria	..	..	..	0	0	..	..	..	0.0	0.0
Belgium	..	..	5	4	..	..	..	0.1	0.1	..
Denmark	..	..	..	2	1	..	..	..	0.0	0.0
Finland	..	..	..	..	..	..	..	..	..	..
France	90	50	41	70	52	1.6	1.0	0.8	1.0	0.8
Germany	452	244	266	405	394	8.2	4.7	5.3	6.0	5.8
Greece	..	..	..	..	..	..	..	..	..	..
Ireland	..	..	1	131	..	..	..	0.0	1.9	..
Italy	..	..	1	1	1	..	..	0.0	0.0	0.0
Luxembourg	..	..	..	0	0	..	..	..	0.0	0.0
Netherlands	194	232	246	268	253	3.5	4.5	4.9	4.0	3.7
Portugal	..	..	..	0	0	..	..	..	0.0	0.0
Spain	..	..	..	0	0	..	..	..	0.0	0.0
Sweden	..	..	80	96	100	..	..	1.6	1.4	1.5
United Kingdom	299	106	172	252	244	5.5	2.0	3.4	3.7	3.6
Czech Republic	..	..	..	0	0	..	..	..	0.0	0.0
Hungary	..	..	..	0	0	..	..	..	0.0	0.0
Iceland	..	..	..	0	0	..	..	..	0.0	0.0
Norway	..	..	..	..	0	..	..	..	..	0.0
Poland	..	..	..	0	0	..	..	..	0.0	0.0
Slovak Republic	..	..	..	0	0	..	..	..	0.0	0.0
Switzerland	201	271	251	205	271	3.7	5.2	5.0	3.0	4.0
Turkey	..	..	..	..	0	..	..	..	..	0.0
Non-OECD Europe, of which:	..	..	..	40	42	..	..	..	0.6	0.6
Baltic countries	..	..	..	0	0	..	..	..	0.0	0.0
Bulgaria	..	..	..	0	0	..	..	..	0.0	0.0
Croatia	..	..	..	0	0	..	..	..	0.0	0.0
Romania	..	..	..	..	..	..	..	..	..	..
Russian Federation	..	..	..	0	0	..	..	..	0.0	0.0
Slovenia	..	..	..	0	0	..	..	..	0.0	0.0
Ukraine	..	..	..	0	0	..	..	..	0.0	0.0
Yugoslavia	..	..	..	0	0	..	..	..	0.0	0.0
Non-OECD Asia, of which:	65	46	70	7	9	1.2	0.9	1.4	0.1	0.1
China	..	..	..	0	0	..	..	..	0.0	0.0
Chinese Taipei	..	..	2	2	7	..	..	0.0	0.0	0.1
Hong Kong (China)	..	..	..	..	..	..	..	..	..	..
India	..	..	..	..	..	..	..	..	..	..
Indonesia	..	..	..	0	0	..	..	..	0.0	0.0
Malaysia	..	..	..	..	0	..	..	..	..	0.0
Philippines	..	..	..	0	0	..	..	..	0.0	0.0
Singapore	..	..	21	3	..	..	..	0.4	0.0	..
Thailand	..	..	..	0	..	..	..	..	0.0	..
Near and Middle East	..	..	..	9	3	..	..	..	0.1	0.0
Africa	..	..	..	..	0	..	..	..	..	0.0
Latin America, of which:	..	..	..	..	..	..	..	..	..	..
Argentina	..	..	..	0	0	..	..	..	0.0	0.0
Brazil	..	..	..	0	0	..	..	..	0.0	0.0
Chile	..	..	..	0	0	..	..	..	0.0	0.0

Note: Majority foreign-owned firms.
Firmes sous contrôle étranger majoritaire.

Table 6A - Tableau 6A

VALUE ADDED / VALEUR AJOUTÉE

| | | Foreign affiliates (Billions of JPY) | | | | | As a % of national total | | | | |
| | | Filiales étrangères (Milliards de JPY) | | | | | En % du total national | | | | |
By industry (ISIC Rev. 3)		1994	1995	1996	1997	1998	1994	1995	1996	1997	1998
10/14	Mining & quarrying	..	..	0	..	0	..	..	0.0	..	..
15/37	**TOTAL MANUFACTURING**	911	1 111	1 053	1 272	1 316	1.0	1.2	1.2	..	..
15/16	Food, beverages, tobacco	85	84	79	85	101	0.9	0.9	1.0	..	..
17/19	Textiles, clothing, leather, footwear	10	9	..	10	11	0.2	0.2	..	..	..
20/22	Wood and paper products	4	5	7	8	8	0.0	0.1	0.1	..	..
20	Wood products	..	..	..	..	..	..	..	..	..	..
21/22	Paper, printing and publishing	..	..	..	..	..	..	..	..	..	..
23/25	Chemicals, Total	431	388	331	451	483	4.6	4.1	3.4	..	..
23	Refined petroleum, nuclear fuel	45	3	3	16	- 4	3.2	0.2	0.3	..	..
24/25	Chemicals, rubber & plastics prod.	387	385	328	435	487	4.8	4.7	3.8	..	..
24	Chemical products	373	374	300	408	466	..	..	..	..	..
2423	Pharmaceuticals	240	215	190	255	298	..	..	..	..	..
25	Rubber and plastics products	14	11	28	26	21	..	..	..	..	..
26	Non-metallic mineral products	5	2	..	7	7	0.2	0.1	..	..	..
27/28	Basic & fabricated metals	12	48	51	35	2	0.1	0.4	0.4	..	..
27	Basic metals	10	47	47	29	0	0.2	0.9	0.9	..	..
28	Fabricated metal products	2	1	4	6	2	0.0	0.0	0.1	..	..
29/32	Machinery, Total	300	501	516	619	541	1.3	2.1	2.2	..	..
29/30	Non-electrical machinery	41	394	419	455	402	0.5	5.4	5.1	..	..
29	Non-electrical machinery nec	41	40	41	450	399	..	..	..	..	..
30	Office and computing machinery	0	354	378	5	3	..	..	..	..	..
31/32	Electrical & electronic equipment	258	108	97	164	139	1.7	0.6	0.6	..	..
31	Electrical machinery nec	10	16	12	29	3	..	..	..	..	..
32	Radio, TV & communications eq.	248	92	86	135	135	..	..	..	..	..
33	Scientific instruments	30	25	34	44	31	1.2	1.0	1.4	..	..
34/35	Transportation equipment	14	8	6	8	131	0.1	0.1	0.1	..	..
34	Motor vehicles	14	7	4	7	129	..	..	..	..	..
35	Other transport equipment	1	1	2	2	2	..	..	..	..	..
351	Shipbuilding & repairing	0	0	0	0	..	0.0	0.0	0.0	..	..
353	Aircraft and spacecraft	..	..	..	..	..	..	..	..	..	..
36/37	Other manufacturing	20	41	19	4	2	0.2	0.5	0.2	..	..
40/45	Construction, electricity, gas & water	..	..	..	..	9	..	..	..	..	..
50/55	Trade, repair, hotels & restaurants	455	532	539	578	515	0.7	0.8	0.8	..	..
65/74	Finance, insurance, business services	49	44	39	41	60	0.2	0.3	0.3	..	..
	OTHER ACTIVITIES	29	38	51	57	50	0.1	0.1	0.1	..	..
01/99	**GRAND TOTAL**	1 445	1 726	1 682	1 955	1 950	0.5	0.6	0.6	..	..

| Total manufacturing by investing country | 1994 | 1995 | 1996 | 1997 | 1998 | As a % of total manufacturing by foreign affiliates | | | | |
						1994	1995	1996	1997	1998
All countries	911	1 111	1 053	1 272	1 316	100.0	100.0	100.0	100.0	100.0
United States	623	794	764	896	915	68.3	71.4	72.5	70.4	69.5
Canada	..	..	..	..	..	..	..	..	..	..
Mexico	..	..	..	..	..	..	..	..	..	..
Japan	..	..	..	..	..	..	..	..	..	..
Europe	..	..	..	..	..	..	..	..	..	..
European Union (15)	218	183	159	283	260	23.9	16.5	15.1	22.2	19.7
Belgium	..	..	..	..	..	..	..	..	..	..
France	11	3	1	3	2	1.2	0.3	0.1	0.2	0.2
Germany	97	60	66	65	87	10.7	5.4	6.3	5.1	6.6
Italy	..	..	..	..	..	..	..	..	..	..
Netherlands	34	42	49	50	54	3.7	3.8	4.6	3.9	4.1
Spain	..	..	..	..	..	..	..	..	..	..
Sweden	..	..	..	..	..	..	..	..	..	..
United Kingdom	48	14	32	42	41	5.3	1.3	3.0	3.3	3.1
Switzerland	41	61	56	38	90	4.5	5.5	5.3	3.0	6.8
Australia and New Zealand	..	..	..	..	..	..	..	..	..	..
Asia (non-OECD)	5	3	4	1	1	0.5	0.3	0.3	0.1	0.0
Latin America	..	..	..	..	..	..	..	..	..	..

Note: Majority foreign-owned firms.
Firmes sous contrôle étranger majoritaire.

Inward investments   *Investissements entrants*

Table 7A - Tableau 7A

COMPENSATION OF EMPLOYEES / SALAIRES ET CHARGES SOCIALES

		Foreign affiliates *(Billions of JPY)* Filiales étrangères *(Milliards de JPY)*					As a % of national total En % du total national				
By industry (ISIC Rev. 3)		1994	1995	1996	1997	1998	1994	1995	1996	1997	1998
10/14	Mining & quarrying	..	..	0	..	0	..	..	0.0	..	..
15/37	**TOTAL MANUFACTURING**	**447**	**629**	**591**	**668**	**782**	**0.7**	**1.1**	**1.0**	**..**	**..**
15/16	Food, beverages, tobacco	10	12	10	11	14	0.2	0.2	0.2	..	..
17/19	Textiles, clothing, leather, footwear	7	7	..	8	9	0.2	0.2	..	..	..
20/22	Wood and paper products	2	4	4	3	4	0.0	0.1	0.1	..	..
20	Wood products	..	..	..	..	..	..	..	..	..	..
21/22	Paper, printing and publishing	..	..	..	..	..	..	..	..	..	..
23/25	Chemicals, Total	246	236	196	255	269	5.1	5.0	4.0	..	..
23	Refined petroleum, nuclear fuel	15	2	2	10	6	3.8	0.4	0.4	..	..
24/25	Chemicals, rubber & plastics prod.	230	234	194	245	263	5.2	5.4	4.3	..	..
24	Chemical products	218	229	177	229	247	..	..	..	..	..
2423	Pharmaceuticals	140	127	110	133	170	..	..	..	..	..
25	Rubber and plastics products	13	5	17	17	16	..	..	..	..	..
26	Non-metallic mineral products	3	1	..	5	5	0.2	0.1	..	..	..
27/28	Basic & fabricated metals	9	34	37	19	7	0.1	0.4	0.5	..	..
27	Basic metals	7	33	34	15	5	0.2	1.0	1.2	..	..
28	Fabricated metal products	2	1	3	4	2	0.0	0.0	0.1	..	..
29/32	Machinery, Total	136	295	299	329	331	0.9	1.9	2.0	..	..
29/30	Non-electrical machinery	23	235	239	251	257	0.4	4.7	4.7	..	..
29	Non-electrical machinery nec	23	23	26	249	255	..	..	..	..	..
30	Office and computing machinery	0	212	213	2	2	..	..	..	..	..
31/32	Electrical & electronic equipment	113	60	60	78	74	1.1	0.6	0.6	..	..
31	Electrical machinery nec	6	3	6	6	3	..	..	..	..	..
32	Radio, TV & communications eq.	107	56	54	72	71	..	..	..	..	..
33	Scientific instruments	17	15	20	29	24	1.0	0.9	1.3	..	..
34/35	Transportation equipment	9	7	4	5	117	0.1	0.1	0.1	..	..
34	Motor vehicles	8	6	2	4	116	..	..	..	..	..
35	Other transport equipment	1	1	1	1	1	..	..	..	..	..
351	Shipbuilding & repairing	0	0	0	0	..	0.0	0.0	0.0	..	..
353	Aircraft and spacecraft	..	..	..	..	..	..	..	..	..	..
36/37	Other manufacturing	8	19	13	3	2	0.1	0.4	0.2	..	..
40/45	Construction, electricity, gas & water	..	..	..	..	7	..	..	..	..	..
50/55	Trade, repair, hotels & restaurants	198	268	252	292	256	0.4	0.6	0.6	..	..
65/74	Finance, insurance, business services	39	24	29	32	40	0.3	0.2	0.3	..	..
	OTHER ACTIVITIES	19	29	35	36	27	0.1	0.1	0.1	..	..
01/99	**GRAND TOTAL**	**702**	**951**	**906**	**1 035**	**1 112**	**0.4**	**0.5**	**0.5**	**..**	**..**

Total manufacturing by investing country							As a % of total manufacturing by foreign affiliates				
All countries	447	629	591	668	782	100.0	100.0	100.0	100.0	100.0	
United States	274	438	395	457	561	61.3	69.6	66.8	68.4	71.7	
Canada	..	..	..	..	..	..	..	..	..	..	
Mexico	..	..	..	..	..	..	..	..	..	..	
Japan	..	..	..	..	..	..	..	..	..	..	
Europe											
European Union (15)	121	105	104	146	169	27.0	16.8	17.5	21.9	21.6	
Belgium	..	..	..	..	..	..	..	..	..	..	
France	5	3	1	2	1	1.2	0.5	0.1	0.3	0.1	
Germany	63	40	45	44	67	14.1	6.4	7.6	6.5	8.5	
Italy	..	..	..	..	..	..	..	..	..	..	
Netherlands	10	17	32	31	40	2.3	2.7	5.3	4.7	5.1	
Spain	..	..	..	..	..	..	..	..	..	..	
Sweden	..	..	..	..	..	..	..	..	..	..	
United Kingdom	26	12	21	22	24	5.9	1.9	3.5	3.3	3.1	
Switzerland	28	32	38	31	38	6.3	5.1	6.4	4.7	4.8	
Australia and New Zealand	..	..	..	..	..	..	..	..	..	..	
Asia (non-OECD)	4	2	3	1	0	0.8	0.4	0.5	0.1	0.0	
Latin America	..	..	..	..	..	..	..	..	..	..	

Note: Majority foreign-owned firms.
Firmes sous contrôle étranger majoritaire.

Table 8A - Tableau 8A
R&D EXPENDITURE / DÉPENSES DE R-D

		Foreign affiliates (Billions of JPY) Filiales étrangères (Milliards de JPY)					As a % of national total En % du total national				
By industry (ISIC Rev. 3)		1994	1995	1996	1997	1998	1994	1995	1996	1997	1998
10/14	Mining & quarrying	..	..	0.0	..	0.0	..	..	0.0	..	0.0
15/37	**TOTAL MANUFACTURING**	126.6	118.5	88.0	128.8	175.3	1.5	1.4	1.0	1.3	1.8
15/16	Food, beverages, tobacco	0.5	0.5	0.4	0.4	1.2	0.2	0.2	0.2	0.1	0.5
17/19	Textiles, clothing, leather, footwear	0.0	0.0	..	0.0	0.0	0.0	0.0	..	0.0	0.0
20/22	Wood and paper products	0.0	0.1	0.1	0.1	0.1	0.0	0.1	0.1	0.0	0.1
20	Wood products	..	..	..	..	..	..	..	..	..	..
21/22	Paper, printing and publishing	..	..	..	..	..	..	..	..	..	..
23/25	Chemicals, Total	66.9	61.3	61.6	70.5	91.9	3.6	3.3	3.2	3.6	4.7
23	Refined petroleum, nuclear fuel	2.6	0.9	1.2	0.9	0.8	3.3	1.3	1.9	1.4	1.7
24/25	Chemicals, rubber & plastics prod.	64.3	60.4	60.4	69.6	91.0	3.6	3.4	3.3	3.7	4.8
24	Chemical products	63.3	59.9	58.8	68.2	89.5	4.1	3.9	3.7	4.2	5.5
2423	Pharmaceuticals	42.4	37.4	45.4	38.8	59.5	6.7	5.8	6.8	6.0	8.7
25	Rubber and plastics products	1.0	0.5	1.6	1.4	1.5	0.4	0.2	0.6	0.5	0.6
26	Non-metallic mineral products	0.4	0.2	..	0.1	0.1	0.2	0.1	..	0.0	0.0
27/28	Basic & fabricated metals	1.0	2.8	2.9	3.5	3.7	0.2	0.6	0.6	0.7	0.8
27	Basic metals	0.9	2.8	2.8	3.2	3.7	0.2	0.8	0.8	0.8	1.1
28	Fabricated metal products	0.1	0.0	0.1	0.3	0.0	0.1	0.0	0.1	0.2	0.0
29/32	Machinery, Total	55.1	51.0	20.7	51.9	51.4	1.5	1.3	0.5	1.2	1.1
29/30	Non-electrical machinery	2.1	39.5	6.6	39.7	40.1	..	..	..	..	..
29	Non-electrical machinery nec	2.1	1.9	1.9	39.7	40.1	..	..	..	..	..
30	Office and computing machinery	0.0	37.6	4.7	0.0	0.0	..	..	..	..	..
31/32	Electrical & electronic equipment	52.9	11.6	14.1	12.2	11.4	..	..	..	..	..
31	Electrical machinery nec	0.2	0.6	1.0	0.1	0.4	0.0	0.1	0.1	0.0	0.0
32	Radio, TV & communications eq.	52.8	10.9	13.1	12.1	11.0	..	..	..	..	..
33	Scientific instruments	1.8	1.2	1.7	1.6	1.7	0.5	0.3	0.5	0.4	0.3
34/35	Transportation equipment	0.8	0.5	0.4	0.8	25.2	0.1	0.0	0.0	0.0	1.5
34	Motor vehicles	0.8	0.5	0.4	0.7	25.2	0.1	0.0	0.0	0.1	1.8
35	Other transport equipment	0.0	0.0	0.0	0.0	0.0	0.0	0.0	0.0	0.0	0.0
351	Shipbuilding & repairing	0.0	0.0	0.0	0.0	..	..	..	..	..	..
353	Aircraft and spacecraft	..	..	..	..	..	..	..	..	..	..
36/37	Other manufacturing	0.1	1.1	0.2	0.0	0.0	0.1	1.3	0.2	0.0	0.0
40/45	Construction, electricity, gas & water	..	..	..	..	0.0	..	..	..	..	0.0
50/55	Trade, repair, hotels & restaurants	6.5	8.4	4.4	5.2	4.5	..	..	..	..	..
65/74	Finance, insurance, business services	1.2	0.4	0.4	2.3	0.5	..	..	..	..	..
	OTHER ACTIVITIES	0.6	1.0	0.9	1.7	1.1	0.2	0.3	0.4	0.5	0.3
01/99	**GRAND TOTAL**	134.8	128.4	93.8	138.0	181.5	1.5	1.4	0.9	1.3	1.7

Total manufacturing by investing country							As a % of total manufacturing by foreign affiliates				
All countries		126.6	118.5	88.0	128.8	175.3	100.0	100.0	100.0	100.0	100.0
United States		94.5	77.2	46.1	80.6	122.9	74.6	65.1	52.4	62.5	70.1
Canada		..	..	..	..	..	..	..	..	..	..
Mexico		..	..	..	..	..	..	..	..	..	..
Japan		..	..	..	..	..	..	..	..	..	..
Europe											
European Union (15)		21.8	25.2	19.9	39.4	46.8	17.2	21.2	22.5	30.6	26.7
Belgium		..	..	..	..	..	..	..	..	..	..
France		2.9	0.4	0.4	0.8	1.0	2.3	0.4	0.4	0.6	0.6
Germany		14.2	11.0	9.7	12.5	16.6	11.2	9.3	11.0	9.7	9.5
Italy		..	..	..	..	..	..	..	..	..	..
Netherlands		0.8	4.2	6.6	6.6	9.3	0.6	3.6	7.5	5.1	5.3
Spain		..	..	..	..	..	..	..	..	..	..
Sweden		..	..	..	..	..	..	..	..	..	..
United Kingdom		3.3	1.3	3.0	5.0	3.7	2.6	1.1	3.4	3.9	2.1
Switzerland		7.6	9.2	14.8	1.6	3.5	6.0	7.7	16.8	1.2	2.0
Australia and New Zealand		..	..	..	..	..	..	..	..	..	..
Asia (non-OECD)		0.1	0.5	0.6	0.0	0.0	0.1	0.4	0.6	0.0	0.0
Latin America		..	..	..	..	..	..	..	..	..	..

Note: Majority foreign-owned firms.
Firmes sous contrôle étranger majoritaire.

Inward investments   *Investissements entrants*

Table 9A - Tableau 9A
NUMBER OF RESEARCHERS / NOMBRE DE CHERCHEURS

By industry (ISIC Rev. 3)	Foreign affiliates (Units) Filiales étrangères (Unités)					As a % of national total En % du total national				
	1994	1995	1996	1997	1998	1994	1995	1996	1997	1998
10/14 Mining & quarrying	..	..	..	..	..	..	..	..	..	..
15/37 **TOTAL MANUFACTURING**	3 903	..	..	3 785	..	1.1	..	..	1.0	..
15/16 Food, beverages, tobacco	28	..	..	11	..	0.2	..	..	0.1	..
17/19 Textiles, clothing, leather, footwear	0	..	..	0	..	0.0	..	..	0.0	..
20/22 Wood and paper products	6	..	..	2	..	0.1	..	..	0.0	..
20 Wood products	..	..	..	..	..	..	..	..	..	..
21/22 Paper, printing and publishing	..	..	..	..	..	..	..	..	..	..
23/25 Chemicals, Total	1 838	..	..	2 916	..	2.4	..	..	4.0	..
23 Refined petroleum, nuclear fuel	120	..	..	60	..	5.7	..	..	2.9	..
24/25 Chemicals, rubber & plastics prod.	1 718	..	..	2 856	..	2.3	..	..	4.0	..
24 Chemical products	1 701	..	..	2 776	..	2.8	..	..	4.7	..
2423 Pharmaceuticals	1 184	..	..	1 043	..	5.9	..	..	5.8	..
25 Rubber and plastics products	17	..	..	80	..	0.1	..	..	0.7	..
26 Non-metallic mineral products	10	..	..	4	..	0.1	..	..	0.0	..
27/28 Basic & fabricated metals	76	..	..	127	..	0.4	..	..	0.7	..
27 Basic metals	76	..	..	127	..	0.7	..	..	1.1	..
28 Fabricated metal products	0	..	..	0	..	0.0	..	..	0.0	..
29/32 Machinery, Total	1 884	..	..	641	..	1.1	..	..	0.4	..
29/30 Non-electrical machinery	104	..	..	378	..	..	..	..	..	..
29 Non-electrical machinery nec	104	..	..	378	..	..	..	..	..	..
30 Office and computing machinery	0	..	..	0	..	..	..	..	..	..
31/32 Electrical & electronic equipment	1 780	..	..	263	..	..	..	..	..	..
31 Electrical machinery nec	29	..	..	72	..	0.1	..	..	0.2	..
32 Radio, TV & communications eq.	1 751	..	..	191	..	..	..	..	..	..
33 Scientific instruments	21	..	..	5	..	0.1	..	..	0.0	..
34/35 Transportation equipment	29	..	..	74	..	0.1	..	..	0.2	..
34 Motor vehicles	26	..	..	74	..	0.1	..	..	0.2	..
35 Other transport equipment	3	..	..	0	..	0.1	..	..	0.0	..
351 Shipbuilding & repairing	0	..	..	0	..	..	..	..	..	..
353 Aircraft and spacecraft	..	..	..	..	..	..	..	..	..	..
36/37 Other manufacturing	11	..	..	5	..	0.2	..	..	0.1	..
40/45 Construction, electricity, gas & water	..	..	..	..	..	..	..	..	..	..
50/55 Trade, repair, hotels & restaurants	306	..	..	230	..	..	..	..	..	..
65/74 Finance, insurance, business services	186	..	..	142	..	..	..	..	..	..
OTHER ACTIVITIES	5	..	..	10	..	0.1	..	..	0.2	..
01/99 **GRAND TOTAL**	4 400	..	..	4 167	..	1.2	..	..	1.0	..

Total manufacturing by investing country						As a % of total manufacturing by foreign affiliates				
All countries	3 903	..	..	3 785	..	100.0	..	..	100.0	..
United States	3 084	..	..	1 971	..	79.0	..	..	52.1	..
Canada	..	..	..	..	..	..	..	..	..	..
Mexico	..	..	..	..	..	..	..	..	..	..
Japan	..	..	..	..	..	..	..	..	..	..
Europe	..	..	..	..	..	..	..	..	..	..
European Union (15)	524	..	..	1 224	..	13.4	..	..	32.3	..
Belgium	..	..	..	..	..	..	..	..	..	..
France	62	..	..	15	..	1.6	..	..	0.4	..
Germany	294	..	..	474	..	7.5	..	..	12.5	..
Italy	..	..	..	..	..	..	..	..	..	..
Netherlands	43	..	..	215	..	1.1	..	..	5.7	..
Spain	..	..	..	..	..	..	..	..	..	..
Sweden	..	..	..	..	..	..	..	..	..	..
United Kingdom	119	..	..	101	..	3.0	..	..	2.7	..
Switzerland	181	..	..	317	..	4.6	..	..	8.4	..
Australia and New Zealand	..	..	..	..	..	..	..	..	..	..
Asia (non-OECD)	11	..	..	9	..	0.3	..	..	0.2	..
Latin America	..	..	..	..	..	..	..	..	..	..

Note: Majority foreign-owned firms.
Firmes sous contrôle étranger majoritaire.

Table 10A - Tableau 10A

GROSS FIXED CAPITAL FORMATION / FORMATION BRUTE DE CAPITAL FIXE

| | | Foreign affiliates (Billions of JPY) | | | | | As a % of national total | | | | |
| | | Filiales étrangères (Milliards de JPY) | | | | | En % du total national | | | | |
By industry (ISIC Rev. 3)		1994	1995	1996	1997	1998	1994	1995	1996	1997	1998
10/14	Mining & quarrying	..	..	0	..	0	..	..	..	..	..
15/37	**TOTAL MANUFACTURING**	203	231	304	301	300	1.6	1.7	2.1	1.9	2.3
15/16	Food, beverages, tobacco	2	1	8	15	7	0.1	0.0	0.7	1.2	0.7
17/19	Textiles, clothing, leather, footwear	3	2	..	0	3	..	..	..	..	..
20/22	Wood and paper products	0	0	0	0	4	..	..	..	..	..
20	Wood products	..	..	..	..	..	..	..	..	..	..
21/22	Paper, printing and publishing	..	..	..	..	..	..	..	..	..	..
23/25	Chemicals, Total	51	39	53	60	88	2.6	2.3	2.9	3.0	5.1
23	Refined petroleum, nuclear fuel	13	2	0	4	0	3.2	0.5	0.1	2.3	0.3
24/25	Chemicals, rubber & plastics prod.	38	37	52	56	88	2.5	3.0	3.5	3.1	5.5
24	Chemical products	36	36	49	54	85	..	..	..	..	..
2423	Pharmaceuticals	14	15	27	25	67	..	..	..	..	..
25	Rubber and plastics products	2	1	3	3	3	..	..	..	..	..
26	Non-metallic mineral products	11	0	..	0	1	..	..	..	..	..
27/28	Basic & fabricated metals	2	14	19	31	13	..	..	..	..	..
27	Basic metals	1	13	19	28	10	..	..	..	..	..
28	Fabricated metal products	1	0	0	2	2	..	..	..	..	..
29/32	Machinery, Total	130	171	219	189	155	4.3	4.3	5.8	4.5	4.3
29/30	Non-electrical machinery	3	101	131	150	126	0.4	14.3	19.7	19.1	17.2
29	Non-electrical machinery nec	3	3	4	150	125	..	..	..	..	..
30	Office and computing machinery	0	98	127	0	0	..	..	..	..	..
31/32	Electrical & electronic equipment	127	70	88	39	30	5.2	2.1	2.9	1.2	1.0
31	Electrical machinery nec	0	1	1	7	0	..	..	..	..	..
32	Radio, TV & communications eq.	127	69	87	32	29	..	..	..	..	..
33	Scientific instruments	1	2	2	4	4	..	..	..	..	..
34/35	Transportation equipment	3	1	1	1	25	..	..	..	..	..
34	Motor vehicles	1	1	0	1	25	..	..	..	..	..
35	Other transport equipment	2	0	0	0	0	..	..	..	..	..
351	Shipbuilding & repairing	0	0	0	0	..	..	..	..	..	..
353	Aircraft and spacecraft	..	..	..	..	..	..	..	..	..	..
36/37	Other manufacturing	1	1	1	1	0	..	..	..	..	..
40/45	Construction, electricity, gas & water	..	..	..	..	0	..	..	..	..	..
50/55	Trade, repair, hotels & restaurants	54	78	55	82	52	..	..	..	..	..
65/74	Finance, insurance, business services	3	15	1	2	3	..	..	..	..	..
	OTHER ACTIVITIES	0	2	5	3	2	..	..	..	..	..
01/99	**GRAND TOTAL**	261	326	365	389	357	..	..	..	..	..

Total manufacturing by investing country	1994	1995	1996	1997	1998	As a % of total manufacturing by foreign affiliates				
						1994	1995	1996	1997	1998
All countries	203	231	304	301	300	100.0	100.0	100.0	100.0	100.0
United States	175	171	238	237	215	85.8	73.7	78.3	78.5	71.8
Canada	..	..	..	..	..	..	..	..	..	..
Mexico	..	..	..	..	..	..	..	..	..	..
Japan	..	..	..	..	..	..	..	..	..	..
Europe	..	..	..	..	..	..	..	..	..	..
European Union (15)	22	40	31	29	70	10.9	17.2	10.2	9.6	23.3
Belgium	..	..	..	..	..	..	..	..	..	..
France	0	0	0	0	0	0.1	0.0	0.0	0.1	0.1
Germany	12	7	6	4	7	5.9	2.9	2.1	1.3	2.4
Italy	..	..	..	..	..	..	..	..	..	..
Netherlands	1	28	22	8	11	0.4	12.1	7.1	2.5	3.6
Spain	..	..	..	..	..	..	..	..	..	..
Sweden	..	..	..	..	..	..	..	..	..	..
United Kingdom	8	0	2	3	2	3.8	0.2	0.5	1.1	0.8
Switzerland	2	6	18	16	9	1.2	2.4	6.0	5.2	3.0
Australia and New Zealand	..	..	..	..	..	..	..	..	..	..
Asia (non-OECD)	0	0	0	1	3	0.2	0.2	0.1	0.2	0.9
Latin America	..	..	..	..	..	..	..	..	..	..

Note: Majority foreign-owned firms.
Firmes sous contrôle étranger majoritaire.

Table 11A - Tableau 11A

TOTAL EXPORTS BY INDUSTRY

EXPORTATIONS TOTALES PAR INDUSTRIE

		Foreign affiliates *(Billions of JPY)* Filiales étrangères *(Milliards de JPY)*					As a % of national total En % du total national				
ISIC Revision 3		1994	1995	1996	1997	1998	1994	1995	1996	1997	1998
10/14	Mining & quarrying	..	..	0	..	0	..	..	..	..	..
15/37	**TOTAL MANUFACTURING**	657	591	652	790	1 271	..	..	..	..	..
15/16	Food, beverages, tobacco	2	2	3	5	0	..	..	..	..	..
17/19	Textiles, clothing, leather, footwear	0	0	..	1	0	..	..	..	..	..
20/22	Wood and paper products	0	3	3	3	4	..	..	..	..	..
20	Wood products	..	..	..	..	..	..	..	..	..	..
21/22	Paper, printing and publishing	..	..	..	..	..	..	..	..	..	..
23/25	Chemicals, Total	130	92	96	123	145	..	..	..	..	..
23	Refined petroleum, nuclear fuel	39	1	3	1	2	..	..	..	..	..
24/25	Chemicals, rubber & plastics prod.	90	91	93	122	144	..	..	..	..	..
24	Chemical products	75	89	67	102	129	..	..	..	..	..
2423	Pharmaceuticals	34	42	22	27	63	..	..	..	..	..
25	Rubber and plastics products	16	3	25	20	14	..	..	..	..	..
26	Non-metallic mineral products	3	2	..	4	4	..	..	..	..	..
27/28	Basic & fabricated metals	7	23	27	34	3	..	..	..	..	..
27	Basic metals	6	23	27	30	1	..	..	..	..	..
28	Fabricated metal products	1	0	0	3	2	..	..	..	..	..
29/32	Machinery, Total	497	436	481	585	512	..	..	..	..	..
29/30	Non-electrical machinery	29	325	319	347	342	..	..	..	..	..
29	Non-electrical machinery nec	29	23	22	346	341	..	..	..	..	..
30	Office and computing machinery	0	302	297	1	1	..	..	..	..	..
31/32	Electrical & electronic equipment	468	112	162	237	170	..	..	..	..	..
31	Electrical machinery nec	17	13	12	32	8	..	..	..	..	..
32	Radio, TV & communications eq.	451	99	150	205	162	..	..	..	..	..
33	Scientific instruments	13	3	7	9	11	..	..	..	..	..
34/35	Transportation equipment	5	28	33	27	592	..	..	..	..	..
34	Motor vehicles	5	26	31	24	591	..	..	..	..	..
35	Other transport equipment	1	2	2	2	1	..	..	..	..	..
351	Shipbuilding & repairing	0	0	0	0	..	..	..	..	..	..
353	Aircraft and spacecraft	..	..	..	..	..	..	..	..	..	..
36/37	Other manufacturing	1	1	2	0	0	..	..	..	..	..
40/45	Construction, electricity, gas & water	..	..	..	..	0	..	..	..	..	..
50/55	Trade, repair, hotels & restaurants	537	444	411	448	437	..	..	..	..	..
65/74	Finance, insurance, business services	14	12	13	6	10	..	..	..	..	..
	OTHER ACTIVITIES	37	88	96	95	71	..	..	..	..	..
01/99	**GRAND TOTAL**	**1 245**	**1 135**	**1 173**	**1 339**	**1 789**	..	..	..	..	..

Note: Majority foreign-owned firms.
Firmes sous contrôle étranger majoritaire.

Table 12A - Tableau 12A

TOTAL EXPORTS BY COUNTRY OF ORIGIN IN THE MANUFACTURING SECTOR

EXPORTATIONS TOTALES PAR PAYS D'ORIGINE DANS L'INDUSTRIE MANUFACTURIÈRE

	Total exports (Billions of JPY) Exportations totales (Milliards de JPY)					As a % of all countries En % du total des pays				
Country of origin (immediate controller)	1994	1995	1996	1997	1998	1994	1995	1996	1997	1998
All countries	657	591	652	790	1 271	100.0	100.0	100.0	100.0	100.0
Total OECD	..	..	646	784	1 266	..	..	99.1	99.3	99.6
United States	505	425	483	603	1 102	76.8	71.9	74.2	76.4	86.7
Canada	..	..	33	38	13	..	..	5.1	4.8	1.0
Mexico	..	..	..	0	0	..	..	..	0.0	0.0
Japan	..	..	..	..	..	..	..	..	..	..
Korea	..	..	28	22	..	..	..	4.3	2.8	..
Australia	..	..	..	0	..	..	..	..	0.0	..
New Zealand	..	..	..	0	0	..	..	..	0.0	0.0
Europe	..	..	99	121	151	..	..	15.2	15.3	11.9
European Union (15)	73	68	66	86	123	11.1	11.5	10.1	10.9	9.7
Austria	..	..	..	0	0	..	..	..	0.0	0.0
Belgium	..	..	0	0	..	..	..	0.0	0.0	..
Denmark	..	..	..	0	0	..	..	..	0.0	..
Finland	..	..	..	..	..	..	..	..	..	..
France	1	1	0	1	0	0.2	0.2	0.1	0.1	0.0
Germany	14	7	10	6	45	2.1	1.2	1.6	0.7	3.6
Greece	..	..	..	..	..	..	..	..	..	..
Ireland	..	..	..	8	..	..	..	..	1.1	..
Italy	..	..	..	0	0	..	..	..	0.0	0.0
Luxembourg	..	..	..	0	0	..	..	..	0.0	0.0
Netherlands	12	38	43	50	47	1.8	6.5	6.5	6.4	3.7
Portugal	..	..	..	0	0	..	..	..	0.0	0.0
Spain	..	..	..	0	0	..	..	..	0.0	0.0
Sweden	..	..	1	3	2	..	..	0.2	0.4	0.2
United Kingdom	14	8	8	17	17	2.1	1.4	1.2	2.2	1.3
Czech Republic	..	..	..	0	0	..	..	..	0.0	0.0
Hungary	..	..	..	0	0	..	..	..	0.0	0.0
Iceland	..	..	..	0	0	..	..	..	0.0	0.0
Norway	..	..	..	..	0	..	..	..	..	0.0
Poland	..	..	..	0	0	..	..	..	0.0	0.0
Slovak Republic	..	..	..	0	0	..	..	..	0.0	0.0
Switzerland	32	37	32	33	28	4.9	6.3	4.9	4.2	2.2
Turkey	..	..	..	..	0	..	..	..	..	0.0
Non-OECD Europe, of which:	..	..	..	0	0	..	..	..	0.0	0.0
Baltic countries	..	..	..	0	0	..	..	..	0.0	0.0
Bulgaria	..	..	..	0	0	..	..	..	0.0	0.0
Croatia	..	..	..	0	0	..	..	..	0.0	0.0
Romania	..	..	..	..	..	..	..	..	..	..
Russian Federation	..	..	..	0	0	..	..	..	0.0	0.0
Slovenia	..	..	..	0	0	..	..	..	0.0	0.0
Ukraine	..	..	..	0	0	..	..	..	0.0	0.0
Yugoslavia	..	..	..	0	0	..	..	..	0.0	0.0
Non-OECD Asia, of which:	41	26	33	3	2	6.2	4.3	5.1	0.4	0.2
China	..	..	..	0	0	..	..	..	0.0	0.0
Chinese Taipei	..	..	1	2	1	..	..	0.2	0.2	0.1
Hong Kong (China)	..	..	..	..	..	..	..	..	..	..
India	..	..	..	..	..	..	..	..	..	..
Indonesia	..	..	..	0	0	..	..	..	0.0	0.0
Malaysia	..	..	..	..	0	..	..	..	..	0.0
Philippines	..	..	..	0	0	..	..	..	0.0	0.0
Singapore	..	..	0	0	..	..	..	0.1	0.1	..
Thailand	..	..	..	0	..	..	..	..	0.0	..
Near and Middle East	..	..	..	2	3	..	..	..	0.2	0.2
Africa	..	..	..	..	0	..	..	..	..	0.0
Latin America, of which:	..	..	..	..	..	..	..	..	..	..
Argentina	..	..	..	0	0	..	..	..	0.0	0.0
Brazil	..	..	..	0	0	..	..	..	0.0	0.0
Chile	..	..	..	0	0	..	..	..	0.0	0.0

Note: Majority foreign-owned firms.
Firmes sous contrôle étranger majoritaire.

Inward investments

Investissements entrants

Table 13A - Tableau 13A

TOTAL IMPORTS BY INDUSTRY

IMPORTATIONS TOTALES PAR INDUSTRIE

| | | Foreign affiliates (Billions of JPY) | | | | | As a % of national total | | | | |
| | | Filiales étrangères (Milliards de JPY) | | | | | En % du total national | | | | |
ISIC Revision 3		1994	1995	1996	1997	1998	1994	1995	1996	1997	1998
10/14	Mining & quarrying	..	..	0	..	0	..	..	..	..	..
15/37	**TOTAL MANUFACTURING**	**1 113**	**944**	**1 125**	**1 758**	**1 502**	..	..	..	..	..
15/16	Food, beverages, tobacco	17	6	8	11	9	..	..	..	..	..
17/19	Textiles, clothing, leather, footwear	15	16	..	16	12	..	..	..	..	..
20/22	Wood and paper products	3	4	6	3	4	..	..	..	..	..
20	Wood products	..	..	..	..	..	..	..	..	..	..
21/22	Paper, printing and publishing	..	..	..	..	..	..	..	..	..	..
23/25	Chemicals, Total	547	384	398	522	567	..	..	..	..	..
23	Refined petroleum, nuclear fuel	68	7	9	67	51	..	..	..	..	..
24/25	Chemicals, rubber & plastics prod.	479	377	389	455	516	..	..	..	..	..
24	Chemical products	468	371	367	427	483	..	..	..	..	..
2423	Pharmaceuticals	307	211	224	220	304	..	..	..	..	..
25	Rubber and plastics products	11	5	22	28	32	..	..	..	..	..
26	Non-metallic mineral products	10	2	..	13	13	..	..	..	..	..
27/28	Basic & fabricated metals	14	62	66	257	15	..	..	..	..	..
27	Basic metals	11	61	64	252	9	..	..	..	..	..
28	Fabricated metal products	3	1	2	5	6	..	..	..	..	..
29/32	Machinery, Total	396	436	565	821	726	..	..	..	..	..
29/30	Non-electrical machinery	42	324	431	466	386	..	..	..	..	..
29	Non-electrical machinery nec	42	20	30	463	383	..	..	..	..	..
30	Office and computing machinery	0	304	401	3	2	..	..	..	..	..
31/32	Electrical & electronic equipment	354	112	134	355	340	..	..	..	..	..
31	Electrical machinery nec	24	1	2	21	2	..	..	..	..	..
32	Radio, TV & communications eq.	330	111	132	334	338	..	..	..	..	..
33	Scientific instruments	68	27	49	93	77	..	..	..	..	..
34/35	Transportation equipment	27	6	6	5	76	..	..	..	..	..
34	Motor vehicles	27	5	4	3	74	..	..	..	..	..
35	Other transport equipment	1	1	2	2	1	..	..	..	..	..
351	Shipbuilding & repairing	0	0	0	0	..	..	..	..	..	..
353	Aircraft and spacecraft	..	..	..	..	..	..	..	..	..	..
36/37	Other manufacturing	16	2	12	18	2	..	..	..	..	..
40/45	Construction, electricity, gas & water	..	..	..	..	1	..	..	..	..	..
50/55	Trade, repair, hotels & restaurants	1 478	1 627	1 803	1 843	1 683	..	..	..	..	..
65/74	Finance, insurance, business services	29	16	4	17	6	..	..	..	..	..
	OTHER ACTIVITIES	4	52	89	63	48	..	..	..	..	..
01/99	**GRAND TOTAL**	**2 625**	**2 639**	**3 021**	**3 682**	**3 240**	..	..	..	..	..

Note: Majority foreign-owned firms.
Firmes sous contrôle étranger majoritaire.

Inward investments   *Investissements entrants*

Table 14A - Tableau 14A

TOTAL IMPORTS BY COUNTRY OF ORIGIN IN THE MANUFACTURING SECTOR

IMPORTATIONS TOTALES PAR PAYS D'ORIGINE DANS L'INDUSTRIE MANUFACTURIÈRE

Country of origin (immediate controller)	Total imports (Billions of JPY) Importations totales (Milliards de JPY)					As a % of all countries En % du total des pays				
	1994	1995	1996	1997	1998	1994	1995	1996	1997	1998
All countries	1 113	944	1 125	1 758	1 502	100.0	100.0	100.0	100.0	100.0
Total OECD	..	..	1 091	1 726	1 483	..	..	96.9	98.1	98.8
United States	649	636	773	1 164	1 118	58.3	67.3	68.7	66.2	74.4
Canada	..	..	57	244	2	..	..	5.1	13.9	0.2
Mexico	..	..	..	0	0	..	..	..	0.0	0.0
Japan	..	..	..	..	..	..	..	..	..	..
Korea	..	..	8	7	..	..	..	0.7	0.4	..
Australia	..	..	..	0	..	..	..	..	0.0	..
New Zealand	..	..	..	0	0	..	..	..	0.0	0.0
Europe	..	..	261	323	374	..	..	23.2	18.3	24.9
European Union (15)	351	143	159	268	293	31.5	15.1	14.2	15.2	19.5
Austria	..	..	..	0	0	..	..	..	0.0	0.0
Belgium	..	..	1	1	..	..	..	0.1	0.1	..
Denmark	..	..	..	1	1	..	..	..	0.1	0.0
Finland	..	..	..	..	..	..	..	..	..	..
France	23	2	2	2	2	2.1	0.2	0.1	0.1	0.1
Germany	153	72	78	78	105	13.7	7.6	6.9	4.4	7.0
Greece	..	..	..	..	..	..	..	..	..	..
Ireland	..	..	0	32	..	..	..	0.0	1.8	..
Italy	..	..	0	0	0	..	..	0.0	0.0	0.0
Luxembourg	..	..	..	0	0	..	..	..	0.0	0.0
Netherlands	35	14	29	45	23	3.1	1.5	2.6	2.5	1.6
Portugal	..	..	..	0	0	..	..	..	0.0	0.0
Spain	..	..	..	0	0	..	..	..	0.0	0.0
Sweden	..	..	5	40	54	..	..	0.4	2.3	3.6
United Kingdom	112	29	42	68	66	10.1	3.1	3.8	3.9	4.4
Czech Republic	..	..	..	0	0	..	..	..	0.0	0.0
Hungary	..	..	..	0	0	..	..	..	0.0	0.0
Iceland	..	..	..	0	0	..	..	..	0.0	0.0
Norway	..	..	..	..	0	..	..	..	..	0.0
Poland	..	..	..	0	0	..	..	..	0.0	0.0
Slovak Republic	..	..	..	0	0	..	..	..	0.0	0.0
Switzerland	59	82	93	42	70	5.3	8.7	8.2	2.4	4.7
Turkey	..	..	..	..	0	..	..	..	..	0.0
Non-OECD Europe, of which:	..	..	..	12	12	..	..	..	0.7	0.8
Baltic countries	..	..	..	0	0	..	..	..	0.0	0.0
Bulgaria	..	..	..	0	0	..	..	..	0.0	0.0
Croatia	..	..	..	0	0	..	..	..	0.0	0.0
Romania	..	..	..	..	..	..	..	..	..	..
Russian Federation	..	..	..	0	0	..	..	..	0.0	0.0
Slovenia	..	..	..	0	0	..	..	..	0.0	0.0
Ukraine	..	..	..	0	0	..	..	..	0.0	0.0
Yugoslavia	..	..	..	0	0	..	..	..	0.0	0.0
Non-OECD Asia, of which:	30	14	24	2	7	2.7	1.5	2.2	0.1	0.4
China	..	..	..	0	0	..	..	..	0.0	0.0
Chinese Taipei	..	..	1	0	5	..	..	0.1	0.0	0.3
Hong Kong (China)	..	..	..	..	..	..	..	..	..	..
India	..	..	..	..	..	..	..	..	..	..
Indonesia	..	..	..	0	0	..	..	..	0.0	0.0
Malaysia	..	..	..	..	0	..	..	..	..	0.0
Philippines	..	..	..	0	0	..	..	..	0.0	0.0
Singapore	..	..	12	1	..	..	..	1.0	0.1	..
Thailand	..	..	..	0	..	..	..	..	0.0	..
Near and Middle East	..	..	..	7	0	..	..	..	0.4	0.0
Africa	..	..	..	..	0	..	..	..	..	0.0
Latin America, of which:	..	..	..	..	..	..	..	..	..	..
Argentina	..	..	..	0	0	..	..	..	0.0	0.0
Brazil	..	..	..	0	0	..	..	..	0.0	0.0
Chile	..	..	..	0	0	..	..	..	0.0	0.0

Note: Majority foreign-owned firms.
Firmes sous contrôle étranger majoritaire.

Table 15A - Tableau 15A

INTRA-FIRM EXPORTS BY INDUSTRY

EXPORTATIONS INTRA-FIRME PAR INDUSTRIE

		Foreign affiliates *(Billions of JPY)*									
		Filiales étrangères *(Milliards de JPY)*									
ISIC Revision 3		1989	1990	1991	1992	1993	1994	1995	1996	1997	1998
10/14	Mining & quarrying	..	..	0.0	0.0	..	..	..	0.0	..	0.0
15/37	**TOTAL MANUFACTURING**	..	..	320.7	341.5	362.5	337.7	331.0	177.7	367.1	558.6
15/16	Food, beverages, tobacco	..	..	0.9	0.2	0.0	1.0	0.3	2.3	0.0	0.0
17/19	Textiles, clothing, leather, footwear	..	..	0.0	..	0.0	0.0	0.3	..	0.1	0.0
20/22	Wood and paper products	..	..	0.2	0.0	0.0	0.0	0.5	0.8	0.7	0.8
20	Wood products	..	..	..	..	..	..	..	..	..	..
21/22	Paper, printing and publishing	..	..	..	..	..	..	..	..	..	..
23/25	Chemicals, Total	..	..	32.4	35.1	70.8	80.3	45.2	55.0	47.0	67.8
23	Refined petroleum, nuclear fuel	..	..	0.0	0.0	39.1	33.7	0.2	2.7	1.1	1.6
24/25	Chemicals, rubber & plastics prod.	..	..	32.4	35.1	31.7	46.7	45.0	52.2	45.9	66.2
24	Chemical products	..	..	31.3	32.2	31.4	38.6	44.8	33.5	30.2	52.9
2423	Pharmaceuticals	..	..	15.1	19.3	16.5	19.1	26.2	18.0	9.1	17.1
25	Rubber and plastics products	..	..	1.1	2.9	0.3	8.1	0.3	18.7	15.7	13.3
26	Non-metallic mineral products	..	..	0.3	0.5	0.2	0.4	0.9	..	0.9	1.2
27/28	Basic & fabricated metals	..	..	0.9	0.1	0.2	1.4	7.7	1.9	5.1	0.4
27	Basic metals	..	..	0.7	0.0	0.1	1.3	7.6	1.8	3.4	0.0
28	Fabricated metal products	..	..	0.3	0.1	0.1	0.1	0.1	0.2	1.7	0.4
29/32	Machinery, Total	..	..	257.6	..	288.4	248.1	254.2	89.8	291.2	226.4
29/30	Non-electrical machinery	..	..	8.6	..	8.1	1.8	208.4	32.6	191.2	139.0
29	Non-electrical machinery nec	..	..	8.6	11.4	8.1	1.8	3.0	11.4	191.1	138.9
30	Office and computing machinery	..	..	0.0	..	0.0	0.0	205.5	21.3	0.1	0.1
31/32	Electrical & electronic equipment	..	..	249.1	261.9	280.3	246.3	45.8	57.1	100.0	87.4
31	Electrical machinery nec	..	..	1.1	2.2	20.2	7.4	2.1	2.0	6.2	2.2
32	Radio, TV & communications eq.	..	..	248.0	259.8	260.2	238.9	43.7	55.1	93.8	85.2
33	Scientific instruments	..	..	27.8	31.1	1.4	2.1	2.6	2.8	4.5	4.9
34/35	Transportation equipment	..	..	0.0	0.6	1.1	4.3	19.3	24.7	17.8	257.2
34	Motor vehicles	..	..	0.0	0.6	1.1	4.1	19.1	24.6	17.6	257.2
35	Other transport equipment	..	..	0.0	0.0	0.0	0.1	0.2	0.2	0.2	0.0
351	Shipbuilding & repairing	..	..	0.0	0.0	..	0.0	..	0.0	0.0	..
353	Aircraft and spacecraft	..	..	..	..	..	..	..	..	..	..
36/37	Other manufacturing	..	..	0.5	0.4	0.4	0.1	0.0	0.0	0.0	0.0
40/45	Construction, electricity, gas & water	..	..	0.0	..	..	..	..	..	..	0.0
50/55	Trade, repair, hotels & restaurants	..	..	483.2	347.6	206.1	153.1	228.8	135.6	115.0	128.4
65/74	Finance, insurance, business services	..	..	7.9	13.6	11.5	3.8	9.4	6.7	2.9	4.5
	OTHER ACTIVITIES	..	..	5.0	..	6.8	3.5	67.9	52.8	51.7	31.7
01/99	**GRAND TOTAL**	..	..	816.9	712.3	586.9	498.1	637.0	372.8	536.7	723.1

Note: Majority foreign-owned firms.
Firmes sous contrôle étranger majoritaire.

Table 16A - Tableau 16A

INTRA-FIRM EXPORTS BY COUNTRY OF ORIGIN IN THE MANUFACTURING SECTOR

EXPORTATIONS INTRA-FIRME PAR PAYS D'ORIGINE DANS L'INDUSTRIE MANUFACTURIÈRE

Country of origin (immediate controller)	Intra-firm exports (Billions of JPY) Exportations intra-firme (Milliards de JPY)					As a % of all countries En % du total des pays				
	1994	1995	1996	1997	1998	1994	1995	1996	1997	1998
All countries	337.7	331.0	177.7	367.1	558.6	100.0	100.0	100.0	100.0	100.0
Total OECD	303.3	329.1	173.5	366.0	557.6	89.8	99.4	97.7	99.7	99.8
United States	245.6	242.8	75.0	276.1	471.9	72.7	73.4	42.2	75.2	84.5
Canada	0.5	12.6	4.5	3.5	3.2	0.1	3.8	2.5	0.9	0.6
Mexico	0.0	0.0	..	0.0	0.0	0.0	0.0	..	0.0	0.0
Japan	..	..	..	..	..	..	..	..	..	..
Korea	0.5	18.5	23.6	16.8	..	0.1	5.6	13.3	4.6	..
Australia	1.0	..	..	0.2	..	0.3	..	..	0.0	..
New Zealand	0.0	0.0	..	0.0	0.0	0.0	0.0	..	0.0	0.0
Europe	55.8	55.3	70.3	69.5	82.5	16.5	16.7	39.6	18.9	14.8
European Union (15)	36.7	37.0	45.0	57.5	65.0	10.9	11.2	25.3	15.7	11.6
Austria	0.0	0.0	..	0.0	0.0	0.0	0.0	..	0.0	0.0
Belgium	0.0	0.1	0.1	0.0	..	0.0	0.0	0.1	0.0	..
Denmark	0.3	0.1	..	0.0	0.0	0.1	0.0	..	0.0	0.0
Finland	..	..	..	..	..	..	..	..	..	..
France	0.0	0.5	0.4	0.8	0.5	0.0	0.1	0.2	0.2	0.1
Germany	5.4	0.9	1.1	0.9	10.3	1.6	0.3	0.6	0.2	1.8
Greece	..	0.0	..	..	..	..	0.0	..	..	..
Ireland	0.0	..	..	8.1	..	0.0	..	..	2.2	..
Italy	0.2	0.0	..	0.0	0.0	0.1	0.0	..	0.0	0.0
Luxembourg	0.0	..	..	0.0	0.0	0.0	..	..	0.0	0.0
Netherlands	1.8	27.4	40.3	44.4	41.8	0.5	8.3	22.7	12.1	7.5
Portugal	0.0	0.0	..	0.0	0.0	0.0	0.0	..	0.0	0.0
Spain	0.0	0.0	..	0.0	0.0	0.0	0.0	..	0.0	0.0
Sweden	0.1	0.0	0.0	1.8	1.4	0.0	0.0	0.0	0.5	0.2
United Kingdom	5.4	1.1	0.8	1.1	0.8	1.6	0.3	0.5	0.3	0.1
Czech Republic	0.0	0.0	..	0.0	0.0	0.0	0.0	..	0.0	0.0
Hungary	0.0	0.0	..	0.0	0.0	0.0	0.0	..	0.0	0.0
Iceland	0.0	0.0	..	0.0	0.0	0.0	0.0	..	0.0	0.0
Norway	..	..	..	..	0.0	..	..	..	..	0.0
Poland	0.0	0.0	..	0.0	0.0	0.0	0.0	..	0.0	0.0
Slovak Republic	0.0	0.0	..	0.0	0.0	0.0	0.0	..	0.0	0.0
Switzerland	19.1	..	25.3	12.0	17.5	5.7	..	14.2	3.3	3.1
Turkey	..	0.0	..	..	0.0	..	0.0	..	..	0.0
Non-OECD Europe, of which:	0.0	..	..	0.1	0.0	0.0	..	..	0.0	0.0
Baltic countries	0.0	0.0	..	0.0	0.0	0.0	0.0	..	0.0	0.0
Bulgaria	0.0	0.0	..	0.0	0.0	0.0	0.0	..	0.0	0.0
Croatia	0.0	0.0	..	0.0	0.0	0.0	0.0	..	0.0	0.0
Romania	..	..	..	..	..	..	..	..	..	..
Russian Federation	0.0	0.0	..	0.0	0.0	0.0	0.0	..	0.0	0.0
Slovenia	0.0	0.0	..	0.0	0.0	0.0	0.0	..	0.0	0.0
Ukraine	0.0	0.0	..	0.0	0.0	0.0	0.0	..	0.0	0.0
Yugoslavia	0.0	0.0	..	0.0	0.0	0.0	0.0	..	0.0	0.0
Non-OECD Asia, of which:	34.8	0.7	26.5	1.1	0.9	10.3	0.2	14.9	0.3	0.2
China	32.9	0.1	..	0.0	0.0	9.7	0.0	..	0.0	0.0
Chinese Taipei	1.3	0.5	0.6	0.7	0.7	0.4	0.2	0.3	0.2	0.1
Hong Kong (China)	..	0.1	..	..	..	..	0.0	..	..	..
India	..	..	..	..	..	..	..	..	..	..
Indonesia	0.0	0.0	..	0.0	0.0	0.0	0.0	..	0.0	0.0
Malaysia	..	0.0	..	..	0.0	..	0.0	..	..	0.0
Philippines	0.0	0.0	..	0.0	0.0	0.0	0.0	..	0.0	0.0
Singapore	0.1	..	0.3	0.3	..	0.0	..	0.2	0.1	..
Thailand	0.0	0.0	..	0.0	..	0.0	0.0	..	0.0	..
Near and Middle East	0.0	..	..	0.0	0.0	0.0	..	..	0.0	0.0
Africa	..	0.0	..	..	0.0	..	0.0	..	..	0.0
Latin America, of which:	..	..	..	..	..	..	..	..	..	..
Argentina	0.0	0.0	..	0.0	0.0	0.0	0.0	..	0.0	0.0
Brazil	0.0	0.0	..	0.0	0.0	0.0	0.0	..	0.0	0.0
Chile	0.0	0.0	..	0.0	0.0	0.0	0.0	..	0.0	0.0

Note: Majority foreign-owned firms.
Firmes sous contrôle étranger majoritaire.

Inward investments   *Investissements entrants*

Table 17A - Tableau 17A

INTRA-FIRM IMPORTS BY INDUSTRY

IMPORTATIONS INTRA-FIRME PAR INDUSTRIE

| | | **Foreign affiliates** *(Billions of JPY)* | | | | | | | | |
| | | **Filiales étrangères** *(Milliards de JPY)* | | | | | | | | |
ISIC Revision 3		1989	1990	1991	1992	1993	1994	1995	1996	1997	1998
10/14	Mining & quarrying	..	..	0.0	0.0	..	..	..	0.0	..	0.0
15/37	**TOTAL MANUFACTURING**	..	..	929.4	1 114.9	725.2	746.8	629.5	670.9	861.6	770.5
15/16	Food, beverages, tobacco	..	..	5.4	1.8	0.4	14.7	3.7	0.8	0.8	5.7
17/19	Textiles, clothing, leather, footwear	..	..	11.1	..	6.2	12.0	13.9	..	13.0	10.2
20/22	Wood and paper products	..	..	6.4	30.2	4.3	1.7	2.6	4.0	1.7	2.1
20	Wood products	..	..	..	..	..	..	..	..	..	..
21/22	Paper, printing and publishing	..	..	..	..	..	..	..	..	..	..
23/25	Chemicals, Total	..	..	483.7	599.8	281.8	351.6	258.2	304.2	279.5	290.9
23	Refined petroleum, nuclear fuel	..	..	62.4	0.1	2.6	20.5	4.8	6.6	65.2	9.7
24/25	Chemicals, rubber & plastics prod.	..	..	421.3	599.7	279.2	331.1	253.3	297.7	214.3	281.2
24	Chemical products	..	..	414.3	588.8	277.7	322.6	249.3	276.6	189.5	249.5
2423	Pharmaceuticals	..	..	260.0	462.8	146.2	215.8	152.0	186.3	117.6	176.7
25	Rubber and plastics products	..	..	7.0	10.9	1.5	8.5	4.0	21.1	24.8	31.7
26	Non-metallic mineral products	..	..	11.0	9.3	4.6	7.7	1.5	..	11.1	9.8
27/28	Basic & fabricated metals	..	..	9.7	6.4	21.1	6.9	24.6	12.1	19.9	5.7
27	Basic metals	..	..	8.6	5.8	21.1	6.5	23.7	11.6	19.4	0.8
28	Fabricated metal products	..	..	1.1	0.6	0.0	0.4	1.0	0.6	0.6	4.9
29/32	Machinery, Total	..	..	298.8	..	297.9	270.1	307.0	305.8	467.5	341.5
29/30	Non-electrical machinery	..	..	28.9	..	26.5	29.9	274.6	257.6	367.6	286.5
29	Non-electrical machinery nec	..	..	28.7	26.5	26.4	29.9	15.1	28.3	365.6	284.3
30	Office and computing machinery	..	..	0.2	0.0	0.0	0.0	259.6	229.4	2.1	2.1
31/32	Electrical & electronic equipment	..	..	269.9	256.6	271.4	240.2	32.4	48.1	99.9	55.0
31	Electrical machinery nec	..	..	7.4	7.3	5.5	22.7	0.9	0.6	20.5	0.9
32	Radio, TV & communications eq.	..	..	262.5	249.3	265.9	217.6	31.5	47.6	79.4	54.1
33	Scientific instruments	..	..	89.0	101.1	44.2	43.5	12.7	19.5	49.9	60.2
34/35	Transportation equipment	..	..	12.3	54.1	51.7	23.6	4.2	3.9	1.7	42.4
34	Motor vehicles	..	..	10.6	52.9	50.7	23.2	4.1	3.2	1.4	41.7
35	Other transport equipment	..	..	1.6	1.2	1.0	0.4	0.2	0.7	0.3	0.7
351	Shipbuilding & repairing	..	..	0.0	0.0	0.0	0.0	0.0	0.0	0.0	..
353	Aircraft and spacecraft	..	..	..	..	..	..	..	..	..	..
36/37	Other manufacturing	..	..	2.1	21.6	12.9	15.1	1.0	8.3	16.5	2.1
40/45	Construction, electricity, gas & water	..	..	0.0	..	..	..	..	..	..	1.1
50/55	Trade, repair, hotels & restaurants	..	..	1 306.0	737.4	739.1	1 040.7	1 226.7	1 356.7	1 429.3	1 184.1
65/74	Finance, insurance, business services	..	..	19.2	23.8	21.2	22.9	14.6	2.2	3.0	4.8
	OTHER ACTIVITIES	..	..	1.3	..	4.2	2.9	29.9	71.7	44.4	31.6
01/99	**GRAND TOTAL**	..	..	2 255.9	1 880.0	1 504.4	1 813.2	1 900.7	2 101.4	2 339.3	1 992.1

Note: Majority foreign-owned firms.
Firmes sous contrôle étranger majoritaire.

Inward investments
Investissements entrants

Table 18A - Tableau 18A

INTRA-FIRM IMPORTS BY COUNTRY OF ORIGIN IN THE MANUFACTURING SECTOR

IMPORTATIONS INTRA-FIRME PAR PAYS D'ORIGINE DANS L'INDUSTRIE MANUFACTURIÈRE

Country of origin (immediate controller)	Intra-firm imports (Billions of JPY) Importations intra-firme (Milliards de JPY)					As a % of all countries En % du total des pays				
	1994	1995	1996	1997	1998	1994	1995	1996	1997	1998
All countries	**746.8**	**629.5**	**670.9**	**861.6**	**770.5**	**100.0**	**100.0**	**100.0**	**100.0**	**100.0**
Total OECD	**721.9**	**612.4**	**641.6**	**831.5**	**755.7**	**96.7**	**97.3**	**95.6**	**96.5**	**98.1**
United States	425.2	445.5	462.6	669.3	565.1	56.9	70.8	69.0	77.7	73.3
Canada	1.5	10.6	0.3	5.6	2.4	0.2	1.7	0.0	0.6	0.3
Mexico	0.0	0.0	..	0.0	0.0	0.0	0.0	..	0.0	0.0
Japan	..	..	..	..	..	..	..	..	..	..
Korea	8.0	9.5	7.8	6.4	..	1.1	1.5	1.2	0.7	..
Australia	0.4	..	..	0.0	..	0.1	..	..	0.0	..
New Zealand	0.0	0.0	..	0.0	0.0	0.0	0.0	..	0.0	0.0
Europe	**291.5**	**155.7**	**177.8**	**160.9**	**197.7**	**39.0**	**24.7**	**26.5**	**18.7**	**25.7**
European Union (15)	**234.3**	**89.7**	**98.7**	**127.8**	**134.8**	**31.4**	**14.3**	**14.7**	**14.8**	**17.5**
Austria	0.0	0.0	..	0.0	0.0	0.0	0.0	..	0.0	0.0
Belgium	0.6	1.4	1.0	1.1	..	0.1	0.2	0.1	0.1	..
Denmark	0.3	0.7	..	0.8	0.4	0.0	0.1	..	0.1	0.0
Finland	..	..	..	..	..	..	..	..	..	..
France	17.7	0.6	1.0	1.0	0.6	2.4	0.1	0.1	0.1	0.1
Germany	98.9	48.0	46.2	62.6	61.2	13.2	7.6	6.9	7.3	7.9
Greece	..	0.0	..	..	..	..	0.0	..	..	..
Ireland	0.0	..	0.3	28.7	..	0.0	..	0.0	3.3	..
Italy	0.5	0.3	0.3	0.2	0.2	0.1	0.0	0.0	0.0	0.0
Luxembourg	0.0	..	..	0.0	0.0	0.0	..	..	0.0	0.0
Netherlands	14.1	7.4	21.4	21.4	6.2	1.9	1.2	3.2	2.5	0.8
Portugal	0.0	0.0	..	0.0	0.0	0.0	0.0	..	0.0	0.0
Spain	0.0	0.0	..	0.0	0.0	0.0	0.0	..	0.0	0.0
Sweden	13.5	2.9	3.7	8.7	24.2	1.8	0.5	0.5	1.0	3.1
United Kingdom	85.7	9.4	23.9	2.6	3.1	11.5	1.5	3.6	0.3	0.4
Czech Republic	0.0	0.0	..	0.0	0.0	0.0	0.0	..	0.0	0.0
Hungary	0.0	0.0	..	0.0	0.0	0.0	0.0	..	0.0	0.0
Iceland	0.0	0.0	..	0.0	0.0	0.0	0.0	..	0.0	0.0
Norway	..	..	..	..	0.0	..	..	..	..	0.0
Poland	0.0	0.0	..	0.0	0.0	0.0	0.0	..	0.0	0.0
Slovak Republic	0.0	0.0	..	0.0	0.0	0.0	0.0	..	0.0	0.0
Switzerland	52.5	..	72.2	22.4	53.3	7.0	..	10.8	2.6	6.9
Turkey	..	0.0	..	..	0.0	..	0.0	..	..	0.0
Non-OECD Europe, of which:	**4.8**	..	..	**10.6**	**9.6**	**0.6**	..	..	**1.2**	**1.2**
Baltic countries	0.0	0.0	..	0.0	0.0	0.0	0.0	..	0.0	0.0
Bulgaria	0.0	0.0	..	0.0	0.0	0.0	0.0	..	0.0	0.0
Croatia	0.0	0.0	..	0.0	0.0	0.0	0.0	..	0.0	0.0
Romania	..	..	..	..	..	..	..	..	..	..
Russian Federation	0.0	0.0	..	0.0	0.0	0.0	0.0	..	0.0	0.0
Slovenia	0.0	0.0	..	0.0	0.0	0.0	0.0	..	0.0	0.0
Ukraine	0.0	0.0	..	0.0	0.0	0.0	0.0	..	0.0	0.0
Yugoslavia	0.0	0.0	..	0.0	0.0	0.0	0.0	..	0.0	0.0
Non-OECD Asia, of which:	**27.0**	**2.0**	**20.9**	**1.3**	**5.2**	**3.6**	**0.3**	**3.1**	**0.2**	**0.7**
China	16.8	0.1	..	0.0	0.2	2.3	0.0	..	0.0	0.0
Chinese Taipei	0.2	0.1	0.7	0.1	4.0	0.0	0.0	0.1	0.0	0.5
Hong Kong (China)	..	1.7	..	..	..	..	0.3	..	..	..
India	..	..	..	..	..	..	..	..	..	..
Indonesia	0.0	0.0	..	0.0	0.0	0.0	0.0	..	0.0	0.0
Malaysia	..	0.0	..	..	0.0	..	0.0	..	..	0.0
Philippines	0.0	0.0	..	0.0	0.0	0.0	0.0	..	0.0	0.0
Singapore	0.8	..	11.4	0.9	..	0.1	..	1.7	0.1	..
Thailand	0.0	0.0	..	0.0	..	0.0	0.0	..	0.0	..
Near and Middle East	**0.0**	..	..	**6.5**	**0.1**	**0.0**	..	..	**0.8**	**0.0**
Africa	..	**0.0**	..	..	**0.0**	..	**0.0**	..	..	**0.0**
Latin America, of which:	..	..	..	..	..	..	..	..	..	..
Argentina	0.0	0.0	..	0.0	0.0	0.0	0.0	..	0.0	0.0
Brazil	0.0	0.0	..	0.0	0.0	0.0	0.0	..	0.0	0.0
Chile	0.0	0.0	..	0.0	0.0	0.0	0.0	..	0.0	0.0

Note: Majority foreign-owned firms.
Firmes sous contrôle étranger majoritaire.

Inward investments   *Investissements entrants*

Table 19A - Tableau 19A

GROSS OPERATING SURPLUS / EXCÉDENT BRUT D'EXPLOITATION

| | Foreign affiliates *(Billions of JPY)* | | | | | As a % of national total | | | | |
| | Filiales étrangères *(Milliards de JPY)* | | | | | En % du total national | | | | |
By industry (ISIC Rev. 3)	1994	1995	1996	1997	1998	1994	1995	1996	1997	1998
10/14 Mining & quarrying	..	..	0	..	0	..	..	..	..	..
15/37 TOTAL MANUFACTURING	**411**	**570**	**583**	**548**	**537**	..	..	..	..	..
15/16 Food, beverages, tobacco	63	69	70	77	86	..	..	..	..	..
17/19 Textiles, clothing, leather, footwear	6	1	..	1	2	..	..	..	..	..
20/22 Wood and paper products	2	2	3	1	2	..	..	..	..	..
20 Wood products	..	..	..	..	..	..	..	..	..	..
21/22 Paper, printing and publishing	..	..	..	..	..	..	..	..	..	..
23/25 Chemicals, Total	156	146	137	154	166	..	..	..	..	..
23 Refined petroleum, nuclear fuel	33	2	1	11	- 1	..	..	..	..	..
24/25 Chemicals, rubber & plastics prod.	123	144	135	142	167	..	..	..	..	..
24 Chemical products	121	138	123	131	161	..	..	..	..	..
2423 Pharmaceuticals	87	85	84	75	114	..	..	..	..	..
25 Rubber and plastics products	1	5	13	11	7	..	..	..	..	..
26 Non-metallic mineral products	2	1	..	1	1	..	..	..	..	..
27/28 Basic & fabricated metals	3	18	22	10	1	..	..	..	..	..
27 Basic metals	2	18	20	8	1	..	..	..	..	..
28 Fabricated metal products	1	0	1	2	0	..	..	..	..	..
29/32 Machinery, Total	161	302	328	288	231	..	..	..	..	..
29/30 Non-electrical machinery	15	241	263	176	143	..	..	..	..	..
29 Non-electrical machinery nec	15	18	14	173	142	..	..	..	..	..
30 Office and computing machinery	0	223	249	3	1	..	..	..	..	..
31/32 Electrical & electronic equipment	146	61	65	112	88	..	..	..	..	..
31 Electrical machinery nec	2	2	4	11	0	..	..	..	..	..
32 Radio, TV & communications eq.	144	59	61	101	88	..	..	..	..	..
33 Scientific instruments	11	8	15	16	12	..	..	..	..	..
34/35 Transportation equipment	5	5	2	4	36	..	..	..	..	..
34 Motor vehicles	5	4	2	3	36	..	..	..	..	..
35 Other transport equipment	0	2	0	1	1	..	..	..	..	..
351 Shipbuilding & repairing	0	0	0	0	..	..	..	..	..	..
353 Aircraft and spacecraft	..	..	..	..	..	..	..	..	..	..
36/37 Other manufacturing	3	18	5	- 5	0	..	..	..	..	..
40/45 Construction, electricity, gas & water	..	..	..	..	1	..	..	..	..	..
50/55 Trade, repair, hotels & restaurants	191	221	239	197	159	..	..	..	..	..
65/74 Finance, insurance, business services	8	8	2	2	13	..	..	..	..	..
OTHER ACTIVITIES	5	15	15	10	8	..	..	..	..	..
01/99 GRAND TOTAL	**615**	**814**	**839**	**758**	**717**	..	..	..	..	..

Total manufacturing by investing country						As a % of total manufacturing by foreign affiliates				
All countries	411	570	583	548	537	100.0	100.0	100.0	100.0	100.0
United States	330	452	475	426	418	80.2	79.3	81.5	77.7	77.9
Canada	..	..	..	..	..	..	..	..	..	..
Mexico	..	..	..	..	..	..	..	..	..	..
Japan	..	..	..	..	..	..	..	..	..	..
Europe	..	..	..	..	..	..	..	..	..	..
European Union (15)	70	63	61	95	98	16.9	11.1	10.5	17.4	18.3
Belgium	..	..	..	..	..	..	..	..	..	..
France	4	0	0	0	1	1.0	0.0	0.0	0.0	0.2
Germany	35	19	25	20	24	8.6	3.4	4.3	3.6	4.6
Italy	..	..	..	..	..	..	..	..	..	..
Netherlands	2	19	22	25	18	0.6	3.3	3.7	4.6	3.4
Spain	..	..	..	..	..	..	..	..	..	..
Sweden	..	..	..	..	..	..	..	..	..	..
United Kingdom	17	3	11	17	15	4.1	0.5	1.8	3.2	2.7
Switzerland	12	29	22	8	11	2.8	5.0	3.8	1.5	2.1
Australia and New Zealand	..	..	..	..	..	..	..	..	..	..
Asia (non-OECD)	- 3	1	0	0	0	-0.7	0.2	0.0	0.0	0.1
Latin America	..	..	..	..	..	..	..	..	..	..

Note: Majority foreign-owned firms.
Firmes sous contrôle étranger majoritaire.

Inward investments　　　　　　　　　　　　　　　　　　　　　　　　*Investissements entrants*

Table 20A - Tableau 20A

TECHNOLOGICAL PAYMENTS / PAIEMENTS TECHNOLOGIQUES

By industry (ISIC Rev. 3)		Foreign affiliates *(Billions of JPY)* Filiales étrangères *(Milliards de JPY)*					As a % of national total *En % du total national*				
		1994	1995	1996	1997	1998	1994	1995	1996	1997	1998
10/14	Mining & quarrying	..	..	0	..	0	..	..	0.0	..	0.0
15/37	**TOTAL MANUFACTURING**	139	174	193	231	234	37.7	44.7	44.0	53.7	57.5
15/16	Food, beverages, tobacco	1	0	1	33	36	6.1	5.6	8.2	..	..
17/19	Textiles, clothing, leather, footwear	1	1	..	1	0	19.0	7.2	..	10.9	0.6
20/22	Wood and paper products	1	1	1	0	1	93.2	46.8	71.7	11.3	43.1
20	Wood products	..	..	..	..	..	..	..	..	..	..
21/22	Paper, printing and publishing	..	..	..	..	..	..	..	..	..	..
23/25	Chemicals, Total	20	24	25	21	33	29.4	31.8	32.6	26.4	41.3
23	Refined petroleum, nuclear fuel	0	0	0	0	0	12.9	15.1	16.5	9.8	12.0
24/25	Chemicals, rubber & plastics prod.	20	23	25	20	32	30.4	32.4	33.1	27.4	42.4
24	Chemical products	19	23	23	18	30	31.4	34.4	32.6	26.7	41.7
2423	Pharmaceuticals	9	12	10	6	18	28.8	31.5	26.0	15.3	45.6
25	Rubber and plastics products	1	1	2	2	2	20.2	9.2	40.3	35.6	54.1
26	Non-metallic mineral products	1	0	..	1	0	25.8	4.0	..	13.5	5.2
27/28	Basic & fabricated metals	0	0	0	0	0	0.1	0.8	3.4	1.7	3.9
27	Basic metals	0	0	0	0	0	0.2	0.2	3.7	1.6	4.1
28	Fabricated metal products	0	0	0	0	0	0.0	3.0	2.4	3.5	2.9
29/32	Machinery, Total	102	132	149	163	154	50.8	59.6	60.8	67.8	67.3
29/30	Non-electrical machinery	2	131	139	145	141	..	..	..	..	..
29	Non-electrical machinery nec	2	4	4	144	141	..	..	..	..	..
30	Office and computing machinery	0	126	135	0	0	..	..	..	..	..
31/32	Electrical & electronic equipment	100	1	11	19	13	..	..	..	..	..
31	Electrical machinery nec	0	0	3	4	0	..	..	..	..	..
32	Radio, TV & communications eq.	100	1	8	15	13	..	..	..	..	..
33	Scientific instruments	1	2	4	5	5	6.5	16.5	28.4	31.6	54.7
34/35	Transportation equipment	1	1	0	1	1	2.7	2.8	0.9	2.3	2.9
34	Motor vehicles	1	1	0	1	1	11.1	12.0	4.6	10.6	16.7
35	Other transport equipment	0	0	0	0	0	0.0	0.0	0.0	0.0	0.1
351	Shipbuilding & repairing	0	0	0	0	..	..	..	..	..	..
353	Aircraft and spacecraft	..	..	..	..	..	..	..	..	..	..
36/37	Other manufacturing	12	14	12	7	4	44.7	71.9	44.4	38.2	18.6
40/45	Construction, electricity, gas & water	..	..	..	..	0	..	..	..	..	..
50/55	Trade, repair, hotels & restaurants	9	16	13	17	19	..	..	..	..	..
65/74	Finance, insurance, business services	7	12	7	7	20	..	..	..	..	..
	OTHER ACTIVITIES	2	2	17	21	21	..	..	..	..	..
01/99	**GRAND TOTAL**	157	204	231	277	294	42.5	52.0	51.1	63.1	68.4

Total manufacturing by investing country	1994	1995	1996	1997	1998	As a % of total manufacturing by foreign affiliates				
						1994	1995	1996	1997	1998
All countries	139	174	193	231	234	100.0	100.0	100.0	100.0	100.0
United States	124	150	173	209	211	89.4	86.3	89.4	90.4	90.3
Canada	..	..	..	..	..	..	..	..	..	..
Mexico	..	..	..	..	..	..	..	..	..	..
Japan	..	..	..	..	..	..	..	..	..	..
Europe	..	..	..	..	..	..	..	..	..	..
European Union (15)	13	18	14	18	17	9.4	10.6	7.3	7.8	7.2
Belgium	..	..	..	..	..	..	..	..	..	..
France	0	0	0	1	1	0.1	0.2	0.0	0.3	0.3
Germany	6	6	2	2	3	4.0	3.7	1.3	0.9	1.2
Italy	..	..	..	..	..	..	..	..	..	..
Netherlands	6	9	11	10	9	4.0	5.2	5.7	4.4	3.9
Spain	..	..	..	..	..	..	..	..	..	..
Sweden	..	..	..	..	..	..	..	..	..	..
United Kingdom	1	0	1	0	0	1.0	0.0	0.3	0.1	0.1
Switzerland	1	4	5	3	5	0.5	2.2	2.6	1.3	2.0
Australia and New Zealand	..	..	..	..	..	..	..	..	..	..
Asia (non-OECD)	0	0	0	0	0	0.1	0.0	0.0	0.0	0.0
Latin America	..	..	..	..	..	..	..	..	..	..

Note: Majority foreign-owned firms.
Firmes sous contrôle étranger majoritaire.

Table 21A - Tableau 21A

STOCK OF FOREIGN DIRECT INVESTMENT / STOCK D'INVESTISSEMENT DIRECT ÉTRANGER

By industry (ISIC Rev. 3)		1989	1990	1991	1992	1993	1994	1995	1996	1997	1998
				Foreign affiliates *(Billions of JPY)*							
				Filiales étrangères *(Milliards de JPY)*							
10/14	Mining & quarrying	..	..	..	0.0	..	..	..	0.0	..	0.0
15/37	**TOTAL MANUFACTURING**	..	..	..	**581.1**	**576.3**	**524.2**	**510.4**	**522.8**	**534.2**	**648.1**
15/16	Food, beverages, tobacco	..	..	..	8.3	6.1	9.9	9.7	9.5	11.0	10.5
17/19	Textiles, clothing, leather, footwear	..	..	..	..	2.7	7.1	2.8	..	3.2	3.7
20/22	Wood and paper products	..	..	..	3.0	1.8	5.9	5.5	4.7	1.7	12.7
20	Wood products	..	..	..	..	..	..	..	..	..	..
21/22	Paper, printing and publishing	..	..	..	..	..	..	..	..	..	..
23/25	Chemicals, Total	..	..	..	233.5	238.7	242.3	221.9	243.0	216.2	311.5
23	Refined petroleum, nuclear fuel	..	..	..	0.1	0.1	11.8	1.4	1.0	10.2	10.2
24/25	Chemicals, rubber & plastics prod.	..	..	..	233.4	238.6	230.5	220.6	242.1	206.0	301.2
24	Chemical products	..	..	..	230.4	211.5	196.1	216.9	196.3	152.9	239.4
2423	Pharmaceuticals	..	..	..	127.6	102.3	113.1	122.1	118.3	61.5	105.4
25	Rubber and plastics products	..	..	..	3.0	27.1	34.4	3.7	45.8	53.1	61.8
26	Non-metallic mineral products	..	..	..	6.9	5.7	7.4	3.5	..	6.5	6.0
27/28	Basic & fabricated metals	..	..	..	24.4	23.2	11.0	24.1	24.9	26.5	11.8
27	Basic metals	..	..	..	23.1	22.4	4.1	23.4	24.0	24.3	9.8
28	Fabricated metal products	..	..	..	1.3	0.8	6.9	0.7	0.9	2.2	1.9
29/32	Machinery, Total	..	..	..	..	243.3	217.0	223.7	214.9	245.2	231.6
29/30	Non-electrical machinery	..	..	..	..	20.9	16.2	165.3	154.5	167.5	153.8
29	Non-electrical machinery nec	..	..	..	21.5	19.5	16.2	17.9	12.1	166.6	153.0
30	Office and computing machinery	..	..	..	..	1.4	0.0	147.4	142.4	0.9	0.8
31/32	Electrical & electronic equipment	..	..	..	219.4	222.4	200.7	58.4	60.4	77.7	77.8
31	Electrical machinery nec	..	..	..	4.0	17.1	4.2	1.5	2.8	6.4	3.7
32	Radio, TV & communications eq.	..	..	..	215.4	205.3	196.5	56.9	57.5	71.3	74.2
33	Scientific instruments	..	..	..	27.8	19.9	14.0	6.8	8.5	12.0	11.5
34/35	Transportation equipment	..	..	..	23.0	26.8	6.5	3.5	3.0	3.2	46.5
34	Motor vehicles	..	..	..	21.2	26.3	5.5	3.2	2.5	2.7	45.9
35	Other transport equipment	..	..	..	1.8	0.5	1.1	0.3	0.5	0.5	0.6
351	Shipbuilding & repairing	..	..	..	0.0	0.0	0.0	0.0	0.0	0.0	..
353	Aircraft and spacecraft	..	..	..	..	..	..	..	..	..	..
36/37	Other manufacturing	..	..	..	9.9	8.3	3.2	8.9	9.5	8.7	2.5
40/45	Construction, electricity, gas & water	..	..	..	..	..	..	..	..	..	0.5
50/55	Trade, repair, hotels & restaurants	..	..	..	239.9	154.0	232.4	242.4	259.2	259.1	266.3
65/74	Finance, insurance, business services	..	..	..	49.5	20.4	26.6	9.3	15.3	18.5	28.5
	OTHER ACTIVITIES	..	..	..	..	18.5	119.8	32.5	39.5	34.8	33.7
01/99	**GRAND TOTAL**	..	..	..	**878.3**	**770.4**	**903.1**	**794.9**	**837.2**	**847.1**	**977.0**

Total manufacturing by investing country

	1989	1990	1991	1992	1993	1994	1995	1996	1997	1998
All countries	..	..	..	**581.1**	**576.3**	**524.2**	**510.4**	**522.8**	**534.2**	**648.1**
United States	..	..	..	416.1	392.0	377.7	359.4	341.1	314.5	421.3
Canada	..	..	..	..	..	..	..	..	..	..
Mexico	..	..	..	..	..	..	..	..	..	..
Japan	..	..	..	..	..	..	..	..	..	..
Europe	..	..	..	..	..	..	..	..	..	..
European Union (15)	..	..	..	97.7	99.4	83.8	97.4	91.6	120.8	128.8
Belgium	..	..	..	..	..	..	..	..	..	..
France	..	..	..	2.4	1.4	3.3	1.4	0.7	3.2	2.5
Germany	..	..	..	39.6	45.0	25.5	21.6	30.8	43.0	47.4
Italy	..	..	..	..	..	..	..	..	..	..
Netherlands	..	..	..	6.9	11.0	8.4	21.0	21.0	24.3	28.6
Spain	..	..	..	..	..	..	..	..	..	..
Sweden	..	..	..	..	..	..	..	..	..	..
United Kingdom	..	..	..	25.1	25.8	31.8	21.0	36.0	18.9	19.9
Switzerland	..	..	..	30.8	56.2	48.0	21.1	55.5	67.0	74.7
Australia and New Zealand	..	..	..	..	..	..	..	..	..	..
Asia (non-OECD)	..	..	..	5.2	3.9	4.0	4.1	6.0	2.4	3.3
Latin America	..	..	..	7.2	..	..	..	..	..	..

Note: Majority foreign-owned firms.
Firmes sous contrôle étranger majoritaire.

Inward investments   *Investissements entrants*

Table 22A - Tableau 22A

CAPITAL UNDER FOREIGN INFLUENCE / CAPITAL SOUS INFLUENCE ÉTRANGÈRE

By industry (ISIC Rev. 3)		1989	1990	1991	1992	1993	1994	1995	1996	1997	1998
		Foreign affiliates *(Billions of JPY)*									
		Filiales étrangères *(Milliards de JPY)*									
10/14	Mining & quarrying	..	..	0.0	0.0	..	..	..	0.0	..	0.0
15/37	**TOTAL MANUFACTURING**	..	..	**701.4**	**590.7**	**600.7**	**540.7**	**530.8**	**552.2**	**547.3**	**665.1**
15/16	Food, beverages, tobacco	..	..	11.3	8.3	6.1	9.9	9.7	9.5	11.0	10.5
17/19	Textiles, clothing, leather, footwear	..	..	7.9	..	2.7	7.4	2.8	..	3.2	5.0
20/22	Wood and paper products	..	..	2.7	3.0	1.8	5.9	5.5	4.7	1.7	12.7
20	Wood products	..	..	..	..	..	..	..	..	..	..
21/22	Paper, printing and publishing	..	..	..	..	..	..	..	..	..	..
23/25	Chemicals, Total	..	..	390.3	236.2	254.8	255.0	233.3	262.9	220.7	321.8
23	Refined petroleum, nuclear fuel	..	..	4.6	0.1	0.1	12.5	1.4	1.0	10.5	10.5
24/25	Chemicals, rubber & plastics prod.	..	..	385.7	236.1	254.7	242.5	231.9	262.0	210.2	311.3
24	Chemical products	..	..	383.3	233.1	227.6	208.1	228.2	216.2	157.1	249.4
2423	Pharmaceuticals	..	..	225.7	127.6	113.0	123.8	131.3	135.8	63.9	114.0
25	Rubber and plastics products	..	..	2.4	3.0	27.1	34.4	3.7	45.8	53.1	61.8
26	Non-metallic mineral products	..	..	4.4	6.9	5.7	7.4	3.5	..	6.5	6.0
27/28	Basic & fabricated metals	..	..	26.3	28.2	29.6	11.3	33.5	33.7	34.8	11.9
27	Basic metals	..	..	25.2	26.9	28.8	4.4	32.8	32.7	32.6	10.0
28	Fabricated metal products	..	..	1.2	1.4	0.8	6.9	0.7	0.9	2.3	1.9
29/32	Machinery, Total	..	..	206.1	..	244.7	220.2	223.0	215.3	245.5	232.9
29/30	Non-electrical machinery	..	..	23.7	..	22.2	16.3	164.3	154.6	167.5	154.3
29	Non-electrical machinery nec	..	..	23.4	22.4	20.9	16.3	18.0	12.1	166.6	153.5
30	Office and computing machinery	..	..	0.3	..	1.4	0.0	146.3	142.4	0.9	0.8
31/32	Electrical & electronic equipment	..	..	182.4	220.0	222.4	203.9	58.8	60.7	78.1	78.7
31	Electrical machinery nec	..	..	2.7	4.0	17.2	4.3	1.5	2.9	6.4	3.7
32	Radio, TV & communications eq.	..	..	179.8	216.0	205.3	199.6	57.2	57.9	71.6	75.0
33	Scientific instruments	..	..	26.9	29.0	20.3	14.0	6.8	8.5	12.0	11.6
34/35	Transportation equipment	..	..	18.5	23.0	26.8	6.5	3.5	3.0	3.2	49.8
34	Motor vehicles	..	..	18.1	21.2	26.3	5.5	3.2	2.5	2.7	49.3
35	Other transport equipment	..	..	0.3	1.8	0.5	1.1	0.3	0.5	0.5	0.6
351	Shipbuilding & repairing	..	..	0.0	0.0	0.0	0.0	0.0	0.0	0.0	..
353	Aircraft and spacecraft	..	..	..	..	..	..	..	..	..	..
36/37	Other manufacturing	..	..	7.0	10.3	8.3	3.2	9.2	9.8	8.7	2.9
40/45	Construction, electricity, gas & water	..	..	0.0	..	..	..	..	..	..	0.5
50/55	Trade, repair, hotels & restaurants	..	..	193.9	254.3	164.6	239.7	253.3	270.2	269.7	280.3
65/74	Finance, insurance, business services	..	..	21.8	49.8	20.9	26.8	9.6	15.4	18.9	28.8
	OTHER ACTIVITIES	..	..	14.7	..	18.6	190.3	32.7	40.3	34.9	34.1
01/99	**GRAND TOTAL**	..	..	**931.7**	**902.7**	**806.0**	**997.5**	**826.6**	**878.4**	**871.3**	**1 008.7**

Total manufacturing by investing country

		1989	1990	1991	1992	1993	1994	1995	1996	1997	1998
All countries		..	..	**701.4**	**590.7**	**600.7**	**540.7**	**530.8**	**552.2**	**547.3**	**665.1**
United States		..	..	413.5	420.7	408.2	393.8	368.7	349.8	316.3	433.2
Canada		..	..	..	..	..	..	..	..	..	..
Mexico		..	..	..	..	..	..	..	..	..	..
Japan		..	..	..	..	..	..	..	..	..	..
Europe		..	..	..	..	..	..	..	..	..	..
European Union (15)		..	..	217.2	98.7	101.0	84.1	99.1	103.2	123.4	131.9
Belgium		..	..	..	..	..	..	..	..	..	..
France		..	..	3.7	2.4	1.5	3.3	1.4	0.7	3.2	2.5
Germany		..	..	162.7	40.1	45.9	25.7	21.6	30.9	43.0	47.9
Italy		..	..	..	..	..	..	..	..	..	..
Netherlands		..	..	5.3	7.2	11.4	8.5	21.2	21.0	24.3	28.6
Spain		..	..	..	..	..	..	..	..	..	..
Sweden		..	..	..	..	..	..	..	..	..	..
United Kingdom		..	..	25.7	25.1	25.9	31.7	23.6	47.5	19.0	19.9
Switzerland		..	..	32.0	30.8	56.5	48.0	21.1	55.9	67.4	75.1
Australia and New Zealand		..	..	..	..	..	..	..	..	..	..
Asia (non-OECD)		..	..	3.2	5.6	4.0	4.0	4.3	6.1	2.4	4.7
Latin America		..	..	6.1	7.2	..	..	..	..	..	..

Note: Majority foreign-owned firms.
Firmes sous contrôle étranger majoritaire.

JAPAN

Source

The data are prepared by the Enterprise Statistics Division, Research and Statistics Department and the International Business Affairs Division, Industrial Policy Bureau, MITI, based on the annual survey on *Trends in Business Activities of Foreign Affiliates in Japan*. The data presented in this publication refer to majority foreign-owned firms. The period covered is the fiscal year ending on the 31 March.

National totals:

- *Number of enterprises*, *Number of employees*, *Turnover*, *Value added*, *Wages and salaries* and *Gross fixed capital formation:* the results come from a survey conducted by the Ministry of Finance (Financial statements of incorporated businesses).

- *R&D expenditure:* data are extracted from the OECD's ANBERD database.

- *Number of researchers:* data come from the OECD's ANRSE database and are converted from ISIC Revision 2 to ISIC Revision 3.

- *Technological payments*: data come from the R&D survey conducted by the Management and Coordination Agency (MCA).

Industrial classification

For all variables, the data are classified according to the principal industrial activity of the affiliate.

The industrial classification used for these tables is ISIC Revision 3, based on the classification used for the survey. Firms in the finance, insurance and real estate sector are excluded from the survey as from 1995. Up to and including 1994, part of *Office and computing machinery* (30) is included in *Radio, TV and communications equipment* (32). The following notes apply to all years and variables:

- *Food, beverages, tobacco* (15/16) includes parts of *Growing of cereals* (0111) and *Growing of vegetables* (0112).

- *Textiles, clothing, leather, footwear* (17/19) includes part of *Manufacture of other general purpose machinery* (2919) (*e.g.* gasket).

- *Refined petroleum and coal products* (23) includes parts of *Mining and agglomeration of hard coal* (1010) and *Mining of lignite* (1020).

- *Rubber and plastic products* (25) includes parts of *Tanning and dressing of leather* (1911) and *Manufacture of footwear* (1920).

- *Non-metallic mineral products* (26) includes parts of *Manufacture of other fabricated metal products nec* (2899) and *Other manufacturing nec* (3699).

- *Basic metals* (27) includes parts of *Processing of nuclear fuel* (2330), *Forging, pressing and roll-forming of metal* (2891), *Manufacture of insulated wire and cable* (3130) and *Recycling of metal waste and scrap* (3710).

- *Fabricated metal products* (28) includes parts of *Manufacture of ovens, furnaces and furnace burners* (2914), *Manufacture of other general purpose machinery* (2919) and *Manufacture of domestic appliances nec* (2930).

- *Non-electrical machinery* (29) includes parts of *Manufacture of cutlery, handtools and general hardware* (2893), *Manufacture of other fabricated metal products nec* (2899) and *Manufacture of parts and accessories for motor vehicles* (3430).

- *Office and computing machinery* (30) includes parts of *Manufacture of other general purpose machinery* (2919), *Manufacture of machinery for textile, apparel and leather production* (2926) and *Manufacture of other special purpose machinery* (2929).

- *Electrical machinery nec* (31) includes parts of *Manufacture of ovens, furnaces and furnace burners* (2914), *Manufacture of machine-tools* (2922), *Manufacture of television and radio receivers, sound and video recording* (3230), *Manufacture of medical and surgical equipment* (3311), *Manufacture of instruments* (3312), *Manufacture of industrial process control equipment* (3313).

- *Radio, TV and communications equipment* (32) includes parts of *Manufacture of other electrical equipment nec* (3190), *Manufacture of medical and surgical equipment* (3311) (*e.g.* x-ray equipment) and *Manufacture of instruments* (3312).

- *Scientific instruments* (33) includes parts of *Manufacture of luggage, handbags and the like* (1912), *Manufacture of pharmaceuticals* (2423) and *Manufacture of other general purpose machinery* (2919).

- *Motor vehicles* (34) includes part of *Manufacture of motorcycles* (3591).

- *Other transport equipment* (35) includes parts of *Manufacture of engines and turbines* (2911) and *Manufacture of lifting and handling equipment* (2915).

- *Other manufacturing* (36/37) includes parts of *Manufacture of made-up textiles* (1721), *Manufacture of builder's carpentry and joinery* (2022), *Manufacture of articles of cork, straw and plaiting materials* (2029), *Manufacture of other chemical products nec* (2429), *Manufacture of articles of concrete, cement and plaster* (2695) and *Manufacture of watches and clocks* (3330).

- *Construction, electricity gas & water* (40/45) includes parts of *Agricultural and animal husbandry service activities* (0140) and *Sewage and refuse disposal, sanitation and similar activities* (9000).

- *Trade, repair, hotels and restaurants* (50/55) includes part of *Dramatic arts, music and other activities* (9214).

- *Finance, insurance, real estate and business services* (65/74) includes part of *News agency activities* (9220).

- *Other activities* (01/05; 60/64; 75/99) includes parts of *Repair of personal and household goods* (5260) and *Photographic activities* (7494).

Variables

- *Number of employees* is calculated on a full-time equivalent basis.

- *Intra-firm exports* and *imports* only refer to trade with the parent company.

- *Gross operating surplus* includes the value of fixed capital consumption.

- *Technological payments* refer to payments for royalties and licence fees.

Geographical breakdown

The investor's country is the country of the immediate controller.

JAPON

Source

Les données émanent de la Division des statistiques d'entreprise, Département de la recherche et des statistiques et de la Division des affaires commerciales internationales, Bureau de la politique industrielle, MITI. Elles s'appuient sur l'enquête annuelle concernant les activités industrielles des filiales étrangères au Japon. Les données présentées dans cette publication se rapportent aux entreprises sous contrôle étranger majoritaire. La période couverte est l'exercice budgétaire se terminant le 31 mars. Les résultats sont publiés dans *Trends in Business Activities of Foreign Affiliates in Japan.*

Totaux nationaux :

- *Nombre d'entreprises*, *Nombre de salariés*, *Chiffre d'affaires*, *Valeur ajoutée*, *Salaires* et *Formation brute de capital fixe* : les résultats proviennent d'une enquête réalisée par le Ministère des Finances (*Financial statements of incorporated businesses*).

- *Dépenses de R-D* : les données sont extraites de la base de données ANBERD de l'OCDE.

- *Nombre de chercheurs* : les données proviennent de la base de données ANRSE de l'OCDE et sont converties de la CITI révision 2 vers la CITI révision 3.

- *Paiements technologiques* : les données proviennent de l'enquête sur la R-D menée par l'Agence de gestion et de coordination (MCA).

Classification industrielle

Pour toutes les variables, les données sont classées selon l'activité industrielle principale de l'entreprise affiliée.

La classification industrielle utilisée pour ces tableaux est la CITI révision 3, sur la base de la classification utilisée pour l'enquête. Les entreprises des domaines suivants : finance, assurance et immobilier sont exclues de l'enquête à partir de 1995. A compter de 1994, une partie de *Machines de bureau et ordinateurs* (30) est comprise dans *Appareils de radio, télévision et télécommunication* (32). Les notes suivantes concernent toutes les variables et toutes les années :

- *Alimentation, boissons, tabac* (15/16) comprend une partie de *Culture de céréales* (0111) et *Culture de légumes* (0112).

- *Textiles, habillement, cuir, chaussures* (17/19) comprend une partie de *Fabrication d'autres machines d'usage général* (2919) (exemple : joints d'étanchéité).

- *Fabrication de produits pétroliers raffinés et de produits du charbon* (23) comprend une partie de *Extraction et agglomération de la houille* (1010) et *Extraction de lignite* (1020).

- *Caoutchouc et plastiques* (25) comprend une partie de *Apprêt et tannage des cuirs* (1911) et *Fabrication de chaussures* (1920).

- *Produits minéraux non métalliques* (26) comprend une partie de *Fabrication d'autres ouvrages en métaux* (2899) et *Autres industriesmanufacturières nca* (3699).

- *Métallurgie de base* (27) comprend une partie de *Traitement de matières nucléaires* (2330), *Forge, emboutissage, estampage ; métallurgie des poudres* (2891), *Fabrication de fils et câbles isolés* (3130) et *Récupération de matières métalliques recyclables* (3710).

- *Ouvrages en métaux* (28) comprend une partie de *Fabrication de fours et brûleurs* (2914), *Fabrication d'autres machines d'usage général* (2919) et *Fabrication d'appareils domestiques* (2930).

- *Machines et matériel non électriques* (29) comprend une partie de *Fabrication de coutellerie, d'outillage et de quincaillerie* (2893), *Fabrication d'autres ouvrages en métaux* (2899) et *Fabrication d'équipements automobiles* (3430).

- *Machines de bureau et ordinateurs* (30) comprend une partie de *Fabrication d'autres machines d'usage général* (2919), *Fabrication de machines pour les industries textiles* (2926) et *Fabrication d'autres machines d'usage spécifique* (2929).

- *Machines et appareils électriques* (31) comprend une partie de *Fabrication de fours et brûleurs* (2914), *Fabrication de machines-outils* (2922), *Fabrication d'appareils de réception, enregistrement ou reproduction du son et de l'image* (3230), *Fabrication de matériel médico-chirurgical et d'orthopédie* (3311), *Fabrication d'instruments de mesure et de contrôle* (3312), *Fabrication d'équipements de contrôle des processus industriels* (3313).

- *Appareils de radio, télévision et télécommunication* (32) comprend une partie de *Fabrication d'autres matériels électriques* (3190), *Fabrication de matériel médico-chirurgical et d'orthopédie* (3311) (exemple : équipements radiologiques) et *Fabrication d'instruments de mesure et de contrôle* (3312).

- *Instruments scientifiques* (33) comprend une partie de *Fabrication d'articles de voyage et de maroquinerie* (1912), *Fabrication de produits pharmaceutiques* (2423) et *Fabrication d'autres machines d'usage général* (2919).

- *Véhicules automobiles* (34) comprend une partie de *Fabrication de motocycles* (3591).

- *Autres matériels de transport* (35) comprend une partie de *Fabrication de moteurs et turbines* (2911) et *Fabrication de matériel de levage et de manutention* (2915).

- *Autres industries manufacturières* (36/37) comprend une partie de *Fabrication d'articles textiles* (1721), *Fabrication de charpentes et de menuiserie* (2022), *Fabrication d'objets en bois, liège et vannerie* (2029), *Fabrication d'autres produits chimiques nca* (2429), *Fabrication d'ouvrages en béton, ciment ou plâtre* (2695) et *Horlogerie* (3330).

- *Construction, electricité gaz et eau* (40/45) comprend une partie de *Services annexes à l'agriculture* (0140) et *Assainissement, voirie et gestion des déchets* (9000).

- *Commerce, réparation, hôtels et restaurants* (50/55) comprend une partie de *Art dramatique, musique et autres activités* (9214).

- *Finance, assurance, immobilier et services aux entreprises* (65/74) comprend une partie de *Agences de presse* (9220).

- *Autres activités* (01/05 ; 60/64 ; 75/99) comprend une partie de *Réparation d'articles personnels et domestiques* (5260) et *Activités photographiques* (7494).

Variables

- Le *Nombre de salariés* est calculé sur la base d'un équivalent plein-temps.

- Les *Exportations* et *Importations intra-firme* concernent seulement les échanges avec la maison mère.

- L'*Excédent brut d'exploitation* comprend la valeur de la consommation de capital fixe.

- Les *Paiements technologiques* concernent les paiements au titre des redevances et droits de licence.

Ventilation géographique

Le pays investisseur est celui où se situe le contrôle immédiat.

LUXEMBOURG

A. Inward investments

B. Outward investments

Sources and Methods

LUXEMBOURG

A. Investissements entrants

B. Investissements sortants

Sources et méthodes

Table 1A - Tableau 1A

NUMBER OF ENTERPRISES / NOMBRE D'ENTREPRISES

By industry (ISIC Rev. 3)		Foreign affiliates (Units) Filiales étrangères (Unités)					As a % of national total En % du total national				
		1995	1996	1997	1998	1999	1995	1996	1997	1998	1999
10/14	Mining & quarrying	..	..	0	..	..	..	..	0.0	..	..
15/37	**TOTAL MANUFACTURING**	**51**	**50**	**51**	**59**	..	..	..	**5.8**	..	..
15/16	Food, beverages, tobacco	..	..	..	..	..	..	..	..	..	..
17/19	Textiles, clothing, leather, footwear	..	..	..	..	..	..	..	..	..	..
20/22	Wood and paper products	..	..	..	..	..	..	..	..	..	..
20	Wood products	..	..	..	..	..	..	..	..	..	..
21/22	Paper, printing and publishing	..	..	..	..	..	..	..	..	..	..
23/25	Chemicals, Total	..	..	..	..	..	..	..	..	..	..
23	Refined petroleum, nuclear fuel	..	..	..	..	..	..	..	..	..	..
24/25	Chemicals, rubber & plastics prod.	..	..	..	..	..	..	..	..	..	..
24	Chemical products	..	..	..	..	..	..	..	..	..	..
2423	Pharmaceuticals	..	..	..	..	..	..	..	..	..	..
25	Rubber and plastics products	..	..	..	..	..	..	..	..	..	..
26	Non-metallic mineral products	..	..	..	..	..	..	..	..	..	..
27/28	Basic & fabricated metals	..	..	..	..	..	..	..	..	..	..
27	Basic metals	..	..	..	..	..	..	..	..	..	..
28	Fabricated metal products	..	..	..	..	..	..	..	..	..	..
29/32	Machinery, Total	..	..	..	..	..	..	..	..	..	..
29/30	Non-electrical machinery	..	..	..	..	..	..	..	..	..	..
29	Non-electrical machinery nec	..	..	..	..	..	..	..	..	..	..
30	Office and computing machinery	..	..	..	..	..	..	..	..	..	..
31/32	Electrical & electronic equipment	..	..	..	..	..	..	..	..	..	..
31	Electrical machinery nec	..	..	..	..	..	..	..	..	..	..
32	Radio, TV & communications eq.	..	..	..	..	..	..	..	..	..	..
33	Scientific instruments	..	..	..	..	..	..	..	..	..	..
34/35	Transportation equipment	..	..	..	..	..	..	..	..	..	..
34	Motor vehicles	..	..	..	..	..	..	..	..	..	..
35	Other transport equipment	..	..	..	..	..	..	..	..	..	..
351	Shipbuilding & repairing	..	..	..	..	..	..	..	..	..	..
353	Aircraft and spacecraft	..	..	..	..	..	..	..	..	..	..
36/37	Other manufacturing	..	..	..	..	..	..	..	..	..	..
40/45	Construction, electricity, gas & water	..	..	7	..	..	..	..	0.4	..	..
50/55	Trade, repair, hotels & restaurants	..	..	29	..	..	..	..	0.3	..	..
65/74	Finance, insurance, business services	..	..	416	..	..	..	..	8.1	..	..
	OTHER ACTIVITIES	..	..	6	..	..	..	..	0.3	..	..
01/99	**GRAND TOTAL**	..	..	**509**	..	..	..	..	**2.7**	..	..

Total manufacturing by investing country						As a % of total manufacturing by foreign affiliates				
All countries	**51**	**50**	**51**	**59**	..	**100.0**	**100.0**	**100.0**	**100.0**	..
United States	..	..	18	..	..	..	..	35.3	..	..
Canada	..	..	..	..	..	..	..	..	..	..
Mexico	..	..	0	..	..	..	..	0.0	..	..
Japan	..	..	1	..	..	..	..	2.0	..	..
Europe	..	..	31	..	..	..	..	60.8	..	..
European Union (15)	..	..	31	..	..	..	..	60.8	..	..
Belgium	..	..	..	..	..	..	..	..	..	..
France	..	..	12	..	..	..	..	23.5	..	..
Germany	..	..	5	..	..	..	..	9.8	..	..
Italy	..	..	..	..	..	..	..	..	..	..
Netherlands	..	..	3	..	..	..	..	5.9	..	..
Spain	..	..	0	..	..	..	..	0.0	..	..
Sweden	..	..	..	..	..	..	..	..	..	..
United Kingdom	..	..	3	..	..	..	..	5.9	..	..
Switzerland	..	..	0	..	..	..	..	0.0	..	..
Australia and New Zealand	..	..	0	..	..	..	..	0.0	..	..
Asia (non-OECD)	..	..	0	..	..	..	..	0.0	..	..
Latin America	..	..	0	..	..	..	..	0.0	..	..

Note: Majority foreign-owned enterprises.
Entreprises sous contrôle étranger majoritaire.

Table 2A - Tableau 2A

NUMBER OF EMPLOYEES / NOMBRE DE SALARIÉS

By industry (ISIC Rev. 3)		Foreign affiliates *(Units)* Filiales étrangères *(Unités)*					As a % of national total En % du total national				
		1995	1996	1997	1998	1999	1995	1996	1997	1998	1999
10/14	Mining & quarrying	..	..	0	0	..	..	..	0.0	..	..
15/37	**TOTAL MANUFACTURING**	**13 350**	**13 294**	**13 508**	**14 677**	**..**	**41.2**	**41.8**	**42.7**	**46.3**	**..**
15/16	Food, beverages, tobacco	..	..	..	..	..	..	..	..	..	..
17/19	Textiles, clothing, leather, footwear	..	..	..	..	..	..	..	..	..	..
20/22	Wood and paper products	..	..	..	..	..	..	..	..	..	..
20	Wood products	..	..	..	..	..	..	..	..	..	..
21/22	Paper, printing and publishing	..	..	..	..	..	..	..	..	..	..
23/25	Chemicals, Total	..	..	..	..	..	..	..	..	..	..
23	Refined petroleum, nuclear fuel	..	..	..	..	..	..	..	..	..	..
24/25	Chemicals, rubber & plastics prod.	..	..	..	..	..	..	..	..	..	..
24	Chemical products	..	..	..	..	..	..	..	..	..	..
2423	Pharmaceuticals	..	..	..	..	..	..	..	..	..	..
25	Rubber and plastics products	..	..	..	..	..	..	..	..	..	..
26	Non-metallic mineral products	..	..	..	..	..	..	..	..	..	..
27/28	Basic & fabricated metals	..	..	..	..	..	..	..	..	..	..
27	Basic metals	..	..	..	..	..	..	..	..	..	..
28	Fabricated metal products	..	..	..	..	..	..	..	..	..	..
29/32	Machinery, Total	..	..	..	..	..	..	..	..	..	..
29/30	Non-electrical machinery	..	..	..	..	..	..	..	..	..	..
29	Non-electrical machinery nec	..	..	..	..	..	..	..	..	..	..
30	Office and computing machinery	..	..	..	..	..	..	..	..	..	..
31/32	Electrical & electronic equipment	..	..	..	..	..	..	..	..	..	..
31	Electrical machinery nec	..	..	..	..	..	..	..	..	..	..
32	Radio, TV & communications eq.	..	..	..	..	..	..	..	..	..	..
33	Scientific instruments	..	..	..	..	..	..	..	..	..	..
34/35	Transportation equipment	..	..	..	..	..	..	..	..	..	..
34	Motor vehicles	..	..	..	..	..	..	..	..	..	..
35	Other transport equipment	..	..	..	..	..	..	..	..	..	..
351	Shipbuilding & repairing	..	..	..	..	..	..	..	..	..	..
353	Aircraft and spacecraft	..	..	..	..	..	..	..	..	..	..
36/37	Other manufacturing	..	..	..	..	..	..	..	..	..	..
40/45	Construction, electricity, gas & water	..	..	797	795	..	..	..	3.2	3.1	..
50/55	Trade, repair, hotels & restaurants	..	..	2 084	2 237	..	..	..	5.2	5.3	..
65/74	Finance, insurance, business services	..	..	14 027	20 870	..	..	..	30.1	40.8	..
	OTHER ACTIVITIES	..	..	360	372	..	..	..	0.5	0.5	..
01/99	**GRAND TOTAL**	**..**	**..**	**30 776**	**38 951**	**..**	**..**	**..**	**14.6**	**17.7**	**..**

Total manufacturing by investing country	1995	1996	1997	1998	1999	As a % of total manufacturing by foreign affiliates				
All countries	**13 350**	**13 294**	**13 508**	**14 677**	**..**	**100.0**	**100.0**	**100.0**	**100.0**	**..**
United States	..	..	7 381	7 613	..	..	..	54.6	51.9	..
Canada	..	..	..	..	..	..	..	..	..	..
Mexico	..	..	0	..	..	..	..	0.0	..	..
Japan	..	..	..	..	..	..	..	..	..	..
Europe	..	..	4 992	..	..	..	..	37.0	..	..
European Union (15)	..	..	4 992	5 587	..	..	..	37.0	38.1	..
Belgium	..	..	81	103	..	..	..	0.6	0.7	..
France	..	..	1 540	..	..	..	..	11.4	..	..
Germany	..	..	1 328	..	..	..	..	9.8	..	..
Italy	..	..	..	..	..	..	..	..	..	..
Netherlands	..	..	435	..	..	..	..	3.2	..	..
Spain	..	..	0	..	..	..	..	0.0	..	..
Sweden	..	..	..	..	..	..	..	..	..	..
United Kingdom	..	..	326	445	..	..	..	2.4	3.0	..
Switzerland	..	..	0	..	..	..	..	0.0	..	..
Australia and New Zealand	..	..	0	..	..	..	..	0.0	..	..
Asia (non-OECD)	..	..	0	..	..	..	..	0.0	..	..
Latin America	..	..	0	..	..	..	..	0.0	..	..

Note: Majority foreign-owned enterprises.
Entreprises sous contrôle étranger majoritaire.

Inward investments

Investissements entrants

Table 3A - Tableau 3A

TURNOVER / CHIFFRE D'AFFAIRES

By industry (ISIC Rev. 3)		Foreign affiliates *(Millions of LUF)* Filiales étrangères *(Millions de LUF)*					As a % of national total En % du total national				
		1995	1996	1997	1998	1999	1995	1996	1997	1998	1999
10/14	Mining & quarrying	..	..	0	0	..	..	..	..	..	..
15/37	**TOTAL MANUFACTURING**	**109 860**	**109 092**	**123 258**	**138 345**	**..**	**46.5**	**48.4**	**49.4**	**52.4**	**..**
15/16	Food, beverages, tobacco	..	..	..	..	..	..	..	..	..	..
17/19	Textiles, clothing, leather, footwear	..	..	..	..	..	..	..	..	..	..
20/22	Wood and paper products	..	..	..	..	..	..	..	..	..	..
20	Wood products	..	..	..	..	..	..	..	..	..	..
21/22	Paper, printing and publishing	..	..	..	..	..	..	..	..	..	..
23/25	Chemicals, Total	..	..	..	..	..	..	..	..	..	..
23	Refined petroleum, nuclear fuel	..	..	..	..	..	..	..	..	..	..
24/25	Chemicals, rubber & plastics prod.	..	..	..	..	..	..	..	..	..	..
24	Chemical products	..	..	..	..	..	..	..	..	..	..
2423	Pharmaceuticals	..	..	..	..	..	..	..	..	..	..
25	Rubber and plastics products	..	..	..	..	..	..	..	..	..	..
26	Non-metallic mineral products	..	..	..	..	..	..	..	..	..	..
27/28	Basic & fabricated metals	..	..	..	..	..	..	..	..	..	..
27	Basic metals	..	..	..	..	..	..	..	..	..	..
28	Fabricated metal products	..	..	..	..	..	..	..	..	..	..
29/32	Machinery, Total	..	..	..	..	..	..	..	..	..	..
29/30	Non-electrical machinery	..	..	..	..	..	..	..	..	..	..
29	Non-electrical machinery nec	..	..	..	..	..	..	..	..	..	..
30	Office and computing machinery	..	..	..	..	..	..	..	..	..	..
31/32	Electrical & electronic equipment	..	..	..	..	..	..	..	..	..	..
31	Electrical machinery nec	..	..	..	..	..	..	..	..	..	..
32	Radio, TV & communications eq.	..	..	..	..	..	..	..	..	..	..
33	Scientific instruments	..	..	..	..	..	..	..	..	..	..
34/35	Transportation equipment	..	..	..	..	..	..	..	..	..	..
34	Motor vehicles	..	..	..	..	..	..	..	..	..	..
35	Other transport equipment	..	..	..	..	..	..	..	..	..	..
351	Shipbuilding & repairing	..	..	..	..	..	..	..	..	..	..
353	Aircraft and spacecraft	..	..	..	..	..	..	..	..	..	..
36/37	Other manufacturing	..	..	..	..	..	..	..	..	..	..
40/45	Construction, electricity, gas & water	..	..	5 207	3 283	..	..	..	5.8	3.5	..
50/55	Trade, repair, hotels & restaurants	..	..	59 760	58 726	..	..	..	47.6	45.0	..
65/74	Finance, insurance, business services	..	..	129 951	178 371	..	..	..	26.2	33.1	..
	OTHER ACTIVITIES	..	..	7 531	11 140	..	..	..	2.9	4.1	..
01/99	**GRAND TOTAL**	**..**	**..**	**325 707**	**389 865**	**..**	**..**	**..**	**26.6**	**29.9**	**..**

Total manufacturing by investing country	1995	1996	1997	1998	1999	As a % of total manufacturing by foreign affiliates				
All countries	**109 860**	**109 092**	**123 258**	**138 345**	**..**	**100.0**	**100.0**	**100.0**	**100.0**	**..**
United States	..	..	65 092	69 971	..	..	..	52.8	50.6	..
Canada	..	..	..	..	..	..	..	..	..	..
Mexico	..	..	0	..	..	..	..	0.0	..	..
Japan	..	..	..	..	..	..	..	..	..	..
Europe	..	..	38 410	..	..	..	..	31.2	..	..
European Union (15)	..	..	38 410	46 333	..	..	..	31.2	33.5	..
Belgium	..	..	403	1 224	..	..	..	0.3	0.9	..
France	..	..	14 219	..	..	..	..	11.5	..	..
Germany	..	..	9 736	..	..	..	..	7.9	..	..
Italy	..	..	..	..	..	..	..	..	..	..
Netherlands	..	..	2 552	..	..	..	..	2.1	..	..
Spain	..	..	0	..	..	..	..	0.0	..	..
Sweden	..	..	..	..	..	..	..	..	..	..
United Kingdom	..	..	3 064	4 470	..	..	..	2.5	3.2	..
Switzerland	..	..	0	..	..	..	..	0.0	..	..
Australia and New Zealand	..	..	0	..	..	..	..	0.0	..	..
Asia (non-OECD)	..	..	0	..	..	..	..	0.0	..	..
Latin America	..	..	0	..	..	..	..	0.0	..	..

Note: Majority foreign-owned enterprises.
Entreprises sous contrôle étranger majoritaire.

Table 4A - Tableau 4A

STOCK OF FOREIGN DIRECT INVESTMENT / STOCK D'INVESTISSEMENT DIRECT ÉTRANGER

By industry (ISIC Rev. 3)		Foreign affiliates (Millions of LUF) Filiales étrangères (Millions de LUF)									
		1990	1991	1992	1993	1994	1995	1996	1997	1998	1999
10/14	Mining & quarrying	..	..	..	..	..	..	..	0	..	..
15/37	**TOTAL MANUFACTURING**	..	..	..	..	..	57 786	67 753	71 678	98 528	..
15/16	Food, beverages, tobacco	..	..	..	..	..	..	..	..	..	..
17/19	Textiles, clothing, leather, footwear	..	..	..	..	..	..	..	..	..	..
20/22	Wood and paper products	..	..	..	..	..	..	..	..	..	..
20	Wood products	..	..	..	..	..	..	..	..	..	..
21/22	Paper, printing and publishing	..	..	..	..	..	..	..	..	..	..
23/25	Chemicals, Total	..	..	..	..	..	..	..	..	..	..
23	Refined petroleum, nuclear fuel	..	..	..	..	..	..	..	..	..	..
24/25	Chemicals, rubber & plastics prod.	..	..	..	..	..	..	..	..	..	..
24	Chemical products	..	..	..	..	..	..	..	..	..	..
2423	Pharmaceuticals	..	..	..	..	..	..	..	..	..	..
25	Rubber and plastics products	..	..	..	..	..	..	..	..	..	..
26	Non-metallic mineral products	..	..	..	..	..	..	..	..	..	..
27/28	Basic & fabricated metals	..	..	..	..	..	..	..	..	..	..
27	Basic metals	..	..	..	..	..	..	..	..	..	..
28	Fabricated metal products	..	..	..	..	..	..	..	..	..	..
29/32	Machinery, Total	..	..	..	..	..	..	..	..	..	..
29/30	Non-electrical machinery	..	..	..	..	..	..	..	..	..	..
29	Non-electrical machinery nec	..	..	..	..	..	..	..	..	..	..
30	Office and computing machinery	..	..	..	..	..	..	..	..	..	..
31/32	Electrical & electronic equipment	..	..	..	..	..	..	..	..	..	..
31	Electrical machinery nec	..	..	..	..	..	..	..	..	..	..
32	Radio, TV & communications eq.	..	..	..	..	..	..	..	..	..	..
33	Scientific instruments	..	..	..	..	..	..	..	..	..	..
34/35	Transportation equipment	..	..	..	..	..	..	..	..	..	..
34	Motor vehicles	..	..	..	..	..	..	..	..	..	..
35	Other transport equipment	..	..	..	..	..	..	..	..	..	..
351	Shipbuilding & repairing	..	..	..	..	..	..	..	..	..	..
353	Aircraft and spacecraft	..	..	..	..	..	..	..	..	..	..
36/37	Other manufacturing	..	..	..	..	..	..	..	..	..	..
40/45	Construction, electricity, gas & water	..	..	..	..	..	..	..	918	..	..
50/55	Trade, repair, hotels & restaurants	..	..	..	..	..	..	..	4 448	..	..
65/74	Finance, insurance, business services	..	..	..	..	..	..	..	397 476	..	..
	OTHER ACTIVITIES	..	..	..	..	..	..	..	3 626	..	..
01/99	**GRAND TOTAL**	..	..	..	..	..	..	..	478 146	..	..

Total manufacturing by investing country

	1990	1991	1992	1993	1994	1995	1996	1997	1998	1999
All countries	..	..	..	..	..	57 786	67 753	71 678	98 528	..
United States	..	..	..	..	..	..	..	48 595	..	..
Canada	..	..	..	..	..	..	..	..	..	..
Mexico	..	..	..	..	..	..	..	0	..	..
Japan	..	..	..	..	..	..	..	..	..	..
Europe	..	..	..	..	..	..	..	17 804	..	..
European Union (15)	..	..	..	..	..	..	..	17 804	..	..
Belgium	..	..	..	..	..	..	..	..	..	..
France	..	..	..	..	..	..	..	7 329	..	..
Germany	..	..	..	..	..	..	..	3 290	..	..
Italy	..	..	..	..	..	..	..	..	..	..
Netherlands	..	..	..	..	..	..	..	..	..	..
Spain	..	..	..	..	..	..	..	0	..	..
Sweden	..	..	..	..	..	..	..	..	..	..
United Kingdom	..	..	..	..	..	..	..	1 254	..	..
Switzerland	..	..	..	..	..	..	..	0	..	..
Australia and New Zealand	..	..	..	..	..	..	..	0	..	..
Asia (non-OECD)	..	..	..	..	..	..	..	0	..	..
Latin America	..	..	..	..	..	..	..	0	..	..

Note: Majority foreign-owned firms.
Firmes sous contrôle étranger majoritaire.

Outward investments

Investissements sortants

Table 1B - Tableau 1B

NUMBER OF ENTERPRISES / NOMBRE D'ENTREPRISES

| | | Foreign affiliates *(Units)* | | | | | As a % of national total | | | | |
| | | Filiales étrangères *(Unités)* | | | | | En % du total national | | | | |
By industry (ISIC Rev. 3)		1995	1996	1997	1998	1999	1995	1996	1997	1998	1999
10/14	Mining & quarrying	..	..	0	..	..	..	..	0.0	..	..
15/37	**TOTAL MANUFACTURING**	**76**	**92**	**102**	**112**	..	..	..	**11.6**	..	..
15/16	Food, beverages, tobacco	..	..	..	..	..	..	..	..	..	..
17/19	Textiles, clothing, leather, footwear	..	..	..	..	..	..	..	..	..	..
20/22	Wood and paper products	..	..	..	..	..	..	..	..	..	..
20	Wood products	..	..	..	..	..	..	..	..	..	..
21/22	Paper, printing and publishing	..	..	..	..	..	..	..	..	..	..
23/25	Chemicals, Total	..	..	..	..	..	..	..	..	..	..
23	Refined petroleum, nuclear fuel	..	..	..	..	..	..	..	..	..	..
24/25	Chemicals, rubber & plastics prod.	..	..	..	..	..	..	..	..	..	..
24	Chemical products	..	..	..	..	..	..	..	..	..	..
2423	Pharmaceuticals	..	..	..	..	..	..	..	..	..	..
25	Rubber and plastics products	..	..	..	..	..	..	..	..	..	..
26	Non-metallic mineral products	..	..	..	..	..	..	..	..	..	..
27/28	Basic & fabricated metals	..	..	..	..	..	..	..	..	..	..
27	Basic metals	..	..	..	..	..	..	..	..	..	..
28	Fabricated metal products	..	..	..	..	..	..	..	..	..	..
29/32	Machinery, Total	..	..	..	..	..	..	..	..	..	..
29/30	Non-electrical machinery	..	..	..	..	..	..	..	..	..	..
29	Non-electrical machinery nec	..	..	..	..	..	..	..	..	..	..
30	Office and computing machinery	..	..	..	..	..	..	..	..	..	..
31/32	Electrical & electronic equipment	..	..	..	..	..	..	..	..	..	..
31	Electrical machinery nec	..	..	..	..	..	..	..	..	..	..
32	Radio, TV & communications eq.	..	..	..	..	..	..	..	..	..	..
33	Scientific instruments	..	..	..	..	..	..	..	..	..	..
34/35	Transportation equipment	..	..	..	..	..	..	..	..	..	..
34	Motor vehicles	..	..	..	..	..	..	..	..	..	..
35	Other transport equipment	..	..	..	..	..	..	..	..	..	..
351	Shipbuilding & repairing	..	..	..	..	..	..	..	..	..	..
353	Aircraft and spacecraft	..	..	..	..	..	..	..	..	..	..
36/37	Other manufacturing	..	..	..	..	..	..	..	..	..	..
40/45	Construction, electricity, gas & water	..	..	2	..	..	..	..	0.1	..	..
50/55	Trade, repair, hotels & restaurants	..	..	43	..	..	..	..	0.5	..	..
65/74	Finance, insurance, business services	..	..	86	..	..	..	..	1.7	..	..
	OTHER ACTIVITIES	..	..	47	..	..	..	..	2.1	..	..
01/99	**GRAND TOTAL**	..	..	**280**	..	..	..	..	**1.5**	..	..

Total manufacturing by country of location						As a % of total manufacturing by foreign affiliates				
All countries	**76**	**92**	**102**	**112**	..	**100.0**	**100.0**	**100.0**	**100.0**	..
United States	..	..	4	..	..	..	..	3.9	..	..
Canada	..	..	..	..	..	..	..	..	..	..
Mexico	..	..	..	..	..	..	..	..	..	..
Japan	..	..	1	..	..	..	..	1.0	..	..
Europe	..	..	..	..	..	..	..	..	..	..
European Union (15)	..	..	72	..	..	..	..	70.6	..	..
Belgium	..	..	..	..	..	..	..	..	..	..
France	..	..	12	..	..	..	..	11.8	..	..
Germany	..	..	22	..	..	..	..	21.6	..	..
Italy	..	..	..	..	..	..	..	..	..	..
Netherlands	..	..	..	..	..	..	..	..	..	..
Spain	..	..	..	..	..	..	..	..	..	..
Sweden	..	..	..	..	..	..	..	..	..	..
United Kingdom	..	..	6	..	..	..	..	5.9	..	..
Switzerland	..	..	..	..	..	..	..	..	..	..
Australia and New Zealand	..	..	..	..	..	..	..	..	..	..
Asia (non-OECD)	..	..	4	..	..	..	..	3.9	..	..
Latin America	..	..	2	..	..	..	..	2.0	..	..

Note: Foreign affiliates majority-owned by national firms.
Filiales étrangères détenues majoritairement par des firmes nationales.

Table 2B - Tableau 2B

NUMBER OF EMPLOYEES / NOMBRE DE SALARIÉS

		Foreign affiliates *(Units)* Filiales étrangères *(Unités)*					As a % of national total En % du total national				
By industry (ISIC Rev. 3)		1995	1996	1997	1998	1999	1995	1996	1997	1998	1999
10/14	Mining & quarrying	..	..	0	..	..	..	..	0.0	..	..
15/37	**TOTAL MANUFACTURING**	**17 725**	**17 807**	**23 763**	**32 018**	..	..	..	**75.2**	..	..
15/16	Food, beverages, tobacco	..	..	..	..	..	..	..	..	..	..
17/19	Textiles, clothing, leather, footwear	..	..	..	..	..	..	..	..	..	..
20/22	Wood and paper products	..	..	..	..	..	..	..	..	..	..
20	Wood products	..	..	..	..	..	..	..	..	..	..
21/22	Paper, printing and publishing	..	..	..	..	..	..	..	..	..	..
23/25	Chemicals, Total	..	..	..	..	..	..	..	..	..	..
23	Refined petroleum, nuclear fuel	..	..	..	..	..	..	..	..	..	..
24/25	Chemicals, rubber & plastics prod.	..	..	..	..	..	..	..	..	..	..
24	Chemical products	..	..	..	..	..	..	..	..	..	..
2423	Pharmaceuticals	..	..	..	..	..	..	..	..	..	..
25	Rubber and plastics products	..	..	..	..	..	..	..	..	..	..
26	Non-metallic mineral products	..	..	..	..	..	..	..	..	..	..
27/28	Basic & fabricated metals	..	..	..	..	..	..	..	..	..	..
27	Basic metals	..	..	..	..	..	..	..	..	..	..
28	Fabricated metal products	..	..	..	..	..	..	..	..	..	..
29/32	Machinery, Total	..	..	..	..	..	..	..	..	..	..
29/30	Non-electrical machinery	..	..	..	..	..	..	..	..	..	..
29	Non-electrical machinery nec	..	..	..	..	..	..	..	..	..	..
30	Office and computing machinery	..	..	..	..	..	..	..	..	..	..
31/32	Electrical & electronic equipment	..	..	..	..	..	..	..	..	..	..
31	Electrical machinery nec	..	..	..	..	..	..	..	..	..	..
32	Radio, TV & communications eq.	..	..	..	..	..	..	..	..	..	..
33	Scientific instruments	..	..	..	..	..	..	..	..	..	..
34/35	Transportation equipment	..	..	..	..	..	..	..	..	..	..
34	Motor vehicles	..	..	..	..	..	..	..	..	..	..
35	Other transport equipment	..	..	..	..	..	..	..	..	..	..
351	Shipbuilding & repairing	..	..	..	..	..	..	..	..	..	..
353	Aircraft and spacecraft	..	..	..	..	..	..	..	..	..	..
36/37	Other manufacturing	..	..	..	..	..	..	..	..	..	..
40/45	Construction, electricity, gas & water	..	..	..	..	..	..	..	..	..	..
50/55	Trade, repair, hotels & restaurants	..	..	700	..	..	..	..	1.7	..	..
65/74	Finance, insurance, business services	..	..	2 090	..	..	..	..	4.5	..	..
	OTHER ACTIVITIES	..	..	..	..	..	..	..	..	..	..
01/99	**GRAND TOTAL**	..	..	**27 162**	..	..	..	..	**12.9**	..	..

Total manufacturing by country of location						As a % of total manufacturing by foreign affiliates				
All countries	**17 725**	**17 807**	**23 763**	**32 018**	..	**100.0**	**100.0**	**100.0**	**100.0**	..
United States	..	..	601	..	..	..	..	2.5	..	..
Canada	..	..	..	..	..	..	..	..	..	..
Mexico	..	..	0	..	..	..	..	0.0	..	..
Japan	..	..	..	..	..	..	..	..	..	..
Europe	..	..	22 780	..	..	..	..	95.9	..	..
European Union (15)	..	..	21 812	..	..	..	..	91.8	..	..
Belgium	..	..	7 310	..	..	..	..	30.8	..	..
France	..	..	246	..	..	..	..	1.0	..	..
Germany	..	..	7 287	..	..	..	..	30.7	..	..
Italy	..	..	151	..	..	..	..	0.6	..	..
Netherlands	..	..	..	..	..	..	..	..	..	..
Spain	..	..	..	..	..	..	..	..	..	..
Sweden	..	..	..	..	..	..	..	..	..	..
United Kingdom	..	..	..	..	..	..	..	..	..	..
Switzerland	..	..	178	..	..	..	..	0.7	..	..
Australia and New Zealand	..	..	..	..	..	..	..	..	..	..
Asia (non-OECD)	..	..	..	..	..	..	..	..	..	..
Latin America	..	..	..	..	..	..	..	..	..	..

Note: Foreign affiliates majority-owned by national firms.
Filiales étrangères détenues majoritairement par des firmes nationales.

Outward investments

Investissements sortants

Table 3B - Tableau 3B
TURNOVER / CHIFFRE D'AFFAIRES

By industry (ISIC Rev. 3)	Foreign affiliates (Millions of LUF) Filiales étrangères (Millions de LUF)					As a % of national total En % du total national				
	1995	1996	1997	1998	1999	1995	1996	1997	1998	1999
10/14 Mining & quarrying	..	..	0	..	..	..	..	..	..	..
15/37 **TOTAL MANUFACTURING**	167 381	204 064	268 826	315 343	..	..	..	..	..	..
15/16 Food, beverages, tobacco	..	..	..	..	..	..	..	..	..	..
17/19 Textiles, clothing, leather, footwear	..	..	..	..	..	..	..	..	..	..
20/22 Wood and paper products	..	..	..	..	..	..	..	..	..	..
20 Wood products	..	..	..	..	..	..	..	..	..	..
21/22 Paper, printing and publishing	..	..	..	..	..	..	..	..	..	..
23/25 Chemicals, Total	..	..	..	..	..	..	..	..	..	..
23 Refined petroleum, nuclear fuel	..	..	..	..	..	..	..	..	..	..
24/25 Chemicals, rubber & plastics prod.	..	..	..	..	..	..	..	..	..	..
24 Chemical products	..	..	..	..	..	..	..	..	..	..
2423 Pharmaceuticals	..	..	..	..	..	..	..	..	..	..
25 Rubber and plastics products	..	..	..	..	..	..	..	..	..	..
26 Non-metallic mineral products	..	..	..	..	..	..	..	..	..	..
27/28 Basic & fabricated metals	..	..	..	..	..	..	..	..	..	..
27 Basic metals	..	..	..	..	..	..	..	..	..	..
28 Fabricated metal products	..	..	..	..	..	..	..	..	..	..
29/32 Machinery, Total	..	..	..	..	..	..	..	..	..	..
29/30 Non-electrical machinery	..	..	..	..	..	..	..	..	..	..
29 Non-electrical machinery nec	..	..	..	..	..	..	..	..	..	..
30 Office and computing machinery	..	..	..	..	..	..	..	..	..	..
31/32 Electrical & electronic equipment	..	..	..	..	..	..	..	..	..	..
31 Electrical machinery nec	..	..	..	..	..	..	..	..	..	..
32 Radio, TV & communications eq.	..	..	..	..	..	..	..	..	..	..
33 Scientific instruments	..	..	..	..	..	..	..	..	..	..
34/35 Transportation equipment	..	..	..	..	..	..	..	..	..	..
34 Motor vehicles	..	..	..	..	..	..	..	..	..	..
35 Other transport equipment	..	..	..	..	..	..	..	..	..	..
351 Shipbuilding & repairing	..	..	..	..	..	..	..	..	..	..
353 Aircraft and spacecraft	..	..	..	..	..	..	..	..	..	..
36/37 Other manufacturing	..	..	..	..	..	..	..	..	..	..
40/45 Construction, electricity, gas & water	..	..	..	..	..	..	..	..	..	..
50/55 Trade, repair, hotels & restaurants	..	..	15 854	..	..	..	..	3.1	..	..
65/74 Finance, insurance, business services	..	..	66 917	..	..	..	..	..	..	..
OTHER ACTIVITIES	..	..	..	..	..	..	..	..	..	..
01/99 **GRAND TOTAL**	..	..	362 147	..	..	..	..	..	..	..

Total manufacturing by country of location						As a % of total manufacturing by foreign affiliates				
All countries	167 381	204 064	268 826	315 343	..	100.0	100.0	100.0	100.0	..
United States	..	..	3 608	..	..	..	..	1.3	..	..
Canada	..	..	..	..	..	..	..	..	..	..
Mexico	..	..	0	..	..	..	..	0.0	..	..
Japan	..	..	..	..	..	..	..	..	..	..
Europe	..	..	263 621	..	..	..	..	98.1	..	..
European Union (15)	..	..	257 875	..	..	..	..	95.9	..	..
Belgium	..	..	88 322	..	..	..	..	32.9	..	..
France	..	..	3 750	..	..	..	..	1.4	..	..
Germany	..	..	107 045	..	..	..	..	39.8	..	..
Italy	..	..	392	..	..	..	..	0.1	..	..
Netherlands	..	..	..	..	..	..	..	..	..	..
Spain	..	..	..	..	..	..	..	..	..	..
Sweden	..	..	..	..	..	..	..	..	..	..
United Kingdom	..	..	..	..	..	..	..	..	..	..
Switzerland	..	..	2 532	..	..	..	..	0.9	..	..
Australia and New Zealand	..	..	..	..	..	..	..	..	..	..
Asia (non-OECD)	..	..	..	..	..	..	..	..	..	..
Latin America	..	..	..	..	..	..	..	..	..	..

Note: Foreign affiliates majority-owned by national firms.
Filiales étrangères détenues majoritairement par des firmes nationales.

Outward investments

Investissements sortants

Table 4B - Tableau 4B

STOCK OF FOREIGN DIRECT INVESTMENT / STOCK D'INVESTISSEMENT DIRECT ÉTRANGER

| By industry (ISIC Rev. 3) | | Foreign affiliates *(Millions of LUF)* | | | | | | | | | |
| | | Filiales étrangères *(Millions de LUF)* | | | | | | | | | |
		1990	1991	1992	1993	1994	1995	1996	1997	1998	1999
10/14	Mining & quarrying	..	..	..	..	..	..	..	0	..	..
15/37	**TOTAL MANUFACTURING**	..	..	..	..	..	58 911	61 500	66 684	73 946	..
15/16	Food, beverages, tobacco	..	..	..	..	..	..	..	..	..	..
17/19	Textiles, clothing, leather, footwear	..	..	..	..	..	..	..	..	..	..
20/22	Wood and paper products	..	..	..	..	..	..	..	..	..	..
20	Wood products	..	..	..	..	..	..	..	..	..	..
21/22	Paper, printing and publishing	..	..	..	..	..	..	..	..	..	..
23/25	Chemicals, Total	..	..	..	..	..	..	..	..	..	..
23	Refined petroleum, nuclear fuel	..	..	..	..	..	..	..	..	..	..
24/25	Chemicals, rubber & plastics prod.	..	..	..	..	..	..	..	..	..	..
24	Chemical products	..	..	..	..	..	..	..	..	..	..
2423	Pharmaceuticals	..	..	..	..	..	..	..	..	..	..
25	Rubber and plastics products	..	..	..	..	..	..	..	..	..	..
26	Non-metallic mineral products	..	..	..	..	..	..	..	..	..	..
27/28	Basic & fabricated metals	..	..	..	..	..	..	..	..	..	..
27	Basic metals	..	..	..	..	..	..	..	..	..	..
28	Fabricated metal products	..	..	..	..	..	..	..	..	..	..
29/32	Machinery, Total	..	..	..	..	..	..	..	..	..	..
29/30	Non-electrical machinery	..	..	..	..	..	..	..	..	..	..
29	Non-electrical machinery nec	..	..	..	..	..	..	..	..	..	..
30	Office and computing machinery	..	..	..	..	..	..	..	..	..	..
31/32	Electrical & electronic equipment	..	..	..	..	..	..	..	..	..	..
31	Electrical machinery nec	..	..	..	..	..	..	..	..	..	..
32	Radio, TV & communications eq.	..	..	..	..	..	..	..	..	..	..
33	Scientific instruments	..	..	..	..	..	..	..	..	..	..
34/35	Transportation equipment	..	..	..	..	..	..	..	..	..	..
34	Motor vehicles	..	..	..	..	..	..	..	..	..	..
35	Other transport equipment	..	..	..	..	..	..	..	..	..	..
351	Shipbuilding & repairing	..	..	..	..	..	..	..	..	..	..
353	Aircraft and spacecraft	..	..	..	..	..	..	..	..	..	..
36/37	Other manufacturing	..	..	..	..	..	..	..	..	..	..
40/45	Construction, electricity, gas & water	..	..	..	..	..	..	..	..	..	..
50/55	Trade, repair, hotels & restaurants	..	..	..	..	..	..	..	2 058	..	..
65/74	Finance, insurance, business services	..	..	..	..	..	..	..	34 482	..	..
	OTHER ACTIVITIES	..	..	..	..	..	..	..	..	..	..
01/99	**GRAND TOTAL**	..	..	..	..	..	..	..	118 509	..	..

Total manufacturing by country of location

	1990	1991	1992	1993	1994	1995	1996	1997	1998	1999
All countries	..	..	..	..	..	58 911	61 500	66 684	73 946	..
United States	..	..	..	..	..	..	..	1 325	..	..
Canada	..	..	..	..	..	..	..	..	..	..
Mexico	..	..	..	..	..	..	..	..	..	..
Japan	..	..	..	..	..	..	..	..	..	..
Europe	..	..	..	..	..	..	..	..	..	..
European Union (15)	..	..	..	..	..	..	..	63 435	..	..
Belgium	..	..	..	..	..	..	..	..	..	..
France	..	..	..	..	..	..	..	679	..	..
Germany	..	..	..	..	..	..	..	9 193	..	..
Italy	..	..	..	..	..	..	..	..	..	..
Netherlands	..	..	..	..	..	..	..	..	..	..
Spain	..	..	..	..	..	..	..	..	..	..
Sweden	..	..	..	..	..	..	..	..	..	..
United Kingdom	..	..	..	..	..	..	..	..	..	..
Switzerland	..	..	..	..	..	..	..	..	..	..
Australia and New Zealand	..	..	..	..	..	..	..	..	..	..
Asia (non-OECD)	..	..	..	..	..	..	..	..	..	..
Latin America	..	..	..	..	..	..	..	..	..	..

Note: Foreign affiliates majority-owned by national firms.
Filiales étrangères détenues majoritairement par des firmes nationales.

LUXEMBOURG

A. Inward investments

Source

The data are prepared by the *Service central de la statistique et des études économiques* (STATEC). They are based on the annual survey on direct investments, which is a joint survey with the *Institut belgo-luxembourgeois du change* (IBLC). Bank statistics are collected by the Central Bank. The survey is only exhaustive in the bank and insurance sectors. However, all large enterprises in the non-financial sector are included. Holding companies are not covered.

A resident enterprise included in the sample is surveyed if the parent company is located abroad or if one or several foreign shareholders holds directly or indirectly at least 10% of its shares or voting rights.

The data in this publication refer to majority foreign-owned enterprises (foreign participating interests of more than 50%).

National totals: provided by the STATEC and fully compatible with foreign affiliates' data.

Industrial classification

For all variables, the data are classified according to the principal industrial activity of the affiliate.

The data are compiled in NACE Revision 1.

For *Turnover* only, banks are not included in *Finance, insurance, real estate and business services* (ISIC 65/74).

Variables

- *Number of employees* is the number of full-time and part-time employees at the end of the year. It is not calculated on a full-time equivalent basis.

Geographical breakdown

The country of origin is in general that of the immediate controller.

B. Outward investments

Source

The data are prepared by the *Service central de la statistique et des études économiques* (STATEC). They are based on the annual survey on direct investments, which is a joint survey with the *Institut belgo-luxembourgeois du change* (IBLC). Bank statistics are collected by the Central Bank. The survey is only exhaustive in the bank and insurance sectors. However, all large enterprises in the non-financial sector are included. Holding companies are not covered.

A resident enterprise included in the sample is surveyed if it holds directly or indirectly one or several subsidiaries, associate companies or branches abroad.

The data in this publication refer to foreign affiliates majority-owned by national firms.

National totals: provided by the STATEC and fully compatible with foreign affiliates' data.

Industrial classification

For all variables, the data are classified according to the principal industrial activity of the resident investing company.

The data are compiled in NACE Revision 1.

For *Turnover* only, banks are not included in *Finance, insurance, real estate and business services* (ISIC 65/74).

Variables

- *Number of employees* is the number of full-time and part-time employees at the end of the year. It is not calculated on a full-time equivalent basis.

Geographical breakdown

The country of destination is in general that of immediate control.

LUXEMBOURG

A. Investissements entrants

Source

Les données sont fournies par le Service central de la statistique et des études économiques (STATEC). Elles sont fondées sur l'enquête annuelle sur les investissements directs, qui est conjointe avec l'Institut belgo-luxembourgeois du change (IBLC). La Banque centrale collecte les données du secteur bancaire. L'enquête est exhaustive uniquement dans les secteurs des banques et assurances. Toutefois, toutes les grandes entreprises du secteur non financier sont couvertes. Les sociétés holding ainsi que les sociétés à participations financières sont exclues.

Une entreprise résidente incluse dans l'échantillon est enquêtée si sa maison mère est établie à l'étranger ou si un ou plusieurs actionnaires étrangers détiennent directement ou indirectement au moins 10 % de ses actions ou de ses droits de vote.

Les données de cette publication se rapportent aux entreprises sous contrôle étranger majoritaire (participation de plus de 50 %).

Totaux nationaux : fournis par le STATEC et entièrement compatibles avec les données relatives aux filiales étrangères.

Classification industrielle

Pour toutes les variables, les données sont classées selon l'activité industrielle principale de l'entreprise affiliée.

La classification industrielle utilisée la NACE Révision 1.

Pour le *Chiffre d'affaires* seulement, les banques ne sont pas incluses dans *Finance, assurance, immobilier et services aux entreprises* (CITI 65/74).

Variables

- Le *Nombre de salariés* est le nombre de salariés à temps plein et à temps partiel à la fin de l'année considérée. Il n'est pas calculé en équivalent plein-temps.

Ventilation géographique

Le pays d'origine est en général le pays où s'exerce le contrôle immédiat.

B. Investissements sortants

Source

Les données sont fournies par le Service central de la statistique et des études économiques (STATEC). Elles sont fondées sur l'enquête annuelle sur les investissements directs, qui est conjointe avec l'Institut belgo-luxembourgeois du change (IBLC). La Banque centrale collecte les données du secteur bancaire. L'enquête est exhaustive uniquement dans les secteurs des banques et assurances. Toutefois, toutes les grandes entreprises du secteur non financier sont couvertes. Les sociétés holding ainsi que les sociétés à participations financières sont exclues.

Une entreprise résidente incluse dans l'échantillon est enquêtée si elle détient directement ou indirectement une ou plusieurs filiales, sociétés affiliées ou succursales à l'étranger.

Les données de cette publication se rapportent aux filiales étrangères dans lesquelles l'investisseur luxembourgeois détient une participation majoritaire.

Totaux nationaux : fournis par le STATEC et entièrement compatibles avec les données relatives aux filiales étrangères.

Classification industrielle

Pour toutes les variables, les données sont classées selon l'activité industrielle principale de l'entreprise d'investissement résidente.

La classification industrielle utilisée la NACE Révision 1.

Pour le *Chiffre d'affaires* seulement, les banques ne sont pas incluses dans *Finance, assurance, immobilier et services aux entreprises* (CITI 65/74).

Variables

- Le *Nombre de salariés* est le nombre de salariés à temps plein et à temps partiel à la fin de l'année considérée. Il n'est pas calculé en équivalent plein-temps.

Ventilation géographique

Le pays de destination est en général le pays où s'exerce le contrôle immédiat.

NETHERLANDS

Sources and Methods

PAYS-BAS

Sources et méthodes

Inward investments　　　　　　　　　　　　　　　*Investissements entrants*

Table 1A - Tableau 1A

NUMBER OF ENTERPRISES / NOMBRE D'ENTREPRISES

	Foreign affiliates (Units) Filiales étrangères (Unités)					As a % of national total En % du total national				
By industry (ISIC Rev. 3)	1994	1995	1996	1997	1998	1994	1995	1996	1997	1998
10/14 Mining & quarrying	..	96	64	46	71	..	38.2	22.1	37.4	26.8
15/37 TOTAL MANUFACTURING	..	**827**	**844**	**859**	**836**	..	**2.4**	**2.6**	**1.4**	**1.8**
15/16 Food, beverages, tobacco	..	125	112	105	94	..	2.2	2.0	1.5	1.7
17/19 Textiles, clothing, leather, footwear	..	36	34	29	23	..	1.5	1.5	0.5	0.6
20/22 Wood and paper products	..	93	108	106	100	..	1.3	1.6	0.7	1.0
20 Wood products	..	..	..	13	12	..	..	..	0.4	0.5
21/22 Paper, printing and publishing	..	..	..	93	88	..	..	..	0.8	1.1
23/25 Chemicals, Total	..	192	218	228	207	..	10.2	12.2	8.3	9.5
23 Refined petroleum, nuclear fuel	..	9	10	10	11	..	40.9	35.7	21.7	31.4
24/25 Chemicals, rubber & plastics prod.	..	183	208	218	196	..	9.9	11.9	8.1	9.1
24 Chemical products	..	123	131	141	130	..	16.0	18.2	12.4	16.0
2423 Pharmaceuticals	..	15	14	15	12	..	13.4	13.1	8.4	10.4
25 Rubber and plastics products	..	60	77	77	66	..	5.5	7.5	4.9	4.9
26 Non-metallic mineral products	..	89	89	88	84	..	7.5	8.0	3.9	4.8
27/28 Basic & fabricated metals	..	92	83	81	90	..	1.7	1.7	0.9	1.2
27 Basic metals	..	24	22	18	16	..	10.8	10.6	5.6	6.0
28 Fabricated metal products	..	68	61	63	74	..	1.3	1.3	0.7	1.1
29/32 Machinery, Total	..	131	128	147	153	..	3.0	3.1	2.0	3.0
29/30 Non-electrical machinery	..	110	108	119	126	..	3.3	3.4	2.1	3.1
29 Non-electrical machinery nec	..	105	103	114	121	..	3.3	3.4	2.3	3.3
30 Office and computing machinery	..	5	5	5	5	..	2.6	3.4	0.9	1.4
31/32 Electrical & electronic equipment	..	21	20	28	27	..	2.1	2.1	1.5	2.3
31 Electrical machinery nec	..	17	17	24	22	..	2.2	2.3	1.7	2.8
32 Radio, TV & communications eq.	..	4	3	4	5	..	2.0	1.6	0.8	1.4
33 Scientific instruments	..	27	28	31	30	..	2.1	2.3	1.3	1.5
34/35 Transportation equipment	..	26	28	25	31	..	1.6	1.8	0.8	1.1
34 Motor vehicles	..	16	21	18	22	..	2.5	3.4	2.0	2.4
35 Other transport equipment	..	10	7	7	9	..	1.0	0.8	0.3	0.5
351 Shipbuilding & repairing	..	1	1	1	..	..	0.1	0.1	0.1	..
353 Aircraft and spacecraft	..	7	3	3	..	..	43.8	7.5	3.8	..
36/37 Other manufacturing	..	16	16	19	24	..	0.5	0.6	0.2	0.4
40/45 Construction, electricity, gas & water	..	70	79	68	67	..	0.2	0.3	0.2	0.1
50/55 Trade, repair, hotels & restaurants	..	1 140	1 102	1 138	1 060	..	0.5	0.4	0.5	0.5
65/74 Finance, insurance, business services	..	629	566	856	770	..	0.6	0.5	0.7	0.6
OTHER ACTIVITIES	..	243	266	320	328	..	0.5	0.4	0.5	0.1
01/99 GRAND TOTAL	..	**3 005**	**2 921**	**3 288**	**3 132**	..	**0.7**	**0.6**	**0.7**	**0.5**

Total manufacturing by investing country						As a % of total manufacturing by foreign affiliates				
All countries	..	827	844	859	836	..	100.0	100.0	100.0	100.0
United States	..	175	180	188	194	..	21.2	21.3	21.9	23.2
Canada	..	..	..	..	..	..	..	..	..	..
Mexico	..	0	0	0	..	..	0.0	0.0	0.0	..
Japan	..	15	21	24	28	..	1.8	2.5	2.8	3.3
Europe	..	..	..	..	..	..	..	..	..	..
European Union (15)	..	483	492	527	492	..	58.4	58.3	61.4	58.9
Belgium	..	..	..	..	..	..	..	..	..	..
France	..	42	37	49	50	..	5.1	4.4	5.7	6.0
Germany	..	108	99	113	110	..	13.1	11.7	13.2	13.2
Italy	..	..	..	..	..	..	..	..	..	..
Netherlands	..	..	..	..	..	..	..	..	..	..
Spain	..	0	0	0	..	..	0.0	0.0	0.0	..
Sweden	..	..	..	..	..	..	..	..	..	..
United Kingdom	..	157	163	183	153	..	19.0	19.3	21.3	18.3
Switzerland	..	54	52	48	39	..	6.5	6.2	5.6	4.7
Australia and New Zealand	..	..	..	..	..	..	..	..	..	..
Asia (non-OECD)	..	0	1	1	..	..	0.0	0.1	0.1	..
Latin America	..	66	77	53	61	..	8.0	9.1	6.2	7.3

Note: Majority foreign-owned firms. Up to 1996, the investor's country is the country of the immediate controller. As from 1997, it is that of the "ultimate beneficial owner".

Firmes sous contrôle étranger majoritaire. Jusqu'en 1996, le pays d'origine est celui où s'exerce le contrôle immédiat. A partir de 1997, il s'agit du "bénéficiaire ultime de l'investissement".

Table 2A - Tableau 2A

NUMBER OF EMPLOYEES BY INDUSTRY

NOMBRE DE SALARIÉS PAR INDUSTRIE

ISIC Revision 3		Foreign affiliates / Filiales étrangères					As a % of national total / En % du total national				
		1994	1995	1996	1997	1998	1994	1995	1996	1997	1998
10/14	Mining & quarrying	..	61	381	2 789	2 205	..	5.7	17.3	30.2	34.9
15/37	**TOTAL MANUFACTURING**	..	**168 401**	**160 487**	**161 296**	**160 651**	..	**20.1**	**19.0**	**19.7**	**21.9**
15/16	Food, beverages, tobacco	..	29 008	29 486	25 573	25 376	..	19.9	19.8	18.4	22.4
17/19	Textiles, clothing, leather, footwear	..	4 595	3 945	3 582	3 180	..	14.2	12.2	12.2	13.0
20/22	Wood and paper products	..	15 673	15 754	16 027	16 614	..	12.6	12.4	13.3	15.0
20	Wood products	..	..	..	1 354	1 424	..	..	..	7.8	8.2
21/22	Paper, printing and publishing	..	..	..	14 673	15 191	..	..	..	14.2	16.3
23/25	Chemicals, Total	..	39 782	39 674	42 356	38 320	..	34.6	34.9	36.8	38.4
23	Refined petroleum, nuclear fuel	..	4 226	4 087	3 796	3 741	..	60.3	59.4	56.5	57.9
24/25	Chemicals, rubber & plastics prod.	..	35 556	35 587	38 560	34 579	..	32.9	33.3	35.6	37.0
24	Chemical products	..	29 652	28 583	31 189	27 995	..	39.2	38.3	41.3	43.2
2423	Pharmaceuticals	..	3 990	3 039	3 591	3 178	..	28.9	22.7	26.0	27.9
25	Rubber and plastics products	..	5 904	7 004	7 371	6 584	..	18.3	21.8	22.6	23.0
26	Non-metallic mineral products	..	13 031	14 277	13 618	13 586	..	39.8	43.8	42.8	45.2
27/28	Basic & fabricated metals	..	16 975	16 454	14 950	15 579	..	14.3	13.8	12.6	13.9
27	Basic metals	..	7 804	7 315	5 970	5 039	..	28.9	28.5	23.6	21.3
28	Fabricated metal products	..	9 171	9 139	8 980	10 541	..	10.0	9.7	9.6	11.9
29/32	Machinery, Total	..	25 573	25 246	28 684	28 588	..	16.1	15.6	18.0	19.6
29/30	Non-electrical machinery	..	17 340	17 526	19 531	19 390	..	19.1	18.9	21.5	22.1
29	Non-electrical machinery nec	..	15 326	15 659	17 440	17 480	..	18.5	18.4	20.9	21.6
30	Office and computing machinery	..	2 014	1 867	2 091	1 910	..	25.4	24.2	29.4	28.4
31/32	Electrical & electronic equipment	..	8 233	7 720	9 153	9 198	..	12.2	11.2	13.3	15.8
31	Electrical machinery nec	..	..	..	..	5 379	..	..	..	..	30.2
32	Radio, TV & communications eq.	..	..	..	..	3 819	..	..	..	..	9.5
33	Scientific instruments	..	7 167	7 594	8 396	7 396	..	32.2	32.1	37.3	38.6
34/35	Transportation equipment	..	14 768	6 011	6 200	9 881	..	27.9	12.3	13.0	20.4
34	Motor vehicles	..	4 770	5 171	5 251	8 982	..	19.4	20.1	20.0	35.2
35	Other transport equipment	..	9 998	840	949	899	..	35.2	3.6	4.4	3.9
351	Shipbuilding & repairing	..	..	..	..	..	..	..	..	..	..
353	Aircraft and spacecraft	..	9 413	..	..	..	..	95.8	..	..	..
36/37	Other manufacturing	..	1 829	2 047	1 910	2 131	..	5.3	5.7	5.6	7.0
40/45	Construction, electricity, gas & water	..	8 403	9 645	9 842	9 598	..	2.1	2.4	2.4	2.4
50/55	Trade, repair, hotels & restaurants	..	101 179	101 052	97 181	104 719	..	8.2	7.9	10.9	10.5
65/74	Finance, insurance, business services	..	31 268	36 568	40 938	95 763	..	6.0	6.0	7.5	19.1
	OTHER ACTIVITIES	..	15 145	18 805	23 967	30 976	..	4.6	4.4	5.9	7.2
01/99	**GRAND TOTAL**	..	**324 458**	**326 939**	**336 013**	**403 912**	..	**9.8**	**9.1**	**10.9**	**13.2**

Note: Majority foreign-owned firms. From 1997 onwards, data expressed on a full-time equivalent basis.
Firmes sous contrôle étranger majoritaire. Données exprimées en équivalent plein-temps à partir de 1997.

Table 3A - Tableau 3A

NUMBER OF EMPLOYEES BY COUNTRY OF ORIGIN IN THE MANUFACTURING SECTOR
NOMBRE DE SALARIÉS PAR PAYS D'ORIGINE DANS L'INDUSTRIE MANUFACTURIÈRE

Country of origin	\multicolumn{5}{c}{Number of employees / Nombre de salariés}					\multicolumn{5}{c}{As a % of all countries / En % du total des pays}				
	1994	1995	1996	1997	1998	1994	1995	1996	1997	1998
All countries	..	168 401	160 487	161 296	160 651	..	100.0	100.0	100.0	100.0
Total OECD	..	160 369	151 434	154 681	153 398	..	95.2	94.4	95.9	95.5
United States	..	49 781	49 189	53 301	58 168	..	29.6	30.6	33.0	36.2
Canada	..	424	328	1 197	532	..	0.3	0.2	0.7	0.3
Mexico	..	0	0	0	0	..	0.0	0.0	0.0	0.0
Japan	..	3 021	3 555	4 579	4 556	..	1.8	2.2	2.8	2.8
Korea	..	0	0	0	0	..	0.0	0.0	0.0	0.0
Australia	..	3 185	3 045	776	746	..	1.9	1.9	0.5	0.5
New Zealand	..	0	0	0	0	..	0.0	0.0	0.0	0.0
Europe	..	103 958	95 316	94 828	89 396	..	61.7	59.4	58.8	55.6
European Union (15)	..	90 627	81 566	80 587	78 408	..	53.8	50.8	50.0	48.8
Austria	..	268	261	418	801	..	0.2	0.2	0.3	0.5
Belgium	..	11 843	13 192	8 040	9 210	..	7.0	8.2	5.0	5.7
Denmark	..	1 546	2 046	2 762	2 573	..	0.9	1.3	1.7	1.6
Finland	..	5 544	4 634	4 596	5 214	..	3.3	2.9	2.8	3.2
France	..	9 411	9 305	10 571	10 331	..	5.6	5.8	6.6	6.4
Germany	..	28 249	18 495	16 610	15 045	..	16.8	11.5	10.3	9.4
Greece	..	0	0	0	0	..	0.0	0.0	0.0	0.0
Ireland	..	3 410	3 397	3 515	3 387	..	2.0	2.1	2.2	2.1
Italy	..	..	..	..	207	..	..	..	..	0.1
Luxembourg	..	2 619	2 211	570	334	..	1.6	1.4	0.4	0.2
Netherlands	..	..	..	..	..	..	..	..	..	..
Portugal	..	0	0	0	0	..	0.0	0.0	0.0	0.0
Spain	..	0	0	0	0	..	0.0	0.0	0.0	0.0
Sweden	..	7 574	7 985	7 942	7 555	..	4.5	5.0	4.9	4.7
United Kingdom	..	20 134	20 035	25 560	23 750	..	12.0	12.5	15.8	14.8
Czech Republic	..	0	0	0	0	..	0.0	0.0	0.0	0.0
Hungary	..	0	0	0	0	..	0.0	0.0	0.0	0.0
Iceland	..	0	0	0	0	..	0.0	0.0	0.0	0.0
Norway	..	1 390	1 432	1 446	1 850	..	0.8	0.9	0.9	1.2
Poland	..	0	0	0	0	..	0.0	0.0	0.0	0.0
Slovak Republic	..	0	0	0	9 137	..	0.0	0.0	0.0	0.0
Switzerland	..	11 941	12 318	12 795	9 137	..	7.1	7.7	7.9	5.7
Turkey	..	0	0	0	0	..	0.0	0.0	0.0	0.0
Non-OECD Europe, of which:	..	0	0	0	0	..	0.0	0.0	0.0	0.0
Baltic countries	..	0	0	0	0	..	0.0	0.0	0.0	0.0
Bulgaria	..	0	0	0	0	..	0.0	0.0	0.0	0.0
Croatia	..	0	0	0	0	..	0.0	0.0	0.0	0.0
Romania	..	0	0	0	0	..	0.0	0.0	0.0	0.0
Russian Federation	..	0	0	0	0	..	0.0	0.0	0.0	5.7
Slovenia	..	0	0	0	0	..	0.0	0.0	0.0	0.0
Ukraine	..	0	0	0	0	..	0.0	0.0	0.0	0.0
Yugoslavia	..	0	0	0	0	..	0.0	0.0	0.0	0.0
Non-OECD Asia, of which:	..	0	..	..	..	..	0.0	..	..	..
China	..	0	0	0	0	..	0.0	0.0	0.0	0.0
Chinese Taipei	..	0	3	108	92	..	0.0	0.0	0.1	0.1
Hong Kong (China)	..	0	0	0	0	..	0.0	0.0	0.0	0.0
India	..	0	0	0	0	..	0.0	0.0	0.0	0.0
Indonesia	..	0	0	0	0	..	0.0	0.0	0.0	0.0
Malaysia	..	0	0	0	0	..	0.0	0.0	0.0	0.0
Philippines	..	0	0	0	0	..	0.0	0.0	0.0	0.0
Singapore	..	0	0	0	0	..	0.0	0.0	0.0	0.0
Thailand	..	0	0	0	0	..	0.0	0.0	0.0	0.0
Near and Middle East	..	329	1 077	909	847	..	0.2	0.7	0.6	0.5
Africa	..	0	0	0	1 408	..	0.0	0.0	0.0	0.9
Latin America, of which:	..	7 703	7 973	5 598	4 906	..	4.6	5.0	3.5	3.1
Argentina	..	0	0	0	0	..	0.0	0.0	0.0	0.0
Brazil	..	0	0	0	0	..	0.0	0.0	0.0	0.0
Chile	..	0	0	0	0	..	0.0	0.0	0.0	0.0

Note: Majority foreign-owned firms. From 1997 onwards, data expressed on a full-time equivalent basis. Up to 1996, the investor's country is the country of the immediate controller. As from 1997, it is that of the "ultimate beneficial owner".

Firmes sous contrôle étranger majoritaire. Données exprimées en équivalent plein-temps à partir de 1997. Jusqu'en 1996, le pays d'origine est celui où s'exerce le contrôle immédiat. A partir de 1997, il s'agit du "bénéficiaire ultime de l'investissement".

Inward investments

Investissements entrants

Table 4A - Tableau 4A

PRODUCTION

By industry (ISIC Rev. 3)	Foreign affiliates (Millions of NLG) Filiales étrangères (Millions de NLG)					As a % of national total En % du total national				
	1994	1995	1996	1997	1998	1994	1995	1996	1997	1998
10/14 Mining & quarrying	..	..	20 083	3 373	4 373	..	..	46.3	7.5	10.7
15/37 **TOTAL MANUFACTURING**	..	..	**113 020**	**127 461**	**138 608**	..	..	**29.7**	**30.4**	**31.7**
15/16 Food, beverages, tobacco	..	..	29 322	31 528	34 839	..	..	29.3	29.8	32.1
17/19 Textiles, clothing, leather, footwear	..	..	1 757	1 745	1 696	..	..	20.5	18.6	17.2
20/22 Wood and paper products	..	..	7 874	8 156	9 509	..	..	20.3	19.8	21.3
20 Wood products	..	..	..	324	341	..	..	..	6.4	6.1
21/22 Paper, printing and publishing	..	..	..	7 832	9 169	..	..	..	21.7	23.5
23/25 Chemicals, Total	..	..	45 322	52 940	51 380	..	..	48.7	50.3	51.2
23 Refined petroleum, nuclear fuel	..	..	13 546	14 867	13 961	..	..	59.5	60.1	65.8
24/25 Chemicals, rubber & plastics prod.	..	..	31 777	38 073	37 419	..	..	45.2	47.3	47.3
24 Chemical products	..	..	28 970	34 811	34 207	..	..	48.5	50.6	51.2
2423 Pharmaceuticals	..	..	4 790	6 474	6 960	..	..	49.6	57.4	58.6
25 Rubber and plastics products	..	..	2 807	3 263	3 212	..	..	26.4	27.9	26.1
26 Non-metallic mineral products	..	..	5 131	5 210	5 584	..	..	45.4	41.8	42.4
27/28 Basic & fabricated metals	..	..	7 302	7 212	8 268	..	..	20.9	19.0	20.1
27 Basic metals	..	..	3 371	3 162	3 132	..	..	32.9	27.5	25.8
28 Fabricated metal products	..	..	3 931	4 050	5 136	..	..	15.9	15.3	17.7
29/32 Machinery, Total	..	..	10 394	14 350	15 723	..	..	17.8	21.2	21.9
29/30 Non-electrical machinery	..	..	7 053	10 496	11 467	..	..	23.7	30.3	30.5
29 Non-electrical machinery nec	..	..	5 512	6 607	7 227	..	..	21.3	23.1	23.5
30 Office and computing machinery	..	..	1 541	3 889	4 240	..	..	39.6	64.0	61.7
31/32 Electrical & electronic equipment	..	..	3 341	3 853	4 256	..	..	11.7	11.7	12.4
31 Electrical machinery nec	..	..	..	..	2 571	..	..	..	..	32.5
32 Radio, TV & communications eq.	..	..	..	..	1 685	..	..	..	..	6.4
33 Scientific instruments	..	..	3 166	3 589	3 910	..	..	45.9	50.4	51.7
34/35 Transportation equipment	..	..	1 870	1 943	6 498	..	..	9.4	8.7	22.8
34 Motor vehicles	..	..	1 487	1 500	5 955	..	..	12.4	10.5	34.8
35 Other transport equipment	..	..	384	443	544	..	..	4.9	5.4	4.8
351 Shipbuilding & repairing	..	..	..	..	..	..	..	..	..	..
353 Aircraft and spacecraft	..	..	..	..	..	..	..	..	..	..
36/37 Other manufacturing	..	..	881	788	1 200	..	..	10.1	7.4	10.6
40/45 Construction, electricity, gas & water	..	..	4 765	5 020	4 938	..	..	3.3	3.2	3.1
50/55 Trade, repair, hotels & restaurants	..	..	109 114	135 266	143 931	..	..	17.8	20.1	19.7
65/74 Finance, insurance, business services	..	..	10 996	13 874	17 992	..	..	10.4	11.1	13.3
OTHER ACTIVITIES	..	..	6 439	10 087	11 287	..	..	5.8	8.0	8.4
01/99 **GRAND TOTAL**	..	..	**264 416**	**295 081**	**321 129**	..	..	**18.9**	**19.1**	**19.6**

Total manufacturing by investing country						As a % of total manufacturing by foreign affiliates				
All countries	..	..	113 020	127 461	138 608	..	..	100.0	100.0	100.0
United States	..	..	51 795	67 840	74 824	..	..	45.8	53.2	54.0
Canada	..	..	91	478	358	..	..	0.1	0.4	0.3
Mexico	..	..	0	0	0	..	..	0.0	0.0	0.0
Japan	..	..	2 184	2 957	3 486	..	..	1.9	2.3	2.5
Europe	..	..	51 434	50 279	53 159	..	..	45.5	39.4	38.4
European Union (15)	..	..	38 534	40 870	46 455	..	..	34.1	32.1	33.5
Belgium	..	..	7 805	4 091	5 191	..	..	6.9	3.2	3.7
France	..	..	4 292	4 912	5 183	..	..	3.8	3.9	3.7
Germany	..	..	7 576	8 144	8 331	..	..	6.7	6.4	6.0
Italy	..	..	..	..	140	..	..	..	..	0.1
Netherlands	..	..	..	..	..	..	..	..	..	..
Spain	..	..	0	0	0	..	..	0.0	0.0	0.0
Sweden	..	..	3 364	3 667	3 931	..	..	3.0	2.9	2.8
United Kingdom	..	..	9 668	14 866	17 633	..	..	8.6	11.7	12.7
Switzerland	..	..	11 513	8 104	5 344	..	..	10.2	6.4	3.9
Australia and New Zealand	..	..	2 015	540	666	..	..	1.8	0.4	0.5
Asia (non-OECD)	..	..	..	..	..	..	..	..	..	..
Latin America	..	..	4 652	2 815	2 776	..	..	4.1	2.2	2.0

Note: Majority foreign-owned firms. Up to 1996, the investor's country is the country of the immediate controller. As from 1997, it is that of the "ultimate beneficial owner".

Firmes sous contrôle étranger majoritaire. Jusqu'en 1996, le pays d'origine est celui où s'exerce le contrôle immédiat. A partir de 1997, il s'agit du "bénéficiaire ultime de l'investissement".

Inward investments

Investissements entrants

Table 5A - Tableau 5A

TURNOVER BY INDUSTRY

CHIFFRE D'AFFAIRES PAR INDUSTRIE

ISIC Revision 3		Foreign affiliates (Millions of NLG) Filiales étrangères (Millions de NLG)					As a % of national total En % du total national				
		1994	1995	1996	1997	1998	1994	1995	1996	1997	1998
10/14	Mining & quarrying	..	1 561	20 065	3 371	3 168	..	4.1	46.3	7.5	8.0
15/37	**TOTAL MANUFACTURING**	..	**110 225**	**111 438**	**125 798**	**137 045**	..	**30.3**	**29.7**	**30.4**	**32.1**
15/16	Food, beverages, tobacco	..	27 407	28 822	31 159	34 575	..	28.8	29.4	30.1	32.5
17/19	Textiles, clothing, leather, footwear	..	1 932	1 755	1 716	1 665	..	21.6	20.6	18.5	17.1
20/22	Wood and paper products	..	7 637	7 761	8 070	9 432	..	19.8	20.1	19.7	21.2
20	Wood products	..	..	..	319	341	..	..	..	6.3	6.1
21/22	Paper, printing and publishing	..	..	..	7 751	9 091	..	..	..	21.5	23.3
23/25	Chemicals, Total	..	40 620	44 597	52 173	50 614	..	47.3	49.1	50.6	51.7
23	Refined petroleum, nuclear fuel	..	10 807	13 397	14 810	13 987	..	60.9	59.9	60.3	66.3
24/25	Chemicals, rubber & plastics prod.	..	29 813	31 201	37 362	36 626	..	43.8	45.6	47.5	47.6
24	Chemical products	..	27 360	28 430	34 154	33 508	..	47.7	49.1	50.9	51.7
2423	Pharmaceuticals	..	3 546	4 524	6 230	6 574	..	46.1	49.8	57.6	59.0
25	Rubber and plastics products	..	2 453	2 771	3 209	3 118	..	23.0	26.4	28.0	25.9
26	Non-metallic mineral products	..	4 515	5 087	5 248	5 485	..	41.2	45.4	42.2	42.4
27/28	Basic & fabricated metals	..	7 207	7 388	7 151	8 148	..	21.4	21.2	18.8	20.1
27	Basic metals	..	3 633	3 392	3 104	3 159	..	33.7	33.3	27.4	26.0
28	Fabricated metal products	..	3 574	3 997	4 047	4 988	..	15.6	16.2	15.1	17.6
29/32	Machinery, Total	..	11 200	10 267	14 167	15 720	..	20.4	17.9	21.3	22.6
29/30	Non-electrical machinery	..	6 300	6 970	10 350	11 384	..	22.9	24.0	30.6	31.2
29	Non-electrical machinery nec	..	4 644	5 457	6 469	7 152	..	19.8	21.6	23.3	24.1
30	Office and computing machinery	..	1 656	1 513	3 881	4 232	..	40.6	39.7	64.4	62.4
31/32	Electrical & electronic equipment	..	4 900	3 297	3 817	4 336	..	17.8	11.7	11.7	13.1
31	Electrical machinery nec	..	..	..	..	2 581	..	..	..	..	32.5
32	Radio, TV & communications eq.	..	..	..	..	1 756	..	..	..	..	7.0
33	Scientific instruments	..	2 841	3 060	3 423	3 756	..	45.9	45.9	49.7	50.9
34/35	Transportation equipment	..	6 210	1 833	1 914	6 448	..	29.8	9.1	8.8	24.6
34	Motor vehicles	..	2 999	1 458	1 482	5 910	..	25.2	12.6	10.5	34.9
35	Other transport equipment	..	3 212	375	432	537	..	36.0	4.4	5.6	5.8
351	Shipbuilding & repairing	..	..	..	..	..	..	..	..	..	..
353	Aircraft and spacecraft	..	2 955	..	..	..	..	95.2	..	..	..
36/37	Other manufacturing	..	656	868	778	1 202	..	7.6	10.0	7.4	10.7
40/45	Construction, electricity, gas & water	..	2 992	4 736	4 987	4 922	..	2.2	3.4	3.3	3.1
50/55	Trade, repair, hotels & restaurants	..	94 106	108 160	135 079	142 408	..	16.6	17.8	19.0	19.6
65/74	Finance, insurance, business services	..	8 906	10 537	13 497	17 415	..	9.7	10.3	11.2	13.4
	OTHER ACTIVITIES	..	4 898	6 321	9 912	10 914	..	6.4	6.1	8.4	8.7
01/99	**GRAND TOTAL**	..	**222 688**	**261 257**	**292 645**	**315 873**	..	**17.5**	**19.0**	**18.8**	**19.7**

Note: Majority foreign-owned firms.
Firmes sous contrôle étranger majoritaire.

Table 6A - Tableau 6A

TURNOVER BY COUNTRY OF ORIGIN IN THE MANUFACTURING SECTOR

CHIFFRE D'AFFAIRES PAR PAYS D'ORIGINE DANS L'INDUSTRIE MANUFACTURIÈRE

Country of origin	**Turnover** *(Millions of NLG)* / **Chiffre d'affaires** *(Millions de NLG)*					*As a % of all countries* / *En % du total des pays*				
	1994	1995	1996	1997	1998	1994	1995	1996	1997	1998
All countries	..	110 225	111 438	125 798	137 045	..	100.0	100.0	100.0	100.0
Total OECD	..	105 458	105 864	120 442	130 990	..	95.7	95.0	95.7	95.6
United States	..	47 706	51 123	67 214	74 432	..	43.3	45.9	53.4	54.3
Canada	..	111	90	476	346	..	0.1	0.1	0.4	0.3
Mexico	..	0	0	0	0	..	0.0	0.0	0.0	0.0
Japan	..	1 640	2 174	2 901	3 454	..	1.5	2.0	2.3	2.5
Korea	..	0	0	0	0	..	0.0	0.0	0.0	0.0
Australia	..	1 796	1 942	544	675	..	1.6	1.7	0.4	0.5
New Zealand	..	0	0	0	0	..	0.0	0.0	0.0	0.0
Europe	..	54 205	50 534	49 306	52 083	..	49.2	45.3	39.2	38.0
European Union (15)	..	42 423	38 097	40 171	45 600	..	38.5	34.2	31.9	33.3
Austria	..	158	134	213	386	..	0.1	0.1	0.2	0.3
Belgium	..	6 642	7 747	4 010	5 064	..	6.0	7.0	3.2	3.7
Denmark	..	440	563	1 056	1 132	..	0.4	0.5	0.8	0.8
Finland	..	2 690	2 475	2 370	2 953	..	2.4	2.2	1.9	2.2
France	..	3 868	4 199	4 720	4 956	..	3.5	3.8	3.8	3.6
Germany	..	10 483	7 513	8 017	8 179	..	9.5	6.7	6.4	6.0
Greece	..	0	0	0	0	..	0.0	0.0	0.0	0.0
Ireland	..	1 322	1 300	1 380	1 353	..	1.2	1.2	1.1	1.0
Italy	..	..	..	..	140	..	..	..	..	0.1
Luxembourg	..	3 151	1 318	171	153	..	2.9	1.2	0.1	0.1
Netherlands	..	..	..	..	..	..	..	..	..	..
Portugal	..	0	0	0	0	..	0.0	0.0	0.0	0.0
Spain	..	0	0	0	0	..	0.0	0.0	0.0	0.0
Sweden	..	4 962	3 326	3 619	3 899	..	4.5	3.0	2.9	2.8
United Kingdom	..	8 693	9 521	14 613	17 384	..	7.9	8.5	11.6	12.7
Czech Republic	..	0	0	0	0	..	0.0	0.0	0.0	0.0
Hungary	..	0	0	0	0	..	0.0	0.0	0.0	0.0
Iceland	..	0	0	0	0	..	0.0	0.0	0.0	0.0
Norway	..	1 270	1 284	1 282	1 302	..	1.2	1.2	1.0	1.0
Poland	..	0	0	0	0	..	0.0	0.0	0.0	0.0
Slovak Republic	..	0	0	0	5 181	..	0.0	0.0	0.0	0.0
Switzerland	..	10 512	11 153	7 852	5 181	..	9.5	10.0	6.2	3.8
Turkey	..	0	0	0	0	..	0.0	0.0	0.0	0.0
Non-OECD Europe, of which:	..	0	0	0	0	..	0.0	0.0	0.0	0.0
Baltic countries	..	0	0	0	0	..	0.0	0.0	0.0	0.0
Bulgaria	..	0	0	0	0	..	0.0	0.0	0.0	0.0
Croatia	..	0	0	0	0	..	0.0	0.0	0.0	0.0
Romania	..	0	0	0	0	..	0.0	0.0	0.0	0.0
Russian Federation	..	0	0	0	0	..	0.0	0.0	0.0	3.8
Slovenia	..	0	0	0	0	..	0.0	0.0	0.0	0.0
Ukraine	..	0	0	0	0	..	0.0	0.0	0.0	0.0
Yugoslavia	..	0	0	0	0	..	0.0	0.0	0.0	0.0
Non-OECD Asia, of which:	..	0	1	..	..	..	0.0	0.0	..	..
China	..	0	0	0	0	..	0.0	0.0	0.0	0.0
Chinese Taipei	..	0	1	15	69	..	0.0	0.0	0.0	0.1
Hong Kong (China)	..	0	0	0	0	..	0.0	0.0	0.0	0.0
India	..	0	0	0	0	..	0.0	0.0	0.0	0.0
Indonesia	..	0	0	0	0	..	0.0	0.0	0.0	0.0
Malaysia	..	0	0	0	0	..	0.0	0.0	0.0	0.0
Philippines	..	0	0	0	0	..	0.0	0.0	0.0	0.0
Singapore	..	0	0	0	0	..	0.0	0.0	0.0	0.0
Thailand	..	0	0	0	0	..	0.0	0.0	0.0	0.0
Near and Middle East	..	346	833	2 484	2 434	..	0.3	0.7	2.0	1.8
Africa	..	0	0	0	821	..	0.0	0.0	0.0	0.6
Latin America, of which:	..	4 421	4 741	2 858	2 730	..	4.0	4.3	2.3	2.0
Argentina	..	0	0	0	0	..	0.0	0.0	0.0	0.0
Brazil	..	0	0	0	0	..	0.0	0.0	0.0	0.0
Chile	..	0	0	0	0	..	0.0	0.0	0.0	0.0

Note: Majority foreign-owned firms. Up to 1996, the investor's country is the country of the immediate controller. As from 1997, it is that of the "ultimate beneficial owner".

Firmes sous contrôle étranger majoritaire. Jusqu'en 1996, le pays d'origine est celui où s'exerce le contrôle immédiat. A partir de 1997, il s'agit du "bénéficiaire ultime de l'investissement".

Table 7A - Tableau 7A
VALUE ADDED / VALEUR AJOUTÉE

By industry (ISIC Rev. 3)		Foreign affiliates (Millions of NLG) Filiales étrangères (Millions de NLG)					As a % of national total En % du total national				
		1994	1995	1996	1997	1998	1994	1995	1996	1997	1998
10/14	Mining & quarrying	..	1 541	19 887	1 616	1 671	..	4.1	47.1	19.4	15.3
15/37	**TOTAL MANUFACTURING**	..	**28 103**	**28 624**	**30 404**	**32 235**	..	**27.3**	**28.5**	**27.9**	**28.7**
15/16	Food, beverages, tobacco	..	5 939	6 532	6 667	7 213	..	31.5	34.3	32.8	34.9
17/19	Textiles, clothing, leather, footwear	..	551	518	463	454	..	22.4	21.0	17.6	16.2
20/22	Wood and paper products	..	2 525	2 612	2 703	2 974	..	17.3	17.9	17.2	18.0
20	Wood products	..	..	..	124	134	..	..	..	7.8	7.1
21/22	Paper, printing and publishing	..	..	..	2 579	2 840	..	..	..	18.2	19.4
23/25	Chemicals, Total	..	10 048	9 852	10 815	10 306	..	44.0	46.3	47.1	47.4
23	Refined petroleum, nuclear fuel	..	1 191	1 414	1 582	1 665	..	62.7	58.3	59.7	64.2
24/25	Chemicals, rubber & plastics prod.	..	8 857	8 438	9 233	8 642	..	42.4	44.8	45.5	45.2
24	Chemical products	..	8 167	7 496	8 172	7 523	..	46.8	49.1	49.7	50.2
2423	Pharmaceuticals	..	893	708	1 019	718	..	35.3	30.9	38.5	30.7
25	Rubber and plastics products	..	690	942	1 061	1 118	..	19.9	26.4	27.5	27.0
26	Non-metallic mineral products	..	1 947	2 162	2 147	2 287	..	44.2	52.6	46.2	47.8
27/28	Basic & fabricated metals	..	2 030	1 955	1 859	2 086	..	16.1	15.6	14.0	14.7
27	Basic metals	..	1 012	886	787	757	..	24.8	24.6	20.1	19.1
28	Fabricated metal products	..	1 018	1 070	1 073	1 329	..	12.0	12.0	11.5	13.1
29/32	Machinery, Total	..	3 137	3 024	3 668	3 964	..	18.3	18.1	20.1	21.0
29/30	Non-electrical machinery	..	1 945	1 949	2 360	2 649	..	21.0	21.2	23.1	24.0
29	Non-electrical machinery nec	..	1 601	1 644	1 946	2 134	..	19.1	19.7	21.2	21.8
30	Office and computing machinery	..	343	304	414	515	..	38.5	35.9	40.3	40.5
31/32	Electrical & electronic equipment	..	1 192	1 075	1 308	1 315	..	15.1	14.3	16.3	16.7
31	Electrical machinery nec	..	..	..	..	774	..	..	..	..	30.8
32	Radio, TV & communications eq.	..	..	..	..	541	..	..	..	..	10.1
33	Scientific instruments	..	952	1 044	1 077	1 120	..	40.6	43.0	41.8	42.1
34/35	Transportation equipment	..	744	649	711	1 501	..	16.3	14.3	13.4	23.3
34	Motor vehicles	..	510	525	573	1 351	..	19.2	19.6	18.3	37.4
35	Other transport equipment	..	235	124	138	151	..	12.3	6.7	6.4	5.3
351	Shipbuilding & repairing	..	..	..	..	..	..	..	..	..	..
353	Aircraft and spacecraft	..	164	..	..	..	..	75.2	..	..	..
36/37	Other manufacturing	..	229	276	294	330	..	7.3	10.5	8.6	8.9
40/45	Construction, electricity, gas & water	..	821	967	1 053	1 159	..	2.0	2.2	2.3	2.4
50/55	Trade, repair, hotels & restaurants	..	12 019	11 897	13 756	15 830	..	14.2	13.9	11.3	15.0
65/74	Finance, insurance, business services	..	3 757	4 185	5 375	6 249	..	7.8	8.2	9.4	10.1
	OTHER ACTIVITIES	..	1 774	2 084	2 827	3 237	..	5.2	4.5	5.5	5.9
01/99	**GRAND TOTAL**	..	**48 016**	**67 645**	**55 030**	**60 381**	..	**13.7**	**18.3**	**14.0**	**15.3**

Total manufacturing by investing country						As a % of total manufacturing by foreign affiliates				
All countries	..	**28 103**	**28 624**	**30 404**	**32 235**	..	**100.0**	**100.0**	**100.0**	**100.0**
United States	..	11 141	10 908	14 171	15 111	..	39.6	38.1	46.6	46.9
Canada	..	..	..	..	..	..	..	..	..	..
Mexico	..	0	0	0	..	..	0.0	0.0	0.0	..
Japan	..	564	614	847	975	..	2.0	2.1	2.8	3.0
Europe	..	..	..	..	..	..	..	..	..	..
European Union (15)	..	11 583	11 565	11 824	13 015	..	41.2	40.4	38.9	40.4
Belgium	..	..	..	..	..	..	..	..	..	..
France	..	1 419	1 367	1 511	1 486	..	5.0	4.8	5.0	4.6
Germany	..	2 554	2 377	2 374	2 360	..	9.1	8.3	7.8	7.3
Italy	..	..	..	..	..	..	..	..	..	..
Netherlands	..	..	..	..	..	..	..	..	..	..
Spain	..	0	0	0	..	..	0.0	0.0	0.0	..
Sweden	..	..	..	..	..	..	..	..	..	..
United Kingdom	..	2 770	2 958	4 008	4 649	..	9.9	10.3	13.2	14.4
Switzerland	..	2 942	3 282	1 997	1 435	..	10.5	11.5	6.6	4.5
Australia and New Zealand	..	..	..	..	..	..	..	..	..	..
Asia (non-OECD)	..	0	..	..	..	..	0.0	..	..	..
Latin America	..	891	979	669	647	..	3.2	3.4	2.2	2.0

Note: Majority foreign-owned firms. Up to 1996, the investor's country is the country of the immediate controller. As from 1997, it is that of the "ultimate beneficial owner".
Firmes sous contrôle étranger majoritaire. Jusqu'en 1996, le pays d'origine est celui où s'exerce le contrôle immédiat. A partir de 1997, il s'agit du "bénéficiaire ultime de l'investissement".

Table 8A - Tableau 8A

COMPENSATION OF EMPLOYEES / SALAIRES ET CHARGES SOCIALES

By industry (ISIC Rev. 3)	Foreign affiliates (Millions of NLG) Filiales étrangères (Millions de NLG)					As a % of national total En % du total national				
	1994	1995	1996	1997	1998	1994	1995	1996	1997	1998
10/14 Mining & quarrying	..	4	31	350	311	..	4.1	11.7	29.5	37.8
15/37 TOTAL MANUFACTURING	..	**15 763**	**15 634**	**14 317**	**15 449**	..	**23.8**	**23.4**	**23.1**	**23.6**
15/16 Food, beverages, tobacco	..	2 778	2 964	2 358	2 509	..	25.2	26.5	23.4	24.0
17/19 Textiles, clothing, leather, footwear	..	364	318	280	269	..	18.8	17.5	16.0	14.8
20/22 Wood and paper products	..	1 403	1 475	1 330	1 525	..	14.8	15.1	14.3	15.3
20 Wood products	..	..	..	86	97	..	..	..	7.7	8.1
21/22 Paper, printing and publishing	..	..	..	1 244	1 428	..	..	..	15.2	16.3
23/25 Chemicals, Total	..	4 377	4 535	4 389	4 359	..	39.0	39.7	41.4	40.9
23 Refined petroleum, nuclear fuel	..	576	562	510	526	..	57.6	53.4	56.8	56.1
24/25 Chemicals, rubber & plastics prod.	..	3 801	3 974	3 879	3 833	..	37.2	38.3	40.0	39.5
24 Chemical products	..	3 293	3 377	3 284	3 271	..	42.2	42.5	44.4	45.0
2423 Pharmaceuticals	..	419	332	363	355	..	31.5	25.4	29.2	28.4
25 Rubber and plastics products	..	507	596	595	562	..	21.0	24.5	25.9	23.0
26 Non-metallic mineral products	..	1 175	1 285	1 117	1 192	..	45.2	49.9	46.5	46.8
27/28 Basic & fabricated metals	..	1 468	1 443	1 194	1 335	..	16.4	16.1	13.9	14.4
27 Basic metals	..	656	637	484	463	..	27.0	26.9	20.8	19.4
28 Fabricated metal products	..	812	806	710	872	..	12.4	12.3	11.4	12.7
29/32 Machinery, Total	..	2 239	2 275	2 393	2 562	..	17.3	17.3	19.8	20.0
29/30 Non-electrical machinery	..	1 493	1 532	1 611	1 702	..	21.2	21.0	23.7	22.9
29 Non-electrical machinery nec	..	1 288	1 343	1 364	1 524	..	20.2	20.2	22.4	22.4
30 Office and computing machinery	..	205	189	246	178	..	31.0	28.7	37.0	28.1
31/32 Electrical & electronic equipment	..	746	743	783	860	..	12.6	12.6	14.8	15.9
31 Electrical machinery nec	..	..	..	..	511	..	..	..	..	31.6
32 Radio, TV & communications eq.	..	..	..	..	349	..	..	..	..	9.2
33 Scientific instruments	..	628	679	677	699	..	37.8	38.1	42.1	40.7
34/35 Transportation equipment	..	1 178	483	431	827	..	27.8	11.9	12.4	20.4
34 Motor vehicles	..	372	417	368	752	..	19.2	19.3	19.8	36.5
35 Other transport equipment	..	806	66	63	75	..	35.1	3.5	3.9	3.8
351 Shipbuilding & repairing	..	..	..	..	..	..	..	..	..	..
353 Aircraft and spacecraft	..	765	..	..	..	..	94.7	..	..	..
36/37 Other manufacturing	..	153	176	149	172	..	7.2	8.4	7.0	7.5
40/45 Construction, electricity, gas & water	..	691	789	799	865	..	2.5	2.7	2.9	2.7
50/55 Trade, repair, hotels & restaurants	..	7 538	7 470	7 824	8 503	..	14.8	14.2	15.1	14.8
65/74 Finance, insurance, business services	..	2 990	3 362	3 818	4 523	..	8.5	8.6	9.7	11.0
OTHER ACTIVITIES	..	1 176	1 515	1 705	2 019	..	5.2	5.2	6.0	6.2
01/99 GRAND TOTAL	..	**28 162**	**28 800**	**28 813**	**31 670**	..	**13.9**	**13.3**	**13.7**	**13.8**

Total manufacturing by investing country						As a % of total manufacturing by foreign affiliates				
All countries	..	**15 763**	**15 634**	**14 317**	**15 449**	..	**100.0**	**100.0**	**100.0**	**100.0**
United States	..	5 075	5 262	5 224	5 882	..	32.2	33.7	36.5	38.1
Canada	..	..	..	..	..	..	..	..	..	..
Mexico	..	0	0	0	..	..	0.0	0.0	0.0	..
Japan	..	287	340	384	448	..	1.8	2.2	2.7	2.9
Europe	..	..	..	..	..	..	..	..	..	..
European Union (15)	..	8 047	7 495	6 759	7 318	..	51.0	47.9	47.2	47.4
Belgium	..	..	..	..	..	..	..	..	..	..
France	..	900	927	937	987	..	5.7	5.9	6.5	6.4
Germany	..	2 400	1 591	1 356	1 368	..	15.2	10.2	9.5	8.9
Italy	..	..	..	..	..	..	..	..	..	..
Netherlands	..	..	..	..	..	..	..	..	..	..
Spain	..	0	0	0	..	..	0.0	0.0	0.0	..
Sweden	..	..	..	..	..	..	..	..	..	..
United Kingdom	..	1 647	1 766	2 183	2 306	..	10.4	11.3	15.2	14.9
Switzerland	..	1 173	1 257	1 132	856	..	7.4	8.0	7.9	5.5
Australia and New Zealand	..	..	..	..	..	..	..	..	..	..
Asia (non-OECD)	..	0	..	..	..	..	0.0	..	..	..
Latin America	..	695	697	412	408	..	4.4	4.5	2.9	2.6

Note: Majority foreign-owned firms. Up to 1996, the investor's country is the country of the immediate controller. As from 1997, it is that of the "ultimate beneficial owner".
Firmes sous contrôle étranger majoritaire. Jusqu'en 1996, le pays d'origine est celui où s'exerce le contrôle immédiat. A partir de 1997, il s'agit du "bénéficiaire ultime de l'investissement".

Inward investments

Investissements entrants

Table 9A - Tableau 9A

R&D EXPENDITURE / DÉPENSES DE R-D

By industry (ISIC Rev. 3)	Foreign affiliates (Millions of NLG) Filiales étrangères (Millions de NLG)					As a % of national total En % du total national				
	1994	1995	1996	1997	1998	1994	1995	1996	1997	1998
10/14 Mining & quarrying	..	..	..	0	6	..	..	..	0.0	1.8
15/37 **TOTAL MANUFACTURING**	..	..	..	**1 273**	**1 274**	..	..	..	**23.4**	**22.6**
15/16 Food, beverages, tobacco	..	..	..	59	51	..	..	..	20.1	12.6
17/19 Textiles, clothing, leather, footwear	..	..	..	3	4	..	..	..	10.0	17.4
20/22 Wood and paper products	..	..	..	15	20	..	..	..	34.1	38.5
20 Wood products	..	..	..	1	0	..	..	..	12.5	0.0
21/22 Paper, printing and publishing	..	..	..	14	19	..	..	..	38.9	38.8
23/25 Chemicals, Total	..	..	..	312	392	..	..	..	22.4	24.4
23 Refined petroleum, nuclear fuel	..	..	..	56	1	..	..	..	68.3	0.9
24/25 Chemicals, rubber & plastics prod.	..	..	..	256	390	..	..	..	19.5	26.0
24 Chemical products	..	..	..	230	378	..	..	..	19.0	26.1
2423 Pharmaceuticals	..	..	..	68	142	..	..	..	28.7	19.7
25 Rubber and plastics products	..	..	..	26	12	..	..	..	25.2	22.6
26 Non-metallic mineral products	..	..	..	17	17	..	..	..	44.7	58.6
27/28 Basic & fabricated metals	..	..	..	80	12	..	..	..	35.9	6.8
27 Basic metals	..	..	..	60	2	..	..	..	48.0	1.9
28 Fabricated metal products	..	..	..	20	10	..	..	..	20.4	14.1
29/32 Machinery, Total	..	..	..	457	393	..	..	..	16.7	14.4
29/30 Non-electrical machinery	..	..	..	180	113	..	..	..	23.5	15.5
29 Non-electrical machinery nec	..	..	..	70	112	..	..	..	13.0	21.4
30 Office and computing machinery	..	..	..	109	1	..	..	..	47.8	0.5
31/32 Electrical & electronic equipment	..	..	..	278	280	..	..	..	14.1	14.0
31 Electrical machinery nec	..	..	..	..	69	..	..	..	..	51.5
32 Radio, TV & communications eq.	..	..	..	..	211	..	..	..	..	11.3
33 Scientific instruments	..	..	..	257	260	..	..	..	77.4	75.6
34/35 Transportation equipment	..	..	..	64	115	..	..	..	20.7	48.1
34 Motor vehicles	..	..	..	64	112	..	..	..	32.2	60.5
35 Other transport equipment	..	..	..	0	3	..	..	..	0.0	5.6
351 Shipbuilding & repairing	..	..	..	..	..	..	..	..	..	..
353 Aircraft and spacecraft	..	..	..	..	..	..	..	..	..	..
36/37 Other manufacturing	..	..	..	8	10	..	..	..	20.0	35.7
40/45 Construction, electricity, gas & water	..	..	..	2	78	..	..	..	1.6	43.3
50/55 Trade, repair, hotels & restaurants	..	..	..	51	176	..	..	..	14.6	46.0
65/74 Finance, insurance, business services	..	..	..	328	182	..	..	..	20.0	13.7
OTHER ACTIVITIES	..	..	..	12	23	..	..	..	6.3	17.0
01/99 **GRAND TOTAL**	..	..	..	**1 666**	**1 738**	..	..	..	**20.6**	**21.8**

Total manufacturing by investing country						As a % of total manufacturing by foreign affiliates				
All countries	..	..	..	**1 273**	**1 274**	..	..	..	**100.0**	**100.0**
United States	..	..	..	599	611	..	..	..	47.1	48.0
Canada	..	..	..	..	..	..	..	..	..	..
Mexico	..	..	..	0	..	..	..	..	0.0	..
Japan	..	..	..	31	42	..	..	..	2.4	3.3
Europe	..	..	..	..	..	..	..	..	..	..
European Union (15)	..	..	..	557	544	..	..	..	43.8	42.7
Belgium	..	..	..	..	..	..	..	..	..	..
France	..	..	..	207	187	..	..	..	16.3	14.7
Germany	..	..	..	91	73	..	..	..	7.1	5.7
Italy	..	..	..	..	..	..	..	..	..	..
Netherlands	..	..	..	..	..	..	..	..	..	..
Spain	..	..	..	0	..	..	..	..	0.0	..
Sweden	..	..	..	..	..	..	..	..	..	..
United Kingdom	..	..	..	107	66	..	..	..	8.4	5.2
Switzerland	..	..	..	57	44	..	..	..	4.5	3.5
Australia and New Zealand	..	..	..	..	..	..	..	..	..	..
Asia (non-OECD)	..	..	..	..	..	..	..	..	..	..
Latin America	..	..	..	17	18	..	..	..	1.3	1.4

Note: Majority foreign-owned firms.
Firmes sous contrôle étranger majoritaire.

Table 10A - Tableau 10A

GROSS FIXED CAPITAL FORMATION / FORMATION BRUTE DE CAPITAL FIXE

By industry (ISIC Rev. 3)		Foreign affiliates (Millions of NLG) Filiales étrangères (Millions de NLG)					As a % of national total En % du total national				
		1994	1995	1996	1997	1998	1994	1995	1996	1997	1998
10/14	Mining & quarrying	..	616	463	813	505	..	35.8	28.8	19.8	20.3
15/37	**TOTAL MANUFACTURING**	..	**3 379**	**4 200**	**4 198**	**5 617**	..	**24.4**	**27.9**	**21.3**	**29.6**
15/16	Food, beverages, tobacco	..	695	812	782	798	..	27.2	29.0	22.5	25.3
17/19	Textiles, clothing, leather, footwear	..	60	62	34	45	..	26.5	27.4	12.7	14.9
20/22	Wood and paper products	..	337	350	317	611	..	17.7	17.0	13.3	20.5
20	Wood products	..	..	..	15	12	..	..	..	5.8	4.3
21/22	Paper, printing and publishing	..	..	..	302	599	..	..	..	14.3	22.2
23/25	Chemicals, Total	..	1 239	1 767	1 760	2 657	..	35.1	42.7	23.6	49.4
23	Refined petroleum, nuclear fuel	..	160	254	402	534	..	35.8	52.3	11.2	66.7
24/25	Chemicals, rubber & plastics prod.	..	1 079	1 513	1 357	2 122	..	35.0	41.5	35.0	46.4
24	Chemical products	..	984	1 277	1 206	1 888	..	38.9	43.6	37.3	49.9
2423	Pharmaceuticals	..	132	71	68	195	..	30.9	21.5	23.6	43.6
25	Rubber and plastics products	..	95	236	151	235	..	17.1	32.6	23.5	29.6
26	Non-metallic mineral products	..	373	362	374	376	..	48.5	50.8	45.0	44.3
27/28	Basic & fabricated metals	..	218	254	319	298	..	18.4	18.9	18.1	14.5
27	Basic metals	..	94	149	201	124	..	26.1	30.6	39.6	18.7
28	Fabricated metal products	..	123	106	118	174	..	14.9	12.4	9.4	12.5
29/32	Machinery, Total	..	292	360	370	537	..	17.0	13.4	16.4	20.1
29/30	Non-electrical machinery	..	164	272	246	299	..	20.6	26.7	22.0	21.4
29	Non-electrical machinery nec	..	151	243	202	230	..	21.8	27.1	20.3	18.8
30	Office and computing machinery	..	13	29	44	69	..	12.9	23.8	36.1	39.7
31/32	Electrical & electronic equipment	..	128	88	124	238	..	13.8	5.3	10.9	18.8
31	Electrical machinery nec	..	..	..	..	191	..	..	..	..	47.5
32	Radio, TV & communications eq.	..	..	..	..	46	..	..	..	..	5.3
33	Scientific instruments	..	67	89	93	98	..	40.4	37.6	38.8	40.8
34/35	Transportation equipment	..	75	84	63	151	..	4.7	14.7	11.0	18.9
34	Motor vehicles	..	54	76	56	140	..	3.7	17.7	18.4	27.8
35	Other transport equipment	..	21	8	7	12	..	15.9	5.7	2.6	4.1
351	Shipbuilding & repairing	..	..	..	..	..	..	..	..	..	..
353	Aircraft and spacecraft	..	16	..	..	..	..	100.0	..	..	..
36/37	Other manufacturing	..	24	60	86	47	..	10.6	20.2	17.7	8.5
40/45	Construction, electricity, gas & water	..	72	122	75	77	..	1.2	1.2	0.9	1.0
50/55	Trade, repair, hotels & restaurants	..	1 948	2 511	1 298	1 559	..	14.3	45.0	10.3	10.8
65/74	Finance, insurance, business services	..	974	10	1 308	2 229	..	10.4	11.5	10.3	10.4
	OTHER ACTIVITIES	..	330	167	571	1 127	..	3.5	0.6	3.6	6.1
01/99	**GRAND TOTAL**	..	**7 319**	**7 473**	**8 263**	**11 113**	..	**13.5**	**12.6**	**11.4**	**13.3**

Total manufacturing by investing country							*As a % of total manufacturing by foreign affiliates*				
All countries		..	**3 379**	**4 200**	**4 198**	**5 617**	..	**100.0**	**100.0**	**100.0**	**100.0**
United States		..	1 121	1 360	1 639	2 293	..	33.2	32.4	39.0	40.8
Canada		..	..	..	..	..	..	..	..	..	..
Mexico		..	0	0	0	..	..	0.0	0.0	0.0	..
Japan		..	136	110	121	143	..	4.0	2.6	2.9	2.5
Europe		..	..	..	..	..	..	..	..	..	..
European Union (15)		..	1 657	1 995	1 829	2 675	..	49.0	47.5	43.6	47.6
Belgium		..	..	..	..	..	..	..	..	..	..
France		..	151	206	156	228	..	4.5	4.9	3.7	4.1
Germany		..	299	308	339	526	..	8.8	7.3	8.1	9.4
Italy		..	..	..	..	..	..	..	..	..	..
Netherlands		..	..	..	..	..	..	..	..	..	..
Spain		..	0	0	0	..	..	0.0	0.0	0.0	..
Sweden		..	..	..	..	..	..	..	..	..	..
United Kingdom		..	404	568	607	1 176	..	12.0	13.5	14.5	20.9
Switzerland		..	295	382	284	231	..	8.7	9.1	6.8	4.1
Australia and New Zealand		..	..	..	..	..	..	..	..	..	..
Asia (non-OECD)		..	0	..	..	..	..	0.0	..	..	..
Latin America		..	81	94	74	96	..	2.4	2.2	1.8	1.7

Note: Majority foreign-owned firms. Up to 1996, the investor's country is the country of the immediate controller. As from 1997, it is that of the "ultimate beneficial owner".

Firmes sous contrôle étranger majoritaire. Jusqu'en 1996, le pays d'origine est celui où s'exerce le contrôle immédiat. A partir de 1997, il s'agit du "bénéficiaire ultime de l'investissement".

Inward investments   *Investissements entrants*

Table 11A - Tableau 11A

TOTAL EXPORTS BY INDUSTRY

EXPORTATIONS TOTALES PAR INDUSTRIE

| | | Foreign affiliates *(Millions of NLG)* | | | | | As a % of national total | | | | |
| | | Filiales étrangères *(Millions de NLG)* | | | | | En % du total national | | | | |
ISIC Revision 3		1994	1995	1996	1997	1998	1994	1995	1996	1997	1998
10/14	Mining & quarrying	..	..	739	1 045	455	..	..	4.4	8.3	6.2
15/37	**TOTAL MANUFACTURING**	..	..	**72 421**	**72 616**	**76 713**	..	..	**42.4**	**42.8**	**47.4**
15/16	Food, beverages, tobacco	..	..	12 684	12 248	13 625	..	..	37.4	38.5	43.2
17/19	Textiles, clothing, leather, footwear	..	..	1 321	1 346	1 343	..	..	33.5	35.8	35.1
20/22	Wood and paper products	..	..	3 025	3 300	4 174	..	..	26.2	34.9	43.1
20	Wood products	..	..	..	10	8	..	..	..	0.9	0.7
21/22	Paper, printing and publishing	..	..	..	3 290	4 166	..	..	..	39.7	48.3
23/25	Chemicals, Total	..	..	35 710	33 958	32 275	..	..	61.6	60.6	63.7
23	Refined petroleum, nuclear fuel	..	..	10 139	7 426	6 238	..	..	75.1	62.6	69.9
24/25	Chemicals, rubber & plastics prod.	..	..	25 571	26 532	26 037	..	..	57.5	60.1	62.4
24	Chemical products	..	..	23 757	24 583	24 139	..	..	59.6	61.5	63.9
2423	Pharmaceuticals	..	..	3 130	2 766	3 228	..	..	52.9	53.9	52.7
25	Rubber and plastics products	..	..	1 814	1 949	1 898	..	..	39.1	46.8	47.4
26	Non-metallic mineral products	..	..	1 078	1 491	1 567	..	..	45.2	54.7	61.3
27/28	Basic & fabricated metals	..	..	3 951	4 466	4 630	..	..	26.0	29.9	31.7
27	Basic metals	..	..	1 873	2 325	2 099	..	..	35.0	35.2	32.6
28	Fabricated metal products	..	..	2 077	2 141	2 531	..	..	21.0	25.8	31.0
29/32	Machinery, Total	..	..	9 521	10 469	10 772	..	..	29.3	28.3	30.7
29/30	Non-electrical machinery	..	..	5 161	6 162	6 437	..	..	36.7	41.3	42.4
29	Non-electrical machinery nec	..	..	2 649	2 889	3 051	..	..	25.4	28.1	29.8
30	Office and computing machinery	..	..	2 512	3 273	3 386	..	..	69.5	70.8	68.5
31/32	Electrical & electronic equipment	..	..	4 360	4 308	4 335	..	..	23.6	19.6	21.8
31	Electrical machinery nec	..	..	..	..	3 520	..	..	..	..	79.1
32	Radio, TV & communications eq.	..	..	..	..	815	..	..	..	..	5.3
33	Scientific instruments	..	..	2 348	2 047	1 732	..	..	61.5	70.1	66.5
34/35	Transportation equipment	..	..	2 654	2 989	6 321	..	..	36.4	34.6	69.8
34	Motor vehicles	..	..	2 380	2 693	6 010	..	..	43.0	43.6	84.3
35	Other transport equipment	..	..	273	296	311	..	..	15.4	12.0	16.1
351	Shipbuilding & repairing	..	..	..	..	..	..	..	..	..	..
353	Aircraft and spacecraft	..	..	..	..	..	..	..	..	..	..
36/37	Other manufacturing	..	..	129	302	273	..	..	5.5	11.8	12.7
40/45	Construction, electricity, gas & water	..	..	186	189	272	..	..	0.7	1.0	1.8
50/55	Trade, repair, hotels & restaurants	..	..	64 502	40 911	56 086	..	..	45.7	26.5	40.6
65/74	Finance, insurance, business services	..	..	6 832	3 523	2 623	..	..	13.4	13.6	12.5
	OTHER ACTIVITIES	..	..	11 033	7 665	3 501	..	..	21.1	16.4	14.2
01/99	**GRAND TOTAL**	..	..	**155 712**	**125 949**	**139 650**	..	..	**34.0**	**29.4**	**38.0**

Note: Majority foreign-owned firms. For 1998, exports of goods only.

Firmes sous contrôle étranger majoritaire. Pour 1998, exportations de biens seulement.

Table 12A - Tableau 12A

TOTAL EXPORTS BY COUNTRY OF ORIGIN IN THE MANUFACTURING SECTOR

EXPORTATIONS TOTALES PAR PAYS D'ORIGINE DANS L'INDUSTRIE MANUFACTURIÈRE

Country of origin	Total exports (Millions of NLG) Exportations totales (Millions de NLG)					As a % of all countries En % du total des pays				
	1994	1995	1996	1997	1998	1994	1995	1996	1997	1998
All countries	..	..	72 421	72 616	76 713	..	..	100.0	100.0	100.0
Total OECD	..	..	69 779	70 490	73 878	..	..	96.4	97.1	96.3
United States	..	..	37 837	39 338	43 638	..	..	52.2	54.2	56.9
Canada	..	..	9	268	11	..	..	0.0	0.4	0.0
Mexico	..	..	0	0	0	..	..	0.0	0.0	0.0
Japan	..	..	2 228	2 668	2 790	..	..	3.1	3.7	3.6
Korea	..	..	0	0	0	..	..	0.0	0.0	0.0
Australia	..	..	264	443	449	..	..	0.4	0.6	0.6
New Zealand	..	..	0	0	0	..	..	0.0	0.0	0.0
Europe	..	..	29 440	27 774	26 990	..	..	40.7	38.2	35.2
European Union (15)	..	..	22 648	23 246	24 189	..	..	31.3	32.0	31.5
Austria	..	..	115	135	155	..	..	0.2	0.2	0.2
Belgium	..	..	4 707	2 047	2 454	..	..	6.5	2.8	3.2
Denmark	..	..	225	655	670	..	..	0.3	0.9	0.9
Finland	..	..	1 747	1 641	1 806	..	..	2.4	2.3	2.4
France	..	..	2 777	3 119	2 786	..	..	3.8	4.3	3.6
Germany	..	..	3 401	3 294	3 134	..	..	4.7	4.5	4.1
Greece	..	..	0	0	0	..	..	0.0	0.0	0.0
Ireland	..	..	157	271	301	..	..	0.2	0.4	0.4
Italy	..	..	0	0	66	..	..	0.0	0.0	0.1
Luxembourg	..	..	1 960	39	70	..	..	2.7	0.1	0.1
Netherlands	..	..	..	..	..	..	..	..	..	..
Portugal	..	..	0	0	0	..	..	0.0	0.0	0.0
Spain	..	..	0	0	0	..	..	0.0	0.0	0.0
Sweden	..	..	3 011	3 521	4 094	..	..	4.2	4.8	5.3
United Kingdom	..	..	4 548	8 524	8 651	..	..	6.3	11.7	11.3
Czech Republic	..	..	0	0	0	..	..	0.0	0.0	0.0
Hungary	..	..	0	0	0	..	..	0.0	0.0	0.0
Iceland	..	..	0	0	0	..	..	0.0	0.0	0.0
Norway	..	..	575	994	789	..	..	0.8	1.4	1.0
Poland	..	..	0	0	0	..	..	0.0	0.0	0.0
Slovak Republic	..	..	0	0	2 012	..	..	0.0	0.0	0.0
Switzerland	..	..	6 217	3 534	2 012	..	..	8.6	4.9	2.6
Turkey	..	..	0	0	0	..	..	0.0	0.0	0.0
Non-OECD Europe, of which:	..	..	0	0	0	..	..	0.0	0.0	0.0
Baltic countries	..	..	0	0	0	..	..	0.0	0.0	0.0
Bulgaria	..	..	0	0	0	..	..	0.0	0.0	0.0
Croatia	..	..	0	0	0	..	..	0.0	0.0	0.0
Romania	..	..	0	0	0	..	..	0.0	0.0	0.0
Russian Federation	..	..	0	0	0	..	..	0.0	0.0	2.6
Slovenia	..	..	0	0	0	..	..	0.0	0.0	0.0
Ukraine	..	..	0	0	0	..	..	0.0	0.0	0.0
Yugoslavia	..	..	0	0	0	..	..	0.0	0.0	0.0
Non-OECD Asia, of which:	..	..	..	..	..	..	..	..	..	..
China	..	..	0	0	0	..	..	0.0	0.0	0.0
Chinese Taipei	..	..	..	15	47	..	..	..	0.0	0.1
Hong Kong (China)	..	..	0	0	0	..	..	0.0	0.0	0.0
India	..	..	0	0	0	..	..	0.0	0.0	0.0
Indonesia	..	..	0	0	0	..	..	0.0	0.0	0.0
Malaysia	..	..	0	0	0	..	..	0.0	0.0	0.0
Philippines	..	..	0	0	0	..	..	0.0	0.0	0.0
Singapore	..	..	0	0	0	..	..	0.0	0.0	0.0
Thailand	..	..	0	0	0	..	..	0.0	0.0	0.0
Near and Middle East	..	..	562	1 099	906	..	..	0.8	1.5	1.2
Africa	..	..	0	0	731	..	..	0.0	0.0	1.0
Latin America, of which:	..	..	2 080	1 013	1 152	..	..	2.9	1.4	1.5
Argentina	..	..	0	0	0	..	..	0.0	0.0	0.0
Brazil	..	..	0	0	0	..	..	0.0	0.0	0.0
Chile	..	..	0	0	0	..	..	0.0	0.0	0.0

Note: Majority foreign-owned firms. Up to 1996, the investor's country is the country of the immediate controller. As from 1997, it is that of the "ultimate beneficial owner". For 1998, exports of goods only.
Firmes sous contrôle étranger majoritaire. Jusqu'en 1996, le pays d'origine est celui où s'exerce le contrôle immédiat. A partir de 1997, il s'agit du "bénéficiaire ultime de l'investissement". Pour 1998, exportations de biens seulement.

Inward investments   *Investissements entrants*

Table 13A - Tableau 13A

TOTAL IMPORTS BY INDUSTRY

IMPORTATIONS TOTALES PAR INDUSTRIE

		Foreign affiliates (Millions of NLG) Filiales étrangères (Millions de NLG)					As a % of national total En % du total national				
ISIC Revision 3		1994	1995	1996	1997	1998	1994	1995	1996	1997	1998
10/14	Mining & quarrying	..	..	1 049	98	254	..	..	10.5	37.7	18.7
15/37	**TOTAL MANUFACTURING**	..	..	**57 163**	**46 395**	**49 368**	..	..	**43.2**	**41.8**	**46.9**
15/16	Food, beverages, tobacco	..	..	10 052	8 434	9 587	..	..	45.5	40.6	47.4
17/19	Textiles, clothing, leather, footwear	..	..	775	886	853	..	..	24.5	30.8	30.9
20/22	Wood and paper products	..	..	2 251	2 234	2 309	..	..	21.6	30.6	33.9
20	Wood products	..	..	..	22	21	..	..	..	2.1	2.1
21/22	Paper, printing and publishing	..	..	..	2 213	2 288	..	..	..	35.3	39.2
23/25	Chemicals, Total	..	..	28 350	19 671	16 748	..	..	65.4	66.1	67.7
23	Refined petroleum, nuclear fuel	..	..	10 235	2 984	1 924	..	..	76.8	68.6	72.0
24/25	Chemicals, rubber & plastics prod.	..	..	18 115	16 687	14 824	..	..	60.3	65.6	67.2
24	Chemical products	..	..	16 899	15 612	13 989	..	..	63.4	68.5	71.2
2423	Pharmaceuticals	..	..	2 660	2 907	3 319	..	..	65.5	73.2	68.5
25	Rubber and plastics products	..	..	1 216	1 075	835	..	..	35.7	40.8	34.4
26	Non-metallic mineral products	..	..	874	841	844	..	..	40.8	41.1	46.7
27/28	Basic & fabricated metals	..	..	3 087	3 300	3 591	..	..	25.0	34.8	36.7
27	Basic metals	..	..	1 105	985	990	..	..	32.7	35.4	33.2
28	Fabricated metal products	..	..	1 982	2 315	2 602	..	..	22.1	34.6	38.3
29/32	Machinery, Total	..	..	7 145	8 231	8 213	..	..	29.0	32.2	35.0
29/30	Non-electrical machinery	..	..	4 193	4 753	4 296	..	..	38.5	46.2	46.8
29	Non-electrical machinery nec	..	..	1 864	1 806	1 775	..	..	22.9	26.4	29.2
30	Office and computing machinery	..	..	2 329	2 947	2 521	..	..	84.8	85.5	81.1
31/32	Electrical & electronic equipment	..	..	2 952	3 478	3 917	..	..	21.5	22.8	27.4
31	Electrical machinery nec	..	..	..	..	3 311	..	..	..	..	76.5
32	Radio, TV & communications eq.	..	..	..	..	605	..	..	..	..	6.1
33	Scientific instruments	..	..	1 854	1 846	1 238	..	..	59.8	75.7	68.4
34/35	Transportation equipment	..	..	2 463	758	5 538	..	..	28.4	9.6	48.1
34	Motor vehicles	..	..	2 230	436	5 194	..	..	31.6	6.9	51.0
35	Other transport equipment	..	..	232	322	344	..	..	14.3	20.8	25.6
351	Shipbuilding & repairing	..	..	..	..	..	..	..	..	..	..
353	Aircraft and spacecraft	..	..	..	..	..	..	..	..	..	..
36/37	Other manufacturing	..	..	312	193	446	..	..	13.3	7.0	20.2
40/45	Construction, electricity, gas & water	..	..	734	972	1 444	..	..	2.9	4.9	8.7
50/55	Trade, repair, hotels & restaurants	..	..	75 866	53 965	65 341	..	..	47.5	26.3	37.8
65/74	Finance, insurance, business services	..	..	6 686	3 629	2 345	..	..	14.0	19.5	13794.1
	OTHER ACTIVITIES	..	..	9 644	5 824	5 374	..	..	21.6	22.8	18531.0
01/99	**GRAND TOTAL**	..	..	**151 142**	**110 883**	**124 125**	..	..	**36.0**	**29.1**	**36293.9**

Note: Majority foreign-owned firms. For 1998, imports of goods only.
Firmes sous contrôle étranger majoritaire. Pour 1998, importations de biens seulement.

Inward investments　　　　　　　　　　　　　　　　　　　　　　　　*Investissements entrants*

Table 14A - Tableau 14A

TOTAL IMPORTS BY COUNTRY OF ORIGIN IN THE MANUFACTURING SECTOR
IMPORTATIONS TOTALES PAR PAYS D'ORIGINE DANS L'INDUSTRIE MANUFACTURIÈRE

Country of origin	Total imports (Millions of NLG) Importations totales (Millions de NLG)					As a % of all countries En % du total des pays				
	1994	1995	1996	1997	1998	1994	1995	1996	1997	1998
All countries	..	..	57 163	46 395	49 368	..	..	100.0	100.0	100.0
Total OECD	..	..	54 732	44 537	47 583	..	..	95.7	96.0	96.4
United States	..	..	30 510	27 187	29 397	..	..	53.4	58.6	59.5
Canada	..	..	15	101	10	..	..	0.0	0.2	0.0
Mexico	..	..	0	0	0	..	..	0.0	0.0	0.0
Japan	..	..	1 555	1 410	1 330	..	..	2.7	3.0	2.7
Korea	..	..	0	0	0	..	..	0.0	0.0	0.0
Australia	..	..	604	19	224	..	..	1.1	0.0	0.5
New Zealand	..	..	0	0	0	..	..	0.0	0.0	0.0
Europe	..	..	22 049	15 820	16 623	..	..	38.6	34.1	33.7
European Union (15)	..	..	17 652	13 009	14 643	..	..	30.9	28.0	29.7
Austria	..	..	29	62	113	..	..	0.1	0.1	0.2
Belgium	..	..	3 936	1 086	1 085	..	..	6.9	2.3	2.2
Denmark	..	..	202	362	351	..	..	0.4	0.8	0.7
Finland	..	..	1 062	1 264	1 216	..	..	1.9	2.7	2.5
France	..	..	2 064	1 995	1 730	..	..	3.6	4.3	3.5
Germany	..	..	2 641	1 992	1 748	..	..	4.6	4.3	3.5
Greece	..	..	0	0	0	..	..	0.0	0.0	0.0
Ireland	..	..	204	220	216	..	..	0.4	0.5	0.4
Italy	..	..	0	0	64	..	..	0.0	0.0	0.1
Luxembourg	..	..	1 115	55	50	..	..	2.0	0.1	0.1
Netherlands	..	..	..	..	..	..	..	..	..	..
Portugal	..	..	0	0	0	..	..	0.0	0.0	0.0
Spain	..	..	0	0	0	..	..	0.0	0.0	0.0
Sweden	..	..	2 935	1 188	3 898	..	..	5.1	2.6	7.9
United Kingdom	..	..	3 464	4 784	4 172	..	..	6.1	10.3	8.5
Czech Republic	..	..	0	0	0	..	..	0.0	0.0	0.0
Hungary	..	..	0	0	0	..	..	0.0	0.0	0.0
Iceland	..	..	0	0	0	..	..	0.0	0.0	0.0
Norway	..	..	306	403	350	..	..	0.5	0.9	0.7
Poland	..	..	0	0	0	..	..	0.0	0.0	0.0
Slovak Republic	..	..	0	0	1 630	..	..	0.0	0.0	0.0
Switzerland	..	..	4 091	2 408	1 630	..	..	7.2	5.2	3.3
Turkey	..	..	0	0	0	..	..	0.0	0.0	0.0
Non-OECD Europe, of which:	..	..	0	0	0	..	..	0.0	0.0	0.0
Baltic countries	..	..	0	0	0	..	..	0.0	0.0	0.0
Bulgaria	..	..	0	0	0	..	..	0.0	0.0	0.0
Croatia	..	..	0	0	0	..	..	0.0	0.0	0.0
Romania	..	..	0	0	0	..	..	0.0	0.0	0.0
Russian Federation	..	..	0	0	0	..	..	0.0	0.0	3.3
Slovenia	..	..	0	0	0	..	..	0.0	0.0	0.0
Ukraine	..	..	0	0	0	..	..	0.0	0.0	0.0
Yugoslavia	..	..	0	0	0	..	..	0.0	0.0	0.0
Non-OECD Asia, of which:	..	..	..	..	..	..	..	..	..	..
China	..	..	0	0	0	..	..	0.0	0.0	0.0
Chinese Taipei	..	..	..	0	8	..	..	..	0.0	0.0
Hong Kong (China)	..	..	0	0	0	..	..	0.0	0.0	0.0
India	..	..	0	0	0	..	..	0.0	0.0	0.0
Indonesia	..	..	0	0	0	..	..	0.0	0.0	0.0
Malaysia	..	..	0	0	0	..	..	0.0	0.0	0.0
Philippines	..	..	0	0	0	..	..	0.0	0.0	0.0
Singapore	..	..	0	0	0	..	..	0.0	0.0	0.0
Thailand	..	..	0	0	0	..	..	0.0	0.0	0.0
Near and Middle East	..	..	313	882	595	..	..	0.5	1.9	1.2
Africa	..	..	0	0	304	..	..	0.0	0.0	0.6
Latin America, of which:	..	..	2 118	976	878	..	..	3.7	2.1	1.8
Argentina	..	..	0	0	0	..	..	0.0	0.0	0.0
Brazil	..	..	0	0	0	..	..	0.0	0.0	0.0
Chile	..	..	0	0	0	..	..	0.0	0.0	0.0

Note: Majority foreign-owned firms. Up to 1996, the investor's country is the country of the immediate controller. As from 1997, it is that of the "ultimate beneficial owner". For 1998, imports of goods only.
Firmes sous contrôle étranger majoritaire. Jusqu'en 1996, le pays d'origine est celui où s'exerce le contrôle immédiat. A partir de 1997, il s'agit du "bénéficiaire ultime de l'investissement". Pour 1998, importations de biens seulement.

Inward investments

Investissements entrants

Table 15A - Tableau 15A

INTRA-FIRM EXPORTS BY INDUSTRY

EXPORTATIONS INTRA-FIRME PAR INDUSTRIE

| | | Foreign affiliates *(Millions of NLG)* | | | | | | | | | |
| | | Filiales étrangères *(Millions de NLG)* | | | | | | | | | |
ISIC Revision 3		1989	1990	1991	1992	1993	1994	1995	1996	1997	1998
10/14	Mining & quarrying	..	..	..	..	..	..	..	..	202	318
15/37	**TOTAL MANUFACTURING**	..	..	..	..	..	..	..	..	**36 420**	**40 037**
15/16	Food, beverages, tobacco	..	..	..	..	..	..	..	..	3 888	5 560
17/19	Textiles, clothing, leather, footwear	..	..	..	..	..	..	..	..	662	711
20/22	Wood and paper products	..	..	..	..	..	..	..	..	1 370	1 615
20	Wood products	..	..	..	..	..	..	..	..	4	2
21/22	Paper, printing and publishing	..	..	..	..	..	..	..	..	1 367	1 613
23/25	Chemicals, Total	..	..	..	..	..	..	..	..	19 774	19 076
23	Refined petroleum, nuclear fuel	..	..	..	..	..	..	..	..	4 141	3 621
24/25	Chemicals, rubber & plastics prod.	..	..	..	..	..	..	..	..	15 632	15 455
24	Chemical products	..	..	..	..	..	..	..	..	14 526	14 639
2423	Pharmaceuticals	..	..	..	..	..	..	..	..	1 831	2 431
25	Rubber and plastics products	..	..	..	..	..	..	..	..	1 106	816
26	Non-metallic mineral products	..	..	..	..	..	..	..	..	344	462
27/28	Basic & fabricated metals	..	..	..	..	..	..	..	..	1 575	1 835
27	Basic metals	..	..	..	..	..	..	..	..	549	537
28	Fabricated metal products	..	..	..	..	..	..	..	..	1 025	1 298
29/32	Machinery, Total	..	..	..	..	..	..	..	..	5 307	4 721
29/30	Non-electrical machinery	..	..	..	..	..	..	..	..	4 394	3 734
29	Non-electrical machinery nec	..	..	..	..	..	..	..	..	1 195	871
30	Office and computing machinery	..	..	..	..	..	..	..	..	3 199	2 863
31/32	Electrical & electronic equipment	..	..	..	..	..	..	..	..	913	987
31	Electrical machinery nec	..	..	..	..	..	..	..	..	..	629
32	Radio, TV & communications eq.	..	..	..	..	..	..	..	..	..	358
33	Scientific instruments	..	..	..	..	..	..	..	..	1 211	1 082
34/35	Transportation equipment	..	..	..	..	..	..	..	..	2 144	4 820
34	Motor vehicles	..	..	..	..	..	..	..	..	2 121	4 776
35	Other transport equipment	..	..	..	..	..	..	..	..	23	44
351	Shipbuilding & repairing	..	..	..	..	..	..	..	..	..	..
353	Aircraft and spacecraft	..	..	..	..	..	..	..	..	..	..
36/37	Other manufacturing	..	..	..	..	..	..	..	..	146	156
40/45	Construction, electricity, gas & water	..	..	..	..	..	..	..	..	57	139
50/55	Trade, repair, hotels & restaurants	..	..	..	..	..	..	..	..	19 789	33 559
65/74	Finance, insurance, business services	..	..	..	..	..	..	..	..	1 579	2 318
	OTHER ACTIVITIES	..	..	..	..	..	..	..	..	3 668	1 714
01/99	**GRAND TOTAL**	..	..	..	..	..	..	..	..	**61 716**	**78 084**

Note: Majority foreign-owned firms.
Firmes sous contrôle étranger majoritaire.

Inward investments

Investissements entrants

Table 16A - Tableau 16A

INTRA-FIRM EXPORTS BY COUNTRY OF ORIGIN IN THE MANUFACTURING SECTOR
EXPORTATIONS INTRA-FIRME PAR PAYS D'ORIGINE DANS L'INDUSTRIE MANUFACTURIÈRE

Country of origin (UBO)	Intra-firm exports *(Millions of NLG)* Exportations intra-firme *(Millions de NLG)*					As a % of all countries En % du total des pays				
	1994	1995	1996	1997	1998	1994	1995	1996	1997	1998
All countries	..	..	..	36 420	40 037	..	..	..	100.0	100.0
Total OECD	..	..	..	35 643	39 344	..	..	..	97.9	98.3
United States	..	..	..	20 745	24 290	..	..	..	57.0	60.7
Canada	..	..	..	260	11	..	..	..	0.7	0.0
Mexico	..	..	..	0	0	..	..	..	0.0	0.0
Japan	..	..	..	1 351	1 378	..	..	..	3.7	3.4
Korea	..	..	..	0	0	..	..	..	0.0	0.0
Australia	..	..	..	0	8	..	..	..	0.0	0.0
New Zealand	..	..	..	0	0	..	..	..	0.0	0.0
Europe	..	..	..	13 288	13 657	..	..	..	36.5	34.1
European Union (15)	..	..	..	11 142	11 693	..	..	..	30.6	29.2
Austria	..	..	..	3	31	..	..	..	0.0	0.1
Belgium	..	..	..	1 352	1 367	..	..	..	3.7	3.4
Denmark	..	..	..	141	310	..	..	..	0.4	0.8
Finland	..	..	..	762	864	..	..	..	2.1	2.2
France	..	..	..	2 182	1 725	..	..	..	6.0	4.3
Germany	..	..	..	1 093	834	..	..	..	3.0	2.1
Greece	..	..	..	0	0	..	..	..	0.0	0.0
Ireland	..	..	..	27	28	..	..	..	0.1	0.1
Italy	..	..	..	0	34	..	..	..	0.0	0.1
Luxembourg	..	..	..	18	22	..	..	..	0.0	0.1
Netherlands	..	..	..	..	..	..	..	..	..	..
Portugal	..	..	..	0	0	..	..	..	0.0	0.0
Spain	..	..	..	0	0	..	..	..	0.0	0.0
Sweden	..	..	..	2 812	3 481	..	..	..	7.7	8.7
United Kingdom	..	..	..	2 751	2 997	..	..	..	7.6	7.5
Czech Republic	..	..	..	0	0	..	..	..	0.0	0.0
Hungary	..	..	..	0	0	..	..	..	0.0	0.0
Iceland	..	..	..	0	0	..	..	..	0.0	0.0
Norway	..	..	..	590	579	..	..	..	1.6	1.4
Poland	..	..	..	0	0	..	..	..	0.0	0.0
Slovak Republic	..	..	..	0	1 384	..	..	..	0.0	0.0
Switzerland	..	..	..	1 556	1 384	..	..	..	4.3	3.5
Turkey	..	..	..	0	0	..	..	..	0.0	0.0
Non-OECD Europe, of which:	..	..	..	0	0	..	..	..	0.0	0.0
Baltic countries	..	..	..	0	0	..	..	..	0.0	0.0
Bulgaria	..	..	..	0	0	..	..	..	0.0	0.0
Croatia	..	..	..	0	0	..	..	..	0.0	0.0
Romania	..	..	..	0	0	..	..	..	0.0	0.0
Russian Federation	..	..	..	0	0	..	..	..	0.0	3.5
Slovenia	..	..	..	0	0	..	..	..	0.0	0.0
Ukraine	..	..	..	0	0	..	..	..	0.0	0.0
Yugoslavia	..	..	..	0	0	..	..	..	0.0	0.0
Non-OECD Asia, of which:	..	..	..	..	..	..	..	..	..	..
China	..	..	..	0	0	..	..	..	0.0	0.0
Chinese Taipei	..	..	..	0	33	..	..	..	0.0	0.1
Hong Kong (China)	..	..	..	0	0	..	..	..	0.0	0.0
India	..	..	..	0	0	..	..	..	0.0	0.0
Indonesia	..	..	..	0	0	..	..	..	0.0	0.0
Malaysia	..	..	..	0	0	..	..	..	0.0	0.0
Philippines	..	..	..	0	0	..	..	..	0.0	0.0
Singapore	..	..	..	0	0	..	..	..	0.0	0.0
Thailand	..	..	..	0	0	..	..	..	0.0	0.0
Near and Middle East	..	..	..	422	281	..	..	..	1.2	0.7
Africa	..	..	..	0	223	..	..	..	0.0	0.6
Latin America, of which:	..	..	..	356	157	..	..	..	1.0	0.4
Argentina	..	..	..	0	0	..	..	..	0.0	0.0
Brazil	..	..	..	0	0	..	..	..	0.0	0.0
Chile	..	..	..	0	0	..	..	..	0.0	0.0

Note: Majority foreign-owned firms.
Firmes sous contrôle étranger majoritaire.

Table 17A - Tableau 17A

INTRA-FIRM IMPORTS BY INDUSTRY

IMPORTATIONS INTRA-FIRME PAR INDUSTRIE

ISIC Revision 3		Foreign affiliates *(Millions of NLG)* Filiales étrangères *(Millions de NLG)*									
		1989	1990	1991	1992	1993	1994	1995	1996	1997	1998
10/14	Mining & quarrying	..	..	..	..	..	..	..	..	17	233
15/37	**TOTAL MANUFACTURING**	..	..	..	..	..	..	..	..	**27 387**	**26 270**
15/16	Food, beverages, tobacco	..	..	..	..	..	..	..	..	4 430	5 894
17/19	Textiles, clothing, leather, footwear	..	..	..	..	..	..	..	..	502	490
20/22	Wood and paper products	..	..	..	..	..	..	..	..	1 270	847
20	Wood products	..	..	..	..	..	..	..	..	3	0
21/22	Paper, printing and publishing	..	..	..	..	..	..	..	..	1 266	847
23/25	Chemicals, Total	..	..	..	..	..	..	..	..	13 332	11 846
23	Refined petroleum, nuclear fuel	..	..	..	..	..	..	..	..	2 378	1 776
24/25	Chemicals, rubber & plastics prod.	..	..	..	..	..	..	..	..	10 954	10 070
24	Chemical products	..	..	..	..	..	..	..	..	10 486	9 763
2423	Pharmaceuticals	..	..	..	..	..	..	..	..	2 525	2 378
25	Rubber and plastics products	..	..	..	..	..	..	..	..	468	307
26	Non-metallic mineral products	..	..	..	..	..	..	..	..	442	497
27/28	Basic & fabricated metals	..	..	..	..	..	..	..	..	1 420	1 147
27	Basic metals	..	..	..	..	..	..	..	..	465	390
28	Fabricated metal products	..	..	..	..	..	..	..	..	955	757
29/32	Machinery, Total	..	..	..	..	..	..	..	..	5 298	2 178
29/30	Non-electrical machinery	..	..	..	..	..	..	..	..	3 211	1 294
29	Non-electrical machinery nec	..	..	..	..	..	..	..	..	835	339
30	Office and computing machinery	..	..	..	..	..	..	..	..	2 376	955
31/32	Electrical & electronic equipment	..	..	..	..	..	..	..	..	2 087	884
31	Electrical machinery nec	..	..	..	..	..	..	..	..	..	368
32	Radio, TV & communications eq.	..	..	..	..	..	..	..	..	..	516
33	Scientific instruments	..	..	..	..	..	..	..	..	394	730
34/35	Transportation equipment	..	..	..	..	..	..	..	..	208	2 529
34	Motor vehicles	..	..	..	..	..	..	..	..	39	2 404
35	Other transport equipment	..	..	..	..	..	..	..	..	168	125
351	Shipbuilding & repairing	..	..	..	..	..	..	..	..	..	..
353	Aircraft and spacecraft	..	..	..	..	..	..	..	..	..	..
36/37	Other manufacturing	..	..	..	..	..	..	..	..	92	111
40/45	Construction, electricity, gas & water	..	..	..	..	..	..	..	..	700	1 045
50/55	Trade, repair, hotels & restaurants	..	..	..	..	..	..	..	..	35 085	38 991
65/74	Finance, insurance, business services	..	..	..	..	..	..	..	..	1 938	1 928
	OTHER ACTIVITIES	..	..	..	..	..	..	..	..	1 082	1 444
01/99	**GRAND TOTAL**	..	..	..	..	..	..	..	..	**66 210**	**69 911**

Note: Majority foreign-owned firms.
Firmes sous contrôle étranger majoritaire.

Inward investments *Investissements entrants*

Table 18A - Tableau 18A

INTRA-FIRM IMPORTS BY COUNTRY OF ORIGIN IN THE MANUFACTURING SECTOR

IMPORTATIONS INTRA-FIRME PAR PAYS D'ORIGINE DANS L'INDUSTRIE MANUFACTURIÈRE

Country of origin (UBO)	Intra-firm imports (Millions of NLG) Importations intra-firme (Millions de NLG)					As a % of all countries En % du total des pays				
	1994	1995	1996	1997	1998	1994	1995	1996	1997	1998
All countries	..	..	..	27 387	26 270	..	..	..	100.0	100.0
Total OECD	..	..	..	26 433	25 776	..	..	..	96.5	98.1
United States	..	..	..	17 859	16 492	..	..	..	65.2	62.8
Canada	..	..	..	82	10	..	..	..	0.3	0.0
Mexico	..	..	..	0	0	..	..	..	0.0	0.0
Japan	..	..	..	534	327	..	..	..	1.9	1.2
Korea	..	..	..	0	0	..	..	..	0.0	0.0
Australia	..	..	..	0	5	..	..	..	0.0	0.0
New Zealand	..	..	..	0	0	..	..	..	0.0	0.0
Europe	..	..	..	7 958	8 943	..	..	..	29.1	34.0
European Union (15)	..	..	..	6 442	7 576	..	..	..	23.5	28.8
Austria	..	..	..	34	45	..	..	..	0.1	0.2
Belgium	..	..	..	536	603	..	..	..	2.0	2.3
Denmark	..	..	..	138	234	..	..	..	0.5	0.9
Finland	..	..	..	448	316	..	..	..	1.6	1.2
France	..	..	..	1 358	1 132	..	..	..	5.0	4.3
Germany	..	..	..	702	579	..	..	..	2.6	2.2
Greece	..	..	..	0	0	..	..	..	0.0	0.0
Ireland	..	..	..	39	78	..	..	..	0.1	0.3
Italy	..	..	..	0	1	..	..	..	0.0	0.0
Luxembourg	..	..	..	55	24	..	..	..	0.2	0.1
Netherlands	..	..	..	..	..	..	..	..	..	..
Portugal	..	..	..	0	0	..	..	..	0.0	0.0
Spain	..	..	..	0	0	..	..	..	0.0	0.0
Sweden	..	..	..	433	2 084	..	..	..	1.6	7.9
United Kingdom	..	..	..	2 699	2 479	..	..	..	9.9	9.4
Czech Republic	..	..	..	0	0	..	..	..	0.0	0.0
Hungary	..	..	..	0	0	..	..	..	0.0	0.0
Iceland	..	..	..	0	0	..	..	..	0.0	0.0
Norway	..	..	..	131	143	..	..	..	0.5	0.5
Poland	..	..	..	0	0	..	..	..	0.0	0.0
Slovak Republic	..	..	..	0	1 223	..	..	..	0.0	0.0
Switzerland	..	..	..	1 384	1 223	..	..	..	5.1	4.7
Turkey	..	..	..	0	0	..	..	..	0.0	0.0
Non-OECD Europe, of which:	..	..	..	0	0	..	..	..	0.0	0.0
Baltic countries	..	..	..	0	0	..	..	..	0.0	0.0
Bulgaria	..	..	..	0	0	..	..	..	0.0	0.0
Croatia	..	..	..	0	0	..	..	..	0.0	0.0
Romania	..	..	..	0	0	..	..	..	0.0	0.0
Russian Federation	..	..	..	0	0	..	..	..	0.0	4.7
Slovenia	..	..	..	0	0	..	..	..	0.0	0.0
Ukraine	..	..	..	0	0	..	..	..	0.0	0.0
Yugoslavia	..	..	..	0	0	..	..	..	0.0	0.0
Non-OECD Asia, of which:	..	..	..	..	..	..	..	..	..	..
China	..	..	..	0	0	..	..	..	0.0	0.0
Chinese Taipei	..	..	..	0	4	..	..	..	0.0	0.0
Hong Kong (China)	..	..	..	0	0	..	..	..	0.0	0.0
India	..	..	..	0	0	..	..	..	0.0	0.0
Indonesia	..	..	..	0	0	..	..	..	0.0	0.0
Malaysia	..	..	..	0	0	..	..	..	0.0	0.0
Philippines	..	..	..	0	0	..	..	..	0.0	0.0
Singapore	..	..	..	0	0	..	..	..	0.0	0.0
Thailand	..	..	..	0	0	..	..	..	0.0	0.0
Near and Middle East	..	..	..	654	458	..	..	..	2.4	1.7
Africa	..	..	..	0	0	..	..	..	0.0	0.0
Latin America, of which:	..	..	..	301	32	..	..	..	1.1	0.1
Argentina	..	..	..	0	0	..	..	..	0.0	0.0
Brazil	..	..	..	0	0	..	..	..	0.0	0.0
Chile	..	..	..	0	0	..	..	..	0.0	0.0

Note: Majority foreign-owned firms.
Firmes sous contrôle étranger majoritaire.

Table 19A - Tableau 19A

GROSS OPERATING SURPLUS / EXCÉDENT BRUT D'EXPLOITATION

By industry (ISIC Rev. 3)		Foreign affiliates (Millions of NLG) / Filiales étrangères (Millions de NLG)					As a % of national total / En % du total national				
		1994	1995	1996	1997	1998	1994	1995	1996	1997	1998
10/14	Mining & quarrying	..	1 537	19 813	1 266	1 360	..	4.1	47.3	17.8	13.5
15/37	**TOTAL MANUFACTURING**	..	**13 950**	**14 734**	**16 086**	**16 786**	..	**33.1**	**37.3**	**34.2**	**35.9**
15/16	Food, beverages, tobacco	..	3 424	3 898	4 309	4 704	..	38.8	43.3	42.1	46.2
17/19	Textiles, clothing, leather, footwear	..	217	226	183	185	..	34.2	30.1	20.8	19.0
20/22	Wood and paper products	..	1 246	1 302	1 373	1 449	..	22.1	23.9	21.6	22.0
20	Wood products	..	..	..	37	37	..	..	..	7.7	5.5
21/22	Paper, printing and publishing	..	..	..	1 336	1 412	..	..	..	22.7	23.9
23/25	Chemicals, Total	..	6 067	5 792	6 426	5 947	..	48.3	53.0	52.0	53.7
23	Refined petroleum, nuclear fuel	..	648	881	1 072	1 138	..	62.9	57.4	61.3	68.7
24/25	Chemicals, rubber & plastics prod.	..	5 419	4 911	5 354	4 809	..	47.0	52.3	50.5	51.1
24	Chemical products	..	5 185	4 502	4 888	4 253	..	50.5	56.2	54.1	55.2
2423	Pharmaceuticals	..	515	418	656	364	..	39.9	38.3	46.7	33.4
25	Rubber and plastics products	..	234	409	466	556	..	18.3	29.7	29.9	32.7
26	Non-metallic mineral products	..	893	1 008	1 030	1 095	..	44.2	57.1	45.9	48.9
27/28	Basic & fabricated metals	..	778	699	665	751	..	17.9	16.3	14.1	15.4
27	Basic metals	..	438	314	303	294	..	24.3	22.9	19.0	18.7
28	Fabricated metal products	..	340	385	362	457	..	13.4	13.2	11.5	13.8
29/32	Machinery, Total	..	1 148	1 008	1 275	1 402	..	21.7	21.2	20.9	23.0
29/30	Non-electrical machinery	..	603	583	750	947	..	21.2	22.4	22.0	26.1
29	Non-electrical machinery nec	..	442	446	582	610	..	17.4	19.0	19.1	20.4
30	Office and computing machinery	..	162	137	168	337	..	54.7	52.5	46.5	52.7
31/32	Electrical & electronic equipment	..	545	425	525	455	..	22.3	19.8	19.4	18.5
31	Electrical machinery nec	..	..	..	..	263	..	..	..	..	29.2
32	Radio, TV & communications eq.	..	..	..	..	192	..	..	..	..	12.3
33	Scientific instruments	..	383	436	400	421	..	48.7	55.7	41.5	44.6
34/35	Transportation equipment	..	- 294	241	280	675	..	-32.7	21.6	15.3	28.2
34	Motor vehicles	..	195	177	205	599	..	19.9	20.0	16.0	38.6
35	Other transport equipment	..	- 489	64	75	76	..	626.9	27.8	13.8	9.1
351	Shipbuilding & repairing	..	..	..	..	..	..	..	..	..	..
353	Aircraft and spacecraft	..	- 520	..	..	..	..	102.8	..	..	..
36/37	Other manufacturing	..	89	123	145	157	..	7.8	17.7	11.3	11.2
40/45	Construction, electricity, gas & water	..	143	187	254	294	..	1.5	1.7	1.4	1.7
50/55	Trade, repair, hotels & restaurants	..	5 193	5 169	5 932	7 326	..	14.0	14.4	8.5	15.2
65/74	Finance, insurance, business services	..	1 161	1 301	1 557	1 726	..	7.8	8.8	8.9	8.2
	OTHER ACTIVITIES	..	731	797	1 122	1 218	..	5.4	3.9	4.8	5.5
01/99	**GRAND TOTAL**	..	**22 714**	**42 002**	**26 217**	**28 711**	..	**14.6**	**25.7**	**14.3**	**17.4**

Total manufacturing by investing country							As a % of total manufacturing by foreign affiliates				
		1994	1995	1996	1997	1998	1994	1995	1996	1997	1998
All countries		..	**13 950**	**14 734**	**16 086**	**16 786**	..	**100.0**	**100.0**	**100.0**	**100.0**
United States		..	6 524	6 167	8 947	9 229	..	46.8	41.9	55.6	55.0
Canada		..	..	..	..	..	..	..	..	..	..
Mexico		..	0	0	0	..	..	0.0	0.0	0.0	..
Japan		..	306	320	463	527	..	2.2	2.2	2.9	3.1
Europe		..	..	..	..	..	..	..	..	..	..
European Union (15)		..	4 396	4 934	5 066	5 696	..	31.5	33.5	31.5	33.9
Belgium		..	..	..	..	..	..	..	..	..	..
France		..	610	543	574	499	..	4.4	3.7	3.6	3.0
Germany		..	403	938	1 018	991	..	2.9	6.4	6.3	5.9
Italy		..	..	..	..	..	..	..	..	..	..
Netherlands		..	..	..	..	..	..	..	..	..	..
Spain		..	0	0	0	..	..	0.0	0.0	0.0	..
Sweden		..	..	..	..	..	..	..	..	..	..
United Kingdom		..	1 292	1 411	1 826	2 342	..	9.3	9.6	11.4	14.0
Switzerland		..	1 871	2 177	865	579	..	13.4	14.8	5.4	3.4
Australia and New Zealand		..	..	..	..	..	..	..	..	..	..
Asia (non-OECD)		..	0	..	..	..	..	0.0	..	..	..
Latin America		..	316	382	257	239	..	2.3	2.6	1.6	1.4

Note: Majority foreign-owned firms. Up to 1996, the investor's country is the country of the immediate controller. As from 1997, it is that of the "ultimate beneficial owner".
Firmes sous contrôle étranger majoritaire. Jusqu'en 1996, le pays d'origine est celui où s'exerce le contrôle immédiat. A partir de 1997, il s'agit du "bénéficiaire ultime de l'investissement".

Inward investments

Investissements entrants

Table 20A - Tableau 20A

CAPITAL UNDER FOREIGN INFLUENCE / CAPITAL SOUS INFLUENCE ÉTRANGÈRE

| By industry (ISIC Rev. 3) | | Foreign affiliates *(Millions of NLG)* | | | | | | | | | |
| | | Filiales étrangères *(Millions de NLG)* | | | | | | | | | |
		1989	1990	1991	1992	1993	1994	1995	1996	1997	1998
10/14	Mining & quarrying	..	..	..	..	..	..	..	..	6 416	7 266
15/37	**TOTAL MANUFACTURING**	..	..	..	..	..	..	..	..	**123 580**	**129 957**
15/16	Food, beverages, tobacco	..	..	..	..	..	..	..	..	23 102	26 895
17/19	Textiles, clothing, leather, footwear	..	..	..	..	..	..	..	..	2 156	2 313
20/22	Wood and paper products	..	..	..	..	..	..	..	..	12 993	12 547
20	Wood products	..	..	..	..	..	..	..	..	227	197
21/22	Paper, printing and publishing	..	..	..	..	..	..	..	..	12 766	12 350
23/25	Chemicals, Total	..	..	..	..	..	..	..	..	57 589	57 074
23	Refined petroleum, nuclear fuel	..	..	..	..	..	..	..	..	8 239	8 325
24/25	Chemicals, rubber & plastics prod.	..	..	..	..	..	..	..	..	49 350	48 749
24	Chemical products	..	..	..	..	..	..	..	..	45 785	44 720
2423	Pharmaceuticals	..	..	..	..	..	..	..	..	5 308	5 521
25	Rubber and plastics products	..	..	..	..	..	..	..	..	3 565	4 029
26	Non-metallic mineral products	..	..	..	..	..	..	..	..	5 553	5 811
27/28	Basic & fabricated metals	..	..	..	..	..	..	..	..	7 062	6 589
27	Basic metals	..	..	..	..	..	..	..	..	2 872	2 109
28	Fabricated metal products	..	..	..	..	..	..	..	..	4 190	4 480
29/32	Machinery, Total	..	..	..	..	..	..	..	..	10 917	11 837
29/30	Non-electrical machinery	..	..	..	..	..	..	..	..	7 512	8 046
29	Non-electrical machinery nec	..	..	..	..	..	..	..	..	6 056	6 639
30	Office and computing machinery	..	..	..	..	..	..	..	..	1 455	1 407
31/32	Electrical & electronic equipment	..	..	..	..	..	..	..	..	3 405	3 791
31	Electrical machinery nec	..	..	..	..	..	..	..	..	..	1 740
32	Radio, TV & communications eq.	..	..	..	..	..	..	..	..	..	2 051
33	Scientific instruments	..	..	..	..	..	..	..	..	2 233	2 366
34/35	Transportation equipment	..	..	..	..	..	..	..	..	1 465	3 968
34	Motor vehicles	..	..	..	..	..	..	..	..	1 201	3 554
35	Other transport equipment	..	..	..	..	..	..	..	..	263	414
351	Shipbuilding & repairing	..	..	..	..	..	..	..	..	..	..
353	Aircraft and spacecraft	..	..	..	..	..	..	..	..	..	..
36/37	Other manufacturing	..	..	..	..	..	..	..	..	511	554
40/45	Construction, electricity, gas & water	..	..	..	..	..	..	..	..	3 357	3 751
50/55	Trade, repair, hotels & restaurants	..	..	..	..	..	..	..	..	90 335	102 498
65/74	Finance, insurance, business services	..	..	..	..	..	..	..	..	15 338	22 180
	OTHER ACTIVITIES	..	..	..	..	..	..	..	..	13 190	15 307
01/99	**GRAND TOTAL**	..	..	..	..	..	..	..	..	**252 217**	**280 960**

Total manufacturing by investing country

	1989	1990	1991	1992	1993	1994	1995	1996	1997	1998
All countries	..	..	..	..	..	..	..	..	**123 580**	**129 957**
United States	..	..	..	..	..	..	..	..	59 190	65 600
Canada	..	..	..	..	..	..	..	..	..	..
Mexico	..	..	..	..	..	..	..	..	..	..
Japan	..	..	..	..	..	..	..	..	6 841	6 658
Europe	..	..	..	..	..	..	..	..	..	..
European Union (15)	..	..	..	..	..	..	..	..	42 549	43 645
Belgium	..	..	..	..	..	..	..	..	..	..
France	..	..	..	..	..	..	..	..	3 945	3 963
Germany	..	..	..	..	..	..	..	..	6 571	6 226
Italy	..	..	..	..	..	..	..	..	..	..
Netherlands	..	..	..	..	..	..	..	..	..	..
Spain	..	..	..	..	..	..	..	..	..	..
Sweden	..	..	..	..	..	..	..	..	..	..
United Kingdom	..	..	..	..	..	..	..	..	18 542	19 252
Switzerland	..	..	..	..	..	..	..	..	5 987	3 317
Australia and New Zealand	..	..	..	..	..	..	..	..	..	..
Asia (non-OECD)	..	..	..	..	..	..	..	..	..	..
Latin America	..	..	..	..	..	..	..	..	3 463	4 143

Note: Majority foreign-owned firms.
Firmes sous contrôle étranger majoritaire.

NETHERLANDS

Source

The data are prepared by the Division Business Statistics of Statistics Netherlands (CBS). They refer to majority foreign-owned enterprises and are based on several sources:

- For *Number of enterprises*, *Number of employees*, *Production*, *Turnover*, *Value added*, *Compensation of employees* and *Gross operating surplus*, the data come from a few surveys on non-financial enterprises. The divisions 11 to 64, 71, 72, 74, 90 and 93 of ISIC Revision 3 are covered.

- For *Gross fixed capital formation*, a survey on tangible investments is used to produce the results. The divisions 10 to 45, 50 to 55, 71, 72, 74, 90 and 93 of ISIC Revision 3 are covered.

- For *R&D expenditure*, data come from the R&D investments survey, covering the following ISIC Revision 3 divisions: 10 to 45, 50 to 64, 70 to 72, 74, 90 and 93.

- For *Total exports* and *imports*, data come from Statistics Netherlands for trade in goods and from De Nederlandsche Bank, the Dutch Central Bank for trade in services. The 1996 and 1997 data comprise both goods and services, the 1998 data comprise trade in goods only.

- For *Intra-firm exports* and *imports*, data are based on an annual questionnaire on the 2 500 large non-financial enterprise groups, with a balance sheet total of at least NLG 25 million. Information on the country of origin comes also from this source. All enterprise groups with a balance sheet total of less than NLG 25 millions are considered to be Dutch enterprise groups.

National totals: provided by Statistics Netherlands and fully compatible with foreign affiliates' data.

Industrial classification

For all variables, the data are classified according to the principal industrial activity of the affiliate.

The industrial classification used for the tables is the national classification converted to ISIC Revision 3.

No information is available for financial enterprises (ISIC 65/67).

Variables

- *Number of enterprises* is defined as the number of non-financial enterprises with a foreign shareholding of more than 50%.

- *Number of employees* is the number of employees at the end of September. From 1997, it is expressed in full-time equivalent.

- *Turnover* is defined as net turnover.

- *Value added* is valued at factor cost.

- *Compensation of employees* consists of wages, salaries, social security and pension contributions.

- *R&D expenditure* refer to expenditure by the affiliate itself.

- *Total exports* and *imports* refer to trade in goods and services for 1996 and 1997, and to trade in goods only for 1998.

- *Gross operating surplus* is in fact net income.

Geographical breakdown

Up to 1996, the investor's country is the country of the immediate controller. As from 1997, it is that of the "ultimate beneficial owner".

PAYS-BAS

Source

Les données émanent de la Division des statistiques des entreprises du Bureau des statistiques néerlandais (CBS). Elles concernent les entreprises sous contrôle étranger majoritaire et sont fondées sur plusieurs sources :

- Pour le *Nombre d'entreprises*, le *Nombre de salariés*, la *Production*, le *Chiffre d'affaires*, la *Valeur ajoutée*, les *Salaires et charges sociales* et l'*Excédent brut d'exploitation*, les données proviennent d'enquêtes sur les entreprises non financières. Les divisions 11 à 64, 71, 72, 74, 90 et 93 de la CITI révision 3 sont couvertes.

- Pour la *Formation brute de capital fixe*, les résultats proviennent d'une enquête sur les investissements tangibles. Les divisions 10 à 45, 50 à 55, 71, 72, 74, 90 et 93 de la CITI révision 3 sont couvertes.

- Pour les *Dépenses de R-D*, les données sont tirées de l'enquête sur les investissements de R-D, couvrant les divisions suivantes de la CITI révision 3 : 10 à 45, 50 à 64, 70 à 72, 74, 90 et 93.

- Pour les *Exportations* et *importations totales*, les données proviennent du Bureau des statistiques néerlandais pour le commerce de biens et de la Banque des Pays-Bas, banque centrale néerlandaise pour le commerce des services. Les données pour 1996 et 1997 comprennent les biens et les services, les données pour 1998 ne comprennent que le commerce des biens.

- Pour les *Exportations* et *importations intra-firme*, les données sont tirées du questionnaire annuel sur les 2 500 groupes d'entreprises non financiers les plus importants, dont le total du bilan dépasse NLG 25 millions. Les informations sur le pays d'origine proviennent également de cette enquête. Tous les groupes d'entreprises faisant apparaître un total au bilan de moins de NLG 25 millions, sont considérées comme étant des groupes néerlandais.

Totaux nationaux : fournis par le Bureau des statistiques néerlandais, et entièrement compatibles avec les données relatives aux filiales étrangères.

Classification industrielle

Pour toutes les variables, les données sont classées selon l'activité industrielle principale de l'entreprise affiliée.

La classification industrielle utilisée pour les tableaux est la classification nationale adaptée de façon à correspondre à la CITI révision 3.

Aucune information n'est disponible pour les entreprises financières (CITI 65/67).

Variables

- Le *Nombre d'entreprises* est défini comme le nombre d'entreprises non financières pour lesquelles la participation étrangère dans le capital est de plus de 50 %.

- Le *Nombre de salariés* correspond aux effectifs à fin septembre. Il est exprimé en équivalent plein-temps à partir de 1997.

- Le *Chiffre d'affaires* est défini comme le chiffre d'affaires net.

- La *Valeur ajoutée* est évaluée au coût des facteurs.

- Les *Salaires et charges sociales* se composent des traitements, salaires, cotisations à la sécurité sociale et au système de retraite.

- Les *Dépenses de R-D* concernent les dépenses effectuées par les filiales pour elles-mêmes.

- L'*Excédent brut d'exploitation* est en fait le revenu net.

Ventilation géographique

Jusqu'en 1996, le pays d'origine est celui où s'exerce le contrôle immédiat. A partir de 1997, il s'agit du "bénéficiaire ultime de l'investissement".

NORWAY

Sources and Methods

NORVÈGE

Sources et méthodes

Inward investments

Investissements entrants

Table 1A - Tableau 1A

NUMBER OF ESTABLISHMENTS / NOMBRE D'ÉTABLISSEMENTS

By industry (ISIC Rev. 3)		Foreign affiliates (Units) Filiales étrangères (Unités)					As a % of national total En % du total national				
		1994	1995	1996	1997	1998	1994	1995	1996	1997	1998
10/14	Mining & quarrying	9	11	19	21	28	10.8	11.8	5.3	6.0	7.6
15/37	**TOTAL MANUFACTURING**	232	348	516	535	586	5.7	8.4	4.7	4.6	5.0
15/16	Food, beverages, tobacco	23	39	44	39	53	2.5	4.3	2.5	2.3	3.2
17/19	Textiles, clothing, leather, footwear	5	6	10	14	13	2.6	3.2	1.9	2.5	2.4
20/22	Wood and paper products	30	51	75	84	83	3.5	5.7	2.5	2.6	2.6
20	Wood products	4	4	..	8	3	1.3	1.2	..	0.8	0.3
21/22	Paper, printing and publishing	26	47	..	76	80	4.6	8.4	..	3.4	3.7
23/25	Chemicals, Total	49	57	66	77	79	15.8	18.9	12.2	13.9	14.2
23	Refined petroleum, nuclear fuel	12	11	3	7	3	18.5	18.3	37.5	77.8	50.0
24/25	Chemicals, rubber & plastics prod.	37	46	63	70	76	15.0	19.0	11.8	12.9	13.8
24	Chemical products	18	26	36	44	49	17.6	25.0	20.3	24.3	24.9
2423	Pharmaceuticals	3	..	6	13	14	21.4	..	26.1	56.5	58.3
25	Rubber and plastics products	19	20	27	26	27	13.2	14.5	7.6	7.2	7.6
26	Non-metallic mineral products	22	35	61	69	78	12.7	18.7	10.2	11.4	12.7
27/28	Basic & fabricated metals	24	30	48	55	61	5.3	6.3	3.7	3.9	4.2
27	Basic metals	9	11	16	17	22	10.8	14.7	13.2	14.2	18.2
28	Fabricated metal products	15	19	32	38	39	4.1	4.7	2.7	2.9	2.9
29/32	Machinery, Total	47	..	144	127	133	9.7	..	9.1	7.4	7.6
29/30	Non-electrical machinery	26	..	87	76	80	8.0	..	7.3	5.9	6.1
29	Non-electrical machinery nec	26	34	85	76	80	8.2	10.0	7.3	6.0	6.2
30	Office and computing machinery	0	..	2	0	0	0.0	..	8.0	0.0	0.0
31/32	Electrical & electronic equipment	21	..	57	51	53	13.0	..	14.6	11.9	12.2
31	Electrical machinery nec	15	..	46	44	43	12.8	..	14.6	12.4	12.3
32	Radio, TV & communications eq.	6	..	11	7	10	13.6	..	14.7	9.6	11.8
33	Scientific instruments	6	..	19	19	20	10.9	..	5.7	5.9	6.0
34/35	Transportation equipment	20	34	34	36	50	5.8	9.3	4.8	4.9	6.9
34	Motor vehicles	2	..	4	3	4	3.7	..	4.1	2.9	3.7
35	Other transport equipment	18	..	30	33	46	6.2	..	4.9	5.2	7.5
351	Shipbuilding & repairing	15	..	26	28	40	5.7	..	4.6	4.8	6.8
353	Aircraft and spacecraft	0	..	0	0	0	0.0	..	0.0	0.0	0.0
36/37	Other manufacturing	6	11	15	15	16	2.5	4.3	2.0	1.8	1.8
40/45	Construction, electricity, gas & water	..	..	..	..	..	..	..	..	..	..
50/55	Trade, repair, hotels & restaurants	..	..	..	..	..	..	..	..	..	..
65/74	Finance, insurance, business services	..	..	..	..	..	..	..	..	..	..
	OTHER ACTIVITIES	..	..	..	..	..	..	..	..	..	..
01/99	**GRAND TOTAL**	..	..	..	..	..	..	..	..	..	..

Total manufacturing by investing country	1994	1995	1996	1997	1998	As a % of total manufacturing by foreign affiliates				
						1994	1995	1996	1997	1998
All countries	232	348	516	535	586	100.0	100.0	100.0	100.0	100.0
United States	23	..	..	40	42	9.9	..	..	7.5	7.2
Canada	3	..	..	1	..	1.3	..	..	0.2	..
Mexico	0	..	..	..	..	0.0	..	..	..	..
Japan	0	..	..	0	0	0.0	..	..	0.0	0.0
Europe	206	..	..	484	..	88.8	..	..	90.5	..
European Union (15)	187	..	..	460	509	80.6	..	..	86.0	86.9
Belgium	5	..	..	13	..	2.2	..	..	2.4	..
France	5	..	..	9	8	2.2	..	..	1.7	1.4
Germany	10	..	..	29	24	4.3	..	..	5.4	4.1
Italy	1	..	..	2	..	0.4	..	..	0.4	..
Netherlands	14	..	..	27	69	6.0	..	..	5.0	11.8
Spain	1	..	..	0	..	0.4	..	..	0.0	..
Sweden	73	..	..	228	..	31.5	..	..	42.6	..
United Kingdom	17	..	..	31	33	7.3	..	..	5.8	5.6
Switzerland	19	..	..	21	23	8.2	..	..	3.9	3.9
Australia and New Zealand	0	..	..	1	..	0.0	..	..	0.2	..
Asia (non-OECD)	0	..	..	1	1	0.0	..	..	0.2	0.2
Latin America	0	..	..	8	4	0.0	..	..	1.5	0.7

Note: Majority foreign-owned establishments. *Crude petroleum and natural gas extraction* (ISIC 11) is excluded from *Mining and quarrying* (10/14). From 1995 onwards data include indirectly from abroad owned establishments. From 1996, change in the coverage of the survey. See country notes.

Etablissements sous contrôle étranger majoritaire. L'*Extraction de pétrole et de gaz naturel* (CITI 11) est exclue des *Industries extractives* (10/14). Les données à partir de 1995 comprennent les établissements contrôlés indirectement par l'étranger. A partir de 1996, changement dans la couverture de l'enquête. Voir les notes par pays.

Inward investments

Investissements entrants

Table 2A - Tableau 2A

NUMBER OF EMPLOYEES BY INDUSTRY

NOMBRE DE SALARIÉS PAR INDUSTRIE

| | | Foreign affiliates (Units) | | | | | As a % of national total | | | | |
| | | Filiales étrangères (Unités) | | | | | En % du total national | | | | |
ISIC Revision 3		1994	1995	1996	1997	1998	1994	1995	1996	1997	1998
10/14	Mining & quarrying	457	807	889	868	773	13.3	23.8	20.6	21.2	19.3
15/37	**TOTAL MANUFACTURING**	**21 664**	**37 237**	**40 348**	**41 572**	**51 606**	**9.0**	**15.0**	**14.3**	**14.2**	**17.4**
15/16	Food, beverages, tobacco	1 908	6 787	6 697	5 908	7 142	4.1	14.5	12.8	11.3	13.4
17/19	Textiles, clothing, leather, footwear	462	276	431	583	485	6.5	4.1	5.2	7.0	6.1
20/22	Wood and paper products	1 904	3 654	3 059	3 434	4 047	3.7	6.9	5.0	5.4	6.4
20	Wood products	181	190	..	247	175	1.6	1.6	..	1.6	1.1
21/22	Paper, printing and publishing	1 723	3 464	..	3 187	3 872	4.3	8.4	..	6.6	8.1
23/25	Chemicals, Total	3 832	4 883	5 031	6 997	6 980	18.8	23.8	23.2	32.1	31.8
23	Refined petroleum, nuclear fuel	485	478	392	405	376	29.6	32.0	32.5	35.0	31.6
24/25	Chemicals, rubber & plastics prod.	3 347	4 405	4 639	6 592	6 604	17.9	23.2	22.7	31.9	31.8
24	Chemical products	2 303	3 052	3 198	5 159	5 198	17.4	22.4	23.1	37.7	37.8
2423	Pharmaceuticals	386	..	737	2 358	2 394	16.1	..	28.2	90.7	90.3
25	Rubber and plastics products	1 044	1 353	1 441	1 433	1 406	19.1	25.0	21.8	20.6	20.0
26	Non-metallic mineral products	1 569	2 561	3 326	2 719	3 146	23.5	36.2	35.2	28.2	31.5
27/28	Basic & fabricated metals	4 076	4 799	5 098	5 758	6 190	15.0	16.7	15.5	16.7	17.3
27	Basic metals	2 953	3 135	3 293	3 407	3 622	20.2	21.0	21.8	22.8	24.7
28	Fabricated metal products	1 123	1 664	1 805	2 351	2 568	9.0	12.1	10.1	12.1	12.2
29/32	Machinery, Total	4 654	..	10 063	9 336	10 194	14.9	..	26.7	23.4	25.2
29/30	Non-electrical machinery	1 943	..	3 411	3 370	4 026	10.2	..	14.4	13.5	15.8
29	Non-electrical machinery nec	1 943	2 742	3 377	3 370	4 026	10.6	14.5	14.8	13.9	16.4
30	Office and computing machinery	0	..	34	0	0	0.0	..	4.6	0.0	0.0
31/32	Electrical & electronic equipment	2 711	..	6 652	5 966	6 168	22.4	..	47.3	40.3	41.2
31	Electrical machinery nec	1 491	..	4 724	4 600	4 607	18.6	..	49.3	46.2	44.2
32	Radio, TV & communications eq.	1 220	..	1 928	1 366	1 561	29.8	..	43.1	28.1	34.5
33	Scientific instruments	559	..	1 107	757	834	15.7	..	20.5	13.6	13.7
34/35	Transportation equipment	2 381	5 298	4 998	5 494	11 796	6.4	13.5	12.5	13.0	28.0
34	Motor vehicles	109	..	413	391	405	3.4	..	8.5	8.1	8.5
35	Other transport equipment	2 272	..	4 585	5 103	11 391	6.7	..	13.1	13.6	30.5
351	Shipbuilding & repairing	1 854	..	3 913	4 454	10 687	6.4	..	12.9	13.5	29.9
353	Aircraft and spacecraft	0	..	0	0	0	0.0	..	0.0	0.0	0.0
36/37	Other manufacturing	319	468	538	586	792	3.3	4.5	4.2	4.0	5.1
40/45	Construction, electricity, gas & water	..	..	..	..	..	..	..	..	..	..
50/55	Trade, repair, hotels & restaurants	..	..	..	..	..	..	..	..	..	..
65/74	Finance, insurance, business services	..	..	..	..	..	..	..	..	..	..
	OTHER ACTIVITIES	..	..	..	..	..	..	..	..	..	..
01/99	**GRAND TOTAL**	..	..	..	..	..	..	..	..	..	..

Note: Majority foreign-owned establishments. *Crude petroleum and natural gas extraction* (ISIC 11) is excluded from *Mining and quarrying* (10/14). From 1995 onwards data include indirectly from abroad owned establishments.
Etablissements sous contrôle étranger majoritaire. L'*Extraction de pétrole et de gaz naturel* (CITI 11) est exclue des *Industries extractives* (10/14). Les données à partir de 1995 comprennent les établissements contrôlés indirectement par l'étranger.

Inward investments   *Investissements entrants*

Table 3A - Tableau 3A

NUMBER OF EMPLOYEES BY COUNTRY OF ORIGIN IN THE MANUFACTURING SECTOR

NOMBRE DE SALARIÉS PAR PAYS D'ORIGINE DANS L'INDUSTRIE MANUFACTURIÈRE

| | Number of employees (Units) | | | | | As a % of all countries | | | | |
| | Nombre de salariés (Unités) | | | | | En % du total des pays | | | | |
Country of origin (immediate controller)	1994	1995	1996	1997	1998	1994	1995	1996	1997	1998
All countries	21 664	37 237	40 348	41 572	51 606	100.0	100.0	100.0	100.0	100.0
Total OECD	..	..	..	..	51 355	..	..	..	..	99.5
United States	2 518	..	..	4 939	5 514	11.6	..	..	11.9	10.7
Canada	694	..	..	603	608	3.2	..	..	1.5	1.2
Mexico	0	..	..	..	0	0.0	..	..	..	0.0
Japan	0	..	..	0	0	0.0	..	..	0.0	0.0
Korea	..	..	..	..	0	..	..	..	..	0.0
Australia	..	..	..	..	64	..	..	..	..	0.1
New Zealand	..	..	..	..	0	..	..	..	..	0.0
Europe	18 452	..	..	35 413	45 275	85.2	..	..	85.2	87.7
European Union (15)	15 692	..	..	33 243	42 704	72.4	..	..	80.0	82.8
Austria	..	..	..	21	23	..	..	..	0.1	0.0
Belgium	416	..	..	986	891	1.9	..	..	2.4	1.7
Denmark	..	..	..	3 916	4 246	..	..	..	9.4	8.2
Finland	..	..	..	1 258	1 343	..	..	..	3.0	2.6
France	270	..	..	850	903	1.2	..	..	2.0	1.7
Germany	481	..	..	2 799	1 864	2.2	..	..	6.7	3.6
Greece	..	..	..	..	0	..	..	..	..	0.0
Ireland	..	..	..	..	0	..	..	..	..	0.0
Italy	39	..	..	55	54	0.2	..	..	0.1	0.1
Luxembourg	..	..	..	..	..	..	..	..	..	..
Netherlands	1 491	..	..	2 501	11 085	6.9	..	..	6.0	21.5
Portugal	..	..	..	0	0	..	..	..	0.0	0.0
Spain	29	..	..	0	10	0.1	..	..	0.0	0.0
Sweden	6 887	..	..	17 389	18 873	31.8	..	..	41.8	36.6
United Kingdom	1 884	..	..	3 468	3 412	8.7	..	..	8.3	6.6
Czech Republic	..	..	..	..	0	..	..	..	..	0.0
Hungary	..	..	..	..	0	..	..	..	..	0.0
Iceland	..	..	..	..	0	..	..	..	..	0.0
Norway	..	..	..	..	0	..	..	..	..	0.0
Poland	..	..	..	0	0	..	..	..	0.0	0.0
Slovak Republic	..	..	..	..	0	..	..	..	0.0	0.0
Switzerland	2 760	..	..	2 129	2 465	12.7	..	..	5.1	4.8
Turkey	..	..	..	..	0	..	..	..	..	0.0
Non-OECD Europe, of which:	..	..	..	..	106	..	..	..	..	0.2
Baltic countries	..	..	..	..	0	..	..	..	..	0.0
Bulgaria	..	..	..	..	0	..	..	..	..	0.0
Croatia	..	..	..	..	0	..	..	..	..	0.0
Romania	..	..	..	..	0	..	..	..	..	0.0
Russian Federation	..	..	..	0	0	..	..	..	..	0.0
Slovenia	..	..	..	..	0	..	..	..	..	0.0
Ukraine	..	..	..	..	0	..	..	..	..	0.0
Yugoslavia	..	..	..	..	0	..	..	..	..	0.0
Non-OECD Asia, of which:	0	..	..	3	6	0.0	..	..	0.0	0.0
China	0	..	..	..	0	0.0	..	..	..	0.0
Chinese Taipei	0	..	..	..	0	0.0	..	..	..	0.0
Hong Kong (China)	0	..	..	..	0	0.0	..	..	..	0.0
India	0	..	..	..	0	0.0	..	..	..	0.0
Indonesia	0	..	..	..	0	0.0	..	..	..	0.0
Malaysia	0	..	..	..	0	0.0	..	..	..	0.0
Philippines	0	..	..	..	0	0.0	..	..	..	0.0
Singapore	0	..	..	..	0	0.0	..	..	..	0.0
Thailand	0	..	..	..	0	0.0	..	..	..	0.0
Near and Middle East	..	..	..	..	0	..	..	..	..	0.0
Africa	..	..	..	0	0	..	..	..	0.0	0.0
Latin America, of which:	0	..	..	550	139	0.0	..	..	1.3	0.3
Argentina	0	..	..	..	0	0.0	..	..	..	0.0
Brazil	0	..	..	..	0	0.0	..	..	..	0.0
Chile	0	..	..	..	0	0.0	..	..	..	0.0

Note: Majority foreign-owned establishments. From 1995 onwards data include indirectly from abroad owned establishments. Data for Belgium include those for Luxembourg.

Etablissements sous contrôle étranger majoritaire. Les données à partir de 1995 comprennent les établissements contrôlés indirectement par l'étranger. Les données pour la Belgique comprennent celles du Luxembourg.

Inward investments

Investissements entrants

Table 4A - Tableau 4A

PRODUCTION BY INDUSTRY

PRODUCTION PAR INDUSTRIE

ISIC Revision 3		Foreign affiliates *(Millions of NOK)* Filiales étrangères *(Millions de NOK)*					As a % of national total En % du total national				
		1994	1995	1996	1997	1998	1994	1995	1996	1997	1998
10/14	Mining & quarrying	445	964	1 232	1 237	1 287	12.7	26.3	23.9	22.5	22.0
15/37	**TOTAL MANUFACTURING**	**41 395**	**66 988**	**74 264**	**84 893**	**111 008**	**13.0**	**19.5**	**19.0**	**19.8**	**24.1**
15/16	Food, beverages, tobacco	3 242	11 526	11 206	11 145	17 452	3.8	13.2	11.6	11.0	16.3
17/19	Textiles, clothing, leather, footwear	378	233	327	458	439	7.4	4.9	5.6	7.6	7.2
20/22	Wood and paper products	2 273	5 153	4 717	5 257	6 355	4.6	9.2	7.5	8.0	9.1
20	Wood products	207	224	..	377	257	1.7	1.8	..	2.3	1.5
21/22	Paper, printing and publishing	2 066	4 929	..	4 879	6 098	5.5	11.4	..	10.0	11.6
23/25	Chemicals, Total	13 304	14 866	17 248	..	22 296	27.8	31.0	30.8	..	38.5
23	Refined petroleum, nuclear fuel	6 837	6 490	9 229	..	6 933	43.6	49.1	49.0	..	46.4
24/25	Chemicals, rubber & plastics prod.	6 467	8 376	8 019	14 585	15 363	20.1	24.1	21.6	35.6	35.8
24	Chemical products	5 368	6 932	6 296	12 848	13 648	19.9	23.8	20.9	38.4	38.9
2423	Pharmaceuticals	..	..	972	5 246	6 291	..	..	17.3	94.2	94.4
25	Rubber and plastics products	1 099	1 444	1 723	1 737	1 715	21.4	25.8	24.4	23.1	22.0
26	Non-metallic mineral products	2 018	2 996	5 247	4 284	4 689	26.6	35.0	42.0	33.2	34.8
27/28	Basic & fabricated metals	10 266	11 928	12 342	15 039	15 556	24.6	24.7	24.6	27.4	25.7
27	Basic metals	9 130	10 222	10 225	12 022	12 018	28.8	27.9	28.8	31.7	29.9
28	Fabricated metal products	1 136	1 706	2 117	3 017	3 538	11.4	14.7	14.4	17.8	17.3
29/32	Machinery, Total	6 206	..	..	14 425	17 232	18.3	..	..	29.7	31.9
29/30	Non-electrical machinery	2 146	..	..	5 113	7 708	10.7	..	..	17.7	22.5
29	Non-electrical machinery nec	2 146	3 889	4 472	5 113	7 708	11.6	18.1	17.0	18.6	24.0
30	Office and computing machinery	0	..	..	0	0	0.0	..	..	0.0	0.0
31/32	Electrical & electronic equipment	4 060	..	9 273	9 312	9 524	29.2	..	52.5	47.6	48.0
31	Electrical machinery nec	2 224	..	6 392	6 365	7 035	23.8	..	56.7	51.7	50.8
32	Radio, TV & communications eq.	1 836	..	2 881	2 947	2 489	40.3	..	44.9	40.7	41.6
33	Scientific instruments	656	..	..	1 992	2 082	15.5	..	..	25.5	23.7
34/35	Transportation equipment	2 735	7 272	6 513	8 467	23 999	7.5	18.5	14.7	14.4	35.5
34	Motor vehicles	..	..	422	479	539	..	..	8.6	9.4	10.2
35	Other transport equipment	..	..	6 091	7 988	23 460	..	..	15.4	14.9	37.7
351	Shipbuilding & repairing	2 313	..	5 439	7 188	22 781	8.0	..	15.7	14.7	37.6
353	Aircraft and spacecraft	0	..	0	0	0	0.0	..	0.0	0.0	0.0
36/37	Other manufacturing	318	470	580	..	909	4.3	5.5	5.5	..	6.4
40/45	Construction, electricity, gas & water	..	..	..	..	..	..	..	..	..	..
50/55	Trade, repair, hotels & restaurants	..	..	..	..	..	..	..	..	..	..
65/74	Finance, insurance, business services	..	..	..	..	..	..	..	..	..	..
	OTHER ACTIVITIES	..	..	..	..	..	..	..	..	..	..
01/99	**GRAND TOTAL**	..	..	..	..	..	..	..	..	..	..

Note: Majority foreign-owned establishments. *Crude petroleum and natural gas extraction* (ISIC 11) is excluded from *Mining and quarrying* (10/14). From 1995 onwards data include indirectly from abroad owned establishments.

Etablissements sous contrôle étranger majoritaire. L'*Extraction de pétrole et de gaz naturel* (CITI 11) est exclue des *Industries extractives* (10/14). Les données à partir de 1995 comprennent les établissements contrôlés indirectement par l'étranger.

Table 5A - Tableau 5A

PRODUCTION BY COUNTRY OF ORIGIN IN THE MANUFACTURING SECTOR

PRODUCTION PAR PAYS D'ORIGINE DANS L'INDUSTRIE MANUFACTURIÈRE

Country of origin (immediate controller)	Production (Millions of NOK) / Production (Millions de NOK)					As a % of all countries / En % du total des pays				
	1994	1995	1996	1997	1998	1994	1995	1996	1997	1998
All countries	41 395	66 988	74 264	84 893	111 008	100.0	100.0	100.0	100.0	100.0
Total OECD	..	..	..	..	110 744	..	..	..	..	99.8
United States	7 859	..	..	12 552	13 329	19.0	..	..	14.8	12.0
Canada	5 121	..	..	..	4 517	12.4	..	..	..	4.1
Mexico	0	..	..	..	0	0.0	..	..	..	0.0
Japan	0	..	..	0	0	0.0	..	..	0.0	0.0
Korea	..	..	..	..	0	..	..	..	..	0.0
Australia	..	..	..	..	..	..	..	..	..	..
New Zealand	..	..	..	..	0	..	..	..	..	0.0
Europe	28 414	..	..	65 917	92 895	68.6	..	..	77.6	83.7
European Union (15)	24 870	..	..	61 189	87 493	60.1	..	..	72.1	78.8
Austria	..	..	..	..	..	..	..	..	..	..
Belgium	394	..	..	765	711	1.0	..	..	0.9	0.6
Denmark	..	..	..	8 438	13 266	..	..	..	9.9	12.0
Finland	..	..	..	1 394	1 644	..	..	..	1.6	1.5
France	327	..	..	2 072	1 793	0.8	..	..	2.4	1.6
Germany	567	..	..	2 950	2 904	1.4	..	..	3.5	2.6
Greece	..	..	..	..	0	..	..	..	..	0.0
Ireland	..	..	..	..	0	..	..	..	..	0.0
Italy	..	..	..	..	..	..	..	..	..	..
Luxembourg	..	..	..	..	..	..	..	..	..	..
Netherlands	2 472	..	..	5 666	23 832	6.0	..	..	6.7	21.5
Portugal	..	..	..	0	0	..	..	..	0.0	0.0
Spain	..	..	..	0	..	..	..	..	0.0	..
Sweden	8 313	..	..	28 609	30 696	20.1	..	..	33.7	27.7
United Kingdom	5 797	..	..	11 108	12 447	14.0	..	..	13.1	11.2
Czech Republic	..	..	..	..	0	..	..	..	..	0.0
Hungary	..	..	..	..	0	..	..	..	..	0.0
Iceland	..	..	..	..	0	..	..	..	..	0.0
Norway	..	..	..	..	0	..	..	..	..	0.0
Poland	..	..	..	0	0	..	..	..	0.0	0.0
Slovak Republic	..	..	..	..	0	..	..	..	0.0	0.0
Switzerland	3 544	..	..	4 679	5 245	8.6	..	..	5.5	4.7
Turkey	..	..	..	..	0	..	..	..	..	0.0
Non-OECD Europe, of which:	..	..	..	..	157	..	..	..	..	0.1
Baltic countries	..	..	..	..	0	..	..	..	..	0.0
Bulgaria	..	..	..	..	0	..	..	..	..	0.0
Croatia	..	..	..	..	0	..	..	..	..	0.0
Romania	..	..	..	..	0	..	..	..	..	0.0
Russian Federation	..	..	..	0	0	..	..	..	..	0.0
Slovenia	..	..	..	..	0	..	..	..	..	0.0
Ukraine	..	..	..	..	0	..	..	..	..	0.0
Yugoslavia	..	..	..	..	0	..	..	..	..	0.0
Non-OECD Asia, of which:	0	..	..	..	..	0.0	..	..	..	..
China	0	..	..	..	0	0.0	..	..	..	0.0
Chinese Taipei	0	..	..	..	0	0.0	..	..	..	0.0
Hong Kong (China)	0	..	..	..	0	0.0	..	..	..	0.0
India	0	..	..	..	0	0.0	..	..	..	0.0
Indonesia	0	..	..	..	0	0.0	..	..	..	0.0
Malaysia	0	..	..	..	0	0.0	..	..	..	0.0
Philippines	0	..	..	..	0	0.0	..	..	..	0.0
Singapore	0	..	..	..	0	0.0	..	..	..	0.0
Thailand	0	..	..	..	0	0.0	..	..	..	0.0
Near and Middle East	..	..	..	..	0	..	..	..	..	0.0
Africa	..	..	..	0	0	..	..	..	0.0	0.0
Latin America, of which:	0	..	..	1 024	106	0.0	..	..	1.2	0.1
Argentina	0	..	..	..	0	0.0	..	..	..	0.0
Brazil	0	..	..	..	0	0.0	..	..	..	0.0
Chile	0	..	..	..	0	0.0	..	..	..	0.0

Note: Majority foreign-owned establishments. From 1995 onwards data include indirectly from abroad owned establishments. Data for Belgium include those for Luxembourg.

Etablissements sous contrôle étranger majoritaire. Les données à partir de 1995 comprennent les établissements contrôlés indirectement par l'étranger. Les données pour la Belgique comprennent celles du Luxembourg.

Inward investments

Investissements entrants

Table 6A - Tableau 6A
TURNOVER / CHIFFRE D'AFFAIRES

By industry (ISIC Rev. 3)	Foreign affiliates (Millions of NOK) Filiales étrangères (Millions de NOK)					As a % of national total En % du total national				
	1994	1995	1996	1997	1998	1994	1995	1996	1997	1998
10/14 Mining & quarrying	..	..	1 186	1 247	1 272	..	..	22.9	22.6	21.6
15/37 TOTAL MANUFACTURING	..	..	74 690	85 697	111 738	..	..	18.9	19.9	23.9
15/16 Food, beverages, tobacco	..	..	11 290	11 173	17 482	..	..	11.5	10.6	15.6
17/19 Textiles, clothing, leather, footwear	..	..	346	469	443	..	..	5.7	7.5	6.9
20/22 Wood and paper products	..	..	4 791	5 350	6 412	..	..	7.5	8.1	9.2
20 Wood products	..	..	..	366	241	..	..	..	2.1	1.4
21/22 Paper, printing and publishing	..	..	..	4 984	6 170	..	..	..	10.2	11.8
23/25 Chemicals, Total	..	..	17 142	..	21 788	..	..	30.8	..	38.4
23 Refined petroleum, nuclear fuel	..	..	9 026	..	7 203	..	..	48.3	..	47.2
24/25 Chemicals, rubber & plastics prod.	..	..	8 116	14 203	14 585	..	..	21.9	35.2	35.1
24 Chemical products	..	..	6 396	12 418	12 827	..	..	21.5	38.1	38.4
2423 Pharmaceuticals	..	..	970	4 717	5 376	..	..	19.5	93.2	92.9
25 Rubber and plastics products	..	..	1 721	1 785	1 758	..	..	23.7	23.0	21.8
26 Non-metallic mineral products	..	..	5 285	4 547	4 898	..	..	41.4	33.8	35.2
27/28 Basic & fabricated metals	..	..	12 542	15 420	15 927	..	..	24.8	27.8	26.1
27 Basic metals	..	..	10 436	12 182	12 259	..	..	29.1	31.9	30.5
28 Fabricated metal products	..	..	2 106	3 238	3 668	..	..	14.3	18.7	17.6
29/32 Machinery, Total	..	..	13 823	14 600	17 967	..	..	30.3	29.8	32.7
29/30 Non-electrical machinery	..	..	..	5 176	7 729	..	..	..	17.7	22.6
29 Non-electrical machinery nec	..	..	4 396	5 176	7 729	..	..	16.6	18.6	24.0
30 Office and computing machinery	..	..	..	0	0	..	..	..	0.0	0.0
31/32 Electrical & electronic equipment	..	..	..	9 424	10 238	..	..	..	48.1	49.4
31 Electrical machinery nec	..	..	6 560	6 617	7 036	..	..	56.5	54.0	50.5
32 Radio, TV & communications eq.	..	..	..	2 807	3 202	..	..	..	38.2	47.2
33 Scientific instruments	..	..	2 248	1 861	1 972	..	..	34.5	25.2	22.7
34/35 Transportation equipment	..	..	6 620	8 739	23 867	..	..	14.5	15.6	34.5
34 Motor vehicles	..	..	390	434	558	..	..	8.0	8.5	10.4
35 Other transport equipment	..	..	6 230	8 305	23 309	..	..	15.3	16.3	36.6
351 Shipbuilding & repairing	..	..	5 519	7 568	22 499	..	..	15.5	16.4	36.4
353 Aircraft and spacecraft	..	..	0	0	0	..	..	0.0	0.0	0.0
36/37 Other manufacturing	..	..	603	..	981	..	..	5.6	..	6.7
40/45 Construction, electricity, gas & water	..	..	..	..	..	..	..	..	..	..
50/55 Trade, repair, hotels & restaurants	..	..	..	..	..	..	..	..	..	..
65/74 Finance, insurance, business services	..	..	..	..	..	..	..	..	..	..
OTHER ACTIVITIES	..	..	..	..	..	..	..	..	..	..
01/99 GRAND TOTAL	..	..	..	..	..	..	..	..	..	..

Total manufacturing by investing country						As a % of total manufacturing by foreign affiliates				
All countries	..	..	74 690	85 697	111 738	..	..	100.0	100.0	100.0
United States	..	..	..	12 618	13 099	..	..	..	14.7	11.7
Canada	..	..	..	..	..	..	..	..	..	..
Mexico	..	..	..	..	..	..	..	..	..	..
Japan	..	..	..	0	0	..	..	..	0.0	0.0
Europe	..	..	..	66 591	..	..	..	..	77.7	..
European Union (15)	..	..	..	61 812	88 347	..	..	..	72.1	79.1
Belgium	..	..	..	771	..	..	..	..	0.9	..
France	..	..	..	2 234	1 976	..	..	..	2.6	1.8
Germany	..	..	..	3 214	2 873	..	..	..	3.8	2.6
Italy	..	..	..	..	..	..	..	..	..	..
Netherlands	..	..	..	5 745	23 865	..	..	..	6.7	21.4
Spain	..	..	..	0	..	..	..	..	0.0	..
Sweden	..	..	..	29 025	..	..	..	..	33.9	..
United Kingdom	..	..	..	10 575	11 522	..	..	..	12.3	10.3
Switzerland	..	..	..	4 719	5 226	..	..	..	5.5	4.7
Australia and New Zealand	..	..	..	..	..	..	..	..	..	..
Asia (non-OECD)	..	..	..	..	..	..	..	..	..	..
Latin America	..	..	..	1 088	107	..	..	..	1.3	0.1

Note: Majority foreign-owned establishments. *Crude petroleum and natural gas extraction* (ISIC 11) is excluded from *Mining and quarrying* (10/14).
Etablissements sous contrôle étranger majoritaire. L'*Extraction de pétrole et de gaz naturel* (CITI 11) est exclue des *Industries extractives* (10/14).

Inward investments   *Investissements entrants*

Table 7A - Tableau 7A

VALUE ADDED / VALEUR AJOUTÉE

	Foreign affiliates *(Millions of NOK)*					As a % of national total				
	Filiales étrangères *(Millions de NOK)*					En % du total national				
By industry (ISIC Rev. 3)	1994	1995	1996	1997	1998	1994	1995	1996	1997	1998
10/14 Mining & quarrying	224	435	449	495	472	15.0	28.9	23.9	23.6	23.0
15/37 **TOTAL MANUFACTURING**	**9 867**	**20 775**	**21 497**	**24 198**	**34 397**	**10.4**	**19.5**	**18.6**	**19.3**	**25.7**
15/16 Food, beverages, tobacco	923	5 940	5 507	4 884	9 497	4.5	27.0	23.3	19.0	35.9
17/19 Textiles, clothing, leather, footwear	100	77	91	168	160	5.4	4.5	4.2	7.6	6.9
20/22 Wood and paper products	704	1 775	1 429	1 605	1 975	4.0	8.6	6.5	7.1	8.2
20 Wood products	72	55	..	54	59	2.0	1.5	..	1.2	1.2
21/22 Paper, printing and publishing	632	1 720	..	1 551	1 915	4.5	10.1	..	8.6	10.1
23/25 Chemicals, Total	2 492	3 412	3 516	..	5 131	20.5	25.4	24.3	..	35.5
23 Refined petroleum, nuclear fuel	702	394	839	..	262	45.0	47.4	51.6	..	18.5
24/25 Chemicals, rubber & plastics prod.	1 790	3 018	2 677	4 565	4 869	16.9	24.0	20.9	35.2	37.4
24 Chemical products	1 424	2 511	2 157	4 069	4 293	16.3	23.7	20.8	39.0	41.7
2423 Pharmaceuticals	..	..	381	1 709	2 018	..	..	13.7	93.0	92.8
25 Rubber and plastics products	365	507	521	495	576	19.5	25.5	21.1	19.4	21.2
26 Non-metallic mineral products	820	1 216	1 819	1 511	1 634	27.2	35.8	43.6	35.0	34.9
27/28 Basic & fabricated metals	1 886	2 281	2 275	3 285	3 618	16.3	15.9	15.6	20.8	20.1
27 Basic metals	1 355	1 665	1 500	2 259	2 345	18.0	17.0	17.9	25.5	23.6
28 Fabricated metal products	531	616	775	1 026	1 273	13.1	13.6	12.5	14.8	15.7
29/32 Machinery, Total	1 732	..	4 381	4 633	6 260	14.8	..	29.6	27.5	33.4
29/30 Non-electrical machinery	672	..	..	1 512	2 320	10.0	..	..	15.3	20.5
29 Non-electrical machinery nec	672	1 100	1 351	1 512	2 320	10.6	15.6	16.0	16.3	21.3
30 Office and computing machinery	0	..	..	0	0	0.0	..	..	0.0	0.0
31/32 Electrical & electronic equipment	1 060	..	..	3 121	3 940	21.3	..	..	44.6	53.2
31 Electrical machinery nec	542	..	2 128	2 297	2 762	16.3	..	55.9	49.3	54.1
32 Radio, TV & communications eq.	518	..	..	824	1 178	31.2	..	..	35.2	51.2
33 Scientific instruments	266	..	528	370	593	16.7	..	24.2	14.9	20.0
34/35 Transportation equipment	826	1 866	1 733	2 337	5 210	6.8	14.2	12.5	14.7	30.1
34 Motor vehicles	..	..	122	137	176	..	..	7.8	8.5	9.6
35 Other transport equipment	..	..	1 611	2 200	5 034	..	..	13.1	15.5	32.5
351 Shipbuilding & repairing	672	..	1 462	1 960	4 886	7.1	..	14.2	15.9	32.6
353 Aircraft and spacecraft	0	..	0	0	0	0.0	..	0.0	0.0	0.0
36/37 Other manufacturing	117	170	218	..	319	4.1	5.3	5.9	..	6.7
40/45 Construction, electricity, gas & water	..	..	..	..	..	..	..	..	..	..
50/55 Trade, repair, hotels & restaurants	..	..	..	..	..	..	..	..	..	..
65/74 Finance, insurance, business services	..	..	..	..	..	..	..	..	..	..
OTHER ACTIVITIES	..	..	..	..	..	..	..	..	..	..
01/99 **GRAND TOTAL**	..	..	..	..	..	..	..	..	..	..

Total manufacturing by investing country						As a % of total manufacturing by foreign affiliates				
All countries	9 867	20 775	21 497	24 198	34 397	100.0	100.0	100.0	100.0	100.0
United States	1 499	..	..	2 489	3 283	15.2	..	..	10.3	9.5
Canada	322	..	..	..	..	3.3	..	..	..	..
Mexico	0	..	..	..	..	0.0	..	..	..	..
Japan	0	..	..	0	0	0.0	..	..	0.0	0.0
Europe	8 046	..	..	..	..	81.5	..	..	..	..
European Union (15)	6 812	..	..	19 729	28 961	69.0	..	..	81.5	84.2
Belgium	145	..	..	..	..	1.5	..	..	..	..
France	104	..	..	587	682	1.1	..	..	2.4	2.0
Germany	208	..	..	1 222	1 060	2.1	..	..	5.1	3.1
Italy	..	..	..	..	..	..	..	..	..	..
Netherlands	820	..	..	1 366	4 799	8.3	..	..	5.6	14.0
Spain	..	..	..	0	..	..	..	..	0.0	..
Sweden	2 713	..	..	..	..	27.5	..	..	..	..
United Kingdom	1 078	..	..	2 479	2 856	10.9	..	..	10.2	8.3
Switzerland	1 234	..	..	1 381	1 638	12.5	..	..	5.7	4.8
Australia and New Zealand	0	..	..	..	..	0.0	..	..	..	..
Asia (non-OECD)	0	..	..	..	..	0.0	..	..	..	..
Latin America	0	..	..	186	54	0.0	..	..	0.8	0.2

Note: Majority foreign-owned establishments. *Crude petroleum and natural gas extraction* (ISIC 11) is excluded from *Mining and quarrying* (10/14). From 1995 onwards data include indirectly from abroad owned establishments.

Etablissements sous contrôle étranger majoritaire. L'*Extraction de pétrole et de gaz naturel* (CITI 11) est exclue des *Industries extractives* (10/14). Les données à partir de 1995 comprennent les établissements contrôlés indirectement par l'étranger.

Inward investments   *Investissements entrants*

Table 8A - Tableau 8A

COMPENSATION OF EMPLOYEES / SALAIRES ET CHARGES SOCIALES

By industry (ISIC Rev. 3)		Foreign affiliates (Millions of NOK) Filiales étrangères (Millions de NOK)					As a % of national total En % du total national				
		1994	1995	1996	1997	1998	1994	1995	1996	1997	1998
10/14	Mining & quarrying	115	237	276	273	273	11.3	24.4	22.9	21.9	21.0
15/37	**TOTAL MANUFACTURING**	6 335	11 488	13 101	14 546	18 907	10.0	17.0	16.8	17.1	20.7
15/16	Food, beverages, tobacco	445	1 894	1 976	1 781	2 027	4.1	17.0	15.5	13.3	14.3
17/19	Textiles, clothing, leather, footwear	119	61	95	127	114	8.8	4.6	5.8	7.1	6.3
20/22	Wood and paper products	496	1 186	984	1 122	1 382	4.1	9.1	6.3	6.6	7.7
20	Wood products	43	45	..	63	43	1.8	1.7	..	1.7	1.1
21/22	Paper, printing and publishing	453	1 141	..	1 059	1 339	4.7	11.1	..	8.0	9.5
23/25	Chemicals, Total	1 304	1 665	1 759	..	2 878	20.7	24.6	24.5	..	36.1
23	Refined petroleum, nuclear fuel	186	193	179	..	167	29.8	32.3	36.1	..	31.6
24/25	Chemicals, rubber & plastics prod.	1 118	1 472	1 580	2 522	2 711	19.7	23.8	23.6	35.5	36.4
24	Chemical products	838	1 105	1 169	2 085	2 274	19.3	23.1	23.7	40.5	42.1
2423	Pharmaceuticals	..	..	267	937	1 038	..	..	28.7	92.0	91.9
25	Rubber and plastics products	280	367	411	438	437	21.1	26.3	23.5	22.5	21.3
26	Non-metallic mineral products	423	715	1 018	857	1 037	23.9	36.9	38.9	30.3	33.5
27/28	Basic & fabricated metals	1 148	1 345	1 509	1 869	2 109	15.0	16.2	15.6	17.7	18.2
27	Basic metals	839	920	990	1 128	1 255	18.5	19.4	19.9	22.0	23.3
28	Fabricated metal products	309	425	519	741	854	9.9	12.0	11.0	13.7	13.7
29/32	Machinery, Total	1 432	..	3 580	3 576	4 197	15.5	..	30.4	27.6	30.0
29/30	Non-electrical machinery	566	..	..	1 261	1 592	10.2	..	..	16.0	18.4
29	Non-electrical machinery nec	566	872	1 123	1 261	1 592	10.7	15.5	16.4	16.6	19.1
30	Office and computing machinery	0	..	..	0	0	0.0	..	..	0.0	0.0
31/32	Electrical & electronic equipment	866	..	..	2 315	2 605	23.5	..	..	45.9	48.7
31	Electrical machinery nec	457	..	1 711	1 721	1 856	18.9	..	56.2	52.4	50.3
32	Radio, TV & communications eq.	409	..	..	594	749	32.2	..	..	33.8	45.2
33	Scientific instruments	176	..	446	340	389	14.2	..	24.2	16.2	17.3
34/35	Transportation equipment	716	1 613	1 603	1 997	4 538	6.8	14.1	13.5	14.9	31.6
34	Motor vehicles	..	..	110	123	139	..	..	8.4	8.7	9.7
35	Other transport equipment	..	..	1 493	1 874	4 399	..	..	14.1	15.6	34.0
351	Shipbuilding & repairing	591	..	1 299	1 660	4 176	7.2	..	14.3	15.7	33.7
353	Aircraft and spacecraft	0	..	0	0	0	0.0	..	0.0	0.0	0.0
36/37	Other manufacturing	76	110	131	..	235	3.6	4.7	4.5	..	6.0
40/45	Construction, electricity, gas & water	..	..	..	..	..	..	..	..	..	..
50/55	Trade, repair, hotels & restaurants	..	..	..	..	..	..	..	..	..	..
65/74	Finance, insurance, business services	..	..	..	..	..	..	..	..	..	..
	OTHER ACTIVITIES	..	..	..	..	..	..	..	..	..	..
01/99	**GRAND TOTAL**	..	..	..	..	..	..	..	..	..	..

Total manufacturing by investing country	1994	1995	1996	1997	1998	As a % of total manufacturing by foreign affiliates				
						1994	1995	1996	1997	1998
All countries	6 335	11 488	13 101	14 546	18 907	100.0	100.0	100.0	100.0	100.0
United States	774	..	..	1 735	2 067	12.2	..	..	11.9	10.9
Canada	216	..	..	..	..	3.4	..	..	..	..
Mexico	0	..	..	..	..	0.0	..	..	..	..
Japan	0	..	..	0	0	0.0	..	..	0.0	0.0
Europe	5 344	..	..	..	..	84.4	..	..	..	..
European Union (15)	4 555	..	..	11 702	15 723	71.9	..	..	80.4	83.2
Belgium	125	..	..	..	..	2.0	..	..	..	..
France	66	..	..	345	382	1.0	..	..	2.4	2.0
Germany	137	..	..	976	712	2.2	..	..	6.7	3.8
Italy	..	..	..	..	..	..	..	..	..	..
Netherlands	391	..	..	792	3 937	6.2	..	..	5.4	20.8
Spain	..	..	..	0	..	..	..	..	0.0	..
Sweden	1 969	..	..	..	..	31.1	..	..	..	..
United Kingdom	643	..	..	1 376	1 472	10.1	..	..	9.5	7.8
Switzerland	789	..	..	717	828	12.5	..	..	4.9	4.4
Australia and New Zealand	0	..	..	..	..	0.0	..	..	..	..
Asia (non-OECD)	0	..	..	..	..	0.0	..	..	..	..
Latin America	0	..	..	148	32	0.0	..	..	1.0	0.2

Note: Majority foreign-owned establishments. *Crude petroleum and natural gas extraction* (ISIC 11) is excluded from *Mining and quarrying* (10/14). From 1995 onwards data include indirectly from abroad owned establishments.

Etablissements sous contrôle étranger majoritaire. L'*Extraction de pétrole et de gaz naturel* (CITI 11) est exclue des *Industries extractives* (10/14). Les données à partir de 1995 comprennent les établissements contrôlés indirectement par l'étranger.

Inward investments *Investissements entrants*

Table 9A - Tableau 9A

GROSS FIXED CAPITAL FORMATION / FORMATION BRUTE DE CAPITAL FIXE

	Foreign affiliates (Millions of NOK) Filiales étrangères (Millions de NOK)					As a % of national total En % du total national				
By industry (ISIC Rev. 3)	1994	1995	1996	1997	1998	1994	1995	1996	1997	1998
10/14 Mining & quarrying	16	82	63	63	70	6.6	24.2	17.3	25.9	20.1
15/37 **TOTAL MANUFACTURING**	**1 513**	**2 773**	**2 942**	**3 200**	**4 299**	**14.8**	**22.2**	**16.7**	**18.3**	**20.5**
15/16 Food, beverages, tobacco	123	522	543	337	1 079	4.8	20.2	15.6	10.8	27.6
17/19 Textiles, clothing, leather, footwear	30	3	4	11	4	16.3	1.4	1.9	5.4	2.2
20/22 Wood and paper products	65	145	200	101	247	3.1	4.9	5.4	2.7	4.8
20 Wood products	6	3	..	- 12	5	1.1	0.5	..	-1.5	0.8
21/22 Paper, printing and publishing	59	142	..	113	243	3.9	6.2	..	3.8	5.4
23/25 Chemicals, Total	430	531	580	..	1 569	25.3	32.3	14.4	..	36.0
23 Refined petroleum, nuclear fuel	138	154	72	..	170	52.9	87.5	14.9	..	23.5
24/25 Chemicals, rubber & plastics prod.	292	377	508	1 240	1 399	20.3	25.6	14.4	37.9	38.4
24 Chemical products	238	276	428	1 152	1 285	20.3	24.7	13.5	41.0	40.7
2423 Pharmaceuticals	..	..	101	324	201	..	..	41.1	94.5	89.3
25 Rubber and plastics products	53	101	80	88	114	19.7	28.7	21.9	19.0	23.7
26 Non-metallic mineral products	256	506	648	175	325	54.3	65.6	66.7	29.4	40.6
27/28 Basic & fabricated metals	318	514	723	724	564	28.2	32.9	26.8	24.9	22.9
27 Basic metals	255	411	581	653	469	28.4	36.2	27.9	28.3	30.4
28 Fabricated metal products	63	103	142	71	95	27.2	24.0	23.2	11.9	10.3
29/32 Machinery, Total	176	..	97	336	182	22.3	..	14.3	29.3	10.7
29/30 Non-electrical machinery	62	..	..	145	145	14.8	..	..	23.5	14.8
29 Non-electrical machinery nec	62	116	87	145	145	15.8	17.9	18.8	26.5	15.1
30 Office and computing machinery	0	..	..	0	0	0.0	..	..	0.0	0.0
31/32 Electrical & electronic equipment	114	..	..	191	37	30.8	..	..	36.2	5.1
31 Electrical machinery nec	42	..	- 41	141	- 5	21.0	..	-33.9	42.0	-0.8
32 Radio, TV & communications eq.	72	..	..	50	42	42.4	..	..	26.2	31.3
33 Scientific instruments	87	..	28	28	37	50.1	..	9.7	16.7	12.7
34/35 Transportation equipment	22	158	57	134	262	2.4	15.3	5.5	8.8	16.6
34 Motor vehicles	..	..	7	15	43	..	..	2.6	3.4	10.1
35 Other transport equipment	..	..	50	119	219	..	..	6.5	11.1	19.0
351 Shipbuilding & repairing	17	..	102	114	214	2.6	..	14.2	12.4	20.1
353 Aircraft and spacecraft	0	..	0	0	0	0.0	..	0.0	0.0	0.0
36/37 Other manufacturing	6	10	62	..	29	2.3	2.9	12.3	..	6.2
40/45 Construction, electricity, gas & water	..	..	..	..	..	..	..	..	..	..
50/55 Trade, repair, hotels & restaurants	..	..	..	..	..	..	..	..	..	..
65/74 Finance, insurance, business services	..	..	..	..	..	..	..	..	..	..
OTHER ACTIVITIES	..	..	..	..	..	..	..	..	..	..
01/99 **GRAND TOTAL**	..	..	..	..	..	..	..	..	..	..

Total manufacturing by investing country						As a % of total manufacturing by foreign affiliates				
All countries	**1 513**	**2 773**	**2 942**	**3 200**	**4 299**	**100.0**	**100.0**	**100.0**	**100.0**	**100.0**
United States	143	..	..	313	1 102	9.5	..	..	9.8	25.6
Canada	101	..	..	..	..	6.7	..	..	..	..
Mexico	0	..	..	..	..	0.0	..	..	..	..
Japan	0	..	..	0	0	0.0	..	..	0.0	0.0
Europe	1 269	..	..	..	..	83.9	..	..	..	..
European Union (15)	977	..	..	1 722	2 164	64.6	..	..	53.8	50.3
Belgium	6	..	..	..	..	0.4	..	..	..	..
France	2	..	..	30	40	0.1	..	..	0.9	0.9
Germany	53	..	..	108	133	3.5	..	..	3.4	3.1
Italy	..	..	..	..	..	..	..	..	..	..
Netherlands	108	..	..	146	487	7.1	..	..	4.6	11.3
Spain	..	..	..	0	..	..	..	..	0.0	..
Sweden	398	..	..	..	..	26.3	..	..	..	..
United Kingdom	155	..	..	348	315	10.2	..	..	10.9	7.3
Switzerland	292	..	..	780	823	19.3	..	..	24.4	19.1
Australia and New Zealand	0	..	..	..	..	0.0	..	..	..	..
Asia (non-OECD)	0	..	..	..	..	0.0	..	..	..	..
Latin America	0	..	..	7	0	0.0	..	..	0.2	0.0

Note: Majority foreign-owned establishments. *Crude petroleum and natural gas extraction* (ISIC 11) is excluded from *Mining and quarrying* (10/14). From 1995 onwards data include indirectly from abroad owned establishments.
Etablissements sous contrôle étranger majoritaire. L'*Extraction de pétrole et de gaz naturel* (CITI 11) est exclue des *Industries extractives* (10/14). Les données à partir de 1995 comprennent les établissements contrôlés indirectement par l'étranger.

Inward investments   *Investissements entrants*

Table 10A - Tableau 10A

GROSS OPERATING SURPLUS / EXCÉDENT BRUT D'EXPLOITATION

| | | Foreign affiliates *(Millions of NOK)* | | | | As a % of national total | | | | |
| | | Filiales étrangères *(Millions de NOK)* | | | | En % du total national | | | | |
By industry (ISIC Rev. 3)		1994	1995	1996	1997	1998	1994	1995	1996	1997	1998
10/14	Mining & quarrying	109	198	174	223	199	..	27.0	20.8	24.4	24.3
15/37	**TOTAL MANUFACTURING**	**3 460**	**6 692**	**5 440**	**7 051**	**8 927**	..	**19.1**	**16.8**	**20.1**	**24.4**
15/16	Food, beverages, tobacco	361	1 412	551	478	680	..	22.6	10.7	8.9	12.1
17/19	Textiles, clothing, leather, footwear	- 18	16	- 4	41	46	..	4.0	-0.7	9.6	9.0
20/22	Wood and paper products	208	589	446	484	593	..	7.4	6.8	7.9	9.6
20	Wood products	28	10	..	- 8	16	..	1.1	..	-0.9	1.5
21/22	Paper, printing and publishing	179	579	..	492	577	..	8.3	..	9.5	11.3
23/25	Chemicals, Total	1 217	1 756	1 762	..	2 260	..	26.3	24.1	..	34.9
23	Refined petroleum, nuclear fuel	524	201	660	..	95	..	83.4	58.4	..	10.7
24/25	Chemicals, rubber & plastics prod.	693	1 555	1 102	2 047	2 165	..	24.1	17.8	34.7	38.7
24	Chemical products	606	1 413	990	1 984	2 020	..	24.2	18.2	37.5	41.1
2423	Pharmaceuticals	..	..	115	771	980	..	..	6.2	94.3	94.0
25	Rubber and plastics products	87	142	112	63	145	..	23.6	15.3	10.3	21.5
26	Non-metallic mineral products	408	502	801	655	598	..	34.4	51.2	44.0	37.5
27/28	Basic & fabricated metals	739	937	767	1 418	1 512	..	15.5	15.6	27.0	23.4
27	Basic metals	517	745	510	1 132	1 092	..	14.8	15.0	30.4	23.9
28	Fabricated metal products	222	192	257	286	420	..	18.8	16.9	18.7	22.3
29/32	Machinery, Total	302	..	806	1 061	2 072	..	..	26.0	26.7	43.5
29/30	Non-electrical machinery	107	..	..	252	728	..	..	..	12.7	27.1
29	Non-electrical machinery nec	107	228	229	252	728	..	15.8	14.3	14.9	28.2
30	Office and computing machinery	0	..	..	0	0	..	..	..	0.0	0.0
31/32	Electrical & electronic equipment	195	..	..	809	1 344	..	..	..	40.8	64.9
31	Electrical machinery nec	86	..	421	578	914	..	..	54.4	41.9	64.1
32	Radio, TV & communications eq.	109	..	..	231	430	..	..	..	38.2	66.5
33	Scientific instruments	90	..	83	30	203	..	..	23.6	7.9	28.1
34/35	Transportation equipment	111	277	141	355	879	..	14.8	6.4	9.4	25.6
34	Motor vehicles	..	..	12	14	37	..	..	4.5	5.7	8.9
35	Other transport equipment	..	..	129	341	842	..	..	6.6	9.7	27.9
351	Shipbuilding & repairing	81	..	172	316	917	..	..	12.4	15.8	30.0
353	Aircraft and spacecraft	0	..	0	0	0	..	..	0.0	0.0	0.0
36/37	Other manufacturing	41	60	87	..	84	..	7.2	11.1	..	10.0
40/45	Construction, electricity, gas & water	..	..	..	..	..	..	..	..	..	..
50/55	Trade, repair, hotels & restaurants	..	..	..	..	..	..	..	..	..	..
65/74	Finance, insurance, business services	..	..	..	..	..	..	..	..	..	..
	OTHER ACTIVITIES	..	..	..	..	..	..	..	..	..	..
01/99	**GRAND TOTAL**	..	..	..	..	..	..	..	..	..	..

Total manufacturing by investing country	1994	1995	1996	1997	1998	As a % of total manufacturing by foreign affiliates				
						1994	1995	1996	1997	1998
All countries	**3 460**	**6 692**	**5 440**	**7 051**	**8 927**	**100.0**	**100.0**	**100.0**	**100.0**	**100.0**
United States	733	..	..	560	1 003	21.2	..	..	7.9	11.2
Canada	114	..	..	..	..	3.3	..	..	..	..
Mexico	0	..	..	..	..	0.0	..	..	..	..
Japan	0	..	..	0	0	0.0	..	..	0.0	0.0
Europe	2 612	..	..	..	..	75.5	..	..	..	..
European Union (15)	2 167	..	..	5 579	6 833	62.6	..	..	79.1	76.5
Belgium	20	..	..	..	..	0.6	..	..	..	..
France	38	..	..	242	304	1.1	..	..	3.4	3.4
Germany	71	..	..	247	349	2.1	..	..	3.5	3.9
Italy	..	..	..	..	..	..	..	..	..	..
Netherlands	429	..	..	575	1 070	12.4	..	..	8.2	12.0
Spain	..	..	..	0	..	..	..	..	0.0	..
Sweden	637	..	..	..	..	18.4	..	..	..	..
United Kingdom	438	..	..	1 102	1 385	12.7	..	..	15.6	15.5
Switzerland	446	..	..	690	864	12.9	..	..	9.8	9.7
Australia and New Zealand	0	..	..	..	..	0.0	..	..	..	..
Asia (non-OECD)	0	..	..	..	0	0.0	..	..	..	0.0
Latin America	0	..	..	54	22	0.0	..	..	0.8	0.2

Note: Majority foreign-owned establishments. *Crude petroleum and natural gas extraction* (ISIC 11) is excluded from *Mining and quarrying* (10/14). From 1995 onwards data include indirectly from abroad owned establishments.

Etablissements sous contrôle étranger majoritaire. L'*Extraction de pétrole et de gaz naturel* (CITI 11) est exclue des *Industries extractives* (10/14). Les données à partir de 1995 comprennent les établissements contrôlés indirectement par l'étranger.

NORWAY

Source

The data are prepared by Statistics Norway (*Statistik sentralbyrå*). They are based on a yearly survey of mining and manufacturing industries, which covers all manufacturing establishments from 1996. Previous surveys covered all establishments employing five or more persons up to 1991, and employing more than ten persons for the period 1992-95. The SIFON register, which includes Norwegian joint-stock companies where the entire share capital or parts of it are in foreign hands, is also used. Data from 1995 onwards are not comparable with those for previous years as they include indirectly foreign-owned establishments. The results are published every year in *Industristatistikk*.

National totals: provided by Statistics Norway and fully compatible with foreign affiliates' data.

Industrial classification

For all variables, the data are classified according to the principal industrial activity of the establishment.

Data are provided in ISIC Revision 3, from the equivalent NACE Revision 1.

Crude petroleum and natural gas extraction (ISIC 11) is excluded.

Variables

- *Number of establishments*: all majority foreign-controlled establishments in the mining and manufacturing industries, except *Crude petroleum and natural gas extraction*.

- *Number of employees* is the number of persons employed (owners and employees) not expressed on a full-time equivalent basis. Figures are annual averages.

- *Value added* is valued in market prices and equals gross value of production less costs of goods and services consumed, excluding VAT.

- *Compensation of employees* comprises salaries and wages in cash and kind, employers' contributions to private pension and family allowance schemes and social expenses levied by law.

- *Gross fixed capital formation* is defined as the acquisition of new and used fixed durable assets, with an expected productive life of more than one year, less receipts from sales of such assets.

- *Gross operating surplus* is defined as gross value added at factor cost less compensation of employees.

Geographical breakdown

The investor's country is the country of the immediate controller.

Data for Belgium include those for Luxembourg.

NORVÈGE

Source

Les données émanent de l'Office norvégien de statistiques (*Statistik sentralbyrå*). Elles proviennent de l'enquête annuelle sur les industries extractives et manufacturières, qui couvre à partir de 1996 tous les établissements manufacturiers. Les enquêtes précédentes couvraient tous les établissements de plus de cinq salariés jusqu'en 1991, et plus de dix personnes pour la période 1992-95. Le registre SIFON, qui recense les entreprises norvégiennes dans lesquelles tout le capital ou une partie de celui-ci est en mains étrangères, est également utilisé. Les données à partir de 1995 ne sont pas comparables avec celles des années précédentes car elles comprennent également les établissements détenus ou contrôlés indirectement par l'étranger. Les résultats sont publiés chaque année dans *Industristatistikk*.

Totaux nationaux : fournis par l'Office norvégien de statistiques et entièrement compatibles avec les données relatives aux filiales étrangères.

Classification industrielle

Pour toutes les variables, les données sont classées selon l'activité industrielle principale de l'établissement.

Les données sont fournies en CITI révision 3, à partir de la classification équivalente NACE révision 1.

Extraction de pétrole brut et de gaz naturel (CITI 11) ne figure pas dans les résultats.

Variables

- *Nombre d'établissements* : tous les établissements sous contrôle étranger majoritaire dans les industries extractives et manufacturières, à l'exception de l'*Extraction de pétrole brut et de gaz naturel*.

- *Nombre de salariés* : nombre de personnes employées (patrons et salariés) non exprimé en équivalent plein-temps. Les chiffres sont une moyenne annuelle.

- La *Valeur ajoutée* est évaluée au prix du marché, et correspond à la valeur brute de la production moins le coût des biens et services consommés hors TVA.

- Les *Salaires et charges sociales* comprennent les traitements et salaires en espèces et en nature, les cotisations patronales aux régimes de retraite et d'allocations familiales et les dépenses sociales légales.

- La *Formation brute de capital fixe* est définie comme la valeur des acquisitions d'actifs fixes neufs et usagés dont la durée de vie productive est supérieure à un an, déduction faite de la valeur des ventes de ces mêmes actifs.

- L'*Excédent brut d'exploitation* est défini comme la valeur ajoutée brute au coût des facteurs, moins les salaires et charges sociales.

Ventilation géographique

Le pays de l'investisseur est celui où se situe le contrôle immédiat.

Les données pour la Belgique comprennent celles du Luxembourg.

POLAND

POLOGNE

Inward investments

Investissements entrants

Table 1A - Tableau 1A

NUMBER OF ENTERPRISES / NOMBRE D'ENTREPRISES

| | | Foreign affiliates *(Units)* | | | | | As a % of national total | | | | |
| | | Filiales étrangères *(Unités)* | | | | | En % du total national | | | | |
By industry (ISIC Rev. 3)		1995	1996	1997	1998	1999	1995	1996	1997	1998	1999
10/14	Mining & quarrying	..	..	41	..	26	..	..	13.3	..	10.0
15/37	**TOTAL MANUFACTURING**	**2 381**	**2 424**	**2 566**	**2 578**	**1 999**	**..**	**..**	**12.8**	**..**	**13.4**
15/16	Food, beverages, tobacco	..	..	298	..	243	..	..	7.6	..	7.8
17/19	Textiles, clothing, leather, footwear	..	..	324	..	253	..	..	14.2	..	14.3
20/22	Wood and paper products	..	..	371	..	246	..	..	13.4	..	14.3
20	Wood products	..	..	178	..	99	..	..	16.6	..	13.3
21/22	Paper, printing and publishing	..	..	193	..	147	..	..	11.4	..	15.0
23/25	Chemicals, Total	..	..	354	..	290	..	..	18.3	..	18.6
23	Refined petroleum, nuclear fuel	..	..	4	..	4	..	..	11.4	..	12.9
24/25	Chemicals, rubber & plastics prod.	..	..	350	..	286	..	..	18.5	..	18.7
24	Chemical products	..	..	125	..	102	..	..	18.4	..	19.7
2423	Pharmaceuticals	..	..	..	..	7	..	..	..	..	25.0
25	Rubber and plastics products	..	..	225	..	184	..	..	18.5	..	18.3
26	Non-metallic mineral products	..	..	170	..	152	..	..	12.9	..	15.4
27/28	Basic & fabricated metals	..	..	276	..	229	..	..	12.5	..	13.0
27	Basic metals	..	..	21	..	21	..	..	8.0	..	8.4
28	Fabricated metal products	..	..	255	..	208	..	..	13.1	..	13.8
29/32	Machinery, Total	..	..	394	..	271	..	..	12.9	..	12.1
29/30	Non-electrical machinery	..	..	250	..	144	..	..	12.0	..	9.3
29	Non-electrical machinery nec	..	..	231	..	139	..	..	11.7	..	9.3
30	Office and computing machinery	..	..	19	..	5	..	..	18.4	..	10.4
31/32	Electrical & electronic equipment	..	..	144	..	127	..	..	14.7	..	18.5
31	Electrical machinery nec	..	..	92	..	95	..	..	15.0	..	19.4
32	Radio, TV & communications eq.	..	..	52	..	32	..	..	14.2	..	16.2
33	Scientific instruments	..	..	72	..	32	..	..	13.1	..	10.1
34/35	Transportation equipment	..	..	105	..	127	..	..	14.6	..	21.0
34	Motor vehicles	..	..	74	..	98	..	..	20.3	..	28.2
35	Other transport equipment	..	..	31	..	29	..	..	8.7	..	11.2
351	Shipbuilding & repairing	..	..	16	..	11	..	..	6.8	..	7.2
353	Aircraft and spacecraft	..	..	4	..	5	..	..	20.0	..	25.0
36/37	Other manufacturing	..	..	202	..	156	..	..	16.1	..	17.2
40/45	Construction, electricity, gas & water	..	..	347	..	151	..	..	3.7	..	2.4
50/55	Trade, repair, hotels & restaurants	..	..	2 942	..	1 088	..	..	10.8	..	7.0
65/74	Finance, insurance, business services	..	..	1 002	..	419	..	..	7.5	..	8.3
	OTHER ACTIVITIES	..	..	786	..	372	..	..	7.5	..	6.3
01/99	**GRAND TOTAL**	**..**	**..**	**7 684**	**..**	**4 055**	**..**	**..**	**9.5**	**..**	**8.4**

Total manufacturing by investing country						As a % of total manufacturing by foreign affiliates				
All countries	2 381	2 424	2 566	2 578	1 999	100.0	100.0	100.0	100.0	100.0
United States	..	..	121	..	103	..	..	4.7	..	5.2
Canada	..	..	..	..	..	..	..	..	..	..
Mexico	..	..	..	..	..	..	..	..	..	..
Japan	..	..	7	..	4	..	..	0.3	..	0.2
Europe	..	..	..	..	..	..	..	..	..	..
European Union (15)	..	..	2 146	..	1 678	..	..	83.6	..	83.9
Belgium	..	..	..	..	..	..	..	..	..	..
France	..	..	133	..	124	..	..	5.2	..	6.2
Germany	..	..	1 181	..	842	..	..	46.0	..	42.1
Italy	..	..	..	..	..	..	..	..	..	..
Netherlands	..	..	215	..	223	..	..	8.4	..	11.2
Spain	..	..	..	..	..	..	..	..	..	..
Sweden	..	..	..	..	..	..	..	..	..	..
United Kingdom	..	..	71	..	58	..	..	2.8	..	2.9
Switzerland	..	..	75	..	59	..	..	2.9	..	3.0
Australia and New Zealand	..	..	..	..	..	..	..	..	..	..
Asia (non-OECD)	..	..	31	..	24	..	..	1.2	..	1.2
Latin America	..	..	12	..	6	..	..	0.5	..	0.3

Note: Majority foreign-owned enterprises.
Entreprises sous contrôle étranger majoritaire.

Inward investments

Investissements entrants

Table 2A - Tableau 2A

NUMBER OF EMPLOYEES BY INDUSTRY

NOMBRE DE SALARIÉS PAR INDUSTRIE

| | | Foreign affiliates *(Units)* | | | | | As a % of national total | | | | |
| | | Filiales étrangères *(Unités)* | | | | | En % du total national | | | | |
ISIC Revision 3		1995	1996	1997	1998	1999	1995	1996	1997	1998	1999
10/14	Mining & quarrying	..	..	1 777	..	2 460	..	..	0.5	..	1.0
15/37	**TOTAL MANUFACTURING**	**226 826**	**249 734**	**287 073**	**325 460**	**379 129**	..	..	**12.5**	..	**18.6**
15/16	Food, beverages, tobacco	..	..	48 507	..	58 797	..	..	11.7	..	15.7
17/19	Textiles, clothing, leather, footwear	..	..	35 418	..	37 661	..	..	10.7	..	14.6
20/22	Wood and paper products	..	..	23 805	..	31 615	..	..	14.1	..	19.4
20	Wood products	..	..	9 032	..	10 191	..	..	11.2	..	13.4
21/22	Paper, printing and publishing	..	..	14 773	..	21 424	..	..	16.9	..	24.7
23/25	Chemicals, Total	..	..	35 681	..	47 011	..	..	15.3	..	20.9
23	Refined petroleum, nuclear fuel	..	..	138	..	158	..	..	0.6	..	0.6
24/25	Chemicals, rubber & plastics prod.	..	..	35 543	..	46 853	..	..	16.9	..	23.6
24	Chemical products	..	..	16 173	..	24 292	..	..	12.7	..	21.6
2423	Pharmaceuticals	..	..	..	..	896	..	..	..	..	7.7
25	Rubber and plastics products	..	..	19 370	..	22 561	..	..	23.2	..	26.1
26	Non-metallic mineral products	..	..	20 443	..	26 720	..	..	15.2	..	21.8
27/28	Basic & fabricated metals	..	..	13 755	..	17 771	..	..	5.1	..	7.4
27	Basic metals	..	..	4 819	..	3 773	..	..	3.6	..	3.5
28	Fabricated metal products	..	..	8 936	..	13 998	..	..	6.5	..	10.6
29/32	Machinery, Total	..	..	51 646	..	67 877	..	..	13.3	..	20.6
29/30	Non-electrical machinery	..	..	16 624	..	24 448	..	..	6.4	..	11.5
29	Non-electrical machinery nec	..	..	16 078	..	24 067	..	..	6.3	..	11.5
30	Office and computing machinery	..	..	546	..	381	..	..	14.2	..	9.6
31/32	Electrical & electronic equipment	..	..	35 022	..	43 429	..	..	27.5	..	37.4
31	Electrical machinery nec	..	..	22 546	..	30 483	..	..	24.8	..	36.0
32	Radio, TV & communications eq.	..	..	12 476	..	12 946	..	..	34.0	..	41.0
33	Scientific instruments	..	..	3 355	..	4 075	..	..	9.8	..	13.6
34/35	Transportation equipment	..	..	27 841	..	52 810	..	..	14.7	..	31.0
34	Motor vehicles	..	..	23 945	..	48 182	..	..	24.2	..	52.2
35	Other transport equipment	..	..	3 896	..	4 628	..	..	4.3	..	5.9
351	Shipbuilding & repairing	..	..	764	..	761	..	..	1.9	..	2.0
353	Aircraft and spacecraft	..	..	700	..	944	..	..	3.5	..	5.9
36/37	Other manufacturing	..	..	26 622	..	34 792	..	..	20.8	..	27.3
40/45	Construction, electricity, gas & water	..	..	9 322	..	14 894	..	..	1.3	..	2.2
50/55	Trade, repair, hotels & restaurants	..	..	79 335	..	138 585	..	..	10.2	..	17.9
65/74	Finance, insurance, business services	..	..	21 195	..	33 506	..	..	6.0	..	8.9
	OTHER ACTIVITIES	..	..	17 691	..	22 211	..	..	1.8	..	2.7
01/99	**GRAND TOTAL**	..	..	**416 393**	..	**590 785**	..	..	**7.6**	..	**11.9**

Note: Majority foreign-owned firms.
Firmes sous contrôle étranger majoritaire.

Inward investments

Investissements entrants

Table 3A - Tableau 3A

NUMBER OF EMPLOYEES BY COUNTRY OF ORIGIN IN THE MANUFACTURING SECTOR

NOMBRE DE SALARIÉS PAR PAYS D'ORIGINE DANS L'INDUSTRIE MANUFACTURIÈRE

Country of origin (immediate controller)	Number of employees (Units) Nombre de salariés (Unités)					As a % of all countries En % du total des pays				
	1995	1996	1997	1998	1999	1995	1996	1997	1998	1999
All countries	226 826	249 734	287 073	325 460	379 129	100.0	100.0	100.0	100.0	100.0
Total OECD	..	..	278 346	..	370 559	..	..	97.0	..	97.7
United States	..	..	23 671	..	33 604	..	..	8.2	..	8.9
Canada	..	..	1 371	..	1 474	..	..	0.5	..	0.4
Mexico	..	..	0	..	0	..	..	0.0	..	0.0
Japan	..	..	68	..	824	..	..	0.0	..	0.2
Korea	..	..	1 821	..	15 654	..	..	0.6	..	4.1
Australia	..	..	988	..	564	..	..	0.3	..	0.1
New Zealand	..	..	0	..	0	..	..	0.0	..	0.0
Europe	..	..	253 039	..	321 827	..	..	88.1	..	84.9
European Union (15)	..	..	232 725	..	296 743	..	..	81.1	..	78.3
Austria	..	..	7 272	..	11 060	..	..	2.5	..	2.9
Belgium	..	..	2 532	..	5 095	..	..	0.9	..	1.3
Denmark	..	..	8 560	..	14 488	..	..	3.0	..	3.8
Finland	..	..	1 528	..	2 479	..	..	0.5	..	0.7
France	..	..	29 830	..	39 262	..	..	10.4	..	10.4
Germany	..	..	93 701	..	103 442	..	..	32.6	..	27.3
Greece	..	..	263	..	197	..	..	0.1	..	0.1
Ireland	..	..	396	..	117	..	..	0.1	..	0.0
Italy	..	..	20 648	..	17 718	..	..	7.2	..	4.7
Luxembourg	..	..	2 713	..	3 881	..	..	0.9	..	1.0
Netherlands	..	..	43 828	..	67 914	..	..	15.3	..	17.9
Portugal	..	..	365	..	394	..	..	0.1	..	0.1
Spain	..	..	668	..	3 858	..	..	0.2	..	1.0
Sweden	..	..	11 102	..	13 703	..	..	3.9	..	3.6
United Kingdom	..	..	9 319	..	13 135	..	..	3.2	..	3.5
Czech Republic	..	..	604	..	538	..	..	0.2	..	0.1
Hungary	..	..	58	..	..	..	..	0.0	..	..
Iceland	..	..	396	..	..	..	..	0.1	..	..
Norway	..	..	4 627	..	6 213	..	..	1.6	..	1.6
Poland	..	..	..	..	..	..	..	0.0	..	0.1
Slovak Republic	..	..	..	..	..	..	..	..	..	..
Switzerland	..	..	11 126	..	14 042	..	..	3.9	..	3.7
Turkey	..	..	891	..	570	..	..	0.3	..	0.2
Non-OECD Europe, of which:	..	..	3 503	..	3 388	..	..	1.2	..	0.9
Baltic countries	..	..	..	..	..	..	..	..	..	..
Bulgaria	..	..	..	..	..	..	..	..	..	..
Croatia	..	..	..	..	..	..	..	..	..	..
Romania	..	..	..	..	0	..	..	..	..	0.0
Russian Federation	..	..	84	..	357	..	..	..	..	..
Slovenia	..	..	98	..	249	..	..	0.0	..	0.1
Ukraine	..	..	9	..	..	..	..	0.0	..	..
Yugoslavia	..	..	..	..	..	..	..	..	..	..
Non-OECD Asia, of which:	..	..	3 849	..	4 454	..	..	1.3	..	1.2
China	..	..	17	..	62	..	..	0.0	..	0.0
Chinese Taipei	..	..	0	..	0	..	..	0.0	..	0.0
Hong Kong (China)	..	..	..	..	..	..	..	..	..	..
India	..	..	0	..	0	..	..	0.0	..	0.0
Indonesia	..	..	0	..	0	..	..	0.0	..	0.0
Malaysia	..	..	0	..	..	..	..	0.0	..	..
Philippines	..	..	0	..	0	..	..	0.0	..	0.0
Singapore	..	..	..	..	..	..	..	..	..	..
Thailand	..	..	0	..	0	..	..	0.0	..	0.0
Near and Middle East	..	..	..	..	1 147	..	..	..	..	0.3
Africa	..	..	73	..	244	..	..	0.0	..	0.1
Latin America, of which:	..	..	725	..	288	..	..	0.3	..	0.1
Argentina	..	..	0	..	0	..	..	0.0	..	0.0
Brazil	..	..	265	..	..	..	..	0.1	..	..
Chile	..	..	0	..	..	..	..	0.0	..	..

Note: Majority foreign-owned firms.
Firmes sous contrôle étranger majoritaire.

Table 4A - Tableau 4A

TURNOVER BY INDUSTRY

CHIFFRE D'AFFAIRES PAR INDUSTRIE

ISIC Revision 3		Foreign affiliates *(Millions of PLN)* Filiales étrangères *(Millions de PLN)*					As a % of national total En % du total national				
		1995	1996	1997	1998	1999	1995	1996	1997	1998	1999
10/14	Mining & quarrying	..	..	163	..	494	..	..	0.6	..	2.0
15/37	**TOTAL MANUFACTURING**	**23 631**	**38 886**	**57 274**	**75 896**	**123 674**	**..**	**..**	**19.4**	**..**	**33.8**
15/16	Food, beverages, tobacco	..	..	16 060	..	29 347	..	..	19.8	..	31.5
17/19	Textiles, clothing, leather, footwear	..	..	1 591	..	2 520	..	..	10.1	..	15.9
20/22	Wood and paper products	..	..	5 414	..	11 792	..	..	26.9	..	41.0
20	Wood products	..	..	1 597	..	3 425	..	..	21.4	..	34.2
21/22	Paper, printing and publishing	..	..	3 818	..	8 367	..	..	30.2	..	44.6
23/25	Chemicals, Total	..	..	7 394	..	17 049	..	..	13.4	..	24.0
23	Refined petroleum, nuclear fuel	..	..	53	..	110	..	..	0.3	..	0.4
24/25	Chemicals, rubber & plastics prod.	..	..	7 341	..	16 939	..	..	21.0	..	39.8
24	Chemical products	..	..	4 141	..	10 903	..	..	17.1	..	39.2
2423	Pharmaceuticals	..	..	..	..	530	..	..	..	..	23.8
25	Rubber and plastics products	..	..	3 201	..	6 037	..	..	29.5	..	41.0
26	Non-metallic mineral products	..	..	2 818	..	6 929	..	..	21.9	..	38.6
27/28	Basic & fabricated metals	..	..	2 297	..	4 741	..	..	7.3	..	13.0
27	Basic metals	..	..	945	..	1 115	..	..	4.9	..	5.5
28	Fabricated metal products	..	..	1 352	..	3 626	..	..	11.3	..	22.1
29/32	Machinery, Total	..	..	8 576	..	17 829	..	..	23.1	..	40.1
29/30	Non-electrical machinery	..	..	2 299	..	5 517	..	..	10.4	..	23.8
29	Non-electrical machinery nec	..	..	2 249	..	5 213	..	..	10.8	..	24.6
30	Office and computing machinery	..	..	50	..	304	..	..	4.1	..	15.4
31/32	Electrical & electronic equipment	..	..	6 277	..	12 311	..	..	41.7	..	58.0
31	Electrical machinery nec	..	..	2 691	..	5 664	..	..	28.7	..	44.4
32	Radio, TV & communications eq.	..	..	3 586	..	6 647	..	..	63.2	..	78.4
33	Scientific instruments	..	..	916	..	1 373	..	..	26.6	..	36.2
34/35	Transportation equipment	..	..	9 932	..	27 731	..	..	33.8	..	68.5
34	Motor vehicles	..	..	9 704	..	27 094	..	..	46.3	..	85.9
35	Other transport equipment	..	..	228	..	638	..	..	3.1	..	7.1
351	Shipbuilding & repairing	..	..	81	..	115	..	..	1.7	..	2.0
353	Aircraft and spacecraft	..	..	33	..	85	..	..	4.0	..	8.3
36/37	Other manufacturing	..	..	2 275	..	4 364	..	..	21.7	..	31.4
40/45	Construction, electricity, gas & water	..	..	2 229	..	6 577	..	..	2.1	..	4.8
50/55	Trade, repair, hotels & restaurants	..	..	3 658	..	80 118	..	..	1.3	..	23.6
65/74	Finance, insurance, business services	..	..	5 404	..	12 616	..	..	11.7	..	20.3
	OTHER ACTIVITIES	..	..	2 566	..	4 605	..	..	3.9	..	5.6
01/99	**GRAND TOTAL**	**..**	**..**	**71 295**	**..**	**228 084**	**..**	**..**	**8.7**	**..**	**22.6**

Note: Majority foreign-owned firms.
        Firmes sous contrôle étranger majoritaire.

Inward investments

Investissements entrants

Table 5A - Tableau 5A

TURNOVER BY COUNTRY OF ORIGIN IN THE MANUFACTURING SECTOR

CHIFFRE D'AFFAIRES PAR PAYS D'ORIGINE DANS L'INDUSTRIE MANUFACTURIÈRE

Country of origin (immediate controller)	Turnover (Millions of PLN) Chiffre d'affaires (Millions de PLN)					As a % of all countries En % du total des pays				
	1995	1996	1997	1998	1999	1995	1996	1997	1998	1999
All countries	23 631	38 886	57 274	75 896	123 674	100.0	100.0	100.0	100.0	100.0
Total OECD	..	..	55 396	..	120 561	..	..	96.7	..	97.5
United States	..	..	5 031	..	9 920	..	..	8.8	..	8.0
Canada	..	..	75	..	124	..	..	0.1	..	0.1
Mexico	..	..	0	..	0	..	..	0.0	..	0.0
Japan	..	..	7	..	119	..	..	0.0	..	0.1
Korea	..	..	519	..	6 702	..	..	0.9	..	5.4
Australia	..	..	192	..	79	..	..	0.3	..	0.1
New Zealand	..	..	0	..	0	..	..	0.0	..	0.0
Europe	..	..	50 076	..	104 679	..	..	87.4	..	84.6
European Union (15)	..	..	46 891	..	97 662	..	..	81.9	..	79.0
Austria	..	..	1 523	..	2 831	..	..	2.7	..	2.3
Belgium	..	..	196	..	733	..	..	0.3	..	0.6
Denmark	..	..	1 391	..	4 457	..	..	2.4	..	3.6
Finland	..	..	166	..	743	..	..	0.3	..	0.6
France	..	..	6 378	..	14 133	..	..	11.1	..	11.4
Germany	..	..	16 110	..	29 246	..	..	28.1	..	23.6
Greece	..	..	6	..	33	..	..	0.0	..	0.0
Ireland	..	..	68	..	21	..	..	0.1	..	0.0
Italy	..	..	6 722	..	9 856	..	..	11.7	..	8.0
Luxembourg	..	..	212	..	743	..	..	0.4	..	0.6
Netherlands	..	..	10 497	..	26 820	..	..	18.3	..	21.7
Portugal	..	..	11	..	21	..	..	0.0	..	0.0
Spain	..	..	207	..	1 509	..	..	0.4	..	1.2
Sweden	..	..	1 881	..	3 591	..	..	3.3	..	2.9
United Kingdom	..	..	1 522	..	2 925	..	..	2.7	..	2.4
Czech Republic	..	..	81	..	92	..	..	0.1	..	0.1
Hungary	..	..	5	..	..	..	..	0.0	..	..
Iceland	..	..	68	..	..	..	..	0.1	..	..
Norway	..	..	537	..	1 215	..	..	0.9	..	1.0
Poland	..	..	..	..	..	..	..	0.0	..	0.0
Slovak Republic	..	..	..	..	..	..	..	..	..	..
Switzerland	..	..	1 938	..	4 503	..	..	3.4	..	3.6
Turkey	..	..	53	..	70	..	..	0.1	..	0.1
Non-OECD Europe, of which:	..	..	557	..	1 064	..	..	1.0	..	0.9
Baltic countries	..	..	..	..	..	..	..	..	..	..
Bulgaria	..	..	..	..	..	..	..	..	..	..
Croatia	..	..	..	..	..	..	..	..	..	..
Romania	..	..	..	..	0	..	..	..	..	0.0
Russian Federation	..	..	8	..	45	..	..	..	..	..
Slovenia	..	..	100	..	200	..	..	0.2	..	0.2
Ukraine	..	..	0	..	..	..	..	0.0	..	..
Yugoslavia	..	..	..	..	..	..	..	..	..	..
Non-OECD Asia, of which:	..	..	1 121	..	1 946	..	..	2.0	..	1.6
China	..	..	0	..	2	..	..	0.0	..	0.0
Chinese Taipei	..	..	0	..	0	..	..	0.0	..	0.0
Hong Kong (China)	..	..	..	..	..	..	..	..	..	..
India	..	..	0	..	0	..	..	0.0	..	0.0
Indonesia	..	..	0	..	0	..	..	0.0	..	0.0
Malaysia	..	..	0	..	..	..	..	0.0	..	..
Philippines	..	..	0	..	0	..	..	0.0	..	0.0
Singapore	..	..	..	..	..	..	..	..	..	..
Thailand	..	..	0	..	0	..	..	0.0	..	0.0
Near and Middle East	..	..	..	..	170	..	..	..	..	0.1
Africa	..	..	11	..	19	..	..	0.0	..	0.0
Latin America, of which:	..	..	33	..	44	..	..	0.1	..	0.0
Argentina	..	..	0	..	0	..	..	0.0	..	0.0
Brazil	..	..	7	..	..	..	..	0.0	..	..
Chile	..	..	0	..	..	..	..	0.0	..	..

Note: Majority foreign-owned firms.

Firmes sous contrôle étranger majoritaire.

Inward investments   *Investissements entrants*

Table 6A - Tableau 6A

R&D EXPENDITURE BY INDUSTRY

DÉPENSES DE R-D PAR INDUSTRIE

		Foreign affiliates (Millions of PLN) Filiales étrangères (Millions de PLN)					As a % of national total En % du total national				
ISIC Revision 3		1995	1996	1997	1998	1999	1995	1996	1997	1998	1999
10/14	Mining & quarrying	..	..	..	..	..	..	..	..	..	..
15/37	**TOTAL MANUFACTURING**	..	..	135	205	429	..	..	13.9	16.1	29.5
15/16	Food, beverages, tobacco	..	..	6	5	13	..	..	18.5	20.1	38.2
17/19	Textiles, clothing, leather, footwear	..	..	0	0	0	..	..	0.0	0.0	0.0
20/22	Wood and paper products	..	..	0	0	12	..	..	0.0	0.0	52.5
20	Wood products	..	..	0	0	12	..	..	0.0	0.0	64.6
21/22	Paper, printing and publishing	..	..	0	0	0	..	..	0.0	0.0	0.0
23/25	Chemicals, Total	..	..	48	46	40	..	..	18.6	15.4	14.3
23	Refined petroleum, nuclear fuel	..	..	0	0	0	..	..	0.0	0.0	0.0
24/25	Chemicals, rubber & plastics prod.	..	..	48	46	40	..	..	19.5	16.2	15.0
24	Chemical products	..	..	10	26	39	..	..	5.7	11.9	17.4
2423	Pharmaceuticals	..	..	0	0	0	..	..	0.0	0.0	0.0
25	Rubber and plastics products	..	..	38	20	1	..	..	48.7	30.7	2.1
26	Non-metallic mineral products	..	..	0	0	1	..	..	0.0	0.0	6.1
27/28	Basic & fabricated metals	..	..	0	0	0	..	..	0.0	0.0	0.0
27	Basic metals	..	..	0	0	0	..	..	0.0	0.0	0.0
28	Fabricated metal products	..	..	0	0	0	..	..	0.0	0.0	0.0
29/32	Machinery, Total	..	..	26	58	203	..	..	7.8	11.2	34.6
29/30	Non-electrical machinery	..	..	5	9	89	..	..	3.3	3.6	27.2
29	Non-electrical machinery nec	..	..	5	9	89	..	..	3.4	3.6	27.3
30	Office and computing machinery	..	..	0	0	0	..	..	0.0	0.0	0.0
31/32	Electrical & electronic equipment	..	..	20	49	114	..	..	12.1	18.1	44.0
31	Electrical machinery nec	..	..	3	10	70	..	..	2.4	6.2	45.2
32	Radio, TV & communications eq.	..	..	18	39	44	..	..	29.3	34.9	42.1
33	Scientific instruments	..	..	0	0	1	..	..	0.0	0.0	3.3
34/35	Transportation equipment	..	..	56	92	154	..	..	26.4	35.8	43.5
34	Motor vehicles	..	..	51	89	141	..	..	53.6	62.4	72.1
35	Other transport equipment	..	..	5	2	13	..	..	4.1	2.0	8.1
351	Shipbuilding & repairing	..	..	0	0	0	..	..	0.0	0.0	0.0
353	Aircraft and spacecraft	..	..	0	0	11	..	..	0.0	0.0	14.1
36/37	Other manufacturing	..	..	0	4	4	..	..	0.0	20.5	30.9
40/45	Construction, electricity, gas & water	..	..	..	..	..	..	..	..	..	..
50/55	Trade, repair, hotels & restaurants	..	..	..	..	..	..	..	..	..	..
65/74	Finance, insurance, business services	..	..	..	..	..	..	..	..	..	..
	OTHER ACTIVITIES	..	..	..	..	..	..	..	..	..	..
01/99	**GRAND TOTAL**	..	..	..	..	..	..	..	..	..	..

Note: All foreign-owned firms.
Toutes les firmes sous contrôle étranger.

Table 7A - Tableau 7A

R&D EXPENDITURE BY COUNTRY OF ORIGIN IN THE MANUFACTURING SECTOR

DÉPENSES DE R-D PAR PAYS D'ORIGINE DANS L'INDUSTRIE MANUFACTURIÈRE

Country of origin	R&D expenditure (Millions of PLN) Dépenses de R-D (Millions de PLN)					As a % of all countries En % du total des pays				
	1995	1996	1997	1998	1999	1995	1996	1997	1998	1999
All countries	..	..	135	205	429	..	..	100.0	100.0	100.0
Total OECD	..	..	130	200	425	..	..	96.5	97.4	99.0
United States	..	..	34	31	30	..	..	25.5	15.3	7.0
Canada	..	..	1	..	1	..	..	0.6	..	0.2
Mexico	..	..	0	0	0	..	..	0.0	0.0	0.0
Japan	..	..	0	0	0	..	..	0.1	0.0	0.0
Korea	..	..	43	84	130	..	..	32.0	40.9	30.3
Australia	..	..	..	0	0	..	..	..	0.0	0.0
New Zealand	..	..	..	0	0	..	..	..	0.0	0.0
Europe	..	..	56	..	269	..	..	41.8	..	62.6
European Union (15)	..	..	51	82	258	..	..	37.9	40.2	60.2
Austria	..	..	..	..	4	..	..	..	..	1.0
Belgium	..	..	..	..	0	..	..	..	..	0.0
Denmark	..	..	..	..	1	..	..	..	..	0.3
Finland	..	..	..	0	0	..	..	..	0.0	0.0
France	..	..	14	3	6	..	..	10.4	1.5	1.4
Germany	..	..	5	11	29	..	..	3.8	5.1	6.8
Greece	..	..	..	0	0	..	..	..	0.0	0.0
Ireland	..	..	..	0	0	..	..	..	0.0	0.0
Italy	..	..	..	0	0	..	..	..	0.0	0.0
Luxembourg	..	..	..	0	0	..	..	..	0.0	0.0
Netherlands	..	..	29	46	127	..	..	21.2	22.5	29.6
Portugal	..	..	..	0	0	..	..	..	0.0	0.0
Spain	..	..	..	0	0	..	..	..	0.0	0.0
Sweden	..	..	1	0	1	..	..	0.4	0.0	0.2
United Kingdom	..	..	2	16	89	..	..	1.5	7.9	20.8
Czech Republic	..	..	..	..	0	..	..	..	..	0.0
Hungary	..	..	..	0	0	..	..	..	0.0	0.0
Iceland	..	..	..	0	0	..	..	..	0.0	0.0
Norway	..	..	..	..	0	..	..	..	..	0.1
Poland	..	..	..	..	0	..	..	..	0.0	0.0
Slovak Republic	..	..	..	0	0	..	..	..	..	0.0
Switzerland	..	..	0	0	6	..	..	0.0	0.0	1.4
Turkey	..	..	..	0	0	..	..	..	0.0	0.0
Non-OECD Europe, of which:	..	..	..	5	4	..	..	..	2.6	1.0
Baltic countries	..	..	..	0	0	..	..	..	0.0	0.0
Bulgaria	..	..	..	0	0	..	..	..	0.0	0.0
Croatia	..	..	..	..	4	..	..	..	..	1.0
Romania	..	..	..	0	0	..	..	..	0.0	0.0
Russian Federation	..	..	..	0	0	..	..	..	0.0	0.0
Slovenia	..	..	..	0	0	..	..	..	0.0	0.0
Ukraine	..	..	..	0	0	..	..	..	0.0	0.0
Yugoslavia	..	..	..	0	0	..	..	..	0.0	0.0
Non-OECD Asia, of which:	..	..	0	0	0	..	..	0.0	0.0	0.0
China	..	..	0	0	0	..	..	0.0	0.0	0.0
Chinese Taipei	..	..	0	0	0	..	..	0.0	0.0	0.0
Hong Kong (China)	..	..	0	0	0	..	..	0.0	0.0	0.0
India	..	..	0	0	0	..	..	0.0	0.0	0.0
Indonesia	..	..	0	0	0	..	..	0.0	0.0	0.0
Malaysia	..	..	0	0	0	..	..	0.0	0.0	0.0
Philippines	..	..	0	0	0	..	..	0.0	0.0	0.0
Singapore	..	..	0	0	0	..	..	0.0	0.0	0.0
Thailand	..	..	0	0	0	..	..	0.0	0.0	0.0
Near and Middle East	..	..	..	0	0	..	..	..	0.0	0.0
Africa	..	..	..	0	0	..	..	..	0.0	0.0
Latin America, of which:	..	..	0	0	0	..	..	0.0	0.0	0.0
Argentina	..	..	0	0	0	..	..	0.0	0.0	0.0
Brazil	..	..	0	0	0	..	..	0.0	0.0	0.0
Chile	..	..	0	0	0	..	..	0.0	0.0	0.0

Note: All foreign-owned firms.
Toutes les firmes sous contrôle étranger.

Inward investments

Investissements entrants

Table 8A - Tableau 8A

NUMBER OF RESEARCHERS / NOMBRE DE CHERCHEURS

		Foreign affiliates *(FTE)* Filiales étrangères *(EPT)*					As a % of national total En % du total national				
By industry (ISIC Rev. 3)		1995	1996	1997	1998	1999	1995	1996	1997	1998	1999
10/14	Mining & quarrying	..	..	..	..	..	..	..	..	..	..
15/37	**TOTAL MANUFACTURING**	..	..	**697**	**914**	**946**	..	..	**9.2**	**12.7**	**12.9**
15/16	Food, beverages, tobacco	..	..	17	30	46	..	..	7.2	15.0	20.8
17/19	Textiles, clothing, leather, footwear	..	..	0	0	0	..	..	0.0	0.0	0.0
20/22	Wood and paper products	..	..	0	0	0	..	..	0.0	0.0	0.0
20	Wood products	..	..	0	0	0	..	..	0.0	0.0	0.0
21/22	Paper, printing and publishing	..	..	0	0	0	..	..	0.0	0.0	0.0
23/25	Chemicals, Total	..	..	146	172	165	..	..	7.6	9.8	9.7
23	Refined petroleum, nuclear fuel	..	..	0	0	0	..	..	0.0	0.0	0.0
24/25	Chemicals, rubber & plastics prod.	..	..	146	172	165	..	..	8.1	10.4	10.3
24	Chemical products	..	..	83	124	164	..	..	5.1	8.4	11.7
2423	Pharmaceuticals	..	..	0	0	0	..	..	0.0	0.0	0.0
25	Rubber and plastics products	..	..	64	47	1	..	..	30.8	26.3	0.5
26	Non-metallic mineral products	..	..	0	0	5	..	..	0.0	0.0	3.6
27/28	Basic & fabricated metals	..	..	0	0	0	..	..	0.0	0.0	0.0
27	Basic metals	..	..	0	0	0	..	..	0.0	0.0	0.0
28	Fabricated metal products	..	..	0	0	0	..	..	0.0	0.0	0.0
29/32	Machinery, Total	..	..	177	278	347	..	..	7.1	11.8	13.9
29/30	Non-electrical machinery	..	..	11	14	82	..	..	0.9	1.3	6.4
29	Non-electrical machinery nec	..	..	11	14	82	..	..	0.9	1.3	6.5
30	Office and computing machinery	..	..	0	0	0	..	..	0.0	0.0	0.0
31/32	Electrical & electronic equipment	..	..	166	264	264	..	..	13.7	20.2	21.8
31	Electrical machinery nec	..	..	24	58	78	..	..	3.8	9.9	12.8
32	Radio, TV & communications eq.	..	..	142	206	186	..	..	24.4	28.6	31.1
33	Scientific instruments	..	..	0	0	5	..	..	0.0	0.0	1.6
34/35	Transportation equipment	..	..	357	425	371	..	..	21.5	26.8	23.3
34	Motor vehicles	..	..	330	406	325	..	..	40.7	47.1	42.3
35	Other transport equipment	..	..	27	20	46	..	..	3.2	2.7	5.6
351	Shipbuilding & repairing	..	..	0	0	0	..	..	0.0	0.0	0.0
353	Aircraft and spacecraft	..	..	0	0	16	..	..	0.0	0.0	4.1
36/37	Other manufacturing	..	..	0	10	7	..	..	0.0	11.9	7.9
40/45	Construction, electricity, gas & water	..	..	..	..	..	..	..	..	..	..
50/55	Trade, repair, hotels & restaurants	..	..	..	..	..	..	..	..	..	..
65/74	Finance, insurance, business services	..	..	..	..	..	..	..	..	..	..
	OTHER ACTIVITIES	..	..	..	..	..	..	..	..	..	..
01/99	**GRAND TOTAL**	..	..	..	..	..	..	..	..	..	..

Total manufacturing by investing country							As a % of total manufacturing by foreign affiliates				
All countries		..	..	697	914	946	..	..	100.0	100.0	100.0
United States		..	..	84	116	86	..	..	12.0	12.6	9.1
Canada		..	..	11	..	4	..	..	1.5	..	0.4
Mexico		..	..	0	0	0	..	..	0.0	0.0	0.0
Japan		..	..	0	0	0	..	..	0.0	0.0	0.0
Europe		..	..	312	..	567	..	..	44.7	..	59.9
European Union (15)		..	..	284	377	540	..	..	40.7	41.2	57.1
Belgium		..	..	..	..	0	..	..	..	..	0.0
France		..	..	48	23	99	..	..	6.9	2.5	10.5
Germany		..	..	29	52	61	..	..	4.1	5.7	6.4
Italy		..	..	..	0	0	..	..	..	0.0	0.0
Netherlands		..	..	179	238	276	..	..	25.6	26.1	29.2
Spain		..	..	..	0	0	..	..	..	0.0	0.0
Sweden		..	..	2	0	6	..	..	0.3	0.0	0.6
United Kingdom		..	..	16	50	86	..	..	2.3	5.5	9.1
Switzerland		..	..	0	0	5	..	..	0.0	0.0	0.6
Australia and New Zealand		..	..	..	0	0	..	..	..	0.0	0.0
Asia (non-OECD)		..	..	0	0	0	..	..	0.0	0.0	0.0
Latin America		..	..	0	0	0	..	..	0.0	0.0	0.0

Note: All foreign-owned firms.
Toutes les firmes sous contrôle étranger.

Inward investments

Investissements entrants

Table 9A - Tableau 9A

GROSS FIXED CAPITAL FORMATION / FORMATION BRUTE DE CAPITAL FIXE

| | | Foreign affiliates *(Millions of PLN)* | | | | | As a % of national total | | | | |
| | | Filiales étrangères *(Millions de PLN)* | | | | | En % du total national | | | | |
By industry (ISIC Rev. 3)		1995	1996	1997	1998	1999	1995	1996	1997	1998	1999
10/14	Mining & quarrying	..	..	60	..	171	..	..	3.1	..	8.6
15/37	**TOTAL MANUFACTURING**	3 034	4 181	7 830	10 059	14 442	..	..	36.7	..	55.3
15/16	Food, beverages, tobacco	..	..	1 448	..	2 543	..	..	33.2	..	50.4
17/19	Textiles, clothing, leather, footwear	..	..	161	..	195	..	..	18.6	..	24.3
20/22	Wood and paper products	..	..	1 171	..	1 827	..	..	46.7	..	63.5
20	Wood products	..	..	579	..	496	..	..	54.3	..	57.6
21/22	Paper, printing and publishing	..	..	592	..	1 331	..	..	41.0	..	66.0
23/25	Chemicals, Total	..	..	1 187	..	2 002	..	..	24.1	..	34.4
23	Refined petroleum, nuclear fuel	..	..	44	..	2	..	..	3.0	..	0.1
24/25	Chemicals, rubber & plastics prod.	..	..	1 143	..	2 000	..	..	33.1	..	56.1
24	Chemical products	..	..	636	..	1 294	..	..	26.9	..	55.4
2423	Pharmaceuticals	..	..	..	..	26	..	..	..	..	..
25	Rubber and plastics products	..	..	508	..	706	..	..	46.5	..	57.3
26	Non-metallic mineral products	..	..	911	..	1 627	..	..	59.0	..	66.1
27/28	Basic & fabricated metals	..	..	355	..	603	..	..	16.2	..	28.3
27	Basic metals	..	..	159	..	118	..	..	11.1	..	9.9
28	Fabricated metal products	..	..	196	..	486	..	..	26.0	..	51.6
29/32	Machinery, Total	..	..	839	..	1 353	..	..	39.9	..	52.6
29/30	Non-electrical machinery	..	..	306	..	395	..	..	30.6	..	37.1
29	Non-electrical machinery nec	..	..	302	..	388	..	..	31.0	..	39.6
30	Office and computing machinery	..	..	4	..	7	..	..	15.3	..	8.4
31/32	Electrical & electronic equipment	..	..	534	..	958	..	..	48.3	..	63.5
31	Electrical machinery nec	..	..	233	..	622	..	..	32.7	..	60.6
32	Radio, TV & communications eq.	..	..	301	..	336	..	..	76.5	..	69.6
33	Scientific instruments	..	..	44	..	57	..	..	24.2	..	31.1
34/35	Transportation equipment	..	..	1 223	..	3 980	..	..	57.6	..	112.4
34	Motor vehicles	..	..	1 157	..	3 884	..	..	62.4	..	120.7
35	Other transport equipment	..	..	66	..	97	..	..	24.6	..	30.1
351	Shipbuilding & repairing	..	..	7	..	5	..	..	..	..	1.5
353	Aircraft and spacecraft	..	..	14	..	12	..	..	..	..	18.2
36/37	Other manufacturing	..	..	491	..	256	..	..	85.9	..	38.8
40/45	Construction, electricity, gas & water	..	..	393	..	835	..	..	3.5	..	6.3
50/55	Trade, repair, hotels & restaurants	..	..	2 532	..	6 948	..	..	39.8	..	61.5
65/74	Finance, insurance, business services	..	..	739	..	3 282	..	..	9.1	..	22.9
	OTHER ACTIVITIES	..	..	548	..	1 169	..	..	4.7	..	8.0
01/99	**GRAND TOTAL**	..	..	12 100	..	26 846	..	..	19.9	..	32.9

Total manufacturing by investing country						As a % of total manufacturing by foreign affiliates				
All countries	3 034	4 181	7 830	10 059	14 442	100.0	100.0	100.0	100.0	100.0
United States	..	..	594	..	1 405	..	..	7.6	..	9.7
Canada	..	..	..	..	..	..	..	..	..	..
Mexico	..	..	..	..	..	..	..	..	..	..
Japan	..	..	25	..	162	..	..	0.3	..	1.1
Europe	..	..	..	..	..	..	..	..	..	..
European Union (15)	..	..	6 106	..	10 025	..	..	78.0	..	69.4
Belgium	..	..	..	..	..	..	..	..	..	..
France	..	..	912	..	1 051	..	..	11.7	..	7.3
Germany	..	..	2 458	..	3 462	..	..	31.4	..	24.0
Italy	..	..	..	..	..	..	..	..	..	..
Netherlands	..	..	1 060	..	2 779	..	..	13.5	..	19.2
Spain	..	..	..	..	..	..	..	..	..	..
Sweden	..	..	..	..	..	..	..	..	..	..
United Kingdom	..	..	149	..	525	..	..	1.9	..	3.6
Switzerland	..	..	397	..	490	..	..	5.1	..	3.4
Australia and New Zealand	..	..	..	..	..	..	..	..	..	..
Asia (non-OECD)	..	..	346	..	244	..	..	4.4	..	1.7
Latin America	..	..	1	..	4	..	..	0.0	..	0.0

Note: Majority foreign-owned enterprises.
Entreprises sous contrôle étranger majoritaire.

Inward investments

Investissements entrants

Table 10A - Tableau 10A

TOTAL EXPORTS BY COUNTRY OF ORIGIN IN THE MANUFACTURING SECTOR
EXPORTATIONS TOTALES PAR PAYS D'ORIGINE DANS L'INDUSTRIE MANUFACTURIÈRE

Country of origin (immediate controller)	Total exports (Millions of PLN) Exportations totales (Millions de PLN)					As a % of all countries En % du total des pays				
	1995	1996	1997	1998	1999	1995	1996	1997	1998	1999
All countries	..	..	..	..	32 837	..	..	..	..	100.0
Total OECD	..	..	..	..	32 283	..	..	..	..	98.3
United States	..	..	..	..	2 651	..	..	..	..	8.1
Canada	..	..	..	..	75	..	..	..	..	0.2
Mexico	..	..	..	..	0	..	..	..	..	0.0
Japan	..	..	..	..	135	..	..	..	..	0.4
Korea	..	..	..	..	1 022	..	..	..	..	3.1
Australia	..	..	..	..	18	..	..	..	..	0.1
New Zealand	..	..	..	..	0	..	..	..	..	0.0
Europe	..	..	..	..	28 435	..	..	..	..	86.6
European Union (15)	..	..	..	..	27 049	..	..	..	..	82.4
Austria	..	..	..	..	864	..	..	..	..	2.6
Belgium	..	..	..	..	295	..	..	..	..	0.9
Denmark	..	..	..	..	786	..	..	..	..	2.4
Finland	..	..	..	..	138	..	..	..	..	0.4
France	..	..	..	..	4 198	..	..	..	..	12.8
Germany	..	..	..	..	7 558	..	..	..	..	23.0
Greece	..	..	..	..	1	..	..	..	..	0.0
Ireland	..	..	..	..	9	..	..	..	..	0.0
Italy	..	..	..	..	4 341	..	..	..	..	13.2
Luxembourg	..	..	..	..	294	..	..	..	..	0.9
Netherlands	..	..	..	..	6 288	..	..	..	..	19.1
Portugal	..	..	..	..	17	..	..	..	..	0.1
Spain	..	..	..	..	341	..	..	..	..	1.0
Sweden	..	..	..	..	1 218	..	..	..	..	3.7
United Kingdom	..	..	..	..	703	..	..	..	..	2.1
Czech Republic	..	..	..	..	5	..	..	..	..	0.0
Hungary	..	..	..	..	..	..	..	..	..	..
Iceland	..	..	..	..	..	..	..	..	..	..
Norway	..	..	..	..	277	..	..	..	..	0.8
Poland	..	..	..	..	..	..	..	..	..	0.0
Slovak Republic	..	..	..	..	..	..	..	..	..	..
Switzerland	..	..	..	..	1 016	..	..	..	..	3.1
Turkey	..	..	..	..	5	..	..	..	..	0.0
Non-OECD Europe, of which:	..	..	..	..	52	..	..	..	..	0.2
Baltic countries	..	..	..	..	..	..	..	..	..	..
Bulgaria	..	..	..	..	..	..	..	..	..	..
Croatia	..	..	..	..	..	..	..	..	..	..
Romania	..	..	..	..	0	..	..	..	..	0.0
Russian Federation	..	..	..	..	4	..	..	..	..	..
Slovenia	..	..	..	..	13	..	..	..	..	0.0
Ukraine	..	..	..	..	..	..	..	..	..	..
Yugoslavia	..	..	..	..	..	..	..	..	..	..
Non-OECD Asia, of which:	..	..	..	..	461	..	..	..	..	1.4
China	..	..	..	..	0	..	..	..	..	0.0
Chinese Taipei	..	..	..	..	0	..	..	..	..	0.0
Hong Kong (China)	..	..	..	..	..	..	..	..	..	..
India	..	..	..	..	0	..	..	..	..	0.0
Indonesia	..	..	..	..	0	..	..	..	..	0.0
Malaysia	..	..	..	..	..	..	..	..	..	..
Philippines	..	..	..	..	0	..	..	..	..	0.0
Singapore	..	..	..	..	..	..	..	..	..	..
Thailand	..	..	..	..	0	..	..	..	..	0.0
Near and Middle East	..	..	..	..	92	..	..	..	..	0.3
Africa	..	..	..	..	18	..	..	..	..	0.1
Latin America, of which:	..	..	..	..	9	..	..	..	..	0.0
Argentina	..	..	..	..	0	..	..	..	..	0.0
Brazil	..	..	..	..	..	..	..	..	..	..
Chile	..	..	..	..	..	..	..	..	..	..

Note: Majority foreign-owned firms.
Firmes sous contrôle étranger majoritaire.

Table 11A - Tableau 11A

TOTAL IMPORTS BY COUNTRY OF ORIGIN IN THE MANUFACTURING SECTOR

IMPORTATIONS TOTALES PAR PAYS D'ORIGINE DANS L'INDUSTRIE MANUFACTURIÈRE

Country of origin (immediate controller)	Total imports (Millions of PLN) Importations totales (Millions de PLN)					As a % of all countries En % du total des pays				
	1995	1996	1997	1998	1999	1995	1996	1997	1998	1999
All countries	..	..	..	..	**32 268**	..	..	..	..	**100.0**
Total OECD	..	..	..	..	**31 392**	..	..	..	..	**97.3**
United States	..	..	..	..	3 476	..	..	..	..	10.8
Canada	..	..	..	..	41	..	..	..	..	0.1
Mexico	..	..	..	..	0	..	..	..	..	0.0
Japan	..	..	..	..	304	..	..	..	..	0.9
Korea	..	..	..	..	703	..	..	..	..	2.2
Australia	..	..	..	..	17	..	..	..	..	0.1
New Zealand	..	..	..	..	0	..	..	..	..	0.0
Europe	..	..	..	..	**27 351**	..	..	..	..	**84.8**
European Union (15)	..	..	..	..	**25 108**	..	..	..	..	**77.8**
Austria	..	..	..	..	861	..	..	..	..	2.7
Belgium	..	..	..	..	237	..	..	..	..	0.7
Denmark	..	..	..	..	978	..	..	..	..	3.0
Finland	..	..	..	..	297	..	..	..	..	0.9
France	..	..	..	..	5 190	..	..	..	..	16.1
Germany	..	..	..	..	6 831	..	..	..	..	21.2
Greece	..	..	..	..	9	..	..	..	..	0.0
Ireland	..	..	..	..	3	..	..	..	..	0.0
Italy	..	..	..	..	857	..	..	..	..	2.7
Luxembourg	..	..	..	..	346	..	..	..	..	1.1
Netherlands	..	..	..	..	6 801	..	..	..	..	21.1
Portugal	..	..	..	..	2	..	..	..	..	0.0
Spain	..	..	..	..	37	..	..	..	..	0.1
Sweden	..	..	..	..	1 832	..	..	..	..	5.7
United Kingdom	..	..	..	..	829	..	..	..	..	2.6
Czech Republic	..	..	..	..	43	..	..	..	..	0.1
Hungary	..	..	..	..	..	..	..	..	..	..
Iceland	..	..	..	..	..	..	..	..	..	..
Norway	..	..	..	..	275	..	..	..	..	0.9
Poland	..	..	..	..		..	..	..	..	0.0
Slovak Republic	..	..	..	..	..	..	..	..	..	..
Switzerland	..	..	..	..	1 376	..	..	..	..	4.3
Turkey	..	..	..	..	4	..	..	..	..	0.0
Non-OECD Europe, of which:	..	..	..	..	**499**	..	..	..	..	**1.5**
Baltic countries	..	..	..	..		..	..	..	..	..
Bulgaria	..	..	..	..	..	..	..	..	..	..
Croatia	..	..	..	..	..	..	..	..	..	..
Romania	..	..	..	..	0	..	..	..	..	0.0
Russian Federation	..	..	..	..	6	..	..	..	..	
Slovenia	..	..	..	..	194	..	..	..	..	0.6
Ukraine	..	..	..	..	..	..	..	..	..	..
Yugoslavia	..	..	..	..	..	..	..	..	..	..
Non-OECD Asia, of which:	..	..	..	..	**351**	..	..	..	..	**1.1**
China	..	..	..	..	0	..	..	..	..	0.0
Chinese Taipei	..	..	..	..	0	..	..	..	..	0.0
Hong Kong (China)	..	..	..	..	..	..	..	..	..	..
India	..	..	..	..	0	..	..	..	..	0.0
Indonesia	..	..	..	..	0	..	..	..	..	0.0
Malaysia	..	..	..	..	..	..	..	..	..	..
Philippines	..	..	..	..	0	..	..	..	..	0.0
Singapore	..	..	..	..	..	..	..	..	..	..
Thailand	..	..	..	..	0	..	..	..	..	100.0
Near and Middle East	..	..	..	..	**47**	..	..	..	..	**0.1**
Africa	..	..	..	..	**1**	..	..	..	..	**0.0**
Latin America, of which:	..	..	..	..	**11**	..	..	..	..	**0.0**
Argentina	..	..	..	..	0	..	..	..	..	0.0
Brazil	..	..	..	..	..	..	..	..	..	..
Chile	..	..	..	..	..	..	..	..	..	..

Note: Majority foreign-owned firms.
Firmes sous contrôle étranger majoritaire.

Inward investments

Investissements entrants

Table 12A - Tableau 12A

CAPITAL UNDER FOREIGN INFLUENCE / CAPITAL SOUS INFLUENCE ÉTRANGÈRE

By industry (ISIC Rev. 3)		1990	1991	1992	1993	1994	1995	1996	1997	1998	1999
		Foreign affiliates *(Millions of PLN)*									
		Filiales étrangères *(Millions de PLN)*									
10/14	Mining & quarrying	..	..	..	..	..	..	..	159	..	321
15/37	**TOTAL MANUFACTURING**	..	..	..	3 257	3 860	6 195	7 895	10 386	25 105	22 728
15/16	Food, beverages, tobacco	..	..	..	..	..	..	..	2 565	..	5 930
17/19	Textiles, clothing, leather, footwear	..	..	..	..	..	..	..	305	..	461
20/22	Wood and paper products	..	..	..	..	..	..	..	624	..	1 413
20	Wood products	..	..	..	..	..	..	..	111	..	275
21/22	Paper, printing and publishing	..	..	..	..	..	..	..	513	..	1 139
23/25	Chemicals, Total	..	..	..	..	..	..	..	2 022	..	3 863
23	Refined petroleum, nuclear fuel	..	..	..	..	..	..	..	14	..	15
24/25	Chemicals, rubber & plastics prod.	..	..	..	..	..	..	..	2 008	..	3 847
24	Chemical products	..	..	..	..	..	..	..	1 484	..	2 499
2423	Pharmaceuticals	..	..	..	..	..	..	..	..	..	30
25	Rubber and plastics products	..	..	..	..	..	..	..	524	..	1 349
26	Non-metallic mineral products	..	..	..	..	..	..	..	1 258	..	2 448
27/28	Basic & fabricated metals	..	..	..	..	..	..	..	586	..	981
27	Basic metals	..	..	..	..	..	..	..	195	..	312
28	Fabricated metal products	..	..	..	..	..	..	..	391	..	670
29/32	Machinery, Total	..	..	..	..	..	..	..	1 191	..	1 921
29/30	Non-electrical machinery	..	..	..	..	..	..	..	315	..	685
29	Non-electrical machinery nec	..	..	..	..	..	..	..	257	..	633
30	Office and computing machinery	..	..	..	..	..	..	..	57	..	52
31/32	Electrical & electronic equipment	..	..	..	..	..	..	..	876	..	1 236
31	Electrical machinery nec	..	..	..	..	..	..	..	405	..	636
32	Radio, TV & communications eq.	..	..	..	..	..	..	..	471	..	601
33	Scientific instruments	..	..	..	..	..	..	..	106	..	127
34/35	Transportation equipment	..	..	..	..	..	..	..	1 471	..	5 212
34	Motor vehicles	..	..	..	..	..	..	..	1 339	..	4 951
35	Other transport equipment	..	..	..	..	..	..	..	132	..	262
351	Shipbuilding & repairing	..	..	..	..	..	..	..	9	..	4
353	Aircraft and spacecraft	..	..	..	..	..	..	..	50	..	79
36/37	Other manufacturing	..	..	..	..	..	..	..	259	..	371
40/45	Construction, electricity, gas & water	..	..	..	..	..	..	..	343	..	578
50/55	Trade, repair, hotels & restaurants	..	..	..	..	..	..	..	4 799	..	11 208
65/74	Finance, insurance, business services	..	..	..	..	..	..	..	2 026	..	2 949
	OTHER ACTIVITIES	..	..	..	..	..	..	..	539	..	1 250
01/99	**GRAND TOTAL**	..	..	..	..	..	..	..	18 252	..	39 033

Total manufacturing by investing country

	1990	1991	1992	1993	1994	1995	1996	1997	1998	1999
All countries	..	..	..	3 257	3 860	6 195	7 895	10 386	25 105	22 728
United States	..	..	..	..	..	..	..	1 176	..	1 742
Canada	..	..	..	..	..	..	..	..	..	..
Mexico	..	..	..	..	..	..	..	..	..	..
Japan	..	..	..	..	..	..	..	28	..	608
Europe	..	..	..	..	..	..	..	..	..	..
European Union (15)	..	..	..	..	..	..	..	7 851	..	15 878
Belgium	..	..	..	..	..	..	..	..	..	..
France	..	..	..	..	..	..	..	1 155	..	2 869
Germany	..	..	..	..	..	..	..	2 436	..	3 992
Italy	..	..	..	..	..	..	..	..	..	..
Netherlands	..	..	..	..	..	..	..	1 879	..	5 041
Spain	..	..	..	..	..	..	..	..	..	..
Sweden	..	..	..	..	..	..	..	..	..	..
United Kingdom	..	..	..	..	..	..	..	255	..	733
Switzerland	..	..	..	..	..	..	..	659	..	692
Australia and New Zealand	..	..	..	..	..	..	..	..	..	..
Asia (non-OECD)	..	..	..	..	..	..	..	35	..	181
Latin America	..	..	..	..	..	..	..	2	..	30

Note: Majority foreign-owned firms.
Firmes sous contrôle étranger majoritaire.

POLAND

Source

For all variables except *R&D expenditure* and *Number of researchers*, the data are prepared by the Department of Enterprises of the Central Statistical Office (GUS). These data are collected on an annual basis since 1993 and refer to majority foreign-owned firms, *i.e.* where more than 50% of the capital is held by non-residents. From 1999, all enterprises employing more than nine persons are covered. Public administration and defence (ISIC 75), as well as banks and insurance companies, are not covered. The results are published in the report *Economic Activity of Companies with Foreign Capital*.

For *R&D expenditure* and *Number of researchers*, the data come from the R&D Section of GUS. They refer to all foreign-owned firms according to the national register Regon. Only enterprises with more than 50 employees are covered.

National totals: data come from the Central Statistical Office and are fully compatible with foreign affiliates' data.

Industrial classification

For all variables, the data are classified according to the principal industrial activity of the affiliate.

The industrial classification used is the national classification (PKD) which is based on NACE Revision 1.

Variables

- *Number of employees* is the number of persons on the payroll at the end of the year. It is not calculated on a full-time equivalent basis.

- *R&D expenditure* refer to expenditure by the affiliate itself.

- *Number of researchers* is expressed on a full-time equivalent basis.

Geographical breakdown

The investor's country is the country of the immediate controller.

POLOGNE

Source

Pour toutes les variables, sauf les *Dépenses de R-D* et le *Nombre de chercheurs*, les données sont fournies par le Département des entreprises de l'Office central de statistique de Pologne (GUS). Ces données sont recueillies annuellement depuis 1993 et font référence aux entreprises sous contrôle étranger majoritaire, c'est-à-dire pour lesquelles plus de 50 % du capital est détenu par des non résidents. A partir de 1999, toutes les entreprises employant plus de neuf personnes sont couvertes. Le secteur de l'administration publique et de la défense (CITI 75) ainsi que les banques et les assurances ne sont pas couverts. Les résultats sont publiés dans le rapport *Economic Activity of Companies with Foreign Capital*.

Pour les *Dépenses de R-D* et le *Nombre de chercheurs*, les données proviennent de la Section R-D de GUS. Elles concernent toutes les entreprises sous contrôle étranger selon le registre national Regon. Seules les entreprises de plus de 50 salariés sont couvertes.

Totaux nationaux : les données sont fournies par l'Office polonais de statistiques et sont entièrement compatibles avec les données relatives aux filiales étrangères.

Classification industrielle

Pour toutes les variables, les données sont classées selon l'activité industrielle principale de l'entreprise affiliée.

La classification industrielle utilisée est la classification nationale (PKD) qui est fondée sur la NACE Révision 1.

Variables

- Le *Nombre de salariés* est le nombre de personnes employées à la fin de l'année. Il n'est pas calculé en équivalent plein-temps.

- Les *Dépenses de R-D* se rapportent aux dépenses de la filiale pour elle-même.

- Le *Nombre de chercheurs* est exprimé en équivalent plein-temps.

Ventilation géographique

Le pays de l'investisseur est celui où se situe le contrôle immédiat.

SWEDEN

A. Inward investments

B. Outward investments

Sources and Methods

SUÈDE

A. Investissements entrants

B. Investissements sortants

Sources et méthodes

Table 1A - Tableau 1A
NUMBER OF ENTERPRISES / NOMBRE D'ENTREPRISES

| | | Foreign affiliates (Units) | | | | | As a % of national total | | | | |
| | | Filiales étrangères (Unités) | | | | | En % du total national | | | | |
By industry (ISIC Rev. 3)		1994	1995	1996	1997	1998	1994	1995	1996	1997	1998
10/14	Mining & quarrying	9	12	13	13	16	1.6	2.0	2.2	2.1	2.7
15/37	**TOTAL MANUFACTURING**	**684**	**780**	**789**	**822**	**876**	**1.6**	**1.8**	**1.7**	**1.7**	**1.7**
15/16	Food, beverages, tobacco	52	53	48	46	47	2.0	2.0	1.8	1.6	1.6
17/19	Textiles, clothing, leather, footwear	26	25	22	19	15	1.0	0.9	0.7	0.5	0.4
20/22	Wood and paper products	112	114	126	130	148	0.9	0.9	1.0	0.9	1.0
20	Wood products	15	15	17	22	22	0.3	0.3	0.3	0.4	0.4
21/22	Paper, printing and publishing	97	99	109	108	126	1.4	1.3	1.4	1.3	1.4
23/25	Chemicals, Total	112	129	126	134	146	5.3	6.0	5.7	6.0	6.3
23	Refined petroleum, nuclear fuel	4	5	6	5	8	10.8	14.7	16.7	13.2	18.6
24/25	Chemicals, rubber & plastics prod.	108	124	120	129	138	5.2	5.9	5.6	5.8	6.1
24	Chemical products	71	82	79	78	85	11.1	12.0	10.7	10.2	10.7
2423	Pharmaceuticals	10	12	9	5	6	11.6	12.8	8.5	5.6	6.2
25	Rubber and plastics products	37	42	41	51	53	2.6	2.9	2.9	3.5	3.6
26	Non-metallic mineral products	28	34	31	37	33	2.4	2.8	2.4	2.6	2.3
27/28	Basic & fabricated metals	79	97	96	103	104	0.9	1.1	1.0	1.1	1.1
27	Basic metals	26	38	31	33	33	7.6	10.3	8.2	10.0	9.8
28	Fabricated metal products	53	59	65	70	71	0.7	0.7	0.7	0.8	0.8
29/32	Machinery, Total	188	219	212	209	233	2.9	3.4	3.2	3.0	3.3
29/30	Non-electrical machinery	140	161	156	154	167	2.9	3.3	3.1	3.0	3.2
29	Non-electrical machinery nec	132	153	148	148	161	3.0	3.4	3.2	3.1	3.3
30	Office and computing machinery	8	8	8	6	6	1.8	1.9	1.9	1.4	1.4
31/32	Electrical & electronic equipment	48	58	56	55	66	3.1	3.6	3.4	3.1	3.5
31	Electrical machinery nec	39	44	45	42	55	3.6	3.9	3.9	3.4	4.3
32	Radio, TV & communications eq.	9	14	11	13	11	2.0	2.9	2.2	2.3	1.9
33	Scientific instruments	21	25	53	64	62	1.3	1.4	2.8	3.3	3.2
34/35	Transportation equipment	35	43	38	45	53	2.2	2.6	2.1	2.4	2.7
34	Motor vehicles	24	32	26	32	38	4.6	5.6	4.3	5.0	5.7
35	Other transport equipment	11	11	12	13	15	1.0	1.0	1.0	1.1	1.2
351	Shipbuilding & repairing	3	3	..	3	..	0.3	0.3	..	0.3	..
353	Aircraft and spacecraft	..	..	..	2	..	..	..	..	1.8	..
36/37	Other manufacturing	31	41	37	35	35	0.9	1.1	0.9	0.7	0.7
40/45	Construction, electricity, gas & water	93	78	122	128	129	0.2	0.2	0.2	0.2	0.3
50/55	Trade, repair, hotels & restaurants	1 304	1 369	1 461	1 438	1 486	1.0	1.1	1.1	1.0	1.1
65/74	Finance, insurance, business services	660	756	830	900	1 022	0.6	0.6	0.6	0.6	0.6
	OTHER ACTIVITIES	324	349	398	324	355	0.2	0.2	0.2	0.1	0.1
01/99	**GRAND TOTAL**	**3 074**	**3 344**	**3 613**	**3 687**	**3 954**	**0.6**	**0.6**	**0.6**	**0.6**	**0.6**

Total manufacturing by investing country						As a % of total manufacturing by foreign affiliates				
All countries	684	780	789	822	876	100.0	100.0	100.0	100.0	100.0
United States	69	85	98	110	134	10.1	10.9	12.4	13.4	15.3
Canada	..	..	..	..	..	..	..	..	..	..
Mexico	0	0	0	0	0	0.0	0.0	0.0	0.0	0.0
Japan	7	12	11	13	16	1.0	1.5	1.4	1.6	1.8
Europe	589	663	662	..	..	86.1	85.0	83.9	..	..
European Union (15)	446	484	491	497	517	65.2	62.1	62.2	60.5	59.0
Belgium	..	..	..	..	..	..	..	..	..	..
France	25	24	29	30	31	3.7	3.1	3.7	3.6	3.5
Germany	51	52	60	64	78	7.5	6.7	7.6	7.8	8.9
Italy	..	..	..	..	..	..	..	..	..	..
Netherlands	117	122	110	124	116	17.1	15.6	13.9	15.1	13.2
Spain	..	..	..	..	..	..	..	..	..	..
Sweden										
United Kingdom	72	96	92	81	74	10.5	12.3	11.7	9.9	8.4
Switzerland	73	90	77	74	75	10.7	11.5	9.8	9.0	8.6
Australia and New Zealand	..	..	..	0	0	..	..	..	0.0	0.0
Asia (non-OECD)	..	..	6	7	8	..	..	0.8	0.9	0.9
Latin America	..	0	0	3	4	..	0.0	0.0	0.4	0.5

Note: **All** majority foreign-owned firms. Source: ITPS's Statistics on Foreign-owned Enterprises.
Toutes les firmes sous contrôle étranger majoritaire. Source : Statistiques d'ITPS sur les entreprises à capitaux étrangers.

Table 2A - Tableau 2A

NUMBER OF EMPLOYEES BY INDUSTRY

NOMBRE DE SALARIÉS PAR INDUSTRIE

| | | Foreign affiliates *(Units)* | | | | | As a % of national total | | | | |
| | | Filiales étrangères *(Unités)* | | | | | En % du total national | | | | |
ISIC Revision 3		1994	1995	1996	1997	1998	1994	1995	1996	1997	1998
10/14	Mining & quarrying	389	712	819	729	867	4.1	7.5	8.6	7.5	9.5
15/37	**TOTAL MANUFACTURING**	**108 648**	**132 239**	**137 097**	**141 629**	**155 672**	**16.2**	**19.2**	**19.3**	**20.0**	**21.8**
15/16	Food, beverages, tobacco	13 127	14 098	18 040	17 153	16 509	20.0	21.2	26.9	26.2	25.0
17/19	Textiles, clothing, leather, footwear	2 272	2 425	2 418	2 340	2 327	13.6	14.4	15.2	14.9	14.3
20/22	Wood and paper products	8 379	9 705	10 776	12 100	21 908	6.1	7.1	7.8	9.0	16.5
20	Wood products	894	969	2 630	3 232	4 128	2.6	2.7	7.2	8.9	11.2
21/22	Paper, printing and publishing	7 485	8 736	8 146	8 868	17 780	7.4	8.6	8.0	9.0	18.5
23/25	Chemicals, Total	18 214	25 319	25 272	26 076	26 596	34.5	46.8	45.8	46.0	45.1
23	Refined petroleum, nuclear fuel	1 844	2 073	1 517	1 514	1 685	69.7	78.1	91.8	91.4	84.4
24/25	Chemicals, rubber & plastics prod.	16 370	23 246	23 755	24 562	24 911	32.7	45.2	44.4	44.7	43.7
24	Chemical products	12 529	18 847	18 928	18 611	18 681	44.8	66.0	64.9	58.5	56.5
2423	Pharmaceuticals	542	6 023	6 655	6 490	6 008	6.4	63.0	63.7	60.4	54.8
25	Rubber and plastics products	3 841	4 399	4 827	5 951	6 230	17.4	19.3	19.8	25.7	26.0
26	Non-metallic mineral products	5 637	6 318	6 272	7 522	6 820	31.4	34.9	35.4	42.7	40.0
27/28	Basic & fabricated metals	8 497	14 434	13 404	14 635	14 434	8.0	12.8	11.2	12.4	12.4
27	Basic metals	5 152	10 584	9 453	9 988	9 553	16.0	32.0	28.0	30.8	29.8
28	Fabricated metal products	3 345	3 850	3 951	4 647	4 881	4.5	4.9	4.6	5.5	5.8
29/32	Machinery, Total	38 278	42 009	41 378	40 600	42 297	25.8	27.5	26.0	24.9	26.0
29/30	Non-electrical machinery	28 166	31 584	31 114	30 106	30 010	28.6	31.7	30.1	30.3	30.6
29	Non-electrical machinery nec	26 243	30 571	30 145	29 191	29 295	28.7	32.3	30.4	30.7	30.9
30	Office and computing machinery	1 923	1 013	969	915	715	26.5	20.5	22.7	22.2	22.3
31/32	Electrical & electronic equipment	10 112	10 425	10 264	10 494	12 287	20.3	19.7	18.4	16.5	19.0
31	Electrical machinery nec	8 230	8 348	8 335	7 306	8 457	44.6	42.7	35.9	31.3	38.8
32	Radio, TV & communications eq.	1 882	2 077	1 929	3 188	3 830	6.0	6.2	5.9	7.9	8.9
33	Scientific instruments	6 499	6 385	7 043	8 070	8 569	32.4	29.5	32.5	35.4	35.3
34/35	Transportation equipment	5 126	7 451	8 253	8 846	10 252	6.1	8.8	9.1	10.2	11.7
34	Motor vehicles	3 177	5 375	6 070	6 735	7 984	5.1	8.3	8.7	10.0	11.8
35	Other transport equipment	1 949	2 076	2 183	2 111	2 268	9.1	10.5	10.5	10.8	11.3
351	Shipbuilding & repairing	158	157	..	133	..	3.6	3.5	..	3.4	..
353	Aircraft and spacecraft	..	..	..	..	..	..	..	..	..	..
36/37	Other manufacturing	2 619	4 095	4 241	4 287	5 960	11.7	16.4	16.7	14.9	19.9
40/45	Construction, electricity, gas & water	8 136	8 547	9 833	9 282	9 639	4.3	4.5	5.1	4.7	4.7
50/55	Trade, repair, hotels & restaurants	49 671	54 284	61 047	65 717	74 562	10.6	11.3	12.5	13.4	14.9
65/74	Finance, insurance, business services	27 113	29 237	40 403	54 225	57 833	8.0	8.3	10.9	13.0	13.1
	OTHER ACTIVITIES	20 057	20 999	28 816	29 431	34 815	5.4	5.5	7.5	1.8	2.2
01/99	**GRAND TOTAL**	**214 014**	**246 018**	**278 016**	**301 013**	**333 395**	**10.5**	**11.7**	**12.9**	**8.7**	**9.6**

Note: **All** majority foreign-owned firms. Source: ITPS's Statistics on Foreign-owned Enterprises.

Toutes les firmes sous contrôle étranger majoritaire. Source : Statistiques d'ITPS sur les entreprises à capitaux étrangers.

Inward investments

Investissements entrants

Table 3A - Tableau 3A

NUMBER OF EMPLOYEES BY COUNTRY OF ORIGIN IN THE MANUFACTURING SECTOR
NOMBRE DE SALARIÉS PAR PAYS D'ORIGINE DANS L'INDUSTRIE MANUFACTURIÈRE

Country of origin (UBO)	Number of employees *(Units)* Nombre de salariés *(Unités)*					As a % of all countries *En % du total des pays*				
	1994	1995	1996	1997	1998	1994	1995	1996	1997	1998
All countries	**108 648**	**132 239**	**137 097**	**141 629**	**155 672**	**100.0**	**100.0**	**100.0**	**100.0**	**100.0**
Total OECD	..	..	..	139 197	152 357	..	..	..	98.3	97.9
United States	10 852	20 062	24 067	24 398	28 257	10.0	15.2	17.6	17.2	18.2
Canada	..	..	..	696	1 003	..	..	..	0.5	0.6
Mexico	0	0	0	0	0	0.0	0.0	0.0	0.0	0.0
Japan	411	528	618	779	896	0.4	0.4	0.5	0.6	0.6
Korea	..	..	..	0	0	..	..	..	0.0	0.0
Australia	..	..	..	0	0	..	..	..	0.0	0.0
New Zealand	..	..	..	0	0	..	..	..	0.0	0.0
Europe	**95 597**	**110 081**	**110 929**	**113 324**	**123 227**	**88.0**	**83.2**	**80.9**	**80.0**	**79.2**
European Union (15)	**65 689**	**73 391**	**71 963**	**77 147**	**84 087**	**60.5**	**55.5**	**52.5**	**54.5**	**54.0**
Austria	..	..	..	1 816	1 837	..	..	..	1.3	1.2
Belgium	..	..	..	506	464	..	..	..	0.4	0.3
Denmark	..	..	..	7 004	8 194	..	..	..	4.9	5.3
Finland	..	..	..	18 815	27 674	..	..	..	13.3	17.8
France	4 606	4 907	5 000	7 003	7 282	4.2	3.7	3.6	4.9	4.7
Germany	6 171	5 955	7 538	7 970	7 998	5.7	4.5	5.5	5.6	5.1
Greece	..	..	..	0	0	..	..	..	0.0	0.0
Ireland	..	..	..	88	0	..	..	..	0.1	0.0
Italy	..	..	..	535	513	..	..	..	0.4	0.3
Luxembourg	..	..	..	302	302	..	..	..	0.2	0.2
Netherlands	23 600	20 980	16 910	18 813	16 497	21.7	15.9	12.3	13.3	10.6
Portugal	..	..	..	0	0	..	..	..	0.0	0.0
Spain	..	..	..	72	52	..	..	..	0.1	0.0
Sweden	..	..	..	..	..	..	..	..	..	..
United Kingdom	7 059	13 439	13 560	14 223	13 274	6.5	10.2	9.9	10.0	8.5
Czech Republic	..	..	..	0	0	..	..	..	0.0	0.0
Hungary	..	..	..	0	0	..	..	..	0.0	0.0
Iceland	..	..	0	0	0	..	..	0.0	0.0	0.0
Norway	..	..	..	14 992	16 156	..	..	..	10.6	10.4
Poland	..	..	..	0	0	..	..	..	0.0	0.0
Slovak Republic	..	..	..	0	0	..	..	..	0.0	0.0
Switzerland	23 892	25 766	23 707	21 185	21 958	22.0	19.5	17.3	15.0	14.1
Turkey	..	..	..	0	0	..	..	..	0.0	0.0
Non-OECD Europe, of which:	..	..	..	0	1 026	..	..	..	0.0	0.7
Baltic countries	..	..	..	0	0	..	..	..	0.0	0.0
Bulgaria	..	..	..	0	0	..	..	..	0.0	0.0
Croatia	..	..	..	0	0	..	..	..	0.0	0.0
Romania	..	..	..	0	0	..	..	..	0.0	0.0
Russian Federation	..	..	..	0	0	..	..	..	0.0	0.0
Slovenia	..	..	..	0	0	..	..	..	0.0	0.0
Ukraine	..	..	..	0	0	..	..	..	0.0	0.0
Yugoslavia	..	..	..	0	0	..	..	..	0.0	0.0
Non-OECD Asia, of which:	..	..	949	1 390	1 557	..	..	0.7	1.0	1.0
China	..	..	..	..	0	..	..	..	..	0.0
Chinese Taipei	..	..	..	..	0	..	..	..	..	0.0
Hong Kong (China)	..	..	..	..	0	..	..	..	..	0.0
India	..	..	..	..	0	..	..	..	..	0.0
Indonesia	..	..	..	..	0	..	..	..	..	0.0
Malaysia	..	..	..	..	86	..	..	..	..	0.1
Philippines	..	..	..	..	0	..	..	..	..	0.0
Singapore	..	..	..	..	1 471	..	..	..	..	0.9
Thailand	..	..	..	..	0	..	..	..	..	0.0
Near and Middle East	..	..	..	..	550	..	..	..	..	0.4
Africa	..	..	..	0	0	..	..	..	0.0	0.0
Latin America, of which:	..	0	0	114	177	..	0.0	0.0	0.1	0.1
Argentina	..	0	0	0	0	..	0.0	0.0	0.0	0.0
Brazil	..	0	0	0	0	..	0.0	0.0	0.0	0.0
Chile	..	0	0	0	0	..	0.0	0.0	0.0	0.0

Note: **All** majority foreign-owned firms. Source: ITPS's Statistics on Foreign-owned Enterprises.
Toutes les firmes sous contrôle étranger majoritaire. Source : Statistiques d'ITPS sur les entreprises à capitaux étrangers.

Inward investments

Investissements entrants

Table 4A - Tableau 4A

PRODUCTION

By industry (ISIC Rev. 3)	Foreign affiliates (Millions of SEK) Filiales étrangères (Millions de SEK)					As a % of national total En % du total national				
	1994	1995	1996	1997	1998	1994	1995	1996	1997	1998
10/14 Mining & quarrying	..	..	..	1 389	1 269	..	..	..	8.1	7.7
15/37 TOTAL MANUFACTURING	**..**	**..**	**..**	**220 478**	**258 080**	**..**	**..**	**..**	**19.7**	**21.9**
15/16 Food, beverages, tobacco	..	..	..	31 137	28 187	..	..	..	27.8	25.5
17/19 Textiles, clothing, leather, footwear	..	..	..	2 459	2 335	..	..	..	19.0	17.9
20/22 Wood and paper products	..	..	..	17 053	41 242	..	..	..	8.1	19.0
20 Wood products	..	..	..	4 465	6 032	..	..	..	7.6	9.9
21/22 Paper, printing and publishing	..	..	..	12 588	35 210	..	..	..	8.3	22.6
23/25 Chemicals, Total	..	..	..	50 614	55 409	..	..	..	43.2	44.1
23 Refined petroleum, nuclear fuel	..	..	..	3 006	3 346	..	..	..	49.1	56.5
24/25 Chemicals, rubber & plastics prod.	..	..	..	47 608	52 063	..	..	..	42.9	43.5
24 Chemical products	..	..	..	41 218	44 944	..	..	..	49.5	49.6
2423 Pharmaceuticals	..	..	..	12 918	14 277	..	..	..	36.0	35.0
25 Rubber and plastics products	..	..	..	6 390	7 119	..	..	..	23.0	24.5
26 Non-metallic mineral products	..	..	..	7 850	7 214	..	..	..	38.1	34.4
27/28 Basic & fabricated metals	..	..	..	29 335	25 844	..	..	..	21.7	18.8
27 Basic metals	..	..	..	23 535	18 489	..	..	..	40.4	34.4
28 Fabricated metal products	..	..	..	5 800	7 355	..	..	..	7.6	8.8
29/32 Machinery, Total	..	..	..	52 435	61 312	..	..	..	18.3	19.9
29/30 Non-electrical machinery	..	..	..	38 515	41 503	..	..	..	27.4	28.4
29 Non-electrical machinery nec	..	..	..	36 780	39 081	..	..	..	27.2	28.1
30 Office and computing machinery	..	..	..	1 735	2 422	..	..	..	32.6	35.7
31/32 Electrical & electronic equipment	..	..	..	13 920	19 809	..	..	..	9.5	12.2
31 Electrical machinery nec	..	..	..	10 138	14 226	..	..	..	32.4	51.6
32 Radio, TV & communications eq.	..	..	..	3 782	5 583	..	..	..	3.3	4.1
33 Scientific instruments	..	..	..	11 285	12 836	..	..	..	35.5	34.9
34/35 Transportation equipment	..	..	..	13 183	16 292	..	..	..	7.9	9.1
34 Motor vehicles	..	..	..	9 101	13 041	..	..	..	6.4	8.5
35 Other transport equipment	..	..	..	4 082	3 251	..	..	..	15.8	12.4
351 Shipbuilding & repairing	..	..	..	151	170	..	..	..	2.9	3.4
353 Aircraft and spacecraft	..	..	..	..	..	..	..	..	..	..
36/37 Other manufacturing	..	..	..	5 122	7 409	..	..	..	19.6	24.2
40/45 Construction, electricity, gas & water	..	..	..	18 117	19 389	..	..	..	5.6	5.9
50/55 Trade, repair, hotels & restaurants	..	..	..	76 158	88 856	..	..	..	21.2	22.8
65/74 Finance, insurance, business services	..	..	..	67 774	68 950	..	..	..	16.8	15.1
OTHER ACTIVITIES	..	..	..	42 780	44 635	..	..	..	10.1	10.0
01/99 GRAND TOTAL	**..**	**..**	**..**	**426 691**	**481 181**	**..**	**..**	**..**	**16.1**	**17.1**

Total manufacturing by investing country						As a % of total manufacturing by foreign affiliates				
All countries	**..**	**..**	**..**	**220 478**	**258 080**	**..**	**..**	**..**	**100.0**	**100.0**
United States	..	..	..	41 549	51 429	..	..	..	18.8	19.9
Canada	..	..	..	..	..	..	..	..	..	..
Mexico	..	..	..	0	0	..	..	..	0.0	0.0
Japan	..	..	..	1 513	1 637	..	..	..	0.7	0.6
Europe	..	..	..	..	..	..	..	..	..	..
European Union (15)	..	..	..	117 336	137 652	..	..	..	53.2	53.3
Belgium	..	..	..	..	..	..	..	..	..	..
France	..	..	..	9 290	9 889	..	..	..	4.2	3.8
Germany	..	..	..	12 980	12 787	..	..	..	5.9	5.0
Italy	..	..	..	..	..	..	..	..	..	..
Netherlands	..	..	..	23 690	22 991	..	..	..	10.7	8.9
Spain	..	..	..	..	..	..	..	..	..	..
Sweden	..	..	..	..	..	..	..	..	..	..
United Kingdom	..	..	..	27 440	21 393	..	..	..	12.4	8.3
Switzerland	..	..	..	30 255	34 108	..	..	..	13.7	13.2
Australia and New Zealand	..	..	..	0	0	..	..	..	0.0	0.0
Asia (non-OECD)	..	..	..	605	3 215	..	..	..	0.3	1.2
Latin America	..	..	..	212	223	..	..	..	0.1	0.1

Note: Majority foreign-owned **non-financial** firms. Source: Statistics Sweden's Structural Business Statistics.
Firmes **non financières** sous contrôle étranger majoritaire. Source : Statistiques structurelles d'entreprises de l'office suédois de statistiques.

Inward investments

Investissements entrants

Table 5A - Tableau 5A

TURNOVER BY INDUSTRY

CHIFFRE D'AFFAIRES PAR INDUSTRIE

		Foreign affiliates *(Millions of SEK)* Filiales étrangères *(Millions de SEK)*					As a % of national total *En % du total national*				
ISIC Revision 3		1994	1995	1996	1997	1998	1994	1995	1996	1997	1998
10/14	Mining & quarrying	633	1 115	1 017	1 364	1 407	4.6	7.0	6.7	8.2	8.8
15/37	**TOTAL MANUFACTURING**	**164 535**	**235 987**	**229 976**	**230 954**	**273 534**	**17.4**	**21.6**	**20.8**	**19.6**	**21.9**
15/16	Food, beverages, tobacco	20 128	23 517	32 277	32 034	30 688	17.4	19.9	26.9	26.4	25.8
17/19	Textiles, clothing, leather, footwear	2 600	2 544	2 768	2 741	2 848	20.5	17.6	20.9	20.4	20.4
20/22	Wood and paper products	11 671	16 034	16 658	17 336	41 658	6.1	7.5	8.2	8.3	19.3
20	Wood products	1 493	1 640	3 907	4 604	6 301	3.1	3.1	8.0	7.9	10.3
21/22	Paper, printing and publishing	10 178	14 394	12 751	12 732	35 357	7.1	8.9	8.3	8.5	22.7
23/25	Chemicals, Total	36 808	54 971	54 731	54 379	60 325	36.8	49.5	49.1	45.5	48.4
23	Refined petroleum, nuclear fuel	1 949	2 719	4 561	2 957	3 137	42.1	57.3	88.9	48.3	55.0
24/25	Chemicals, rubber & plastics prod.	34 859	52 252	50 170	51 422	57 188	36.6	49.1	47.2	45.4	48.0
24	Chemical products	29 221	46 094	44 514	44 300	48 096	42.0	59.5	58.0	52.3	53.9
2423	Pharmaceuticals	1 072	10 799	11 256	12 522	13 512	3.9	36.3	36.6	38.5	37.7
25	Rubber and plastics products	5 639	6 158	5 657	7 122	9 092	21.8	21.3	19.1	24.9	30.5
26	Non-metallic mineral products	6 546	7 825	7 314	8 625	8 156	33.6	37.1	34.4	40.6	37.2
27/28	Basic & fabricated metals	15 346	33 774	28 392	29 655	26 660	14.1	25.8	22.3	21.7	18.9
27	Basic metals	11 034	27 501	22 286	23 214	18 905	21.5	44.2	40.4	39.6	34.3
28	Fabricated metal products	4 312	6 273	6 106	6 441	7 755	7.5	9.2	8.5	8.3	9.0
29/32	Machinery, Total	53 517	71 411	61 378	54 472	64 501	25.4	28.9	22.1	18.5	20.2
29/30	Non-electrical machinery	36 962	54 292	44 096	39 575	42 937	28.6	37.7	29.3	26.5	27.4
29	Non-electrical machinery nec	34 901	52 961	42 621	37 741	40 459	29.2	38.3	29.4	26.2	27.0
30	Office and computing machinery	2 061	1 331	1 475	1 834	2 478	20.9	23.5	25.8	34.0	36.1
31/32	Electrical & electronic equipment	16 555	17 119	17 282	14 897	21 564	20.3	16.6	13.6	10.2	13.2
31	Electrical machinery nec	14 230	14 532	14 956	10 997	15 123	56.5	53.4	45.7	32.7	52.2
32	Radio, TV & communications eq.	2 325	2 587	2 326	3 900	6 441	4.1	3.4	2.5	3.5	4.8
33	Scientific instruments	7 616	9 480	10 738	12 390	14 409	34.4	34.1	39.4	38.5	37.6
34/35	Transportation equipment	7 054	11 340	10 656	13 831	16 533	4.8	6.2	5.9	6.8	7.4
34	Motor vehicles	3 509	7 437	7 359	9 810	13 693	2.7	4.7	4.7	5.5	6.9
35	Other transport equipment	3 545	3 903	3 297	4 021	2 840	19.6	17.3	13.5	14.6	10.9
351	Shipbuilding & repairing	..	..	..	156	181	..	..	..	2.5	3.4
353	Aircraft and spacecraft	..	..	..	..	..	..	..	..	..	..
36/37	Other manufacturing	3 249	5 091	5 066	5 489	7 756	16.4	21.1	20.3	20.6	25.1
40/45	Construction, electricity, gas & water	8 770	8 485	20 493	18 077	19 092	3.1	2.9	6.3	5.7	6.1
50/55	Trade, repair, hotels & restaurants	174 316	206 163	247 602	270 336	286 958	16.3	17.6	20.6	21.6	21.8
65/74	Finance, insurance, business services	31 846	38 068	43 334	71 000	75 271	15.8	17.3	18.2	18.4	17.0
	OTHER ACTIVITIES	27 659	34 341	40 837	42 582	46 472	8.3	9.5	9.5	10.2	10.6
01/99	**GRAND TOTAL**	**407 760**	**524 159**	**583 258**	**634 311**	**702 737**	**14.3**	**16.6**	**17.6**	**17.8**	**18.6**

Note: Majority foreign-owned **non-financial** firms. Source: Statistics Sweden's Structural Business Statistics.
Firmes **non financières** sous contrôle étranger majoritaire. Source : Statistiques structurelles d'entreprises de l'office suédois de statistiques.

Table 6A - Tableau 6A

TURNOVER BY COUNTRY OF ORIGIN IN THE MANUFACTURING SECTOR

CHIFFRE D'AFFAIRES PAR PAYS D'ORIGINE DANS L'INDUSTRIE MANUFACTURIÈRE

| | **Turnover** (Millions of SEK) | | | | | **As a % of all countries** | | | | |
| | **Chiffre d'affaires** (Millions de SEK) | | | | | **En % du total des pays** | | | | |
Country of origin (UBO)	1994	1995	1996	1997	1998	1994	1995	1996	1997	1998
All countries	164 535	235 987	229 976	230 954	273 534	100.0	100.0	100.0	100.0	100.0
Total OECD	..	234 386	228 399	228 830	268 677	..	99.3	99.3	99.1	98.2
United States	17 514	35 445	39 720	42 777	53 717	10.6	15.0	17.3	18.5	19.6
Canada	..	564	515	900	1 322	..	0.2	0.2	0.4	0.5
Mexico	..	..	0	0	0	..	..	..	0.0	0.0
Japan	..	1 460	1 124	1 728	1 768	..	0.6	0.5	0.7	0.6
Korea	..	..	..	0	0	..	..	..	0.0	0.0
Australia	..	..	..	0	0	..	..	..	0.0	0.0
New Zealand	..	..	..	0	0	..	..	..	0.0	0.0
Europe	143 837	196 977	187 236	183 425	213 298	87.4	83.5	81.4	79.4	78.0
European Union (15)	97 607	133 861	120 211	123 151	147 736	59.3	56.7	52.3	53.3	54.0
Austria	..	..	..	1 997	2 300	..	..	..	0.9	0.8
Belgium	..	736	683	600	729	..	0.3	0.3	0.3	0.3
Denmark	..	..	..	10 597	12 854	..	..	..	4.6	4.7
Finland	..	35 579	29 498	32 240	57 345	..	15.1	12.8	14.0	21.0
France	6 274	7 570	7 357	9 723	11 968	3.8	3.2	3.2	4.2	4.4
Germany	10 497	12 102	12 222	14 115	14 059	6.4	5.1	5.3	6.1	5.1
Greece	..	..	..	0	0	..	..	..	0.0	0.0
Ireland	..	73	80	75	0	..	0.0	0.0	0.0	0.0
Italy	..	729	1 064	690	715	..	0.3	0.5	0.3	0.3
Luxembourg	..	..	..	322	326	..	..	..	0.1	0.1
Netherlands	33 320	40 527	30 263	25 088	24 886	20.3	17.2	13.2	10.9	9.1
Portugal	..	..	..	0	0	..	..	..	0.0	0.0
Spain	..	..	161	90	94	..	..	0.1	0.0	0.0
Sweden	..	..	..	..	..	..	..	..	..	..
United Kingdom	8 605	25 689	25 907	27 614	22 459	5.2	10.9	11.3	12.0	8.2
Czech Republic	..	..	..	0	0	..	..	..	0.0	0.0
Hungary	..	..	..	0	0	..	..	..	0.0	0.0
Iceland	..	..	..	0	0	..	..	..	0.0	0.0
Norway	..	..	..	28 199	28 822	..	..	..	12.2	10.5
Poland	..	..	..	0	0	..	..	..	0.0	0.0
Slovak Republic	..	..	..	0	0	..	..	..	0.0	0.0
Switzerland	36 196	42 933	40 785	32 075	35 323	22.0	18.2	17.7	13.9	12.9
Turkey	..	..	..	0	0	..	..	..	0.0	0.0
Non-OECD Europe, of which:	..	..	..	0	1 417	..	..	..	0.0	0.5
Baltic countries	..	..	..	0	0	..	..	..	0.0	0.0
Bulgaria	..	..	..	0	0	..	..	..	0.0	0.0
Croatia	..	..	..	0	0	..	..	..	0.0	0.0
Romania	..	..	..	0	0	..	..	..	0.0	0.0
Russian Federation	..	..	..	0	0	..	..	..	0.0	0.0
Slovenia	..	..	..	0	0	..	..	..	0.0	0.0
Ukraine	..	..	..	0	0	..	..	..	0.0	0.0
Yugoslavia	..	..	..	0	0	..	..	..	0.0	0.0
Non-OECD Asia, of which:	..	..	1 111	594	2 761	..	..	0.5	0.3	1.0
China	..	..	..	..	0	..	..	..	..	0.0
Chinese Taipei	..	..	..	..	0	..	..	..	..	0.0
Hong Kong (China)	..	..	..	..	0	..	..	..	..	0.0
India	..	..	..	..	0	..	..	..	..	0.0
Indonesia	..	..	..	..	0	..	..	..	..	0.0
Malaysia	..	..	..	..	145	..	..	..	..	0.1
Philippines	..	..	..	..	0	..	..	..	..	0.0
Singapore	..	..	..	..	2 616	..	..	..	..	1.0
Thailand	..	..	..	..	0	..	..	..	..	0.0
Near and Middle East	..	..	..	..	457	..	..	..	..	0.2
Africa	..	..	..	0	0	..	..	..	0.0	0.0
Latin America, of which:	..	0	0	211	212	..	0.0	0.0	0.1	0.1
Argentina	..	0	0	0	0	..	0.0	0.0	0.0	0.0
Brazil	..	0	0	0	0	..	0.0	0.0	0.0	0.0
Chile	..	0	0	0	0	..	0.0	0.0	0.0	0.0

Note: Majority foreign-owned **non-financial** firms. Source: Statistics Sweden's Structural Business Statistics.

Firmes **non financières** sous contrôle étranger majoritaire. Source : Statistiques structurelles d'entreprises de l'office suédois de statistiques.

Table 7A - Tableau 7A
VALUE ADDED / VALEUR AJOUTÉE

By industry (ISIC Rev. 3)	Foreign affiliates *(Millions of SEK)* Filiales étrangères *(Millions de SEK)*					As a % of national total En % du total national				
	1994	1995	1996	1997	1998	1994	1995	1996	1997	1998
10/14 Mining & quarrying	282	516	417	671	650	5.7	8.7	7.9	10.1	10.7
15/37 TOTAL MANUFACTURING	**48 824**	**69 534**	**68 281**	**75 050**	**86 125**	**15.6**	**21.2**	**21.8**	**19.9**	**22.5**
15/16 Food, beverages, tobacco	6 008	5 763	9 192	10 611	8 753	24.0	23.3	33.9	35.9	30.0
17/19 Textiles, clothing, leather, footwear	1 119	969	1 124	1 122	1 197	25.6	19.6	24.5	24.0	25.0
20/22 Wood and paper products	3 497	4 655	4 960	5 203	12 757	5.0	6.1	8.2	7.5	18.2
20 Wood products	422	425	1 166	1 354	1 521	2.9	2.9	10.6	8.3	9.6
21/22 Paper, printing and publishing	3 075	4 230	3 794	3 849	11 236	5.6	6.9	7.6	7.3	20.7
23/25 Chemicals, Total	10 836	18 000	16 474	19 510	21 437	30.1	48.1	45.6	45.8	46.3
23 Refined petroleum, nuclear fuel	1 054	1 369	1 750	1 173	1 275	62.0	81.9	92.5	55.1	55.4
24/25 Chemicals, rubber & plastics prod.	9 782	16 631	14 724	18 337	20 162	28.5	46.5	43.0	45.3	45.8
24 Chemical products	8 317	14 770	12 901	15 641	17 145	32.8	56.5	52.4	52.0	51.9
2423 Pharmaceuticals	368	5 115	4 298	6 726	7 463	2.7	39.0	35.4	46.2	45.1
25 Rubber and plastics products	1 465	1 861	1 823	2 696	3 017	16.4	19.4	18.9	25.9	27.5
26 Non-metallic mineral products	2 103	2 589	2 600	3 097	2 952	31.9	36.1	34.7	40.5	37.9
27/28 Basic & fabricated metals	3 705	8 638	5 932	7 200	6 678	9.7	18.5	13.9	15.0	13.4
27 Basic metals	2 513	6 984	4 289	5 175	4 390	16.5	36.9	29.4	31.9	29.2
28 Fabricated metal products	1 192	1 654	1 643	2 025	2 288	5.2	6.0	5.8	6.4	6.5
29/32 Machinery, Total	16 237	21 385	19 821	18 275	20 385	24.1	28.7	25.3	16.5	22.6
29/30 Non-electrical machinery	11 191	16 203	14 613	13 533	13 969	24.7	33.3	29.8	26.2	26.7
29 Non-electrical machinery nec	10 515	15 757	14 191	12 976	13 227	25.0	33.5	30.2	26.1	26.5
30 Office and computing machinery	676	446	422	557	742	21.0	28.5	20.9	27.6	31.9
31/32 Electrical & electronic equipment	5 046	5 182	5 208	4 742	6 416	22.9	20.1	17.7	8.0	17.0
31 Electrical machinery nec	4 436	4 407	4 613	3 564	4 749	53.0	49.2	42.1	31.0	49.0
32 Radio, TV & communications eq.	610	775	595	1 178	1 667	4.4	4.6	3.2	2.5	5.9
33 Scientific instruments	2 705	3 341	3 679	4 513	4 923	31.1	32.1	33.7	33.6	34.6
34/35 Transportation equipment	2 085	3 005	2 924	3 847	5 070	4.0	7.8	7.8	9.0	8.3
34 Motor vehicles	1 088	2 170	2 004	2 878	4 202	3.9	6.9	6.6	7.7	8.2
35 Other transport equipment	997	835	920	969	868	4.1	12.3	12.4	18.8	9.1
351 Shipbuilding & repairing	70	..	..	63	73	5.4	..	..	4.1	4.4
353 Aircraft and spacecraft	43	..	..	..	..	0.2	..	..	..	..
36/37 Other manufacturing	528	1 189	1 574	1 667	1 973	8.4	15.8	19.8	18.8	20.9
40/45 Construction, electricity, gas & water	2 822	3 217	6 281	5 391	5 183	3.2	3.5	6.4	5.3	4.8
50/55 Trade, repair, hotels & restaurants	26 011	28 387	32 060	34 166	40 099	16.8	17.2	18.6	18.9	20.6
65/74 Finance, insurance, business services	10 507	12 586	14 524	23 890	26 961	13.0	13.3	14.9	12.8	12.9
OTHER ACTIVITIES	5 579	4 686	8 213	9 947	12 227	5.0	3.9	6.1	6.8	7.7
01/99 GRAND TOTAL	**94 025**	**118 926**	**129 776**	**149 110**	**171 246**	**12.5**	**14.8**	**15.8**	**14.9**	**16.2**

Total manufacturing by investing country						*As a % of total manufacturing by foreign affiliates*				
All countries	**48 824**	**69 534**	**68 281**	**75 050**	**86 125**	**100.0**	**100.0**	**100.0**	**100.0**	**100.0**
United States	4 899	11 247	13 053	16 727	19 542	10.0	16.2	19.1	22.3	22.7
Canada	..	..	..	..	..	..	..	..	..	..
Mexico	..	..	..	0	0	..	..	..	0.0	0.0
Japan	..	471	322	471	533	..	0.7	0.5	0.6	0.6
Europe	42 616	56 795	54 029	..	..	87.3	81.7	79.1	..	..
European Union (15)	29 067	38 941	34 760	36 980	43 421	59.5	56.0	50.9	49.3	50.4
Belgium	..	..	..	..	..	..	..	..	..	..
France	2 136	2 321	2 405	3 312	3 655	4.4	3.3	3.5	4.4	4.2
Germany	3 283	3 763	3 746	4 119	3 860	6.7	5.4	5.5	5.5	4.5
Italy	..	..	..	..	..	..	..	..	..	..
Netherlands	9 938	11 810	9 465	8 672	8 300	20.4	17.0	13.9	11.6	9.6
Spain	..	..	..	..	..	..	..	..	..	..
Sweden	..	..	..	..	..	..	..	..	..	..
United Kingdom	2 822	7 979	6 463	7 151	6 212	5.8	11.5	9.5	9.5	7.2
Switzerland	10 782	11 855	12 371	10 814	11 811	22.1	17.0	18.1	14.4	13.7
Australia and New Zealand	..	..	..	0	0	..	..	..	0.0	0.0
Asia (non-OECD)	..	..	683	277	1 011	..	..	1.0	0.4	1.2
Latin America	..	0	0	76	90	..	0.0	0.0	0.1	0.1

Note: Majority foreign-owned **non-financial** firms. Source: Statistics Sweden's Structural Business Statistics.
Firmes **non financières** sous contrôle étranger majoritaire. Source : Statistiques structurelles d'entreprises de l'office suédois de statistiques.

Inward investments

Investissements entrants

Table 8A - Tableau 8A

COMPENSATION OF EMPLOYEES / SALAIRES ET CHARGES SOCIALES

| | | Foreign affiliates *(Millions of SEK)* | | | | | As a % of national total | | | | |
| | | Filiales étrangères *(Millions de SEK)* | | | | | En % du total national | | | | |
By industry (ISIC Rev. 3)		1994	1995	1996	1997	1998	1994	1995	1996	1997	1998
10/14	Mining & quarrying	103	235	271	237	291	3.4	7.2	8.4	6.7	8.3
15/37	**TOTAL MANUFACTURING**	**31 466**	**44 003**	**47 441**	**48 166**	**56 952**	**17.2**	**21.6**	**21.4**	**20.3**	**22.9**
15/16	Food, beverages, tobacco	3 567	4 021	5 643	5 692	5 665	22.0	23.1	30.7	29.5	28.4
17/19	Textiles, clothing, leather, footwear	712	680	739	742	734	23.5	20.5	21.8	19.9	18.0
20/22	Wood and paper products	2 130	3 094	3 454	3 591	7 569	5.7	7.8	8.2	8.3	17.0
20	Wood products	225	263	771	882	1 308	2.7	3.0	8.8	8.6	11.8
21/22	Paper, printing and publishing	1 905	2 831	2 683	2 709	6 261	6.5	9.2	8.1	8.2	18.8
23/25	Chemicals, Total	5 656	8 894	9 888	9 732	10 901	32.4	46.9	46.9	41.5	43.0
23	Refined petroleum, nuclear fuel	563	745	974	455	566	66.0	80.6	95.6	41.6	46.5
24/25	Chemicals, rubber & plastics prod.	5 093	8 149	8 914	9 277	10 335	30.6	45.2	44.4	41.5	42.9
24	Chemical products	3 992	6 942	7 627	7 454	8 283	37.5	59.3	58.1	48.3	49.7
2423	Pharmaceuticals	172	2 431	2 808	2 780	2 993	3.8	47.6	47.6	41.6	41.1
25	Rubber and plastics products	1 101	1 207	1 287	1 823	2 052	18.4	19.1	18.5	26.3	27.5
26	Non-metallic mineral products	1 468	1 816	1 886	2 306	2 147	31.0	35.3	34.7	43.3	39.3
27/28	Basic & fabricated metals	2 366	4 402	4 343	4 957	5 115	9.9	15.9	14.5	14.2	13.7
27	Basic metals	1 477	3 221	3 124	3 435	3 361	17.7	35.6	32.4	35.2	33.8
28	Fabricated metal products	889	1 181	1 219	1 522	1 754	5.7	6.3	6.0	6.0	6.4
29/32	Machinery, Total	11 630	15 691	15 371	13 810	15 475	25.3	30.4	26.6	22.7	24.1
29/30	Non-electrical machinery	8 024	11 653	11 159	10 364	10 624	26.3	35.0	30.8	28.8	28.3
29	Non-electrical machinery nec	7 426	11 322	10 860	9 990	10 206	26.4	35.8	31.3	28.9	28.3
30	Office and computing machinery	598	331	299	374	418	25.2	20.7	19.4	27.1	27.5
31/32	Electrical & electronic equipment	3 606	4 038	4 212	3 446	4 851	23.3	22.1	19.5	13.9	18.3
31	Electrical machinery nec	3 107	3 396	3 623	2 627	3 644	52.3	51.0	43.9	30.1	50.5
32	Radio, TV & communications eq.	499	642	589	819	1 207	5.2	5.5	4.4	5.1	6.2
33	Scientific instruments	1 822	2 149	2 451	3 053	3 533	31.0	30.1	32.5	34.9	35.3
34/35	Transportation equipment	1 454	2 258	2 524	3 016	3 889	6.1	8.1	8.3	9.7	13.0
34	Motor vehicles	788	1 561	1 723	2 173	3 011	4.4	7.2	7.3	9.1	13.4
35	Other transport equipment	666	697	801	843	878	11.6	11.3	11.7	11.7	11.8
351	Shipbuilding & repairing	..	..	..	50	57	..	..	..	4.0	4.0
353	Aircraft and spacecraft	..	..	..	..	..	..	..	..	..	..
36/37	Other manufacturing	661	998	1 143	1 267	1 924	13.9	18.8	19.7	17.8	23.3
40/45	Construction, electricity, gas & water	2 347	2 627	3 571	3 385	3 089	4.5	4.9	6.1	5.8	5.0
50/55	Trade, repair, hotels & restaurants	16 265	18 674	21 029	24 183	28 180	14.7	15.7	17.0	18.5	19.8
65/74	Finance, insurance, business services	7 303	8 495	11 996	18 174	20 881	12.1	12.3	15.6	17.6	17.3
	OTHER ACTIVITIES	3 828	4 012	6 841	7 630	9 168	4.7	4.5	6.7	7.0	7.7
01/99	**GRAND TOTAL**	**61 311**	**78 046**	**91 148**	**101 775**	**118 561**	**12.5**	**14.5**	**15.5**	**15.8**	**17.0**

Total manufacturing by investing country							As a % of total manufacturing by foreign affiliates				
All countries		**31 466**	**44 003**	**47 441**	**48 166**	**56 952**	**100.0**	**100.0**	**100.0**	**100.0**	**100.0**
United States		3 201	6 948	8 812	9 091	11 343	10.2	15.8	18.6	18.9	19.9
Canada		..	..	..	..	..	..	..	..	..	..
Mexico		..	..	..	0	0	..	..	..	0.0	0.0
Japan		..	278	219	286	329	..	0.6	0.5	0.6	0.6
Europe		27 554	36 249	37 942	..	..	87.6	82.4	80.0	..	..
European Union (15)		18 030	23 993	23 955	24 736	28 914	57.3	54.5	50.5	51.4	50.8
Belgium		..	..	..	..	..	..	..	..	..	..
France		1 268	1 443	1 596	2 205	2 589	4.0	3.3	3.4	4.6	4.5
Germany		1 945	2 330	2 459	2 858	2 888	6.2	5.3	5.2	5.9	5.1
Italy		..	..	..	..	..	..	..	..	..	..
Netherlands		5 961	7 558	6 516	5 266	5 082	18.9	17.2	13.7	10.9	8.9
Spain		..	..	..	..	..	..	..	..	..	..
Sweden		..	..	..	..	..	..	..	..	..	..
United Kingdom		1 966	4 053	4 476	4 862	4 632	6.2	9.2	9.4	10.1	8.1
Switzerland		7 713	8 890	9 371	8 088	8 965	24.5	20.2	19.8	16.8	15.7
Australia and New Zealand		..	..	..	0	0	..	..	..	0.0	0.0
Asia (non-OECD)		..	..	314	268	781	..	..	0.7	0.6	1.4
Latin America		..	0	0	47	56	..	0.0	0.0	0.1	0.1

Note: Majority foreign-owned **non-financial** firms. Source: Statistics Sweden's Structural Business Statistics.

Firmes **non financières** sous contrôle étranger majoritaire. Source : Statistiques structurelles d'entreprises de l'office suédois de statistiques.

Inward investments   *Investissements entrants*

Table 9A - Tableau 9A

R&D EXPENDITURE / DÉPENSES DE R-D

		Foreign affiliates (Millions of SEK) Filiales étrangères (Millions de SEK)					As a % of national total En % du total national				
By industry (ISIC Rev. 3)		1994	1995	1996	1997	1998	1994	1995	1996	1997	1998
10/14	Mining & quarrying	..	..	3	1	1	..	..	3.5	5.3	0.4
15/37	**TOTAL MANUFACTURING**	3 933	7 725	7 517	7 413	8 293	9.1	19.0	18.7	14.1	16.0
15/16	Food, beverages, tobacco	66	76	91	124	127	25.0	28.3	29.3	43.4	30.5
17/19	Textiles, clothing, leather, footwear	33	50	48	51	49	60.0	71.4	55.2	75.0	62.8
20/22	Wood and paper products	18	25	35	55	315	2.4	3.2	3.5	7.2	29.9
20	Wood products	1	1	..	25	34	1.6	1.8	..	41.7	47.2
21/22	Paper, printing and publishing	17	24	..	30	281	2.5	3.3	..	4.2	28.6
23/25	Chemicals, Total	648	2 606	2 730	2 793	2 920	11.4	34.0	31.5	28.3	26.3
23	Refined petroleum, nuclear fuel	78	89	18	0	0	100.0	87.3	85.7	0.0	0.0
24/25	Chemicals, rubber & plastics prod.	570	2 517	2 712	2 793	2 920	10.1	33.3	31.4	28.3	26.6
24	Chemical products	410	2 440	2 617	2 709	2 830	7.9	34.1	31.8	28.1	26.4
2423	Pharmaceuticals	50	1 953	2 060	2 308	2 221	1.1	30.3	27.8	26.6	23.4
25	Rubber and plastics products	160	77	96	84	90	37.0	18.6	23.0	37.8	35.9
26	Non-metallic mineral products	51	60	57	80	73	35.7	33.9	31.1	51.9	45.3
27/28	Basic & fabricated metals	80	116	146	185	182	8.7	22.5	13.0	16.2	14.3
27	Basic metals	58	95	109	150	162	18.0	29.3	28.6	46.2	38.9
28	Fabricated metal products	22	21	37	35	20	3.7	10.9	5.0	4.3	2.3
29/32	Machinery, Total	2 000	3 517	2 867	1 933	2 207	7.7	19.8	14.0	7.8	7.6
29/30	Non-electrical machinery	1 296	2 642	1 942	1 360	1 603	8.0	49.9	36.5	27.9	33.6
29	Non-electrical machinery nec	1 121	2 493	1 797	1 279	1 533	29.8	50.0	35.6	27.8	34.5
30	Office and computing machinery	174	149	145	81	70	1.4	48.4	54.3	30.1	21.6
31/32	Electrical & electronic equipment	704	875	925	573	604	7.3	7.0	6.1	2.9	2.5
31	Electrical machinery nec	603	733	865	431	471	89.9	90.6	52.7	23.0	70.4
32	Radio, TV & communications eq.	101	142	60	142	133	1.1	1.2	0.4	0.8	0.6
33	Scientific instruments	885	1 040	1 165	1 593	1 804	36.6	38.2	40.9	53.9	45.1
34/35	Transportation equipment	132	175	234	405	515	1.8	1.6	4.4	3.3	11.4
34	Motor vehicles	36	74	91	64	498	0.7	0.9	2.5	0.6	12.4
35	Other transport equipment	96	101	143	341	17	5.2	5.1	8.2	18.4	3.5
351	Shipbuilding & repairing	..	..	..	0	1	..	..	..	0.0	2.7
353	Aircraft and spacecraft	..	..	..	0	..	..	..	..	0.0	..
36/37	Other manufacturing	20	60	146	194	101	21.1	51.7	74.1	80.5	65.6
40/45	Construction, electricity, gas & water	84	..	297	112	98	13.8	..	35.8	23.8	13.9
50/55	Trade, repair, hotels & restaurants	128	267	285	337	443	40.1	58.7	59.9	62.1	59.0
65/74	Finance, insurance, business services	762	511	1 001	1 708	1 924	26.8	13.5	18.5	35.7	32.8
	OTHER ACTIVITIES	84	9	3	1	1	9.2	0.7	0.2	0.1	0.0
01/99	**GRAND TOTAL**	4 990	8 512	9 106	9 572	10 760	10.4	18.4	18.7	15.9	17.5

Total manufacturing by investing country						As a % of total manufacturing by foreign affiliates				
All countries	3 933	7 725	7 517	7 413	8 293	100.0	100.0	100.0	100.0	100.0
United States	267	2 362	2 758	2 879	2 986	6.8	30.6	36.7	38.8	36.0
Canada	1	1	..	..	..	0.0	0.0	..	..	..
Mexico	..	..	..	0	0	..	..	..	0.0	0.0
Japan	14	7	4	4	30	0.4	0.1	0.1	0.1	0.4
Europe	3 608	5 349	4 676	..	..	91.7	69.2	62.2	..	..
European Union (15)	1 719	2 917	2 103	2 018	2 660	43.7	37.8	28.0	27.2	32.1
Belgium	4	4	..	..	..	0.1	0.1	..	..	..
France	63	84	109	104	107	1.6	1.1	1.5	1.4	1.3
Germany	405	336	441	761	469	10.3	4.3	5.9	10.3	5.7
Italy	11	6	..	..	..	0.3	0.1	..	..	..
Netherlands	773	1 805	923	399	831	19.7	23.4	12.3	5.4	10.0
Spain	..	..	..	..	..	..	..	..	..	..
Sweden										
United Kingdom	76	279	295	337	402	1.9	3.6	3.9	4.5	4.8
Switzerland	1 825	2 249	2 482	2 273	2 315	46.4	29.1	33.0	30.7	27.9
Australia and New Zealand	..	..	..	0	0	..	..	..	0.0	0.0
Asia (non-OECD)	..	..	0	3	20	..	..	0.0	0.0	0.2
Latin America	..	0	0	0	0	..	0.0	0.0	0.0	0.0

Note: Majority foreign-owned **non-financial** firms with 50 or more employees. Source: Statistics Sweden's Structural Business Statistics.

Firmes **non financières** sous contrôle étranger majoritaire de plus de 50 salariés. Source : Statistiques structurelles d'entreprises de l'office suédois de statistiques.

Inward investments   *Investissements entrants*

Table 10A - Tableau 10A

GROSS FIXED CAPITAL FORMATION / FORMATION BRUTE DE CAPITAL FIXE

	Foreign affiliates *(Millions of SEK)* Filiales étrangères *(Millions de SEK)*					As a % of national total En % du total national				
By industry (ISIC Rev. 3)	1994	1995	1996	1997	1998	1994	1995	1996	1997	1998
10/14 Mining & quarrying	56	101	90	147	203	3.3	5.2	5.3	6.8	8.1
15/37 TOTAL MANUFACTURING	**5 560**	**10 973**	**12 536**	**9 233**	**11 036**	**14.4**	**20.4**	**20.1**	**16.6**	**20.4**
15/16 Food, beverages, tobacco	1 020	1 171	1 045	1 218	1 586	29.4	28.5	30.5	31.9	42.6
17/19 Textiles, clothing, leather, footwear	118	71	89	147	138	27.8	13.4	13.3	37.4	26.1
20/22 Wood and paper products	476	583	795	584	3 308	4.6	3.6	4.4	4.0	24.1
20 Wood products	51	107	..	222	321	2.0	3.6	..	7.3	9.9
21/22 Paper, printing and publishing	425	476	..	362	2 987	5.5	3.6	..	3.1	28.5
23/25 Chemicals, Total	1 666	4 675	5 942	2 982	1 922	28.5	55.2	55.5	35.8	26.2
23 Refined petroleum, nuclear fuel	449	764	1 430	- 765	715	73.7	85.4	98.7	..	84.4
24/25 Chemicals, rubber & plastics prod.	1 217	3 911	4 512	3 747	1 207	23.2	51.6	48.7	41.8	18.6
24 Chemical products	1 024	3 652	4 270	3 323	723	26.0	58.8	57.2	45.8	15.4
2423 Pharmaceuticals	49	1 125	1 674	1 259	-1 450	2.0	36.5	41.0	34.6	..
25 Rubber and plastics products	193	258	242	424	484	14.8	18.9	13.5	24.6	27.0
26 Non-metallic mineral products	184	383	344	279	478	37.2	48.7	38.7	40.3	43.1
27/28 Basic & fabricated metals	284	1 298	1 045	998	970	7.4	19.9	14.8	12.4	10.8
27 Basic metals	236	1 119	894	764	723	16.5	39.5	31.0	21.8	19.8
28 Fabricated metal products	48	179	151	234	247	2.0	4.8	3.6	5.2	4.6
29/32 Machinery, Total	1 379	2 014	2 244	1 881	1 482	18.8	24.3	26.4	22.7	18.8
29/30 Non-electrical machinery	906	1 416	1 667	1 166	1 075	22.4	31.9	32.2	25.4	24.4
29 Non-electrical machinery nec	760	1 400	1 641	1 131	1 047	20.9	32.7	33.0	25.7	25.2
30 Office and computing machinery	146	16	26	35	28	36.8	10.3	12.1	19.1	11.9
31/32 Electrical & electronic equipment	473	598	577	715	407	14.4	15.5	17.4	19.4	11.7
31 Electrical machinery nec	383	406	424	457	356	55.8	48.0	35.0	38.3	32.9
32 Radio, TV & communications eq.	90	192	153	258	51	3.5	6.4	7.2	10.4	2.1
33 Scientific instruments	153	320	414	307	169	25.7	34.2	40.4	29.6	19.0
34/35 Transportation equipment	214	363	501	666	735	3.7	5.2	4.6	7.2	8.4
34 Motor vehicles	101	225	435	619	515	2.0	3.5	4.2	7.5	6.8
35 Other transport equipment	113	138	66	47	220	19.8	23.5	10.4	4.4	19.7
351 Shipbuilding & repairing	..	..	..	5	6	..	..	..	4.0	3.2
353 Aircraft and spacecraft	..	..	..	..	..	..	..	..	..	..
36/37 Other manufacturing	65	96	118	171	248	8.8	10.6	13.6	15.8	22.7
40/45 Construction, electricity, gas & water	87	93	147	977	1 310	0.7	0.6	0.9	5.4	6.7
50/55 Trade, repair, hotels & restaurants	1 930	2 617	3 330	4 932	4 194	15.6	17.2	18.8	24.1	21.4
65/74 Finance, insurance, business services	1 761	1 826	612	3 326	3 186	24.6	22.0	6.6	5.5	4.4
OTHER ACTIVITIES	1 657	1 201	1 615	2 470	2 656	8.7	4.9	5.0	7.4	9.1
01/99 GRAND TOTAL	**11 050**	**16 811**	**18 337**	**21 085**	**22 588**	**12.2**	**14.2**	**13.1**	**11.1**	**11.5**

Total manufacturing by investing country						As a % of total manufacturing by foreign affiliates				
All countries	**5 560**	**10 973**	**12 536**	**9 233**	**11 036**	**100.0**	**100.0**	**100.0**	**100.0**	**100.0**
United States	903	1 962	2 853	2 048	- 64	16.2	17.9	22.8	22.2	-0.6
Canada	..	..	..	..	..	..	..	..	..	..
Mexico	..	..	..	0	0	..	..	..	0.0	0.0
Japan	..	55	129	73	35	..	0.5	1.0	0.8	0.3
Europe	4 183	8 252	8 090	..	..	75.2	75.2	64.5	..	..
European Union (15)	2 681	6 064	6 009	5 601	8 125	48.2	55.3	47.9	60.7	73.6
Belgium	..	..	..	..	..	..	..	..	..	..
France	256	198	389	570	603	4.6	1.8	3.1	6.2	5.5
Germany	191	254	492	454	670	3.4	2.3	3.9	4.9	6.1
Italy	..	..	..	..	..	..	..	..	..	..
Netherlands	1 065	1 926	2 137	1 596	1 209	19.2	17.6	17.0	17.3	11.0
Spain	..	..	..	..	..	..	..	..	..	..
Sweden	..	..	..	..	..	..	..	..	..	..
United Kingdom	259	1 519	1 006	840	730	4.7	13.8	8.0	9.1	6.6
Switzerland	1 135	1 340	1 233	965	840	20.4	12.2	9.8	10.5	7.6
Australia and New Zealand	..	..	..	0	0	..	..	..	0.0	0.0
Asia (non-OECD)	..	..	1 111	107	88	..	..	8.9	1.2	0.8
Latin America	..	0	0	21	14	..	0.0	0.0	0.2	0.1

Note: Majority foreign-owned **non-financial** firms. Source: Statistics Sweden's Structural Business Statistics.
Firmes **non financières** sous contrôle étranger majoritaire. Source : Statistiques structurelles d'entreprises de l'office suédois de statistiques.

Table 11A - Tableau 11A

TOTAL EXPORTS BY INDUSTRY

EXPORTATIONS TOTALES PAR INDUSTRIE

		Foreign affiliates *(Millions of SEK)* Filiales étrangères *(Millions de SEK)*					As a % of national total En % du total national				
ISIC Revision 3		1994	1995	1996	1997	1998	1994	1995	1996	1997	1998
10/14	Mining & quarrying	272	610	715	786	675	4.4	9.6	10.1	9.7	8.8
15/37	**TOTAL MANUFACTURING**	**78 415**	**107 290**	**108 892**	**111 385**	**133 930**	**17.8**	**20.6**	**20.7**	**21.8**	**26.8**
15/16	Food, beverages, tobacco	2 929	3 442	3 963	4 631	4 389	35.4	33.8	36.8	40.4	40.9
17/19	Textiles, clothing, leather, footwear	1 442	1 463	1 528	1 610	1 805	33.0	31.9	31.7	32.0	32.5
20/22	Wood and paper products	3 694	4 352	6 105	8 838	25 290	4.6	4.7	7.6	10.6	36.1
20	Wood products	..	944	..	2 630	2 325	..	..	..	12.4	11.7
21/22	Paper, printing and publishing	..	3 408	..	6 208	22 966	..	..	..	10.0	45.9
23/25	Chemicals, Total	18 288	30 366	29 218	28 546	30 900	35.1	53.0	53.4	46.1	47.9
23	Refined petroleum, nuclear fuel	680	622	1 568	677	1 037	48.3	43.1	96.5	40.3	62.7
24/25	Chemicals, rubber & plastics prod.	17 608	29 744	27 650	27 869	29 863	34.8	53.3	52.0	46.3	47.5
24	Chemical products	15 042	28 010	25 289	24 602	25 887	36.8	62.1	60.1	49.8	50.0
2423	Pharmaceuticals	709	8 601	8 734	8 702	9 313	3.2	39.5	39.8	36.0	33.8
25	Rubber and plastics products	2 566	1 734	2 360	3 268	3 976	26.1	16.1	21.4	30.3	35.8
26	Non-metallic mineral products	1 852	2 655	2 624	3 450	2 878	51.0	59.2	58.4	64.5	56.0
27/28	Basic & fabricated metals	8 966	19 846	17 565	17 634	15 447	18.3	34.7	31.8	30.4	28.7
27	Basic metals	7 603	18 305	15 197	15 438	13 236	25.0	50.9	46.2	43.6	40.9
28	Fabricated metal products	1 363	1 541	2 368	2 196	2 211	7.3	7.3	10.6	9.7	10.3
29/32	Machinery, Total	32 281	33 112	35 596	32 713	35 214	25.6	22.2	21.1	19.4	22.9
29/30	Non-electrical machinery	25 806	26 168	27 229	24 496	25 815	34.2	31.0	32.3	31.5	39.5
29	Non-electrical machinery nec	25 039	25 038	25 979	23 206	24 630	34.7	30.7	32.0	30.9	39.5
30	Office and computing machinery	767	1 130	1 250	1 290	1 185	23.7	37.9	40.0	47.1	38.4
31/32	Electrical & electronic equipment	6 475	6 944	8 367	8 217	9 399	12.8	10.7	9.9	9.0	10.6
31	Electrical machinery nec	4 889	5 343	6 686	5 291	6 749	62.5	58.3	54.5	40.8	62.2
32	Radio, TV & communications eq.	1 586	1 601	1 681	2 926	2 650	3.7	2.9	2.3	3.8	3.4
33	Scientific instruments	5 576	6 447	6 558	6 773	8 493	41.8	47.2	44.8	42.8	42.8
34/35	Transportation equipment	2 754	4 702	4 658	5 822	7 878	2.7	3.7	3.7	6.2	7.3
34	Motor vehicles	1 335	2 805	2 669	3 817	6 185	1.4	2.4	2.3	4.8	6.7
35	Other transport equipment	1 419	1 897	1 989	2 005	1 693	23.2	21.1	20.1	13.7	10.6
351	Shipbuilding & repairing	..	..	..	14	32	..	..	..	1.8	1.6
353	Aircraft and spacecraft	..	..	..	..	..	..	..	..	..	..
36/37	Other manufacturing	634	905	1 077	1 367	1 638	12.6	16.0	16.9	18.7	20.4
40/45	Construction, electricity, gas & water	485	0	313	537	888	17.9	..	9.3	12.9	23.0
50/55	Trade, repair, hotels & restaurants	25 967	24 749	36 119	36 293	35 413	41.8	48.4	53.3	51.3	51.1
65/74	Finance, insurance, business services	2 751	13 190	3 117	6 178	3 885	35.6	..	37.1	63.1	47.5
	OTHER ACTIVITIES	2 081	672	2 039	2 060	3 940	34.7	7.8	24.2	33.7	59.5
01/99	**GRAND TOTAL**	**109 972**	**146 511**	**151 199**	**157 242**	**178 731**	**20.9**	**24.6**	**24.4**	**25.8**	**30.0**

Note: Majority foreign-owned **non-financial** firms. Source: Statistics Sweden's Structural Business Statistics and Trade Statistics.
Firmes **non financières** sous contrôle étranger majoritaire. Source : office suédois de statistiques, Statistiques structurelles d'entreprises et Statistiques du commerce.

Inward investments   *Investissements entrants*

Table 12A - Tableau 12A

TOTAL EXPORTS BY COUNTRY OF ORIGIN IN THE MANUFACTURING SECTOR
EXPORTATIONS TOTALES PAR PAYS D'ORIGINE DANS L'INDUSTRIE MANUFACTURIÈRE

Country of origin (UBO)	Total exports (Millions of SEK) Exportations totales (Millions de SEK)					As a % of all countries En % du total des pays				
	1994	1995	1996	1997	1998	1994	1995	1996	1997	1998
All countries	78 415	107 290	108 892	111 385	133 930	100.0	100.0	100.0	100.0	100.0
Total OECD	..	107 013	108 540	111 150	133 277	..	99.7	99.7	99.8	99.5
United States	6 433	18 862	21 270	20 840	24 282	8.2	17.6	19.5	18.7	18.1
Canada	..	..	296	603	594	..	..	0.3	0.5	0.4
Mexico	..	..	..	0	0	..	..	..	0.0	0.0
Japan	..	301	623	1 003	987	..	0.3	0.6	0.9	0.7
Korea	..	..	..	0	0	..	..	..	0.0	0.0
Australia	..	..	..	0	0	..	..	..	0.0	0.0
New Zealand	..	..	..	0	0	..	..	..	0.0	0.0
Europe	68 555	87 450	86 601	88 704	107 935	87.4	81.5	79.5	79.6	80.6
European Union (15)	48 595	56 252	56 885	65 524	82 803	62.0	52.4	52.2	58.8	61.8
Austria	..	1 748	..	1 502	1 717	..	1.6	..	1.3	1.3
Belgium	..	159	268	222	246	..	0.1	0.2	0.2	0.2
Denmark	..	1 087	..	2 304	2 482	..	1.0	..	2.1	1.9
Finland	..	18 365	14 222	16 010	34 870	..	17.1	13.1	14.4	26.0
France	2 513	3 243	2 927	4 401	4 393	3.2	3.0	2.7	4.0	3.3
Germany	5 078	4 809	6 844	7 300	7 590	6.5	4.5	6.3	6.6	5.7
Greece	..	..	..	0	0	..	..	..	0.0	0.0
Ireland	..	..	44	47	0	..	..	0.0	0.0	0.0
Italy	..	542	597	316	333	..	0.5	0.5	0.3	0.2
Luxembourg	..	..	..	38	51	..	..	..	0.0	0.0
Netherlands	17 241	10 374	12 210	16 046	16 910	22.0	9.7	11.2	14.4	12.6
Portugal	..	..	..	0	0	..	..	..	0.0	0.0
Spain	..	..	91	116	85	..	..	0.1	0.1	0.1
Sweden	..	..	..	..	..	..	..	..	..	..
United Kingdom	5 078	15 850	16 874	17 222	14 125	6.5	14.8	15.5	15.5	10.5
Czech Republic	..	..	..	0	0	..	..	..	0.0	0.0
Hungary	..	..	..	0	0	..	..	..	0.0	0.0
Iceland	..	..	..	0	0	..	..	..	0.0	0.0
Norway	..	10 705	..	9 816	9 570	..	10.0	..	8.8	7.1
Poland	..	..	..	0	0	..	..	..	0.0	0.0
Slovak Republic	..	..	..	0	0	..	..	..	0.0	0.0
Switzerland	16 279	20 456	20 498	13 364	15 042	20.8	19.1	18.8	12.0	11.2
Turkey	..	..	..	0	0	..	..	..	0.0	0.0
Non-OECD Europe, of which:	..	..	..	0	525	..	..	..	0.0	0.4
Baltic countries	..	..	..	0	0	..	..	..	0.0	0.0
Bulgaria	..	..	..	0	0	..	..	..	0.0	0.0
Croatia	..	..	..	0	0	..	..	..	0.0	0.0
Romania	..	..	..	0	0	..	..	..	0.0	0.0
Russian Federation	..	..	..	0	0	..	..	..	0.0	0.0
Slovenia	..	..	..	0	0	..	..	..	0.0	0.0
Ukraine	..	..	..	0	0	..	..	..	0.0	0.0
Yugoslavia	..	..	..	0	0	..	..	..	0.0	0.0
Non-OECD Asia, of which:	..	..	185	24	62	..	..	0.2	0.0	0.0
China	..	..	..	..	0	..	..	..	..	0.0
Chinese Taipei	..	..	..	..	0	..	..	..	..	0.0
Hong Kong (China)	..	..	..	..	0	..	..	..	..	0.0
India	..	..	..	..	0	..	..	..	..	0.0
Indonesia	..	..	..	..	0	..	..	..	..	0.0
Malaysia	..	..	..	..	31	..	..	..	..	0.0
Philippines	..	..	..	..	0	..	..	..	..	0.0
Singapore	..	..	..	..	31	..	..	..	..	0.0
Thailand	..	..	..	..	0	..	..	..	..	0.0
Near and Middle East	..	..	..	..	6	..	..	..	..	0.0
Africa	..	..	..	0	0	..	..	..	0.0	0.0
Latin America, of which:	..	0	0	56	60	..	0.0	0.0	0.1	0.0
Argentina	..	0	0	0	0	..	0.0	0.0	0.0	0.0
Brazil	..	0	0	0	0	..	0.0	0.0	0.0	0.0
Chile	..	0	0	0	0	..	0.0	0.0	0.0	0.0

Note: Majority foreign-owned **non-financial** firms. Source: Statistics Sweden's Structural Business Statistics and Trade Statistics.
Firmes **non financières** sous contrôle étranger majoritaire. Source : office suédois de statistiques, Statistiques structurelles d'entreprises et Statistiques du commerce.

Table 13A - Tableau 13A

TOTAL IMPORTS BY INDUSTRY

IMPORTATIONS TOTALES PAR INDUSTRIE

		Foreign affiliates *(Millions of SEK)* Filiales étrangères *(Millions de SEK)*					As a % of national total *En % du total national*				
ISIC Revision 3		1994	1995	1996	1997	1998	1994	1995	1996	1997	1998
10/14	Mining & quarrying	..	59	80	159	138	..	3.3	4.8	8.0	6.8
15/37	**TOTAL MANUFACTURING**	**34 503**	**50 423**	**50 334**	**58 126**	**62 234**	**28.2**	**29.4**	**30.3**	**29.1**	**30.8**
15/16	Food, beverages, tobacco	..	5 246	5 877	7 219	7 551	..	44.3	49.7	53.8	52.8
17/19	Textiles, clothing, leather, footwear	..	704	859	815	880	..	15.5	23.2	20.2	21.2
20/22	Wood and paper products	..	2 121	2 299	2 597	3 887	..	19.7	24.4	20.8	35.6
20	Wood products	..	..	..	668	884	..	..	..	29.6	33.2
21/22	Paper, printing and publishing	..	..	..	1 929	3 003	..	..	..	18.9	36.3
23/25	Chemicals, Total	..	14 513	15 706	16 290	16 843	..	54.5	58.2	51.2	53.2
23	Refined petroleum, nuclear fuel	..	1 762	2 457	1 014	1 151	..	87.2	96.8	53.2	55.4
24/25	Chemicals, rubber & plastics prod.	..	12 751	13 249	15 276	15 692	..	51.8	54.2	51.1	53.1
24	Chemical products	..	11 301	11 736	13 439	12 444	..	58.7	61.4	54.3	50.6
2423	Pharmaceuticals	..	1 333	1 444	1 955	1 957	..	20.6	21.0	21.9	19.3
25	Rubber and plastics products	..	1 449	1 513	1 837	3 248	..	27.1	28.3	35.6	65.8
26	Non-metallic mineral products	..	1 524	1 368	1 575	1 621	..	51.9	54.9	50.4	51.4
27/28	Basic & fabricated metals	..	10 237	8 749	10 833	9 356	..	45.8	44.1	41.3	38.1
27	Basic metals	..	8 520	7 382	9 239	7 476	..	57.5	56.0	55.4	50.3
28	Fabricated metal products	..	1 717	1 367	1 594	1 880	..	22.8	20.6	16.6	19.4
29/32	Machinery, Total	..	10 566	9 686	10 737	12 086	..	27.4	25.2	20.4	24.3
29/30	Non-electrical machinery	..	6 652	6 146	6 676	7 350	..	33.5	33.7	29.5	34.6
29	Non-electrical machinery nec	..	6 432	5 918	6 371	7 008	..	33.5	34.0	29.2	34.9
30	Office and computing machinery	..	220	228	305	342	..	33.8	28.4	39.0	29.4
31/32	Electrical & electronic equipment	..	3 914	3 540	4 061	4 736	..	21.0	17.5	13.5	16.6
31	Electrical machinery nec	..	2 711	2 431	2 275	2 864	..	55.8	44.4	37.6	54.5
32	Radio, TV & communications eq.	..	1 203	1 109	1 786	1 872	..	8.7	7.5	7.4	8.0
33	Scientific instruments	..	2 318	2 513	3 222	3 988	..	45.5	51.0	53.4	55.0
34/35	Transportation equipment	..	2 192	2 288	3 422	4 176	..	4.7	5.0	7.3	8.0
34	Motor vehicles	..	1 816	1 855	2 819	3 747	..	4.9	5.1	7.5	8.6
35	Other transport equipment	..	376	433	603	429	..	4.2	4.7	6.6	4.9
351	Shipbuilding & repairing	..	..	..	14	26	..	..	..	6.1	7.2
353	Aircraft and spacecraft	..	..	..	..	..	..	..	..	..	..
36/37	Other manufacturing	..	1 001	989	1 417	1 846	..	35.2	36.4	44.7	47.4
40/45	Construction, electricity, gas & water	..	369	351	339	878	..	10.9	6.5	5.7	15.1
50/55	Trade, repair, hotels & restaurants	..	92 001	103 800	124 887	123 091	..	47.5	50.6	51.0	49.8
65/74	Finance, insurance, business services	..	3 431	2 382	4 450	3 384	..	71.9	42.7	75.4	36.9
	OTHER ACTIVITIES	..	363	438	4 490	6 469	..	3.4	3.8	30.6	45.0
01/99	**GRAND TOTAL**	**..**	**146 645**	**157 385**	**192 452**	**196 195**	**..**	**38.0**	**39.8**	**40.7**	**40.8**

Note: Majority foreign-owned **non-financial** firms. Imports of goods. Source: Statistics Sweden's Structural Business Statistics and Trade Statistics.

Firmes **non financières** sous contrôle étranger majoritaire. Importations de biens. Source : office suédois de statistiques, Statistiques structurelles d'entreprises et Statistiques du commerce.

Inward investments

Investissements entrants

Table 14A - Tableau 14A

TOTAL IMPORTS BY COUNTRY OF ORIGIN IN THE MANUFACTURING SECTOR

IMPORTATIONS TOTALES PAR PAYS D'ORIGINE DANS L'INDUSTRIE MANUFACTURIÈRE

Country of origin (UBO)	Total imports (Millions of SEK) Importations totales (Millions de SEK)					As a % of all countries En % du total des pays				
	1994	1995	1996	1997	1998	1994	1995	1996	1997	1998
All countries	34 503	50 423	50 334	58 126	62 234	100.0	100.0	100.0	100.0	100.0
Total OECD	..	..	49 785	57 422	61 432	..	..	98.9	98.8	98.7
United States	..	7 505	7 766	10 486	12 829	..	14.9	15.4	18.0	20.6
Canada	..	119	92	198	215	..	0.2	0.2	0.3	0.3
Mexico	..	..	..	0	0	..	..	..	0.0	0.0
Japan	..	419	374	496	552	..	0.8	0.7	0.9	0.9
Korea	..	..	..	0	0	..	..	..	0.0	0.0
Australia	..	..	..	0	0	..	..	..	0.0	0.0
New Zealand	..	..	..	0	0	..	..	..	0.0	0.0
Europe	..	42 114	42 020	46 242	48 062	..	83.5	83.5	79.6	77.2
European Union (15)	..	28 027	27 383	32 144	34 589	..	55.6	54.4	55.3	55.6
Austria	..	..	..	430	534	..	..	..	0.7	0.9
Belgium	..	102	152	178	206	..	0.2	0.3	0.3	0.3
Denmark	..	..	..	1 673	2 333	..	..	..	2.9	3.7
Finland	..	8 062	6 685	7 608	9 381	..	16.0	13.3	13.1	15.1
France	..	1 988	1 748	2 356	4 148	..	3.9	3.5	4.1	6.7
Germany	..	3 087	3 311	3 902	3 864	..	6.1	6.6	6.7	6.2
Greece	..	..	..	0	0	..	..	..	0.0	0.0
Ireland	..	16	18	13	0	..	0.0	0.0	0.0	0.0
Italy	..	47	149	136	165	..	0.1	0.3	0.2	0.3
Luxembourg	..	..	..	16	16	..	..	..	0.0	0.0
Netherlands	..	5 249	4 955	5 763	6 027	..	10.4	9.8	9.9	9.7
Portugal	..	..	..	0	0	..	..	..	0.0	0.0
Spain	..	..	47	9	7	..	..	0.1	0.0	0.0
Sweden	..	..	..	..	..	..	..	..	..	..
United Kingdom	..	7 964	8 623	10 060	7 907	..	15.8	17.1	17.3	12.7
Czech Republic	..	..	..	0	0	..	..	..	0.0	0.0
Hungary	..	..	..	0	0	..	..	..	0.0	0.0
Iceland	..	..	..	0	0	..	..	..	0.0	0.0
Norway	..	..	..	8 688	7 689	..	..	..	14.9	12.4
Poland	..	..	..	0	0	..	..	..	0.0	0.0
Slovak Republic	..	..	..	0	0	..	..	..	0.0	0.0
Switzerland	..	8 330	6 976	5 410	5 559	..	16.5	13.9	9.3	8.9
Turkey	..	..	..	0	0	..	..	..	0.0	0.0
Non-OECD Europe, of which:	..	..	..	0	226	..	..	..	0.0	0.4
Baltic countries	..	..	..	0	0	..	..	..	0.0	0.0
Bulgaria	..	..	..	0	0	..	..	..	0.0	0.0
Croatia	..	..	..	0	0	..	..	..	0.0	0.0
Romania	..	..	..	0	0	..	..	..	0.0	0.0
Russian Federation	..	..	..	0	0	..	..	..	0.0	0.0
Slovenia	..	..	..	0	0	..	..	..	0.0	0.0
Ukraine	..	..	..	0	0	..	..	..	0.0	0.0
Yugoslavia	..	..	..	0	0	..	..	..	0.0	0.0
Non-OECD Asia, of which:	..	..	432	402	515	..	..	0.9	0.7	0.8
China	..	..	..	..	0	..	..	..	..	0.0
Chinese Taipei	..	..	..	..	0	..	..	..	..	0.0
Hong Kong (China)	..	..	..	..	0	..	..	..	..	0.0
India	..	..	..	..	0	..	..	..	..	0.0
Indonesia	..	..	..	..	0	..	..	..	..	0.0
Malaysia	..	..	..	..	10	..	..	..	..	0.0
Philippines	..	..	..	..	0	..	..	..	..	0.0
Singapore	..	..	..	..	505	..	..	..	..	0.8
Thailand	..	..	..	..	0	..	..	..	..	0.0
Near and Middle East	..	..	..	..	2	..	..	..	..	0.0
Africa	..	..	..	0	0	..	..	..	0.0	0.0
Latin America, of which:	..	0	0	68	59	..	0.0	0.0	0.1	0.1
Argentina	..	0	0	0	0	..	0.0	0.0	0.0	0.0
Brazil	..	0	0	0	0	..	0.0	0.0	0.0	0.0
Chile	..	0	0	0	0	..	0.0	0.0	0.0	0.0

Note: Majority foreign-owned **non-financial** firms. Imports of goods. Source: Statistics Sweden's Structural Business Statistics and Trade Statistics.

Firmes **non financières** sous contrôle étranger majoritaire. Importations de biens. Source : office suédois de statistiques, Statistiques structurelles d'entreprises et Statistiques du commerce.

Table 15A - Tableau 15A

INTRA-FIRM EXPORTS BY INDUSTRY

EXPORTATIONS INTRA-FIRME PAR INDUSTRIE

| | | **Foreign affiliates** *(Millions of SEK)* | | | | | | | | | |
| | | **Filiales étrangères** *(Millions de SEK)* | | | | | | | | | |
ISIC Revision 3		1989	1990	1991	1992	1993	1994	1995	1996	1997	1998
10/14	Mining & quarrying	..	152	164	174	161	20	373	418	36	67
15/37	**TOTAL MANUFACTURING**	..	**23 911**	**24 357**	**26 700**	**27 114**	**33 021**	**56 208**	**58 275**	**62 838**	**74 431**
15/16	Food, beverages, tobacco	..	409	549	667	809	1 670	2 325	2 484	2 863	2 996
17/19	Textiles, clothing, leather, footwear	..	22	287	308	243	251	432	328	374	420
20/22	Wood and paper products	..	350	327	241	465	620	544	1 820	1 499	10 843
20	Wood products	..	..	..	..	60	79	94	..	654	507
21/22	Paper, printing and publishing	..	..	..	..	405	541	450	..	845	10 336
23/25	Chemicals, Total	..	2 504	3 026	5 259	5 470	8 786	15 740	15 792	19 012	20 750
23	Refined petroleum, nuclear fuel	..	4	3	2	..	32	67	355	219	238
24/25	Chemicals, rubber & plastics prod.	..	2 500	3 023	5 257	5 443	8 754	15 673	15 437	18 793	20 512
24	Chemical products	..	2 369	2 646	4 576	4 311	7 961	14 956	14 071	16 812	17 761
2423	Pharmaceuticals	..	28	19	20	17	429	5 657	5 868	7 515	8 220
25	Rubber and plastics products	..	131	377	681	1 149	1 221	717	1 366	1 981	2 751
26	Non-metallic mineral products	..	558	338	408	400	500	863	859	1 059	1 034
27/28	Basic & fabricated metals	..	1 638	2 425	2 041	2 118	3 029	9 874	9 967	11 511	8 535
27	Basic metals	..	1 069	1 434	1 368	1 856	2 780	9 398	9 090	10 476	7 640
28	Fabricated metal products	..	569	991	673	262	249	476	877	1 035	895
29/32	Machinery, Total	..	17 271	16 495	14 367	13 932	13 609	19 979	20 579	18 614	20 793
29/30	Non-electrical machinery	..	11 874	11 065	10 577	10 107	9 636	15 923	15 361	14 047	15 982
29	Non-electrical machinery nec	..	6 394	6 408	6 276	9 743	8 940	15 102	14 523	12 872	14 250
30	Office and computing machinery	..	5 480	4 657	4 301	364	696	821	838	1 175	1 732
31/32	Electrical & electronic equipment	..	5 397	5 430	3 790	3 825	3 973	4 056	5 218	4 567	4 811
31	Electrical machinery nec	..	2 723	3 670	3 692	3 385	2 798	3 043	4 093	3 220	3 924
32	Radio, TV & communications eq.	..	2 674	1 760	98	440	1 175	1 013	1 125	1 317	887
33	Scientific instruments	..	500	405	2 811	2 848	3 606	4 295	4 627	5 404	6 419
34/35	Transportation equipment	..	585	461	524	702	712	1 675	1 319	1 997	2 150
34	Motor vehicles	..	164	141	151	370	236	966	642	1 798	1 651
35	Other transport equipment	..	421	320	373	332	476	709	677	699	499
351	Shipbuilding & repairing	..	..	..	..	16	43	..	..	7	16
353	Aircraft and spacecraft	..	..	..	..	..	..	..	..	..	..
36/37	Other manufacturing	..	73	46	75	129	239	481	502	506	491
40/45	Construction, electricity, gas & water	..	0	0	0	0	0	0	1	311	107
50/55	Trade, repair, hotels & restaurants	..	1 831	1 922	3 027	5 117	4 775	6 900	7 278	12 318	12 477
65/74	Finance, insurance, business services	..	313	696	482	555	1 298	1 659	1 581	7 180	8 392
	OTHER ACTIVITIES	..	414	172	274	659	1 048	504	1 218	1 865	4 832
01/99	**GRAND TOTAL**	..	**26 620**	**27 311**	**30 656**	**33 606**	**40 161**	**65 644**	**68 771**	**84 548**	**100 306**

Note: Majority foreign-owned **non-financial** firms. Source: Statistics Sweden's Structural Business Statistics.
Firmes **non financières** sous contrôle étranger majoritaire. Source : Statistiques structurelles d'entreprises de l'office suédois de statistiques.

Table 16A - Tableau 16A

INTRA-FIRM EXPORTS BY COUNTRY OF ORIGIN IN THE MANUFACTURING SECTOR

EXPORTATIONS INTRA-FIRME PAR PAYS D'ORIGINE DANS L'INDUSTRIE MANUFACTURIÈRE

Country of origin (UBO)	Intra-firm exports *(Millions of SEK)* Exportations intra-firme *(Millions de SEK)*					As a % of all countries En % du total des pays				
	1994	1995	1996	1997	1998	1994	1995	1996	1997	1998
All countries	33 021	56 209	58 275	62 838	74 431	100.0	100.0	100.0	100.0	100.0
Total OECD	32 778	56 103	58 248	62 528	74 383	99.3	99.8	100.0	99.5	99.9
United States	3 152	11 245	12 690	13 768	15 682	9.5	20.0	21.8	21.9	21.1
Canada	..	0	23	226	218	..	0.0	0.0	0.4	0.3
Mexico	0	0	0	0	0	0.0	0.0	0.0	0.0	0.0
Japan	47	49	134	301	296	0.1	0.1	0.2	0.5	0.4
Korea	0	0	0	0	0	0.0	0.0	0.0	0.0	0.0
Australia	0	0	0	0	0	0.0	0.0	0.0	0.0	0.0
New Zealand	0	0	0	0	0	0.0	0.0	0.0	0.0	0.0
Europe	29 552	44 809	45 415	48 233	58 210	89.5	79.7	77.9	76.8	78.2
European Union (15)	19 918	28 257	29 201	32 422	41 864	60.3	50.3	50.1	51.6	56.2
Austria	1 336	1 366	..	1 353	1 472	4.0	2.4	..	2.2	2.0
Belgium	..	49	35	23	32	..	0.1	0.1	0.0	0.0
Denmark	262	345	..	1 299	1 378	0.8	0.6	..	2.1	1.9
Finland	6 999	6 507	5 761	5 544	16 493	21.2	11.6	9.9	8.8	22.2
France	1 412	1 713	1 699	2 428	2 850	4.3	3.0	2.9	3.9	3.8
Germany	3 142	2 841	4 437	3 866	4 913	9.5	5.1	7.6	6.2	6.6
Greece	0	0	0	0	0	0.0	0.0	0.0	0.0	0.0
Ireland	..	0	..	0	0	..	0.0	..	0.0	0.0
Italy	..	63	95	136	93	..	0.1	0.2	0.2	0.1
Luxembourg	..	44	..	1	0	..	0.1	..	0.0	0.0
Netherlands	4 955	5 848	5 678	6 224	6 887	15.0	10.4	9.7	9.9	9.3
Portugal	0	0	0	0	0	0.0	0.0	0.0	0.0	0.0
Spain	..	0	..	2	6	..	0.0	..	0.0	0.0
Sweden	..	..	..	..	..	..	..	..	..	..
United Kingdom	1 707	9 481	9 873	11 546	7 738	5.2	16.9	16.9	18.4	10.4
Czech Republic	0	0	..	0	0	0.0	0.0	..	0.0	0.0
Hungary	0	0	..	0	0	0.0	0.0	..	0.0	0.0
Iceland	0	0	..	0	0	0.0	0.0	..	0.0	0.0
Norway	887	4 847	..	5 498	4 668	2.7	8.6	..	8.7	6.3
Poland	0	0	..	0	0	0.0	0.0	..	0.0	0.0
Slovak Republic	0	0	..	0	0	0.0	0.0	..	0.0	0.0
Switzerland	8 747	11 705	11 621	10 313	11 658	26.5	20.8	19.9	16.4	15.7
Turkey	0	0	..	0	0	0.0	0.0	..	0.0	0.0
Non-OECD Europe, of which:	0	0	..	0	0	0.0	0.0	..	0.0	0.0
Baltic countries	0	0	..	0	0	0.0	0.0	..	0.0	0.0
Bulgaria	0	0	..	0	0	0.0	0.0	..	0.0	0.0
Croatia	0	0	..	0	0	0.0	0.0	..	0.0	0.0
Romania	0	0	..	0	0	0.0	0.0	..	0.0	0.0
Russian Federation	0	0	..	0	0	0.0	0.0	..	0.0	0.0
Slovenia	0	0	..	0	0	0.0	0.0	..	0.0	0.0
Ukraine	0	0	..	0	0	0.0	0.0	..	0.0	0.0
Yugoslavia	0	0	..	0	0	0.0	0.0	..	0.0	0.0
Non-OECD Asia, of which:	..	0	0	270	23	..	0.0	0.0	0.4	0.0
China	..	0	0	..	0	..	0.0	0.0	..	0.0
Chinese Taipei	..	0	0	..	0	..	0.0	0.0	..	0.0
Hong Kong (China)	..	0	0	..	0	..	0.0	0.0	..	0.0
India	..	0	0	..	0	..	0.0	0.0	..	0.0
Indonesia	..	0	0	..	0	..	0.0	0.0	..	0.0
Malaysia	..	0	0	..	12	..	0.0	0.0	..	0.0
Philippines	..	0	0	..	0	..	0.0	0.0	..	0.0
Singapore	..	0	0	..	2	..	0.0	0.0	..	0.0
Thailand	..	0	0	..	0	..	0.0	0.0	..	0.0
Near and Middle East	..	0	..	..	0	..	0.0	..	..	0.0
Africa	0	0	0	0	0	0.0	0.0	0.0	0.0	0.0
Latin America, of which:	..	0	0	86	0	..	0.0	0.0	0.1	0.0
Argentina	..	0	0	0	0	..	0.0	0.0	0.0	0.0
Brazil	..	0	0	0	0	..	0.0	0.0	0.0	0.0
Chile	..	0	0	0	0	..	0.0	0.0	0.0	0.0

Note: Majority foreign-owned **non-financial** firms. Source: Statistics Sweden's Structural Business Statistics.

Firmes **non financières** sous contrôle étranger majoritaire. Source : Statistiques structurelles d'entreprises de l'office suédois de statistiques.

Table 17A - Tableau 17A

GROSS OPERATING SURPLUS / EXCÉDENT BRUT D'EXPLOITATION

| | | Foreign affiliates *(Millions of SEK)* | | | | | As a % of national total | | | | |
| | | Filiales étrangères *(Millions de SEK)* | | | | | En % du total national | | | | |
By industry (ISIC Rev. 3)		1994	1995	1996	1997	1998	1994	1995	1996	1997	1998
10/14	Mining & quarrying	179	275	146	435	350	9.3	10.1	7.2	13.8	13.7
15/37	**TOTAL MANUFACTURING**	17 358	25 915	20 840	24 695	26 401	13.3	20.7	22.7	20.2	22.9
15/16	Food, beverages, tobacco	2 441	2 496	3 549	4 602	2 933	27.5	28.6	40.6	46.9	32.3
17/19	Textiles, clothing, leather, footwear	406	306	386	310	435	30.2	18.7	32.4	26.7	35.3
20/22	Wood and paper products	1 367	1 634	1 506	1 406	4 780	4.3	4.3	8.0	6.0	19.9
20	Wood products	197	161	..	407	144	3.1	2.8	..	7.5	3.4
21/22	Paper, printing and publishing	1 170	1 473	..	999	4 636	4.6	4.6	..	5.5	23.4
23/25	Chemicals, Total	5 180	8 334	6 586	9 345	9 798	28.0	44.8	43.7	51.7	50.0
23	Refined petroleum, nuclear fuel	491	611	776	657	573	57.9	82.9	88.8	68.9	61.4
24/25	Chemicals, rubber & plastics prod.	4 689	7 723	5 810	8 688	9 225	26.5	43.3	41.0	50.7	49.5
24	Chemical products	4 325	7 061	5 273	7 887	8 444	29.3	51.5	45.9	56.3	54.9
2423	Pharmaceuticals	197	1 810	1 491	3 832	4 415	2.2	25.3	23.9	50.6	49.6
25	Rubber and plastics products	364	662	536	801	781	12.4	16.0	19.9	25.7	24.0
26	Non-metallic mineral products	635	788	714	685	659	34.2	37.5	34.7	31.3	31.2
27/28	Basic & fabricated metals	1 339	4 438	1 589	1 792	1 215	9.5	23.1	12.4	13.1	8.8
27	Basic metals	1 036	3 953	1 165	1 361	734	15.0	39.0	23.6	25.8	17.0
28	Fabricated metal products	303	485	424	431	481	4.2	5.4	5.4	5.1	5.1
29/32	Machinery, Total	4 608	5 669	4 449	4 102	4 425	21.5	26.3	21.6	10.7	18.6
29/30	Non-electrical machinery	3 167	4 382	3 454	2 758	3 036	21.4	33.2	26.9	19.5	22.6
29	Non-electrical machinery nec	3 089	4 246	3 331	2 582	2 720	22.1	32.2	27.0	19.0	21.5
30	Office and computing machinery	78	136	123	176	316	9.3	..	26.0	29.8	38.9
31/32	Electrical & electronic equipment	1 441	1 287	995	1 344	1 389	21.9	15.4	12.8	5.6	13.4
31	Electrical machinery nec	1 329	1 146	989	851	982	54.8	37.8	36.7	34.6	42.9
32	Radio, TV & communications eq.	112	141	6	493	407	2.7	2.6	0.1	2.3	5.0
33	Scientific instruments	884	1 267	1 228	1 383	1 189	31.3	33.5	36.4	31.3	30.9
34/35	Transportation equipment	631	766	401	683	969	2.2	8.0	5.6	7.7	6.0
34	Motor vehicles	300	620	281	574	1 003	3.0	7.1	4.3	5.2	7.0
35	Other transport equipment	331	146	120	109	- 34	1.8	17.6	20.6	..	..
351	Shipbuilding & repairing	..	..	..	12	16	..	..	..	4.6	8.8
353	Aircraft and spacecraft	..	..	..	..	..	..	..	..	..	..
36/37	Other manufacturing	- 132	217	431	387	- 2	..	9.6	19.9	17.8	..
40/45	Construction, electricity, gas & water	475	608	2 710	1 876	1 899	1.3	1.4	6.7	4.4	4.8
50/55	Trade, repair, hotels & restaurants	9 746	9 247	11 031	9 218	11 010	21.9	19.4	22.7	18.9	21.4
65/74	Finance, insurance, business services	3 205	3 645	2 529	6 407	7 483	15.7	14.2	12.2	7.1	7.4
	OTHER ACTIVITIES	1 751	633	1 372	2 155	3 576	5.8	2.0	4.2	4.6	6.7
01/99	**GRAND TOTAL**	32 714	40 323	38 628	44 786	50 712	12.4	14.6	16.4	12.7	14.0

Total manufacturing by investing country						As a % of total manufacturing by foreign affiliates				
All countries	17 358	25 915	20 840	24 695	26 401	100.0	100.0	100.0	100.0	100.0
United States	1 699	4 247	4 241	7 251	7 766	9.8	16.4	20.4	29.4	29.4
Canada	..	..	..	..	..	..	..	..	..	..
Mexico	..	..	..	0	0	..	..	..	0.0	0.0
Japan	..	195	103	162	181	..	0.8	0.5	0.7	0.7
Europe	15 063	20 998	15 121	..	..	86.8	81.0	72.6	..	..
European Union (15)	11 036	15 180	10 805	10 942	12 940	63.6	58.6	51.8	44.3	49.0
Belgium	..	..	..	..	..	..	..	..	..	..
France	868	989	809	952	923	5.0	3.8	3.9	3.9	3.5
Germany	1 339	1 533	1 286	1 207	909	7.7	5.9	6.2	4.9	3.4
Italy	..	..	..	..	..	..	..	..	..	..
Netherlands	3 977	4 074	2 948	3 087	2 885	22.9	15.7	14.1	12.5	10.9
Spain	..	..	..	..	..	..	..	..	..	..
Sweden										
United Kingdom	855	3 917	1 987	1 975	1 393	4.9	15.1	9.5	8.0	5.3
Switzerland	3 069	3 126	3 000	2 423	2 502	17.7	12.1	14.4	9.8	9.5
Australia and New Zealand	..	..	..	0	0	..	..	..	0.0	0.0
Asia (non-OECD)	..	..	370	121	215	..	..	1.8	0.5	0.8
Latin America	..	0	0	22	28	..	0.0	0.0	0.1	0.1

Note: Majority foreign-owned **non-financial** firms. Source: Statistics Sweden's Structural Business Statistics.
Firmes **non financières** sous contrôle étranger majoritaire. Source : Statistiques structurelles d'entreprises de l'office suédois de statistiques.

Inward investments   *Investissements entrants*

Table 18A - Tableau 18A

CAPITAL UNDER FOREIGN INFLUENCE / CAPITAL SOUS INFLUENCE ÉTRANGÈRE

By industry (ISIC Rev. 3)		1989	1990	1991	1992	1993	1994	1995	1996	1997	1998
							Foreign affiliates *(Millions of SEK)*				
							Filiales étrangères *(Millions de SEK)*				
10/14	Mining & quarrying	..	418	344	326	615	737	1 094	1 061	2 018	2 414
15/37	**TOTAL MANUFACTURING**	..	**117 375**	**149 412**	**140 980**	**137 635**	**166 307**	**238 636**	**229 865**	**201 007**	**256 090**
15/16	Food, beverages, tobacco	..	8 069	9 699	14 708	18 832	19 133	21 420	26 134	22 749	26 175
17/19	Textiles, clothing, leather, footwear	..	1 736	2 057	2 013	2 016	2 473	2 353	2 763	2 843	3 115
20/22	Wood and paper products	..	9 373	9 081	10 290	10 732	7 704	11 244	11 422	16 470	54 621
20	Wood products	..	..	..	..	616	794	888	3 000	7 635	10 223
21/22	Paper, printing and publishing	..	..	..	..	10 116	6 910	10 356	8 422	8 835	44 398
23/25	Chemicals, Total	..	18 723	25 766	21 864	23 383	51 531	67 502	68 831	60 469	64 733
23	Refined petroleum, nuclear fuel	..	504	569	650	..	3 331	4 732	6 911	4 276	5 045
24/25	Chemicals, rubber & plastics prod.	..	18 219	25 197	21 214	23 380	48 200	62 770	61 920	56 193	59 688
24	Chemical products	..	16 020	22 408	19 057	18 152	44 873	59 540	58 696	49 688	52 591
2423	Pharmaceuticals	..	762	426	469	451	864	21 926	22 284	22 539	21 453
25	Rubber and plastics products	..	2 200	2 789	2 157	3 498	3 327	3 230	3 224	6 505	7 097
26	Non-metallic mineral products	..	5 681	5 203	5 133	5 270	5 230	5 886	5 711	6 862	6 747
27/28	Basic & fabricated metals	..	7 533	8 330	9 024	7 256	8 391	23 154	22 852	24 022	23 524
27	Basic metals	..	2 373	3 752	4 982	4 787	5 765	19 703	19 322	20 189	18 675
28	Fabricated metal products	..	5 160	4 578	4 042	2 469	2 626	3 451	3 530	3 833	4 849
29/32	Machinery, Total	..	60 587	82 405	67 067	58 653	59 230	89 765	72 989	43 877	46 025
29/30	Non-electrical machinery	..	30 318	51 861	36 492	27 580	32 200	44 661	34 272	30 594	32 804
29	Non-electrical machinery nec	..	21 988	41 664	29 344	26 536	30 357	43 496	33 237	29 370	31 508
30	Office and computing machinery	..	8 330	10 197	7 148	1 044	1 843	1 165	1 035	1 224	1 296
31/32	Electrical & electronic equipment	..	30 269	30 544	30 575	31 073	27 030	45 104	38 717	13 283	13 221
31	Electrical machinery nec	..	25 305	26 855	29 626	29 454	25 409	43 186	36 731	9 685	10 471
32	Radio, TV & communications eq.	..	4 964	3 689	949	1 619	1 621	1 918	1 986	3 598	2 750
33	Scientific instruments	..	1 093	968	4 365	4 418	5 833	7 360	8 879	10 923	13 245
34/35	Transportation equipment	..	3 890	5 383	5 812	5 840	5 205	7 529	7 407	9 381	12 494
34	Motor vehicles	..	1 434	1 660	1 988	2 238	1 649	3 923	3 743	5 693	8 611
35	Other transport equipment	..	2 456	3 723	3 824	3 602	3 556	3 606	3 664	3 688	3 883
351	Shipbuilding & repairing	..	..	..	..	..	..	..	..	97	93
353	Aircraft and spacecraft	..	..	..	..	..	..	..	..	..	..
36/37	Other manufacturing	..	690	520	704	1 235	1 577	2 423	2 877	3 411	5 411
40/45	Construction, electricity, gas & water	..	..	..	..	5 284	13 492	6 141	36 598	42 910	70 966
50/55	Trade, repair, hotels & restaurants	..	65 233	63 688	62 245	71 096	91 411	103 215	121 400	130 312	135 146
65/74	Finance, insurance, business services	..	20 285	21 793	20 735	57 034	78 843	86 807	99 121	210 825	316 065
	OTHER ACTIVITIES	..	11 669	11 904	21 657	13 048	15 979	14 050	20 578	26 207	34 521
01/99	**GRAND TOTAL**	..	**214 981**	**247 141**	**245 942**	**284 712**	**366 770**	**449 943**	**508 623**	**613 279**	**818 595**

Total manufacturing by investing country

	1989	1990	1991	1992	1993	1994	1995	1996	1997	1998
All countries	..	**117 375**	**149 412**	**140 980**	**137 635**	**166 307**	**238 636**	**229 865**	**201 007**	**256 090**
United States	..	..	..	..	..	12 394	39 382	44 325	44 550	54 764
Canada	..	..	..	..	..	..	..	..	..	..
Mexico	..	..	..	0	0	..	..	..	0	0
Japan	..	..	..	..	..	965	1 397	1 098	1 387	1 436
Europe	..	104 052	134 435	125 498	126 612	149 757	193 883	173 079	..	..
European Union (15)	..	51 310	80 426	69 207	75 240	100 972	117 192	105 405	107 043	145 496
Belgium	..	..	..	..	..	..	..	..	..	..
France	..	..	..	..	..	4 774	5 257	5 531	12 504	14 968
Germany	..	..	..	..	..	7 267	9 025	9 051	11 441	12 128
Italy	..	..	..	..	..	..	..	..	..	..
Netherlands	..	..	..	..	..	51 442	47 419	34 155	21 651	21 910
Spain	..	..	..	..	..	..	..	..	..	..
Sweden	..	..	..	..	..	..	..	..	..	..
United Kingdom	..	..	..	..	..	6 542	22 109	24 232	24 749	24 122
Switzerland	..	..	..	..	..	42 093	62 987	55 922	23 261	25 239
Australia and New Zealand	..	..	..	0	0	..	..	..	0	0
Asia (non-OECD)	..	..	..	0	0	2 133	..	4 106	1 352	1 538
Latin America	..	..	..	0	0	..	0	0	237	265

Note: Majority foreign-owned **non-financial** firms. Source: Statistics Sweden's Structural Business Statistics. Up to 1992, ISIC 20/22 includes part of *Furniture* (361), small part of ISIC 353 and 35 is included in ISIC 29/32 and ISIC 40/45 is included in *Other activities*. See country notes.
Firmes **non financières** sous contrôle étranger majoritaire. Source : Statistiques structurelles d'entreprises de l'office suédois de statistiques. Jusqu'en 1992, la CITI 20/22 comprend une partie de *Meubles* (361), une petite partie de la CITI 353 et 35 est comprise dans la CITI 29/32 et la CITI 40/45 est comprise dans *Autres activités*. Voir les notes par pays.

Outward investments   *Investissements sortants*

Table 1B - Tableau 1B

NUMBER OF EMPLOYEES BY INDUSTRY

NOMBRE DE SALARIÉS PAR INDUSTRIE

ISIC Revision 3		Foreign affiliates *(FTE)* Filiales étrangères *(EPT)*					As a % of national total En % du total national				
		1993	1994	1995	1996	1997	1993	1994	1995	1996	1997
10/14	Mining & quarrying	..	..	..	317	339	..	..	..	9.0	9.6
15/37	**TOTAL MANUFACTURING**	**458 257**	**..**	**..**	**476 939**	**485 195**	**54.7**	**..**	**..**	**56.1**	**58.1**
15/16	Food, beverages, tobacco	1 888	..	..	8 773	7 768	12.3	..	..	37.1	30.2
17/19	Textiles, clothing, leather, footwear	1 864	..	..	7 167	8 433	39.8	..	..	65.9	67.8
20/22	Wood and paper products	74 304	..	..	71 988	71 358	48.0	..	..	51.3	54.8
20	Wood products	3 270	..	..	5 260	2 526	41.4	..	..	36.9	29.8
21/22	Paper, printing and publishing	71 034	..	..	66 728	68 832	48.4	..	..	53.0	56.5
23/25	Chemicals, Total	51 125	..	..	38 109	42 435	65.9	..	..	61.1	65.3
23	Refined petroleum, nuclear fuel	..	..	..	..	0	..	..	..	..	..
24/25	Chemicals, rubber & plastics prod.	..	..	..	..	42 435	..	..	..	..	65.3
24	Chemical products	..	..	..	..	27 818	..	..	..	..	72.9
2423	Pharmaceuticals	..	..	..	..	0	..	..	..	..	..
25	Rubber and plastics products	6 517	..	..	13 329	14 617	51.7	..	..	48.0	54.5
26	Non-metallic mineral products	10 744	..	..	8 704	10 524	57.8	..	..	59.5	64.8
27/28	Basic & fabricated metals	43 923	..	..	42 000	41 458	38.4	..	..	39.9	41.1
27	Basic metals	25 600	..	..	28 693	26 358	49.0	..	..	50.5	50.8
28	Fabricated metal products	18 323	..	..	13 307	15 100	29.5	..	..	27.4	30.7
29/32	Machinery, Total	213 390	..	..	243 493	238 570	69.5	..	..	71.0	70.7
29/30	Non-electrical machinery	175 448	..	..	192 120	181 489	74.6	..	..	78.2	76.9
29	Non-electrical machinery nec	..	..	..	189 622	181 087	..	..	..	78.8	77.1
30	Office and computing machinery	..	..	..	2 498	402	..	..	..	49.9	36.0
31/32	Electrical & electronic equipment	37 942	..	..	51 373	57 081	52.7	..	..	52.8	56.3
31	Electrical machinery nec	905	..	..	1 456	1 523	19.5	..	..	23.6	39.8
32	Radio, TV & communications eq.	37 037	..	..	49 917	55 558	55.0	..	..	54.7	57.0
33	Scientific instruments	15 917	..	..	5 924	20 022	75.3	..	..	61.6	81.0
34/35	Transportation equipment	43 058	..	..	49 837	43 284	36.6	..	..	36.7	36.9
34	Motor vehicles	42 917	..	..	47 839	42 692	36.8	..	..	41.8	39.3
35	Other transport equipment	141	..	..	1 998	592	14.1	..	..	9.4	6.7
351	Shipbuilding & repairing	..	..	..	..	..	..	..	..	..	..
353	Aircraft and spacecraft	..	..	..	..	..	..	..	..	..	..
36/37	Other manufacturing	2 044	..	..	944	1 343	34.2	..	..	19.2	26.7
40/45	Construction, electricity, gas & water	..	..	..	..	28 962	..	..	..	..	35.8
50/55	Trade, repair, hotels & restaurants	29 591	..	..	29 331	27 788	24.4	..	..	30.4	31.7
65/74	Finance, insurance, business services	23 886	..	..	47 205	55 816	45.6	..	..	37.6	40.9
	OTHER ACTIVITIES	..	..	..	..	30 401	..	..	..	..	20.2
01/99	**GRAND TOTAL**	**535 147**	**..**	**..**	**605 603**	**628 501**	**46.7**	**..**	**..**	**46.3**	**48.6**

Note: Foreign affiliates majority-owned by national firms.
Filiales étrangères détenues majoritairement par des firmes nationales.

Outward investments *Investissements sortants*

Table 2B - Tableau 2B

NUMBER OF EMPLOYEES BY COUNTRY OF LOCATION IN THE MANUFACTURING SECTOR

NOMBRE DE SALARIÉS PAR PAYS D'IMPLANTATION DANS L'INDUSTRIE MANUFACTURIÈRE

Country of location	Number of employees *(FTE)* Nombre de salariés *(EPT)*					As a % of all countries En % du total des pays				
	1993	1994	1995	1996	1997	1993	1994	1995	1996	1997
All countries	**458 257**	..	..	**476 939**	**485 195**	**100.0**	..	..	**100.0**	**100.0**
Total OECD	**395 813**	..	..	..	**398 716**	**86.4**	..	..	..	**82.2**
United States	79 127	..	..	80 816	87 598	17.3	..	..	16.9	18.1
Canada	7 302	..	..	8 219	9 828	1.6	..	..	1.7	2.0
Mexico	9 742	..	..	6 708	6 311	2.1	..	..	1.4	1.3
Japan	4 197	..	..	4 385	4 408	0.9	..	..	0.9	0.9
Korea	614	..	..	789	729	0.1	..	..	0.2	0.2
Australia	7 218	..	..	7 691	7 487	1.6	..	..	1.6	1.5
New Zealand	736	..	..	1 111	1 105	0.2	..	..	0.2	0.2
Europe	**288 940**	..	..	**296 940**	**294 134**	**63.1**	..	..	**62.3**	**60.6**
European Union (15)	**264 842**	..	..	**255 066**	**245 149**	**57.8**	..	..	**53.5**	**50.5**
Austria	6 869	..	..	8 217	8 144	1.5	..	..	1.7	1.7
Belgium	16 220	..	..	17 514	16 825	3.5	..	..	3.7	3.5
Denmark	20 101	..	..	17 697	16 978	4.4	..	..	3.7	3.5
Finland	7 481	..	..	10 392	11 650	1.6	..	..	2.2	2.4
France	30 705	..	..	31 425	30 852	6.7	..	..	6.6	6.4
Germany	52 296	..	..	60 501	54 838	11.4	..	..	12.7	11.3
Greece	829	..	..	682	772	0.2	..	..	0.1	0.2
Ireland	2 485	..	..	2 185	2 308	0.5	..	..	0.5	0.5
Italy	34 719	..	..	32 147	32 616	7.6	..	..	6.7	6.7
Luxembourg	0	..	..	..	665	0.0	..	..	..	0.1
Netherlands	16 998	..	..	15 869	15 231	3.7	..	..	3.3	3.1
Portugal	4 026	..	..	2 195	2 195	0.9	..	..	0.5	0.5
Spain	14 108	..	..	12 674	11 480	3.1	..	..	2.7	2.4
Sweden	..	..	..	..	..	..	..	..	..	..
United Kingdom	58 005	..	..	43 568	40 595	12.7	..	..	9.1	8.4
Czech Republic	1 286	..	..	2 618	3 534	0.3	..	..	0.5	0.7
Hungary	5 190	..	..	6 017	6 338	1.1	..	..	1.3	1.3
Iceland	27	..	..	..	36	0.0	..	..	..	0.0
Norway	11 216	..	..	12 924	10 969	2.4	..	..	2.7	2.3
Poland	1 097	..	..	6 222	7 867	0.0	..	..	0.4	0.4
Slovak Republic	0	..	..	..	2 883	0.2	..	..	1.3	1.6
Switzerland	3 967	..	..	3 359	3 554	0.9	..	..	0.7	0.7
Turkey	455	..	..	712	920	0.1	..	..	0.1	0.2
Non-OECD Europe, of which:	**7 354**	..	..	..	**12 884**	**1.6**	..	..	..	**2.7**
Baltic countries	471	..	..	7 369	9 152	0.1	..	..	1.5	1.9
Bulgaria	11	..	..	..	341	0.0	..	..	..	0.1
Croatia	0	..	..	..	23	0.0	..	..	..	0.0
Romania	2	..	..	..	252	0.0	..	..	..	0.1
Russian Federation	106	..	..	1 979	2 107	0.0	..	..	..	0.6
Slovenia	4	..	..	..	79	0.0	..	..	..	0.0
Ukraine	1	..	..	..	428	0.0	..	..	..	0.1
Yugoslavia	19	..	..	..	65	0.0	..	..	..	0.0
Non-OECD Asia, of which:	**24 988**	..	..	**33 562**	**37 051**	**5.5**	..	..	**7.0**	**7.6**
China	477	..	..	7 256	8 673	0.1	..	..	1.5	1.8
Chinese Taipei	1 029	..	..	891	979	0.2	..	..	0.2	0.2
Hong Kong (China)	901	..	..	767	817	0.2	..	..	0.2	0.2
India	5 754	..	..	7 595	8 251	1.3	..	..	1.6	1.7
Indonesia	2 585	..	..	3 738	4 310	0.6	..	..	0.8	0.9
Malaysia	4 557	..	..	3 750	3 325	1.0	..	..	0.8	0.7
Philippines	3 393	..	..	1 852	1 815	0.7	..	..	0.4	0.4
Singapore	1 308	..	..	1 226	1 306	0.3	..	..	0.3	0.3
Thailand	4 358	..	..	5 171	5 406	1.0	..	..	1.1	1.1
Near and Middle East	**1 143**	..	..	..	**494**	**0.2**	..	..	..	**0.1**
Africa	**2 789**	..	..	**5 185**	**5 477**	**0.6**	..	..	**1.1**	**1.1**
Latin America, of which:	**29 953**	..	..	**29 747**	**30 569**	**6.5**	..	..	**6.2**	**6.3**
Argentina	3 262	..	..	3 243	3 319	0.7	..	..	0.7	0.7
Brazil	18 350	..	..	19 530	18 381	4.0	..	..	4.1	3.8
Chile	1 170	..	..	..	1 342	0.3	..	..	..	0.3

Note: Foreign affiliates majority-owned by national firms. For 1996, data for Belgium include those for Luxembourg and data for the Czech Republic include those for the Slovak Republic.
Filiales étrangères détenues majoritairement par des firmes nationales. Pour 1996, les données de la Belgique comprennent celles du Luxembourg et celles de la République tchèque comprennent celles de la République slovaque.

Outward investments

Investissements sortants

Table 3B - Tableau 3B

R&D EXPENDITURE / DÉPENSES DE R-D

By industry (ISIC Rev. 3)	Foreign affiliates (Millions of SEK) Filiales étrangères (Millions de SEK)					As a % of national total En % du total national				
	1995	1996	1997	1998	1999	1995	1996	1997	1998	1999
10/14 Mining & quarrying	..	..	..	..	..	..	..	..	..	..
15/37 TOTAL MANUFACTURING	7 936	..	16 565	..	19 053	21.8	..	40.7	..	41.0
15/16 Food, beverages, tobacco	..	..	..	..	..	..	..	..	..	..
17/19 Textiles, clothing, leather, footwear	..	..	..	..	..	..	..	..	..	..
20/22 Wood and paper products	..	..	..	..	..	..	..	..	..	..
20 Wood products	..	..	..	..	..	..	..	..	..	..
21/22 Paper, printing and publishing	..	..	..	..	..	..	..	..	..	..
23/25 Chemicals, Total	..	..	..	..	..	..	..	..	..	..
23 Refined petroleum, nuclear fuel	..	..	..	..	..	..	..	..	..	..
24/25 Chemicals, rubber & plastics prod.	..	..	..	..	..	..	..	..	..	..
24 Chemical products	..	..	..	..	..	..	..	..	..	..
2423 Pharmaceuticals	..	..	..	..	..	..	..	..	..	..
25 Rubber and plastics products	..	..	..	..	..	..	..	..	..	..
26 Non-metallic mineral products	..	..	..	..	..	..	..	..	..	..
27/28 Basic & fabricated metals	..	..	..	..	..	..	..	..	..	..
27 Basic metals	..	..	..	..	..	..	..	..	..	..
28 Fabricated metal products	..	..	..	..	..	..	..	..	..	..
29/32 Machinery, Total	..	..	..	..	..	..	..	..	..	..
29/30 Non-electrical machinery	..	..	..	..	..	..	..	..	..	..
29 Non-electrical machinery nec	..	..	..	..	..	..	..	..	..	..
30 Office and computing machinery	..	..	..	..	..	..	..	..	..	..
31/32 Electrical & electronic equipment	..	..	..	..	..	..	..	..	..	..
31 Electrical machinery nec	..	..	..	..	..	..	..	..	..	..
32 Radio, TV & communications eq.	..	..	..	..	..	..	..	..	..	..
33 Scientific instruments	..	..	..	..	..	..	..	..	..	..
34/35 Transportation equipment	..	..	..	..	..	..	..	..	..	..
34 Motor vehicles	..	..	..	..	..	..	..	..	..	..
35 Other transport equipment	..	..	..	..	..	..	..	..	..	..
351 Shipbuilding & repairing	..	..	..	..	..	..	..	..	..	..
353 Aircraft and spacecraft	..	..	..	..	..	..	..	..	..	..
36/37 Other manufacturing	..	..	..	..	..	..	..	..	..	..
40/45 Construction, electricity, gas & water	..	..	..	..	..	..	..	..	..	..
50/55 Trade, repair, hotels & restaurants	..	..	..	..	..	..	..	..	..	..
65/74 Finance, insurance, business services	..	..	..	..	..	..	..	..	..	..
OTHER ACTIVITIES	..	..	..	..	..	..	..	..	..	..
01/99 GRAND TOTAL	..	..	..	..	..	..	..	..	..	..

Total manufacturing by country of location						As a % of total manufacturing by foreign affiliates				
All countries	7 936	..	16 565	..	19 053	100.0	..	100.0	..	100.0
United States	2 419	..	5 034	..	5 716	30.5	..	30.4	..	30.0
Canada	158	..	962	..	1 536	2.0	..	5.8	..	8.1
Mexico	0	..	92	..	173	0.0	..	0.6	..	0.9
Japan	140	..	..	..	..	1.8	..	..	..	..
Europe	..	..	..	..	..	..	..	..	..	..
European Union (15)	4 515	..	8 760	..	9 055	56.9	..	52.9	..	47.5
Belgium	554	..	512	..	..	7.0	..	3.1	..	..
France	388	..	477	..	673	4.9	..	2.9	..	3.5
Germany	952	..	1 866	..	2 257	12.0	..	11.3	..	11.8
Italy	510	..	993	..	1 147	6.4	..	6.0	..	6.0
Netherlands	553	..	828	..	1 063	7.0	..	5.0	..	5.6
Spain	267	..	388	..	439	3.4	..	2.3	..	2.3
Sweden	..	..	..	..	..	..	..	..	..	..
United Kingdom	901	..	2 276	..	1 041	11.4	..	13.7	..	5.5
Switzerland	..	..	..	..	..	..	..	..	..	..
Australia and New Zealand	186	..	..	..	..	2.3	..	..	..	..
Asia (non-OECD)	..	..	..	..	..	..	..	..	..	..
Latin America	..	..	..	..	..	..	..	..	..	..

Note: Data based on a sample of the 20 largest manufacturing enterprise groups.

Données fondées sur un échantillon des 20 plus grands groupes d'entreprises manufacturiers.

Outward investments

Investissements sortants

Table 4B - Tableau 4B

NUMBER OF RESEARCHERS / NOMBRE DE CHERCHEURS

		Foreign affiliates *(FTE)* Filiales étrangères *(EPT)*					As a % of national total En % du total national				
By industry (ISIC Rev. 3)		1995	1996	1997	1998	1999	1995	1996	1997	1998	1999
10/14	Mining & quarrying	..	..	..	..	..	..	..	..	..	..
15/37	**TOTAL MANUFACTURING**	**677**	..	**1 008**	..	**1 872**	**38.4**	..	**40.1**	..	**45.9**
15/16	Food, beverages, tobacco	..	..	..	..	..	..	..	..	..	..
17/19	Textiles, clothing, leather, footwear	..	..	..	..	..	..	..	..	..	..
20/22	Wood and paper products	..	..	..	..	..	..	..	..	..	..
20	Wood products	..	..	..	..	..	..	..	..	..	..
21/22	Paper, printing and publishing	..	..	..	..	..	..	..	..	..	..
23/25	Chemicals, Total	..	..	..	..	..	..	..	..	..	..
23	Refined petroleum, nuclear fuel	..	..	..	..	..	..	..	..	..	..
24/25	Chemicals, rubber & plastics prod.	..	..	..	..	..	..	..	..	..	..
24	Chemical products	..	..	..	..	..	..	..	..	..	..
2423	Pharmaceuticals	..	..	..	..	..	..	..	..	..	..
25	Rubber and plastics products	..	..	..	..	..	..	..	..	..	..
26	Non-metallic mineral products	..	..	..	..	..	..	..	..	..	..
27/28	Basic & fabricated metals	..	..	..	..	..	..	..	..	..	..
27	Basic metals	..	..	..	..	..	..	..	..	..	..
28	Fabricated metal products	..	..	..	..	..	..	..	..	..	..
29/32	Machinery, Total	..	..	..	..	..	..	..	..	..	..
29/30	Non-electrical machinery	..	..	..	..	..	..	..	..	..	..
29	Non-electrical machinery nec	..	..	..	..	..	..	..	..	..	..
30	Office and computing machinery	..	..	..	..	..	..	..	..	..	..
31/32	Electrical & electronic equipment	..	..	..	..	..	..	..	..	..	..
31	Electrical machinery nec	..	..	..	..	..	..	..	..	..	..
32	Radio, TV & communications eq.	..	..	..	..	..	..	..	..	..	..
33	Scientific instruments	..	..	..	..	..	..	..	..	..	..
34/35	Transportation equipment	..	..	..	..	..	..	..	..	..	..
34	Motor vehicles	..	..	..	..	..	..	..	..	..	..
35	Other transport equipment	..	..	..	..	..	..	..	..	..	..
351	Shipbuilding & repairing	..	..	..	..	..	..	..	..	..	..
353	Aircraft and spacecraft	..	..	..	..	..	..	..	..	..	..
36/37	Other manufacturing	..	..	..	..	..	..	..	..	..	..
40/45	Construction, electricity, gas & water	..	..	..	..	..	..	..	..	..	..
50/55	Trade, repair, hotels & restaurants	..	..	..	..	..	..	..	..	..	..
65/74	Finance, insurance, business services	..	..	..	..	..	..	..	..	..	..
	OTHER ACTIVITIES	..	..	..	..	..	..	..	..	..	..
01/99	**GRAND TOTAL**	..	..	..	..	..	..	..	..	..	..

Total manufacturing by country of location							*As a % of total manufacturing by foreign affiliates*				
All countries		**677**	..	**1 008**	..	**1 872**	**100.0**	..	**100.0**	..	**100.0**
United States		185	..	222	..	468	27.3	..	22.0	..	25.0
Canada		..	..	51	..	118	..	..	5.1	..	6.3
Mexico		..	..	8	..	46	..	..	0.8	..	2.5
Japan		..	..	..	..	..	..	..	..	..	..
Europe		..	..	..	..	..	..	..	..	..	..
European Union (15)		389	..	595	..	982	57.5	..	59.0	..	52.5
Belgium		28	..	9	..	..	4.1	..	0.9	..	..
France		27	..	34	..	46	4.0	..	3.4	..	2.5
Germany		58	..	92	..	219	8.6	..	9.1	..	11.7
Italy		18	..	42	..	110	2.7	..	4.2	..	5.9
Netherlands		52	..	25	..	136	7.7	..	2.5	..	7.3
Spain		28	..	19	..	86	4.1	..	1.9	..	4.6
Sweden		..	..	..	..	..	..	..	..	..	..
United Kingdom		173	..	325	..	110	25.6	..	32.2	..	5.9
Switzerland		..	..	..	..	..	..	..	..	..	..
Australia and New Zealand		..	..	..	..	..	..	..	..	..	..
Asia (non-OECD)		..	..	..	..	..	..	..	..	..	..
Latin America		..	..	..	..	..	..	..	..	..	..

Note: Data based on a sample of the 20 largest manufacturing enterprise groups.
Données fondées sur un échantillon des 20 plus grands groupes d'entreprises manufacturiers.

SWEDEN

A. *Inward investments*

Source

As of 1 July 1994, statistics on international business, *i.e.* Swedish groups with subsidiaries abroad and foreign-owned enterprises in Sweden, have an official status and are regularly produced and published. The Swedish National Board for Industrial and Technical Development, NUTEK, was the governmental agency responsible for the production of these official statistics. Since 1 January 2001, a new government authority, the Swedish Institute for Growth Policy Studies (ITPS), was given responsibility for these statistics. The surveys are carried out in co-operation with Statistics Sweden.

From reference year 1996, data on foreign-owned affiliates are based on annual questionnaires to all parent companies, subsidiaries as well as to all branches located in Sweden. Coverage has been extended over time: questionnaires were sent to one in four parent companies in the 1980s and the beginning of the 1990s; and to about one in two in 1995. Greater efforts have also been made to cover new foreign-owned affiliates. The increase in the number of enterprises and the number of employees in 1995 and 1996 is partly the result of this improved coverage.

The data refer to majority foreign-owned enterprises, *i.e.* enterprises in which a foreign investor owns more than 50% of the voting power. The reporting unit is, in most cases, the enterprise. In 1996, 11% of the units were branches.

ITPS's statistics on foreign-owned Enterprises is based on data from three sources (in addition to the survey on ownership):

1) Statistic Sweden's Business Register includes all foreign-owned enterprises and branches, except for the period 1990-92, when branches were not included. The register is used for the variables *Number of enterprises* and *Number of employees*. These tables provide a better coverage on these variables, but should not be mixed with other tables.

2) Statistics Sweden's Structural Business Statistics. All non-financial enterprises with an annual average of 20 or more employees (manufacturing industry) and 50 or more employees (service sector) are surveyed annually. These statistics are based on data from annual reports and questionnaires on exports, revenues and costs, R&D expenditure etc. Since the 1996 reference year, enterprises with less than 20 (manufacturing) / 50 employees (services) are surveyed using tax returns. Collection of these data is mandatory for all Swedish enterprises. Data are not included for real estate management (ISIC 70) or for financial enterprises.

3) Statistics Sweden's Trade Statistics. Exports of goods for small enterprises and all data regarding imports are taken from this register.

Statistics on firms under foreign control are published by ITPS/Statistics Sweden under the title *Foreign-owned Enterprises*. All publications from ITPS are available at ITPS's homepage, www.itps.se.

National totals: data are provided by ITPS/Statistics Sweden and are fully compatible with foreign affiliates' data.

Industrial classification

For all variables, the data are classified according to the principal industrial activity of the affiliate in Sweden. The whole business sector is surveyed.

The industrial classification used for Swedish tables is ISIC Revision 3, equivalent to NACE Revision 1.

Variables

- *Number of employees* is defined as salaried employment in number of persons, *i.e.* no distinction is made between full-time and part-time employees.

- *Turnover* is defined as sales including part of other operating income.

- *Value added* is calculated as the adjusted gross profit before depreciation, plus labour costs.

- *Compensation of employees* includes employer's social insurance contributions on behalf of the employees.

- *R&D expenditure* includes both intramural and extramural R&D as well as depreciation for enterprises having more than 50 employees.

- *Gross fixed capital formation* corresponds to investment in tangible fixed assets, less sales of such assets.

- *Total exports* includes exports of goods and services from foreign affiliates to parent company and other intra-group firms in Sweden. It excludes services for firms with less than 50 employees.

- *Total imports* includes only imports of goods. The transactions are based on "statistical value" and not on the invoiced price. The lack of data for some years relates to uncertainty regarding the quality of the data.

- *Intra-firm exports* includes exports of goods and services from the parent and other intra-group firms in Sweden to the enterprise group abroad.

- *Gross operating surplus* consists of profit or loss before depreciation.

Geographical breakdown

The country of origin is that of the "ultimate beneficial owner".

B. Outward investments

Source

As of 1 July 1994, statistics on international business, *i.e.* Swedish groups with subsidiaries abroad and foreign-owned enterprises in Sweden, have an official status and are regularly produced and published. The Swedish National Board for Industrial and Technical Development, NUTEK, was the governmental agency responsible for the production of these official statistics. Since 1 January 2001, a new government authority, the Swedish Institute for Growth Policy Studies (ITPS), was given responsibility for these statistics. The surveys are carried out in co-operation with MM Partner in Sweden (data on number of employees by country of location) and with Statistics Sweden (data on R&D).

For the variable *Number of employees*, the survey covers all enterprise groups having at least one subsidiary abroad.

For the variables *R&D expenditure* and *Number of researchers*, data come from the survey of R&D in the 20 largest manufacturing groups, which has been carried out every two years from 1995. These 20 groups account for about 80% of the manufacturing industry's R&D in Sweden.

The data refer to foreign affiliates majority-owned by national firms. The reporting unit is the enterprise group.

Statistics on outward investments are published by ITPS under the title *Swedish-owned Enterprises having Subsidiaries Abroad* and *Research and Development in International Enterprises*. All publications from ITPS are available at ITPS's homepage, www.itps.se.

National totals: for the variable *Number of employees*, data are provided by ITPS/Statistics Sweden and are fully compatible with foreign affiliates' data. Data on R&D (*R&D expenditure* and *Number of researchers*) are not fully compatible with foreign affiliates' data. National totals are somewhat underestimated because they only include enterprises having at least 50 employees. The 20 manufacturing groups include all enterprises, irrespective of size. These groups are not active in all industries and they also carry out some service activities.

Industrial classification

For all variables, the data are classified according to the principal industrial activity of the enterprise group in Sweden.

The industrial classification used for Swedish tables is ISIC Revision 3, equivalent to NACE Revision 1.

Variables

- *Number of employees* is calculated on a full-time equivalent basis.

- *R&D expenditure* includes mainly intramural R&D and is defined according to the OECD's Frascati Manual.

- *Number of researchers* is the number of university graduates having a PhD. It is calculated on a full-time equivalent basis.

SUÈDE

A. *Investissements entrants*

Source

Depuis le 1er juillet 1994, les statistiques sur les entreprises internationales, *i.e.* sur les groupes suédois ayant des filiales à l'étranger et sur les entreprises étrangères implantées en Suède, ont un statut officiel et sont produites et diffusées régulièrement. Le Conseil national suédois pour le développement industriel et technique (NUTEK) était l'agence responsable de l'élaboration de ces statistiques officielles. Depuis le 1er janvier 2001, une nouvelle autorité gouvernementale, l'Institut suédois pour les études de politique de la croissance (ITPS), est devenue responsable de ces statistiques. Les enquêtes sont menées en collaboration avec l'Office suédois de statistiques.

A partir de l'année de référence 1996, les données sur les filiales étrangères sont fondées sur des questionnaires annuels envoyés à toutes les maisons mères, à toutes les filiales ainsi qu'à toutes les succursales situées sur le territoire suédois. La couverture a été élargie au fil du temps : les questionnaires étaient envoyés à une entreprise sur quatre dans les années 80 et au début des années 90, puis à environ la moitié des maisons mères en 1995. Des efforts ont également été faits pour recenser de nouvelles filiales étrangères. L'augmentation du nombre d'entreprises et du nombre de salariés en 1995 et 1996 provient donc en partie de l'amélioration de la couverture.

Les données concernent les entreprises sous contrôle étranger majoritaire, *i.e.* dans lesquelles l'investisseur étranger possède plus de 50 % des droits de vote dans l'entreprise. L'unité déclarante est dans la plupart des cas l'entreprise. En 1996, 11 % de ces unités étaient des succursales.

Les statistiques d'ITPS sur les entreprises à capitaux étrangers sont fondées sur des données provenant de trois sources (sans compter l'enquête sur l'origine de l'investissement) :

1) Le Registre des entreprises de l'Office suédois de statistiques. Le registre sur les entreprises à capitaux étrangers prend en compte toutes les entreprises et les succursales à participation étrangère, sauf pour la période 1990-92 où les succursales ne sont pas incluses. Ces registres ont été utilisés pour le *Nombre d'entreprises* et pour le *Nombre de salariés*. Ces tableaux fournissent une meilleure couverture pour ces variables, mais ils ne doivent pas être mélangés aux autres.

2) Les Statistiques structurelles d'entreprises de l'Office suédois de statistiques. Toutes les entreprises non financières employant au moins 20 salariés pour l'industrie manufacturière et au moins 50 salariés pour le secteur des services (en moyenne annuelle) sont enquêtées chaque année. Ces statistiques sont fondées sur des données provenant de rapports annuels et d'enquêtes sur les exportations, les revenus et les coûts, les dépenses de R-D, etc. Depuis l'année de référence 1996, les entreprises de moins de 20 salariés (50 dans le cas des services) sont enquêtées à travers les déclarations fiscales. La collecte de ces données est une obligation légale pour toutes les entreprises suédoises. Les données sur les services immobiliers (CITI 70) et les entreprises financières sont exclues.

3) Les Statistiques du commerce de l'Office suédois de statistiques. Les exportations de biens concernant les petites entreprises et l'ensemble des données sur les importations proviennent de ce registre.

Les statistiques sur les entreprises sous contrôle étranger sont publiées annuellement par ITPS/office suédois de statistiques sous le titre *Foreign-owned Enterprises*. Toutes les publications d'ITPS sont disponibles sur le site Internet, www.itps.se.

Totaux nationaux : les données sont fournies par ITPS/Office suédois de statistiques et sont entièrement compatibles avec les données relatives aux filiales étrangères.

Classification industrielle

Pour toutes les variables, les données sont classées selon l'activité industrielle principale de l'entreprise affiliée établie en Suède. La totalité du secteur des entreprises est enquêtée.

La classification industrielle utilisée pour les tableaux suédois est la CITI révision 3, équivalant à la NACE révision 1.

Variables

- Le *Nombre de salariés* est défini comme l'emploi salarié en nombre de personnes, *i.e.* aucune distinction n'est faite entre les salariés à temps plein et à temps partiel.

- Le *Chiffre d'affaires* représente les ventes y compris une partie du revenu d'exploitation.

- La *Valeur ajoutée* est calculée comme le profit net ajusté avant amortissement, auquel s'ajoutent les coûts salariaux.

- Les *Salaires* comprennent les cotisations patronales d'assurance sociale pour le compte des salariés.

- Les *Dépenses de R-D* comprennent à la fois les dépenses de R-D intra-muros et extra-muros, ainsi que les dépenses d'amortissement pour les entreprises de plus de 50 salariés.

- La *Formation brute de capital fixe* correspond à l'investissement en actifs tangibles fixes diminué des cessions de ces mêmes actifs.

- Les *Exportations totales* comprennent les exportations de biens et services en provenance des filiales étrangères vers la maison mère et les autres firmes du même groupe en Suède. Elles excluent les services pour les entreprises de moins de 50 salariés.

- Les *Importations totales* correspondent aux importations de biens uniquement. Les transactions sont basées sur une "valeur statistique" et non sur le prix facturé. Le manque de données pour certaines années provient de l'incertitude quant à leur qualité.

- Les *Exportations intra-firme* comprennent les exportations de biens et services en provenance de la maison mère et des autres firmes du même groupe en Suède vers l'entreprise ou le groupe à l'étranger.

- L'*Excédent brut d'exploitation* consiste dans les pertes et profits avant amortissement.

Ventilation géographique

Le pays de l'investisseur est le pays du "bénéficiaire ultime de l'investissement".

B. *Investissements sortants*

Source

Depuis le 1er juillet 1994, les statistiques sur les entreprises internationales, *i.e.* les groupes suédois ayant des filiales à l'étranger et sur les entreprises étrangères implantées en Suède, ont un statut officiel et sont produites et diffusées régulièrement. Le Conseil national suédois pour le développement industriel et technique (NUTEK) était l'agence responsable de l'élaboration de ces statistiques officielles. Depuis le 1er janvier 2001, une nouvelle autorité gouvernementale, l'Institut suédois pour les études de politique de la croissance (ITPS), est devenue responsable de ces statistiques. Les enquêtes sont menées en collaboration avec MM Partner en Suède (données sur le nombre de salariés par pays d'implantation) et avec l'office suédois de statistiques (données sur la R-D).

Pour la variable *Nombre de salariés*, l'enquête couvre tous les groupes d'entreprises ayant au moins une filiale à l'étranger.

Pour les variables *Dépenses de R-D* et *Nombre de chercheurs*, les données proviennent de l'enquête sur la R-D dans les 20 plus grands groupes manufacturiers, qui est menée tous les deux ans depuis 1995. Ces 20 groupes totalisent environ 80 % de la R-D manufacturière en Suède.

Les données se rapportent aux filiales étrangères dans lesquelles l'investisseur suédois détient une participation majoritaire. L'unité déclarante est le groupe d'entreprise.

Les statistiques sur les groupes suédois ayant des filiales à l'étranger sont publiées par ITPS/office suédois de statistiques sous le titre *Swedish-owned Enterprises having Subsidiaries Abroad* et *Research and Development in International Enterprises*. Toutes les publications d'ITPS sont disponibles sur le site Internet, www.itps.se.

Totaux nationaux : Pour le *Nombre de salariés*, les données sont fournies par ITPS/Office suédois de statistiques et sont entièrement compatibles avec les données relatives aux filiales étrangères. Les données sur la R-D (*Dépenses de R-D* et *Nombre de chercheurs*) ne sont pas entièrement compatibles avec les données des filiales étrangères. Les totaux nationaux sont quelque peu sous-estimés parce qu'ils incluent seulement les entreprises ayant au moins 50 employés. Les 20 plus grands groupes manufacturiers incluent toutes les entreprises sans tenir compte de la taille. De plus, ces groupes ne sont pas actifs dans toutes les industries et ils effectuent aussi quelques activités de service.

Classification industrielle

Pour toutes les variables, les données sont classées selon l'activité industrielle principale du groupe d'entreprise suédois.

La classification industrielle utilisée pour les tableaux suédois est la CITI révision 3, équivalant à la NACE révision 1.

Variables

- Le *Nombre de salariés* est exprimé en équivalent plein-temps.

- Les *Dépenses de R-D* comprennent principalement les dépenses de R-D intra-muros, et sont définies conformément au Manuel de Frascati de l'OCDE.

- Le *Nombre de chercheurs* est le nombre de diplômés universitaires titulaires d'un doctorat. Il est exprimé en équivalent plein-temps.

TURKEY

TURQUIE

Inward investments

Investissements entrants

Table 1A - Tableau 1A

NUMBER OF ESTABLISHMENTS / NOMBRE D'ÉTABLISSEMENTS

| | | Foreign affiliates *(Units)* | | | | | As a % of national total | | | | |
| | | Filiales étrangères *(Unités)* | | | | | En % du total national | | | | |
By industry (ISIC Rev. 3)		1994	1995	1996	1997	1998	1994	1995	1996	1997	1998
10/14	Mining & quarrying	..	..	..	..	..	..	..	..	..	..
15/37	**TOTAL MANUFACTURING**	156	169	170	170	193	1.5	1.7	1.6	1.5	1.6
15/16	Food, beverages, tobacco	31	34	33	30	37	1.7	1.9	1.8	1.6	1.9
17/19	Textiles, clothing, leather, footwear	21	22	21	18	21	0.7	0.7	0.6	0.5	0.5
20/22	Wood and paper products	4	4	5	5	5	0.7	0.7	0.8	0.8	0.7
20	Wood products	0	0	0	0	0	0.0	0.0	0.0	0.0	0.0
21/22	Paper, printing and publishing	4	4	5	5	5	1.1	1.1	1.3	1.3	1.1
23/25	Chemicals, Total	32	35	39	43	43	3.8	4.1	4.4	4.3	3.9
23	Refined petroleum, nuclear fuel	4	4	5	5	5	17.4	21.1	20.8	16.1	13.5
24/25	Chemicals, rubber & plastics prod.	28	31	34	38	38	3.4	3.7	4.0	3.9	3.6
24	Chemical products	22	24	26	26	22	5.9	6.0	6.5	6.2	4.9
2423	Pharmaceuticals	9	9	9	8	6	12.3	11.4	11.7	10.5	7.6
25	Rubber and plastics products	6	7	8	12	16	1.3	1.6	1.8	2.2	2.6
26	Non-metallic mineral products	11	11	5	6	11	1.3	1.3	0.6	0.7	1.2
27/28	Basic & fabricated metals	12	12	14	15	20	1.1	1.1	1.3	1.2	1.4
27	Basic metals	2	2	3	2	2	0.6	0.5	0.8	0.5	0.4
28	Fabricated metal products	10	10	11	13	18	1.4	1.5	1.5	1.6	1.9
29/32	Machinery, Total	30	32	34	36	38	2.5	2.7	2.7	2.7	2.5
29/30	Non-electrical machinery	13	14	15	16	16	1.5	1.6	1.7	1.7	1.5
29	Non-electrical machinery nec	13	14	15	16	16	1.5	1.6	1.7	1.7	1.5
30	Office and computing machinery	0	0	0	0	0	0.0	0.0	0.0	0.0	0.0
31/32	Electrical & electronic equipment	17	18	19	20	22	5.3	5.3	5.1	5.1	5.0
31	Electrical machinery nec	11	11	13	15	17	4.3	4.1	4.2	4.5	4.6
32	Radio, TV & communications eq.	6	7	6	5	5	9.1	10.3	9.2	8.3	7.4
33	Scientific instruments	1	2	2	2	2	1.4	2.7	2.7	2.8	2.2
34/35	Transportation equipment	10	14	14	10	9	4.0	5.5	5.0	3.4	2.8
34	Motor vehicles	10	13	13	9	8	5.2	6.5	5.9	4.1	3.2
35	Other transport equipment	0	1	1	1	1	0.0	1.9	1.7	1.4	1.4
351	Shipbuilding & repairing	0	1	0	0	0	0.0	3.3	0.0	0.0	0.0
353	Aircraft and spacecraft	0	0	0	0	0	0.0	0.0	0.0	0.0	0.0
36/37	Other manufacturing	4	3	3	5	7	1.2	0.9	0.9	1.3	1.6
40/45	Construction, electricity, gas & water	..	..	..	..	..	..	..	..	..	..
50/55	Trade, repair, hotels & restaurants	..	..	..	..	..	..	..	..	..	..
65/74	Finance, insurance, business services	..	..	..	..	..	..	..	..	..	..
	OTHER ACTIVITIES	..	..	..	..	..	..	..	..	..	..
01/99	**GRAND TOTAL**	..	..	..	..	..	..	..	..	..	..

Total manufacturing by investing country	1994	1995	1996	1997	1998	*As a % of total manufacturing by foreign affiliates*				
All countries	156	169	170	170	193	100.0	100.0	100.0	100.0	100.0
United States	20	20	18	23	26	12.8	11.8	10.6	13.5	13.5
Canada	1	1	0	..	1	0.6	0.6	0.0	..	0.5
Mexico	0	0	0	..	0	0.0	0.0	0.0	..	0.0
Japan	0	0	1	2	3	0.0	0.0	0.6	1.2	1.6
Europe	131	141	142	138	156	84.0	83.4	83.5	81.2	80.8
European Union (15)	120	129	131	126	143	76.9	76.3	77.1	74.1	74.1
Belgium	5	7	9	7	1	3.2	4.1	5.3	4.1	0.5
France	19	19	21	16	24	12.2	11.2	12.4	9.4	12.4
Germany	41	46	42	47	50	26.3	27.2	24.7	27.6	25.9
Italy	15	14	15	17	19	9.6	8.3	8.8	10.0	9.8
Netherlands	15	17	20	18	22	9.6	10.1	11.8	10.6	11.4
Spain	2	1	1	1	1	1.3	0.6	0.6	0.6	0.5
Sweden	4	4	2	2	3	2.6	2.4	1.2	1.2	1.6
United Kingdom	12	15	15	13	11	7.7	8.9	8.8	7.6	5.7
Switzerland	11	12	12	12	12	7.1	7.1	7.1	7.1	6.2
Australia and New Zealand	1	1	1	..	0	0.6	0.6	0.6	..	0.0
Asia (non-OECD)	1	1	2	2	2	0.6	0.6	1.2	1.2	1.0
Latin America	0	0	0	0	0	0.0	0.0	0.0	0.0	0.0

Note: Majority foreign-owned establishments.
Etablissements sous contrôle étranger majoritaire.

Inward investments

Investissements entrants

Table 2A - Tableau 2A

NUMBER OF EMPLOYEES BY INDUSTRY

NOMBRE DE SALARIÉS PAR INDUSTRIE

ISIC Revision 3		Foreign affiliates *(Units)* Filiales étrangères *(Unités)*					As a % of national total En % du total national				
		1994	1995	1996	1997	1998	1994	1995	1996	1997	1998
10/14	Mining & quarrying	..	..	..	..	..	..	..	..	..	..
15/37	**TOTAL MANUFACTURING**	**49 055**	**54 377**	**58 422**	**60 169**	**65 779**	**5.3**	**5.6**	**5.6**	**5.3**	**5.5**
15/16	Food, beverages, tobacco	8 602	9 928	10 808	10 837	10 626	5.1	5.9	6.3	6.2	5.7
17/19	Textiles, clothing, leather, footwear	3 124	3 995	4 433	3 727	4 815	1.1	1.2	1.2	0.9	1.2
20/22	Wood and paper products	455	352	566	505	749	1.0	0.8	1.1	1.1	1.5
20	Wood products	0	0	0	0	0	0.0	0.0	0.0	0.0	0.0
21/22	Paper, printing and publishing	455	352	566	505	749	1.3	1.0	1.5	1.5	2.0
23/25	Chemicals, Total	9 721	10 563	10 745	12 980	10 757	11.4	11.9	11.6	12.5	9.9
23	Refined petroleum, nuclear fuel	697	825	903	718	934	9.5	12.0	13.0	10.6	13.2
24/25	Chemicals, rubber & plastics prod.	9 024	9 738	9 842	12 262	9 823	11.6	11.9	11.5	12.7	9.6
24	Chemical products	6 059	6 778	7 567	8 110	5 404	11.7	12.6	14.0	13.9	9.1
2423	Pharmaceuticals	3 247	3 423	4 061	4 176	1 998	25.8	24.1	28.5	26.2	12.2
25	Rubber and plastics products	2 965	2 960	2 275	4 152	4 419	11.2	10.6	7.2	10.9	10.4
26	Non-metallic mineral products	1 597	1 446	814	863	1 099	2.5	2.2	1.2	1.2	1.4
27/28	Basic & fabricated metals	1 607	1 588	1 786	1 883	2 955	1.6	1.5	1.7	1.5	2.3
27	Basic metals	538	525	558	75	69	0.9	0.8	1.0	0.1	0.1
28	Fabricated metal products	1 069	1 063	1 228	1 808	2 886	2.7	2.7	2.7	3.2	4.9
29/32	Machinery, Total	11 993	13 978	15 039	19 148	23 240	12.1	14.1	14.4	15.6	17.1
29/30	Non-electrical machinery	1 836	4 687	5 233	5 480	4 905	2.9	7.5	8.1	7.2	5.9
29	Non-electrical machinery nec	1 836	4 687	5 233	5 480	4 905	2.9	7.5	8.1	7.3	6.0
30	Office and computing machinery	0	0	0	0	0	0.0	0.0	0.0	0.0	0.0
31/32	Electrical & electronic equipment	10 157	9 291	9 806	13 668	18 335	28.6	25.4	24.8	29.3	34.5
31	Electrical machinery nec	2 985	3 135	3 300	8 479	12 286	14.5	13.7	12.8	24.0	30.7
32	Radio, TV & communications eq.	7 172	6 156	6 506	5 189	6 049	48.2	44.9	46.9	45.8	46.2
33	Scientific instruments	71	86	90	89	89	2.0	2.0	2.0	2.1	1.5
34/35	Transportation equipment	11 713	12 318	13 963	9 459	10 437	21.2	22.3	23.2	15.6	16.6
34	Motor vehicles	11 713	12 240	13 905	9 384	10 345	29.0	30.2	30.9	20.8	21.4
35	Other transport equipment	0	78	58	75	92	0.0	0.5	0.4	0.5	0.6
351	Shipbuilding & repairing	0	78	0	0	0	0.0	2.0	0.0	0.0	0.0
353	Aircraft and spacecraft	0	0	0	0	0	0.0	0.0	0.0	0.0	0.0
36/37	Other manufacturing	172	123	178	678	1 012	1.1	0.7	0.9	2.8	3.5
40/45	Construction, electricity, gas & water	..	..	..	..	..	..	..	..	..	..
50/55	Trade, repair, hotels & restaurants	..	..	..	..	..	..	..	..	..	..
65/74	Finance, insurance, business services	..	..	..	..	..	..	..	..	..	..
	OTHER ACTIVITIES	..	..	..	..	..	..	..	..	..	..
01/99	**GRAND TOTAL**	..	..	..	..	..	..	..	..	..	..

Note: Majority foreign-owned establishments.
Etablissements sous contrôle étranger majoritaire.

Inward investments   Investissements entrants

Table 3A - Tableau 3A

NUMBER OF EMPLOYEES BY COUNTRY OF ORIGIN IN THE MANUFACTURING INDUSTRY

NOMBRE DE SALARIÉS PAR PAYS D'ORIGINE DANS L'INDUSTRIE MANUFACTURIÈRE

Country of origin	Number of employees (Units) Nombre de salariés (Unités)					As a % of all countries En % du total des pays				
	1994	1995	1996	1997	1998	1994	1995	1996	1997	1998
All countries	49 055	54 377	58 422	60 169	65 779	100.0	100.0	100.0	100.0	100.0
Total OECD	..	..	..	59 032	64 633	..	..	..	98.1	98.3
United States	7 350	8 138	7 815	10 880	11 311	15.0	15.0	13.4	18.1	17.2
Canada	1 722	1 507	0	0	302	3.5	2.8	0.0	0.0	0.5
Mexico	0	0	0	0	..	0.0	0.0	0.0	0.0	..
Japan	0	0	58	607	924	0.0	0.0	0.1	1.0	1.4
Korea	..	..	..	0	0	..	..	..	0.0	0.0
Australia	..	..	..	..	..	..	..	..	..	..
New Zealand	..	..	..	..	..	..	..	..	..	..
Europe	39 621	44 114	49 319	47 545	52 096	80.8	81.1	84.4	79.0	79.2
European Union (15)	37 135	40 189	45 177	41 940	48 292	75.7	73.9	77.3	69.7	73.4
Austria	..	..	..	81	104	..	..	..	0.1	0.2
Belgium	2 579	2 458	2 762	1 399	1 234	5.3	4.5	4.7	2.3	1.9
Denmark	..	..	..	0	0	..	..	..	0.0	0.0
Finland	..	..	..	370	278	..	..	..	0.6	0.4
France	8 341	6 425	6 775	5 907	7 211	17.0	11.8	11.6	9.8	11.0
Germany	14 797	18 230	19 274	18 754	20 001	30.2	33.5	33.0	31.2	30.4
Greece	..	..	..	..	424	..	..	..	..	0.6
Ireland	..	..	..	..	0	..	..	..	..	0.0
Italy	3 950	3 678	4 170	4 212	4 826	8.1	6.8	7.1	7.0	7.3
Luxembourg	..	..	..	119	134	..	..	..	0.2	0.2
Netherlands	4 161	5 175	7 337	8 026	10 281	8.5	9.5	12.6	13.3	15.6
Portugal	..	..	..	0	..	..	..	..	0.0	..
Spain	81	36	41	25	25	0.2	0.1	0.1	0.0	0.0
Sweden	118	103	86	97	299	0.2	0.2	0.1	0.2	0.5
United Kingdom	2 348	3 357	3 892	2 950	3 475	4.8	6.2	6.7	4.9	5.3
Czech Republic	..	..	..	..	..	..	..	..	..	..
Hungary	..	..	..	..	..	..	..	..	..	..
Iceland	..	..	..	..	..	..	..	..	..	..
Norway	..	..	..	..	94	..	..	..	..	0.1
Poland	..	..	..	..	..	..	..	..	..	..
Slovak Republic	..	..	..	..	..	..	..	..	..	..
Switzerland	2 464	3 902	4 221	5 605	3 710	5.0	7.2	7.2	9.3	5.6
Turkey	..	..	..	..	..	..	..	..	..	..
Non-OECD Europe, of which:	..	..	..	..	..	..	..	..	..	..
Baltic countries	..	..	..	..	..	..	..	..	..	..
Bulgaria	..	..	..	..	..	..	..	..	..	..
Croatia	..	..	..	..	..	..	..	..	..	..
Romania	..	..	..	..	..	..	..	..	..	..
Russian Federation	..	..	..	..	..	..	..	..	..	..
Slovenia	..	..	..	..	..	..	..	..	..	..
Ukraine	..	..	..	..	..	..	..	..	..	..
Yugoslavia	..	..	..	..	..	..	..	..	..	..
Non-OECD Asia, of which:	31	17	149	145	153	0.1	0.0	0.3	0.2	0.2
China	..	..	..	..	..	..	..	..	..	..
Chinese Taipei	..	..	..	145	16	..	..	..	0.2	0.0
Hong Kong (China)	..	..	..	..	..	..	..	..	..	..
India	..	..	..	..	137	..	..	..	..	0.2
Indonesia	..	..	..	..	..	..	..	..	..	..
Malaysia	..	..	..	..	..	..	..	..	..	..
Philippines	..	..	..	..	..	..	..	..	..	..
Singapore	..	..	..	..	..	..	..	..	..	..
Thailand	..	..	..	..	..	..	..	..	..	..
Near and Middle East	..	..	..	788	611	..	..	..	1.3	0.9
Africa	..	..	..	0	..	..	..	..	0.0	..
Latin America, of which:	0	0	0	0	0	0.0	0.0	0.0	0.0	0.0
Argentina	0	0	0	0	0	0.0	0.0	0.0	0.0	0.0
Brazil	0	0	0	0	0	0.0	0.0	0.0	0.0	0.0
Chile	0	0	0	0	0	0.0	0.0	0.0	0.0	0.0

Note: Majority foreign-owned establishments.
       Etablissements sous contrôle étranger majoritaire.

Inward investments

Investissements entrants

Table 4A - Tableau 4A

PRODUCTION BY INDUSTRY

PRODUCTION PAR INDUSTRIE

ISIC Revision 3		Foreign affiliates (Billions of TRL) Filiales étrangères (Milliards de TRL)					As a % of national total En % du total national				
		1994	1995	1996	1997	1998	1994	1995	1996	1997	1998
10/14	Mining & quarrying	..	..	..	..	..	..	..	..	..	..
15/37	**TOTAL MANUFACTURING**	**243 933**	**545 574**	**963 075**	**1 934 589**	**3 095 517**	**11.1**	**12.1**	**12.7**	**12.0**	**11.2**
15/16	Food, beverages, tobacco	55 030	117 466	227 005	362 255	556 751	13.9	14.9	15.9	13.2	10.8
17/19	Textiles, clothing, leather, footwear	6 128	11 288	17 018	26 574	59 372	1.4	1.3	1.2	0.8	1.1
20/22	Wood and paper products	1 925	3 408	8 327	14 019	99 465	1.9	1.7	2.4	2.0	8.6
20	Wood products	0	0	0	0	0	0.0	0.0	0.0	0.0	0.0
21/22	Paper, printing and publishing	1 925	3 408	8 327	14 019	99 465	2.3	2.0	2.9	2.5	10.5
23/25	Chemicals, Total	83 752	199 310	304 763	672 037	910 487	17.0	19.0	17.5	19.0	15.9
23	Refined petroleum, nuclear fuel	32 600	73 026	126 823	210 309	298 706	15.1	16.6	16.0	13.0	11.9
24/25	Chemicals, rubber & plastics prod.	51 152	126 285	177 941	461 728	611 781	18.5	20.8	18.8	24.0	19.1
24	Chemical products	36 523	89 691	147 024	340 603	426 802	17.4	19.8	21.4	24.4	19.0
2423	Pharmaceuticals	20 445	36 767	65 835	123 899	145 170	42.2	35.6	40.5	38.0	22.2
25	Rubber and plastics products	14 630	36 593	30 917	121 125	184 980	21.9	23.5	11.9	22.7	19.4
26	Non-metallic mineral products	5 776	9 442	11 081	16 039	37 053	4.8	4.3	2.9	2.0	2.6
27/28	Basic & fabricated metals	6 855	16 669	29 814	42 777	138 127	2.3	2.9	3.5	2.0	4.1
27	Basic metals	1 831	3 754	5 682	690	1 194	0.8	0.8	0.9	0.0	0.0
28	Fabricated metal products	5 024	12 915	24 132	42 087	136 933	9.4	10.6	10.1	7.9	14.2
29/32	Machinery, Total	42 694	96 510	176 650	401 563	806 050	20.2	22.0	24.1	26.0	28.1
29/30	Non-electrical machinery	10 063	32 491	50 168	108 585	174 544	8.2	12.5	11.9	12.4	11.0
29	Non-electrical machinery nec	10 063	32 491	50 168	108 585	174 544	8.2	12.6	12.0	12.7	11.4
30	Office and computing machinery	0	0	0	0	0	0.0	0.0	0.0	0.0	0.0
31/32	Electrical & electronic equipment	32 630	64 019	126 482	292 978	631 506	36.8	35.7	40.7	43.6	49.2
31	Electrical machinery nec	11 078	26 421	41 333	153 413	292 960	24.8	25.5	26.1	36.9	40.3
32	Radio, TV & communications eq.	21 552	37 598	85 148	139 565	338 546	49.0	49.5	55.8	54.4	60.8
33	Scientific instruments	91	219	330	607	1 058	2.3	2.2	2.0	2.3	1.4
34/35	Transportation equipment	41 308	90 934	186 763	392 374	472 603	32.8	30.5	34.0	31.1	24.3
34	Motor vehicles	41 308	90 847	185 430	389 984	468 033	36.3	33.1	36.8	33.8	26.2
35	Other transport equipment	0	87	1 333	2 390	4 569	0.0	0.4	2.9	2.3	2.9
351	Shipbuilding & repairing	0	87	0	0	0	0.0	1.2	0.0	0.0	0.0
353	Aircraft and spacecraft	0	0	0	0	0	0.0	0.0	0.0	0.0	0.0
36/37	Other manufacturing	374	328	1 324	6 342	14 552	2.6	0.9	1.7	3.6	4.3
40/45	Construction, electricity, gas & water	..	..	..	..	..	..	..	..	..	..
50/55	Trade, repair, hotels & restaurants	..	..	..	..	..	..	..	..	..	..
65/74	Finance, insurance, business services	..	..	..	..	..	..	..	..	..	..
	OTHER ACTIVITIES	..	..	..	..	..	..	..	..	..	..
01/99	**GRAND TOTAL**	..	..	..	..	..	..	..	..	..	..

Note: Majority foreign-owned establishments.
Etablissements sous contrôle étranger majoritaire.

Table 5A - Tableau 5A

PRODUCTION BY COUNTRY OF ORIGIN IN THE MANUFACTURING INDUSTRY

PRODUCTION PAR PAYS D'ORIGINE DANS L'INDUSTRIE MANUFACTURIÈRE

Country of origin	Production (Billions of TRL) / Production (Milliards de TRL)					As a % of all countries / En % du total des pays				
	1994	1995	1996	1997	1998	1994	1995	1996	1997	1998
All countries	**243 933**	**545 574**	**963 075**	**1 934 589**	**3 095 517**	**100.0**	**100.0**	**100.0**	**100.0**	**100.0**
Total OECD	..	..	..	1 914 359	3 059 001	..	..	..	99.0	98.8
United States	67 751	136 910	210 186	506 933	691 906	27.8	25.1	21.8	26.2	22.4
Canada	5 329	8 842	0	0	67 529	2.2	1.6	0.0	0.0	2.2
Mexico	0	0	0	0	..	0.0	0.0	0.0	0.0	..
Japan	0	0	1 333	4 928	12 310	0.0	0.0	0.1	0.3	0.4
Korea	..	..	..	..	..	..	..	..	..	..
Australia	..	..	..	..	..	..	..	..	..	..
New Zealand	..	..	..	..	..	..	..	..	..	..
Europe	169 427	395 683	740 107	1 402 498	2 287 257	69.5	72.5	76.8	72.5	73.9
European Union (15)	157 892	369 721	690 966	1 268 707	2 123 283	64.7	67.8	71.7	65.6	68.6
Austria	..	..	..	626	1 419	..	..	..	0.0	0.0
Belgium	7 197	12 973	30 792	27 283	100 191	3.0	2.4	3.2	1.4	3.2
Denmark	..	..	..	..	..	..	..	..	..	..
Finland	..	..	..	8 839	15 455	..	..	..	0.5	0.5
France	28 466	56 413	90 869	165 615	325 397	11.7	10.3	9.4	8.6	10.5
Germany	65 660	136 596	263 887	568 055	672 377	26.9	25.0	27.4	29.4	21.7
Greece	..	..	..	..	7 168	..	..	..	..	0.2
Ireland	..	..	..	..	..	..	..	..	..	..
Italy	14 175	32 835	59 868	137 770	333 037	5.8	6.0	6.2	7.1	10.8
Luxembourg	..	..	..	1 759	2 968	..	..	..	0.1	0.1
Netherlands	31 783	110 393	204 632	313 161	570 151	13.0	20.2	21.2	16.2	18.4
Portugal	..	..	..	..	..	..	..	..	..	..
Spain	112	68	103	345	443	0.0	0.0	0.0	0.0	0.0
Sweden	313	646	696	1 395	3 590	0.1	0.1	0.1	0.1	0.1
United Kingdom	8 322	15 765	32 438	43 858	91 090	3.4	2.9	3.4	2.3	2.9
Czech Republic	..	..	..	..	..	..	..	..	..	..
Hungary	..	..	..	..	..	..	..	..	..	..
Iceland	..	..	..	..	..	..	..	..	..	..
Norway	..	..	..	..	5 075	..	..	..	..	0.2
Poland	..	..	..	..	..	..	..	..	..	..
Slovak Republic	..	..	..	..	..	..	..	..	..	..
Switzerland	11 121	25 294	49 520	133 791	158 899	4.6	4.6	5.1	6.9	5.1
Turkey	..	..	..	..	..	..	..	..	..	..
Non-OECD Europe, of which:	..	..	..	..	..	..	..	..	..	..
Baltic countries	..	..	..	..	..	..	..	..	..	..
Bulgaria	..	..	..	..	..	..	..	..	..	..
Croatia	..	..	..	..	..	..	..	..	..	..
Romania	..	..	..	..	..	..	..	..	..	..
Russian Federation	..	..	..	..	..	..	..	..	..	..
Slovenia	..	..	..	..	..	..	..	..	..	..
Ukraine	..	..	..	..	..	..	..	..	..	..
Yugoslavia	..	..	..	..	..	..	..	..	..	..
Non-OECD Asia, of which:	5	14	135	309	666	0.0	0.0	0.0	0.0	0.0
China	..	..	..	..	..	..	..	..	..	..
Chinese Taipei	..	..	..	309	126	..	..	..	..	..
Hong Kong (China)	..	..	..	..	..	..	..	..	..	..
India	..	..	..	..	540	..	..	..	..	0.0
Indonesia	..	..	..	..	..	..	..	..	..	..
Malaysia	..	..	..	..	..	..	..	..	..	..
Philippines	..	..	..	..	..	..	..	..	..	..
Singapore	..	..	..	..	..	..	..	..	0.0	0.0
Thailand	..	..	..	..	..	..	..	..	..	..
Near and Middle East	..	..	..	7 724	11 676	..	..	..	0.4	0.4
Africa	..	..	..	..	..	..	..	..	..	..
Latin America, of which:	0	0	0	0	..	0.0	0.0	0.0	0.0	..
Argentina	0	0	0	0	..	0.0	0.0	0.0	0.0	..
Brazil	0	0	0	0	..	0.0	0.0	0.0	0.0	..
Chile	0	0	0	0	..	0.0	0.0	0.0	0.0	..

Note: Majority foreign-owned establishments.
Etablissements sous contrôle étranger majoritaire.

Inward investments   *Investissements entrants*

Table 6A - Tableau 6A
TURNOVER / CHIFFRE D'AFFAIRES

By industry (ISIC Rev. 3)	Foreign affiliates (Billions of TRL) Filiales étrangères (Milliards de TRL)					As a % of national total En % du total national				
	1994	1995	1996	1997	1998	1994	1995	1996	1997	1998
10/14 Mining & quarrying	..	..	..	..	..	..	..	..	..	..
15/37 **TOTAL MANUFACTURING**	235 323	534 071	935 921	1 887 080	3 043 341	11.1	12.4	12.8	12.3	11.5
15/16 Food, beverages, tobacco	53 226	114 826	218 113	346 442	533 720	14.0	15.4	16.4	13.4	11.0
17/19 Textiles, clothing, leather, footwear	6 004	11 029	16 567	25 565	57 086	1.4	1.3	1.2	0.8	1.1
20/22 Wood and paper products	1 896	3 354	8 194	13 679	90 329	1.9	1.7	2.4	2.1	8.1
20 Wood products	0	0	0	0	0	0.0	0.0	0.0	0.0	0.0
21/22 Paper, printing and publishing	1 896	3 354	8 194	13 679	90 329	2.2	2.0	2.9	2.5	9.7
23/25 Chemicals, Total	80 968	193 957	298 420	661 409	939 285	16.9	18.9	17.5	19.1	16.6
23 Refined petroleum, nuclear fuel	31 725	72 340	126 796	206 259	296 471	15.0	16.6	16.2	13.0	11.8
24/25 Chemicals, rubber & plastics prod.	49 243	121 617	171 624	455 150	642 814	18.4	20.6	18.7	24.4	20.5
24 Chemical products	35 185	87 093	141 624	336 150	464 306	17.3	19.7	21.2	24.9	20.9
2423 Pharmaceuticals	19 606	34 986	62 201	126 353	135 643	41.7	35.2	40.0	39.4	22.0
25 Rubber and plastics products	14 058	34 525	30 000	119 000	178 508	22.0	23.2	12.0	23.1	19.5
26 Non-metallic mineral products	5 673	9 287	10 823	15 687	36 858	4.9	4.3	2.9	2.0	2.6
27/28 Basic & fabricated metals	6 529	16 311	28 915	41 840	135 127	2.3	3.0	3.5	2.1	4.1
27 Basic metals	1 801	3 725	5 451	650	1 099	0.8	0.9	0.9	0.0	0.0
28 Fabricated metal products	4 728	12 586	23 464	41 190	134 028	9.2	10.6	10.2	8.1	14.4
29/32 Machinery, Total	40 594	94 030	168 587	389 577	777 450	19.8	22.0	23.8	26.2	28.1
29/30 Non-electrical machinery	9 505	32 679	48 899	102 788	164 395	8.0	12.8	12.0	12.4	10.8
29 Non-electrical machinery nec	9 505	32 679	48 899	102 788	164 395	8.0	13.0	12.1	12.7	11.2
30 Office and computing machinery	0	0	0	0	0	0.0	0.0	0.0	0.0	0.0
31/32 Electrical & electronic equipment	31 089	61 351	119 688	286 789	613 054	36.3	35.3	40.1	43.7	49.1
31 Electrical machinery nec	10 395	25 667	40 251	147 798	285 037	24.1	25.4	26.1	36.6	40.3
32 Radio, TV & communications eq.	20 695	35 684	79 437	138 991	328 017	48.5	49.0	54.9	55.0	60.7
33 Scientific instruments	98	217	323	596	1 029	2.5	2.3	2.0	2.3	1.4
34/35 Transportation equipment	39 953	90 765	184 804	385 998	458 232	33.0	31.5	34.6	31.4	25.1
34 Motor vehicles	39 953	90 677	183 496	383 720	453 772	36.2	34.0	37.3	34.0	27.0
35 Other transport equipment	0	88	1 308	2 278	4 460	0.0	0.4	3.2	2.3	3.0
351 Shipbuilding & repairing	0	88	0	0	0	0.0	1.7	0.0	0.0	0.0
353 Aircraft and spacecraft	0	0	0	0	0	0.0	0.0	0.0	0.0	0.0
36/37 Other manufacturing	383	294	1 174	6 287	14 224	2.7	0.9	1.6	3.8	4.4
40/45 Construction, electricity, gas & water	..	..	..	..	..	..	..	..	..	..
50/55 Trade, repair, hotels & restaurants	..	..	..	..	..	..	..	..	..	..
65/74 Finance, insurance, business services	..	..	..	..	..	..	..	..	..	..
OTHER ACTIVITIES										
01/99 **GRAND TOTAL**	..	..	..	..	..	..	..	..	..	..

Total manufacturing by investing country						As a % of total manufacturing by foreign affiliates				
All countries	235 323	534 071	935 921	1 887 080	3 043 341	100.0	100.0	100.0	100.0	100.0
United States	64 378	133 538	205 963	504 373	666 237	27.4	25.0	22.0	26.7	21.9
Canada	5 267	8 685	0	..	67 451	2.2	1.6	0.0	..	2.2
Mexico	0	0	0	..	0	0.0	0.0	0.0	..	0.0
Japan	0	0	1 308	4 710	12 007	0.0	0.0	0.1	0.2	0.4
Europe	164 277	387 749	717 482	1 358 555	2 262 583	69.8	72.6	76.7	72.0	74.3
European Union (15)	152 866	364 115	671 436	1 239 568	2 104 568	65.0	68.2	71.7	65.7	69.2
Belgium	6 916	12 539	30 320	26 829	98 381	2.9	2.3	3.2	1.4	3.2
France	27 905	55 798	88 387	163 748	317 483	11.9	10.4	9.4	8.7	10.4
Germany	62 342	133 237	256 348	553 444	706 740	26.5	24.9	27.4	29.3	23.2
Italy	13 936	32 587	58 669	135 183	320 999	5.9	6.1	6.3	7.2	10.5
Netherlands	31 491	110 220	200 199	306 009	544 630	13.4	20.6	21.4	16.2	17.9
Spain	107	68	102	426	422	0.0	0.0	0.0	0.0	0.0
Sweden	311	629	690	1 361	3 545	0.1	0.1	0.1	0.1	0.1
United Kingdom	8 149	15 413	30 605	42 548	83 335	3.5	2.9	3.3	2.3	2.7
Switzerland	10 998	22 979	46 353	118 987	152 983	4.7	4.3	5.0	6.3	5.0
Australia and New Zealand	86	198	307	..	0	0.0	0.0	0.0	..	0.0
Asia (non-OECD)	5	14	98	236	119	0.0	0.0	0.0	0.0	0.0
Latin America	0	0	0	0	0	0.0	0.0	0.0	0.0	0.0

Note: Majority foreign-owned establishments.
Etablissements sous contrôle étranger majoritaire.

Inward investments   *Investissements entrants*

Table 7A - Tableau 7A

VALUE ADDED / VALEUR AJOUTÉE

By industry (ISIC Rev. 3)	Foreign affiliates (Billions of TRL) Filiales étrangères (Milliards de TRL)					As a % of national total En % du total national				
	1994	1995	1996	1997	1998	1994	1995	1996	1997	1998
10/14 Mining & quarrying	..	..	..	..	..	..	..	..	..	..
15/37 **TOTAL MANUFACTURING**	**118 573**	**255 454**	**444 994**	**861 766**	**1 417 872**	**12.9**	**14.7**	**15.4**	**13.8**	**12.9**
15/16 Food, beverages, tobacco	25 247	44 804	97 498	124 255	256 174	18.3	16.5	20.5	16.6	16.0
17/19 Textiles, clothing, leather, footwear	3 742	4 669	7 755	13 137	27 987	2.3	1.6	1.5	1.2	1.5
20/22 Wood and paper products	949	1 565	4 168	7 045	78 566	2.3	2.2	3.3	2.9	17.1
20 Wood products	0	0	0	0	0	0.0	0.0	0.0	0.0	0.0
21/22 Paper, printing and publishing	949	1 565	4 168	7 045	78 566	2.6	2.7	3.8	3.4	20.1
23/25 Chemicals, Total	42 905	116 937	181 521	386 039	451 844	17.8	22.7	22.8	22.0	15.3
23 Refined petroleum, nuclear fuel	17 576	49 935	91 941	140 631	204 655	15.9	19.9	23.4	15.6	12.4
24/25 Chemicals, rubber & plastics prod.	25 328	67 002	89 580	245 408	247 189	19.3	25.3	22.2	28.8	19.0
24 Chemical products	17 429	46 925	75 450	180 478	163 997	17.1	23.5	25.0	28.4	17.6
2423 Pharmaceuticals	10 987	18 414	28 524	47 070	51 653	40.4	36.9	35.8	31.8	15.7
25 Rubber and plastics products	7 899	20 076	14 130	64 931	83 191	26.6	30.8	14.1	29.8	22.5
26 Non-metallic mineral products	3 008	5 145	5 936	9 546	22 755	4.3	4.3	3.0	2.3	3.1
27/28 Basic & fabricated metals	3 951	7 425	10 726	21 568	68 759	3.6	4.5	4.0	2.8	5.0
27 Basic metals	732	1 160	2 056	381	669	0.9	1.0	1.2	0.1	0.1
28 Fabricated metal products	3 219	6 265	8 670	21 187	68 090	13.9	12.6	9.5	9.4	16.4
29/32 Machinery, Total	25 885	45 209	80 633	184 993	360 640	26.4	24.9	27.3	29.0	30.9
29/30 Non-electrical machinery	7 385	14 563	22 136	43 030	71 340	13.1	14.2	13.5	12.1	11.1
29 Non-electrical machinery nec	7 385	14 563	22 136	43 030	71 340	13.2	14.3	13.6	12.2	11.3
30 Office and computing machinery	0	0	0	0	0	0.0	0.0	0.0	0.0	0.0
31/32 Electrical & electronic equipment	18 500	30 646	58 497	141 963	289 300	44.0	38.9	44.3	50.3	55.1
31 Electrical machinery nec	4 198	9 024	17 204	82 898	162 532	22.9	22.6	27.9	44.2	47.9
32 Radio, TV & communications eq.	14 302	21 622	41 293	59 066	126 767	60.3	55.6	58.7	62.5	68.0
33 Scientific instruments	69	80	114	404	584	3.1	1.9	2.0	3.0	1.8
34/35 Transportation equipment	12 596	29 496	55 937	111 565	144 299	24.4	28.2	28.6	23.9	23.2
34 Motor vehicles	12 596	29 432	55 139	110 742	142 776	28.7	33.0	32.5	27.9	27.0
35 Other transport equipment	0	64	798	823	1 523	0.0	0.4	3.0	1.2	1.6
351 Shipbuilding & repairing	0	64	0	0	0	0.0	1.3	0.0	0.0	0.0
353 Aircraft and spacecraft	0	0	0	0	0	0.0	0.0	0.0	0.0	0.0
36/37 Other manufacturing	222	125	705	3 212	6 263	3.3	0.9	2.2	4.1	5.0
40/45 Construction, electricity, gas & water	..	..	..	..	..	..	..	..	..	..
50/55 Trade, repair, hotels & restaurants	..	..	..	..	..	..	..	..	..	..
65/74 Finance, insurance, business services	..	..	..	..	..	..	..	..	..	..
OTHER ACTIVITIES	..	..	..	..	..	..	..	..	..	..
01/99 **GRAND TOTAL**	..	..	..	..	..	..	..	..	..	..

Total manufacturing by investing country						As a % of total manufacturing by foreign affiliates				
All countries	**118 573**	**255 454**	**444 994**	**861 766**	**1 417 872**	**100.0**	**100.0**	**100.0**	**100.0**	**100.0**
United States	42 025	79 811	127 439	261 768	380 741	35.4	31.2	28.6	30.4	26.9
Canada	3 704	4 291	0	..	52 317	3.1	1.7	0.0	..	3.7
Mexico	0	0	0	0	0	0.0	0.0	0.0	0.0	0.0
Japan	0	0	798	101	5 377	0.0	0.0	0.2	0.0	0.4
Europe	72 481	170 200	312 809	592 646	957 835	61.1	66.6	70.3	68.8	67.6
European Union (15)	67 953	161 071	288 247	531 661	871 756	57.3	63.1	64.8	61.7	61.5
Belgium	3 639	5 512	15 288	14 928	44 426	3.1	2.2	3.4	1.7	3.1
France	8 900	19 583	33 596	54 573	110 450	7.5	7.7	7.5	6.3	7.8
Germany	32 655	57 815	92 323	216 807	218 502	27.5	22.6	20.7	25.2	15.4
Italy	5 828	16 232	27 561	73 492	233 330	4.9	6.4	6.2	8.5	16.5
Netherlands	11 409	51 851	99 416	148 019	221 289	9.6	20.3	22.3	17.2	15.6
Spain	38	31	49	151	118	0.0	0.0	0.0	0.0	0.0
Sweden	166	217	359	704	1 577	0.1	0.1	0.1	0.1	0.1
United Kingdom	4 591	8 561	16 986	20 103	30 646	3.9	3.4	3.8	2.3	2.2
Switzerland	4 361	8 901	24 834	60 985	83 360	3.7	3.5	5.6	7.1	5.9
Australia and New Zealand	75	133	272	..	0	0.1	0.1	0.1	..	0.0
Asia (non-OECD)	1	6	74	161	446	0.0	0.0	0.0	0.0	0.0
Latin America	0	0	0	0	0	0.0	0.0	0.0	0.0	0.0

Note: Majority foreign-owned establishments.
Etablissements sous contrôle étranger majoritaire.

Inward investments

Investissements entrants

Table 8A - Tableau 8A

COMPENSATION OF EMPLOYEES / SALAIRES ET CHARGES SOCIALES

By industry (ISIC Rev. 3)	Foreign affiliates (Billions of TRL) Filiales étrangères (Milliards de TRL)					As a % of national total En % du total national				
	1994	1995	1996	1997	1998	1994	1995	1996	1997	1998
10/14 Mining & quarrying	..	..	..	..	..	..	..	..	..	..
15/37 TOTAL MANUFACTURING	**14 522**	**33 536**	**58 983**	**113 518**	**228 932**	**9.8**	**12.6**	**11.9**	**10.8**	**11.3**
15/16 Food, beverages, tobacco	2 249	5 029	9 495	15 452	29 414	8.2	11.1	12.3	9.8	9.4
17/19 Textiles, clothing, leather, footwear	333	879	1 915	2 456	6 556	1.2	1.6	1.7	1.0	1.5
20/22 Wood and paper products	105	222	631	1 077	3 109	1.4	1.7	2.7	2.4	3.5
20 Wood products	0	0	0	0	0	0.0	0.0	0.0	0.0	0.0
21/22 Paper, printing and publishing	105	222	631	1 077	3 109	1.8	2.1	3.2	2.9	4.2
23/25 Chemicals, Total	4 608	10 855	16 228	37 703	63 486	20.4	25.7	22.5	24.3	20.7
23 Refined petroleum, nuclear fuel	351	825	1 499	1 968	6 735	12.0	17.1	26.4	13.5	23.9
24/25 Chemicals, rubber & plastics prod.	4 257	10 030	14 729	35 735	56 751	21.7	26.8	22.2	25.4	20.4
24 Chemical products	2 780	5 964	12 742	25 629	33 989	19.3	22.2	26.2	25.8	17.5
2423 Pharmaceuticals	1 509	2 937	6 269	11 850	12 196	40.6	36.6	41.3	38.1	18.9
25 Rubber and plastics products	1 477	4 066	1 987	10 106	22 762	28.5	38.7	11.2	24.5	26.9
26 Non-metallic mineral products	469	685	791	1 358	3 516	4.5	3.4	2.2	1.8	2.5
27/28 Basic & fabricated metals	548	829	1 998	3 308	8 534	2.5	2.5	3.1	2.4	3.3
27 Basic metals	154	288	551	99	210	0.9	1.1	1.2	0.1	0.1
28 Fabricated metal products	394	541	1 447	3 209	8 324	8.7	6.5	7.7	7.0	9.5
29/32 Machinery, Total	3 451	7 998	15 585	34 703	78 646	19.8	24.7	26.1	25.5	28.0
29/30 Non-electrical machinery	471	2 123	3 718	8 483	15 029	4.6	11.5	11.4	11.0	9.8
29 Non-electrical machinery nec	471	2 123	3 718	8 483	15 029	4.6	11.6	11.4	11.0	10.0
30 Office and computing machinery	0	0	0	0	0	0.0	0.0	0.0	0.0	0.0
31/32 Electrical & electronic equipment	2 980	5 876	11 867	26 220	63 617	41.4	41.9	43.6	44.5	49.9
31 Electrical machinery nec	734	1 670	3 498	15 625	38 363	21.3	24.1	26.3	38.0	44.6
32 Radio, TV & communications eq.	2 246	4 205	8 369	10 596	25 254	59.8	59.5	60.1	59.5	60.8
33 Scientific instruments	13	27	48	86	186	3.2	3.0	2.5	2.5	2.0
34/35 Transportation equipment	2 731	6 999	12 261	16 718	33 660	22.4	29.0	28.5	19.9	21.2
34 Motor vehicles	2 731	6 974	12 175	16 529	33 237	34.4	40.0	38.6	26.9	27.1
35 Other transport equipment	0	25	86	189	423	0.0	0.4	0.7	0.8	1.2
351 Shipbuilding & repairing	0	25	0	0	0	0.0	1.5	0.0	0.0	0.0
353 Aircraft and spacecraft	0	0	0	0	0	0.0	0.0	0.0	0.0	0.0
36/37 Other manufacturing	16	14	31	656	1 826	1.3	0.6	0.5	5.0	6.6
40/45 Construction, electricity, gas & water	..	..	..	..	..	..	..	..	..	..
50/55 Trade, repair, hotels & restaurants	..	..	..	..	..	..	..	..	..	..
65/74 Finance, insurance, business services	..	..	..	..	..	..	..	..	..	..
OTHER ACTIVITIES	..	..	..	..	..	..	..	..	..	..
01/99 GRAND TOTAL	..	..	..	..	..	..	..	..	..	..

Total manufacturing by investing country						As a % of total manufacturing by foreign affiliates				
All countries	14 522	33 536	58 983	113 518	228 932	100.0	100.0	100.0	100.0	100.0
United States	2 638	5 696	7 201	19 827	37 109	18.2	17.0	12.2	17.5	16.2
Canada	760	1 578	0	..	2 707	5.2	4.7	0.0	..	1.2
Mexico	0	0	0	..	0	0.0	0.0	0.0	..	0.0
Japan	0	0	86	676	2 345	0.0	0.0	0.1	0.6	1.0
Europe	11 038	26 049	51 180	91 539	184 316	76.0	77.7	86.8	80.6	80.5
European Union (15)	10 041	23 756	47 390	81 917	169 474	69.1	70.8	80.3	72.2	74.0
Belgium	631	1 419	2 541	2 565	6 549	4.3	4.2	4.3	2.3	2.9
France	2 019	3 163	6 979	11 979	26 832	13.9	9.4	11.8	10.6	11.7
Germany	4 352	10 652	19 342	35 110	61 200	30.0	31.8	32.8	30.9	26.7
Italy	1 328	3 532	4 258	9 787	23 990	9.1	10.5	7.2	8.6	10.5
Netherlands	1 125	3 355	10 804	17 800	37 946	7.7	10.0	18.3	15.7	16.6
Spain	3	4	9	13	27	0.0	0.0	0.0	0.0	0.0
Sweden	35	51	88	182	822	0.2	0.2	0.1	0.2	0.4
United Kingdom	392	1 328	2 851	3 533	9 931	2.7	4.0	4.8	3.1	4.3
Switzerland	984	2 288	3 870	9 622	14 294	6.8	6.8	6.6	8.5	6.2
Australia and New Zealand	16	47	79	..	0	0.1	0.1	0.1	..	0.0
Asia (non-OECD)	1	1	87	131	90	0.0	0.0	0.1	0.1	0.0
Latin America	0	0	0	0	0	0.0	0.0	0.0	0.0	0.0

Note: Majority foreign-owned establishments.
Etablissements sous contrôle étranger majoritaire.

Table 9A - Tableau 9A
R&D EXPENDITURE / DÉPENSES DE R-D

By industry (ISIC Rev. 3)	Foreign affiliates (Billions of TRL) Filiales étrangères (Milliards de TRL)					As a % of national total En % du total national				
	1994	1995	1996	1997	1998	1994	1995	1996	1997	1998
10/14 Mining & quarrying	..	..	..	0	..	..	..	..	0.0	..
15/37 **TOTAL MANUFACTURING**	**1 016**	**2 286**	**3 680**	**6 791**	**6 887**	**29.4**	**32.8**	**21.7**	**18.6**	**10.1**
15/16 Food, beverages, tobacco	21	36	77	130	187	12.7	12.6	13.1	9.9	10.5
17/19 Textiles, clothing, leather, footwear	..	..	..	0	..	..	..	..	0.0	..
20/22 Wood and paper products	..	..	..	0	43	..	..	..	0.0	11.2
20 Wood products	..	..	..	0	43	..	..	..	0.0	47.3
21/22 Paper, printing and publishing	..	..	..	0	0	..	..	..	0.0	0.0
23/25 Chemicals, Total	75	204	165	539	976	20.6	30.8	11.4	12.1	17.0
23 Refined petroleum, nuclear fuel	22	29	..	0	..	97.8	96.7	..	0.0	..
24/25 Chemicals, rubber & plastics prod.	53	175	165	539	976	15.5	27.6	11.5	12.1	21.8
24 Chemical products	53	175	165	539	976	20.1	36.6	16.5	16.3	29.2
2423 Pharmaceuticals	12	39	..	0	..	36.4	42.4	..	0.0	..
25 Rubber and plastics products	..	..	..	0	..	..	..	..	0.0	..
26 Non-metallic mineral products	..	..	..	0	..	..	..	..	0.0	..
27/28 Basic & fabricated metals	..	..	..	0	15	..	..	..	0.0	0.3
27 Basic metals	..	..	..	0	..	..	..	..	0.0	..
28 Fabricated metal products	..	0	..	0	15	..	0.0	..	0.0	1.8
29/32 Machinery, Total	885	1 943	2 754	1 041	2 547	48.0	51.3	37.3	7.3	12.4
29/30 Non-electrical machinery	..	234	70	17	38	..	17.7	2.8	0.3	0.4
29 Non-electrical machinery nec	..	234	70	17	38	..	17.7	3.2	0.3	0.4
30 Office and computing machinery	..	0	..	0	..	..	0.0	..	0.0	..
31/32 Electrical & electronic equipment	885	1 709	2 684	1 023	2 509	74.7	69.4	54.5	11.9	25.6
31 Electrical machinery nec	77	192	391	55	..	63.1	58.2	41.8	2.2	..
32 Radio, TV & communications eq.	808	1 517	2 293	969	2 509	76.0	71.1	57.4	15.9	26.0
33 Scientific instruments	..	..	..	0	..	..	..	..	0.0	..
34/35 Transportation equipment	35	103	684	5 080	3 119	13.0	16.6	31.8	54.2	10.0
34 Motor vehicles	35	103	684	5 080	3 119	15.2	19.7	35.9	58.9	10.7
35 Other transport equipment	..	..	..	0	..	..	..	..	0.0	..
351 Shipbuilding & repairing	..	..	..	0	..	..	..	..	0.0	..
353 Aircraft and spacecraft	..	..	..	0	..	..	..	..	0.0	..
36/37 Other manufacturing	..	..	..	0	..	..	..	..	0.0	..
40/45 Construction, electricity, gas & water	..	..	..	0	..	..	..	..	0.0	..
50/55 Trade, repair, hotels & restaurants	..	..	..	0	0	..	..	..	0.0	0.0
65/74 Finance, insurance, business services	..	..	..	0	..	..	..	..	0.0	..
OTHER ACTIVITIES	..	..	..	0	..	..	..	..	0.0	..
01/99 **GRAND TOTAL**	..	..	..	**6 791**	**6 887**	..	..	..	**14.8**	**8.4**

Total manufacturing by investing country						As a % of total manufacturing by foreign affiliates				
All countries	**1 016**	**2 286**	**3 680**	**6 791**	**6 887**	**100.0**	**100.0**	**100.0**	**100.0**	**100.0**
United States	..	..	..	..	..	..	..	..	..	..
Canada	..	..	..	..	..	..	..	..	..	..
Mexico	..	..	..	..	..	..	..	..	..	..
Japan	..	..	..	..	..	..	..	..	..	..
Europe	..	..	..	..	..	..	..	..	..	..
European Union (15)	..	..	..	..	..	..	..	..	..	..
Belgium	..	..	..	..	..	..	..	..	..	..
France	..	..	..	..	..	..	..	..	..	..
Germany	..	..	..	..	..	..	..	..	..	..
Italy	..	..	..	..	..	..	..	..	..	..
Netherlands	..	..	..	..	..	..	..	..	..	..
Spain	..	..	..	..	..	..	..	..	..	..
Sweden	..	..	..	..	..	..	..	..	..	..
United Kingdom	..	..	..	..	..	..	..	..	..	..
Switzerland	..	..	..	..	..	..	..	..	..	..
Australia and New Zealand	..	..	..	..	..	..	..	..	..	..
Asia (non-OECD)	..	..	..	..	..	..	..	..	..	..
Latin America	..	..	..	..	..	..	..	..	..	..

Note: Majority foreign-owned firms.
Firmes sous contrôle étranger majoritaire.

Inward investments   *Investissements entrants*

Table 10A - Tableau 10A

NUMBER OF RESEARCHERS / NOMBRE DE CHERCHEURS

By industry (ISIC Rev. 3)		Foreign affiliates *(FTE)* Filiales étrangères *(EPT)*					As a % of national total En % du total national				
		1994	1995	1996	1997	1998	1994	1995	1996	1997	1998
10/14	Mining & quarrying	..	..	..	0	..	..	..	..	0.0	..
15/37	**TOTAL MANUFACTURING**	**413**	**498**	**490**	**333**	**304**	**20.7**	**22.5**	**20.0**	**14.6**	**13.0**
15/16	Food, beverages, tobacco	18	22	10	17	20	18.8	20.6	11.2	9.7	11.6
17/19	Textiles, clothing, leather, footwear	..	..	..	0	..	..	..	..	0.0	..
20/22	Wood and paper products	..	..	..	0	3	..	..	..	0.0	14.3
20	Wood products	..	..	..	0	3	..	..	..	0.0	15.0
21/22	Paper, printing and publishing	..	..	..	0	0	..	..	..	0.0	0.0
23/25	Chemicals, Total	18	47	38	48	40	10.8	24.1	14.9	17.6	13.5
23	Refined petroleum, nuclear fuel	..	..	..	0	..	..	..	..	0.0	..
24/25	Chemicals, rubber & plastics prod.	18	47	38	48	40	10.9	24.2	15.0	17.6	16.0
24	Chemical products	18	47	38	48	40	13.8	30.5	18.7	22.7	20.7
2423	Pharmaceuticals	5	7	..	0	..	16.7	18.9	..	0.0	..
25	Rubber and plastics products	..	..	..	0	..	..	..	..	0.0	..
26	Non-metallic mineral products	..	..	..	0	..	..	..	..	0.0	..
27/28	Basic & fabricated metals	..	..	..	0	2	..	..	..	0.0	2.2
27	Basic metals	..	..	..	0	..	..	..	..	0.0	..
28	Fabricated metal products	..	..	..	0	2	..	..	..	0.0	7.1
29/32	Machinery, Total	356	404	401	165	129	36.1	37.0	35.3	14.5	12.1
29/30	Non-electrical machinery	..	19	23	0	2	..	7.1	6.9	0.0	0.5
29	Non-electrical machinery nec	..	19	23	0	2	..	7.1	7.6	0.0	0.5
30	Office and computing machinery	..	..	..	0	..	..	..	..	0.0	..
31/32	Electrical & electronic equipment	356	385	378	165	127	46.2	46.7	47.1	21.5	19.8
31	Electrical machinery nec	6	15	74	66	..	14.6	23.8	48.7	36.9	..
32	Radio, TV & communications eq.	350	370	304	99	127	48.0	48.6	46.7	16.8	23.0
33	Scientific instruments	..	..	..	0	..	..	..	..	0.0	..
34/35	Transportation equipment	21	25	41	103	110	14.8	14.0	21.8	26.7	23.1
34	Motor vehicles	21	25	41	103	110	17.2	17.2	28.1	33.0	30.4
35	Other transport equipment	..	..	..	0	..	..	..	..	0.0	..
351	Shipbuilding & repairing	..	..	..	0	..	..	..	..	0.0	..
353	Aircraft and spacecraft	..	..	..	0	..	..	..	..	0.0	..
36/37	Other manufacturing	..	..	..	0	..	..	..	..	0.0	..
40/45	Construction, electricity, gas & water	..	..	..	0	..	..	..	..	0.0	..
50/55	Trade, repair, hotels & restaurants	..	..	..	0		..	..	..	0.0	..
65/74	Finance, insurance, business services	..	..	..	0	..	..	..	..	0.0	..
	OTHER ACTIVITIES	..	..	..	0	..	..	..	..	0.0	..
01/99	**GRAND TOTAL**	..	..	..	**333**	**304**	..	..	..	**10.3**	**9.9**

Total manufacturing by investing country						As a % of total manufacturing by foreign affiliates				
All countries	**413**	**498**	**490**	**333**	**304**	**100.0**	**100.0**	**100.0**	**100.0**	**100.0**
United States	..	..	..	..	..	..	..	..	..	..
Canada	..	..	..	..	..	..	..	..	..	..
Mexico	..	..	..	..	..	..	..	..	..	..
Japan	..	..	..	..	..	..	..	..	..	..
Europe	..	..	..	..	..	..	..	..	..	..
European Union (15)	..	..	..	..	..	..	..	..	..	..
Belgium	..	..	..	..	..	..	..	..	..	..
France	..	..	..	..	..	..	..	..	..	..
Germany	..	..	..	..	..	..	..	..	..	..
Italy	..	..	..	..	..	..	..	..	..	..
Netherlands	..	..	..	..	..	..	..	..	..	..
Spain	..	..	..	..	..	..	..	..	..	..
Sweden	..	..	..	..	..	..	..	..	..	..
United Kingdom	..	..	..	..	..	..	..	..	..	..
Switzerland	..	..	..	..	..	..	..	..	..	..
Australia and New Zealand	..	..	..	..	..	..	..	..	..	..
Asia (non-OECD)	..	..	..	..	..	..	..	..	..	..
Latin America	..	..	..	..	..	..	..	..	..	..

Note: Majority foreign-owned firms.
        Firmes sous contrôle étranger majoritaire.

Inward investments

Investissements entrants

Table 11A - Tableau 11A

GROSS FIXED CAPITAL FORMATION / FORMATION BRUTE DE CAPITAL FIXE

		Foreign affiliates (Billions of TRL) Filiales étrangères (Milliards de TRL)					As a % of national total En % du total national				
By industry (ISIC Rev. 3)		1994	1995	1996	1997	1998	1994	1995	1996	1997	1998
10/14	Mining & quarrying	..	..	..	..	..	..	..	..	..	..
15/37	**TOTAL MANUFACTURING**	10 280	20 823	53 211	90 329	177 053	10.0	9.8	10.3	9.9	11.7
15/16	Food, beverages, tobacco	2 081	6 607	15 634	23 659	40 576	20.4	31.2	31.9	26.8	19.5
17/19	Textiles, clothing, leather, footwear	150	399	640	1 162	9 217	0.7	0.7	0.5	0.5	2.4
20/22	Wood and paper products	226	229	330	105	1 960	3.5	1.7	1.5	0.2	2.2
20	Wood products	0	0	0	0	0	0.0	0.0	0.0	0.0	0.0
21/22	Paper, printing and publishing	226	229	330	105	1 960	4.3	2.2	2.0	0.3	2.7
23/25	Chemicals, Total	2 045	5 633	11 850	28 056	28 921	12.6	14.0	14.8	20.0	11.7
23	Refined petroleum, nuclear fuel	623	1 346	4 377	6 174	7 294	71.4	10.2	15.2	33.1	14.7
24/25	Chemicals, rubber & plastics prod.	1 422	4 287	7 474	21 883	21 627	9.2	15.8	14.6	18.0	10.9
24	Chemical products	953	2 558	3 574	11 418	11 407	13.1	18.9	13.7	15.6	9.2
2423	Pharmaceuticals	418	1 245	1 546	3 645	2 176	32.3	34.3	21.4	26.9	8.3
25	Rubber and plastics products	468	1 729	3 900	10 465	10 220	5.8	12.7	15.5	21.6	13.7
26	Non-metallic mineral products	868	502	2 552	1 042	4 579	7.1	2.6	5.1	1.0	3.2
27/28	Basic & fabricated metals	704	359	2 595	4 147	3 710	6.0	1.2	2.7	3.8	2.5
27	Basic metals	6	108	455	51	7	0.1	0.5	0.6	0.1	0.0
28	Fabricated metal products	698	251	2 140	4 097	3 703	27.8	3.5	11.8	12.7	8.2
29/32	Machinery, Total	1 674	3 291	9 163	14 544	36 365	16.0	20.0	19.5	20.2	24.0
29/30	Non-electrical machinery	126	527	877	3 948	11 807	2.2	5.7	3.2	9.5	12.2
29	Non-electrical machinery nec	126	527	877	3 948	11 807	2.2	5.7	3.2	9.5	12.2
30	Office and computing machinery	0	0	0	0	0	0.0	0.0	0.0	0.0	0.0
31/32	Electrical & electronic equipment	1 547	2 764	8 286	10 596	24 558	32.8	38.8	42.5	34.8	45.2
31	Electrical machinery nec	656	822	2 053	9 305	8 617	21.5	19.0	19.3	37.4	30.0
32	Radio, TV & communications eq.	891	1 942	6 233	1 291	15 941	53.9	69.4	70.3	23.5	62.3
33	Scientific instruments	2	6	9	3	4	0.5	0.8	0.4	0.3	0.2
34/35	Transportation equipment	2 506	3 786	10 411	17 461	45 705	19.5	27.0	42.4	19.2	37.7
34	Motor vehicles	2 506	3 783	10 295	17 383	45 641	20.3	28.8	47.2	20.2	39.4
35	Other transport equipment	0	3	116	78	63	0.0	0.4	4.2	1.6	1.2
351	Shipbuilding & repairing	0	3	0	0	0	0.0	0.7	0.0	0.0	0.0
353	Aircraft and spacecraft	0	0	0	0	0	0.0	0.0	0.0	0.0	0.0
36/37	Other manufacturing	25	11	27	150	6 016	4.0	0.7	0.7	1.2	22.2
40/45	Construction, electricity, gas & water	..	..	..	..	..	..	..	..	..	..
50/55	Trade, repair, hotels & restaurants	..	..	..	..	..	..	..	..	..	..
65/74	Finance, insurance, business services	..	..	..	..	..	..	..	..	..	..
	OTHER ACTIVITIES	..	..	..	..	..	..	..	..	..	..
01/99	**GRAND TOTAL**	..	..	..	..	..	..	..	..	..	..

Total manufacturing by investing country	1994	1995	1996	1997	1998	As a % of total manufacturing by foreign affiliates				
						1994	1995	1996	1997	1998
All countries	10 280	20 823	53 211	90 329	177 053	100.0	100.0	100.0	100.0	100.0
United States	1 372	2 442	10 342	24 162	23 343	13.3	11.7	19.4	26.7	13.2
Canada	466	539	0	..	- 285	4.5	2.6	0.0	..	-0.2
Mexico	0	0	0	..	0	0.0	0.0	0.0	..	0.0
Japan	0	0	116	1 334	1 006	0.0	0.0	0.2	1.5	0.6
Europe	8 435	17 361	42 319	63 761	143 914	82.1	83.4	79.5	70.6	81.3
European Union (15)	8 222	16 376	41 684	59 432	141 307	80.0	78.6	78.3	65.8	79.8
Belgium	189	1 942	2 694	2 821	5 167	1.8	9.3	5.1	3.1	2.9
France	3 611	3 265	10 462	15 069	43 536	35.1	15.7	19.7	16.7	24.6
Germany	2 384	5 305	13 045	19 627	39 191	23.2	25.5	24.5	21.7	22.1
Italy	989	1 795	2 343	9 071	12 857	9.6	8.6	4.4	10.0	7.3
Netherlands	551	3 563	8 310	8 120	29 842	5.4	17.1	15.6	9.0	16.9
Spain	1	5	22	0	2	0.0	0.0	0.0	0.0	0.0
Sweden	5	9	18	31	4 369	0.1	0.0	0.0	0.0	2.5
United Kingdom	423	335	4 711	4 525	5 632	4.1	1.6	8.9	5.0	3.2
Switzerland	185	987	688	4 329	2 442	1.8	4.7	1.3	4.8	1.4
Australia and New Zealand	1	31	52	..	0	0.0	0.1	0.1	..	0.0
Asia (non-OECD)	0	0	0	0	7 119	0.0	0.0	0.0	0.0	4.0
Latin America	0	0	0	0	0	0.0	0.0	0.0	0.0	0.0

Note: Majority foreign-owned establishments.
Etablissements sous contrôle étranger majoritaire.

TURKEY

Source

The data are prepared by the Turkish State Institute of Statistics. For all variables except *R&D expenditure* and *Number of researchers*, they are derived from the annual manufacturing survey. Prior to 1993, all manufacturing establishments in the public sector and establishments employing 25 or more persons in the private sector were covered; from 1993 onwards, establishments employing ten or more persons in the private sector are covered. Data are available separately for majority foreign-owned firms, minority foreign-owned firms and national firms. The data in this publication refer to majority foreign-owned establishments, which have a foreign capital share of more than 50%. Data on *R&D expenditure* and *Number of researchers* come from the R&D survey and the enterprise is the basic unit.

National totals: data are provided by the State Institute of Statistics and are fully compatible with foreign affiliates' data.

Industrial classification

For all variables, the data are classified according to the principal industrial activity of the affiliate.

Data are only available for manufacturing industries.

The industrial classification used for the Turkish tables is the national industrial classification converted to ISIC Revision 3.

Variables

- *Number of employees* is the number of persons engaged, defined as the arithmetic average of the number of employees in February, May, August and November, plus the number of owners, partners and unpaid family workers active in November.

- *Production* is the value of output calculated by subtracting the value of the beginning-of-year stock (finished and semi-finished goods) from the total of receipts from sales and services rendered to others, receipts from sales of transfers of electricity plus the end-of-year stock (finished and semi-finished goods) and the production value of fixed assets produced by the establishment's staff for own use.

- *Value added* is obtained by subtracting the value of inputs from output. The value of inputs is calculated by subtracting the value of the end-of-year stock (raw materials, supplementary materials, packaging materials and fuel) from the total value of goods and services purchased or transferred, electricity purchased and the beginning-of-year stock (raw materials, supplementary materials, packaging materials and fuel).

- *Turnover* is defined as sales revenue, which includes sales of goods produced plus sales of goods purchased without further processing plus receipts for manufacturing services rendered to others using their materials.

- *Compensation of employees* includes all payments on the payroll and per diems gross of income tax, social security and pension fund premiums. It also includes overtime payments, bonuses, indemnities, payments in kind, and employer's contributions paid to social security, pensions and insurance schemes, as well as the benefits received by employees under these schemes and severance and termination pay.

- *R&D expenditure* is intramural expenditure on R&D performed by foreign affiliates, whatever the source of funds.

- *Gross fixed capital formation* is not available. It is replaced by gross additions to fixed assets, which is calculated by subtracting the sales value of fixed assets sold during the year from total expenditures made on new or used fixed assets purchased from the domestic market, fixed assets imported new or used, fixed assets produced by the establishment's own staff, parts of fixed assets installed during the year and bought at an auction, major repairs and expenditures made on fixed assets, studies and plans, drawings, machinery, equipment, motor vehicle and building, other construction, office equipment and furniture (used by the establishment and expected to have a productive life of more than one year and recorded in the capital accounts) and expenditures on land and land improvements.

Geographical breakdown

The breakdown by foreign investor's country is available for all variables. It is not possible to identify whether the investor's country is that of the immediate controller or that of the "ultimate beneficial owner".

TURQUIE

Source

Les données émanent de l'Institut de statistique de l'État turc. Pour toutes les variables à l'exception des *Dépenses de R-D* et du *Nombre de chercheurs*, les données proviennent de l'enquête annuelle auprès de l'industrie manufacturière. Jusqu'en 1992, tous les établissements du secteur manufacturier public étaient couverts, ainsi que ceux du secteur privé employant au moins 25 personnes ; à partir de 1993, tous les établissements du secteur privé employant dix personnes ou plus sont couverts. Des données sont disponibles séparément pour les entreprises à participation étrangère majoritaire, minoritaire, ainsi que pour les entreprises nationales. Les données de cette publication se rapportent aux établissements sous contrôle étranger où la part du capital en mains étrangères est de plus de 50 %. Pour les *Dépenses de R-D* et le *Nombre de chercheurs*, les données proviennent de l'enquête sur la R-D et l'unité de base est l'entreprise.

Totaux nationaux : fournis par l'Institut national des statistiques et entièrement compatibles avec les données relatives aux filiales étrangères.

Classification industrielle

Pour toutes les variables, les données sont classées selon l'activité industrielle principale de l'entreprise affiliée.

On ne dispose de données que pour l'industrie manufacturière.

La classification industrielle utilisée pour les tableaux turcs est la classification nationale adaptée à la CITI révision 3.

Variables

- Le *Nombre de salariés* est le nombre de personnes employées, défini comme la moyenne arithmétique du nombre de salariés aux mois de février, mai, août et novembre, plus le nombre de propriétaires exploitants, partenaires et travailleurs familiaux non rémunérés actifs au mois de novembre.

- La *Production* est donnée par la valeur totale des ventes de biens et services et des transferts d'électricité, à laquelle on ajoute la valeur des stocks (de produits finis et semi-finis) en fin d'année et celle des actifs fixes produits par l'unité pour son propre usage et dont on déduit la valeur des stocks en début d'année (de produits finis et semi-finis).

- Le *Chiffre d'affaires* est défini comme le revenu des ventes, qui comprennent la vente des biens produits, plus la vente des biens acquis sans traitement complémentaire, plus la vente des services manufacturiers rendus à d'autres unités en utilisant leurs matériaux.

- La *Valeur ajoutée* est donnée par la production déduction faite de la valeur des consommations intermédiaires. Cette dernière correspond à la valeur totale des produits et services achetés ou transférés, de l'électricité achetée et de la valeur des stocks en début d'année après déduction de la valeur des stocks en fin d'année (matières premières, fournitures, matériel d'emballage et combustibles).

- Les *Salaires et charges sociales* comprennent tous les versements qui figurent sur la feuille de paie, les indemnités journalières avant déduction de l'impôt sur le revenu, ainsi que les cotisations de sécurité sociale et de retraite. Cette variable comprend également le paiement des heures supplémentaires, les primes, indemnités, paiements en nature, les cotisations patronales aux régimes de sécurité sociale, de retraite et d'assurance, ainsi que les indemnités de licenciement.

- Les *Dépenses de R-D* sont les dépenses intramuros de R-D réalisées par les filiales étrangères, quelle que soit la source de financement.

- La *Formation brute de capital fixe* n'est pas disponible, et est remplacée par les acquisitions brutes d'actifs fixes. Celles-ci sont calculées par le coût total des actifs fixes neufs ou usagés acquis sur le marché intérieur, des actifs fixes neufs ou usagés importés, des actifs fixes produits par le personnel de l'établissement, des actifs fixes installés pendant l'année et achetés aux enchères, des grosses réparations et des dépenses faites sur les actifs fixes, des études, plans et dessins, des machines, équipement, véhicules et construction, du matériel et mobilier de bureau (à condition qu'ils soient utilisés dans l'établissement, qu'ils aient une espérance de vie productive supérieure à un an et qu'ils soient portés au compte de capital) et aux dépenses d'acquisition et d'amélioration des terrains, déduction faite des ventes.

Ventilation géographique

La ventilation par pays d'origine de l'investissement est disponible pour toutes les variables. Il n'est pas possible d'identifier si le pays de l'investisseur est celui où se situe le contrôle immédiat ou bien si c'est celui du "bénéficiaire ultime de l'investissement".

UNITED KINGDOM

ROYAUME-UNI

Inward investments   *Investissements entrants*

Table 1A - Tableau 1A

NUMBER OF ENTERPRISES / NOMBRE D'ENTREPRISES

| | | Foreign affiliates *(Units)* | | | | As a % of national total | | | | |
| | | Filiales étrangères *(Unités)* | | | | En % du total national | | | | |
By industry (ISIC Rev. 3)		1994	1995	1996	1997	1998	1994	1995	1996	1997	1998
10/14	Mining & quarrying	..	..	26	123	..	..	..	2.0	7.5	..
15/37	**TOTAL MANUFACTURING**	**2 633**	**2 397**	**2 686**	**2 462**	**659**	**1.5**	**1.4**	**1.6**	**1.5**	**22.7**
15/16	Food, beverages, tobacco	..	..	151	134	41	..	..	1.8	1.6	9.7
17/19	Textiles, clothing, leather, footwear	..	..	78	72	..	..	..	0.5	0.5	..
20/22	Wood and paper products	361	316	358	368	39	0.9	0.8	0.9	0.9	12.1
20	Wood products	31	25	..	18	1	0.4	0.3	..	0.2	4.8
21/22	Paper, printing and publishing	330	291	..	350	38	1.1	1.0	..	1.1	12.7
23/25	Chemicals, Total	503	458	514	455	133	4.8	3.8	4.4	3.9	29.5
23	Refined petroleum, nuclear fuel	20	28	25	21	7	8.4	6.0	8.5	8.0	36.8
24/25	Chemicals, rubber & plastics prod.	483	430	489	434	126	4.7	3.7	4.3	3.8	29.2
24	Chemical products	308	281	296	270	86	7.4	6.1	7.0	6.5	35.7
2423	Pharmaceuticals	..	..	53	56	20	..	..	10.4	11.8	37.7
25	Rubber and plastics products	175	149	193	164	40	2.8	2.2	2.7	2.3	20.9
26	Non-metallic mineral products	79	67	90	81	20	1.9	1.3	1.8	1.5	18.9
27/28	Basic & fabricated metals	314	301	305	251	62	1.0	0.9	1.0	0.8	23.1
27	Basic metals	101	95	92	79	27	4.0	3.4	3.3	2.9	24.1
28	Fabricated metal products	213	206	213	172	35	0.7	0.7	0.7	0.6	22.4
29/32	Machinery, Total	699	651	746	681	213	2.7	2.4	3.1	2.7	35.6
29/30	Non-electrical machinery	443	396	455	415	114	2.8	2.2	3.0	2.6	35.2
29	Non-electrical machinery nec	403	355	410	373	95	2.9	2.2	3.0	2.6	33.5
30	Office and computing machinery	40	41	45	42	19	2.2	1.8	3.2	2.6	47.5
31/32	Electrical & electronic equipment	256	255	291	266	99	2.5	2.8	3.4	3.0	36.0
31	Electrical machinery nec	144	144	179	154	53	2.2	2.5	3.2	2.6	31.7
32	Radio, TV & communications eq.	112	111	112	112	46	3.0	3.4	3.8	3.7	42.6
33	Scientific instruments	177	158	175	170	29	3.8	2.3	3.1	2.9	28.7
34/35	Transportation equipment	178	157	171	173	80	3.8	2.2	3.3	3.1	29.3
34	Motor vehicles	122	107	109	113	65	6.4	2.6	4.4	4.1	37.6
35	Other transport equipment	56	50	62	60	15	2.0	1.6	2.3	2.1	15.0
351	Shipbuilding & repairing	..	..	5	7	5	..	..	0.3	0.5	17.9
353	Aircraft and spacecraft	..	..	32	34	7	..	..	4.2	3.5	12.5
36/37	Other manufacturing	94	82	98	79	21	0.4	0.4	0.5	0.4	18.6
40/45	Construction, electricity, gas & water	..	..	203	163	..	..	..	0.1	0.1	..
50/55	Trade, repair, hotels & restaurants	..	..	..	..	4 451	..	..	..	..	0.9
65/74	Finance, insurance, business services	..	..	..	..	2 749	..	..	..	..	0.6
	OTHER ACTIVITIES	..	..	..	..	1 681	..	..	..	..	2.2
01/99	**GRAND TOTAL**	**..**	**..**	**..**	**..**	**9 551**	**..**	**..**	**..**	**..**	**0.9**

Total manufacturing by investing country						As a % of total manufacturing by foreign affiliates				
All countries	2 633	2 397	2 686	2 462	659	100.0	100.0	100.0	100.0	100.0
United States	..	873	1 067	941	276	..	36.4	39.7	38.2	41.9
Canada	..	118	80	..	..	..	4.9	3.0	..	..
Mexico	..	..	..	0	..	..	..	..	0.0	..
Japan	..	138	139	132	61	..	5.8	5.2	5.4	9.3
Europe	..	..	..	..	..	..	..	..	..	..
European Union (15)	..	798	1 044	1 023	230	..	33.3	38.9	41.6	34.9
Belgium	..	..	27	..	..	..	..	1.0	..	..
France	..	151	155	153	51	..	6.3	5.8	6.2	7.7
Germany	..	256	265	268	66	..	10.7	9.9	10.9	10.0
Italy	..	..	25	..	..	..	..	0.9	..	..
Netherlands	..	161	177	163	45	..	6.7	6.6	6.6	6.8
Spain	..	..	..	..	..	..	..	..	..	..
Sweden	..	127	118	..	..	..	5.3	4.4	..	..
United Kingdom	..	..	..	..	..	..	..	..	..	..
Switzerland	..	153	157	136	31	..	6.4	5.8	5.5	4.7
Australia and New Zealand	..	56	63	..	..	..	2.3	2.3	..	..
Asia (non-OECD)	..	..	31	29	12	..	..	1.2	1.2	1.8
Latin America	..	..	0	3	0	..	..	0.0	0.1	0.0

Note: Majority foreign-owned firms. For 1998 data, only enterprises with more than 250 employees are included in the manufacturing industry.
Firmes sous contrôle étranger majoritaire. Pour 1998, seules les entreprises de plus de 250 salariés sont incluses dans les données du secteur manufacturier.

Inward investments

Investissements entrants

Table 2A - Tableau 2A

NUMBER OF EMPLOYEES BY INDUSTRY

NOMBRE DE SALARIÉS PAR INDUSTRIE

ISIC Revision 3		Foreign affiliates *(Units)* Filiales étrangères *(Unités)*					As a % of national total En % du total national				
		1994	1995	1996	1997	1998	1994	1995	1996	1997	1998
10/14	Mining & quarrying	..	..	3 449	14 644	18 210	..	..	..	17.7	32.5
15/37	**TOTAL MANUFACTURING**	**789 000**	**718 400**	**815 161**	**743 251**	**576 824**	**18.1**	**16.3**	**19.2**	**17.8**	**27.3**
15/16	Food, beverages, tobacco	..	..	74 639	62 190	37 317	..	..	15.0	12.7	10.6
17/19	Textiles, clothing, leather, footwear	..	..	21 787	18 271	..	..	..	5.5	4.7	..
20/22	Wood and paper products	67 100	55 700	58 879	57 504	23 863	12.1	9.8	10.6	10.8	12.9
20	Wood products	3 300	2 500	..	1 960	..	4.0	2.9	..	2.3	..
21/22	Paper, printing and publishing	63 800	53 200	..	55 544	..	13.6	11.1	..	12.4	..
23/25	Chemicals, Total	139 600	133 300	151 217	134 048	..	25.9	24.0	27.7	24.2	..
23	Refined petroleum, nuclear fuel	4 600	5 900	6 189	5 547	..	16.4	21.9	22.2	21.7	..
24/25	Chemicals, rubber & plastics prod.	135 000	127 400	145 028	128 502	99 151	26.5	24.1	28.0	24.3	32.8
24	Chemical products	95 100	87 600	97 310	89 907	68 756	35.1	31.2	36.4	33.6	35.8
2423	Pharmaceuticals	..	..	30 419	29 375	19 284	..	..	46.9	43.4	35.5
25	Rubber and plastics products	39 900	39 800	47 718	38 595	30 395	16.7	16.1	19.1	14.9	27.7
26	Non-metallic mineral products	19 100	15 400	19 049	18 830	14 101	12.0	9.3	12.1	12.5	18.8
27/28	Basic & fabricated metals	58 200	54 800	56 737	44 999	41 848	10.8	9.4	10.3	8.7	25.7
27	Basic metals	22 700	22 200	22 129	20 460	16 039	16.0	16.0	15.9	14.8	20.0
28	Fabricated metal products	35 500	32 600	34 608	24 539	25 809	8.9	7.4	8.4	6.4	31.3
29/32	Machinery, Total	208 900	188 000	225 168	213 073	168 849	25.8	23.0	28.4	26.8	40.4
29/30	Non-electrical machinery	124 100	106 100	127 861	117 806	87 204	26.1	21.9	27.9	25.7	39.7
29	Non-electrical machinery nec	86 100	81 500	97 982	86 197	63 497	21.4	19.4	24.5	21.7	35.4
30	Office and computing machinery	38 000	24 600	29 879	31 609	23 707	51.4	39.0	50.8	51.7	59.3
31/32	Electrical & electronic equipment	84 800	81 900	97 307	95 267	81 645	25.4	24.6	29.3	28.5	41.1
31	Electrical machinery nec	39 800	33 300	45 007	37 047	33 895	20.0	17.1	23.1	19.1	32.6
32	Radio, TV & communications eq.	45 000	48 600	52 301	58 220	47 750	33.3	35.2	37.9	41.4	50.5
33	Scientific instruments	24 100	20 900	28 587	25 696	16 994	17.7	15.0	20.2	18.8	27.3
34/35	Transportation equipment	158 900	148 600	163 333	156 573	149 526	38.9	36.5	40.2	38.0	45.6
34	Motor vehicles	126 300	122 300	134 126	130 239	132 375	55.2	51.0	54.7	52.3	68.5
35	Other transport equipment	32 600	26 300	29 207	26 334	17 151	18.2	15.7	18.1	16.2	12.8
351	Shipbuilding & repairing	..	..	1 471	2 852	..	..	..	3.8	7.0	..
353	Aircraft and spacecraft	..	..	16 523	15 633	5 925	..	..	16.1	15.0	6.5
36/37	Other manufacturing	12 400	9 370	15 765	12 065	9 647	5.7	4.3	7.4	5.8	17.1
40/45	Construction, electricity, gas & water	..	..	28 497	46 085	35 977	..	..	2.5	4.6	8.4
50/55	Trade, repair, hotels & restaurants	..	..	..	..	359 145	..	..	..	..	6.7
65/74	Finance, insurance, business services	..	..	..	..	267 338	..	..	..	..	8.0
	OTHER ACTIVITIES	..	..	..	..	110 861	..	..	..	..	9.7
01/99	**GRAND TOTAL**	**..**	**..**	**..**	**..**	**1 368 355**	**..**	**..**	**..**	**..**	**11.0**

Note: Majority foreign-owned firms. For 1998 data, only enterprises with more than 250 employees are included in the manufacturing industry.

Firmes sous contrôle étranger majoritaire. Pour 1998, seules les entreprises de plus de 250 salariés sont incluses dans les données du secteur manufacturier.

Table 3A - Tableau 3A

NUMBER OF EMPLOYEES BY COUNTRY OF ORIGIN IN THE MANUFACTURING INDUSTRY
NOMBRE DE SALARIÉS PAR PAYS D'ORIGINE DANS L'INDUSTRIE MANUFACTURIÈRE

Country of origin (UBO)	Number of employees *(Units)* Nombre de salariés *(Unités)*					As a % of all countries En % du total des pays				
	1994	1995	1996	1997	1998	1994	1995	1996	1997	1998
All countries	**789 000**	**718 400**	**815 161**	**743 251**	**576 824**	**100.0**	**100.0**	**100.0**	**100.0**	**100.0**
Total OECD	..	..	810 500	737 200	..	..	..	99.4	99.2	..
United States	..	323 100	379 370	330 828	261 808	..	45.0	46.5	44.5	45.4
Canada	..	36 400	31 700	34 600	23 449	..	5.1	3.9	4.7	4.1
Mexico	..	..	..	0	0	..	..	..	0.0	0.0
Japan	..	51 700	56 862	61 443	58 958	..	7.2	7.0	8.3	10.2
Korea	..	..	..	..	..	..	..	..	..	..
Australia	..	15 800	..	10 400	6 344	..	2.2	..	1.4	1.1
New Zealand	..	..	..	..	0	..	..	..	..	0.0
Europe	..	..	325 500	297 500	212 442	..	..	39.9	40.0	36.8
European Union (15)	..	208 200	267 606	249 323	186 862	..	29.0	32.8	33.5	32.4
Austria	..	..	..	800	..	..	..	..	0.1	..
Belgium	..	..	5 800	5 600	6 340	..	..	0.7	0.8	1.1
Denmark	..	7 600	..	10 600	6 660	..	1.1	..	1.4	1.2
Finland	..	..	7 300	7 100	..	..	..	0.9	1.0	..
France	..	51 400	56 689	49 841	43 337	..	7.2	7.0	6.7	7.5
Germany	..	78 400	85 106	83 611	74 887	..	10.9	10.4	11.2	13.0
Greece	..	..	..	..	0	..	..	..	..	0.0
Ireland	..	17 000	23 900	19 300	8 970	..	2.4	2.9	2.6	1.6
Italy	..	..	9 800	10 000	5 417	..	..	1.2	1.3	0.9
Luxembourg	..	2 500	..	2 700	1 845	..	0.3	..	0.4	0.3
Netherlands	..	38 800	39 390	36 499	31 535	..	5.4	4.8	4.9	5.5
Portugal	..	..	..	..	0	..	..	..	..	0.0
Spain	..	..	..	..	0	..	..	..	..	0.0
Sweden	..	23 600	20 900	22 900	6 907	..	3.3	2.6	3.1	1.2
United Kingdom	..	..	..	..	..	..	..	..	..	..
Czech Republic	..	..	..	0	0	..	..	..	0.0	0.0
Hungary	..	..	..	0	0	..	..	..	0.0	0.0
Iceland	..	..	..	0	0	..	..	..	0.0	0.0
Norway	..	3 500	..	8 100	5 259	..	0.5	..	1.1	0.9
Poland	..	..	..	0	0	..	..	..	0.0	0.0
Slovak Republic	..	..	..	0	0	..	..	..	0.0	0.0
Switzerland	..	43 100	43 645	37 177	20 016	..	6.0	5.4	5.0	3.5
Turkey	..	..	..	..	0	..	..	..	..	0.0
Non-OECD Europe, of which:	..	..	..	1 800	305	..	..	..	0.2	0.1
Baltic countries	..	..	..	0	0	..	..	..	0.0	0.0
Bulgaria	..	..	..	0	0	..	..	..	0.0	0.0
Croatia	..	..	..	0	0	..	..	..	0.0	0.0
Romania	..	..	..	0	0	..	..	..	0.0	0.0
Russian Federation	..	..	..	0	0	..	..	..	0.0	0.0
Slovenia	..	..	..	0	0	..	..	..	0.0	0.0
Ukraine	..	..	..	0	0	..	..	..	0.0	0.0
Yugoslavia	..	..	..	0	0	..	..	..	0.0	0.0
Non-OECD Asia, of which:	..	..	4 554	5 678	4 187	..	..	0.6	0.8	0.7
China	..	..	..	0	0	..	..	..	0.0	0.0
Chinese Taipei	..	..	..	..	..	..	..	..	..	..
Hong Kong (China)	..	90	1 200	1 700	1 203	..	0.0	0.1	0.2	0.2
India	..	..	..	0	0	..	..	..	0.0	0.0
Indonesia	..	..	..	0	0	..	..	..	0.0	0.0
Malaysia	..	..	..	..	..	..	..	..	..	..
Philippines	..	..	..	..	0	..	..	..	..	0.0
Singapore	..	..	500	..	0	..	..	0.1	..	0.0
Thailand	..	..	..	0	0	..	..	..	0.0	0.0
Near and Middle East	..	..	..	..	..	..	..	..	..	..
Africa	..	..	..	..	0	..	..	..	..	0.0
Latin America, of which:	..	..	0	523	0	..	..	0.0	0.1	0.0
Argentina	..	..	..	0	0	..	..	..	0.0	0.0
Brazil	..	..	..	0	0	..	..	..	0.0	0.0
Chile	..	..	..	0	0	..	..	..	0.0	0.0

Note: Majority foreign-owned firms. For 1998 data, only enterprises with more than 250 employees are included in the manufacturing industry.
Firmes sous contrôle étranger majoritaire. Pour 1998, seules les entreprises de plus de 250 salariés sont incluses dans les données du secteur manufacturier.

Inward investments

Investissements entrants

Table 4A - Tableau 4A
PRODUCTION

By industry (ISIC Rev. 3)	Foreign affiliates (Millions of GBP) Filiales étrangères (Millions de GBP)					As a % of national total En % du total national				
	1994	1995	1996	1997	1998	1994	1995	1996	1997	1998
10/14 Mining & quarrying	..	..	398	11 678	..	..	..	1.5	38.3	..
15/37 TOTAL MANUFACTURING	**116 853**	**123 113**	**146 979**	**141 733**	**..**	**30.3**	**29.4**	**33.2**	**31.4**	**..**
15/16 Food, beverages, tobacco	..	..	17 956	16 693	..	..	..	23.7	21.9	..
17/19 Textiles, clothing, leather, footwear	..	..	1 636	1 475	..	..	..	8.3	7.2	..
20/22 Wood and paper products	7 485	7 133	8 076	7 873	..	18.3	16.0	17.5	17.1	..
20 Wood products	475	465	..	308	..	8.6	8.1	..	5.3	..
21/22 Paper, printing and publishing	7 010	6 668	..	7 565	..	19.8	17.1	..	18.8	..
23/25 Chemicals, Total	29 398	32 416	40 054	36 664	..	37.3	38.3	44.1	40.7	..
23 Refined petroleum, nuclear fuel	10 268	11 578	16 365	14 160	..	47.0	51.8	63.0	59.4	..
24/25 Chemicals, rubber & plastics prod.	19 130	20 838	23 689	22 504	..	33.5	33.5	36.6	33.9	..
24 Chemical products	15 567	16 698	19 009	18 469	..	38.5	37.7	41.7	39.8	..
2423 Pharmaceuticals	..	..	5 069	5 271	..	..	..	52.6	49.5	..
25 Rubber and plastics products	3 562	4 140	4 680	4 035	..	21.4	23.0	24.4	20.2	..
26 Non-metallic mineral products	1 514	1 299	1 617	1 708	..	14.2	11.0	14.2	14.8	..
27/28 Basic & fabricated metals	6 971	7 775	7 348	5 865	..	18.3	18.0	16.8	14.0	..
27 Basic metals	3 741	4 450	3 794	3 442	..	22.2	22.7	19.8	19.4	..
28 Fabricated metal products	3 230	3 325	3 554	2 422	..	15.3	14.1	14.5	10.0	..
29/32 Machinery, Total	25 951	28 987	35 643	36 514	..	39.7	39.2	45.3	43.3	..
29/30 Non-electrical machinery	16 274	18 022	22 731	22 401	..	39.8	38.9	46.5	43.0	..
29 Non-electrical machinery nec	8 061	8 990	11 235	10 354	..	28.1	26.7	32.4	28.3	..
30 Office and computing machinery	8 213	9 032	11 497	12 046	..	67.6	70.9	81.2	77.4	..
31/32 Electrical & electronic equipment	9 677	10 964	12 912	14 114	..	39.4	39.7	43.4	43.8	..
31 Electrical machinery nec	3 061	2 621	3 845	3 240	..	25.2	20.8	28.1	23.0	..
32 Radio, TV & communications eq.	6 616	8 343	9 067	10 874	..	53.2	55.4	56.4	59.9	..
33 Scientific instruments	2 040	1 901	3 129	2 437	..	23.5	19.8	28.8	22.9	..
34/35 Transportation equipment	25 483	25 512	30 071	31 281	..	57.5	55.6	58.0	56.0	..
34 Motor vehicles	23 102	23 417	27 213	28 237	..	75.1	70.5	74.0	73.1	..
35 Other transport equipment	2 381	2 095	2 858	3 044	..	17.6	16.5	19.0	17.6	..
351 Shipbuilding & repairing	..	..	115	338	..	..	..	4.2	11.7	..
353 Aircraft and spacecraft	..	..	1 716	1 798	..	..	..	16.0	14.1	..
36/37 Other manufacturing	1 018	988	1 450	1 223	..	8.2	7.4	10.4	8.3	..
40/45 Construction, electricity, gas & water	..	..	3 946	8 312	..	..	..	3.1	6.2	..
50/55 Trade, repair, hotels & restaurants	..	..	..	..	..	..	..	..	..	..
65/74 Finance, insurance, business services	..	..	..	..	..	..	..	..	..	..
OTHER ACTIVITIES	..	..	..	..	..	..	..	..	..	..
01/99 GRAND TOTAL	**..**	**..**	**..**	**..**	**..**	**..**	**..**	**..**	**..**	**..**

Total manufacturing by investing country						As a % of total manufacturing by foreign affiliates				
All countries	**116 853**	**123 113**	**146 979**	**141 733**	**..**	**100.0**	**100.0**	**100.0**	**100.0**	**..**
United States	..	68 481	83 982	78 051	..	..	55.6	57.1	55.1	..
Canada	..	5 080	4 805	..	..	..	4.1	3.3	..	..
Mexico	..	..	..	0	..	..	..	..	0.0	..
Japan	..	7 881	9 333	10 461	..	..	6.4	6.3	7.4	..
Europe	..	..	..	..	..	..	..	..	..	..
European Union (15)	..	27 791	38 272	37 655	..	..	22.6	26.0	26.6	..
Belgium	..	..	2 138	..	..	..	..	1.5	..	..
France	..	7 589	9 916	9 154	..	..	6.2	6.7	6.5	..
Germany	..	10 006	10 736	11 178	..	..	8.1	7.3	7.9	..
Italy	..	..	2 353	..	..	..	..	1.6	..	..
Netherlands	..	3 741	4 067	4 248	..	..	3.0	2.8	3.0	..
Spain	..	..	..	..	..	..	..	..	..	..
Sweden	..	2 975	2 564	..	..	..	2.4	1.7	..	..
United Kingdom	..	..	..	..	..	..	..	..	..	..
Switzerland	..	5 747	6 215	5 655	..	..	4.7	4.2	4.0	..
Australia and New Zealand	..	..	..	0	..	..	..	..	0.0	..
Asia (non-OECD)	..	..	512	569	..	..	..	0.3	0.4	..
Latin America	..	..	0	113	..	..	..	0.0	0.1	..

Note: Majority foreign-owned firms. For 1998 data, only enterprises with more than 250 employees are included in the manufacturing industry.
Firmes sous contrôle étranger majoritaire. Pour 1998, seules les entreprises de plus de 250 salariés sont incluses dans les données du secteur manufacturier.

Inward investments

Investissements entrants

Table 5A - Tableau 5A

TURNOVER BY INDUSTRY

CHIFFRE D'AFFAIRES PAR INDUSTRIE

ISIC Revision 3		Foreign affiliates (Millions of GBP) Filiales étrangères (Millions de GBP)					As a % of national total En % du total national				
		1994	1995	1996	1997	1998	1994	1995	1996	1997	1998
10/14	Mining & quarrying	..	..	393	11 602	7 235	..	..	..	38.1	47.9
15/37	**TOTAL MANUFACTURING**	**116 363**	**121 872**	**146 969**	**141 883**	**120 593**	**..**	**30.6**	**33.2**	**31.4**	**40.9**
15/16	Food, beverages, tobacco	..	..	17 864	16 629	10 697	..	..	23.7	21.8	19.1
17/19	Textiles, clothing, leather, footwear	..	..	1 626	1 482	..	..	..	8.3	7.3	..
20/22	Wood and paper products	7 436	7 080	8 107	7 876	3 650	..	..	17.5	17.1	18.3
20	Wood products	473	460	..	308	86	..	..	..	5.4	7.9
21/22	Paper, printing and publishing	6 963	6 620	..	7 567	3 564	..	..	..	18.8	18.9
23/25	Chemicals, Total	29 353	32 145	39 884	36 718	..	..	..	44.1	40.8	..
23	Refined petroleum, nuclear fuel	10 255	11 535	16 366	14 245	..	..	..	63.1	59.8	..
24/25	Chemicals, rubber & plastics prod.	19 098	20 609	23 518	22 474	16 296	..	..	36.5	33.9	38.4
24	Chemical products	15 546	16 506	18 825	18 439	13 201	..	..	41.6	39.8	39.5
2423	Pharmaceuticals	..	..	5 062	5 226	4 128	..	..	52.8	49.7	43.4
25	Rubber and plastics products	3 552	4 103	4 693	4 035	3 094	..	..	24.5	20.2	34.1
26	Non-metallic mineral products	1 516	1 298	1 594	1 713	1 571	..	..	14.2	14.9	25.7
27/28	Basic & fabricated metals	6 952	7 681	7 329	5 929	5 390	..	..	16.8	14.1	28.5
27	Basic metals	3 731	4 401	3 790	3 480	2 370	..	..	19.8	19.6	20.1
28	Fabricated metal products	3 221	3 280	3 539	2 449	3 020	..	..	14.4	10.1	42.4
29/32	Machinery, Total	26 081	28 713	35 807	36 454	..	..	..	45.6	43.4	..
29/30	Non-electrical machinery	16 454	17 862	22 871	22 414	..	..	..	46.8	43.2	..
29	Non-electrical machinery nec	8 028	8 887	11 248	10 340	8 037	..	..	32.5	28.4	45.4
30	Office and computing machinery	8 426	8 975	11 623	12 074	..	..	..	81.5	77.6	..
31/32	Electrical & electronic equipment	9 627	10 851	12 936	14 040	12 596	..	..	43.6	43.7	54.0
31	Electrical machinery nec	3 051	2 600	3 850	3 237	3 262	..	..	28.2	23.1	39.8
32	Radio, TV & communications eq.	6 576	8 251	9 086	10 803	9 334	..	..	56.6	59.8	61.7
33	Scientific instruments	2 031	1 899	3 112	2 511	1 617	..	..	28.8	23.4	31.9
34/35	Transportation equipment	25 058	25 019	30 203	31 341	31 217	..	..	57.8	55.5	56.0
34	Motor vehicles	22 729	23 041	27 323	28 460	29 513	..	..	74.1	73.3	83.5
35	Other transport equipment	2 329	1 978	2 880	2 881	1 704	..	..	18.7	16.3	8.3
351	Shipbuilding & repairing	..	..	132	332	..	..	..	5.1	11.1	..
353	Aircraft and spacecraft	..	..	1 705	1 774	693	..	..	15.2	13.4	4.2
36/37	Other manufacturing	1 012	982	1 443	1 229	1 043	..	..	10.5	8.3	24.2
40/45	Construction, electricity, gas & water	..	..	3 918	8 219	4 684	..	..	3.1	6.2	6.2
50/55	Trade, repair, hotels & restaurants	..	..	..	..	139 153	..	..	..	..	19.2
65/74	Finance, insurance, business services	..	..	..	..	22 947	..	..	..	..	11.2
	OTHER ACTIVITIES	..	..	..	..	19 824	..	..	..	..	21.0
01/99	**GRAND TOTAL**	**..**	**..**	**..**	**..**	**314 437**	**..**	**..**	**..**	**..**	**22.3**

Note: Majority foreign-owned firms. For 1998 data, only enterprises with more than 250 employees are included in the manufacturing industry.

Firmes sous contrôle étranger majoritaire. Pour 1998, seules les entreprises de plus de 250 salariés sont incluses dans les données du secteur manufacturier.

Table 6A - Tableau 6A

TURNOVER BY COUNTRY OF ORIGIN IN THE MANUFACTURING INDUSTRY

CHIFFRE D'AFFAIRES PAR PAYS D'ORIGINE DANS L'INDUSTRIE MANUFACTURIÈRE

Country of origin (UBO)	Turnover (Millions of GBP) / Chiffre d'affaires (Millions de GBP)					As a % of all countries / En % du total des pays				
	1994	1995	1996	1997	1998	1994	1995	1996	1997	1998
All countries	116 363	121 872	146 969	141 883	120 593	100.0	100.0	100.0	100.0	100.0
Total OECD	..	..	146 523	140 955	119 399	..	..	99.7	99.3	99.0
United States	..	67 871	84 102	78 260	66 765	..	55.7	57.2	55.2	55.4
Canada	..	5 010	4 760	5 295	3 976	..	4.1	3.2	3.7	3.3
Mexico	..	..	0	0	0	..	..	..	0.0	0.0
Japan	..	7 807	9 303	10 494	10 118	..	6.4	6.3	7.4	8.4
Korea	..	..	..	..	..	..	..	..	..	..
Australia	..	2 912	..	1 945	1 460	..	2.4	..	1.4	1.2
New Zealand	..	..	..	..	0	..	..	..	..	0.0
Europe	..	..	45 808	44 709	36 688	..	..	31.2	31.5	30.4
European Union (15)	..	27 511	37 971	37 607	33 331	..	22.6	25.8	26.5	27.6
Austria	..	..	..	72	..	..	..	..	0.1	..
Belgium	..	..	2 142	2 197	637	..	..	1.5	1.5	0.5
Denmark	..	915	..	1 371	711	..	0.8	..	1.0	0.6
Finland	..	..	1 368	1 361	..	..	..	0.9	1.0	..
France	..	7 622	9 887	9 096	9 338	..	6.3	6.7	6.4	7.7
Germany	..	9 784	10 732	11 282	9 560	..	8.0	7.3	8.0	7.9
Greece	..	..	..	..	0	..	..	..	..	0.0
Ireland	..	1 750	2 431	1 930	1 171	..	1.4	1.7	1.4	1.0
Italy	..	..	2 365	2 302	1 090	..	..	1.6	1.6	0.9
Luxembourg	..	214	..	290	348	..	0.2	..	0.2	0.3
Netherlands	..	3 680	3 942	4 119	9 555	..	3.0	2.7	2.9	7.9
Portugal	..	..	..	..	0	..	..	..	..	0.0
Spain	..	..	..	..	0	..	..	..	..	0.0
Sweden	..	2 949	2 569	3 407	805	..	2.4	1.7	2.4	0.7
United Kingdom	..	..	..	..	..	..	..	..	..	..
Czech Republic	..	..	..	0	0	..	..	..	0.0	0.0
Hungary	..	..	..	0	0	..	..	..	0.0	0.0
Iceland	..	..	..	0	0	..	..	..	0.0	0.0
Norway	..	612	..	1 120	700	..	0.5	..	0.8	0.6
Poland	..	..	..	0	0	..	..	..	0.0	0.0
Slovak Republic	..	..	..	0	0	..	..	..	0.0	0.0
Switzerland	..	5 585	6 298	5 677	2 636	..	4.6	4.3	4.0	2.2
Turkey	..	..	..	..	0	..	..	..	..	0.0
Non-OECD Europe, of which:	..	..	..	305	21	..	..	..	0.2	0.0
Baltic countries	..	..	..	0	0	..	..	..	0.0	0.0
Bulgaria	..	..	..	0	0	..	..	..	0.0	0.0
Croatia	..	..	..	0	0	..	..	..	0.0	0.0
Romania	..	..	..	0	0	..	..	..	0.0	0.0
Russian Federation	..	..	..	0	0	..	..	..	0.0	0.0
Slovenia	..	..	..	0	0	..	..	..	0.0	0.0
Ukraine	..	..	..	0	0	..	..	..	0.0	0.0
Yugoslavia	..	..	..	0	0	..	..	..	0.0	0.0
Non-OECD Asia, of which:	..	..	517	565	349	..	..	0.4	0.4	0.3
China	..	..	..	0	0	..	..	..	0.0	0.0
Chinese Taipei	..	..	..	..	..	..	..	..	..	..
Hong Kong (China)	..	74	212	228	74	..	0.1	0.1	0.2	0.1
India	..	..	..	0	0	..	..	..	0.0	0.0
Indonesia	..	..	..	0	0	..	..	..	0.0	0.0
Malaysia	..	..	..	..	..	..	..	..	..	..
Philippines	..	..	..	..	0	..	..	..	..	0.0
Singapore	..	..	49	..	0	..	..	0.0	..	0.0
Thailand	..	..	..	0	0	..	..	..	0.0	0.0
Near and Middle East	..	..	..	..	..	..	..	..	..	..
Africa	..	..	..	..	0	..	..	..	..	0.0
Latin America, of which:	..	..	0	113	0	..	..	0.0	0.1	0.0
Argentina	..	..	..	0	0	..	..	..	0.0	0.0
Brazil	..	..	..	0	0	..	..	..	0.0	0.0
Chile	..	..	..	0	0	..	..	..	0.0	0.0

Note: Majority foreign-owned firms. For 1998 data, only enterprises with more than 250 employees are included in the manufacturing industry.

Firmes sous contrôle étranger majoritaire. Pour 1998, seules les entreprises de plus de 250 salariés sont incluses dans les données du secteur manufacturier.

Table 7A - Tableau 7A

VALUE ADDED / VALEUR AJOUTÉE

		Foreign affiliates *(Millions of GBP)* Filiales étrangères *(Millions de GBP)*					As a % of national total En % du total national				
By industry (ISIC Rev. 3)		1994	1995	1996	1997	1998	1994	1995	1996	1997	1998
10/14	Mining & quarrying	..	..	253	9 312	4 187	..	..	..	40.3	49.3
15/37	**TOTAL MANUFACTURING**	**40 908**	**42 093**	**50 420**	**48 421**	**27 846**	**..**	**25.7**	**..**	**26.1**	**32.9**
15/16	Food, beverages, tobacco	..	..	6 828	6 435	2 702	..	..	..	23.8	18.1
17/19	Textiles, clothing, leather, footwear	..	..	837	756	..	..	..	..	8.0	..
20/22	Wood and paper products	3 930	3 639	4 126	4 135	1 239	..	..	..	16.6	15.0
20	Wood products	194	201	100	143	..	..	..	..	6.0	..
21/22	Paper, printing and publishing	3 736	3 438	4 026	3 992	..	..	..	..	17.7	..
23/25	Chemicals, Total	9 577	10 207	11 963	10 821	8 617	..	..	..	33.0	46.6
23	Refined petroleum, nuclear fuel	923	1 083	1 167	813	860	..	..	..	27.2	42.4
24/25	Chemicals, rubber & plastics prod.	8 655	9 124	10 796	10 008	7 758	..	..	..	33.5	47.2
24	Chemical products	6 970	7 298	8 607	8 027	4 274	..	..	..	39.6	33.3
2423	Pharmaceuticals	..	..	2 634	2 775	1 706	..	..	..	45.6	42.0
25	Rubber and plastics products	1 685	1 826	2 189	1 982	1 186	..	..	..	20.7	32.9
26	Non-metallic mineral products	793	699	897	952	660	..	..	..	15.0	24.1
27/28	Basic & fabricated metals	2 612	2 844	2 662	2 176	..	..	..	..	11.8	..
27	Basic metals	1 232	1 432	1 202	1 082	..	..	..	..	17.6	..
28	Fabricated metal products	1 380	1 413	1 460	1 094	1 096	..	..	..	8.9	39.1
29/32	Machinery, Total	8 980	9 708	11 891	11 827	7 803	..	..	..	35.2	49.6
29/30	Non-electrical machinery	5 335	5 610	7 134	6 984	4 167	..	..	..	34.1	50.7
29	Non-electrical machinery nec	3 267	3 434	4 353	4 173	2 600	..	..	..	25.4	43.2
30	Office and computing machinery	2 068	2 176	2 781	2 811	1 567	..	..	..	69.6	71.1
31/32	Electrical & electronic equipment	3 645	4 098	4 757	4 843	3 636	..	..	..	36.9	48.5
31	Electrical machinery nec	1 319	1 182	1 654	1 339	999	..	..	..	21.3	36.2
32	Radio, TV & communications eq.	2 326	2 916	3 103	3 504	2 637	..	..	..	51.1	55.6
33	Scientific instruments	1 087	995	1 332	1 209	667	..	..	..	21.8	29.5
34/35	Transportation equipment	7 273	7 448	9 221	9 556	6 229	..	..	..	47.9	43.4
34	Motor vehicles	6 208	6 706	8 191	8 266	6 038	..	..	..	66.4	76.8
35	Other transport equipment	1 065	742	1 030	1 290	190	..	..	..	17.2	2.9
351	Shipbuilding & repairing	..	..	28	215	..	..	..	..	16.5	..
353	Aircraft and spacecraft	..	..	601	765	..	..	..	..	13.7	..
36/37	Other manufacturing	433	409	663	554	318	..	..	..	7.9	18.2
40/45	Construction, electricity, gas & water	..	..	1 775	3 322	1 445	..	..	..	5.7	6.3
50/55	Trade, repair, hotels & restaurants	..	..	..	..	15 868	..	..	..	..	12.5
65/74	Finance, insurance, business services	..	..	..	..	10 824	..	..	..	..	9.5
	OTHER ACTIVITIES	..	..	..	..	4 539	..	..	..	..	10.1
01/99	**GRAND TOTAL**	**..**	**..**	**..**	**..**	**64 709**	**..**	**..**	**..**	**..**	**16.1**

Total manufacturing by investing country						As a % of total manufacturing by foreign affiliates					
All countries	40 908	42 093	50 420	48 421	27 846	100.0	100.0	100.0	100.0	100.0	
United States	..	22 015	27 430	25 113	15 861	..	52.3	54.4	51.9	57.0	
Canada	..	2 142	2 183	..	..	..	5.1	4.3	..	..	
Mexico	..	..	..	0	..	..	..	..	0.0	..	
Japan	..	2 581	2 641	3 346	2 259	..	6.1	5.2	6.9	8.1	
Europe	..	..	..	..	..	..	..	..	..	..	
European Union (15)	..	9 758	13 341	13 006	6 604	..	23.2	26.5	26.9	23.7	
Belgium	..	..	289	..	..	..	..	0.6	..	..	
France	..	2 757	3 399	3 242	1 956	..	6.5	6.7	6.7	7.0	
Germany	..	3 658	3 868	3 877	1 831	..	8.7	7.7	8.0	6.6	
Italy	..	..	761	..	..	..	..	1.5	..	..	
Netherlands	..	1 613	1 771	1 878	1 529	..	3.8	3.5	3.9	5.5	
Spain	..	..	..	..	..	..	..	..	..	..	
Sweden	..	1 099	942	..	..	..	2.6	1.9	..	..	
United Kingdom	..	..	..	..	..	..	..	..	..	..	
Switzerland	..	2 544	2 933	2 712	704	..	6.0	5.8	5.6	2.5	
Australia and New Zealand	..	1 075	892	..	..	..	2.6	1.8	..	..	
Asia (non-OECD)	..	..	152	197	145	..	..	0.3	0.4	0.5	
Latin America	..	..	0	39	0	..	..	0.0	0.1	0.0	

Note: Majority foreign-owned firms. For 1998 data, only enterprises with more than 250 employees are included in the manufacturing industry.
Firmes sous contrôle étranger majoritaire. Pour 1998, seules les entreprises de plus de 250 salariés sont incluses dans les données du secteur manufacturier.

Inward investments

Investissements entrants

Table 8A - Tableau 8A

COMPENSATION OF EMPLOYEES / SALAIRES ET CHARGES SOCIALES

By industry (ISIC Rev. 3)		Foreign affiliates (Millions of GBP) Filiales étrangères (Millions de GBP)					As a % of national total En % du total national				
		1994	1995	1996	1997	1998	1994	1995	1996	1997	1998
10/14	Mining & quarrying	..	..	73	556	667	..	..	..	22.4	37.5
15/37	**TOTAL MANUFACTURING**	**14 463**	**13 791**	**16 356**	**16 048**	**15 211**	**21.9**	**20.4**	**23.4**	**21.8**	**31.4**
15/16	Food, beverages, tobacco	..	..	1 462	1 419	1 088	..	..	19.4	17.5	15.4
17/19	Textiles, clothing, leather, footwear	..	..	300	269	..	..	..	7.0	6.0	..
20/22	Wood and paper products	1 284	1 122	1 262	1 326	676	14.2	12.3	12.9	13.2	14.9
20	Wood products	54	43	..	36	9	5.2	3.9	..	3.2	4.4
21/22	Paper, printing and publishing	1 230	1 079	..	1 291	667	15.3	13.4	..	14.4	15.4
23/25	Chemicals, Total	2 778	2 801	3 333	3 114	..	29.4	28.0	32.5	29.0	..
23	Refined petroleum, nuclear fuel	125	160	182	166	..	18.6	23.8	25.5	24.5	..
24/25	Chemicals, rubber & plastics prod.	2 653	2 641	3 150	2 949	2 722	30.2	28.3	33.0	29.3	36.2
24	Chemical products	1 960	1 920	2 266	2 197	1 984	36.7	33.5	39.7	36.6	37.5
2423	Pharmaceuticals	..	..	761	778	663	..	..	49.4	46.8	37.8
25	Rubber and plastics products	693	721	884	752	738	20.1	20.0	23.0	18.5	33.2
26	Non-metallic mineral products	303	255	319	344	331	13.3	10.5	13.4	14.1	21.2
27/28	Basic & fabricated metals	995	998	1 082	917	925	12.2	11.5	12.2	10.4	25.2
27	Basic metals	405	424	435	431	373	16.9	17.0	16.8	16.2	18.8
28	Fabricated metal products	590	574	647	487	551	10.3	9.3	10.3	7.9	32.7
29/32	Machinery, Total	3 722	3 436	4 293	4 369	..	28.6	25.9	31.6	30.1	..
29/30	Non-electrical machinery	2 345	2 001	2 516	2 457	..	29.2	24.5	30.9	28.0	..
29	Non-electrical machinery nec	1 489	1 488	1 863	1 715	1 462	22.7	21.3	26.6	22.9	36.5
30	Office and computing machinery	856	512	653	742	..	58.6	44.2	56.5	57.4	..
31/32	Electrical & electronic equipment	1 377	1 435	1 777	1 911	1 942	27.5	28.1	32.7	33.2	44.8
31	Electrical machinery nec	630	537	782	683	704	22.5	19.0	26.2	21.9	35.1
32	Radio, TV & communications eq.	747	899	995	1 228	1 238	34.0	39.4	40.6	46.6	53.2
33	Scientific instruments	409	366	550	492	385	18.9	16.5	23.0	19.8	27.1
34/35	Transportation equipment	3 078	3 032	3 506	3 584	4 172	42.5	40.9	44.6	41.7	46.4
34	Motor vehicles	2 497	2 524	2 914	3 002	3 761	61.4	58.2	61.8	59.0	73.1
35	Other transport equipment	581	508	592	581	411	18.3	16.5	18.8	16.6	10.7
351	Shipbuilding & repairing	..	..	25	66	132	..	..	3.6	8.1	17.9
353	Aircraft and spacecraft	..	..	369	362	170	..	..	17.4	15.3	6.0
36/37	Other manufacturing	177	148	249	213	206	6.4	5.4	8.7	6.8	19.5
40/45	Construction, electricity, gas & water	..	..	552	1 072	963	..	..	3.1	5.4	9.0
50/55	Trade, repair, hotels & restaurants	..	..	..	..	7 529	..	..	..	..	11.7
65/74	Finance, insurance, business services	..	..	..	..	6 351	..	..	..	..	11.0
	OTHER ACTIVITIES	..	..	..	..	2 345	..	..	..	..	10.4
01/99	**GRAND TOTAL**	..	..	..	..	**33 066**	..	..	..	..	**16.1**

Total manufacturing by investing country						As a % of total manufacturing by foreign affiliates				
All countries	14 463	13 791	16 356	16 048	15 211	100.0	100.0	100.0	100.0	100.0
United States	..	6 513	7 967	7 398	7 374	..	47.2	48.7	46.1	48.5
Canada	..	717	704	..	..	..	5.2	4.3	..	..
Mexico	..	..	..	0	..	..	..	..	0.0	..
Japan	..	815	952	1 155	1 386	..	5.9	5.8	7.2	9.1
Europe	..	..	..	..	..	..	..	..	..	..
European Union (15)	..	3 824	5 160	5 138	4 576	..	27.7	31.5	32.0	30.1
Belgium	..	..	120	..	..	..	..	0.7	..	..
France	..	987	1 182	1 059	1 094	..	7.2	7.2	6.6	7.2
Germany	..	1 513	1 701	1 769	1 971	..	11.0	10.4	11.0	13.0
Italy	..	..	219	..	..	..	..	1.3	..	..
Netherlands	..	677	731	727	737	..	4.9	4.5	4.5	4.8
Spain	..	..	..	..	..	..	..	..	..	..
Sweden	..	407	372	..	..	..	2.9	2.3	..	..
United Kingdom	..	..	..	..	..	..	..	..	..	..
Switzerland	..	842	885	852	518	..	6.1	5.4	5.3	3.4
Australia and New Zealand	..	387	253	..	..	..	2.8	1.5	..	..
Asia (non-OECD)	..	..	66	99	108	..	..	0.4	0.6	0.7
Latin America	..	..	0	12	0	..	..	0.0	0.1	0.0

Note: Majority foreign-owned firms. For 1998 data, only enterprises with more than 250 employees are included in the manufacturing industry.
Firmes sous contrôle étranger majoritaire. Pour 1998, seules les entreprises de plus de 250 salariés sont incluses dans les données du secteur manufacturier.

Inward investments   *Investissements entrants*

Table 9A - Tableau 9A
R&D EXPENDITURE / DÉPENSES DE R-D

By industry (ISIC Rev. 3)	Foreign affiliates *(Millions of GBP)* Filiales étrangères *(Millions de GBP)*					As a % of national total En % du total national				
	1995	1996	1997	1998	1999	1995	1996	1997	1998	1999
10/14 Mining & quarrying	5	9	8	5	8	7.7	14.1	18.2	12.2	19.0
15/37 TOTAL MANUFACTURING	..	**2 241**	..	**2 530**	**2 837**	..	**30.3**	..	**30.7**	**31.5**
15/16 Food, beverages, tobacco	61	65	61	92	88	32.3	32.8	33.9	38.0	37.1
17/19 Textiles, clothing, leather, footwear	3	3	3	5	4	13.0	11.1	9.1	15.2	14.3
20/22 Wood and paper products	10	14	12	20	11	25.6	24.6	27.3	40.8	24.4
20 Wood products	..	..	..	..	..	..	..	..	..	..
21/22 Paper, printing and publishing	..	..	..	..	..	..	..	..	..	..
23/25 Chemicals, Total	759	876	1 175	1 101	1 319	25.7	30.1	36.3	32.8	37.3
23 Refined petroleum, nuclear fuel	21	25	77	82	85	5.6	6.9	22.1	22.7	40.1
24/25 Chemicals, rubber & plastics prod.	738	851	1 098	1 019	1 234	28.7	33.4	38.0	34.1	37.1
24 Chemical products	709	825	1 081	993	1 205	28.2	33.3	38.2	33.9	37.0
2423 Pharmaceuticals	489	610	824	768	1 066	27.0	32.9	38.3	34.3	42.1
25 Rubber and plastics products	29	26	17	26	29	48.3	38.8	28.3	39.4	40.3
26 Non-metallic mineral products	6	7	5	6	5	11.1	11.7	10.6	10.7	8.5
27/28 Basic & fabricated metals	55	21	..	35	44	33.1	14.5	..	22.3	33.1
27 Basic metals	13	3	..	16	6	19.7	5.6	..	23.9	9.5
28 Fabricated metal products	42	18	17	19	38	42.0	19.8	19.3	21.1	54.3
29/32 Machinery, Total	504	543	511	454	623	27.6	28.7	28.3	23.2	31.5
29/30 Non-electrical machinery	238	233	226	208	198	32.5	31.6	31.2	27.2	26.3
29 Non-electrical machinery nec	135	129	166	144	134	23.2	22.4	26.7	22.5	20.9
30 Office and computing machinery	103	104	60	64	64	68.7	64.6	58.8	51.2	57.7
31/32 Electrical & electronic equipment	266	310	285	246	425	24.3	26.9	26.4	20.6	34.7
31 Electrical machinery nec	87	77	56	63	42	17.6	15.7	13.2	14.9	11.8
32 Radio, TV & communications eq.	179	233	229	183	383	29.7	35.2	35.0	23.7	44.2
33 Scientific instruments	114	98	85	74	72	37.6	31.9	25.3	21.8	15.2
34/35 Transportation equipment	604	611	..	738	660	35.1	34.2	..	36.5	26.7
34 Motor vehicles	489	549	598	690	616	61.5	59.3	64.7	75.6	58.1
35 Other transport equipment	115	62	..	48	44	12.4	7.2	..	4.3	3.1
351 Shipbuilding & repairing	1	0	0	1	0	5.0	0.0	0.0	2.8	0.0
353 Aircraft and spacecraft	103	47	65	28	34	11.6	5.8	7.3	2.7	2.7
36/37 Other manufacturing	..	3	4	5	10	..	17.6	16.0	25.0	29.4
40/45 Construction, electricity, gas & water	2	..	..	1	1	1.1	..	..	0.6	0.6
50/55 Trade, repair, hotels & restaurants	1	1	1	2	16	12.5	25.0	20.0	25.0	64.0
65/74 Finance, insurance, business services	..	429	375	372	446	..	34.1	33.0	31.2	32.9
OTHER ACTIVITIES	..	..	..	174	214	..	..	..	30.0	30.4
01/99 GRAND TOTAL	**2 698**	**2 843**	**3 134**	**3 082**	**3 522**	**29.2**	**30.1**	**32.5**	**30.1**	**31.2**

Grand total by investing country						As a % of total manufacturing by foreign affiliates				
All countries	**2 698**	**2 843**	**3 134**	**3 082**	**3 522**	**100.0**	**100.0**	**100.0**	**100.0**	**100.0**
United States	1 385	1 472	1 640	1 620	..	51.3	51.8	52.3	52.6	..
Canada	..	..	..	..	..	..	..	..	..	..
Mexico	..	..	..	..	..	..	..	..	..	..
Japan	296	323	244	262	..	11.0	11.4	7.8	8.5	..
Europe	..	..	..	..	..	..	..	..	..	..
European Union (15)	736	801	887	827	..	27.3	28.2	28.3	26.8	..
Belgium	..	..	..	..	..	..	..	..	..	..
France	175	151	94	77	..	6.5	5.3	3.0	2.5	..
Germany	288	301	213	309	..	10.7	10.6	6.8	10.0	..
Italy	..	..	..	..	..	..	..	..	..	..
Netherlands	..	..	..	..	..	..	..	..	..	..
Spain	..	..	..	..	..	..	..	..	..	..
Sweden	..	..	..	..	..	..	..	..	..	..
United Kingdom	..	..	..	..	..	..	..	..	..	..
Switzerland	..	..	..	..	..	..	..	..	..	..
Australia and New Zealand	..	..	..	..	..	..	..	..	..	..
Asia (non-OECD)	..	..	..	..	..	..	..	..	..	..
Latin America	..	..	..	..	..	..	..	..	..	..

Note: Majority foreign-owned firms.
Firmes sous contrôle étranger majoritaire.

Inward investments

Investissements entrants

Table 10A - Tableau 10A

GROSS FIXED CAPITAL FORMATION / FORMATION BRUTE DE CAPITAL FIXE

By industry (ISIC Rev. 3)		Foreign affiliates (Millions of GBP) / Filiales étrangères (Millions de GBP)					As a % of national total / En % du total national				
		1994	1995	1996	1997	1998	1994	1995	1996	1997	1998
10/14	Mining & quarrying	..	..	34	2 295	..	..	..	..	0.7	55.3	..
15/37	**TOTAL MANUFACTURING**	**4 175**	**5 340**	**5 859**	**6 781**	**5 205**	**29.8**	**30.7**	**32.8**	**33.8**	**39.9**
15/16	Food, beverages, tobacco	..	..	449	456	365	..	..	19.1	17.8	17.6
17/19	Textiles, clothing, leather, footwear	..	..	73	88	..	..	..	11.7	16.6	..
20/22	Wood and paper products	273	274	311	463	178	14.4	12.0	15.9	20.6	21.0
20	Wood products	32	26	9	29	1	24.7	16.3	5.3	12.3	1.3
21/22	Paper, printing and publishing	240	248	302	434	177	13.6	11.7	16.9	21.6	23.1
23/25	Chemicals, Total	956	1 166	1 488	1 448	1 328	29.6	29.2	33.4	31.1	34.3
23	Refined petroleum, nuclear fuel	122	213	199	131	95	21.1	28.3	27.8	18.7	13.7
24/25	Chemicals, rubber & plastics prod.	834	953	1 289	1 317	1 234	31.4	29.4	34.4	33.3	38.8
24	Chemical products	691	805	1 078	1 133	1 089	36.6	35.2	39.1	40.0	40.5
2423	Pharmaceuticals	..	..	297	340	407	..	..	47.8	49.5	47.8
25	Rubber and plastics products	143	148	211	184	142	18.7	15.6	21.4	16.4	28.8
26	Non-metallic mineral products	71	89	87	102	93	16.8	14.6	12.9	17.6	21.5
27/28	Basic & fabricated metals	204	291	267	252	204	18.1	21.2	17.0	15.2	27.3
27	Basic metals	76	144	136	153	122	19.8	27.5	21.7	22.7	24.5
28	Fabricated metal products	129	147	132	99	81	17.2	17.4	14.0	10.1	32.1
29/32	Machinery, Total	1 057	1 398	1 419	1 635	1 118	45.9	44.9	47.3	46.2	57.8
29/30	Non-electrical machinery	511	495	544	578	352	42.3	34.3	37.0	38.1	60.2
29	Non-electrical machinery nec	276	271	368	305	231	31.6	25.1	31.2	26.7	60.5
30	Office and computing machinery	235	224	177	273	120	70.1	61.5	60.8	72.8	59.1
31/32	Electrical & electronic equipment	546	903	875	1 057	766	49.9	54.2	57.2	52.3	56.8
31	Electrical machinery nec	105	98	164	182	117	30.2	24.1	35.7	25.1	30.2
32	Radio, TV & communications eq.	441	805	711	875	649	59.0	63.9	66.4	67.6	67.5
33	Scientific instruments	87	81	123	133	46	23.8	23.9	32.8	31.1	23.7
34/35	Transportation equipment	1 025	1 564	1 598	2 180	1 830	67.8	67.9	66.2	65.5	69.5
34	Motor vehicles	986	1 448	1 529	2 092	1 789	77.8	74.8	78.7	77.1	88.7
35	Other transport equipment	39	116	70	88	41	16.0	31.4	14.9	14.3	6.6
351	Shipbuilding & repairing	..	..	0	1	..	..	..	0.0	1.3	..
353	Aircraft and spacecraft	..	..	52	71	24	..	..	18.1	14.1	4.5
36/37	Other manufacturing	38	26	42	24	43	11.5	5.9	10.0	4.2	29.3
40/45	Construction, electricity, gas & water	..	..	263	724	..	..	..	..	4.9	10.6	..
50/55	Trade, repair, hotels & restaurants	..	..	..	..	1 630	..	..	..	..	8.2
65/74	Finance, insurance, business services	..	..	..	..	2 178	..	..	..	..	7.8
	OTHER ACTIVITIES	..	..	..	..	1 602	..	..	..	..	10.6
01/99	**GRAND TOTAL**	..	..	..	..	**13 181**	..	..	..	..	**15.4**

Total manufacturing by investing country							As a % of total manufacturing by foreign affiliates				
All countries		4 175	5 340	5 859	6 781	5 205	100.0	100.0	100.0	100.0	100.0
United States		..	2 586	2 829	3 126	2 650	..	48.4	48.3	46.1	50.9
Canada		..	163	187	..	..	..	3.1	3.2	..	..
Mexico		..	..	..	0	..	..	..	..	0.0	..
Japan		..	776	637	913	657	..	14.5	10.9	13.5	12.6
Europe		..	..	..	..	..	..	..	..	..	..
European Union (15)		..	1 305	1 697	1 686	1 437	..	24.4	29.0	24.9	27.6
Belgium		..	..	55	..	..	..	..	0.9	..	..
France		..	268	268	261	193	..	5.0	4.6	3.8	3.7
Germany		..	707	780	818	858	..	13.2	13.3	12.1	16.5
Italy		..	..	63	..	..	..	..	1.1	..	..
Netherlands		..	150	224	145	222	..	2.8	3.8	2.1	4.3
Spain		..	..	..	..	..	..	..	..	..	..
Sweden		..	99	102	..	..	..	1.9	1.7	..	..
United Kingdom		..	..	..	..	..	..	..	..	..	..
Switzerland		..	267	266	272	161	..	5.0	4.5	4.0	3.1
Australia and New Zealand		..	63	28	..	..	..	1.2	0.5	..	..
Asia (non-OECD)		..	..	18	97	10	..	..	0.3	1.4	0.2
Latin America		..	..	0	1	0	..	..	0.0	0.0	0.0

Note: Majority foreign-owned firms. For 1998 data, only enterprises with more than 250 employees are included in the manufacturing industry.

Firmes sous contrôle étranger majoritaire. Pour 1998, seules les entreprises de plus de 250 salariés sont incluses dans les données du secteur manufacturier.

Inward investments   *Investissements entrants*

Table 11A - Tableau 11A
GROSS OPERATING SURPLUS / EXCÉDENT BRUT D'EXPLOITATION

| | | Foreign affiliates (Millions of GBP) | | | | | As a % of national total | | | | |
| | | Filiales étrangères (Millions de GBP) | | | | | En % du total national | | | | |
By industry (ISIC Rev. 3)		1994	1995	1996	1997	1998	1994	1995	1996	1997	1998
10/14	Mining & quarrying	..	..	91	7 357	3 520	..	..	5.8	44.7	52.5
15/37	**TOTAL MANUFACTURING**	16 490	18 544	22 387	20 127	12 636	27.6	27.3	31.5	28.3	35.0
15/16	Food, beverages, tobacco	..	..	3 493	3 134	1 614	..	..	29.6	27.2	20.7
17/19	Textiles, clothing, leather, footwear	..	..	353	279	..	..	..	10.4	8.3	..
20/22	Wood and paper products	1 499	1 524	1 697	1 572	563	20.5	17.1	19.5	18.6	15.1
20	Wood products	97	121	..	81	..	17.4	16.8	..	8.8	..
21/22	Paper, printing and publishing	1 403	1 403	..	1 491	..	20.7	17.2	..	19.8	..
23/25	Chemicals, Total	4 335	4 938	5 792	4 835	..	34.1	33.2	39.0	34.9	..
23	Refined petroleum, nuclear fuel	660	718	716	471	..	41.4	32.0	38.8	33.4	..
24/25	Chemicals, rubber & plastics prod.	3 675	4 221	5 076	4 364	5 036	33.1	33.5	39.0	35.1	56.4
24	Chemical products	3 048	3 423	4 200	3 563	2 291	37.3	35.4	43.1	40.5	30.3
2423	Pharmaceuticals	..	..	1 111	1 137	1 043	..	..	42.2	39.3	45.2
25	Rubber and plastics products	627	798	876	802	447	21.4	27.1	26.7	22.1	32.4
26	Non-metallic mineral products	294	266	358	347	330	13.0	10.5	13.8	14.1	28.1
27/28	Basic & fabricated metals	1 111	1 297	1 070	858	..	20.3	17.9	16.5	12.7	..
27	Basic metals	613	739	555	463	..	24.6	22.7	21.8	20.9	..
28	Fabricated metal products	497	558	514	395	545	16.7	14.0	13.1	8.7	48.8
29/32	Machinery, Total	3 302	4 416	5 083	4 603	..	35.3	38.4	42.3	37.0	..
29/30	Non-electrical machinery	1 789	2 580	3 108	2 646	..	33.2	38.1	42.5	35.6	..
29	Non-electrical machinery nec	1 142	1 333	1 603	1 665	1 138	28.7	26.5	29.2	27.5	56.5
30	Office and computing machinery	648	1 247	1 505	981	..	46.2	71.4	82.1	71.6	..
31/32	Electrical & electronic equipment	1 513	1 837	1 975	1 957	1 694	38.2	38.9	42.0	39.0	53.4
31	Electrical machinery nec	421	434	524	398	295	22.0	21.7	25.5	19.0	39.1
32	Radio, TV & communications eq.	1 092	1 403	1 451	1 559	1 399	53.3	51.5	54.9	53.2	57.9
33	Scientific instruments	498	444	493	473	282	28.3	25.0	25.0	22.3	33.5
34/35	Transportation equipment	2 318	2 572	3 794	3 820	2 056	36.4	42.8	54.5	51.1	38.3
34	Motor vehicles	2 050	2 487	3 555	3 258	2 277	64.9	62.1	72.8	69.0	83.9
35	Other transport equipment	269	85	239	562	- 221	8.3	4.2	11.5	20.4	-8.3
351	Shipbuilding & repairing	..	..	- 2	143	..	..	..	-0.4	45.4	..
353	Aircraft and spacecraft	..	..	112	300	..	..	..	8.2	13.4	..
36/37	Other manufacturing	164	186	255	207	113	10.3	9.7	11.1	8.0	16.3
40/45	Construction, electricity, gas & water	..	..	707	1 564	482	..	..	2.9	6.0	3.9
50/55	Trade, repair, hotels & restaurants	..	..	..	..	8 339	..	..	..	..	13.4
65/74	Finance, insurance, business services	..	..	..	..	4 473	..	..	..	..	8.0
	OTHER ACTIVITIES	..	..	..	..	2 194	..	..	..	..	9.8
01/99	**GRAND TOTAL**	..	..	..	..	31 643	..	..	..	..	16.2

Total manufacturing by investing country							As a % of total manufacturing by foreign affiliates				
All countries		16 490	18 544	22 387	20 127	12 636	100.0	100.0	100.0	100.0	100.0
United States		..	10 290	13 603	11 677	8 488	..	55.5	60.8	58.0	67.2
Canada		..	995	1 006	..	..	..	5.4	4.5	..	..
Mexico		..	..	..	0	..	..	..	..	0.0	..
Japan		..	1 331	1 082	1 220	873	..	7.2	4.8	6.1	6.9
Europe		..	..	..	..	..	..	..	..	..	..
European Union (15)		..	3 480	4 449	4 132	2 027	..	18.8	19.9	20.5	16.0
Belgium		..	..	58	..	..	..	..	0.3	..	..
France		..	1 152	1 205	1 265	862	..	6.2	5.4	6.3	6.8
Germany		..	1 117	1 040	806	- 140	..	6.0	4.6	4.0	-1.1
Italy		..	..	312	..	..	..	..	1.4	..	..
Netherlands		..	551	639	771	792	..	3.0	2.9	3.8	6.3
Spain		..	..	..	..	..	..	..	..	..	..
Sweden		..	434	331	..	..	..	2.3	1.5	..	..
United Kingdom		..	..	..	..	..	..	..	..	..	..
Switzerland		..	1 189	1 402	1 350	186	..	6.4	6.3	6.7	1.5
Australia and New Zealand		..	423	499	..	..	..	2.3	2.2	..	..
Asia (non-OECD)		..	..	51	43	37	..	..	0.2	0.2	0.3
Latin America		..	..	0	14	0	..	..	0.0	0.1	0.0

Note: Majority foreign-owned firms. For 1998 data, only enterprises with more than 250 employees are included in the manufacturing industry.
Firmes sous contrôle étranger majoritaire. Pour 1998, seules les entreprises de plus de 250 salariés sont incluses dans les données du secteur manufacturier.

UNITED KINGDOM

Source

The data are prepared by the Office for National Statistics and are based on the Annual Business Inquiry, which replaced the annual Census of Production in 1993. This inquiry covers United Kingdom (except Channel Islands and Isle of Man) "enterprises" engaged in industrial production, *i.e.* mining and quarrying, manufacturing, construction, and electricity, gas and water supply industries (Sections C to F of SIC92). Up to 1995, data for foreign enterprises, *i.e.* controlled or owned by companies incorporated overseas (majority foreign ownership), are available separately for manufacturing industries only.

The reporting unit is the *company*, with the exception of large mixed activity companies which are asked to make separate returns to the inquiry for each of their production activities on an establishment basis. These reporting units are referred to as "enterprises".

Forms are in general despatched to all businesses with 100 or more employees, samples of one-in-four and one-in-two respectively being taken for businesses in the 20-49 and 50-99 employment size bands. Estimates are made for non-responders, unsatisfactory returns and enterprises not selected for the Inquiry. The data are published every year in *Business Monitor – Production and Construction Inquiry, Summary Volume (PA 1002)* and PACSTAT CD Rom.

For *R&D expenditure*, data come from the Survey of Business Enterprise R&D and are published by the Office for National Statistics in *Research and Development in UK Business*.

National totals: for all variables except *R&D expenditure*, data come from the OECD ISIS database until 1995. From 1996, they have been provided by the NSO and are fully compatible with foreign affiliates' data.

Industrial classification

For all variables, data are classified according to the principal industrial activity of the enterprise.

Since 1993, the inquiry has been conducted on the Standard Industrial Classification Revised (SIC92), based on ISIC Revision 3.

Variables

- *Number of employees* consists of the average number of administrative, technical and clerical employees and operatives on the payroll and the number of working proprietors employed during the year of return. Full-time and part-time employees are included but outworkers and casual employees are excluded.

- *Production* is defined as gross output and is calculated by adjusting the value of total sales and work done by the change during the year of work in progress and goods on hand for sale.

- *Value added* is defined as net output, which is calculated by deducting from gross output the cost of purchases of materials for use in production and packaging and fuel and purchases of goods for merchanting or factoring, the cost of industrial services received, and is adjusted for net duties and levies, etc., where applicable. Purchases are adjusted for changes during the year of stocks of materials, stores and fuel.

- *Wages and salaries* represent amounts paid during the year to administrative, technical and clerical employees and to operatives. All overtime payments, bonuses, commissions, holiday pay and redundancy payments less any amounts reimbursed for this purpose from government sources are included. No deduction is made for income tax or employees' national insurance contributions, etc. Payments to working proprietors, payments in kind, travelling expenses, lodging allowances, etc., and employers' national insurance contributions, etc., are excluded.

- *Gross fixed capital formation* is defined as net capital expenditure, which is calculated by adding to the value of new building work acquisitions less disposals of land and existing buildings, vehicles and plant and machinery.

- *Gross operating surplus* is defined as gross value added at factor cost less wages and salaries.

Geographical breakdown

The country of origin is the country of the "ultimate beneficial owner".

Prior to 1996, the European Union consists of its 12 former member states and the figures for Australia and New Zealand concern Australia only.

For *R&D expenditure*, the breakdown by country of origin is available for the *Grand total* and not for *Total manufacturing* as for other variables.

ROYAUME-UNI

Source

Les données émanent de l'Office national des statistiques et sont basées sur l'Enquête annuelle sur les entreprises qui a remplacé en 1993 le Recensement annuel de la production. Cette enquête couvre au Royaume-Uni (à l'exception des îles anglo-normandes et de l'île de Man) les "entreprises" engagées dans la production industrielle, c'est-à-dire les industries extractives, le secteur manufacturier, la construction, la production et la distribution d'électricité, de gaz et d'eau (Divisions C à F de la SIC92). Jusqu'en 1995, les données concernant les entreprises étrangères, c'est-à-dire contrôlées par ou appartenant à des sociétés immatriculées à l'étranger (participation étrangère majoritaire), sont disponibles séparément pour l'industrie manufacturière seulement.

L'unité employée pour le recensement est la *société*, à l'exception des grandes sociétés à l'activité mixte qui sont tenues, dans ce cadre, de faire des rapports séparés pour chacune de leurs activités de production sur la base de l'établissement. Il est fait référence à ces unités sous le terme d'"entreprises".

Des formulaires sont en général envoyés à toutes les entreprises de 100 salariés ou plus. Pour les autres, on tire un échantillon : un sur quatre dans le groupe des entreprises de 20 à 49 salariés, et un sur deux dans celui des entreprises de 50 à 99 salariés. On fait des estimations pour les non réponses, les déclarations non satisfaisantes et les entreprises non sélectionnées pour l'enquête. Les données sont publiées chaque année dans *Business Monitor – Production and Construction Inquiry, Summary Volume (PA 1002)* et dans le CD-Rom PACSTAT.

Pour les *Dépenses de R-D*, les données proviennent de l'enquête sur la R-D des entreprises et sont publiées par l'ONS dans *Research and Development in UK Business*.

Totaux nationaux : pour toutes les variables à l'exception des *Dépenses de R-D*, les données proviennent de la base de données SISI de l'OCDE jusqu'en 1995. A partir de 1996, elles sont fournies par l'ONS et sont entièrement compatibles avec les données relatives aux filiales étrangères.

Classification industrielle

Pour toutes les variables, les données sont classées selon l'activité industrielle principale de l'entreprise.

Depuis 1993, les données sont classées selon la Classification industrielle standard révisée (SIC92), basée sur la CITI révision 3.

Variables

- Le *Nombre de salariés* est le nombre moyen d'employés de bureau, personnel administratif et technique et d'ouvriers, et le nombre de propriétaires exploitants employés pendant l'exercice considéré. Sont pris en compte les salariés à plein temps et à temps partiel, mais sont exclus les travailleurs à domicile et occasionnels.

- La *Production* est définie en tant que production brute et est calculée en ajustant la valeur des ventes totales et travaux effectués aux variations durant l'année des travaux en cours et biens disponibles à la vente.

- La *Valeur ajoutée* est en fait la production nette qui est calculée en déduisant de la production brute le coût des achats de matériels à utiliser dans la production et l'emballage ainsi que de fuel, et des achats pour courtage sur marchandises ou affacturage, le coût des services industriels reçus, et est ajustée des droits et prélèvements nets, etc., le cas échéant. Les achats sont ajustés des variations survenues pendant l'année des stocks de matériels, approvisionnements et fuel.

- Les *Salaires et traitements* représentent les montants versés pendant l'année aux employés de bureau, au personnel administratif et technique et aux ouvriers. Toutes les heures supplémentaires, primes, commissions, congés payés et indemnités pour perte d'emploi sont inclus, déduction faite de tout montant de source publique remboursé à cette fin. Aucune déduction n'est faite pour l'impôt sur le revenu ou les cotisations salariales au régime national d'assurance. Les versements aux propriétaires exploitants, paiements en nature, frais de voyage, indemnités de logement, etc., et les cotisations patronales au régime d'assurance sociale sont exclus.

- La *Formation brute de capital fixe* est définie comme les dépenses nettes en capital qui sont calculées en ajoutant à la valeur des constructions nouvelles les acquisitions moins les cessions de terrains et bâtiments existants, véhicules, installations et équipements.

- L'*Excédent brut d'exploitation* est défini comme la valeur ajoutée brute au coût des facteurs, moins les salaires et traitements.

Ventilation géographique

Le pays d'origine est le pays du bénéficiaire ultime de l'investissement.

Avant 1996, l'Union européenne ne comprend que les 12 anciens États membres, et les chiffres pour Australie et Nouvelle-Zélande concernent l'Australie seulement.

Pour les *Dépenses de R-D*, la ventilation par pays d'origine est disponible pour le *Total général* et non pour le *Total manufacturier* comme pour les autres variables.

UNITED STATES

A. Inward investments

B. Outward investments

Sources and Methods

ÉTATS-UNIS

A. Investissements entrants

B. Investissements sortants

Sources et méthodes

Inward investments

Investissements entrants

Table 1A - Tableau 1A

NUMBER OF ENTERPRISES / NOMBRE D'ENTREPRISES

By industry (ISIC Rev. 3)	Foreign affiliates (Units) Filiales étrangères (Unités)									
	1989	1990	1991	1992	1993	1994	1995	1996	1997	1998
10/14 Mining & quarrying	109	114	119	110	110	112	113	112	165	157
15/37 **TOTAL MANUFACTURING**	**2 143**	**2 431**	**2 563**	**2 808**	**2 866**	**2 926**	**3 019**	**3 072**	**2 846**	**2 944**
15/16 Food, beverages, tobacco	197	226	231	258	264	260	258	267	267	284
17/19 Textiles, clothing, leather, footwear	95	104	111	131	133	139	139	128	122	121
20/22 Wood and paper products	175	202	216	239	245	252	259	259	138	139
20 Wood products	47	60	67	78	76	75	76	74	34	35
21/22 Paper, printing and publishing	128	142	149	161	169	177	183	185	104	104
23/25 Chemicals, Total	341	392	412	485	498	524	550	559	553	581
23 Refined petroleum, nuclear fuel	..	..	..	..	..	..	..	..	27	34
24/25 Chemicals, rubber & plastics prod.	341	392	412	485	498	524	550	559	526	547
24 Chemical products	214	253	260	304	314	332	346	355	339	355
2423 Pharmaceuticals	49	52	59	62	70	80	85	91	80	84
25 Rubber and plastics products	127	139	152	181	184	192	204	204	187	192
26 Non-metallic mineral products	122	125	129	130	131	129	138	138	131	131
27/28 Basic & fabricated metals	286	345	368	396	399	401	404	424	373	360
27 Basic metals	108	143	147	159	162	170	168	178	169	171
28 Fabricated metal products	178	202	221	237	237	231	236	246	204	189
29/32 Machinery, Total	600	672	708	715	735	745	773	778	712	729
29/30 Non-electrical machinery	360	399	423	430	447	451	466	464	433	435
29 Non-electrical machinery nec	293	312	337	358	360	365	374	373	359	361
30 Office and computing machinery	67	87	86	72	87	86	92	91	74	74
31/32 Electrical & electronic equipment	240	273	285	285	288	294	307	314	279	294
31 Electrical machinery nec	87	85	93	102	104	107	107	111	104	103
32 Radio, TV & communications eq.	153	188	192	183	184	187	200	203	175	191
33 Scientific instruments	128	143	145	163	170	175	175	186	136	142
34/35 Transportation equipment	118	134	146	170	174	190	209	212	260	304
34 Motor vehicles	83	97	102	114	117	134	150	156	220	260
35 Other transport equipment	35	37	44	56	57	56	59	56	40	44
351 Shipbuilding & repairing	..	..	..	..	..	..	..	..	2	5
353 Aircraft and spacecraft	..	..	..	..	..	..	..	..	18	24
36/37 Other manufacturing	81	88	97	121	117	111	114	114	145	141
40/45 Construction, electricity, gas & water	116	130	135	140	141	146	144	147	227	254
50/55 Trade, repair, hotels & restaurants	1 883	1 948	2 014	2 545	2 597	2 602	2 618	2 637	2 258	2 281
65/74 Finance, insurance, business services	3 489	3 804	3 954	4 406	4 488	4 564	4 625	4 680	3 037	3 106
OTHER ACTIVITIES	1 730	1 855	1 962	2 129	2 187	2 256	2 297	2 370	915	969
01/99 **GRAND TOTAL**	**9 470**	**10 282**	**10 747**	**12 138**	**12 389**	**12 606**	**12 816**	**13 018**	**9 474**	**9 738**

Total manufacturing by investing country

All countries	2 143	2 431	2 563	2 808	2 866	2 926	3 019	3 072	2 846	2 944
United States	..	..	..	..	..	..	..	..	..	..
Canada	..	..	..	..	..	..	..	..	..	..
Mexico	..	..	..	..	..	..	..	..	..	..
Japan	..	..	..	..	..	..	..	..	..	..
Europe	..	..	..	..	..	..	..	..	..	..
European Union (15)	..	..	..	..	..	..	..	..	..	..
Belgium	..	..	..	..	..	..	..	..	..	..
France	..	..	..	..	..	..	..	..	..	..
Germany	..	..	..	..	..	..	..	..	..	..
Italy	..	..	..	..	..	..	..	..	..	..
Netherlands	..	..	..	..	..	..	..	..	..	..
Spain	..	..	..	..	..	..	..	..	..	..
Sweden	..	..	..	..	..	..	..	..	..	..
United Kingdom	..	..	..	..	..	..	..	..	..	..
Switzerland	..	..	..	..	..	..	..	..	..	..
Australia and New Zealand	..	..	..	..	..	..	..	..	..	..
Asia (non-OECD)	..	..	..	..	..	..	..	..	..	..
Latin America	..	..	..	..	..	..	..	..	..	..

Note: Majority and minority foreign-owned firms. Change of industrial classification from 1997. See country notes.
Firmes sous contrôle étranger majoritaire et minoritaire. Changement de classification industrielle à partir de 1997. Voir les notes par pays.

Table 2A - Tableau 2A

NUMBER OF EMPLOYEES BY INDUSTRY

NOMBRE DE SALARIÉS PAR INDUSTRIE

ISIC Revision 3		Foreign affiliates (Thousands) Filiales étrangères (Milliers)									
		1989	1990	1991	1992	1993	1994	1995	1996	1997	1998
10/14	Mining & quarrying	44.1	36.0	44.2	48.1	49.3	46.8	42.0	41.7	65.2	67.8
15/37	**TOTAL MANUFACTURING**	**2 138.6**	**2 220.7**	**2 233.6**	**2 252.0**	**2 241.2**	**2 309.5**	**2 281.9**	**2 291.5**	**2 227.0**	**2 539.6**
15/16	Food, beverages, tobacco	251.3	247.3	241.0	242.3	199.9	234.3	234.6	214.0	183.9	197.9
17/19	Textiles, clothing, leather, footwear	58.9	60.3	63.0	76.3	89.3	100.1	89.7	86.5	79.1	68.0
20/22	Wood and paper products	159.3	190.4	194.6	186.9	214.0	220.5	235.2	226.8	114.8	136.7
20	Wood products	13.3	19.9	23.6	23.1	26.1	27.1	23.9	24.3	10.6	11.5
21/22	Paper, printing and publishing	146.0	170.5	171.0	163.8	187.9	193.4	211.3	202.5	104.2	125.2
23/25	Chemicals, Total	525.1	626.0	610.0	622.2	611.7	619.6	537.7	546.3	572.5	601.4
23	Refined petroleum, nuclear fuel	..	..	..	..	..	..	..	..	58.8	82.8
24/25	Chemicals, rubber & plastics prod.	525.1	626.0	610.0	622.2	611.7	619.6	537.7	546.3	513.7	518.6
24	Chemical products	437.1	512.5	508.3	515.6	505.8	508.3	416.7	421.1	389.4	380.0
2423	Pharmaceuticals	93.3	115.0	123.4	127.9	159.8	164.8	151.6	153.2	143.5	144.3
25	Rubber and plastics products	88.0	113.5	101.7	106.6	105.9	111.3	121.0	125.2	124.3	138.6
26	Non-metallic mineral products	115.6	122.8	111.9	114.0	108.9	105.2	120.9	125.6	132.8	139.8
27/28	Basic & fabricated metals	280.2	255.5	270.2	266.0	271.7	261.6	241.4	248.3	219.4	224.1
27	Basic metals	118.4	135.2	149.3	139.5	141.8	123.8	111.2	101.4	95.6	101.8
28	Fabricated metal products	161.8	120.3	120.9	126.5	129.9	137.8	130.1	147.0	123.8	122.3
29/32	Machinery, Total	511.8	509.1	509.0	503.0	498.8	516.3	545.5	557.9	582.9	..
29/30	Non-electrical machinery	245.3	219.0	218.6	210.5	211.1	225.1	240.7	246.4	296.5	245.4
29	Non-electrical machinery nec	199.6	157.6	158.7	168.5	175.0	197.8	198.3	209.2	260.8	209.7
30	Office and computing machinery	45.7	61.3	59.9	42.0	36.1	27.3	42.4	37.2	35.7	35.7
31/32	Electrical & electronic equipment	266.6	290.1	290.4	292.5	287.7	291.3	304.8	311.5	286.4	..
31	Electrical machinery nec	118.1	135.1	154.1	144.8	147.4	164.5	175.5	170.4	129.5	167.6
32	Radio, TV & communications eq.	148.5	155.1	136.2	147.7	140.3	126.8	129.3	141.1	156.9	..
33	Scientific instruments	71.9	90.3	107.4	108.8	110.0	97.8	105.6	100.1	86.3	145.5
34/35	Transportation equipment	74.5	87.8	95.2	101.5	104.4	119.2	141.2	156.6	207.9	368.2
34	Motor vehicles	44.6	57.0	56.2	57.7	64.2	84.2	107.2	115.7	170.0	337.6
35	Other transport equipment	29.9	30.8	39.0	43.8	40.2	35.0	34.0	40.9	37.9	30.6
351	Shipbuilding & repairing	..	..	..	..	..	..	..	..	0.1	1.1
353	Aircraft and spacecraft	..	..	..	..	..	..	..	..	18.0	25.1
36/37	Other manufacturing	89.8	31.2	31.4	31.2	32.5	34.9	30.2	30.9	36.1	..
40/45	Construction, electricity, gas & water	72.5	92.0	82.0	59.1	56.2	54.1	66.6	70.1	85.6	93.4
50/55	Trade, repair, hotels & restaurants	1 202.6	1 174.6	1 245.8	1 149.1	1 191.8	1 150.8	1 224.5	1 301.9	1 497.6	1 537.3
65/74	Finance, insurance, business services	244.6	230.4	252.4	247.7	238.1	226.7	221.0	228.1	350.6	379.1
	OTHER ACTIVITIES	809.0	980.7	1 014.0	959.3	989.0	1 052.6	1 105.7	1 171.8	938.4	1 015.8
01/99	**GRAND TOTAL**	**4 511.5**	**4 734.5**	**4 871.9**	**4 715.4**	**4 765.6**	**4 840.5**	**4 941.8**	**5 105.0**	**5 164.3**	**5 633.0**

Note: Majority and minority foreign-owned firms. Change of industrial classification from 1997. See country notes.
Firmes sous contrôle étranger majoritaire et minoritaire. Changement de classification industrielle à partir de 1997. Voir les notes par pays.

Table 3A - Tableau 3A

NUMBER OF EMPLOYEES BY COUNTRY OF ORIGIN IN THE MANUFACTURING SECTOR
NOMBRE DE SALARIÉS PAR PAYS D'ORIGINE DANS L'INDUSTRIE MANUFACTURIÈRE

Country of origin (UBO)	Number of employees (Thousands) Nombre de salariés (Milliers)					As a % of all countries En % du total des pays				
	1994	1995	1996	1997	1998	1994	1995	1996	1997	1998
All countries	2 309.5	2 281.9	2 291.5	2 227.0	2 539.6	100.0	100.0	100.0	100.0	100.0
Total OECD	..	..	..	..	..	..	..	..	..	..
United States	4.9	6.0	9.7	16.5	21.1	0.2	0.3	0.4	0.7	0.8
Canada	357.3	294.8	263.4	197.0	208.1	15.5	12.9	11.5	8.8	8.2
Mexico	22.3	23.8	22.8	17.2	18.8	1.0	1.0	1.0	0.8	0.7
Japan	333.6	372.4	370.0	389.3	436.0	14.4	16.3	16.1	17.5	17.2
Korea	4.7	7.0	7.8	6.3	6.3	0.2	0.3	0.3	0.3	0.2
Australia	35.3	38.0	39.6	46.8	39.5	1.5	1.7	1.7	2.1	1.6
New Zealand	3.6	2.8	1.5	..	0.2	0.2	0.1	0.1	..	0.0
Europe	1 439.7	1 434.5	1 476.7	1 448.5	1 656.7	62.3	62.9	64.4	65.0	65.2
European Union (15)	1 160.9	1 256.5	1 302.4	1 276.0	1 494.7	50.3	55.1	56.8	57.3	58.9
Austria	5.7	5.5	3.9	3.5	3.9	0.2	0.2	0.2	0.2	0.2
Belgium	12.4	12.8	12.3	..	..	0.5	0.6	0.5	..	..
Denmark	6.8	5.6	6.8	8.2	8.6	0.3	0.2	0.3	0.4	0.3
Finland	23.6	18.1	15.7	13.4	15.1	1.0	0.8	0.7	0.6	0.6
France	195.6	187.9	206.8	194.0	203.7	8.5	8.2	9.0	8.7	8.0
Germany	283.9	290.7	305.4	309.2	441.7	12.3	12.7	13.3	13.9	17.4
Greece	..	..	..	..	..	..	..	..	..	..
Ireland	27.9	33.0	34.0	35.1	59.6	1.2	1.4	1.5	1.6	2.3
Italy	31.1	27.9	24.8	23.3	25.2	1.3	1.2	1.1	1.0	1.0
Luxembourg	4.4	3.9	13.6	3.7	..	0.2	0.2	0.6	0.2	..
Netherlands	88.9	87.9	103.5	109.9	111.1	3.8	3.9	4.5	4.9	4.4
Portugal	..	..	..	..	..	..	..	..	..	..
Spain	2.9	2.8	2.4	..	3.7	0.1	0.1	0.1	..	0.1
Sweden	68.2	81.7	74.6	74.3	73.0	3.0	3.6	3.3	3.3	2.9
United Kingdom	507.0	498.1	498.3	472.0	517.6	22.0	21.8	21.7	21.2	20.4
Czech Republic	..	..	..	..	..	..	..	..	..	..
Hungary	..	..	..	..	..	..	..	..	..	..
Iceland	..	..	..	..	..	..	..	..	..	..
Norway	9.1	8.6	9.0	10.8	10.8	0.4	0.4	0.4	0.5	0.4
Poland	..	..	..	..	..	..	..	..	..	..
Slovak Republic	..	..	..	..	..	..	..	..	..	..
Switzerland	169.0	166.6	162.7	158.9	148.9	7.3	7.3	7.1	7.1	5.9
Turkey	..	..	..	..	..	..	..	..	..	..
Non-OECD Europe, of which:	..	..	..	..	..	..	..	..	..	..
Baltic countries	..	..	..	..	..	..	..	..	..	..
Bulgaria	..	..	..	..	..	..	..	..	..	..
Croatia	..	..	..	..	..	..	..	..	..	..
Romania	..	..	..	..	..	..	..	..	..	..
Russian Federation	..	..	..	..	..	..	..	..	..	..
Slovenia	..	..	..	..	..	..	..	..	..	..
Ukraine	..	..	..	..	..	..	..	..	..	..
Yugoslavia	..	..	..	..	..	..	..	..	..	..
Non-OECD Asia, of which:	49.6	54.4	46.7	46.1	..	2.1	2.4	2.0	2.1	..
China	0.7	1.0	1.2	0.8	1.0	0.0	0.0	0.1	0.0	0.0
Chinese Taipei	12.7	14.1	14.0	14.8	13.2	0.5	0.6	0.6	0.7	0.5
Hong Kong (China)	2.9	2.7	2.5	2.8	2.9	0.1	0.1	0.1	0.1	0.1
India	..	..	..	..	..	..	..	..	..	..
Indonesia	4.7	4.9	4.6	9.0	6.0	0.2	0.2	0.2	0.4	0.2
Malaysia	..	7.3	6.4	5.7	5.1	..	0.3	0.3	0.3	0.2
Philippines	6.4	..	0.7	0.7	0.8	0.3	..	0.0	0.0	0.0
Singapore	3.9	4.1	3.4	2.0	3.3	0.2	0.2	0.1	0.1	0.1
Thailand	..	..	..	..	..	..	..	..	..	..
Near and Middle East	22.3	20.3	27.0	34.2	30.5	1.0	0.9	1.2	1.5	1.2
Africa	6.7	10.9	12.3	12.1	10.1	0.3	0.5	0.5	0.5	0.4
Latin America, of which:	60.0	50.7	46.0	36.5	96.7	2.6	2.2	2.0	1.6	3.8
Argentina	..	..	..	..	..	..	..	..	..	..
Brazil	1.8	1.8	1.7	1.5	1.7	0.1	0.1	0.1	0.1	0.1
Chile	..	..	..	..	..	..	..	..	..	..

Note: Majority and minority foreign-owned firms. Change of industrial classification from 1997. See country notes.
Firmes sous contrôle étranger majoritaire et minoritaire. Changement de classification industrielle à partir de 1997. Voir les notes par pays.

Inward investments

Investissements entrants

Table 4A - Tableau 4A

TURNOVER BY INDUSTRY

CHIFFRE D'AFFAIRES PAR INDUSTRIE

| ISIC Revision 3 | | Foreign affiliates (Billions of USD) | | | | | | | | | |
| | | Filiales étrangères (Milliards de USD) | | | | | | | | | |
		1989	1990	1991	1992	1993	1994	1995	1996	1997	1998
10/14	Mining & quarrying	8.5	8.2	9.7	11.2	11.3	11.8	12.0	12.0	19.6	22.8
15/37	**TOTAL MANUFACTURING**	**353.1**	**396.4**	**405.7**	**431.2**	**468.3**	**524.9**	**559.3**	**587.0**	**667.6**	**834.4**
15/16	Food, beverages, tobacco	42.6	47.1	47.7	47.0	46.8	48.9	51.1	54.0	60.3	65.0
17/19	Textiles, clothing, leather, footwear	5.6	5.8	6.6	8.3	9.3	11.0	10.8	10.2	9.8	8.5
20/22	Wood and paper products	24.1	29.4	29.8	31.0	38.6	41.4	47.3	45.4	25.3	27.9
20	Wood products	1.7	2.9	3.1	3.7	4.8	6.0	4.6	4.8	2.1	2.2
21/22	Paper, printing and publishing	22.4	26.5	26.7	27.4	33.8	35.5	42.6	40.7	23.2	25.7
23/25	Chemicals, Total	104.9	127.2	129.5	140.0	147.5	165.2	155.8	162.9	233.2	263.2
23	Refined petroleum, nuclear fuel	..	..	..	..	..	..	..	..	67.1	95.3
24/25	Chemicals, rubber & plastics prod.	104.9	127.2	129.5	140.0	147.5	165.2	155.8	162.9	166.1	167.9
24	Chemical products	92.7	110.5	115.0	123.5	129.8	145.1	133.4	140.2	141.7	141.9
2423	Pharmaceuticals	17.5	22.1	24.9	27.9	39.0	42.4	45.6	49.7	49.4	52.3
25	Rubber and plastics products	12.2	16.8	14.5	16.5	17.7	20.1	22.4	22.7	24.4	26.0
26	Non-metallic mineral products	16.8	17.9	16.8	17.6	17.9	19.3	22.8	25.7	28.8	30.2
27/28	Basic & fabricated metals	51.7	50.8	51.0	54.0	57.6	64.7	67.3	68.7	65.1	66.6
27	Basic metals	26.5	32.3	32.2	32.8	36.5	39.7	41.3	39.3	39.4	41.6
28	Fabricated metal products	25.2	18.5	18.8	21.2	21.1	25.0	26.0	29.4	25.7	24.9
29/32	Machinery, Total	71.6	80.0	82.5	88.5	99.8	114.6	123.1	135.1	148.2	..
29/30	Non-electrical machinery	35.4	36.7	36.7	36.4	40.9	48.1	58.0	60.5	73.2	67.1
29	Non-electrical machinery nec	27.8	24.7	24.3	27.8	32.2	38.0	39.7	45.1	56.7	49.8
30	Office and computing machinery	7.5	12.1	12.4	8.6	8.8	10.1	18.2	15.4	16.5	17.3
31/32	Electrical & electronic equipment	36.2	43.3	45.8	52.1	58.8	66.6	65.2	74.6	75.0	..
31	Electrical machinery nec	14.2	19.4	23.2	22.8	25.8	32.9	34.5	36.3	26.2	32.9
32	Radio, TV & communications eq.	22.0	23.9	22.6	29.3	33.0	33.7	30.6	38.3	48.8	..
33	Scientific instruments	8.6	10.8	13.4	15.2	16.4	15.7	17.1	17.2	16.2	..
34/35	Transportation equipment	16.4	19.9	21.8	22.9	27.6	36.0	55.9	58.7	72.6	169.7
34	Motor vehicles	12.6	15.8	16.9	16.6	21.4	29.7	50.0	51.6	65.7	163.3
35	Other transport equipment	3.8	4.1	4.9	6.3	6.2	6.2	5.9	7.1	6.9	6.4
351	Shipbuilding & repairing	..	..	..	..	..	..	..	..	..	..
353	Aircraft and spacecraft	..	..	..	..	..	..	..	..	3.8	5.3
36/37	Other manufacturing	10.7	7.6	6.7	6.8	6.9	8.2	8.1	8.4	6.4	5.6
40/45	Construction, electricity, gas & water	13.1	16.8	16.4	15.9	15.2	15.3	16.4	19.5	32.0	54.9
50/55	Trade, repair, hotels & restaurants	419.4	451.5	445.9	457.5	495.7	518.9	559.0	577.4	642.5	606.2
65/74	Finance, insurance, business services	113.3	111.1	122.7	121.7	124.1	127.9	142.9	164.7	212.7	..
	OTHER ACTIVITIES	149.4	191.9	185.5	194.6	214.8	244.7	255.0	307.0	141.8	..
01/99	**GRAND TOTAL**	**1 056.7**	**1 175.9**	**1 185.9**	**1 232.0**	**1 329.4**	**1 443.5**	**1 544.6**	**1 667.6**	**1 717.2**	**1 881.9**

Note: Majority and minority foreign-owned firms. Change of industrial classification from 1997. See country notes.
Firmes sous contrôle étranger majoritaire et minoritaire. Changement de classification industrielle à partir de 1997. Voir les notes par pays.

UNITED STATES
Inward investments

ÉTATS-UNIS
Investissements entrants

Table 5A - Tableau 5A

TURNOVER BY COUNTRY OF ORIGIN IN THE MANUFACTURING SECTOR
CHIFFRE D'AFFAIRES PAR PAYS D'ORIGINE DANS L'INDUSTRIE MANUFACTURIÈRE

Country of origin (UBO)	Turnover (Billions of USD) / Chiffre d'affaires (Milliards de USD)					As a % of all countries / En % du total des pays				
	1994	1995	1996	1997	1998	1994	1995	1996	1997	1998
All countries	524.9	559.3	587.0	667.6	834.4	100.0	100.0	100.0	100.0	100.0
Total OECD	..	..	..	..	..	..	..	..	..	..
United States	1.1	1.5	2.4	5.0	..	0.2	0.3	0.4	0.7	..
Canada	70.5	50.4	48.0	47.5	53.2	13.4	9.0	8.2	7.1	6.4
Mexico	3.5	..	3.9	3.5	4.2	0.7	..	0.7	0.5	0.5
Japan	90.7	123.4	124.7	137.1	161.4	17.3	22.1	21.2	20.5	19.3
Korea	1.7	3.0	3.6	2.9	4.9	0.3	0.5	0.6	0.4	0.6
Australia	8.5	9.1	10.4	12.9	10.6	1.6	1.6	1.8	1.9	1.3
New Zealand	0.9	0.4	0.2	..	0.1	0.2	0.1	0.0	..	0.0
Europe	327.3	344.8	370.7	422.6	554.8	62.4	61.6	63.1	63.3	66.5
European Union (15)	261.7	298.2	323.3	373.7	504.5	49.9	53.3	55.1	56.0	60.5
Austria	1.1	1.1	0.8	0.7	0.8	0.2	0.2	0.1	0.1	0.1
Belgium	3.1	3.6	3.9	..	10.4	0.6	0.6	0.7	..	1.2
Denmark	1.4	1.2	1.5	2.0	1.9	0.3	0.2	0.3	0.3	0.2
Finland	4.6	4.2	4.0	3.2	3.3	0.9	0.7	0.7	0.5	0.4
France	50.0	49.4	54.3	53.7	53.7	9.5	8.8	9.2	8.0	6.4
Germany	67.7	73.5	81.0	83.5	171.8	12.9	13.1	13.8	12.5	20.6
Greece	..	..	..	..	..	..	..	..	..	..
Ireland	5.4	7.0	6.9	7.4	11.2	1.0	1.3	1.2	1.1	1.3
Italy	9.8	8.8	8.2	8.8	9.3	1.9	1.6	1.4	1.3	1.1
Luxembourg	0.6	0.6	2.5	0.9	0.5	0.1	0.1	0.4	0.1	0.1
Netherlands	25.2	26.4	31.6	58.9	76.4	4.8	4.7	5.4	8.8	9.2
Portugal	..	..	..	..	..	..	..	..	..	..
Spain	0.8	0.7	0.8	0.8	0.9	0.1	0.1	0.1	0.1	0.1
Sweden	17.0	18.1	18.3	18.6	19.6	3.2	3.2	3.1	2.8	2.4
United Kingdom	97.7	103.6	109.5	124.2	144.5	18.6	18.5	18.7	18.6	17.3
Czech Republic	..	..	..	..	..	..	..	..	..	..
Hungary	..	..	..	..	..	..	..	..	..	..
Iceland	..	..	..	..	..	..	..	..	..	..
Norway	3.4	3.8	3.7	..	3.7	0.7	0.7	0.6	..	0.4
Poland	..	..	..	..	..	..	..	..	..	..
Slovak Republic	..	..	..	..	..	..	..	..	..	..
Switzerland	39.0	42.3	43.2	44.4	46.0	7.4	7.6	7.4	6.7	5.5
Turkey	..	..	..	..	..	..	..	..	..	..
Non-OECD Europe, of which:	..	..	..	..	..	..	..	..	..	..
Baltic countries	..	..	..	..	..	..	..	..	..	..
Bulgaria	..	..	..	..	..	..	..	..	..	..
Croatia	..	..	..	..	..	..	..	..	..	..
Romania	..	..	..	..	..	..	..	..	..	..
Russian Federation	..	..	..	..	..	..	..	..	..	..
Slovenia	..	..	..	..	..	..	..	..	..	..
Ukraine	..	..	..	..	..	..	..	..	..	..
Yugoslavia	..	..	..	..	..	..	..	..	..	..
Non-OECD Asia, of which:	10.6	12.4	12.0	12.8	..	2.0	2.2	2.1	1.9	..
China	..	..	..	0.4	0.3	..	..	..	0.1	0.0
Chinese Taipei	3.6	4.5	0.4	5.4	5.6	0.7	0.8	0.1	0.8	0.7
Hong Kong (China)	0.5	0.5	0.6	0.7	0.6	0.1	0.1	0.1	0.1	0.1
India	..	..	..	..	..	..	..	..	..	..
Indonesia	0.9	0.9	0.8	1.2	0.8	0.2	0.2	0.1	0.2	0.1
Malaysia	..	0.9	0.9	0.8	0.8	..	0.2	0.1	0.1	0.1
Philippines	0.8	0.8	0.1	0.1	0.1	0.2	0.1	0.0	0.0	0.0
Singapore	0.7	0.7	0.8	0.4	0.6	0.1	0.1	0.1	0.1	0.1
Thailand	..	..	..	..	..	..	..	..	..	..
Near and Middle East	2.8	3.1	3.7	12.4	7.5	0.5	0.5	0.6	1.9	0.9
Africa	3.5	5.9	6.2	6.3	..	0.7	1.1	1.1	0.9	..
Latin America, of which:	10.0	8.6	8.8	11.1	20.1	1.9	1.5	1.5	1.7	2.4
Argentina	..	..	..	..	..	..	..	..	..	..
Brazil	0.8	0.9	0.9	0.9	1.2	0.2	0.2	0.1	0.1	0.1
Chile	..	..	..	..	..	..	..	..	..	..

Note: Majority and minority foreign-owned firms. Change of industrial classification from 1997. See country notes.
Firmes sous contrôle étranger majoritaire et minoritaire. Changement de classification industrielle à partir de 1997. Voir les notes par pays.

Inward investments

Investissements entrants

Table 6A - Tableau 6A

VALUE ADDED / VALEUR AJOUTÉE

		Foreign affiliates (Billions of USD) Filiales étrangères (Milliards de USD)								
By industry (ISIC Rev. 3)		1989	1990	1991	1992	1993	1994	1995	1996	1997	1998
10/14	Mining & quarrying	3.3	3.5	4.9	5.5	5.0	5.9	6.5	5.5	9.8	9.1
15/37	TOTAL MANUFACTURING	109.2	119.9	125.9	134.1	142.5	157.1	155.7	166.6	188.5	224.4
15/16	Food, beverages, tobacco	9.9	11.2	12.3	12.3	11.6	12.3	12.1	12.6	16.9	15.6
17/19	Textiles, clothing, leather, footwear	1.8	1.9	2.2	2.9	3.4	3.9	3.7	3.8	3.5	3.1
20/22	Wood and paper products	7.7	9.8	9.9	10.5	12.5	14.2	15.3	16.3	8.4	9.4
20	Wood products	0.5	0.9	0.8	0.9	1.2	1.5	1.2	1.1	0.6	0.7
21/22	Paper, printing and publishing	7.2	8.9	9.2	9.6	11.3	12.6	14.1	15.2	7.9	8.7
23/25	Chemicals, Total	36.2	42.4	43.3	47.4	50.3	55.5	47.8	51.5	72.3	78.5
23	Refined petroleum, nuclear fuel	..	..	..	..	..	..	..	..	23.4	26.5
24/25	Chemicals, rubber & plastics prod.	36.2	42.4	43.3	47.4	50.3	55.5	47.8	51.5	48.9	52.1
24	Chemical products	32.4	37.2	39.0	41.9	44.3	48.6	40.6	43.8	40.9	42.9
2423	Pharmaceuticals	6.9	8.9	10.0	11.4	14.2	15.1	15.3	16.1	16.1	18.2
25	Rubber and plastics products	3.8	5.2	4.3	5.5	6.0	6.9	7.3	7.7	8.0	9.2
26	Non-metallic mineral products	5.9	5.8	5.7	6.2	6.5	6.8	8.8	9.8	12.0	11.8
27/28	Basic & fabricated metals	15.7	14.6	14.9	15.0	16.5	16.4	16.9	18.3	16.5	17.3
27	Basic metals	7.0	8.4	8.6	8.7	10.0	9.6	9.7	9.2	8.6	9.9
28	Fabricated metal products	8.7	6.2	6.3	6.3	6.5	6.8	7.1	9.1	7.9	7.4
29/32	Machinery, Total	21.8	23.4	24.8	25.9	26.9	31.4	31.9	34.5	36.6	..
29/30	Non-electrical machinery	10.9	10.3	10.5	10.2	10.4	12.9	13.4	14.6	17.6	16.2
29	Non-electrical machinery nec	..	..	..	8.0	9.2	11.3	11.5	13.4	16.6	14.6
30	Office and computing machinery	..	..	..	2.2	1.2	1.6	1.9	1.2	1.0	1.6
31/32	Electrical & electronic equipment	10.9	13.1	14.4	15.7	16.5	18.5	18.5	19.9	19.0	..
31	Electrical machinery nec	..	..	..	7.2	7.8	9.9	10.4	10.3	7.5	9.9
32	Radio, TV & communications eq.	..	..	..	8.5	8.7	8.6	8.2	9.6	11.5	..
33	Scientific instruments	3.2	4.2	5.5	6.1	6.6	6.1	6.3	6.5	6.2	9.6
34/35	Transportation equipment	2.7	3.9	4.7	4.8	5.7	7.5	9.2	9.4	13.6	36.1
34	Motor vehicles	..	..	..	2.7	3.7	5.7	7.3	7.1	11.4	34.2
35	Other transport equipment	..	..	..	2.2	1.9	1.8	1.9	2.3	2.2	1.9
351	Shipbuilding & repairing	..	..	..	..	..	..	..	..	0.0	0.0
353	Aircraft and spacecraft	..	..	..	..	..	..	..	..	1.2	1.6
36/37	Other manufacturing	4.3	2.8	2.7	3.0	2.6	3.2	3.7	3.9	1.8	..
40/45	Construction, electricity, gas & water	3.0	4.0	4.0	3.2	3.0	3.0	3.4	3.6	5.8	7.3
50/55	Trade, repair, hotels & restaurants	39.7	41.6	49.9	50.9	54.2	57.2	62.5	66.5	85.4	86.4
65/74	Finance, insurance, business services	21.3	16.0	17.9	15.3	16.2	17.7	16.1	23.8	41.0	41.3
	OTHER ACTIVITIES	46.9	54.3	55.1	57.3	64.8	72.2	78.3	92.2	53.9	49.7
01/99	GRAND TOTAL	223.4	239.3	257.6	266.3	285.7	313.0	322.6	358.1	384.9	418.1

Total manufacturing by investing country

	1989	1990	1991	1992	1993	1994	1995	1996	1997	1998
All countries	109.2	119.9	125.9	134.1	142.5	157.1	155.7	166.6	188.5	224.4
United States	0.4	0.1	..	0.1	0.1	0.3	0.6	1.0	2.4	2.5
Canada	20.2	20.9	..	20.4	23.5	25.4	14.9	15.8	13.6	14.7
Mexico	..	..	..	0.9	0.8	1.1	1.1	1.0	0.8	0.9
Japan	10.8	15.0	..	16.9	18.9	21.7	25.0	24.8	27.3	33.7
Europe	70.5	75.0	..	88.8	91.4	100.0	105.1	114.7	130.9	157.4
European Union (15)	..	..	..	71.2	73.7	80.3	90.7	99.7	115.3	141.6
Belgium	..	..	..	0.9	0.8	1.0	1.1	1.3	..	..
France	7.8	8.8	..	11.6	12.0	13.6	13.8	16.1	15.7	15.9
Germany	13.4	14.2	..	16.4	19.1	20.6	21.8	25.3	25.3	46.0
Italy	..	..	..	1.5	1.7	2.2	2.0	1.8	1.9	2.0
Netherlands	5.8	6.0	..	6.8	6.2	6.6	7.0	7.8	17.8	15.1
Spain	..	..	..	0.1	0.1	0.2	0.2	0.1	..	0.2
Sweden	..	..	..	3.6	4.1	4.6	5.1	4.6	4.8	5.1
United Kingdom	25.5	27.2	..	32.1	31.8	34.0	35.6	37.9	42.7	48.7
Switzerland	10.4	10.7	..	12.3	11.9	12.8	13.6	14.2	14.5	14.9
Australia and New Zealand	..	..	..	3.1	3.1	2.4	2.7	2.8	..	..
Asia (non-OECD)	1.7	1.5	..	1.4	1.7	2.7	3.0	2.6	2.7	..
Latin America	3.0	2.6	..	2.9	2.8	3.2	2.6	2.6	2.7	6.9

Note: Majority and minority foreign-owned firms. Change of industrial classification from 1997. See country notes.
Firmes sous contrôle étranger majoritaire et minoritaire. Changement de classification industrielle à partir de 1997. Voir les notes par pays.

Inward investments

Investissements entrants

Table 7A - Tableau 7A
COMPENSATION OF EMPLOYEES / SALAIRES ET CHARGES SOCIALES

By industry (ISIC Rev. 3)		Foreign affiliates (Billions of USD) Filiales étrangères (Milliards de USD)									
		1989	1990	1991	1992	1993	1994	1995	1996	1997	1998
10/14	Mining & quarrying	1.8	1.5	2.3	2.5	2.5	2.7	2.6	2.7	4.0	4.7
15/37	**TOTAL MANUFACTURING**	76.5	88.7	92.8	97.6	101.8	107.0	106.2	110.6	111.4	134.9
15/16	Food, beverages, tobacco	6.6	7.3	7.5	7.5	7.1	7.6	7.5	7.2	8.3	9.0
17/19	Textiles, clothing, leather, footwear	1.4	1.5	1.6	2.0	2.3	2.7	2.6	2.6	2.4	2.2
20/22	Wood and paper products	5.5	6.9	7.2	7.7	9.0	9.6	10.5	10.9	5.7	6.1
20	Wood products	0.4	0.6	0.6	0.6	0.7	0.8	0.7	0.7	0.4	0.4
21/22	Paper, printing and publishing	5.2	6.4	6.6	7.0	8.4	8.8	9.8	10.1	5.4	5.7
23/25	Chemicals, Total	22.0	28.2	29.2	31.7	31.9	33.5	30.4	31.1	34.9	38.6
23	Refined petroleum, nuclear fuel	..	..	..	..	..	..	..	..	4.3	6.3
24/25	Chemicals, rubber & plastics prod.	22.0	28.2	29.2	31.7	31.9	33.5	30.4	31.1	30.6	32.3
24	Chemical products	18.9	23.8	25.0	27.0	27.1	28.4	25.1	25.6	25.1	25.8
2423	Pharmaceuticals	4.1	5.4	6.1	6.8	9.0	9.5	10.3	10.5	10.6	11.7
25	Rubber and plastics products	3.1	4.4	4.2	4.8	4.9	5.1	5.3	5.4	5.5	6.5
26	Non-metallic mineral products	4.2	4.8	4.6	4.7	4.6	4.8	5.6	6.0	6.5	6.7
27/28	Basic & fabricated metals	11.5	11.2	11.8	11.6	12.6	12.6	11.7	12.3	10.8	11.4
27	Basic metals	4.7	6.3	6.8	6.8	7.4	6.6	6.2	5.6	5.4	6.2
28	Fabricated metal products	6.8	4.9	5.0	4.8	5.2	6.0	5.5	6.8	5.4	5.2
29/32	Machinery, Total	18.3	21.0	21.7	22.4	23.6	24.8	25.2	27.1	27.7	..
29/30	Non-electrical machinery	8.9	9.0	9.4	9.0	9.5	10.1	10.9	11.6	13.8	12.3
29	Non-electrical machinery nec	6.7	6.0	6.3	6.9	7.4	8.5	8.7	9.8	12.1	10.4
30	Office and computing machinery	2.2	3.0	3.1	2.2	2.0	1.6	2.3	1.8	1.7	1.9
31/32	Electrical & electronic equipment	9.4	12.0	12.3	13.4	14.1	14.8	14.3	15.5	13.9	..
31	Electrical machinery nec	3.7	5.6	6.6	6.4	7.0	8.4	8.3	8.7	5.8	7.3
32	Radio, TV & communications eq.	5.7	6.3	5.7	7.0	7.1	6.4	6.0	6.9	8.1	..
33	Scientific instruments	2.4	3.2	4.0	4.5	4.9	4.5	4.7	4.7	4.5	6.9
34/35	Transportation equipment	2.5	3.3	3.9	4.3	4.6	5.5	6.8	7.3	8.9	21.1
34	Motor vehicles	1.6	2.2	2.4	2.4	2.7	3.8	5.0	5.5	7.4	19.8
35	Other transport equipment	0.9	1.2	1.5	1.9	1.8	1.7	1.8	1.7	1.6	1.4
351	Shipbuilding & repairing	..	..	..	..	..	..	..	..	0.0	0.0
353	Aircraft and spacecraft	..	..	..	..	..	..	..	..	0.8	1.1
36/37	Other manufacturing	2.1	1.4	1.1	1.2	1.2	1.4	1.3	1.4	1.2	..
40/45	Construction, electricity, gas & water	2.7	3.7	3.7	3.0	2.8	2.8	3.4	3.4	4.5	5.2
50/55	Trade, repair, hotels & restaurants	26.1	28.3	32.1	32.2	34.1	34.0	37.6	40.0	46.8	48.8
65/74	Finance, insurance, business services	13.5	11.5	13.4	14.4	14.7	14.4	15.7	18.6	28.9	31.9
	OTHER ACTIVITIES	23.6	29.9	31.6	32.5	37.0	39.6	40.9	45.4	34.5	35.3
01/99	**GRAND TOTAL**	144.2	163.6	176.0	182.1	193.0	200.6	206.4	220.6	230.3	260.7

Total manufacturing by investing country

	1989	1990	1991	1992	1993	1994	1995	1996	1997	1998
All countries	76.5	88.7	92.8	97.6	101.8	107.0	106.2	110.6	111.4	134.9
United States	0.4	0.1	0.1	0.1	0.1	0.2	0.3	0.5	1.0	1.1
Canada	11.8	13.3	13.4	13.7	15.5	15.6	10.7	11.0	8.7	10.0
Mexico	..	..	..	..	..	..	..	..	..	..
Japan	8.1	11.6	12.9	13.6	14.6	15.1	17.0	16.8	17.4	22.0
Europe	50.6	57.9	60.7	64.2	65.3	69.2	71.1	75.1	76.5	92.3
European Union (15)	..	..	..	..	..	..	..	..	..	..
Belgium	..	..	..	..	..	..	..	..	..	..
France	6.0	8.4	9.2	9.1	9.2	10.2	9.7	10.9	11.1	11.9
Germany	9.9	11.0	11.4	12.6	14.2	15.0	16.0	17.2	17.4	28.5
Italy	..	..	..	..	..	..	..	..	..	..
Netherlands	4.7	5.1	5.0	5.2	4.6	4.3	4.5	5.6	7.1	7.1
Spain	..	..	..	..	..	..	..	..	..	..
Sweden	..	..	..	..	..	..	..	..	..	..
United Kingdom	16.9	19.1	19.8	20.6	20.4	21.4	21.9	22.5	21.8	24.8
Switzerland	7.7	8.1	8.3	9.0	8.7	9.1	9.6	9.6	9.6	9.7
Australia and New Zealand	..	..	..	..	..	..	..	..	..	..
Asia (non-OECD)	1.3	1.4	1.1	1.2	1.3	1.8	2.0	1.8	1.9	..
Latin America	2.5	2.3	2.1	2.2	2.3	2.6	2.2	2.1	1.8	4.0

Note: Majority and minority foreign-owned firms. Change of industrial classification from 1997. See country notes.
Firmes sous contrôle étranger majoritaire et minoritaire. Changement de classification industrielle à partir de 1997. Voir les notes par pays.

Table 8A - Tableau 8A

R&D EXPENDITURE / DÉPENSES DE R-D

By industry (ISIC Rev. 3)		Foreign affiliates (Millions of USD) Filiales étrangères (Millions de USD)					As a % of national total En % du total national				
		1994	1995	1996	1997	1998	1994	1995	1996	1997	1998
10/14	Mining & quarrying	46	45	29	210	255	..	..	..	..	..
15/37	**TOTAL MANUFACTURING**	12 970	14 756	14 481	15 627	20 034	13.7	14.4	12.6	12.4	16.0
15/16	Food, beverages, tobacco	294	360	244	317	317	19.9	23.0	15.6	16.6	16.3
17/19	Textiles, clothing, leather, footwear	55	51	56	54	51	15.4	12.9	11.5	10.1	8.8
20/22	Wood and paper products	187	179	181	148	154	9.3	8.9	6.2	6.5	5.7
20	Wood products	34	9	7	5	6	10.8	3.8	0.9	1.3	1.0
21/22	Paper, printing and publishing	153	170	174	143	148	9.0	9.6	8.0	7.5	7.1
23/25	Chemicals, Total	7 254	8 515	7 890	7 605	8 506	38.0	45.1	38.8	34.2	33.3
23	Refined petroleum, nuclear fuel	..	..	..	278	478	..	..	..	16.4	26.4
24/25	Chemicals, rubber & plastics prod.	7 254	8 515	7 890	7 327	8 028	38.0	45.1	38.8	35.6	33.8
24	Chemical products	7 003	8 263	7 604	7 009	7 660	40.1	46.9	40.3	36.6	34.9
2423	Pharmaceuticals	4 506	5 201	6 026	5 398	5 998	46.8	50.9	61.7	45.4	47.4
25	Rubber and plastics products	251	252	286	318	368	15.5	20.1	19.2	22.1	20.0
26	Non-metallic mineral products	153	162	166	214	160	25.9	36.2	35.5	33.8	22.0
27/28	Basic & fabricated metals	348	322	320	316	340	19.3	19.9	13.9	11.3	14.0
27	Basic metals	170	161	165	144	149	24.6	27.2	22.1	14.6	19.0
28	Fabricated metal products	178	161	155	172	190	16.0	15.7	10.0	9.5	11.6
29/32	Machinery, Total	3 567	3 991	4 161	5 157	..	12.3	12.2	9.9	10.5	..
29/30	Non-electrical machinery	954	1 136	997	1 230	..	7.0	8.2	5.2	5.1	..
29	Non-electrical machinery nec	475	541	627	980	906	11.9	10.7	10.3	16.6	14.8
30	Office and computing machinery	479	595	369	250	..	5.0	6.7	2.8	1.4	..
31/32	Electrical & electronic equipment	2 613	2 855	3 164	3 927	..	17.0	15.2	14.1	15.7	..
31	Electrical machinery nec	969	931	1 001	809	930	36.4	26.8	29.8	17.9	19.2
32	Radio, TV & communications eq.	1 643	1 923	2 163	3 118	..	13.0	12.6	11.3	15.2	..
33	Scientific instruments	671	691	791	..	..	5.9	5.8	6.5	..	..
34/35	Transportation equipment	375	424	606	707	2 723	1.3	1.3	1.9	2.2	9.3
34	Motor vehicles	203	309	433	514	2 547	1.5	2.1	2.7	3.4	17.8
35	Other transport equipment	173	115	174	193	176	1.2	0.7	1.0	1.1	1.2
351	Shipbuilding & repairing	..	..	..	..	..	..	..	..	..	..
353	Aircraft and spacecraft	..	..	..	..	..	..	..	..	..	..
36/37	Other manufacturing	66	60	66	..	..	13.0	12.1	13.5	..	..
40/45	Construction, electricity, gas & water	2	7	6	27	52	..	..	..	4.8	6.9
50/55	Trade, repair, hotels & restaurants	1 089	1 437	1 886	1 898	..	..	..	..	22.9	..
65/74	Finance, insurance, business services	11	17	22	773	..	..	..	..	..	..
	OTHER ACTIVITIES	1 448	1 280	1 559	725	..	..	..	..	..	..
01/99	**GRAND TOTAL**	15 566	17 542	17 984	19 260	25 148	13.0	13.3	12.4	12.2	14.9

Total manufacturing by investing country						As a % of total manufacturing by foreign affiliates				
All countries	12 970	14 756	14 481	15 627	20 034	100.0	100.0	100.0	100.0	100.0
United States	..	61	58	62	..	..	0.4	0.4	0.4	..
Canada	2 263	1 205	1 306	1 516	2 138	17.4	8.2	9.0	9.7	10.7
Mexico	..	..	..	..	..	..	..	..	..	..
Japan	1 017	1 199	1 073	1 269	1 765	7.8	8.1	7.4	8.1	8.8
Europe	8 980	11 824	11 491	12 174	15 315	69.2	80.1	79.4	77.9	76.4
European Union (15)	..	..	..	..	..	..	..	..	..	..
Belgium	..	..	..	..	..	..	..	..	..	..
France	1 400	1 551	1 717	1 817	1 905	10.8	10.5	11.9	11.6	9.5
Germany	2 187	3 567	2 817	2 849	4 923	16.9	24.2	19.5	18.2	24.6
Italy	..	..	..	..	..	..	..	..	..	..
Netherlands	510	612	772	948	961	3.9	4.1	5.3	6.1	4.8
Spain	..	..	..	..	..	..	..	..	..	..
Sweden	..	..	..	..	..	..	..	..	..	..
United Kingdom	2 177	2 211	2 424	2 849	3 116	16.8	15.0	16.7	18.2	15.6
Switzerland	2 056	2 735	3 032	2 708	3 401	15.9	18.5	20.9	17.3	17.0
Australia and New Zealand	..	..	..	..	..	..	..	..	..	..
Asia (non-OECD)	..	110	116	121	..	..	0.7	0.8	0.8	..
Latin America	485	148	183	193	162	3.7	1.0	1.3	1.2	0.8

Note: Majority and minority foreign-owned firms. Change of industrial classification from 1997. See country notes.
Firmes sous contrôle étranger majoritaire et minoritaire. Changement de classification industrielle à partir de 1997. Voir les notes par pays.

Table 9A - Tableau 9A

NUMBER OF RESEARCHERS / NOMBRE DE CHERCHEURS

By industry (ISIC Rev. 3)		Foreign affiliates (Thousands) / Filiales étrangères (Milliers)					As a % of national total / En % du total national				
		1994	1995	1996	1997	1998	1994	1995	1996	1997	1998
10/14	Mining & quarrying	0.5	0.4	0.3	2.2	2.0	..	..	..	..	..
15/37	**TOTAL MANUFACTURING**	**84.7**	**84.6**	**89.7**	**92.3**	**106.9**	**15.1**	**13.6**	**13.7**	**12.7**	**14.8**
15/16	Food, beverages, tobacco	1.9	2.0	1.9	2.1	2.2	21.3	20.4	18.3	19.1	21.2
17/19	Textiles, clothing, leather, footwear	0.7	0.6	0.7	0.6	0.5	24.1	15.8	18.9	18.8	17.9
20/22	Wood and paper products	1.7	1.7	1.8	1.0	0.9	13.2	12.2	12.3	7.2	5.8
20	Wood products	0.5	0.1	0.1	0.0	0.0	21.7	3.4	2.9	0.3	0.3
21/22	Paper, printing and publishing	1.2	1.6	1.7	1.0	0.9	11.3	14.5	15.2	9.6	7.3
23/25	Chemicals, Total	41.6	39.6	38.0	38.6	37.3	38.0	37.9	38.4	35.4	33.5
23	Refined petroleum, nuclear fuel	..	..	..	1.7	2.1	..	..	..	21.5	26.3
24/25	Chemicals, rubber & plastics prod.	41.6	39.6	38.0	36.9	35.2	38.0	37.9	38.4	36.5	34.0
24	Chemical products	39.8	37.8	36.1	34.4	32.8	40.0	40.1	40.5	38.4	36.2
2423	Pharmaceuticals	22.6	23.2	23.2	21.1	21.6	44.9	47.3	53.8	46.6	43.2
25	Rubber and plastics products	1.8	1.8	1.9	2.5	2.4	18.4	17.6	19.2	21.7	18.8
26	Non-metallic mineral products	0.7	0.7	0.7	0.7	0.7	16.3	17.9	18.9	17.9	17.5
27/28	Basic & fabricated metals	3.0	2.7	3.0	2.3	2.4	19.1	20.5	19.4	12.0	13.1
27	Basic metals	1.2	1.2	1.1	0.9	1.0	18.5	29.3	20.0	14.1	16.4
28	Fabricated metal products	1.7	1.5	1.9	1.4	1.4	18.5	16.5	19.0	10.9	11.5
29/32	Machinery, Total	26.2	28.9	31.8	34.8	..	13.5	12.2	12.7	10.6	..
29/30	Non-electrical machinery	8.2	9.7	9.0	10.0	10.7	9.1	8.7	7.9	6.4	6.6
29	Non-electrical machinery nec	5.2	5.5	6.0	8.0	6.6	14.1	10.3	13.8	17.4	13.1
30	Office and computing machinery	3.0	4.2	3.0	2.0	4.1	5.6	7.2	4.2	1.8	3.7
31/32	Electrical & electronic equipment	18.0	19.2	22.8	24.8	..	17.4	15.3	16.8	14.5	..
31	Electrical machinery nec	7.9	8.4	8.4	4.9	9.6	39.5	33.2	39.3	14.2	35.7
32	Radio, TV & communications eq.	10.2	10.8	14.4	19.9	..	12.2	10.7	12.6	14.5	..
33	Scientific instruments	5.6	5.3	5.6	..	..	6.6	7.5	8.7	..	..
34/35	Transportation equipment	2.9	2.8	5.7	6.1	15.5	2.4	1.8	3.5	4.2	11.7
34	Motor vehicles	1.7	2.0	2.7	4.6	13.6	3.3	3.5	4.2	7.2	21.7
35	Other transport equipment	1.2	0.9	3.0	1.5	1.9	1.7	0.9	3.1	1.9	2.7
351	Shipbuilding & repairing	..	..	..	..	..	..	..	..	..	..
353	Aircraft and spacecraft	..	..	..	..	..	..	..	..	..	..
36/37	Other manufacturing	0.4	0.4	0.5	..	..	5.3	4.9	1.5	..	..
40/45	Construction, electricity, gas & water	0.0	0.1	0.1	0.1	0.4	..	..	..	..	..
50/55	Trade, repair, hotels & restaurants	9.8	8.9	10.7	10.1	11.8	..	18.7	27.0	21.8	181.7
65/74	Finance, insurance, business services	0.1	0.1	0.0	4.3	6.5	..	..	..	..	..
	OTHER ACTIVITIES	10.2	9.6	11.9	6.1	9.0	..	..	..	..	..
01/99	**GRAND TOTAL**	**105.1**	**103.7**	**112.8**	**115.7**	**136.6**	**14.1**	**12.5**	**12.7**	**12.2**	**13.7**

Total manufacturing by investing country						As a % of total manufacturing by foreign affiliates				
All countries	**84.7**	**84.6**	**89.7**	**92.3**	**106.9**	**100.0**	**100.0**	**100.0**	**100.0**	**100.0**
United States	0.1	0.4	0.4	0.3	0.3	0.1	0.5	0.4	0.3	0.3
Canada	10.2	5.8	7.9	9.1	..	12.0	6.9	8.8	9.9	..
Mexico	..	..	..	..	..	..	..	..	..	..
Japan	7.4	8.3	8.3	11.1	12.2	8.7	9.8	9.3	12.0	11.4
Europe	62.4	66.5	69.0	67.9	79.2	73.7	78.6	76.9	73.6	74.1
European Union (15)	..	..	..	..	..	..	..	..	..	..
Belgium	..	..	..	..	..	..	..	..	..	..
France	9.2	8.8	9.2	9.9	10.9	10.9	10.4	10.3	10.7	10.2
Germany	15.7	16.9	16.3	15.9	28.4	18.5	20.0	18.2	17.2	26.6
Italy	..	..	..	..	..	..	..	..	..	..
Netherlands	4.4	5.1	6.3	6.4	5.8	5.2	6.0	7.0	6.9	5.4
Spain	..	..	..	..	..	..	..	..	..	..
Sweden	..	..	..	..	..	..	..	..	..	..
United Kingdom	15.8	14.7	17.2	17.5	17.1	18.7	17.4	19.2	19.0	16.0
Switzerland	11.5	13.5	13.3	11.8	10.9	13.6	16.0	14.8	12.8	10.2
Australia and New Zealand	..	..	..	..	..	..	..	..	..	..
Asia (non-OECD)	0.5	0.7	0.9	1.0	..	0.6	0.8	1.0	1.1	..
Latin America	2.9	1.0	1.2	0.9	..	3.4	1.2	1.3	1.0	..

Note: Majority and minority foreign-owned firms. Change of industrial classification from 1997. See country notes.
Firmes sous contrôle étranger majoritaire et minoritaire. Changement de classification industrielle à partir de 1997. Voir les notes par pays.

Inward investments   *Investissements entrants*

Table 10A - Tableau 10A

GROSS FIXED CAPITAL FORMATION / FORMATION BRUTE DE CAPITAL FIXE

By industry (ISIC Rev. 3)		**Foreign affiliates** *(Millions of USD)*									
		Filiales étrangères *(Millions de USD)*									
		1989	1990	1991	1992	1993	1994	1995	1996	1997	1998
10/14	Mining & quarrying	1 107	978	1 405	1 176	1 456	1 910	1 642	1 824	3 832	3 865
15/37	**TOTAL MANUFACTURING**	23 268	27 869	26 190	24 505	22 628	24 549	28 001	32 498	38 417	56 812
15/16	Food, beverages, tobacco	1 450	2 100	1 943	1 748	1 582	2 090	2 007	2 149	1 988	2 333
17/19	Textiles, clothing, leather, footwear	771	344	377	476	486	573	572	467	455	415
20/22	Wood and paper products	1 683	1 906	1 776	1 400	1 560	1 963	2 178	2 270	1 424	1 522
20	Wood products	155	193	155	184	87	170	173	154	98	97
21/22	Paper, printing and publishing	1 528	1 713	1 621	1 216	1 473	1 793	2 005	2 116	1 326	1 425
23/25	Chemicals, Total	9 049	12 219	11 221	10 716	9 818	9 654	9 624	11 265	16 414	21 752
23	Refined petroleum, nuclear fuel	..	..	..	..	..	..	..	..	5 163	9 269
24/25	Chemicals, rubber & plastics prod.	9 049	12 219	11 221	10 716	9 818	9 654	9 624	11 265	11 251	12 483
24	Chemical products	8 102	10 498	10 066	9 439	8 508	8 314	8 303	9 898	9 719	10 417
2423	Pharmaceuticals	1 188	1 694	1 976	2 022	2 077	2 339	2 730	3 134	2 646	2 883
25	Rubber and plastics products	947	1 721	1 155	1 277	1 310	1 340	1 321	1 367	1 532	2 066
26	Non-metallic mineral products	1 278	1 295	1 212	1 064	1 031	1 267	1 742	2 532	2 905	2 553
27/28	Basic & fabricated metals	3 138	3 352	3 329	2 897	2 449	2 989	3 465	4 086	4 622	4 217
27	Basic metals	2 144	2 400	2 393	1 934	1 598	1 935	2 340	2 750	3 388	2 852
28	Fabricated metal products	995	952	937	963	851	1 054	1 125	1 336	1 234	1 366
29/32	Machinery, Total	3 792	4 470	3 894	3 903	3 537	3 727	5 570	6 404	6 316	..
29/30	Non-electrical machinery	1 767	1 960	1 597	1 565	1 255	1 337	1 810	1 998	2 116	1 991
29	Non-electrical machinery nec	1 141	1 281	830	970	982	1 108	1 285	1 695	1 842	1 608
30	Office and computing machinery	626	680	766	595	273	229	525	302	274	383
31/32	Electrical & electronic equipment	2 025	2 509	2 298	2 338	2 283	2 390	3 760	4 406	4 200	..
31	Electrical machinery nec	695	845	1 098	1 010	1 044	1 204	1 729	1 804	1 073	2 323
32	Radio, TV & communications eq.	1 330	1 664	1 200	1 329	1 238	1 185	2 031	2 602	3 127	..
33	Scientific instruments	524	618	646	520	588	582	603	678	..	..
34/35	Transportation equipment	1 164	1 165	1 498	1 502	1 251	1 370	1 876	2 192	3 137	12 780
34	Motor vehicles	1 036	1 061	1 358	1 312	1 094	1 260	1 718	2 032	2 924	12 519
35	Other transport equipment	128	105	139	190	158	110	158	160	213	261
351	Shipbuilding & repairing	..	..	..	..	..	..	..	..	..	..
353	Aircraft and spacecraft	..	..	..	..	..	..	..	..	..	..
36/37	Other manufacturing	418	401	293	279	326	334	364	378	..	..
40/45	Construction, electricity, gas & water	379	494	328	625	334	537	588	923	1 487	2 416
50/55	Trade, repair, hotels & restaurants	8 076	10 858	12 448	12 332	14 510	17 937	18 726	23 890	30 766	28 750
65/74	Finance, insurance, business services	8 758	10 329	10 005	7 762	7 151	6 735	8 181	10 993	11 384	16 829
	OTHER ACTIVITIES	13 575	19 052	19 440	14 965	17 163	16 512	17 371	20 456	15 038	0
01/99	**GRAND TOTAL**	55 164	69 580	69 816	61 366	63 243	68 179	74 510	90 582	100 756	123 559

Total manufacturing by investing country

	1989	1990	1991	1992	1993	1994	1995	1996	1997	1998
All countries	23 268	27 869	26 190	24 505	22 628	24 549	28 001	32 498	38 417	56 812
United States	82	23	10	7	4	58	151	243	218	224
Canada	4 473	5 202	4 311	3 880	3 275	3 643	2 194	2 102	2 009	2 134
Mexico	..	..	..	..	..	..	..	..	..	..
Japan	5 273	6 042	5 601	5 201	4 251	4 314	5 899	6 983	8 907	10 263
Europe	11 772	14 157	13 865	13 229	13 181	14 646	17 536	20 172	23 976	40 371
European Union (15)	..	..	..	..	..	..	..	..	..	..
Belgium	..	..	..	..	..	..	..	..	..	..
France	1 605	2 281	2 088	2 183	1 893	2 138	2 420	3 260	3 500	3 494
Germany	2 783	3 361	3 456	3 183	3 696	3 727	4 333	5 362	5 259	16 671
Italy	..	..	..	..	..	..	..	..	..	..
Netherlands	1 049	1 027	829	840	913	1 082	1 433	1 433	4 202	5 454
Spain	..	..	..	..	..	..	..	..	..	..
Sweden	..	..	..	..	..	..	..	..	..	..
United Kingdom	3 418	4 078	3 871	3 760	3 354	3 746	4 995	5 470	6 281	9 065
Switzerland	1 283	1 573	1 760	1 763	1 729	2 082	2 036	2 300	2 195	2 205
Australia and New Zealand	..	..	..	..	..	..	..	..	..	..
Asia (non-OECD)	689	1 110	1 034	1 048	872	672	755	1 086	1 169	..
Latin America	332	601	469	478	489	512	511	456	475	1 237

Note: Majority and minority foreign-owned firms. Change of industrial classification from 1997. See country notes.
Firmes sous contrôle étranger majoritaire et minoritaire. Changement de classification industrielle à partir de 1997. Voir les notes par pays.

Table 11A - Tableau 11A

TOTAL EXPORTS / EXPORTATIONS TOTALES

| | **Foreign affiliates** *(Billions of USD)* | | | | | | | | | |
| | **Filiales étrangères** *(Milliards de USD)* | | | | | | | | | |
By industry (ISIC Rev. 3)	**1989**	**1990**	**1991**	**1992**	**1993**	**1994**	**1995**	**1996**	**1997**	**1998**
10/14　Mining & quarrying	1.2	1.2	1.4	2.1	1.5	1.9	2.5	2.1	3.6	3.7
15/37　TOTAL MANUFACTURING	**31.9**	**36.1**	**37.7**	**40.3**	**43.4**	**49.9**	**55.4**	**62.3**	**70.1**	**87.6**
15/16　Food, beverages, tobacco	1.4	1.6	1.8	2.0	2.3	2.5	2.8	3.1	4.2	4.6
17/19　Textiles, clothing, leather, footwear	0.3	0.3	0.3	0.5	0.5	0.6	0.6	0.6	0.5	0.5
20/22　Wood and paper products	1.2	1.5	1.6	1.8	2.3	2.3	2.6	2.6	2.1	2.2
20　　Wood products	0.3	0.3	0.3	0.3	0.4	0.4	0.4	0.3	0.2	0.2
21/22　Paper, printing and publishing	0.9	1.3	1.4	1.5	1.8	1.8	2.2	2.3	1.9	2.0
23/25　Chemicals, Total	10.2	11.9	12.8	13.7	14.3	16.0	15.9	16.8	20.8	20.2
23　　Refined petroleum, nuclear fuel	..	..	..	..	..	..	..	..	3.0	2.9
24/25　Chemicals, rubber & plastics prod.	10.2	11.9	12.8	13.7	14.3	16.0	15.9	16.8	17.8	17.2
24　　Chemical products	9.6	10.7	11.6	12.5	13.0	14.4	14.1	14.8	15.3	14.9
2423　　Pharmaceuticals	1.0	1.1	1.2	1.3	3.0	3.2	4.3	4.3	4.1	4.1
25　　Rubber and plastics products	0.6	1.2	1.2	1.2	1.3	1.6	1.8	2.0	2.5	2.3
26　Non-metallic mineral products	0.5	0.6	0.6	0.7	0.7	0.7	0.9	1.0	0.9	0.9
27/28　Basic & fabricated metals	3.5	2.8	3.7	3.5	3.6	4.0	4.2	4.8	5.1	5.2
27　　Basic metals	1.7	1.8	2.3	2.2	2.2	2.2	2.3	2.5	3.4	3.2
28　　Fabricated metal products	1.9	1.1	1.4	1.3	1.4	1.7	1.8	2.3	1.7	2.1
29/32　Machinery, Total	11.4	13.5	12.2	12.3	13.8	16.8	18.7	22.7	..	..
29/30　Non-electrical machinery	4.8	5.2	5.1	5.1	5.9	6.4	7.5	8.9	12.0	9.4
29　　Non-electrical machinery nec	3.5	3.4	3.2	3.6	4.7	5.2	5.6	7.6	10.4	7.9
30　　Office and computing machinery	1.4	1.8	1.8	1.5	1.3	1.2	1.9	1.3	1.6	1.5
31/32　Electrical & electronic equipment	6.6	8.3	7.2	7.2	7.9	10.4	11.2	13.8	..	..
31　　Electrical machinery nec	1.4	2.9	3.9	3.3	3.3	5.4	5.8	5.5	3.4	5.0
32　　Radio, TV & communications eq.	5.2	5.4	3.3	4.0	4.6	5.0	5.4	8.3	..	..
33　Scientific instruments	1.2	1.5	1.8	2.0	2.3	2.8	2.8	3.2	2.7	..
34/35　Transportation equipment	1.2	1.2	1.7	2.3	2.3	2.7	4.9	5.6	7.6	24.6
34　　Motor vehicles	0.5	0.5	1.0	1.2	1.2	1.8	4.3	4.7	6.5	23.2
35　　Other transport equipment	0.7	0.7	0.7	1.2	1.1	0.9	0.6	1.0	1.1	1.4
351　　Shipbuilding & repairing	..	..	..	..	..	..	..	..	0.0	
353　　Aircraft and spacecraft	..	..	..	..	..	..	..	..	0.8	1.2
36/37　Other manufacturing	0.9	1.1	1.3	1.4	1.4	1.6	2.1	1.8	0.6	0.5
40/45　Construction, electricity, gas & water	0.2	0.2	0.2	0.0	0.0	0.1	..	0.2	..	0.3
50/55　Trade, repair, hotels & restaurants	50.5	51.1	53.4	56.9	57.3	56.3	66.9	65.1	65.2	57.5
65/74　Finance, insurance, business services	0.0	0.0	0.1	0.0	..	0.0	0.0	0.0	..	..
OTHER ACTIVITIES	2.5	3.8	4.1	4.6	4.4	12.5	..	11.2	..	..
01/99　GRAND TOTAL	**86.3**	**92.3**	**96.9**	**103.9**	**106.6**	**120.7**	**135.2**	**140.9**	**140.9**	**150.8**

Total manufacturing by investing country

	1989	1990	1991	1992	1993	1994	1995	1996	1997	1998
All countries	**31.9**	**36.1**	**37.7**	**40.3**	**43.4**	**49.9**	**55.4**	**62.3**	**70.1**	**87.6**
United States	0.1	0.0	0.1	0.0	..	..	0.3	0.4	0.5	0.6
Canada	4.9	5.4	5.5	5.9	5.9	6.0	3.4	3.8	4.6	5.2
Mexico	..	..	..	..	..	..	..	..	..	..
Japan	4.2	5.3	6.2	7.5	8.1	8.1	11.8	12.9	15.1	15.3
Europe	20.3	23.0	23.8	24.5	27.2	32.7	36.4	41.1	45.3	62.0
European Union (15)	..	..	..	..	..	..	..	..	..	..
Belgium	..	..	..	..	..	..	..	..	..	..
France	4.9	5.3	3.5	3.6	4.2	5.7	5.7	7.0	7.1	7.4
Germany	5.2	5.3	5.9	6.1	6.6	7.8	8.9	9.5	10.6	26.6
Italy	..	..	..	..	..	..	..	..	..	..
Netherlands	1.5	1.4	1.8	1.9	2.2	2.7	2.6	2.7	4.3	3.6
Spain	..	..	..	..	..	..	..	..	..	..
Sweden	..	..	..	..	..	..	..	..	..	..
United Kingdom	4.9	5.7	6.2	6.6	6.7	7.4	8.5	10.2	12.2	13.4
Switzerland	2.0	2.8	3.3	2.6	2.9	3.6	4.8	5.0	4.7	4.7
Australia and New Zealand	..	..	..	..	..	..	..	..	..	..
Asia (non-OECD)	1.1	0.9	0.8	0.7	0.8	1.1	1.6	1.6	1.6	..
Latin America	0.7	0.5	0.4	0.7	0.5	0.7	0.7	0.9	0.8	1.2

Note:　Majority and minority foreign-owned firms. Change of industrial classification from 1997. See country notes.
　　Firmes sous contrôle étranger majoritaire et minoritaire. Changement de classification industrielle à partir de 1997. Voir les notes par pays.

Table 12A - Tableau 12A

TOTAL IMPORTS / IMPORTATIONS TOTALES

| | | Foreign affiliates (Billions of USD) | | | | | | | | |
| | | Filiales étrangères (Milliards de USD) | | | | | | | | |
By industry (ISIC Rev. 3)		1989	1990	1991	1992	1993	1994	1995	1996	1997	1998
10/14	Mining & quarrying	0.2	0.3	0.2	0.2	0.3	0.1	0.1	0.3	0.5	0.6
15/37	**TOTAL MANUFACTURING**	**40.9**	**47.2**	**47.0**	**53.3**	**59.6**	**68.4**	**81.6**	**83.9**	**99.3**	**126.9**
15/16	Food, beverages, tobacco	2.5	2.4	2.9	3.0	3.2	3.2	3.2	3.5	3.8	3.7
17/19	Textiles, clothing, leather, footwear	0.7	0.4	0.4	0.7	0.8	0.8	0.8	0.7	0.8	0.6
20/22	Wood and paper products	1.0	1.2	1.4	1.4	1.7	1.6	1.8	2.2	1.7	1.2
20	Wood products	0.2	0.2	0.2	0.5	0.5	0.3	0.3	0.3	0.3	0.2
21/22	Paper, printing and publishing	0.9	1.0	1.2	1.0	1.2	1.3	1.5	1.8	1.5	0.9
23/25	Chemicals, Total	8.8	11.4	11.5	14.2	15.2	17.3	16.8	18.0	31.2	27.1
23	Refined petroleum, nuclear fuel	..	..	..	..	..	..	..	..	11.6	9.1
24/25	Chemicals, rubber & plastics prod.	8.8	11.4	11.5	14.2	15.2	17.3	16.8	18.0	19.6	18.0
24	Chemical products	7.6	9.1	9.6	11.9	12.6	14.3	13.4	15.0	16.0	14.4
2423	Pharmaceuticals	1.8	2.1	2.4	2.9	5.4	5.5	6.1	6.5	7.7	7.4
25	Rubber and plastics products	1.2	2.4	1.9	2.3	2.5	3.0	3.4	3.0	3.6	3.6
26	Non-metallic mineral products	0.8	1.1	0.9	0.9	1.1	1.2	1.4	1.4	1.6	1.6
27/28	Basic & fabricated metals	5.0	5.0	5.1	6.0	6.4	7.6	7.9	8.4	8.3	8.9
27	Basic metals	3.4	3.8	3.8	4.3	4.8	5.3	5.3	5.4	6.6	6.4
28	Fabricated metal products	1.6	1.3	1.3	1.7	1.6	2.3	2.6	3.0	1.8	2.5
29/32	Machinery, Total	14.4	17.9	16.8	19.8	22.5	26.0	30.0	31.2	31.7	..
29/30	Non-electrical machinery	6.0	8.4	7.7	7.9	9.2	10.7	14.4	13.6	11.2	..
29	Non-electrical machinery nec	4.2	3.9	3.6	5.3	6.5	7.3	7.7	8.7	8.3	7.4
30	Office and computing machinery	1.7	4.5	4.0	2.6	2.7	3.3	6.8	4.9	2.9	..
31/32	Electrical & electronic equipment	8.4	9.5	9.2	12.0	13.3	15.3	15.6	17.7	20.5	..
31	Electrical machinery nec	1.8	2.4	2.9	2.6	2.8	5.9	6.9	6.2	3.4	3.0
32	Radio, TV & communications eq.	6.6	7.2	6.3	9.3	10.5	9.4	8.7	11.5	17.1	..
33	Scientific instruments	0.8	1.0	1.0	1.1	1.3	1.4	1.5	1.7	1.3	1.4
34/35	Transportation equipment	6.1	5.9	5.6	5.5	6.7	8.8	17.6	16.2	18.2	45.2
34	Motor vehicles	5.4	5.5	5.0	4.8	5.9	7.8	17.0	15.6	17.5	44.5
35	Other transport equipment	0.7	0.5	0.6	0.6	0.8	1.0	0.6	0.6	0.7	0.8
351	Shipbuilding & repairing	..	..	..	..	..	..	..	..	0.0	0.0
353	Aircraft and spacecraft	..	..	..	..	..	..	..	..	0.5	0.6
36/37	Other manufacturing	0.9	0.7	1.4	0.8	0.9	0.7	0.5	0.7	0.6	..
40/45	Construction, electricity, gas & water	0.4	..	..	..	..	..	0.1	0.1	0.2	2.0
50/55	Trade, repair, hotels & restaurants	115.9	115.8	114.3	112.5	122.7	145.5	149.3	160.4	159.7	159.3
65/74	Finance, insurance, business services	0.0	0.0	0.0	0.0	0.0	0.0	0.0	0.0	..	0.5
	OTHER ACTIVITIES	14.5	..	..	..	..	..	19.8	24.0	..	0.5
01/99	**GRAND TOTAL**	**171.9**	**182.9**	**178.7**	**184.5**	**200.6**	**232.4**	**250.8**	**268.7**	**261.5**	**289.7**

Total manufacturing by investing country

	1989	1990	1991	1992	1993	1994	1995	1996	1997	1998
All countries	**40.9**	**47.2**	**47.0**	**53.3**	**59.6**	**68.4**	**81.6**	**83.9**	**99.3**	**126.9**
United States	0.1	..	0.0	..	0.0	0.1	..	0.3	0.4	..
Canada	5.8	5.8	5.8	6.4	7.2	7.4	6.4	6.8	6.9	7.0
Mexico	..	..	..	..	..	..	..	..	..	..
Japan	10.1	14.1	12.8	14.7	15.9	17.8	31.2	29.6	31.1	36.5
Europe	22.5	24.3	25.0	29.3	33.0	39.2	39.8	43.0	51.1	76.4
European Union (15)	..	..	..	..	..	..	..	..	..	..
Belgium	..	..	..	..	..	..	..	..	..	..
France	4.1	4.9	4.2	5.4	6.2	8.2	7.3	8.3	8.6	8.8
Germany	6.0	6.7	6.7	8.1	8.4	10.8	11.0	12.3	12.7	38.9
Italy	..	..	..	..	..	..	..	..	..	..
Netherlands	2.5	2.6	2.6	2.9	3.5	3.4	3.8	4.1	7.5	7.0
Spain	..	..	..	..	..	..	..	..	..	..
Sweden	..	..	..	..	..	..	..	..	..	..
United Kingdom	5.1	5.1	5.5	6.0	6.7	7.3	7.6	7.9	11.6	11.1
Switzerland	2.3	2.4	2.7	2.9	3.2	3.5	3.9	4.3	3.5	3.7
Australia and New Zealand	..	..	..	..	..	..	..	..	..	..
Asia (non-OECD)	1.1	1.0	1.2	1.3	1.6	1.4	..	1.5	1.5	..
Latin America	..	..	0.5	0.6	0.8	1.2	..	1.4	2.5	2.3

Note: Majority and minority foreign-owned firms. Change of industrial classification from 1997. See country notes.
Firmes sous contrôle étranger majoritaire et minoritaire. Changement de classification industrielle à partir de 1997. Voir les notes par pays.

Inward investments | *Investissements entrants*

Table 13A - Tableau 13A

INTRA-FIRM EXPORTS / EXPORTATIONS INTRA-FIRME

By industry (ISIC Rev. 3)	Foreign affiliates (Millions of USD) Filiales étrangères (Millions de USD)									
	1989	1990	1991	1992	1993	1994	1995	1996	1997	1998
10/14 Mining & quarrying	567	383	288	420	269	170	213	403	908	1 195
15/37 **TOTAL MANUFACTURING**	**13 352**	**15 002**	**17 294**	**19 534**	**20 863**	**24 616**	**28 872**	**31 282**	**35 707**	**47 820**
15/16 Food, beverages, tobacco	523	579	671	900	1 088	1 175	1 336	1 468	1 797	1 730
17/19 Textiles, clothing, leather, footwear	126	117	148	170	170	188	163	206	187	146
20/22 Wood and paper products	558	481	545	751	882	940	952	1 181	1 021	939
20 Wood products	170	56	65	97	167	186	91	86	94	94
21/22 Paper, printing and publishing	388	425	480	654	715	754	861	1 095	927	845
23/25 Chemicals, Total	5 228	6 171	6 879	7 825	8 172	9 127	8 777	9 184	11 647	11 857
23 Refined petroleum, nuclear fuel	..	..	..	..	..	..	..	..	856	1 457
24/25 Chemicals, rubber & plastics prod.	5 228	6 171	6 879	7 825	8 172	9 127	8 777	9 184	10 791	10 400
24 Chemical products	4 885	5 538	6 306	7 002	7 422	8 228	7 689	7 838	9 138	8 809
2423 Pharmaceuticals	742	973	944	1 006	2 250	2 489	3 283	3 070	3 362	3 518
25 Rubber and plastics products	343	633	573	823	750	899	1 088	1 346	1 653	1 591
26 Non-metallic mineral products	129	205	249	324	350	302	320	468	388	366
27/28 Basic & fabricated metals	1 136	978	1 112	964	1 025	1 179	1 468	1 697	1 727	1 813
27 Basic metals	721	742	828	629	698	835	919	987	1 195	1 099
28 Fabricated metal products	415	236	284	335	328	344	548	710	533	713
29/32 Machinery, Total	4 360	5 073	5 813	6 082	6 662	8 586	9 777	10 975		
29/30 Non-electrical machinery	2 330	2 694	2 604	2 518	2 499	2 614	3 388	3 403	..	3 889
29 Non-electrical machinery nec	1 149	1 280	1 210	1 394	1 670	1 888	2 076	2 492	3 611	3 235
30 Office and computing machinery	1 181	1 414	1 394	1 124	829	728	1 312	911	..	654
31/32 Electrical & electronic equipment	2 030	2 379	3 209	3 565	4 162	5 972	6 389	7 572		
31 Electrical machinery nec	602	837	1 308	1 207	1 296	2 956	3 010	2 793	1 929	1 916
32 Radio, TV & communications eq.	1 429	1 543	1 901	2 357	2 866	3 016	3 379	4 779	..	..
33 Scientific instruments	537	615	856	1 073	1 118	1 345	1 411	1 560	..	..
34/35 Transportation equipment	356	355	511	939	948	1 230	3 611	3 708	4 504	17 705
34 Motor vehicles	258	272	365	668	729	959	3 423	3 526	4 219	17 420
35 Other transport equipment	99	84	146	271	220	272	187	182	284	283
351 Shipbuilding & repairing	..	..	..	..	..	..	..	..	..	..
353 Aircraft and spacecraft	..	..	..	..	..	..	..	..	..	..
36/37 Other manufacturing	402	428	512	504	446	541	1 057	806	..	..
40/45 Construction, electricity, gas & water	55	51	40	21	19	33	..	96	..	118
50/55 Trade, repair, hotels & restaurants	25 712	28 165	30 272	36 403	35 371	33 491	37 639	38 149	38 793	31 474
65/74 Finance, insurance, business services	8	9	105	15	22	11	14	17	..	..
OTHER ACTIVITIES	1 024	1 712	2 357	2 214	1 768	6 515	..	5 189	..	..
01/99 **GRAND TOTAL**	**40 717**	**45 322**	**50 356**	**58 607**	**58 312**	**64 837**	**72 194**	**75 136**	**76 206**	**81 185**

Total manufacturing by investing country

	1989	1990	1991	1992	1993	1994	1995	1996	1997	1998
All countries	**7 926**	**9 067**	**10 445**	**11 574**	**12 092**	**14 067**	**18 215**	**21 809**	**25 661**	**27 125**
United States	..	..	..	9	..	..	115	102	172	129
Canada	..	..	..	1 055	1 139	1 294	1 487	1 953	1 960	2 053
Mexico	..	..	..	..	..	..	..	..	..	..
Japan	..	..	..	2 731	2 830	3 104	4 495	5 715	6 339	7 209
Europe	..	..	..	7 295	7 674	9 108	11 450	13 055	16 234	16 950
European Union (15)	..	..	..	..	..	..	..	..	..	..
Belgium	..	..	..	..	..	..	..	..	..	..
France	..	..	..	1 014	958	1 020	1 223	1 618	..	2 220
Germany	..	..	..	1 934	1 998	2 337	2 794	3 209	4 380	5 277
Italy	..	..	..	..	..	..	..	..	..	..
Netherlands	..	..	..	911	874	979	1 416	1 384	1 970	1 829
Spain	..	..	..	..	..	..	..	..	..	..
Sweden	..	..	..	..	..	..	..	..	..	..
United Kingdom	..	..	..	1 466	1 390	1 557	2 309	2 233	2 939	2 650
Switzerland	..	..	..	1 131	1 290	1 610	1 913	2 130	2 227	2 390
Australia and New Zealand	..	..	..	..	..	..	..	..	..	..
Asia (non-OECD)	..	..	..	168	141	225	234	359	326	348
Latin America	..	..	..	230	194	174	199	308	221	74

Note: Majority and minority foreign-owned firms. Defined as US merchandise exports shipped by affiliates a) to the foreign parent company + b) to foreign affiliates. For Total manufacturing by investing country, a) only. Change of industrial classification from 1997. See country notes.
Firmes sous contrôle étranger majoritaire et minoritaire. Définies comme les exportations à destination a) du groupe-parent étranger + b) des filiales étrangères. a) uniquement pour le total manufacturier par pays investisseur. Changement de classification industrielle à partir de 1997. Voir les notes par pays.

Inward investments   *Investissements entrants*

Table 14A - Tableau 14A
INTRA-FIRM IMPORTS / IMPORTATIONS INTRA-FIRME

| | | **Foreign affiliates** *(Millions of USD)* | | | | | | | | |
| | | **Filiales étrangères** *(Millions de USD)* | | | | | | | | |
By industry (ISIC Rev. 3)		1989	1990	1991	1992	1993	1994	1995	1996	1997	1998
10/14	Mining & quarrying	176	318	214	203	167	90	99	307	380	395
15/37	**TOTAL MANUFACTURING**	30 564	36 670	35 972	42 006	46 221	54 873	68 716	69 478	78 054	101 224
15/16	Food, beverages, tobacco	1 226	1 450	1 697	1 753	2 009	2 033	1 876	1 687	2 191	2 199
17/19	Textiles, clothing, leather, footwear	411	216	226	352	393	431	378	316	358	321
20/22	Wood and paper products	699	739	771	956	1 129	1 041	1 179	1 577	1 309	693
20	Wood products	129	146	110	399	388	213	235	231	214	186
21/22	Paper, printing and publishing	570	593	661	557	741	828	944	1 346	1 095	507
23/25	Chemicals, Total	6 919	9 073	9 286	11 700	12 647	14 346	15 053	16 122	23 381	20 275
23	Refined petroleum, nuclear fuel	..	..	..	..	..	..	..	..	5 439	4 021
24/25	Chemicals, rubber & plastics prod.	6 919	9 073	9 286	11 700	12 647	14 346	15 053	16 122	17 942	16 254
24	Chemical products	5 836	6 836	7 526	9 499	10 244	11 889	12 227	13 382	14 629	12 907
2423	Pharmaceuticals	1 755	2 007	2 300	2 746	5 050	5 058	5 881	5 975	7 354	6 893
25	Rubber and plastics products	1 083	2 237	1 760	2 201	2 403	2 457	2 826	2 740	3 313	3 347
26	Non-metallic mineral products	565	759	624	704	867	1 015	1 039	1 055	1 227	1 080
27/28	Basic & fabricated metals	3 433	2 813	3 166	4 132	4 183	5 351	6 013	5 998	6 372	6 793
27	Basic metals	2 353	2 237	2 553	2 919	3 112	3 491	3 746	3 614	4 884	4 607
28	Fabricated metal products	1 080	575	613	1 213	1 071	1 860	2 267	2 384	1 487	2 186
29/32	Machinery, Total	10 471	14 794	14 383	15 904	17 258	20 874	24 630	25 395	25 114	..
29/30	Non-electrical machinery	4 656	7 807	6 832	6 274	6 671	7 503	10 888	10 324	7 894	..
29	Non-electrical machinery nec	3 317	3 493	3 137	3 934	4 948	5 760	5 936	6 568	6 146	5 614
30	Office and computing machinery	1 339	4 314	3 693	2 340	1 724	1 743	4 951	3 755	1 748	..
31/32	Electrical & electronic equipment	5 815	6 989	7 552	9 631	10 587	13 371	13 742	15 071	17 220	..
31	Electrical machinery nec	1 542	2 075	2 533	2 268	2 467	4 976	5 743	5 213	3 217	2 727
32	Radio, TV & communications eq.	4 273	4 914	5 018	7 362	8 120	8 395	7 999	9 858	14 003	..
33	Scientific instruments	671	805	811	915	977	1 091	1 158	1 391	..	..
34/35	Transportation equipment	5 878	5 724	4 641	5 221	6 346	8 314	17 079	15 705	16 671	39 127
34	Motor vehicles	5 297	5 296	4 062	4 601	5 596	7 337	16 524	15 153	16 024	38 390
35	Other transport equipment	580	428	578	620	750	977	554	552	648	738
351	Shipbuilding & repairing	..	..	..	..	..	..	..	..	..	..
353	Aircraft and spacecraft	..	..	..	..	..	..	..	..	..	..
36/37	Other manufacturing	293	295	370	370	412	378	313	250	..	..
40/45	Construction, electricity, gas & water	312	..	..	..	..	..	55	74	62	1 693
50/55	Trade, repair, hotels & restaurants	94 980	92 861	90 660	91 153	101 923	120 627	123 713	129 934	129 226	127 610
65/74	Finance, insurance, business services	1	4	4	11	2	2	21	16	..	..
	OTHER ACTIVITIES	8 238	..	..	..	..	..	11 071	13 336	..	..
01/99	**GRAND TOTAL**	134 270	141 847	137 043	143 943	158 874	185 960	203 676	213 144	208 739	231 674

Total manufacturing by investing country

	1989	1990	1991	1992	1993	1994	1995	1996	1997	1998
All countries	27 587	33 221	32 730	37 259	39 866	47 243	60 366	61 211	70 042	76 805
United States	..	..	..	..	2	105	..	158	171	..
Canada	..	..	..	3 706	4 110	4 164	5 115	5 846	5 561	5 849
Mexico	..	..	..	..	..	..	..	..	..	..
Japan	..	..	..	12 315	13 143	15 018	25 310	23 838	24 300	29 467
Europe	..	..	..	19 576	20 684	26 088	28 196	29 535	32 367	37 273
European Union (15)	..	..	..	..	..	..	..	..	..	..
Belgium	..	..	..	..	..	..	..	..	..	..
France	..	..	..	2 427	2 269	3 424	3 843	4 098	3 307	3 648
Germany	..	..	..	6 513	6 180	8 244	8 775	9 022	9 771	15 635
Italy	..	..	..	..	..	..	..	..	..	..
Netherlands	..	..	..	1 734	1 759	1 951	2 663	3 087	4 062	4 661
Spain	..	..	..	..	..	..	..	..	..	..
Sweden	..	..	..	..	..	..	..	..	..	..
United Kingdom	..	..	..	3 883	4 229	4 727	4 658	4 738	7 203	5 097
Switzerland	..	..	..	2 532	2 714	3 045	3 425	3 639	2 901	3 024
Australia and New Zealand	..	..	..	..	..	..	..	..	..	..
Asia (non-OECD)	..	..	..	987	1 161	1 035	..	908	1 286	1 279
Latin America	..	..	..	369	450	512	..	483	1 954	1 189

Note: Majority and minority foreign-owned firms. Defined as US merchandise exports shipped by affiliates a) to the foreign parent company + b) to foreign affiliates. For Total manufacturing by investing country, a) only. Change of industrial classification from 1997. See country notes.

Firmes sous contrôle étranger majoritaire et minoritaire. Définies comme les exportations à destination a) du groupe-parent étranger + b) des filiales étrangères. a) uniquement pour le total manufacturier par pays investisseur. Changement de classification industrielle à partir de 1997. Voir les notes par pays.

Inward investments   *Investissements entrants*

Table 15A - Tableau 15A
GROSS OPERATING SURPLUS / EXCÉDENT BRUT D'EXPLOITATION

By industry (ISIC Rev. 3)		1989	1990	1991	1992	1993	1994	1995	1996	1997	1998
					Foreign affiliates *(Millions of USD)*						
					Filiales étrangères *(Millions de USD)*						
10/14	Mining & quarrying	46	597	655	- 80	- 2	381	1 202	703	1 446	-1 573
15/37	**TOTAL MANUFACTURING**	**5 698**	**- 31**	**-3 265**	**-9 171**	**-6 351**	**6 432**	**9 189**	**8 096**	**18 826**	**17 025**
15/16	Food, beverages, tobacco	444	89	210	238	-1 621	- 172	512	3 425	788	1 608
17/19	Textiles, clothing, leather, footwear	- 42	- 188	- 74	4	148	- 41	21	98	207	205
20/22	Wood and paper products	- 76	- 199	- 726	-1 222	- 894	717	819	927	333	- 101
20	Wood products	73	35	- 22	85	490	331	125	535	81	145
21/22	Paper, printing and publishing	- 149	- 234	- 704	-1 307	-1 384	386	694	392	252	- 246
23/25	Chemicals, Total	4 857	4 263	2 586	-2 075	2 939	5 240	4 158	1 347	9 003	3 878
23	Refined petroleum, nuclear fuel	..	..	..	..	..	..	..	..	4 463	261
24/25	Chemicals, rubber & plastics prod.	4 857	4 263	2 586	-2 075	2 939	5 240	4 158	1 347	4 540	3 617
24	Chemical products	4 894	4 923	3 886	-1 281	3 338	5 123	3 834	878	4 280	3 226
2423	Pharmaceuticals	1 166	1 847	2 190	2 291	2 178	2 195	2 748	1 754	1 297	1 134
25	Rubber and plastics products	- 37	- 660	-1 300	- 794	- 399	117	324	469	260	391
26	Non-metallic mineral products	173	- 659	- 918	-1 005	- 563	- 439	801	597	2 225	1 840
27/28	Basic & fabricated metals	791	363	-1 072	-2 029	-1 854	384	1 311	1 411	1 744	1 644
27	Basic metals	557	312	- 770	-2 014	-1 445	1 025	1 210	990	788	692
28	Fabricated metal products	234	51	- 301	- 15	- 408	- 641	101	421	956	951
29/32	Machinery, Total	- 394	-3 659	-3 105	-2 749	-3 970	66	222	- 573	1 422	..
29/30	Non-electrical machinery	297	-1 464	-1 865	-1 638	-2 193	52	- 384	- 254	3	- 375
29	Non-electrical machinery nec	462	- 437	- 582	- 835	- 625	468	614	921	1 390	855
30	Office and computing machinery	- 166	-1 028	-1 283	- 803	-1 568	- 415	- 998	-1 175	-1 387	-1 230
31/32	Electrical & electronic equipment	- 691	-2 195	-1 240	-1 112	-1 778	13	607	- 320	1 419	..
31	Electrical machinery nec	- 327	- 813	- 747	- 672	- 796	- 234	310	- 281	631	1 157
32	Radio, TV & communications eq.	- 364	-1 381	- 493	- 439	- 982	247	297	- 38	788	..
33	Scientific instruments	80	5	416	366	68	132	538	576	667	..
34/35	Transportation equipment	- 708	- 792	- 585	- 920	- 683	408	410	187	2 060	6 957
34	Motor vehicles	- 730	- 614	- 465	- 487	- 515	434	529	- 99	1 883	6 823
35	Other transport equipment	22	- 178	- 120	- 433	- 168	- 26	- 119	285	176	134
351	Shipbuilding & repairing	..	..	..	..	..	..	..	..	..	..
353	Aircraft and spacecraft	..	..	..	..	..	..	..	..	72	144
36/37	Other manufacturing	574	746	1	221	79	137	397	249	275	150
40/45	Construction, electricity, gas & water	- 70	- 243	- 338	- 413	- 393	- 129	- 386	- 315	- 207	267
50/55	Trade, repair, hotels & restaurants	- 643	-2 153	-1 898	-2 421	- 681	2 769	309	1 853	5 578	5 856
65/74	Finance, insurance, business services	3 139	-1 196	-1 607	-1 803	2 905	1 186	2 699	4 994	12 797	..
	OTHER ACTIVITIES	1 117	-1 508	-4 564	-7 444	168	-2 507	2 481	9 048	4 134	..
01/99	**GRAND TOTAL**	**9 286**	**-4 535**	**-11 018**	**-21 331**	**-4 354**	**8 132**	**15 493**	**24 379**	**42 547**	**33 276**

Total manufacturing by investing country

	1989	1990	1991	1992	1993	1994	1995	1996	1997	1998
All countries	**5 698**	**- 31**	**-3 265**	**-9 171**	**-6 351**	**6 432**	**9 189**	**8 096**	**18 826**	**17 025**
United States	- 65	- 44	- 29	- 2	11	48	113	- 25	- 141	..
Canada	3 391	3 116	1 545	-3 421	-1 609	3 206	812	4 232	1 419	2 000
Mexico	..	..	..	..	..	..	..	..	..	..
Japan	- 632	-1 600	-3 526	-4 059	-3 474	558	1 216	132	2 258	1 986
Europe	3 348	- 993	- 837	- 902	- 622	2 547	7 155	4 688	14 985	12 848
European Union (15)	..	..	..	..	..	..	..	..	..	..
Belgium	..	..	..	..	..	..	..	..	..	..
France	0	-1 958	- 759	- 554	-1 007	- 554	559	1 448	808	- 442
Germany	411	53	- 653	- 521	617	1 040	238	1 719	2 210	6 211
Italy	..	..	..	..	..	..	..	..	..	..
Netherlands	- 89	- 831	- 353	10	- 428	574	817	214	3 436	- 500
Spain	..	..	..	..	..	..	..	..	..	..
Sweden	..	..	..	..	..	..	..	..	..	..
United Kingdom	2 321	1 976	2 084	1 201	1 906	1 948	3 680	147	5 820	4 433
Switzerland	317	- 54	- 226	- 126	- 444	- 546	324	757	1 394	2 197
Australia and New Zealand	..	..	..	..	..	..	..	..	..	..
Asia (non-OECD)	- 204	- 489	- 283	- 453	- 267	43	- 146	- 459	- 639	..
Latin America	- 33	16	9	- 46	- 491	- 132	- 145	- 587	108	884

Note: Majority and minority foreign-owned firms. Change of industrial classification from 1997. See country notes.
Firmes sous contrôle étranger majoritaire et minoritaire. Changement de classification industrielle à partir de 1997. Voir les notes par pays.

Table 16A - Tableau 16A

TECHNOLOGICAL PAYMENTS / PAIEMENTS TECHNOLOGIQUES

By industry (ISIC Rev. 3)		Foreign affiliates (Millions of USD) Filiales étrangères (Millions de USD)									
		1990	1991	1992	1993	1994	1995	1996	1997	1998	1999
10/14	Mining & quarrying	..	..	..	..	..	..	..	..	..	..
15/37	**TOTAL MANUFACTURING**	1 317	1 771	2 066	2 063	2 389	3 350	3 241	3 751	4 812	5 213
15/16	Food, beverages, tobacco	155	214	222	227	235	226	267	271	275	542
17/19	Textiles, clothing, leather, footwear	..	..	..	..	..	..	..	..	..	..
20/22	Wood and paper products	..	..	..	..	..	..	..	..	..	..
20	Wood products	..	..	..	..	..	..	..	..	..	..
21/22	Paper, printing and publishing	..	..	..	..	..	..	..	..	..	..
23/25	Chemicals, Total	..	..	..	..	..	..	..	..	..	..
23	Refined petroleum, nuclear fuel	..	..	..	..	..	..	..	..	..	..
24/25	Chemicals, rubber & plastics prod.	..	..	..	..	..	..	..	..	..	..
24	Chemical products	683	1 073	1 267	1 224	1 421	1 949	1 987	2 280	2 300	1 884
2423	Pharmaceuticals	..	..	..	..	..	..	..	..	..	..
25	Rubber and plastics products	..	..	..	..	..	..	..	..	..	..
26	Non-metallic mineral products	..	..	..	..	..	..	..	..	..	..
27/28	Basic & fabricated metals	64	51	64	72	70	103	137	139	158	168
27	Basic metals	..	..	..	..	..	..	..	..	..	..
28	Fabricated metal products	..	..	..	..	..	..	..	..	..	..
29/32	Machinery, Total	222	173	222	228	298	301	339	362	563	599
29/30	Non-electrical machinery	..	..	..	..	..	..	..	..	..	..
29	Non-electrical machinery nec	..	..	..	..	..	..	..	..	..	..
30	Office and computing machinery	..	..	..	..	..	..	..	..	..	..
31/32	Electrical & electronic equipment	..	..	..	..	..	..	..	..	..	..
31	Electrical machinery nec	..	..	..	..	..	..	..	..	..	..
32	Radio, TV & communications eq.	..	..	..	..	..	..	..	..	..	..
33	Scientific instruments	..	..	..	..	..	..	..	..	..	..
34/35	Transportation equipment	..	..	..	..	..	..	..	..	..	..
34	Motor vehicles	..	..	..	..	..	..	..	..	..	..
35	Other transport equipment	..	..	..	..	..	..	..	..	..	..
351	Shipbuilding & repairing	..	..	..	..	..	..	..	..	..	..
353	Aircraft and spacecraft	..	..	..	..	..	..	..	..	..	..
36/37	Other manufacturing	..	..	..	..	..	..	..	..	..	..
40/45	Construction, electricity, gas & water	..	..	..	..	..	..	..	..	..	..
50/55	Trade, repair, hotels & restaurants	382	675	789	680	..	..	729	..	..	1 599
65/74	Finance, insurance, business services	..	..	..	49	44	67	..	64	87	119
	OTHER ACTIVITIES	..	..	..	..	..	..	..	..	..	..
01/99	**GRAND TOTAL**	1 860	2 652	3 049	2 998	3 312	4 411	..	5 581	..	..

Total manufacturing by investing country

	1990	1991	1992	1993	1994	1995	1996	1997	1998	1999
All countries	1 317	1 771	2 066	2 063	2 389	3 350	3 241	3 751	4 812	5 213
United States	..	..	..	..	..	..	..	..	..	..
Canada	9	6	24	..	12	33	53	..	..	146
Mexico	0	0	0	0	2	0	0	..	..	..
Japan	138	185	211	231	276	648	558	592	1 359	1 693
Europe	1 159	1 570	1 820	1 801	2 094	2 661	2 620	3 007	3 287	3 325
European Union (15)	885	1 225	1 434	1 436	1 638	2 220	2 180	2 487	2 759	2 459
Belgium	24	33	31	31	44	63	69	74	95	90
France	110	108	102	106	69	98	98	170	299	291
Germany	209	166	225	230	362	403	403	498	571	572
Italy	15	7	8	8	..	17	16	..	..	19
Netherlands	151	113	157	111	114	283	234	..	309	272
Spain	0	0	0	0	..	..	1	1	2	1
Sweden	15	27	24	29	46	41	39	..	75	91
United Kingdom	374	798	908	945	1 010	1 283	1 294	1 390	1 352	991
Switzerland	240	309	354	318	383	439	438	519	527	858
Australia and New Zealand	4	4	4	3	4	4	4	..	8	..
Asia (non-OECD)	1	1	0	2	1	1	1	..	1	9
Latin America	5	5	8	..	3	3	2	..	..	..

Note: Majority and minority foreign-owned firms.
Firmes sous contrôle étranger majoritaire et minoritaire.

Table 17A - Tableau 17A
TECHNOLOGICAL RECEIPTS / RECETTES TECHNOLOGIQUES

| By industry (ISIC Rev. 3) | | Foreign affiliates (Millions of USD) | | | | | | | | | |
		Filiales étrangères (Millions de USD)									
		1990	1991	1992	1993	1994	1995	1996	1997	1998	1999
10/14	Mining & quarrying	..	..	..	..	..	..	..	..	..	..
15/37	**TOTAL MANUFACTURING**	**165**	**200**	**283**	**261**	**403**	**709**	**1 208**	**811**	**1 456**	**1 120**
15/16	Food, beverages, tobacco	31	30	39	57	46	54	46	58	72	123
17/19	Textiles, clothing, leather, footwear	..	..	..	..	..	..	..	..	..	..
20/22	Wood and paper products	..	..	..	..	..	..	..	..	..	..
20	Wood products	..	..	..	..	..	..	..	..	..	..
21/22	Paper, printing and publishing	..	..	..	..	..	..	..	..	..	..
23/25	Chemicals, Total	..	..	..	..	..	..	..	..	..	..
23	Refined petroleum, nuclear fuel	..	..	..	..	..	..	..	..	..	..
24/25	Chemicals, rubber & plastics prod.	..	..	..	..	..	..	..	..	..	..
24	Chemical products	68	81	58	96	81	149	400	367	783	533
2423	Pharmaceuticals	..	..	..	..	..	..	..	..	..	..
25	Rubber and plastics products	..	..	..	..	..	..	..	..	..	..
26	Non-metallic mineral products	..	..	..	..	..	..	..	..	..	..
27/28	Basic & fabricated metals	7	8	3	9	7	23	27	9	13	9
27	Basic metals	..	..	..	..	..	..	..	..	..	..
28	Fabricated metal products	..	..	..	..	..	..	..	..	..	..
29/32	Machinery, Total	20	36	105	43	222	404	559	244	135	169
29/30	Non-electrical machinery	..	..	..	..	..	..	..	..	..	..
29	Non-electrical machinery nec	..	..	..	..	..	..	..	..	..	..
30	Office and computing machinery	..	..	..	..	..	..	..	..	..	..
31/32	Electrical & electronic equipment	..	..	..	..	..	..	..	..	..	..
31	Electrical machinery nec	..	..	..	..	..	..	..	..	..	..
32	Radio, TV & communications eq.	..	..	..	..	..	..	..	..	..	..
33	Scientific instruments	..	..	..	..	..	..	..	..	..	..
34/35	Transportation equipment	..	..	..	..	..	..	..	..	..	..
34	Motor vehicles	..	..	..	..	..	..	..	..	..	..
35	Other transport equipment	..	..	..	..	..	..	..	..	..	..
351	Shipbuilding & repairing	..	..	..	..	..	..	..	..	..	..
353	Aircraft and spacecraft	..	..	..	..	..	..	..	..	..	..
36/37	Other manufacturing	..	..	..	..	..	..	..	..	..	..
40/45	Construction, electricity, gas & water	..	..	..	..	..	..	..	..	..	..
50/55	Trade, repair, hotels & restaurants	..	..	..	..	..	..	..	..	..	283
65/74	Finance, insurance, business services	..	..	24	19	15	..	..	14	25	23
	OTHER ACTIVITIES	..	..	..	..	..	..	..	..	..	..
01/99	**GRAND TOTAL**	..	**553**	**697**	**714**	**974**	**1 387**	**1 744**	**1 696**	..	..

Total manufacturing by investing country

	1990	1991	1992	1993	1994	1995	1996	1997	1998	1999
All countries	**165**	**200**	**283**	**261**	**403**	**709**	**1 208**	**811**	**1 456**	**1 120**
United States	..	..	..	..	..	..	..	..	..	..
Canada	8	10	10	11	24	18	33	..	..	26
Mexico	1	1	7	6	6	10	8	..	74	11
Japan	25	19	58	57	89	147	172	170	74	88
Europe	119	150	186	161	251	499	956	508	1 139	821
European Union (15)	108	122	146	141	235	486	918	411	955	705
Belgium	10	4	3	..	7	..	59	13	5	5
France	39	19	51	23	67	189	..	56	11	11
Germany	23	40	30	33	44	56	34	42	189	157
Italy	3	2	3	2	8	..	21	..	..	10
Netherlands	2	6	10	10	11	37	10	..	89	47
Spain	0	0	0	5	9	..	0	0	0	0
Sweden	4	5	2	5	2	1	..	..	..	5
United Kingdom	..	49	44	50	89	171	301	183	580	419
Switzerland	6	18	36	14	11	10	38	94	174	104
Australia and New Zealand	1	8	3	7	..	..	2	1	..	..
Asia (non-OECD)	10	13	19	18	..	..	31	76	..	12
Latin America	1	1	7	7	10	11	9	..	..	..

Note: Majority and minority foreign-owned firms.
Firmes sous contrôle étranger majoritaire et minoritaire.

Table 18A - Tableau 18A

STOCK OF FOREIGN DIRECT INVESTMENT / STOCK D'INVESTISSEMENT DIRECT ÉTRANGER

By industry (ISIC Rev. 3)		**Foreign affiliates** *(Billions of USD)* **Filiales étrangères** *(Milliards de USD)*									
		1990	1991	1992	1993	1994	1995	1996	1997	1998	1999
10/14	Mining & quarrying	8.5	7.9	8.5	10.1	10.6	11.3	10.6	12.5	12.1	12.0
15/37	**TOTAL MANUFACTURING**	**152.8**	**157.1**	**160.4**	**168.2**	**189.5**	**214.5**	**245.7**	**271.3**	**334.9**	**391.0**
15/16	Food, beverages, tobacco	22.5	23.9	23.8	22.8	21.4	27.0	28.1	26.2	22.0	16.7
17/19	Textiles, clothing, leather, footwear	1.8	2.1	2.6	2.6	3.2	3.9	3.5	4.0	3.3	3.3
20/22	Wood and paper products	15.4	13.5	14.2	15.7	17.5	20.0	30.3	31.8	37.5	43.1
20	Wood products	0.8	0.5	0.8	2.5	2.8	2.9	1.9	1.0	1.0	1.2
21/22	Paper, printing and publishing	14.7	13.0	13.4	13.2	14.8	17.0	28.4	30.8	36.5	41.9
23/25	Chemicals, Total	51.3	54.7	57.5	63.0	72.7	79.9	89.6	96.3	106.5	115.4
23	Refined petroleum, nuclear fuel	..	..	..	..	..	..	..	..	..	..
24/25	Chemicals, rubber & plastics prod.	51.3	54.7	57.5	63.0	72.7	79.9	89.6	96.3	106.5	115.4
24	Chemical products	45.8	48.6	52.4	56.8	66.0	72.1	79.5	86.6	95.7	103.5
2423	Pharmaceuticals	11.5	11.8	12.2	19.2	24.9	28.6	33.9	38.9	43.7	43.2
25	Rubber and plastics products	5.6	6.1	5.1	6.2	6.6	7.7	10.0	9.8	10.8	12.0
26	Non-metallic mineral products	9.5	9.5	8.1	9.5	10.2	12.0	12.9	13.1	17.0	20.6
27/28	Basic & fabricated metals	13.7	12.9	12.2	12.5	14.3	14.2	18.6	20.5	19.3	21.8
27	Basic metals	7.2	7.9	5.9	5.8	7.6	8.1	9.0	9.3	10.0	11.9
28	Fabricated metal products	6.5	5.0	6.3	6.7	6.7	6.1	9.6	11.1	9.4	9.9
29/32	Machinery, Total	27.6	29.5	30.5	30.2	35.2	37.1	39.1	51.7	62.1	76.6
29/30	Non-electrical machinery	11.5	12.0	11.9	10.8	13.5	15.2	15.4	20.0	20.1	28.2
29	Non-electrical machinery nec	8.9	9.3	10.1	9.6	11.7	12.7	13.0	16.3	16.9	24.2
30	Office and computing machinery	2.6	2.7	1.8	1.3	1.8	2.5	2.4	3.7	3.3	4.0
31/32	Electrical & electronic equipment	16.1	17.6	18.6	19.4	21.7	21.9	23.7	31.7	42.0	48.4
31	Electrical machinery nec	6.8	8.0	7.1	7.4	9.3	10.1	10.6	10.8	10.6	13.2
32	Radio, TV & communications eq.	9.3	9.6	11.5	12.1	12.4	11.8	13.1	20.9	31.3	35.2
33	Scientific instruments	8.1	7.5	7.4	7.7	7.3	8.6	10.3	13.0	27.3	45.5
34/35	Transportation equipment	3.7	4.0	5.1	5.0	7.0	11.1	12.4	13.8	38.1	45.1
34	Motor vehicles	3.1	2.9	3.5	3.4	5.3	8.8	11.0	12.7	36.0	42.4
35	Other transport equipment	0.6	1.2	1.6	1.6	1.7	2.3	1.4	1.1	2.1	2.7
351	Shipbuilding & repairing	..	..	..	..	..	..	..	..	..	..
353	Aircraft and spacecraft	..	..	..	..	..	..	..	..	..	..
36/37	Other manufacturing	-0.8	-0.5	-0.9	-0.8	0.7	0.8	0.9	0.9	1.9	2.9
40/45	Construction, electricity, gas & water	4.1	3.6	1.6	2.0	2.0	2.0	1.1	4.2	2.9	3.6
50/55	Trade, repair, hotels & restaurants	60.2	65.3	70.6	75.2	75.7	79.4	87.3	103.8	111.1	132.3
65/74	Finance, insurance, business services	70.4	78.3	81.6	110.6	95.6	115.6	128.8	154.3	167.2	198.6
	OTHER ACTIVITIES	80.5	81.9	78.2	76.8	80.3	78.9	79.9	104.9	121.8	189.1
01/99	**GRAND TOTAL**	**376.5**	**394.2**	**400.9**	**442.8**	**453.5**	**501.7**	**566.8**	**650.9**	**749.9**	**926.6**

Total manufacturing by investing country

	1990	1991	1992	1993	1994	1995	1996	1997	1998	1999
All countries	**152.8**	**157.1**	**160.4**	**168.2**	**189.5**	**214.5**	**245.7**	**271.3**	**334.9**	**391.0**
United States	..	..	..	..	..	..	..	..	..	..
Canada	9.2	15.7	15.8	16.0	17.4	20.3	23.1	24.3	26.5	26.3
Mexico	0.2	0.2	0.4	0.5	1.1	1.0	0.6	0.6	1.3	2.2
Japan	17.2	18.2	18.8	18.4	20.6	25.5	35.5	37.5	47.4	47.3
Europe	115.8	114.3	116.1	124.7	138.8	156.5	176.3	200.0	251.8	305.5
European Union (15)	98.6	97.5	99.3	105.9	116.7	141.6	158.6	177.4	225.2	274.7
Belgium	1.4	1.4	1.3	1.8	2.3	2.3	2.2	3.5	4.1	4.0
France	13.0	15.1	17.1	17.7	20.0	21.6	26.7	29.3	38.1	39.1
Germany	15.7	15.7	16.5	18.1	22.4	25.0	29.6	33.8	54.4	59.3
Italy	0.8	2.6	0.8	0.9	1.0	0.9	0.7	0.6	0.9	1.1
Netherlands	24.7	19.5	21.5	22.1	19.8	19.1	27.4	31.0	38.0	42.9
Spain	0.1	0.1	0.2	0.1	0.3	0.4	0.4	0.6	0.7	1.0
Sweden	5.0	4.8	5.0	5.4	5.7	7.1	6.4	8.5	7.3	6.9
United Kingdom	42.4	41.9	40.2	43.2	47.3	56.7	58.7	55.7	54.8	68.2
Switzerland	10.7	10.2	10.0	11.8	13.2	13.5	16.2	21.1	24.3	27.8
Australia and New Zealand	2.2	2.4	2.5	2.9	3.2	3.0	3.0	2.4	3.0	..
Asia (non-OECD)	1.7	1.5	1.1	1.8	1.9	2.1	2.0	2.8	2.2	2.3
Latin America	6.5	4.7	5.8	4.0	6.8	6.0	4.5	3.7	4.4	6.0

Note: Majority and minority foreign-owned firms.
Firmes sous contrôle étranger majoritaire et minoritaire.

Table 1B - Tableau 1B

NUMBER OF ENTERPRISES / NOMBRE D'ENTREPRISES

By industry (ISIC Rev. 3)		Foreign affiliates *(Units)* Filiales étrangères *(Unités)*									
		1989	1990	1991	1992	1993	1994	1995	1996	1997	1998
10/14	Mining & quarrying	86	89	89	94	87	101	96	105	108	110
15/37	**TOTAL MANUFACTURING**	**6 314**	**6 382**	**6 390**	**6 494**	**6 435**	**6 955**	**7 075**	**7 310**	**7 589**	**7 833**
15/16	Food, beverages, tobacco	566	559	554	592	627	664	650	659	651	664
17/19	Textiles, clothing, leather, footwear	158	153	153	169	170	203	211	215	229	227
20/22	Wood and paper products	402	414	425	436	437	553	560	565	569	597
20	Wood products	75	74	76	79	87	114	113	125	125	139
21/22	Paper, printing and publishing	327	340	349	357	350	439	447	440	444	458
23/25	Chemicals, Total	1 878	1 895	1 888	1 927	1 879	2 014	2 055	2 164	2 215	2 265
23	Refined petroleum, nuclear fuel	..	..	..	..	..	..	..	..	..	..
24/25	Chemicals, rubber & plastics prod.	1 878	1 895	1 888	1 927	1 879	2 014	2 055	2 164	2 215	2 265
24	Chemical products	1 579	1 588	1 578	1 610	1 559	1 599	1 636	1 727	1 777	1 798
2423	Pharmaceuticals	447	472	457	468	451	418	408	439	442	446
25	Rubber and plastics products	299	307	310	317	320	415	419	437	438	467
26	Non-metallic mineral products	123	128	133	126	127	119	120	122	125	121
27/28	Basic & fabricated metals	569	575	567	572	569	627	643	650	657	668
27	Basic metals	104	106	105	103	107	130	137	138	140	147
28	Fabricated metal products	465	469	462	469	462	497	506	512	517	521
29/32	Machinery, Total	1 636	1 654	1 648	1 630	1 597	1 690	1 724	1 761	1 870	1 941
29/30	Non-electrical machinery	917	921	909	898	875	916	935	953	1 021	1 060
29	Non-electrical machinery nec	773	767	768	759	742	792	802	817	873	895
30	Office and computing machinery	144	154	141	139	133	124	133	136	148	165
31/32	Electrical & electronic equipment	719	733	739	732	722	774	789	808	849	881
31	Electrical machinery nec	260	261	261	255	251	275	274	276	278	284
32	Radio, TV & communications eq.	459	472	478	477	471	499	515	532	571	597
33	Scientific instruments	456	468	472	481	468	474	479	484	515	536
34/35	Transportation equipment	324	327	330	334	334	359	395	437	477	530
34	Motor vehicles	280	280	281	282	285	302	337	378	419	467
35	Other transport equipment	44	47	49	52	49	57	58	59	58	63
351	Shipbuilding & repairing	..	..	..	..	..	..	..	..	..	..
353	Aircraft and spacecraft	..	..	..	..	..	..	..	..	..	..
36/37	Other manufacturing	202	209	220	227	227	252	238	253	281	284
40/45	Construction, electricity, gas & water	104	100	113	129	110	130	134	145	126	132
50/55	Trade, repair, hotels & restaurants	3 991	4 002	4 025	4 101	4 086	5 177	5 078	5 145	5 223	5 319
65/74	Finance, insurance, business services	2 047	2 080	2 110	2 169	2 161	2 476	2 567	2 726	2 907	3 228
	OTHER ACTIVITIES	2 839	2 902	2 983	3 063	2 988	4 090	4 147	4 282	4 524	4 713
01/99	**GRAND TOTAL**	**15 381**	**15 555**	**15 710**	**16 050**	**15 867**	**18 929**	**19 097**	**19 713**	**20 477**	**21 335**

Total manufacturing by country of location

All countries	6 314	6 382	6 390	6 494	6 435	6 955	7 075	7 310	7 589	7 833
United States	..	..	..	..	..	..	..	..	..	..
Canada	..	..	..	..	..	..	..	..	..	..
Mexico	..	..	..	..	..	..	..	..	..	..
Japan	..	..	..	..	..	..	..	..	..	..
Europe	..	..	..	..	..	..	..	..	..	..
European Union (15)	..	..	..	..	..	..	..	..	..	..
Belgium	..	..	..	..	..	..	..	..	..	..
France	..	..	..	..	..	..	..	..	..	..
Germany	..	..	..	..	..	..	..	..	..	..
Italy	..	..	..	..	..	..	..	..	..	..
Netherlands	..	..	..	..	..	..	..	..	..	..
Spain	..	..	..	..	..	..	..	..	..	..
Sweden	..	..	..	..	..	..	..	..	..	..
United Kingdom	..	..	..	..	..	..	..	..	..	..
Switzerland	..	..	..	..	..	..	..	..	..	..
Australia and New Zealand	..	..	..	..	..	..	..	..	..	..
Asia (non-OECD)	..	..	..	..	..	..	..	..	..	..
Latin America	..	..	..	..	..	..	..	..	..	..

Note: Foreign affiliates majority-owned by national firms.
Filiales étrangères détenues majoritairement par des firmes nationales.

Table 2B - Tableau 2B

NUMBER OF EMPLOYEES BY INDUSTRY

NOMBRE DE SALARIÉS PAR INDUSTRIE

| *ISIC Revision 3* | | Foreign affiliates *(Thousands)* | | | | | | | | | |
| | | Filiales étrangères *(Milliers)* | | | | | | | | | |
		1989	1990	1991	1992	1993	1994	1995	1996	1997	1998
10/14	Mining & quarrying	40.0	42.0	39.3	39.6	39.6	43.2	39.6	42.6	39.3	39.3
15/37	**TOTAL MANUFACTURING**	**3 246.7**	**3 376.9**	**3 299.6**	**3 269.1**	**3 225.6**	**3 516.0**	**3 605.8**	**3 666.1**	**3 852.8**	**3 977.3**
15/16	Food, beverages, tobacco	307.5	327.8	346.7	371.3	410.9	421.7	389.1	378.2	378.9	434.9
17/19	Textiles, clothing, leather, footwear	81.7	82.2	85.2	99.2	93.1	92.4	96.5	101.3	116.5	111.4
20/22	Wood and paper products	198.0	216.1	201.3	206.4	201.8	219.7	228.1	237.6	234.0	252.8
20	Wood products	37.0	46.3	42.0	45.9	52.6	60.6	61.1	69.7	71.5	84.7
21/22	Paper, printing and publishing	161.0	169.8	159.3	160.5	149.2	159.1	167.0	167.9	162.5	168.1
23/25	Chemicals, Total	611.1	628.3	627.3	630.4	614.8	629.3	648.1	677.8	698.6	701.4
23	Refined petroleum, nuclear fuel	..	..	..	..	..	..	..	..	..	..
24/25	Chemicals, rubber & plastics prod.	611.1	628.3	627.3	630.4	614.8	629.3	648.1	677.8	698.6	701.4
24	Chemical products	474.6	489.9	501.0	506.9	486.3	497.5	515.1	537.3	545.4	543.6
2423	Pharmaceuticals	152.8	168.7	172.9	176.3	166.8	164.5	179.8	183.5	184.2	191.6
25	Rubber and plastics products	136.5	138.4	126.3	123.5	128.5	131.8	133.0	140.5	153.2	157.8
26	Non-metallic mineral products	65.1	64.1	59.6	52.4	53.4	52.8	54.0	56.5	59.4	53.3
27/28	Basic & fabricated metals	178.8	184.4	168.6	163.3	162.3	162.4	164.4	206.9	181.3	190.0
27	Basic metals	33.6	43.1	39.9	37.3	42.1	48.6	48.5	52.2	52.2	51.9
28	Fabricated metal products	145.2	141.3	128.7	126.0	120.2	113.8	115.9	154.7	129.1	138.1
29/32	Machinery, Total	962.6	1 012.2	958.8	933.3	907.4	1 134.7	1 189.5	1 144.3	1 275.3	1 285.0
29/30	Non-electrical machinery	507.9	513.6	474.4	446.5	422.7	449.3	462.9	498.9	562.2	563.6
29	Non-electrical machinery nec	263.1	252.7	232.2	221.6	208.9	232.9	232.7	257.7	297.8	304.2
30	Office and computing machinery	244.8	261.0	242.1	224.9	213.7	216.3	230.2	241.3	264.6	259.3
31/32	Electrical & electronic equipment	454.7	498.6	484.4	486.8	484.7	685.4	726.6	645.4	713.1	721.4
31	Electrical machinery nec	177.4	181.2	167.9	163.4	165.1	200.7	203.3	204.6	224.2	230.9
32	Radio, TV & communications eq.	277.3	317.4	316.6	323.5	319.5	484.7	523.4	440.7	489.0	490.5
33	Scientific instruments	160.4	167.1	166.6	163.4	157.5	146.3	163.0	165.9	170.9	176.8
34/35	Transportation equipment	596.7	597.7	591.5	538.6	516.3	542.2	555.7	577.5	616.1	642.0
34	Motor vehicles	562.5	563.3	558.9	512.1	491.4	515.6	528.3	547.3	582.3	606.6
35	Other transport equipment	34.2	34.4	32.6	26.5	24.9	26.7	27.4	30.2	33.9	35.4
351	Shipbuilding & repairing	..	..	..	..	..	..	..	..	..	..
353	Aircraft and spacecraft	..	..	..	..	..	..	..	..	..	..
36/37	Other manufacturing	84.7	97.2	94.1	110.7	108.0	114.6	117.3	120.1	121.9	129.7
40/45	Construction, electricity, gas & water	39.6	41.6	53.8	61.4	53.9	50.1	54.9	48.6	31.1	34.5
50/55	Trade, repair, hotels & restaurants	846.3	977.1	1 005.8	941.0	912.0	962.4	1 012.8	1 030.2	1 067.3	1 164.1
65/74	Finance, insurance, business services	119.9	126.0	122.7	124.1	135.0	151.3	164.8	172.8	198.6	222.1
	OTHER ACTIVITIES	821.6	792.4	865.3	847.2	857.4	984.3	1 045.7	1 116.6	1 290.7	1 462.5
01/99	**GRAND TOTAL**	**5 114.0**	**5 356.0**	**5 386.5**	**5 282.4**	**5 223.3**	**5 707.1**	**5 923.5**	**6 076.8**	**6 479.8**	**6 899.9**

Note: Foreign affiliates majority-owned by national firms.
Filiales étrangères détenues majoritairement par des firmes nationales.

Table 3B - Tableau 3B

NUMBER OF EMPLOYEES BY COUNTRY OF LOCATION IN THE MANUFACTURING SECTOR
NOMBRE DE SALARIÉS PAR PAYS D'IMPLANTATION DANS L'INDUSTRIE MANUFACTURIÈRE

Country of location (UBO)	Number of employees (Thousands) Nombre de salariés (Milliers)					As a % of all countries En % du total des pays				
	1994	1995	1996	1997	1998	1994	1995	1996	1997	1998
All countries	3 516.0	3 605.8	3 666.1	3 852.8	3 977.3	100.0	100.0	100.0	100.0	100.0
Total OECD	..	..	..	..	..	..	..	..	..	..
United States	..	..	..	..	..	..	..	..	..	..
Canada	376.8	359.9	363.5	370.5	376.6	10.7	10.0	9.9	9.6	9.5
Mexico	415.2	423.3	424.1	451.5	530.4	11.8	11.7	11.6	11.7	13.3
Japan	86.3	89.1	86.6	64.8	64.4	2.5	2.5	2.4	1.7	1.6
Korea	19.2	18.6	17.9	16.8	16.8	0.5	0.5	0.5	0.4	0.4
Australia	93.4	83.4	100.3	99.9	93.9	2.7	2.3	2.7	2.6	2.4
New Zealand	8.1	8.2	19.5	18.6	19.3	0.2	0.2	0.5	0.5	0.5
Europe	1 590.0	1 636.2	1 683.5	1 740.7	1 794.4	45.2	45.4	45.9	45.2	45.1
European Union (15)	1 463.2	1 527.9	1 551.7	1 590.0	1 632.1	41.6	42.4	42.3	41.3	41.0
Austria	13.0	12.2	14.8	15.8	18.2	0.4	0.3	0.4	0.4	0.5
Belgium	62.4	69.3	63.5	61.8	61.2	1.8	1.9	1.7	1.6	1.5
Denmark	7.8	9.1	9.2	10.4	10.5	0.2	0.3	0.3	0.3	0.3
Finland	3.7	4.1	5.6	6.3	6.8	0.1	0.1	0.2	0.2	0.2
France	215.0	219.7	242.2	241.1	239.1	6.1	6.1	6.6	6.3	6.0
Germany	394.5	386.9	400.7	414.3	414.2	11.2	10.7	10.9	10.8	10.4
Greece	5.5	5.7	6.3	6.6	6.5	0.2	0.2	0.2	0.2	0.2
Ireland	44.5	50.3	49.0	55.3	57.4	1.3	1.4	1.3	1.4	1.4
Italy	113.2	121.5	120.4	123.8	116.4	3.2	3.4	3.3	3.2	2.9
Luxembourg	6.9	7.0	6.9	6.6	7.0	0.2	0.2	0.2	0.2	0.2
Netherlands	70.7	71.3	78.8	80.3	82.3	2.0	2.0	2.1	2.1	2.1
Portugal	16.8	18.7	18.9	21.0	23.2	0.5	0.5	0.5	0.5	0.6
Spain	90.6	91.4	89.6	99.4	102.9	2.6	2.5	2.4	2.6	2.6
Sweden	13.7	31.6	29.9	23.6	26.1	0.4	0.9	0.8	0.6	0.7
United Kingdom	435.3	429.1	416.0	423.8	460.4	12.4	11.9	11.3	11.0	11.6
Czech Republic	..	..	..	..	..	..	..	..	..	..
Hungary	..	..	..	..	..	..	..	..	..	..
Iceland	..	..	..	..	..	..	..	..	..	..
Norway	4.7	4.6	6.2	6.5	6.5	0.1	0.1	0.2	0.2	0.2
Poland	..	..	..	..	..	..	..	..	..	..
Slovak Republic	..	..	..	..	..	..	..	..	..	..
Switzerland	13.9	14.1	16.9	16.6	16.2	0.4	0.4	0.5	0.4	0.4
Turkey	10.5	10.9	12.2	13.1	13.5	0.3	0.3	0.3	0.3	0.3
Non-OECD Europe, of which:	..	..	..	..	..	..	..	..	..	..
Baltic countries	..	..	..	..	..	..	..	..	..	..
Bulgaria	..	..	..	..	..	..	..	..	..	..
Croatia	..	..	..	..	..	..	..	..	..	..
Romania	..	..	..	..	..	..	..	..	..	..
Russian Federation	..	..	..	..	..	..	..	..	..	..
Slovenia	..	..	..	..	..	..	..	..	..	..
Ukraine	..	..	..	..	..	..	..	..	..	..
Yugoslavia	..	..	..	..	..	..	..	..	..	..
Non-OECD Asia, of which:	507.3	565.7	534.9	627.0	622.7	14.4	15.7	14.6	16.3	15.7
China	56.2	72.8	86.4	115.1	142.4	1.6	2.0	2.4	3.0	3.6
Chinese Taipei	38.0	39.2	33.7	34.6	32.4	1.1	1.1	0.9	0.9	0.8
Hong Kong (China)	54.3	57.1	37.2	59.0	43.7	1.5	1.6	1.0	1.5	1.1
India	15.8	19.0	18.9	30.6	33.6	0.4	0.5	0.5	0.8	0.8
Indonesia	22.0	17.7	20.6	21.1	20.7	0.6	0.5	0.6	0.5	0.5
Malaysia	110.2	124.3	98.9	115.3	108.7	3.1	3.4	2.7	3.0	2.7
Philippines	52.2	60.9	50.7	45.0	46.3	1.5	1.7	1.4	1.2	1.2
Singapore	69.1	76.1	77.4	83.4	75.1	2.0	2.1	2.1	2.2	1.9
Thailand	57.2	66.5	68.3	81.0	76.8	1.6	1.8	1.9	2.1	1.9
Near and Middle East	13.7	15.6	13.6	14.9	14.4	0.4	0.4	0.4	0.4	0.4
Africa	40.1	43.3	44.1	55.9	60.1	1.1	1.2	1.2	1.5	1.5
Latin America, of which:	808.3	812.5	839.7	879.0	950.9	23.0	22.5	22.9	22.8	23.9
Argentina	36.8	39.3	45.8	46.1	48.5	1.0	1.1	1.2	1.2	1.2
Brazil	225.3	217.9	236.4	244.4	236.1	6.4	6.0	6.4	6.3	5.9
Chile	12.2	12.6	12.8	13.9	13.3	0.3	0.3	0.3	0.4	0.3

Note: Foreign affiliates majority-owned by national firms.
Filiales étrangères détenues majoritairement par des firmes nationales.

Table 4B - Tableau 4B

TURNOVER BY INDUSTRY

CHIFFRE D'AFFAIRES PAR INDUSTRIE

ISIC Revision 3		Foreign affiliates *(Billions of USD)*									
		Filiales étrangères *(Milliards de USD)*									
		1989	1990	1991	1992	1993	1994	1995	1996	1997	1998
10/14	Mining & quarrying	4.6	4.9	5.1	5.5	5.4	6.8	8.0	9.2	9.6	9.2
15/37	**TOTAL MANUFACTURING**	**509.3**	**581.3**	**596.3**	**622.6**	**614.7**	**697.6**	**829.6**	**899.7**	**941.3**	**954.0**
15/16	Food, beverages, tobacco	50.8	61.6	67.9	72.3	79.9	87.9	95.9	100.2	104.6	108.5
17/19	Textiles, clothing, leather, footwear	5.1	6.2	5.3	6.7	7.3	8.0	8.9	9.6	11.1	10.6
20/22	Wood and paper products	24.1	29.6	29.2	30.3	30.0	34.0	43.2	43.4	43.1	48.5
20	Wood products	2.6	3.4	3.6	4.0	6.0	7.1	8.3	9.8	10.8	12.6
21/22	Paper, printing and publishing	21.4	26.2	25.6	26.3	24.0	26.9	34.9	33.6	32.4	35.9
23/25	Chemicals, Total	110.3	125.6	130.5	141.4	136.4	153.6	188.9	202.5	212.5	208.4
23	Refined petroleum, nuclear fuel	..	..	..	..	..	..	..	..	..	..
24/25	Chemicals, rubber & plastics prod.	110.3	125.6	130.5	141.4	136.4	153.6	188.9	202.5	212.5	208.4
24	Chemical products	94.7	108.0	113.6	123.5	115.6	130.0	161.1	174.4	184.5	179.8
2423	Pharmaceuticals	22.8	29.9	31.9	37.0	34.9	37.4	51.1	55.3	59.9	65.1
25	Rubber and plastics products	15.6	17.6	16.9	17.9	20.8	23.7	27.7	28.1	28.1	28.6
26	Non-metallic mineral products	7.6	9.1	8.4	7.5	7.3	7.9	8.5	9.4	9.4	8.8
27/28	Basic & fabricated metals	21.0	23.4	22.1	23.1	22.1	24.9	29.0	34.4	33.6	35.2
27	Basic metals	5.7	6.2	5.9	6.1	6.4	8.4	10.1	10.3	11.0	10.7
28	Fabricated metal products	15.3	17.2	16.2	17.0	15.7	16.4	18.9	24.1	22.6	24.5
29/32	Machinery, Total	140.0	159.9	160.2	160.6	157.9	183.3	228.1	253.1	261.8	267.3
29/30	Non-electrical machinery	100.3	114.2	112.7	111.7	105.7	118.7	146.0	159.3	160.9	163.8
29	Non-electrical machinery nec	32.3	34.7	31.2	32.3	29.8	36.2	45.0	50.9	57.1	58.9
30	Office and computing machinery	68.0	79.5	81.6	79.5	75.9	82.5	101.0	108.4	103.9	104.9
31/32	Electrical & electronic equipment	39.7	45.6	47.5	48.9	52.2	64.6	82.2	93.8	100.9	103.5
31	Electrical machinery nec	14.6	15.9	15.7	15.0	16.1	17.3	19.6	20.6	21.7	21.5
32	Radio, TV & communications eq.	25.1	29.7	31.8	33.9	36.0	47.3	62.6	73.2	79.1	82.0
33	Scientific instruments	21.9	25.1	26.1	28.6	26.6	27.0	37.1	38.3	39.2	39.4
34/35	Transportation equipment	114.4	123.7	127.6	135.2	131.5	150.6	170.5	188.3	204.0	204.4
34	Motor vehicles	110.9	119.4	123.1	131.6	128.0	146.7	166.0	183.4	198.0	197.9
35	Other transport equipment	3.5	4.3	4.4	3.5	3.4	3.9	4.5	5.0	6.0	6.4
351	Shipbuilding & repairing	..	..	..	..	..	..	..	..	..	..
353	Aircraft and spacecraft	..	..	..	..	..	..	..	..	..	..
36/37	Other manufacturing	14.1	17.2	19.0	17.1	15.9	20.5	19.6	20.6	21.9	22.8
40/45	Construction, electricity, gas & water	4.6	6.2	8.5	8.7	6.9	6.7	8.4	8.6	9.2	11.8
50/55	Trade, repair, hotels & restaurants	227.9	264.3	266.7	275.5	283.0	326.6	385.1	412.7	442.0	477.5
65/74	Finance, insurance, business services	51.1	58.2	66.0	71.3	77.2	82.3	102.4	109.8	124.1	146.2
	OTHER ACTIVITIES	222.5	293.5	300.1	308.0	288.5	316.0	360.4	428.6	446.3	429.1
01/99	**GRAND TOTAL**	**1 020.0**	**1 208.4**	**1 242.6**	**1 291.7**	**1 275.8**	**1 435.9**	**1 693.8**	**1 868.6**	**1 972.5**	**2 027.8**

Note: Foreign affiliates majority-owned by national firms.
Filiales étrangères détenues majoritairement par des firmes nationales.

Table 5B - Tableau 5B

TURNOVER BY COUNTRY OF LOCATION IN THE MANUFACTURING SECTOR

CHIFFRE D'AFFAIRES PAR PAYS D'IMPLANTATION DANS L'INDUSTRIE MANUFACTURIÈRE

| | Turnover *(Billions of USD)* | | | | | As a % of all countries | | | | |
| | Chiffre d'affaires *(Milliards de USD)* | | | | | En % du total des pays | | | | |
Country of location (UBO)	1994	1995	1996	1997	1998	1994	1995	1996	1997	1998
All countries	697.6	829.6	899.7	941.3	954.0	100.0	100.0	100.0	100.0	100.0
Total OECD	..	..	..	..	..	..	..	..	..	..
United States	..	..	..	..	..	..	..	..	..	..
Canada	109.0	118.8	123.0	133.0	131.6	15.6	14.3	13.7	14.1	13.8
Mexico	30.9	29.3	39.8	47.2	52.5	4.4	3.5	4.4	5.0	5.5
Japan	37.4	42.7	43.2	31.3	28.4	5.4	5.2	4.8	3.3	3.0
Korea	3.0	4.0	4.5	4.3	3.5	0.4	0.5	0.5	0.5	0.4
Australia	17.4	18.8	23.6	23.5	21.2	2.5	2.3	2.6	2.5	2.2
New Zealand	1.3	1.6	4.0	3.8	3.6	0.2	0.2	0.4	0.4	0.4
Europe	396.2	489.4	513.2	525.3	536.9	56.8	59.0	57.0	55.8	56.3
European Union (15)	375.1	471.0	491.7	500.8	508.5	53.8	56.8	54.6	53.2	53.3
Austria	4.5	4.7	6.1	6.1	6.4	0.6	0.6	0.7	0.6	0.7
Belgium	20.9	27.0	24.5	23.1	22.0	3.0	3.2	2.7	2.5	2.3
Denmark	1.7	2.1	2.3	2.3	2.3	0.2	0.2	0.3	0.2	0.2
Finland	0.8	1.3	1.8	2.1	2.2	0.1	0.2	0.2	0.2	0.2
France	50.3	64.4	68.7	66.7	66.6	7.2	7.8	7.6	7.1	7.0
Germany	106.3	125.5	128.6	124.1	125.1	15.2	15.1	14.3	13.2	13.1
Greece	1.0	1.4	1.5	1.5	1.6	0.1	0.2	0.2	0.2	0.2
Ireland	13.7	19.2	19.8	22.2	26.5	2.0	2.3	2.2	2.4	2.8
Italy	28.8	34.4	37.4	36.7	32.1	4.1	4.1	4.2	3.9	3.4
Luxembourg	1.4	1.8	1.7	1.6	1.6	0.2	0.2	0.2	0.2	0.2
Netherlands	29.1	36.5	36.9	43.2	42.5	4.2	4.4	4.1	4.6	4.5
Portugal	2.2	2.6	2.9	2.9	2.8	0.3	0.3	0.3	0.3	0.3
Spain	22.4	27.2	29.1	29.2	31.6	3.2	3.3	3.2	3.1	3.3
Sweden	3.2	8.1	6.1	6.6	7.0	0.5	1.0	0.7	0.7	0.7
United Kingdom	97.6	115.0	124.3	132.5	138.2	14.0	13.9	13.8	14.1	14.5
Czech Republic	..	..	..	..	..	..	..	..	..	..
Hungary	..	..	..	..	..	..	..	..	..	..
Iceland	..	..	..	..	..	..	..	..	..	..
Norway	1.0	1.3	1.6	1.7	1.9	0.1	0.2	0.2	0.2	0.2
Poland	..	..	..	..	..	..	..	..	..	..
Slovak Republic	..	..	..	..	..	..	..	..	..	..
Switzerland	5.0	7.4	8.0	8.7	9.7	0.7	0.9	0.9	0.9	1.0
Turkey	1.6	2.3	2.7	3.1	3.0	0.2	0.3	0.3	0.3	0.3
Non-OECD Europe, of which:	..	..	..	..	..	..	..	..	..	..
Baltic countries	..	..	..	..	..	..	..	..	..	..
Bulgaria	..	..	..	..	..	..	..	..	..	..
Croatia	..	..	..	..	..	..	..	..	..	..
Romania	..	..	..	..	..	..	..	..	..	..
Russian Federation	..	..	..	..	..	..	..	..	..	..
Slovenia	..	..	..	..	..	..	..	..	..	..
Ukraine	..	..	..	..	..	..	..	..	..	..
Yugoslavia	..	..	..	..	..	..	..	..	..	..
Non-OECD Asia, of which:	56.1	70.9	86.3	97.5	97.4	8.0	8.5	9.6	10.4	10.2
China	1.9	3.4	5.9	8.4	11.1	0.3	0.4	0.7	0.9	1.2
Chinese Taipei	6.4	8.0	7.4	7.5	8.1	0.9	1.0	0.8	0.8	0.8
Hong Kong (China)	5.7	7.7	8.5	10.5	9.8	0.8	0.9	0.9	1.1	1.0
India	0.7	1.1	1.3	1.7	1.9	0.1	0.1	0.1	0.2	0.2
Indonesia	1.7	1.0	1.3	1.4	0.8	0.2	0.1	0.1	0.1	0.1
Malaysia	6.7	8.3	9.8	12.2	12.7	1.0	1.0	1.1	1.3	1.3
Philippines	3.1	3.9	4.3	4.9	4.9	0.4	0.5	0.5	0.5	0.5
Singapore	21.5	26.4	33.2	36.7	33.9	3.1	3.2	3.7	3.9	3.6
Thailand	3.8	5.1	5.7	5.8	6.6	0.6	0.6	0.6	0.6	0.7
Near and Middle East	1.8	2.3	2.5	2.4	2.4	0.3	0.3	0.3	0.3	0.3
Africa	3.5	4.3	4.7	5.6	5.9	0.5	0.5	0.5	0.6	0.6
Latin America, of which:	76.3	82.5	103.3	122.8	130.2	10.9	9.9	11.5	13.0	13.6
Argentina	7.2	7.4	10.7	12.1	12.7	1.0	0.9	1.2	1.3	1.3
Brazil	25.5	30.0	36.9	42.1	42.3	3.6	3.6	4.1	4.5	4.4
Chile	1.8	2.2	2.3	2.5	2.4	0.3	0.3	0.3	0.3	0.3

Note: Foreign affiliates majority-owned by national firms.
Filiales étrangères détenues majoritairement par des firmes nationales.

Table 6B - Tableau 6B

VALUE ADDED / VALEUR AJOUTÉE

| | | Foreign affiliates *(Billions of USD)* | | | | | | | | |
| | | Filiales étrangères *(Milliards de USD)* | | | | | | | | |
By industry (ISIC Rev. 3)		1989	1990	1991	1992	1993	1994	1995	1996	1997	1998
10/14	Mining & quarrying	..	..	..	..	..	3.3	4.1	4.3	4.5	3.8
15/37	**TOTAL MANUFACTURING**	..	..	..	..	..	205.2	238.9	250.4	254.6	251.4
15/16	Food, beverages, tobacco	..	..	..	..	..	24.8	24.9	24.4	25.6	26.6
17/19	Textiles, clothing, leather, footwear	..	..	..	..	..	2.6	2.9	3.1	3.5	3.3
20/22	Wood and paper products	..	..	..	..	..	10.8	13.2	12.7	12.8	13.1
20	Wood products	..	..	..	..	..	2.3	2.5	2.5	2.8	3.0
21/22	Paper, printing and publishing	..	..	..	..	..	8.4	10.7	10.2	10.1	10.1
23/25	Chemicals, Total	..	..	..	..	..	49.2	55.9	59.6	61.7	63.6
23	Refined petroleum, nuclear fuel	..	..	..	..	..	..	..	..	..	..
24/25	Chemicals, rubber & plastics prod.	..	..	..	..	..	49.2	55.9	59.6	61.7	63.6
24	Chemical products	..	..	..	..	..	41.0	46.6	50.5	52.7	55.0
2423	Pharmaceuticals	..	..	..	..	..	14.2	17.0	18.8	20.7	24.0
25	Rubber and plastics products	..	..	..	..	..	8.2	9.3	9.1	9.0	8.6
26	Non-metallic mineral products	..	..	..	..	..	2.9	3.5	3.8	3.7	3.8
27/28	Basic & fabricated metals	..	..	..	..	..	8.1	9.4	11.0	10.6	10.7
27	Basic metals	..	..	..	..	..	2.4	3.3	3.1	3.3	3.1
28	Fabricated metal products	..	..	..	..	..	5.6	6.1	8.0	7.3	7.7
29/32	Machinery, Total	..	..	..	..	..	47.4	57.7	60.4	61.8	57.5
29/30	Non-electrical machinery	..	..	..	..	..	27.5	34.0	37.0	36.1	34.8
29	Non-electrical machinery nec	..	..	..	..	..	11.2	13.2	14.5	17.1	17.2
30	Office and computing machinery	..	..	..	..	..	16.3	20.8	22.6	19.0	17.6
31/32	Electrical & electronic equipment	..	..	..	..	..	19.9	23.7	23.4	25.7	22.8
31	Electrical machinery nec	..	..	..	..	..	5.8	6.3	6.4	6.7	6.5
32	Radio, TV & communications eq.	..	..	..	..	..	14.1	17.4	16.9	19.0	16.3
33	Scientific instruments	..	..	..	..	..	9.3	12.4	12.5	12.1	12.2
34/35	Transportation equipment	..	..	..	..	..	35.9	35.5	37.8	44.6	41.6
34	Motor vehicles	..	..	..	..	..	34.4	33.7	36.2	42.6	39.5
35	Other transport equipment	..	..	..	..	..	1.5	1.8	1.6	2.0	2.1
351	Shipbuilding & repairing	..	..	..	..	..	..	..	..	..	..
353	Aircraft and spacecraft	..	..	..	..	..	..	..	..	..	..
36/37	Other manufacturing	..	..	..	..	..	14.4	23.6	25.1	18.2	19.1
40/45	Construction, electricity, gas & water	..	..	..	..	..	2.1	2.5	2.5	1.5	1.9
50/55	Trade, repair, hotels & restaurants	..	..	..	..	..	55.4	64.9	66.3	66.9	72.4
65/74	Finance, insurance, business services	..	..	..	..	..	8.5	14.1	17.2	22.5	22.9
	OTHER ACTIVITIES	..	..	..	..	..	129.3	141.1	157.6	170.8	158.3
01/99	**GRAND TOTAL**	..	..	..	..	..	403.7	465.6	498.3	520.9	510.7

Total manufacturing by country of location

		1989	1990	1991	1992	1993	1994	1995	1996	1997	1998
All countries		..	..	..	..	..	205.2	238.9	250.4	254.6	251.4
United States		..	..	..	..	..	..	..	..	..	..
Canada		..	..	..	..	..	25.3	26.9	25.9	27.9	27.5
Mexico		..	..	..	..	..	8.1	6.6	8.9	10.2	11.4
Japan		..	..	..	..	..	10.9	12.6	13.3	8.6	7.5
Europe		..	..	..	..	..	121.5	145.8	149.9	148.5	150.6
European Union (15)		..	..	..	..	..	114.7	139.6	142.6	140.6	142.5
Belgium		..	..	..	..	..	6.8	8.3	7.5	7.2	7.4
France		..	..	..	..	..	16.5	18.9	20.7	20.0	19.3
Germany		..	..	..	..	..	36.7	41.0	40.4	39.4	38.7
Italy		..	..	..	..	..	8.3	8.6	9.1	9.4	8.5
Netherlands		..	..	..	..	..	7.2	9.0	8.9	9.4	9.6
Spain		..	..	..	..	..	5.5	6.4	6.1	6.7	7.5
Sweden		..	..	..	..	..	0.8	2.7	2.4	2.2	2.2
United Kingdom		..	..	..	..	..	26.7	33.6	35.7	32.3	34.6
Switzerland		..	..	..	..	..	2.2	2.8	3.2	3.1	2.8
Australia and New Zealand		..	..	..	..	..	..	..	..	..	..
Asia (non-OECD)		..	..	..	..	..	12.3	14.8	18.7	20.9	18.7
Latin America		..	..	..	..	..	27.6	30.9	33.8	39.5	38.2

Note: Foreign affiliates majority-owned by national firms.
Filiales étrangères détenues majoritairement par des firmes nationales.

Outward investments *Investissements sortants*

Table 7B - Tableau 7B

COMPENSATION OF EMPLOYEES / SALAIRES ET CHARGES SOCIALES

By industry (ISIC Rev. 3)	Foreign affiliates *(Billions of USD)*									
	Filiales étrangères *(Milliards de USD)*									
	1989	1990	1991	1992	1993	1994	1995	1996	1997	1998
10/14 Mining & quarrying	0.8	1.1	0.9	0.9	0.9	1.2	1.0	1.2	1.1	1.0
15/37 TOTAL MANUFACTURING	**81.7**	**93.9**	**98.3**	**103.7**	**100.8**	**109.2**	**117.1**	**122.8**	**122.8**	**124.4**
15/16 Food, beverages, tobacco	6.2	7.2	8.2	9.0	10.1	10.7	11.0	11.0	11.0	11.6
17/19 Textiles, clothing, leather, footwear	1.1	1.2	1.2	1.7	1.6	1.7	1.8	2.1	2.3	2.1
20/22 Wood and paper products	4.9	5.8	6.0	6.5	6.3	6.7	7.2	7.5	7.5	7.7
20 Wood products	0.7	0.9	0.9	1.0	1.3	1.4	1.4	1.6	1.8	1.9
21/22 Paper, printing and publishing	4.2	5.0	5.1	5.5	5.0	5.3	5.8	5.9	5.7	5.8
23/25 Chemicals, Total	16.8	19.2	20.4	22.9	22.4	23.8	26.7	27.7	27.0	26.8
23 Refined petroleum, nuclear fuel	..	..	..	..	..	..	..	..	..	..
24/25 Chemicals, rubber & plastics prod.	16.8	19.2	20.4	22.9	22.4	23.8	26.7	27.7	27.0	26.8
24 Chemical products	13.6	15.5	16.8	19.1	18.4	19.5	21.9	22.8	22.2	22.0
2423 Pharmaceuticals	4.4	5.6	5.9	6.9	6.8	7.0	8.4	8.9	8.0	8.6
25 Rubber and plastics products	3.2	3.7	3.7	3.8	4.0	4.3	4.8	4.9	4.8	4.8
26 Non-metallic mineral products	1.8	2.0	2.0	1.8	1.8	1.8	1.9	2.1	2.1	2.3
27/28 Basic & fabricated metals	4.1	4.6	4.6	4.9	4.7	5.1	5.5	6.8	6.2	6.4
27 Basic metals	0.8	1.0	1.1	1.1	1.2	1.4	1.6	1.8	1.8	1.7
28 Fabricated metal products	3.3	3.6	3.6	3.8	3.5	3.7	3.9	5.0	4.4	4.8
29/32 Machinery, Total	24.3	27.7	28.4	28.4	27.6	31.4	33.0	34.0	33.7	33.9
29/30 Non-electrical machinery	16.7	19.0	19.3	18.9	17.8	19.2	19.6	20.9	20.0	20.3
29 Non-electrical machinery nec	6.4	6.9	6.8	7.0	6.7	7.9	8.6	9.4	11.2	11.1
30 Office and computing machinery	10.3	12.1	12.5	11.9	11.1	11.4	11.0	11.5	8.9	9.1
31/32 Electrical & electronic equipment	7.7	8.8	9.1	9.5	9.8	12.2	13.4	13.1	13.7	13.6
31 Electrical machinery nec	3.4	3.8	3.8	3.7	3.8	4.0	4.3	4.2	4.2	4.2
32 Radio, TV & communications eq.	4.2	5.0	5.3	5.8	6.0	8.2	9.1	8.8	9.5	9.4
33 Scientific instruments	4.5	5.2	5.6	5.9	5.4	5.5	6.9	7.1	7.1	7.1
34/35 Transportation equipment	16.6	19.1	19.8	20.2	18.6	20.0	20.5	21.9	23.5	23.9
34 Motor vehicles	15.4	17.7	18.4	19.2	17.7	18.9	19.4	20.8	22.3	22.6
35 Other transport equipment	1.2	1.4	1.3	1.0	0.9	1.0	1.1	1.1	1.2	1.3
351 Shipbuilding & repairing	..	..	..	..	..	..	..	..	..	..
353 Aircraft and spacecraft	..	..	..	..	..	..	..	..	..	..
36/37 Other manufacturing	1.5	1.9	2.1	2.5	2.5	2.6	2.6	2.7	2.5	2.6
40/45 Construction, electricity, gas & water	0.9	1.4	1.9	2.3	1.9	1.6	2.0	1.9	1.0	1.3
50/55 Trade, repair, hotels & restaurants	22.4	26.1	27.8	28.4	27.6	29.4	31.7	33.0	33.4	34.4
65/74 Finance, insurance, business services	4.9	5.7	5.6	6.4	7.4	8.3	9.8	9.9	12.2	13.4
OTHER ACTIVITIES	21.8	22.9	25.6	27.8	27.9	33.8	38.1	41.9	48.6	53.8
01/99 GRAND TOTAL	**132.6**	**151.1**	**160.1**	**169.6**	**166.5**	**183.6**	**199.7**	**210.7**	**219.1**	**228.3**

Total manufacturing by country of location

	1989	1990	1991	1992	1993	1994	1995	1996	1997	1998
All countries	**81.7**	**93.9**	**98.3**	**103.7**	**100.8**	**109.2**	**117.1**	**122.8**	**122.8**	**124.4**
United States	..	..	..	..	..	..	..	..	..	..
Canada	15.9	16.2	16.3	15.6	15.3	16.1	15.4	15.6	15.6	15.3
Mexico	1.9	2.2	2.8	3.3	3.5	4.2	3.7	3.8	4.3	5.2
Japan	3.8	4.0	4.6	4.7	5.8	6.6	6.7	7.2	4.5	4.2
Europe	48.7	59.2	62.5	67.3	62.1	67.1	73.8	75.8	76.0	77.9
European Union (15)	47.2	57.2	59.9	64.9	59.5	64.2	71.8	73.4	73.5	75.3
Belgium	2.7	3.2	3.2	3.5	3.3	3.4	4.1	3.6	3.4	3.4
France	6.8	8.6	8.7	9.5	9.7	10.9	11.8	12.6	11.9	11.8
Germany	15.0	18.2	19.1	21.9	19.9	21.7	23.7	23.4	22.9	22.4
Italy	4.3	5.4	5.4	5.4	4.5	4.8	5.1	5.3	5.2	5.1
Netherlands	2.6	3.0	3.2	3.3	3.1	3.1	3.4	3.7	3.9	3.9
Spain	2.6	3.2	3.5	3.6	3.3	3.1	3.5	3.7	3.8	3.9
Sweden	0.6	0.7	0.8	0.8	0.6	0.5	1.6	1.7	1.0	1.1
United Kingdom	11.7	13.7	14.8	15.5	13.5	14.8	15.0	15.5	17.3	19.2
Switzerland	0.5	0.7	1.0	0.7	0.8	0.9	1.0	1.2	1.1	1.1
Australia and New Zealand	..	..	..	..	..	..	..	..	..	..
Asia (non-OECD)	2.4	2.7	3.0	3.5	4.0	5.0	5.8	6.7	7.5	7.3
Latin America	7.7	8.5	8.6	9.4	10.6	10.9	11.7	13.2	14.7	15.3

Note: Foreign affiliates majority-owned by national firms.
Filiales étrangères détenues majoritairement par des firmes nationales.

Table 8B - Tableau 8B

R&D EXPENDITURE BY INDUSTRY

DÉPENSES DE R-D PAR INDUSTRIE

ISIC Revision 3		Foreign affiliates *(Millions of USD)* Filiales étrangères *(Millions de USD)*					As a % of national total En % du total national				
		1994	1995	1996	1997	1998	1994	1995	1996	1997	1998
10/14	Mining & quarrying	1	4	6	8	8	..	..	..	..	..
15/37	**TOTAL MANUFACTURING**	**10 053**	**10 791**	**12 205**	**12 505**	**12 746**	**10.7**	**10.5**	**10.6**	**9.9**	**10.2**
15/16	Food, beverages, tobacco	252	354	390	370	366	17.1	22.6	24.9	19.4	18.8
17/19	Textiles, clothing, leather, footwear	25	39	44	50	50	7.0	9.9	9.1	9.3	8.7
20/22	Wood and paper products	188	223	264	269	234	9.4	11.1	9.0	11.8	8.7
20	Wood products	22	65	74	120	87	7.0	27.4	9.9	31.3	14.2
21/22	Paper, printing and publishing	166	158	190	149	147	9.8	8.9	8.7	7.8	7.1
23/25	Chemicals, Total	3 377	3 933	3 951	4 250	4 280	17.7	20.8	19.4	19.1	16.7
23	Refined petroleum, nuclear fuel	..	..	..	..	..	..	..	..	..	..
24/25	Chemicals, rubber & plastics prod.	3 377	3 933	3 951	4 250	4 280	17.7	20.8	19.4	20.7	18.0
24	Chemical products	3 121	3 693	3 673	3 964	4 002	17.9	21.0	19.5	20.7	18.2
2423	Pharmaceuticals	2 094	2 682	2 892	3 253	3 316	21.7	26.3	29.6	27.3	26.2
25	Rubber and plastics products	256	240	278	286	278	15.8	19.1	18.7	19.9	15.1
26	Non-metallic mineral products	40	52	57	50	49	6.8	11.6	12.2	7.9	6.7
27/28	Basic & fabricated metals	111	113	177	123	155	6.2	7.0	7.7	4.4	6.4
27	Basic metals	8	12	15	17	16	1.2	2.0	2.0	1.7	2.0
28	Fabricated metal products	103	101	162	107	140	9.3	9.9	10.4	5.9	8.5
29/32	Machinery, Total	2 690	2 223	2 405	2 251	2 328	9.3	6.8	5.7	4.6	5.0
29/30	Non-electrical machinery	1 891	1 186	1 273	1 013	1 116	13.8	8.5	6.6	4.2	5.5
29	Non-electrical machinery nec	..	..	..	..	..	..	..	..	..	..
30	Office and computing machinery	1 439	563	571	293	276	14.9	6.3	4.3	1.6	2.0
31/32	Electrical & electronic equipment	799	1 037	1 132	1 238	1 212	5.2	5.5	5.0	5.0	4.6
31	Electrical machinery nec	176	271	277	251	267	6.6	7.8	8.2	5.6	5.5
32	Radio, TV & communications eq.	623	766	855	987	946	4.9	5.0	4.5	4.8	4.4
33	Scientific instruments	464	739	791	696	682	4.1	6.2	6.5	5.0	4.6
34/35	Transportation equipment	2 824	3 015	4 024	4 328	4 465	10.1	9.3	12.3	13.5	15.2
34	Motor vehicles	2 675	2 847	3 809	..	..	20.0	19.0	23.8	..	..
35	Other transport equipment	149	168	215	..	..	1.0	1.0	1.3	..	..
351	Shipbuilding & repairing	..	..	..	..	..	..	..	..	..	..
353	Aircraft and spacecraft	..	..	..	..	..	..	..	..	..	..
36/37	Other manufacturing	..	..	..	..	..	..	..	..	..	..
40/45	Construction, electricity, gas & water	3	..	10	4	1	..	..	..	0.7	0.1
50/55	Trade, repair, hotels & restaurants	957	823	741	816	845	..	..	..	9.8	7.0
65/74	Finance, insurance, business services	11	20	12	100	55	..	..	..	..	..
	OTHER ACTIVITIES	853	..	1 064	1 158	1 331	..	..	..	..	..
01/99	**GRAND TOTAL**	**11 877**	**12 582**	**14 039**	**14 593**	**14 986**	**9.9**	**9.5**	**9.7**	**9.3**	**8.9**

Note: Foreign affiliates majority-owned by national firms.
Filiales étrangères détenues majoritairement par des firmes nationales.

Table 9B - Tableau 9B

R&D EXPENDITURE BY COUNTRY OF LOCATION IN THE MANUFACTURING SECTOR

DÉPENSES DE R-D PAR PAYS D'IMPLANTATION DANS L'INDUSTRIE MANUFACTURIÈRE

Country of location (UBO)	R&D expenditure *(Millions of USD)* Dépenses de R-D *(Millions de USD)*					As a % of all countries *En % du total des pays*				
	1994	1995	1996	1997	1998	1994	1995	1996	1997	1998
All countries	10 053	10 791	12 205	12 505	12 746	100.0	100.0	100.0	100.0	100.0
Total OECD	..	..	..	..	..	..	..	..	..	..
United States	..	..	..	..	..	..	..	..	..	..
Canada	..	922	1 445	1 653	1 569	..	8.5	11.8	13.2	12.3
Mexico	179	55	101	108	140	1.8	0.5	0.8	0.9	1.1
Japan	793	932	1 002	766	722	7.9	8.6	8.2	6.1	5.7
Korea	14	22	27	30	26	0.1	0.2	0.2	0.2	0.2
Australia	151	206	318	297	240	1.5	1.9	2.6	2.4	1.9
New Zealand	6	8	15	15	14	0.1	0.1	0.1	0.1	0.1
Europe	7 569	8 092	8 612	8 729	9 154	75.3	75.0	70.6	69.8	71.8
European Union (15)	7 426	7 932	8 409	8 519	8 902	73.9	73.5	68.9	68.1	69.8
Austria	..	16	100	71	83	..	0.1	0.8	0.6	0.7
Belgium	384	239	286	247	232	3.8	2.2	2.3	2.0	1.8
Denmark	..	52	..	..	60	..	0.5	..	..	0.5
Finland	18	27	41	47	58	0.2	0.3	0.3	0.4	0.5
France	1 147	1 076	1 148	1 118	1 143	11.4	10.0	9.4	8.9	9.0
Germany	2 690	2 928	2 927	2 803	2 908	26.8	27.1	24.0	22.4	22.8
Greece	2	3	4	5	5	0.0	0.0	0.0	0.0	0.0
Ireland	369	153	..	..	245	3.7	1.4	..	..	1.9
Italy	337	310	..	514	521	3.4	2.9	..	4.1	4.1
Luxembourg	..	..	..	..	138	..	..	..	..	1.1
Netherlands	343	336	384	306	301	3.4	3.1	3.1	2.4	2.4
Portugal	4	..	87	26	30	0.0	..	0.7	0.2	0.2
Spain	101	270	307	165	181	1.0	2.5	2.5	1.3	1.4
Sweden	33	..	404	359	385	0.3	..	3.3	2.9	3.0
United Kingdom	1 931	1 681	1 864	2 423	2 610	19.2	15.6	15.3	19.4	20.5
Czech Republic	..	..	..	..	..	..	..	..	..	..
Hungary	..	..	..	..	..	..	..	..	..	..
Iceland	..	..	..	..	..	..	..	..	..	..
Norway	3	5	6	14	13	0.0	0.0	0.0	0.1	0.1
Poland	..	..	..	..	..	..	..	..	..	..
Slovak Republic	..	..	..	..	..	..	..	..	..	..
Switzerland	..	130	134	142	164	..	1.2	1.1	1.1	1.3
Turkey	1	4	25	3	3	0.0	0.0	0.2	0.0	0.0
Non-OECD Europe, of which:	..	..	..	..	..	..	..	..	..	..
Baltic countries	..	..	..	..	..	..	..	..	..	..
Bulgaria	..	..	..	..	..	..	..	..	..	..
Croatia	..	..	..	..	..	..	..	..	..	..
Romania	..	..	..	..	..	..	..	..	..	..
Russian Federation	..	..	..	..	..	..	..	..	..	..
Slovenia	..	..	..	..	..	..	..	..	..	..
Ukraine	..	..	..	..	..	..	..	..	..	..
Yugoslavia	..	..	..	..	..	..	..	..	..	..
Non-OECD Asia, of which:	372	229	272	347	305	3.7	2.1	2.2	2.8	2.4
China	5	11	24	33	50	0.0	0.1	0.2	0.3	0.4
Chinese Taipei	..	45	54	66	64	..	0.4	0.4	0.5	0.5
Hong Kong (China)	42	24	23	63	28	0.4	0.2	0.2	0.5	0.2
India	4	4	8	19	21	0.0	0.0	0.1	0.2	0.2
Indonesia	5	9	6	5	3	0.0	0.1	0.0	0.0	0.0
Malaysia	27	21	23	32	30	0.3	0.2	0.2	0.3	0.2
Philippines	12	22	14	11	9	0.1	0.2	0.1	0.1	0.1
Singapore	..	58	74	67	56	..	0.5	0.6	0.5	0.4
Thailand	3	5	5	5	4	0.0	0.0	0.0	0.0	0.0
Near and Middle East	..	27	32	67	63	..	0.3	0.3	0.5	0.5
Africa	13	17	19	23	32	0.1	0.2	0.2	0.2	0.3
Latin America, of which:	462	366	505	624	662	4.6	3.4	4.1	5.0	5.2
Argentina	20	22	40	41	49	0.2	0.2	0.3	0.3	0.4
Brazil	234	240	338	..	435	2.3	2.2	2.8	..	3.4
Chile	1	..	3	..	3	0.0	..	0.0	..	0.0

Note: Foreign affiliates majority-owned by national firms.
Filiales étrangères détenues majoritairement par des firmes nationales.

Outward investments

Investissements sortants

Table 10B - Tableau 10B

TOTAL EXPORTS BY INDUSTRY

EXPORTATIONS TOTALES PAR INDUSTRIE

ISIC Revision 3		Foreign affiliates *(Billions of USD)*									
		Filiales étrangères *(Milliards de USD)*									
		1989	1990	1991	1992	1993	1994	1995	1996	1997	1998
10/14	Mining & quarrying	0.3	0.3	0.3	0.4	0.5	0.6	0.5	0.8	0.9	0.6
15/37	**TOTAL MANUFACTURING**	**66.5**	**65.7**	**73.0**	**76.6**	**80.1**	**100.4**	**110.2**	**120.3**	**135.1**	**131.7**
15/16	Food, beverages, tobacco	2.1	1.5	1.9	2.2	2.4	2.4	2.7	2.6	2.6	3.2
17/19	Textiles, clothing, leather, footwear	0.4	0.5	0.9	0.9	0.6	0.5	0.6	0.6	0.8	1.2
20/22	Wood and paper products	1.4	1.8	1.7	1.8	2.2	2.7	2.8	2.7	2.8	2.8
20	Wood products	0.2	0.4	0.3	0.3	0.4	0.6	0.4	0.5	0.5	0.7
21/22	Paper, printing and publishing	1.2	1.3	1.4	1.5	1.8	2.1	2.4	2.2	2.3	2.2
23/25	Chemicals, Total	8.6	9.5	10.0	10.6	10.8	13.0	15.2	15.9	18.5	17.4
23	Refined petroleum, nuclear fuel	..	..	..	..	..	..	..	..	..	..
24/25	Chemicals, rubber & plastics prod.	8.6	9.5	10.0	10.6	10.8	13.0	15.2	15.9	18.5	17.4
24	Chemical products	7.3	8.0	8.5	8.9	8.8	10.9	12.8	13.5	15.8	14.7
2423	Pharmaceuticals	1.8	2.0	2.2	2.3	2.2	2.5	2.4	2.7	3.6	3.7
25	Rubber and plastics products	1.2	1.5	1.4	1.6	2.0	2.1	2.4	2.4	2.7	2.6
26	Non-metallic mineral products	0.6	0.6	0.6	0.5	0.5	0.5	0.6	0.9	0.8	0.8
27/28	Basic & fabricated metals	1.8	1.5	1.7	1.9	1.8	2.3	2.2	2.7	2.5	3.0
27	Basic metals	0.8	0.6	0.6	0.5	0.6	0.7	0.6	0.8	0.7	0.9
28	Fabricated metal products	1.0	0.9	1.1	1.4	1.2	1.6	1.6	1.9	1.8	2.1
29/32	Machinery, Total	19.8	19.7	22.0	22.1	23.8	29.9	37.2	39.5	44.9	42.7
29/30	Non-electrical machinery	11.7	11.0	12.8	12.7	13.4	14.7	18.1	19.6	23.4	21.2
29	Non-electrical machinery nec	..	..	..	..	..	..	..	..	..	..
30	Office and computing machinery	8.0	7.7	9.9	9.9	10.2	10.7	13.3	13.5	16.5	15.2
31/32	Electrical & electronic equipment	8.1	8.7	9.2	9.4	10.3	15.2	19.1	19.9	21.6	21.5
31	Electrical machinery nec	1.5	1.5	1.6	1.7	1.9	1.9	2.3	2.5	3.0	3.2
32	Radio, TV & communications eq.	6.7	7.2	7.6	7.7	8.4	13.3	16.9	17.4	18.6	18.3
33	Scientific instruments	3.6	3.6	4.3	4.7	4.3	4.5	5.7	6.5	6.8	6.5
34/35	Transportation equipment	27.9	26.8	29.3	31.2	33.0	43.8	42.3	47.7	54.2	52.9
34	Motor vehicles	27.5	26.2	28.7	30.6	32.4	42.8	41.5	46.6	53.0	51.7
35	Other transport equipment	0.4	0.6	0.6	0.5	0.6	1.1	0.8	1.1	1.2	1.3
351	Shipbuilding & repairing	..	..	..	..	..	..	..	..	..	..
353	Aircraft and spacecraft	..	..	..	..	..	..	..	..	..	..
36/37	Other manufacturing	..	..	..	..	..	..	..	..	..	..
40/45	Construction, electricity, gas & water	0.1	0.1	0.1	0.2	0.1	0.2	0.2	0.3	0.3	0.6
50/55	Trade, repair, hotels & restaurants	27.5	30.7	31.6	34.4	40.0	47.6	55.1	61.1	68.0	70.5
65/74	Finance, insurance, business services	0.0	0.0	0.0	0.0	0.0	0.0	0.0	0.0	0.0	0.0
	OTHER ACTIVITIES	3.2	..	..	3.9	3.5	4.7	5.3	5.5	8.4	7.2
01/99	**GRAND TOTAL**	**97.5**	**100.2**	**108.8**	**115.5**	**124.1**	**153.5**	**171.4**	**188.0**	**212.8**	**210.6**

Note: Foreign affiliates majority-owned by national firms.
Filiales étrangères détenues majoritairement par des firmes nationales.

Table 11B - Tableau 11B

TOTAL EXPORTS BY COUNTRY OF LOCATION IN THE MANUFACTURING SECTOR

EXPORTATIONS TOTALES PAR PAYS D'IMPLANTATION DANS L'INDUSTRIE MANUFACTURIÈRE

Country of location (UBO)	Total exports (Billions of USD) Exportations totales (Milliards de USD)					As a % of all countries En % du total des pays				
	1994	1995	1996	1997	1998	1994	1995	1996	1997	1998
All countries	100.4	110.2	120.3	135.1	131.7	100.0	100.0	100.0	100.0	100.0
Total OECD	..	..	..	..	..	..	..	..	..	..
United States	..	..	..	..	..	..	..	..	..	..
Canada	47.2	46.9	49.1	54.7	53.2	47.0	42.5	40.8	40.5	40.4
Mexico	13.4	14.7	18.1	20.8	22.2	13.4	13.3	15.0	15.4	16.8
Japan	3.7	4.8	6.0	4.9	3.6	3.7	4.3	4.9	3.6	2.7
Korea	0.6	0.7	1.1	0.9	0.6	0.6	0.6	0.9	0.6	0.4
Australia	1.6	1.6	2.2	2.0	1.6	1.6	1.4	1.8	1.5	1.2
New Zealand	0.0	0.1	0.1	0.1	0.1	0.0	0.1	0.1	0.1	0.1
Europe	22.4	26.3	26.1	29.8	30.2	22.3	23.9	21.7	22.0	22.9
European Union (15)	21.8	25.6	25.4	28.9	29.0	21.7	23.2	21.1	21.4	22.0
Austria	..	0.1	..	0.7	0.6	..	0.1	..	0.5	0.4
Belgium	1.7	2.2	2.1	2.1	1.9	1.7	2.0	1.7	1.6	1.4
Denmark	..	0.0	..	0.1	0.1	..	0.0	..	0.0	0.1
Finland	0.0	0.0	0.1	0.0	0.1	0.0	0.0	0.0	0.0	0.1
France	2.4	3.7	3.4	3.2	3.6	2.4	3.3	2.8	2.3	2.8
Germany	5.2	5.8	5.5	5.8	5.4	5.2	5.3	4.6	4.3	4.1
Greece	..	..	0.0	0.0	0.0	..	..	0.0	0.0	0.0
Ireland	1.1	1.0	1.0	1.2	1.5	1.1	0.9	0.8	0.9	1.1
Italy	0.9	1.2	1.3	1.6	1.4	0.9	1.1	1.1	1.2	1.0
Luxembourg	..	..	0.1	0.1	0.1	..	..	0.1	0.1	0.1
Netherlands	2.3	2.7	2.5	4.1	4.1	2.3	2.5	2.1	3.1	3.1
Portugal	0.0	0.1	0.1	0.1	0.1	0.0	0.1	0.0	0.1	0.0
Spain	0.7	0.8	0.9	0.9	0.9	0.6	0.7	0.7	0.7	0.6
Sweden	0.1	0.2	0.2	0.2	0.2	0.1	0.1	0.2	0.1	0.2
United Kingdom	7.3	7.8	7.7	8.9	9.2	7.3	7.0	6.4	6.6	7.0
Czech Republic	..	..	..	..	..	..	..	..	..	..
Hungary	..	..	..	..	..	..	..	..	..	..
Iceland	..	..	..	..	..	..	..	..	..	..
Norway	0.1	0.0	0.1	0.2	0.3	0.0	0.0	0.1	0.1	0.2
Poland	..	..	..	..	..	..	..	..	..	..
Slovak Republic	..	..	..	..	..	..	..	..	..	..
Switzerland	0.2	0.5	0.3	0.3	0.5	0.2	0.4	0.3	0.2	0.3
Turkey	0.1	0.1	..	..	..	0.0	0.1	..	..	..
Non-OECD Europe, of which:	..	..	..	..	..	..	..	..	..	..
Baltic countries	..	..	..	..	..	..	..	..	..	..
Bulgaria	..	..	..	..	..	..	..	..	..	..
Croatia	..	..	..	..	..	..	..	..	..	..
Romania	..	..	..	..	..	..	..	..	..	..
Russian Federation	..	..	..	..	..	..	..	..	..	..
Slovenia	..	..	..	..	..	..	..	..	..	..
Ukraine	..	..	..	..	..	..	..	..	..	..
Yugoslavia	..	..	..	..	..	..	..	..	..	..
Non-OECD Asia, of which:	8.4	11.3	13.4	15.4	13.4	8.4	10.2	11.2	11.4	10.2
China	..	0.8	0.8	1.5	1.5	..	0.7	0.6	1.1	1.1
Chinese Taipei	0.8	1.3	1.3	1.6	1.5	0.8	1.2	1.1	1.2	1.1
Hong Kong (China)	0.9	1.2	1.5	1.9	1.3	0.9	1.1	1.2	1.4	0.9
India	0.0	0.0	0.1	0.1	0.1	0.0	0.0	0.0	0.0	0.1
Indonesia	0.1	0.1	0.1	0.1	0.1	0.1	0.1	0.1	0.1	0.1
Malaysia	2.0	2.4	2.7	2.6	1.9	1.9	2.1	2.2	1.9	1.4
Philippines	0.2	0.8	1.0	1.3	1.4	0.2	0.7	0.8	0.9	1.0
Singapore	2.9	3.2	3.6	4.2	4.2	2.9	2.9	3.0	3.1	3.2
Thailand	0.7	0.9	1.3	1.2	1.0	0.7	0.8	1.0	0.9	0.8
Near and Middle East	0.1	0.1	..	0.2	0.3	0.1	0.1	..	0.2	0.2
Africa	0.2	0.2	..	0.3	0.2	0.2	0.2	..	0.2	0.2
Latin America, of which:	16.9	19.1	23.0	27.8	29.1	16.9	17.3	19.1	20.6	22.1
Argentina	0.3	0.5	0.5	0.9	1.1	0.3	0.4	0.4	0.7	0.8
Brazil	1.5	2.4	2.9	3.6	3.4	1.5	2.2	2.4	2.7	2.5
Chile	0.1	0.2	0.2	0.2	0.2	0.1	0.2	0.1	0.1	0.2

Note: Foreign affiliates majority-owned by national firms.
Filiales étrangères détenues majoritairement par des firmes nationales.

Table 12B - Tableau 12B

TOTAL IMPORTS BY INDUSTRY

IMPORTATIONS TOTALES PAR INDUSTRIE

ISIC Revision 3		Foreign affiliates *(Billions of USD)*									
		Filiales étrangères *(Milliards de USD)*									
		1989	1990	1991	1992	1993	1994	1995	1996	1997	1998
10/14	Mining & quarrying	1.0	0.9	0.9	0.8	0.8	1.0	0.9	1.1	1.1	1.1
15/37	**TOTAL MANUFACTURING**	**65.2**	**68.4**	**68.8**	**75.7**	**86.0**	**98.8**	**112.1**	**11.0**	**135.5**	**147.6**
15/16	Food, beverages, tobacco	0.9	1.2	1.2	1.3	1.7	1.9	2.3	12.0	3.2	4.8
17/19	Textiles, clothing, leather, footwear	1.0	1.4	1.1	1.3	0.9	0.8	0.7	1.0	1.1	1.4
20/22	Wood and paper products	3.7	3.6	3.1	3.4	3.5	3.5	3.8	3.3	3.6	4.2
20	Wood products	0.8	0.9	0.7	0.7	1.6	1.7	2.3	2.0	2.2	2.2
21/22	Paper, printing and publishing	3.0	2.7	2.5	2.7	1.9	1.8	1.6	1.3	1.4	2.0
23/25	Chemicals, Total	4.8	4.5	4.8	5.2	5.5	6.5	8.5	1.8	9.8	11.7
23	Refined petroleum, nuclear fuel	..	..	..	..	..	..	..	..	..	..
24/25	Chemicals, rubber & plastics prod.	4.8	4.5	4.8	5.2	5.5	6.5	8.5	1.8	9.8	11.7
24	Chemical products	4.0	3.8	4.1	4.4	4.4	5.1	6.5	0.0	7.8	9.7
2423	Pharmaceuticals	0.6	0.6	0.8	0.9	0.9	1.0	1.6	1.6	1.8	4.0
25	Rubber and plastics products	0.7	0.7	0.7	0.8	1.1	1.5	2.0	1.8	2.0	2.0
26	Non-metallic mineral products	0.4	0.5	0.4	0.4	0.5	0.6	0.7	0.9	0.8	1.0
27/28	Basic & fabricated metals	1.9	1.8	1.5	1.7	1.9	2.5	3.1	0.3	3.7	3.3
27	Basic metals	0.9	0.8	0.6	0.7	0.9	1.4	1.8	1.9	2.1	1.5
28	Fabricated metal products	1.0	1.0	0.9	1.0	1.0	1.1	1.3	1.6	1.6	1.7
29/32	Machinery, Total	21.6	23.3	24.3	26.9	31.0	37.2	41.4	23.0	54.0	59.2
29/30	Non-electrical machinery	12.6	12.8	13.5	14.5	17.3	21.4	24.3	1.8	30.5	34.2
29	Non-electrical machinery nec	..	..	..	..	..	..	..	..	..	..
30	Office and computing machinery	8.7	8.7	10.6	11.6	14.0	17.5	19.9	23.1	23.8	27.0
31/32	Electrical & electronic equipment	9.0	10.5	10.7	12.4	13.7	15.7	17.1	21.2	23.5	25.0
31	Electrical machinery nec	1.3	1.5	1.6	1.5	1.6	1.6	2.0	2.6	3.0	3.2
32	Radio, TV & communications eq.	7.7	8.9	9.2	10.9	12.1	14.1	15.1	18.7	20.4	21.8
33	Scientific instruments	1.7	1.7	1.9	2.2	2.1	2.1	3.3	2.8	2.9	2.9
34/35	Transportation equipment	28.7	29.8	29.8	32.5	37.9	42.9	47.4	188.0	55.4	57.8
34	Motor vehicles	27.4	28.1	27.9	31.1	36.4	41.4	45.9	50.0	53.4	55.5
35	Other transport equipment	1.2	1.7	1.8	1.4	1.5	1.6	1.5	1.8	2.1	2.3
351	Shipbuilding & repairing	..	..	..	..	..	..	..	..	..	..
353	Aircraft and spacecraft	..	..	..	..	..	..	..	..	..	..
36/37	Other manufacturing	..	..	..	..	..	..	..	..	..	..
40/45	Construction, electricity, gas & water	..	..	..	0.0	..	..	..	0.0	..	..
50/55	Trade, repair, hotels & restaurants	7.6	7.3	..	8.9	9.8	11.0	..	26.7	13.6	16.5
65/74	Finance, insurance, business services	0.0	0.0	0.0	0.0	0.0	0.0	0.0	0.0	0.0	..
	OTHER ACTIVITIES	..	..	12.1	12.6	..	..	..	185.8	..	..
01/99	**GRAND TOTAL**	**84.3**	**88.6**	**90.5**	**98.0**	**108.0**	**122.4**	**136.3**	**21.2**	**167.1**	**178.2**

Note: Foreign affiliates majority-owned by national firms.
Filiales étrangères détenues majoritairement par des firmes nationales.

Table 13B - Tableau 13B

TOTAL IMPORTS BY COUNTRY OF LOCATION IN THE MANUFACTURING SECTOR

IMPORTATIONS TOTALES PAR PAYS D'IMPLANTATION DANS L'INDUSTRIE MANUFACTURIÈRE

Country of location (UBO)	Total imports (Billions of USD) Importations totales (Milliards de USD)					As a % of all countries En % du total des pays				
	1994	1995	1996	1997	1998	1994	1995	1996	1997	1998
All countries	98.8	112.1	11.0	135.5	147.6	100.0	100.0	100.0	100.0	100.0
Total OECD	..	..	..	..	..	..	..	..	..	..
United States	..	..	..	..	..	..	..	..	..	..
Canada	46.3	51.1	5.4	55.4	58.5	46.9	45.6	49.0	40.9	39.6
Mexico	14.5	17.3	1.3	24.6	26.0	14.7	15.4	11.8	18.2	17.6
Japan	2.2	2.0	..	1.0	1.1	2.2	1.7	..	0.8	0.7
Korea	0.6	..	0.0	..	..	0.6	..	0.0	..	..
Australia	0.4	0.9	0.1	1.0	0.8	0.4	0.8	0.8	0.7	0.5
New Zealand	0.0	..	..	..	0.0	0.0	..	..	..	0.0
Europe	14.1	18.8	2.7	22.4	28.1	14.3	16.8	24.3	16.5	19.0
European Union (15)	13.0	18.5	2.5	21.7	25.5	13.2	16.5	22.9	16.0	17.2
Austria	..	..	0.0	0.2	0.2	..	..	0.0	0.1	0.1
Belgium	1.1	1.0	0.1	0.9	..	1.1	0.9	0.8	0.7	..
Denmark	..	0.1	..	..	..	..	0.1	..	..	..
Finland	0.1	0.1	0.0	0.1	0.1	0.1	0.1	0.2	0.1	0.1
France	1.4	2.7	0.5	2.5	2.9	1.5	2.4	4.8	1.9	2.0
Germany	2.9	3.8	..	4.4	4.4	3.0	3.4	..	3.2	3.0
Greece	0.0	0.0	..	..	0.0	0.0	0.0	..	..	0.0
Ireland	0.8	..	..	2.8	..	0.9	..	..	2.0	..
Italy	0.8	1.0	0.1	1.1	1.0	0.8	0.9	1.3	0.8	0.7
Luxembourg	..	..	..	..	0.1	..	..	..	..	0.1
Netherlands	0.8	1.1	0.4	1.9	1.9	0.8	1.0	3.4	1.4	1.3
Portugal	..	0.0	0.0	0.1	0.1	..	0.0	0.0	0.1	0.1
Spain	0.4	0.5	0.0	..	..	0.4	0.4	0.3	..	..
Sweden	0.1	0.2	0.1	0.4	0.5	0.1	0.2	0.5	0.3	0.4
United Kingdom	4.5	5.8	0.6	6.5	7.6	4.6	5.2	5.8	4.8	5.2
Czech Republic	..	..	..	..	..	..	..	..	..	..
Hungary	..	..	..	..	..	..	..	..	..	..
Iceland	..	..	..	..	..	..	..	..	..	..
Norway	..	0.0	0.0	0.0	0.0	..	0.0	0.0	0.0	0.0
Poland	..	..	..	..	..	..	..	..	..	..
Slovak Republic	..	..	..	..	..	..	..	..	..	..
Switzerland	0.2	0.2	0.1	0.5	0.5	0.2	0.2	1.2	0.4	0.3
Turkey	0.0	..	..	..	..	0.0	..	..	..	..
Non-OECD Europe, of which:	..	..	..	..	..	..	..	..	..	..
Baltic countries	..	..	..	..	..	..	..	..	..	..
Bulgaria	..	..	..	..	..	..	..	..	..	..
Croatia	..	..	..	..	..	..	..	..	..	..
Romania	..	..	..	..	..	..	..	..	..	..
Russian Federation	..	..	..	..	..	..	..	..	..	..
Slovenia	..	..	..	..	..	..	..	..	..	..
Ukraine	..	..	..	..	..	..	..	..	..	..
Yugoslavia	..	..	..	..	..	..	..	..	..	..
Non-OECD Asia, of which:	17.9	18.5	..	26.8	28.1	18.1	16.5	..	19.8	19.0
China	0.5	0.4	..	1.7	..	0.5	0.3	..	1.2	..
Chinese Taipei	1.3	1.2	0.0	1.3	1.1	1.3	1.1	0.0	1.0	0.7
Hong Kong (China)	..	1.1	0.3	1.6	1.9	..	1.0	2.5	1.2	1.3
India	..	0.0	..	..	0.1	..	0.0	..	..	0.0
Indonesia	..	..	0.0	0.0	0.0	..	..	0.0	0.0	0.0
Malaysia	2.5	3.0	..	5.1	5.6	2.5	2.7	..	3.8	3.8
Philippines	..	0.5	..	1.0	1.2	..	0.4	..	0.8	0.8
Singapore	11.0	11.5	0.0	15.1	14.1	11.1	10.3	0.4	11.1	9.6
Thailand	0.6	0.5	..	0.7	2.2	0.6	0.4	..	0.5	1.5
Near and Middle East	..	..	0.0	..	0.6	..	..	0.0	..	0.4
Africa	..	..	..	..	0.1	..	..	..	..	0.0
Latin America, of which:	17.3	20.2	2.1	28.2	30.5	17.5	18.0	19.2	20.8	20.6
Argentina	0.1	0.1	0.0	0.1	0.2	0.1	0.0	0.1	0.1	0.1
Brazil	1.8	1.6	0.5	2.3	2.7	1.8	1.4	4.4	1.7	1.8
Chile	0.2	0.2	0.0	0.1	..	0.2	0.2	0.1	0.1	..

Note: Foreign affiliates majority-owned by national firms.
Filiales étrangères détenues majoritairement par des firmes nationales.

Outward investments *Investissements sortants*

Table 14B - Tableau 14B

INTRA-FIRM EXPORTS BY INDUSTRY

EXPORTATIONS INTRA-FIRME PAR INDUSTRIE

ISIC Revision 3		**Foreign affiliates** *(Millions of USD)* **Filiales étrangères** *(Millions de USD)*									
		1989	1990	1991	1992	1993	1994	1995	1996	1997	1998
10/14	Mining & quarrying	228	223	241	327	362	466	232	265	323	244
15/37	**TOTAL MANUFACTURING**	**57 707**	**56 662**	**62 915**	**65 272**	**66 051**	**83 633**	**91 932**	**100 117**	**114 374**	**111 499**
15/16	Food, beverages, tobacco	1 465	1 076	1 329	1 776	1 890	1 948	2 123	1 954	2 031	2 389
17/19	Textiles, clothing, leather, footwear	307	361	659	690	305	371	471	420	697	1 064
20/22	Wood and paper products	952	1 127	1 188	1 307	1 709	1 971	2 277	2 263	2 379	2 339
20	Wood products	184	343	238	219	313	345	357	408	446	520
21/22	Paper, printing and publishing	768	784	950	1 088	1 396	1 626	1 920	1 855	1 933	1 819
23/25	Chemicals, Total	7 549	7 877	8 381	8 884	9 276	11 062	13 163	14 028	16 614	15 780
23	Refined petroleum, nuclear fuel	..	..	..	..	..	..	..	..	..	..
24/25	Chemicals, rubber & plastics prod.	7 549	7 877	8 381	8 884	9 276	11 062	13 163	14 028	16 614	15 780
24	Chemical products	6 500	6 622	7 212	7 539	7 589	9 189	11 116	12 005	14 368	13 528
2423	Pharmaceuticals	1 637	1 899	2 009	2 073	2 008	2 082	2 211	2 518	3 370	3 511
25	Rubber and plastics products	1 049	1 255	1 169	1 345	1 687	1 873	2 047	2 023	2 246	2 252
26	Non-metallic mineral products	468	456	505	310	366	352	469	742	613	632
27/28	Basic & fabricated metals	1 409	1 256	1 333	1 307	1 221	1 567	1 658	1 934	1 876	2 257
27	Basic metals	627	519	459	341	360	476	471	466	528	633
28	Fabricated metal products	782	737	874	966	862	1 090	1 186	1 469	1 348	1 624
29/32	Machinery, Total	18 123	17 926	20 375	20 526	21 205	27 433	33 841	35 596	40 440	38 609
29/30	Non-electrical machinery	10 837	9 966	11 862	11 719	11 652	13 035	16 077	17 284	20 641	18 622
29	Non-electrical machinery nec	..	..	..	..	..	..	..	..	..	..
30	Office and computing machinery	7 694	7 322	9 450	9 355	9 150	9 811	12 166	12 028	14 659	13 296
31/32	Electrical & electronic equipment	7 286	7 960	8 513	8 807	9 553	14 398	17 764	18 312	19 799	19 987
31	Electrical machinery nec	1 154	1 209	1 373	1 494	1 643	1 690	2 022	2 149	2 423	2 732
32	Radio, TV & communications eq.	6 132	6 751	7 140	7 313	7 910	12 708	15 742	16 163	17 375	17 255
33	Scientific instruments	3 232	3 204	3 940	4 445	4 123	4 197	5 281	6 092	6 292	6 205
34/35	Transportation equipment	23 841	23 024	24 586	25 323	25 286	34 119	31 774	35 996	42 488	41 093
34	Motor vehicles	23 635	22 802	24 324	25 064	25 051	33 744	31 310	35 499	42 177	40 659
35	Other transport equipment	206	222	262	260	235	375	465	498	311	434
351	Shipbuilding & repairing	..	..	..	..	..	..	..	..	..	..
353	Aircraft and spacecraft	..	..	..	..	..	..	..	..	..	..
36/37	Other manufacturing	..	..	..	..	..	..	..	..	..	..
40/45	Construction, electricity, gas & water	62	25	30	44	37	42	54	35	294	553
50/55	Trade, repair, hotels & restaurants	25 553	28 747	29 520	31 967	37 571	44 786	51 201	56 866	63 383	66 424
65/74	Finance, insurance, business services	0	23	29	21	18	13	15	22	19	25
	OTHER ACTIVITIES	2 499	..	..	3 107	2 789	3 753	4 187	4 055	6 671	5 632
01/99	**GRAND TOTAL**	**86 050**	**88 375**	**95 779**	**100 737**	**106 827**	**132 694**	**147 622**	**161 359**	**185 065**	**184 378**

Note: Foreign affiliates majority-owned by national firms.
Filiales étrangères détenues majoritairement par des firmes nationales.

Table 15B - Tableau 15B

INTRA-FIRM EXPORTS BY COUNTRY OF LOCATION IN THE MANUFACTURING SECTOR

EXPORTATIONS INTRA-FIRME PAR PAYS D'IMPLANTATION DANS L'INDUSTRIE MANUFACTURIÈRE

Country of location (UBO)	Intra-firm exports (Millions of USD) Exportations intra-firme (Millions de USD)					As a % of all countries En % du total des pays				
	1994	1995	1996	1997	1998	1994	1995	1996	1997	1998
All countries	83 633	91 932	100 117	114 374	111 499	100.0	100.0	100.0	100.0	100.0
Total OECD	..	..	..	..	..	..	..	..	..	..
United States	..	..	..	..	..	..	..	..	..	..
Canada	36 710	35 990	37 180	43 310	41 859	43.9	39.1	37.1	37.9	37.5
Mexico	12 132	12 861	16 261	18 453	20 196	14.5	14.0	16.2	16.1	18.1
Japan	3 513	4 568	5 749	4 697	3 454	4.2	5.0	5.7	4.1	3.1
Korea	..	612	1 034	..	476	..	0.7	1.0	..	0.4
Australia	1 364	1 351	1 958	1 835	1 469	1.6	1.5	2.0	1.6	1.3
New Zealand	41	77	94	87	43	0.0	0.1	0.1	0.1	0.0
Europe	19 626	23 509	22 665	26 029	26 601	23.5	25.6	22.6	22.8	23.9
European Union (15)	19 174	22 844	22 025	25 334	25 551	22.9	24.8	22.0	22.2	22.9
Austria	..	75	..	630	514	..	0.1	..	0.6	0.5
Belgium	1 542	2 081	1 940	2 007	1 784	1.8	2.3	1.9	1.8	1.6
Denmark	..	33	..	..	62	..	0.0	..	..	0.1
Finland	19	16	49	35	66	0.0	0.0	0.0	0.0	0.1
France	2 216	3 482	3 161	2 879	3 381	2.6	3.8	3.2	2.5	3.0
Germany	4 658	5 195	4 707	4 957	4 551	5.6	5.7	4.7	4.3	4.1
Greece	..	8	7	6	17	..	0.0	0.0	0.0	0.0
Ireland	961	917	774	1 009	1 294	1.1	1.0	0.8	0.9	1.2
Italy	773	933	1 058	1 474	1 227	0.9	1.0	1.1	1.3	1.1
Luxembourg	..	..	85	..	81	..	..	0.1	..	0.1
Netherlands	2 157	2 507	2 263	3 977	3 913	2.6	2.7	2.3	3.5	3.5
Portugal	22	..	48	57	53	0.0	..	0.0	0.0	0.0
Spain	497	589	629	646	687	0.6	0.6	0.6	0.6	0.6
Sweden	105	153	202	154	224	0.1	0.2	0.2	0.1	0.2
United Kingdom	6 256	6 702	6 477	7 374	7 698	7.5	7.3	6.5	6.4	6.9
Czech Republic	..	..	..	..	..	..	..	..	..	..
Hungary	..	..	..	..	..	..	..	..	..	..
Iceland	..	..	..	..	..	..	..	..	..	..
Norway	14	17	41	96	209	0.0	0.0	0.0	0.1	0.2
Poland	..	..	..	..	..	..	..	..	..	..
Slovak Republic	..	..	..	..	..	..	..	..	..	..
Switzerland	166	425	294	278	380	0.2	0.5	0.3	0.2	0.3
Turkey	15	83	..	..	..	0.0	0.1	..	..	..
Non-OECD Europe, of which:	..	..	..	..	..	..	..	..	..	..
Baltic countries	..	..	..	..	..	..	..	..	..	..
Bulgaria	..	..	..	..	..	..	..	..	..	..
Croatia	..	..	..	..	..	..	..	..	..	..
Romania	..	..	..	..	..	..	..	..	..	..
Russian Federation	..	..	..	..	..	..	..	..	..	..
Slovenia	..	..	..	..	..	..	..	..	..	..
Ukraine	..	..	..	..	..	..	..	..	..	..
Yugoslavia	..	..	..	..	..	..	..	..	..	..
Non-OECD Asia, of which:	7 245	9 907	11 796	13 786	11 546	8.7	10.8	11.8	12.1	10.4
China	..	737	698	1 010	1 034	..	0.8	0.7	0.9	0.9
Chinese Taipei	769	1 123	1 151	1 585	1 447	0.9	1.2	1.1	1.4	1.3
Hong Kong (China)	892	1 177	1 420	1 840	1 197	1.1	1.3	1.4	1.6	1.1
India	13	15	46	41	71	0.0	0.0	0.0	0.0	0.1
Indonesia	69	54	102	130	75	0.1	0.1	0.1	0.1	0.1
Malaysia	1 760	2 197	2 536	2 462	1 599	2.1	2.4	2.5	2.2	1.4
Philippines	144	665	816	1 151	1 230	0.2	0.7	0.8	1.0	1.1
Singapore	2 195	2 632	3 053	3 740	3 492	2.6	2.9	3.0	3.3	3.1
Thailand	583	596	819	893	856	0.7	0.6	0.8	0.8	0.8
Near and Middle East	54	47	..	219	240	0.1	0.1	..	0.2	0.2
Africa	174	154	..	214	200	0.2	0.2	..	0.2	0.2
Latin America, of which:	14 948	16 406	20 325	24 285	26 130	17.9	17.8	20.3	21.2	23.4
Argentina	..	371	396	788	927	..	0.4	0.4	0.7	0.8
Brazil	1 310	1 991	2 341	2 971	2 908	1.6	2.2	2.3	2.6	2.6
Chile	90	162	150	151	182	0.1	0.2	0.1	0.1	0.2

Note: Foreign affiliates majority-owned by national firms.
Filiales étrangères détenues majoritairement par des firmes nationales.

Outward investments   *Investissements sortants*

Table 16B - Tableau 16B

INTRA-FIRM IMPORTS BY INDUSTRY

IMPORTATIONS INTRA-FIRME PAR INDUSTRIE

| ISIC Revision 3 | | Foreign affiliates *(Millions of USD)* | | | | | | | | | |
| | | Filiales étrangères *(Millions de USD)* | | | | | | | | | |
		1989	1990	1991	1992	1993	1994	1995	1996	1997	1998
10/14	Mining & quarrying	336	332	345	372	345	358	441	556	598	628
15/37	**TOTAL MANUFACTURING**	**57 070**	**59 427**	**60 448**	**67 241**	**76 579**	**89 636**	**99 930**	**113 845**	**120 004**	**130 653**
15/16	Food, beverages, tobacco	789	1 076	1 000	1 132	1 218	1 467	1 573	1 628	2 232	3 326
17/19	Textiles, clothing, leather, footwear	761	1 093	829	935	530	372	337	673	867	1 158
20/22	Wood and paper products	1 659	1 727	1 489	1 566	1 629	1 844	1 719	1 650	1 878	2 253
20	Wood products	426	562	398	392	808	924	844	776	895	1 065
21/22	Paper, printing and publishing	1 233	1 165	1 091	1 174	821	920	875	874	983	1 188
23/25	Chemicals, Total	3 827	3 794	3 930	4 341	4 679	5 419	6 837	7 230	7 999	9 939
23	Refined petroleum, nuclear fuel	..	..	..	..	..	..	..	..	..	..
24/25	Chemicals, rubber & plastics prod.	3 827	3 794	3 930	4 341	4 679	5 419	6 837	7 230	7 999	9 939
24	Chemical products	3 231	3 215	3 410	3 775	3 826	4 307	5 377	5 896	6 525	8 405
2423	Pharmaceuticals	611	557	834	888	831	898	1 325	1 401	1 539	3 822
25	Rubber and plastics products	596	579	520	566	853	1 112	1 460	1 334	1 474	1 534
26	Non-metallic mineral products	253	274	251	227	317	477	504	767	640	758
27/28	Basic & fabricated metals	1 090	938	762	879	995	1 374	1 728	1 843	2 112	1 750
27	Basic metals	675	467	327	430	526	881	1 130	1 153	1 341	786
28	Fabricated metal products	415	471	435	449	469	494	598	690	770	964
29/32	Machinery, Total	19 963	21 396	22 451	24 950	28 190	35 061	38 041	46 598	47 968	53 092
29/30	Non-electrical machinery	11 698	11 953	12 825	13 663	15 674	20 046	21 774	26 491	26 021	29 632
29	Non-electrical machinery nec	..	..	..	..	..	..	..	..	..	..
30	Office and computing machinery	8 440	8 329	10 414	11 273	13 185	16 725	18 085	21 702	20 503	23 538
31/32	Electrical & electronic equipment	8 265	9 443	9 626	11 287	12 516	15 015	16 267	20 107	21 947	23 460
31	Electrical machinery nec	1 084	1 318	1 310	1 156	1 394	1 464	1 707	2 185	2 573	2 720
32	Radio, TV & communications eq.	7 181	8 125	8 316	10 132	11 122	13 550	14 561	17 923	19 373	20 740
33	Scientific instruments	1 574	1 566	1 745	2 005	1 969	1 919	3 132	2 645	2 596	2 675
34/35	Transportation equipment	26 799	27 169	27 442	30 521	36 050	40 857	45 218	49 784	52 842	54 621
34	Motor vehicles	26 261	26 410	26 605	29 806	35 277	39 987	44 425	48 737	51 713	53 600
35	Other transport equipment	537	758	837	715	773	870	792	1 047	1 128	1 022
351	Shipbuilding & repairing	..	..	..	..	..	..	..	..	..	..
353	Aircraft and spacecraft	..	..	..	..	..	..	..	..	..	..
36/37	Other manufacturing	..	..	..	..	..	..	..	..	..	..
40/45	Construction, electricity, gas & water	..	..	..	15	..	7	..	15	..	..
50/55	Trade, repair, hotels & restaurants	6 138	5 993	..	7 874	8 733	9 696	..	10 433	11 945	14 439
65/74	Finance, insurance, business services	1	3	2	2	1	0	1	1	1	..
	OTHER ACTIVITIES	..	..	9 524	9 386	..	7 505	7 525	8 538	..	..
01/99	**GRAND TOTAL**	**71 283**	**75 251**	**77 578**	**84 890**	**93 205**	**107 203**	**118 359**	**133 388**	**143 841**	**154 763**

Note: Foreign affiliates majority-owned by national firms.
Filiales étrangères détenues majoritairement par des firmes nationales.

Table 17B - Tableau 17B

INTRA-FIRM IMPORTS BY COUNTRY OF LOCATION IN THE MANUFACTURING SECTOR

IMPORTATIONS INTRA-FIRME PAR PAYS D'IMPLANTATION DANS L'INDUSTRIE MANUFACTURIÈRE

Country of location (UBO)	Intra-firm imports *(Millions of USD)* Importations intra-firme *(Millions de USD)*					As a % of all countries En % du total des pays				
	1994	1995	1996	1997	1998	1994	1995	1996	1997	1998
All countries	89 636	99 930	113 845	120 004	130 653	100.0	100.0	100.0	100.0	100.0
Total OECD	..	..	..	..	..	..	..	..	..	..
United States	..	..	..	..	..	..	..	..	..	..
Canada	40 551	44 670	45 642	47 879	50 142	45.2	44.7	40.1	39.9	38.4
Mexico	14 200	16 636	22 131	24 070	24 996	15.8	16.6	19.4	20.1	19.1
Japan	2 140	1 801	1 214	1 038	1 075	2.4	1.8	1.1	0.9	0.8
Korea	550	..	..	..	..	0.6	..	..	..	..
Australia	218	238	418	364	290	0.2	0.2	0.4	0.3	0.2
New Zealand	3	..	..	..	8	0.0	..	..	..	0.0
Europe	12 808	17 000	18 149	20 107	25 572	14.3	17.0	15.9	16.8	19.6
European Union (15)	11 823	16 785	17 737	19 452	23 039	13.2	16.8	15.6	16.2	17.6
Austria	..	..	..	115	124	..	..	..	0.1	0.1
Belgium	1 002	940	1 012	852	..	1.1	0.9	0.9	0.7	..
Denmark	..	57	93	..	..	..	0.1	0.1	..	..
Finland	97	109	110	133	125	0.1	0.1	0.1	0.1	0.1
France	1 299	2 345	2 178	2 254	2 644	1.4	2.3	1.9	1.9	2.0
Germany	2 744	3 550	3 265	3 945	3 963	3.1	3.6	2.9	3.3	3.0
Greece	0	0	..	..	0	0.0	0.0	..	..	0.0
Ireland	792	..	..	2 688	..	0.9	..	..	2.2	..
Italy	737	888	928	837	704	0.8	0.9	0.8	0.7	0.5
Luxembourg	..	..	..	..	100	..	..	..	..	0.1
Netherlands	700	924	780	1 617	1 670	0.8	0.9	0.7	1.3	1.3
Portugal	..	43	51	100	101	..	0.0	0.0	0.1	0.1
Spain	341	437	..	..	..	0.4	0.4	..	..	..
Sweden	116	131	149	404	510	0.1	0.1	0.1	0.3	0.4
United Kingdom	4 017	5 207	5 607	5 855	6 760	4.5	5.2	4.9	4.9	5.2
Czech Republic	..	..	..	..	..	..	..	..	..	..
Hungary	..	..	..	..	..	..	..	..	..	..
Iceland	..	..	..	..	..	..	..	..	..	..
Norway	..	15	..	37	37	..	0.0	..	0.0	0.0
Poland	..	..	..	..	..	..	..	..	..	..
Slovak Republic	..	..	..	..	..	..	..	..	..	..
Switzerland	119	166	..	444	450	0.1	0.2	..	0.4	0.3
Turkey	6	..	..	..	..	0.0	..	..	..	..
Non-OECD Europe, of which:	..	..	..	..	..	..	..	..	..	..
Baltic countries	..	..	..	..	..	..	..	..	..	..
Bulgaria	..	..	..	..	..	..	..	..	..	..
Croatia	..	..	..	..	..	..	..	..	..	..
Romania	..	..	..	..	..	..	..	..	..	..
Russian Federation	..	..	..	..	..	..	..	..	..	..
Slovenia	..	..	..	..	..	..	..	..	..	..
Ukraine	..	..	..	..	..	..	..	..	..	..
Yugoslavia	..	..	..	..	..	..	..	..	..	..
Non-OECD Asia, of which:	16 674	16 325	22 591	22 640	23 842	18.6	16.3	19.8	18.9	18.2
China	402	286	869	1 316	..	0.4	0.3	0.8	1.1	..
Chinese Taipei	1 264	1 152	1 379	1 326	1 041	1.4	1.2	1.2	1.1	0.8
Hong Kong (China)	..	928	888	1 041	1 489	..	0.9	0.8	0.9	1.1
India	..	21	31	..	57	..	0.0	0.0	..	0.0
Indonesia	..	..	..	26	29	..	..	..	0.0	0.0
Malaysia	2 501	2 978	3 930	5 088	5 425	2.8	3.0	3.5	4.2	4.2
Philippines	..	450	755	972	1 140	..	0.5	0.7	0.8	0.9
Singapore	10 194	9 757	13 827	..	10 983	11.4	9.8	12.1	..	8.4
Thailand	..	458	471	..	..	..	0.5	0.4	..	..
Near and Middle East	..	..	..	..	572	..	..	..	..	0.4
Africa	..	..	..	..	74	..	..	..	..	0.1
Latin America, of which:	16 730	19 269	25 004	27 287	29 086	18.7	19.3	22.0	22.7	22.3
Argentina	52	39	59	..	189	0.1	0.0	0.1	..	0.1
Brazil	1 660	1 503	1 845	2 096	2 538	1.9	1.5	1.6	1.7	1.9
Chile	19	23	14	28	..	0.0	0.0	0.0	0.0	..

Note: Foreign affiliates majority-owned by national firms.
Filiales étrangères détenues majoritairement par des firmes nationales.

Outward investments   *Investissements sortants*

Table 18B - Tableau 18B

GROSS OPERATING SURPLUS / EXCÉDENT BRUT D'EXPLOITATION

| | | **Foreign affiliates** *(Millions of USD)* | | | | | | | | | |
| | | **Filiales étrangères** *(Millions de USD)* | | | | | | | | | |
By industry (ISIC Rev. 3)		1989	1990	1991	1992	1993	1994	1995	1996	1997	1998
10/14	Mining & quarrying	442	289	339	586	394	654	1 232	1 231	1 414	618
15/37	**TOTAL MANUFACTURING**	**34 025**	**31 141**	**25 157**	**22 937**	**24 780**	**35 184**	**47 222**	**49 549**	**57 206**	**52 342**
15/16	Food, beverages, tobacco	2 928	3 787	4 257	5 031	5 720	5 653	6 379	5 962	7 373	6 362
17/19	Textiles, clothing, leather, footwear	358	318	181	250	224	128	269	245	349	387
20/22	Wood and paper products	1 668	1 440	740	636	572	1 020	2 067	1 682	2 061	1 617
20	Wood products	105	33	3	21	168	292	503	198	275	323
21/22	Paper, printing and publishing	1 563	1 407	737	615	404	728	1 564	1 484	1 786	1 294
23/25	Chemicals, Total	8 612	8 061	7 448	8 406	7 983	10 966	14 659	16 314	17 950	19 908
23	Refined petroleum, nuclear fuel	..	..	..	..	..	..	..	..	..	..
24/25	Chemicals, rubber & plastics prod.	8 612	8 061	7 448	8 406	7 983	10 966	14 659	16 314	17 950	19 908
24	Chemical products	7 713	7 479	6 833	7 698	7 131	9 829	12 906	14 741	16 440	18 517
2423	Pharmaceuticals	2 232	3 035	3 954	4 158	3 463	4 336	5 964	6 546	8 745	11 561
25	Rubber and plastics products	899	582	615	708	852	1 137	1 753	1 573	1 510	1 391
26	Non-metallic mineral products	749	540	343	202	308	470	739	711	629	661
27/28	Basic & fabricated metals	1 668	1 083	666	781	562	936	1 565	1 363	1 722	1 546
27	Basic metals	448	- 9	- 143	51	- 80	272	633	214	495	375
28	Fabricated metal products	1 221	1 092	810	730	642	663	932	1 149	1 227	1 171
29/32	Machinery, Total	9 710	9 206	5 867	2 664	3 533	7 630	12 255	14 205	15 649	11 091
29/30	Non-electrical machinery	7 249	7 498	4 287	1 389	1 180	3 882	6 847	9 118	9 405	8 088
29	Non-electrical machinery nec	1 369	668	162	- 388	373	1 275	1 723	2 237	2 658	2 374
30	Office and computing machinery	5 880	6 830	4 125	1 777	807	2 607	5 124	6 880	6 745	5 714
31/32	Electrical & electronic equipment	2 461	1 708	1 580	1 275	2 353	3 748	5 408	5 087	6 244	3 003
31	Electrical machinery nec	641	562	486	196	365	608	838	1 092	1 147	765
32	Radio, TV & communications eq.	1 819	1 146	1 094	1 080	1 988	3 139	4 570	3 995	5 097	2 238
33	Scientific instruments	1 495	1 655	1 310	1 577	1 509	1 586	2 639	2 403	2 060	2 332
34/35	Transportation equipment	5 723	3 817	2 902	1 929	2 721	5 112	4 486	4 058	6 686	5 472
34	Motor vehicles	5 698	3 650	2 808	1 768	2 551	4 804	4 064	3 730	6 283	4 976
35	Other transport equipment	25	166	94	161	169	307	422	328	403	496
351	Shipbuilding & repairing	..	..	..	..	..	..	..	..	..	..
353	Aircraft and spacecraft	..	..	..	..	..	..	..	..	..	..
36/37	Other manufacturing	1 115	1 235	1 443	1 458	1 650	1 685	2 165	2 605	2 727	2 966
40/45	Construction, electricity, gas & water	208	282	288	271	259	252	287	253	321	405
50/55	Trade, repair, hotels & restaurants	8 704	8 691	7 868	7 062	8 107	11 473	14 411	15 702	15 337	17 944
65/74	Finance, insurance, business services	17 542	17 432	16 614	18 995	19 816	24 184	32 553	34 984	43 967	49 514
	OTHER ACTIVITIES	11 220	15 420	15 725	13 098	13 212	9 349	12 954	17 198	22 267	16 133
01/99	**GRAND TOTAL**	**72 142**	**73 254**	**65 990**	**62 948**	**66 570**	**81 095**	**108 662**	**118 918**	**140 512**	**136 957**

Total manufacturing by country of location

	1989	1990	1991	1992	1993	1994	1995	1996	1997	1998
All countries	**34 025**	**31 141**	**25 157**	**22 937**	**24 780**	**35 184**	**47 222**	**49 549**	**57 206**	**52 342**
United States	..	..	..	..	..	..	..	..	..	..
Canada	4 862	2 912	1 748	1 370	1 953	3 940	5 662	4 893	6 097	5 376
Mexico	1 000	1 158	1 578	1 542	1 588	1 718	866	1 957	2 367	2 185
Japan	1 359	1 047	1 036	999	411	1 238	1 781	2 397	1 553	877
Europe	19 459	19 992	16 180	12 174	12 335	17 461	25 307	26 136	30 640	31 814
European Union (15)	18 719	19 206	15 489	11 553	11 500	16 206	23 645	24 357	28 640	30 011
Belgium	731	873	1 147	734	748	1 110	1 045	1 285	1 441	1 571
France	1 686	1 807	1 515	651	775	1 471	2 280	2 726	2 737	2 408
Germany	3 453	3 985	3 643	1 796	1 858	2 150	3 177	3 583	3 917	5 402
Italy	1 362	1 864	1 559	1 349	1 172	1 350	1 463	1 510	1 584	1 244
Netherlands	2 364	2 262	1 888	1 519	1 503	2 076	3 104	3 144	3 556	3 332
Spain	1 642	1 537	1 327	697	152	998	1 209	988	1 321	1 869
Sweden	256	221	76	- 89	55	193	653	383	825	816
United Kingdom	4 771	3 663	1 350	1 389	2 466	3 598	5 624	5 572	5 991	5 157
Switzerland	294	315	342	364	411	566	956	1 099	1 093	872
Australia and New Zealand	..	..	..	..	..	..	..	..	..	..
Asia (non-OECD)	2 484	3 021	2 542	3 054	3 290	4 629	5 842	8 026	8 547	6 174
Latin America	4 097	2 688	2 631	4 147	5 223	6 360	6 947	6 441	8 647	6 874

Note: Foreign affiliates majority-owned by national firms.
Filiales étrangères détenues majoritairement par des firmes nationales.

UNITED STATES

A. Inward investments

Source

The data are prepared by the Bureau of Economic Analysis, US Department of Commerce. Most of the data are based on annual and benchmark surveys which cover US business enterprises in which a foreign person owned (or controlled) a direct (or indirect) interest of 10% or more at the end of the US business enterprise's fiscal year. The last benchmark surveys were conducted in 1987, 1992 and 1997. They provide benchmarks for deriving current universe estimates of direct investment from sample data collected in non-benchmark years. They are published every year in *Foreign Direct Investment in the United States*. The Bureau of Economic Analysis also publishes a limited amount of data on majority-owned affiliates (those in which the foreign parents ownership share exceeds 50%). The tables in this publication use data for all affiliates. The data are electronically released annually and are also available on the Web site of the Bureau of Economic Analysis (www.bea.doc.gov).

The data on technological payments and receipts (royalties and license fees) and on the foreign direct investment position are from quarterly surveys conducted by the Bureau of Economic Analysis.

National totals: except for R&D variables, no data from enterprises on the other variables included in this report are available for the United States.

- *R&D expenditure:* data are extracted from the OECD's ANBERD database.

- *Number of researchers:* data come from the OECD's ANRSE database and are converted from ISIC Revision 2 to ISIC Revision 3. The ratio for number of researchers is overestimated, because ANRSE provides only data for researchers, whereas data for the foreign affiliates refer to total R&D employment (including support staff).

Industrial classification

For all variables, the data are classified according to the principal industrial activity of the affiliate.

Up to 1996, the industrial classification used is ISI (national classification), converted to ISIC Revision 3. The following notes apply to all variables up to 1996 and to *Technological payments, Technological receipts* and *Stock of foreign direct investment* for all years:

- *Mining and quarrying* (10/14) excludes *Petroleum and natural gas extraction* (11), which is included in *Other activities* (01/05; 60/64; 75/99).

- *Total manufacturing* (15/37) excludes *Refined petroleum and coal products* (23), which is included in *Other activities* (01/05; 60/64; 75/99).

- *Food, beverages, tobacco* (15/16) excludes *Tobacco* (16), which is included in *Other manufacturing* (36/37).

- *Textiles, clothing, leather, footwear* (17/19) excludes *Leather* (191), which is included in *Other manufacturing* (36/37).

- *Wood and paper products* (20/22) and *Wood products* (20) include *Furniture* (361), which should be included in *Other manufacturing* (36/37).

- *Chemicals, total* (23/25) excludes *Refined petroleum and coal products* (23), which is included in *Other activities* (01/05; 60/64; 75/99).

- *Refined petroleum and coal products* (23) is not available separately. It is included in *Other activities* (01/05; 60/64; 75/99).

- *Shipbuilding* (351) and *Aircraft and spacecraft* (353) are not available separately.

- *Other manufacturing* (36/37) excludes *Furniture* (361); includes *Tobacco* (16) and *Leather* (191).

- *Construction, electricity gas & water* (40/45) excludes *Electricity, gas & water* (40/41), which is included in *Other activities* (01/05; 60/64; 75/99).

- *Trade, repair, hotels and restaurants* (50/55) excludes *Hotels* (551), *Petroleum wholesale trade* (5141) and *Gasoline service stations* (505), which are included in *Other activities* (01/05; 60/64; 75/99).

- *Finance, insurance, real estate and business services* (65/74) excludes *Business services* (71/74), which is included in *Other activities* (01/05; 60/64; 75/99).

- *Other activities* (01/05; 60/64; 75/99) includes all Petroleum activities (extraction, manufacturing, trade, storage and transportation), *Electricity, gas and water* (40/41), *Hotels* (551), *Business services* (71/74).

From 1997 onwards, data are classified according to NAICS (North American Industrial Classification System), which provides a better comparability with ISIC Revision 3. The following notes apply to all variables as from 1997 (except *Technological payments, Technological receipts* and *Stock of foreign direct investment*):

- *Total manufacturing* (15/37) excludes *Publishing* (221) *and Reproduction of recorded media* (223), which are included in *Other activities* (01/05; 60/64; 75/99).

- *Paper, printing and publishing* (21/22) excludes *Publishing* (221) and *Reproduction of recorded media (223),* which are included in *Other activities* (01/05; 60/64; 75/99).

- *Refined petroleum and coal products* (23) excludes *Processing of nuclear fuel* (233).

- *Chemical products* (24) includes part of *Processing of nuclear fuel* (233).

- *Basic metals* (27) includes part of *Processing of nuclear fuel* (233) and *Recycling of metal waste and scrap* (371).

- *Fabricated metal products* (28) includes part of *Weapons and ammunition* (2927).

- *Non-electrical machinery nec* (29) excludes *Weapons and ammunition* (2927) and parts of *Domestic appliances nec* (293); includes parts of *Office, accounting and computing machinery* (30) and parts of *Optical instruments and photographic equipment* (332).

- *Electrical machinery nec* (31) includes parts of *Domestic appliances nec* (293).

- *Scientific instruments* (33) excludes *Optical instruments and photographic equipment* (332).

- *Aircraft and spacecraft* (353) includes part of *Weapons and ammunition* (2927).

- *Other manufacturing* (36/37) excludes *Recycling* (37).

- *Trade, repair, hotels and restaurants* (50/55) excludes *Repair of motor vehicles* (502), *Repair of motorcycles* (part of 504) and *Repair of personal and household goods* (526); includes part of *Recycling of non-metal waste and scrap* (372).

- *Finance, insurance, real estate and business services* (65/74) excludes *Repair and maintenance of computers* (725), which is included in *Other activities* (01/05; 60/64; 75/99).

- *Other activities* (01/; 60/64; 75/99) includes *Publishing* (221), *Reproduction of recorded media* (223), *Repair of motor vehicles* (502), *Repair of motorcycles* (part of 504), *Repair of personal and household goods* (526) and *Repair and maintenance of computers* (725).

Variables

- *Number of enterprises* is defined as the number of non-bank affiliates, which means the number of business enterprises located in the United States which are directly or indirectly owned or controlled by a foreign person to the extent of 10% or more of its securities for an incorporated business enterprise or an equivalent interest for an unincorporated business enterprise, including a branch. Prior to 1997, the data cover affiliates with total assets, sales, or net income above USD 1 million. Beginning in 1997, this threshold was raised to USD 3 million. Each report covers a fully consolidated US business enterprise, which may consist of a number of individual companies. The number of companies consolidated is substantially higher than the number of affiliates. For example, in 1997, for non-bank affiliates, the figures were 34 900 and 10 090, respectively. The number of establishments, which is not available from the benchmark survey, would be even higher.

- *Number of employees* consists of the number of full-time and part-time employees on the payroll at the end of the fiscal year.

- *Turnover* is defined as sales of goods and services, plus investment income included in "sales or gross operating revenues" in the income statement (mostly finance and insurance affiliates).

- *Value added* is called gross product and is defined as the sum of employee compensation, profit-type return, net interest paid, indirect business taxes and capital consumption allowance.

- *Compensation of employees* consists of wages and salaries of employees and employer expenditures for all employee benefit plans.

- Up to 1996, *R&D expenditure* is defined as the amount of R&D funded by the affiliate. Beginning with 1997, it is defined as the amount of R&D performed by the affiliate.

- *Number of researchers* is called R&D employment, and consists of all employees engaged in research and development, including managers, scientists, engineers, and other professional and technical employees.

- *Gross fixed capital formation* is defined as expenditure for new plant and equipment.

- *Total exports* is defined as the US merchandise exports shipped by affiliates. It excludes exports of services.

- *Total imports* is defined as the US merchandise imports shipped to affiliates. It excludes imports of services.

- *Intra-firm exports* is defined as the US exports shipped by affiliates a) to the foreign parent company + b) to foreign affiliates. For *Total manufacturing* by investing country, a) only. Exports of services are excluded.

- *Intra-firm imports* is defined as the imports shipped to affiliates a) from the foreign parent company + b) from foreign affiliates. For *Total manufacturing* by investing country, a) only. Imports of services are excluded.

- *Gross operating surplus* is called net income, and consists of the difference between total income and total costs and expenses of affiliate.

- *Technological payments:* it is defined as US affiliates' payments to the parent group for royalties and licence fees.

- *Technological receipts:* it is defined as US affiliates' receipts from the parent group for royalties and licence fees.

Geographical breakdown

For *Technological payments, Technological receipts* and *Stock of foreign direct investment*, the breakdown of *Total manufacturing* is by country of foreign parent. For all other variables, the breakdown is by country of the ultimate beneficial owner.

Data for the Asia (non-OECD) area actually correspond to those of Asia-Pacific excluding Japan and Australia. Data for Latin America include those for Mexico.

Prior to 1995, the European Union consists of its 12 former member states.

B. Outward investments

Source

The data are prepared by the Bureau of Economic Analysis, US Department of Commerce. Most of the data are based on annual and benchmark surveys which cover all non-bank affiliates of non-bank US parents. All foreign affiliates in which the combined direct and indirect ownership interest of all US parents exceeds 10% are covered by the survey. However, in order to reduce respondent burden, most of the detailed data are only collected on majority-owned affiliates (those affiliates in which the combined direct and indirect ownership interest of all US parents exceeds 50%). The tables in this publication use data for majority-owned affiliates. The data are published annually in *U.S. Direct Investment Abroad.* and released electronically. They are also available on the Web site of the Bureau of Economic Analysis (www.bea.doc.gov).

National totals: except for *R&D expenditure*, no data from enterprises on the other variables included in this report are available for the United States.

- For *R&D expenditure*, data are extracted from the OECD's ANBERD database.

Industrial classification

For all variables, the data are classified according to the principal industrial activity of the affiliate.

The industrial classification used is ISI (national classification), converted to ISIC Revision 3. The following notes apply to all years and variables:

- *Mining and quarrying* (10/14) excludes *Petroleum and natural gas extraction* (11), which is included in *Other activities* (01/05; 60/64; 75/99).

- *Total manufacturing* (15/37) excludes *Refined petroleum and coal products* (23), which is included in *Other activities* (01/05; 60/64; 75/99).

- *Food, beverages, tobacco* (15/16) excludes *Tobacco* (16), which is included in *Other manufacturing* (36/37).

- *Textiles, clothing, leather, footwear* (17/19) excludes *Leather* (191), which is included in *Other manufacturing* (36/37).

- *Wood and paper products* (20/22) and *Wood products* (20) include *Furniture* (361), which should be included in *Other manufacturing* (36/37).

- *Chemicals, total* (23/25) excludes *Refined petroleum and coal products* (23), which is included in *Other activities* (01/05; 60/64; 75/99).

- *Refined petroleum and coal products* (23) is not available separately. It is included in *Other activities* (01/05; 60/64; 75/99).

- *Shipbuilding* (351) and *Aircraft and spacecraft* (353) are not available separately.

- *Other manufacturing* (36/37) excludes *Furniture* (361); includes *Tobacco* (16) and *Leather* (191).

- *Construction, electricity gas & water* (40/45) excludes *Electricity, gas & water* (40/41), which is included in *Other activities* (01/05; 60/64; 75/99).

- *Trade, repair, hotels and restaurants* (50/55) excludes *Hotels* (551), *Petroleum wholesale trade* (5141) and *Gasoline service stations* (505), which are included in *Other activities* (01/05; 60/64; 75/99).

- *Finance, insurance, real estate and business services* (65/74) excludes *Business services* (71/74), which is included in *Other activities* (01/05; 60/64; 75/99).

- *Other activities* (01/05; 60/64; 75/99) includes all Petroleum activities (extraction, manufacturing, trade, storage and transportation), *Electricity, gas and water* (40/41), *Hotels* (551), *Business services* (71/74).

Variables

- *Number of employees* consists of the number of full-time and part-time employees on the payroll at the end of the fiscal year.

- *Turnover* is defined as sales of goods and services, plus investment income included in "sales or gross operating revenues" in the income statement (mostly finance and insurance affiliates).

- *Value added* is called gross product, and is defined as the sum of employee compensation, profit-type return, net interest paid, indirect business taxes and capital consumption allowance.

- *Compensation of employees* consists of wages and salaries of employees and employer expenditures for all employee benefit plans.

- *R&D expenditure* is defined as expenditures for R&D performed by affiliates. It includes R&D performed by affiliates for themselves or for others.

- *Total exports* is defined as the US exports shipped to affiliates.

- *Total imports* is defined as the US imports shipped by affiliates.

- *Intra-firm exports* is defined as the US exports shipped to affiliates by US parents.

- *Intra-firm imports* is defined as the US imports shipped by affiliates to US parents.

- *Gross operating surplus* is called net income, and consists of the difference between total income and total costs and expenses of affiliate.

ÉTATS-UNIS

A. *Investissements entrants*

Source

Les données émanent du Bureau d'analyse économique du *US Department of Commerce*. La plupart des données sont basées sur des enquêtes annuelles et de référence qui couvrent les entreprises américaines dans lesquelles une personne étrangère possède une participation directe (ou indirecte) de 10 % ou plus à la fin de l'exercice (ou exerce un contrôle équivalent). Les dernières enquêtes de référence ont été menées en 1987, 1992 et 1997. Elles fournissent des repères permettant de faire des estimations d'investissements directs à partir de données recueillies par sondage lors des années autres que celles de référence. Elles sont publiées chaque année dans *Foreign Direct Investment in the United States*. Le Bureau d'analyse économique publie également un nombre limité de données sur les filiales majoritaires (celles dans lesquelles la société mère détient plus de 50 % des parts). Les tableaux de cette publication utilisent des données qui concernent toutes les filiales. Les données sont disponibles annuellement sous forme électronique et sur le site Internet du Bureau d'analyse économique (www.bea.doc.gov).

Les données sur les paiements et recettes technologiques (redevances et droits de licence), ainsi que celles concernant les stocks d'investissements directs sont tirées d'enquêtes trimestrielles menées par le Bureau d'analyse économique.

Totaux nationaux : à l'exception des variables relatives à la R-D, aucune donnée collectée au niveau de l'entreprise n'est disponible pour les États-Unis pour les variables contenues dans cette publication.

- *Dépenses de R-D* : les données sont extraites de la base de données ANBERD de l'OCDE.

- *Nombre de chercheurs* : les données ont été extraites de la base de données ANRSE de l'OCDE, et sont converties de la CITI révision 2 vers la CITI révision 3. Les ratios relatifs au nombre de chercheurs sont surestimés, puisque ANRSE fournit des données sur les chercheurs, tandis que les données des filiales font référence à l'emploi total de R-D (y compris le personnel de soutien).

Classification industrielle

Pour toutes les variables, les données sont classées selon l'activité industrielle principale de l'entreprise affiliée.

Jusqu'en 1996, la classification industrielle utilisée pour les tableaux américains est la classification nationale (ISI) adaptée pour correspondre à la CITI révision 3. Les notes suivantes s'appliquent à toutes les variables jusqu'en 1996 (et au-delà pour les *Paiements* et *Recettes technologiques* et le *Stock d'investissement direct étranger*) :

- *Activités extractives* (10/14) exclut *Extraction de pétrole et de gaz naturel* (11) qui est inclus dans *Autres activités* (01/05 ; 60/64 ; 75/99).

- *Activités de fabrication* (15/37) exclut *Raffineries de pétrole et dérivés du charbon* (23) qui est inclus dans *Autres activités* (01/05 ; 60/64 ; 75/99).

- *Produits alimentaires, boissons, tabac* (15/16) exclut le *Tabac* (16) qui est inclus dans *Autres activités de fabrication* (36/37).

- *Textiles, habillement, cuirs, chaussures* (17/19) exclut les *Cuirs* (191), inclus dans *Autres activités de fabrication* (36/37).

- *Articles en bois et en papier* (20/22) et *Articles en bois* (20) incluent *Meubles* (361) qui devrait être inclus dans *Autres activités de fabrication* (36/37).

- *Produits chimiques* (23/25) exclut *Raffineries de pétrole et dérivés du charbon* (23) qui est inclus dans *Autres activités* (01/05 ; 60/64 ; 75/99).

- *Raffineries de pétrole et dérivés du charbon* (23) n'est pas disponible séparément. Est inclus dans *Autres activités* (01/05 ; 60/64 ; 75/99).

- *Construction navale* (351) et *Construction aéronautique et spatiale* (353) ne sont pas disponibles séparément.

- *Autres activités de fabrication* (36/37) exclut *Meubles* (361) ; inclut *Tabac* (16) et *Cuirs* (191).

- *Construction, électricité, gaz et eau* (40/45) exclut *Electricité, gaz et eau* (40/41) qui est inclus dans *Autres activités* (01/05 ; 60/64 ; 75/99).

- *Commerce, réparation, hôtels et restaurants* (50/55) exclut *Hôtels* (551), *Commerce de gros de combustibles* (5141) et *Stations de distribution de carburants* (505) qui sont inclus dans *Autres activités* (01/05 ; 60/64 ; 75/99).

- *Finance, assurance, immobilier et services aux entreprises* (65/74) exclut *Activités de service aux entreprises* (71/74) qui est inclus dans *Autres activités* (01/05 ; 60/64 ; 75/99).

- *Autres activités* (01/05 ; 60/64 ; 75/99) inclut toutes les activités concernant le pétrole (extraction, fabrication, commerce, stockage et transport), *Electricité, gaz et eau* (40/41), *Hôtels* (551), *Services aux entreprises* (71/74).

A partir de 1997, les données sont classées selon la NAICS (North American Industrial Classification System), qui fournit une meilleure comparabilité avec la CITI révision 3. Les notes suivantes s'appliquent à toutes les variables à partir de 1997 (sauf pour les *Paiements* et les *Recettes technologiques* et le *Stock d'investissement direct étranger*) :

- Le *Total manufacturier* (15/37) exclut *Edition* (221) et *Reproduction de supports enregistrés* (223), qui sont inclus dans *Autres activités* (01/05 ; 60/64 ; 75/99).

- *Papier, imprimerie, édition* (21/22) exclut *Edition* (221) et *Reproduction de supports enregistrés* (223), qui sont inclus dans *Autres activités* (01/05 ; 60/64 ; 75/99).

- *Raffineries de pétrole et dérivés du charbon* (23) exclut *Traitement de combustibles nucléaires* (233).

- *Produits chimiques* (24) comprend une partie de *Traitement de combustibles nucléaires* (233).

- *Métallurgie* (27) comprend une partie de *Traitement de combustibles nucléaires* (233) et *Récupération de matières métalliques recyclables* (371).

- *Travail des métaux* (28) comprend une partie de *Fabrication d'armes et de munitions* (2927).

- *Machines et matériels non électriques nca* (29) exclut *Fabrication d'armes et de munitions* (2927) et des éléments de *Fabrication d'appareils domestiques* (293) ; comprend des éléments de *Machines de bureau et ordinateurs* (30) et des éléments de *Fabrication de matériels optique et photographique* (332).

- *Machines électriques nca* (31) comprend des éléments de *Fabrication d'appareils domestiques* (293).

- *Instruments scientifiques* (33) exclut *Fabrication de matériels optique et photographique* (332).

- *Construction aéronautique et spatiale* (353) comprend une partie de *Fabrication d'armes et de munitions* (2927).

- *Autres industries manufacturières* (36/37) exclut Récupération (37).

- *Commerce, réparation, hôtels et restaurants* (50/55) exclut *Réparation de véhicules automobiles* (502), *Réparation de motocycles* (partie de 504) et *Réparation d'articles personnels et domestiques* (526) ; comprend une partie de *Récupération de matières non métalliques recyclables* (372).

- *Finance, assurance, immobilier et services aux entreprises* (65/74) exclut *Entretien et réparation de matériel informatique* (725), qui est compris dans *Autres activités* (01/05; 60/64; 75/99).

- *Autres activités* (01/; 60/64; 75/99) comprend *Edition* (221), *Réparation de véhicules automobiles* (502), *Réparation de motocycles* (partie de 504), *Réparation d'articles personnels et domestiques* (526) et *Entretien et réparation de matériel informatique* (725).

Variables

- Le *Nombre d'entreprises* est défini comme le nombre d'entreprises affiliées du secteur non bancaire situées aux États-Unis, qui appartiennent directement ou indirectement ou qui sont sous le contrôle d'une personne étrangère à hauteur de 10 % ou plus de ses titres pour une entreprise constituée en société ou avec une participation équivalente pour une entreprise non constituée en société, y compris une succursale. Avant 1997, les données couvrent les filiales de plus de USD 1 million d'actifs, ventes ou de revenus nets. A partir de 1997, ce seuil passe à USD 3 millions. Chaque rapport couvre un groupe américain complet qui peut comprendre plusieurs sociétés individuelles. Le nombre de sociétés membres du groupe est beaucoup plus élevé que le nombre de sociétés affiliées. Par exemple, en 1997, pour les entreprises affiliées du secteur non bancaire, les chiffres étaient respectivement de 34 900 et 10 090. Le nombre d'établissements, qui n'est pas disponible dans l'enquête de référence, serait encore plus élevé.

- Le *Nombre de salariés* représente le nombre de personnes employées à plein temps et à temps partiel à la fin de l'exercice budgétaire.

- Le *Chiffre d'affaires* est défini en tant que ventes de biens et services, plus les revenus d'investissement inclus dans les "ventes ou recettes brutes d'exploitation" de la déclaration de revenus (filiales du secteur de la finance ou des assurances pour la plupart).

- La *Valeur ajoutée* est appelée produit brut, et est définie comme la somme de la rémunération des salariés, des bénéfices, des intérêts nets payés, des impôts indirects sur les sociétés et des provisions pour amortissement.

- Les *Salaires et charges sociales* se composent des traitements et salaires des personnes employées et des dépenses patronales pour tous les régimes de prestations sociales.

- Jusqu'en 1996, les *Dépenses de R-D* sont définies comme le montant de R-D financé par les filiales. A partir de 1997, elles sont définies commes les dépenses pour la R-D exécutées par les filiales américaines.

- Le *Nombre de chercheurs* est appelé emploi de R-D et comprend tous les salariés travaillant dans la recherche et développement, y compris les dirigeants, scientifiques, ingénieurs et autres professionnels et techniciens.

- La *Formation brute de capital fixe* est définie comme les dépenses pour de nouveaux équipements et installations.

- Les *Exportations totales* sont définies comme les exportations américaines de marchandises expédiées par les entreprises affiliées. Sont exclues les exportations de services.

- Les *Importations totales* sont définies comme les importations américaines de marchandises expédiées aux entreprises affiliées. Sont exclues les importations de services.

- Les *Exportations intra-firme* sont définies comme les exportations américaines à destination a) du groupe parent étranger + b) des filiales étrangères. Pour le total manufacturier par pays investisseur, a) uniquement. Sont exclues les exportations de services.

- Les *Importations intra-firme* sont définies comme les importations américaines en provenance a) du groupe parent étranger + b) des filiales étrangères. Pour le total manufacturier par pays investisseur, a) uniquement. Sont exclues les importations de services.

- L'*Excédent brut d'exploitation* est appelé aussi revenu net et résulte de la différence entre le revenu total et l'ensemble des coûts et dépenses de l'entreprise affiliée.

- Les *Paiements technologiques* sont définis comme les paiements de la filiale américaine au groupe parent au titre des redevances et droits de licence.

- Les *Recettes technologiques* sont définies comme les recettes de la filiale américaine provenant du groupe parent au titre des redevances et droits de licence.

Ventilation géographique

Pour les *Paiements technologiques,* les *Recettes technologiques* et le *Stock d'investissement direct étranger*, la ventilation du *Total manufacturier* s'effectue par pays du parent étranger. Pour toutes les autres variables, la ventilation se fait par pays du bénéficiaire ultime de l'investissement.

Les données pour la zone Asie hors OCDE correspondent en fait à celles de l'Asie-Pacifique, à l'exclusion du Japon et de l'Australie. Les données de la zone Amérique latine comprennent celles du Mexique.

Avant 1995, l'Union européenne ne comprend que les 12 anciens États membres.

B. Investissements sortants

Source

Les données émanent du Bureau d'analyse économique du *US Department of Commerce*. La plupart des données sont basées sur des enquêtes annuelles et de référence qui couvrent toutes les filiales non bancaires des sociétés mères américaines du secteur non bancaire. Toutes les filiales étrangères dans lesquelles la participation directe et indirecte combinée de toutes les sociétés mères américaines excède 10 % sont couvertes par l'enquête. Néanmoins, afin de réduire la tâche des répondants, la plupart des données détaillées ne sont collectées que pour les filiales majoritaires (celles pour lesquelles la participation directe et indirecte combinée de toutes les sociétés mères américaines excède 50 %). Les tableaux de cette publication utilisent des données qui concernent les filiales majoritaires. Les données sont publiées chaque année dans *Foreign Direct Investment Abroad* et sous forme électronique, ainsi que sur le site Internet du Bureau d'analyse économique (www.bea.doc.gov).

Totaux nationaux : à l'exception des *Dépenses de R-D*, aucune donnée collectée au niveau de l'entreprise n'est disponible pour les États-Unis pour les variables contenues dans cette publication.

- *Dépenses de R-D* : les données sont extraites de la base de données ANBERD de l'OCDE.

Classification industrielle

Pour toutes les variables, les données sont classées selon l'activité industrielle principale de l'entreprise affiliée.

La classification industrielle utilisée pour les tableaux américains est la classification nationale (ISI) adaptée pour correspondre à la CITI révision 3. Les notes suivantes s'appliquent à toutes les variables et à toutes les années :

- *Activités extractives* (10/14) exclut *Extraction de pétrole et de gaz naturel* (11) qui est inclus dans *Autres activités* (01/05 ; 60/64 ; 75/99).

- *Activités de fabrication* (15/37) exclut *Raffineries de pétrole et dérivés du charbon* (23) qui est inclus dans *Autres activités* (01/05 ; 60/64 ; 75/99).

- *Produits alimentaires, boissons, tabac* (15/16) exclut le *Tabac* (16) qui est inclus dans *Autres activités de fabrication* (36/37).

- *Textiles, habillement, cuirs, chaussures* (17/19) exclut les *Cuirs* (191), inclus dans *Autres activités de fabrication* (36/37).

- *Articles en bois et en papier* (20/22) et *Articles en bois* (20) incluent *Meubles* (361) qui devrait être inclus dans *Autres activités de fabrication* (36/37).

- *Produits chimiques* (23/25) exclut *Raffineries de pétrole et dérivés du charbon* (23) qui est inclus dans *Autres activités* (01/05 ; 60/64 ; 75/99).

- *Raffineries de pétrole et dérivés du charbon* (23) n'est pas disponible séparément. Est inclus dans *Autres activités* (01/05 ; 60/64 ; 75/99).

- *Construction navale* (351) et *Construction aéronautique et spatiale* (353) ne sont pas disponibles séparément.

- *Autres activités de fabrication* (36/37) exclut *Meubles* (361) ; inclut *Tabac* (16) et *Cuirs* (191).

- *Construction, électricité, gaz et eau* (40/45) exclut *Electricité, gaz et eau* (40/41) qui est inclus dans *Autres activités* (01/05 ; 60/64 ; 75/99).

- *Commerce, réparation, hôtels et restaurants* (50/55) exclut *Hôtels* (551), *Commerce de gros de combustibles* (5141) et *Stations de distribution de carburants* (505) qui sont inclus dans *Autres activités* (01/05 ; 60/64 ; 75/99).

- *Finance, assurance, immobilier et services aux entreprises* (65/74) exclut *Activités de service aux entreprises* (71/74) qui est inclus dans *Autres activités* (01/05 ; 60/64 ; 75/99).

- *Autres activités* (01/05 ; 60/64 ; 75/99) inclut toutes les activités concernant le pétrole (extraction, fabrication, commerce, stockage et transport), *Electricité, gaz et eau* (40/41), *Hôtels* (551), *Services aux entreprises* (71/74).

Variables

- Le *Nombre de salariés* représente le nombre de personnes employées à plein temps et à temps partiel à la fin de l'exercice budgétaire.

- Le *Chiffre d'affaires* est défini en tant que ventes de biens et services, plus les revenus d'investissement inclus dans les "ventes ou recettes brutes d'exploitation" de la déclaration de revenus (filiales du secteur de la finance ou des assurances pour la plupart).

- La *Valeur ajoutée* est appelée produit brut, et est définie comme la somme de la rémunération des salariés, des bénéfices, des intérêts nets payés, des impôts indirects sur les sociétés et des provisions pour amortissement.

- Les *Salaires et charges sociales* se composent des traitements et salaires des personnes employées et des dépenses patronales pour tous les régimes de prestations sociales.

- Les *Dépenses de R-D* sont définies comme les dépenses pour la R-D exécutée par les filiales américaines pour elles-mêmes ou pour d'autres.

- Les *Exportations totales* sont définies comme les exportations américaines expédiées aux entreprises affiliées.

- Les *Importations totales* sont définies comme les importations américaines expédiées par les entreprises affiliées.

- Les *Exportations intra-firme* sont définies comme les exportations américaines à destination des filiales étrangères par les sociétés mères américaines.

- Les *Importations intra-firme* sont définies comme les importations américaines en provenance des filiales étrangères vers les sociétés mères américaines.

- L'*Excédent brut d'exploitation* est appelé aussi revenu net et résulte de la différence entre le revenu total et l'ensemble des coûts et dépenses de l'entreprise affiliée.

List of industries in ISIC Revision 3

Liste des industries en CITI révision 3

	Industries in ISIC Revision 3	Industries en CITI révision 3
10/14	Mining and quarrying	Activités extractives
15/37	Total manufacturing	Total manufacturier
15/16	Food, beverages and tobacco	Alimentation, boissons, tabac
17/19	Textiles, wearing apparel, leather, footwear	Textile, habillement, cuir, chaussures
20/22	Wood and paper products, publishing, printing	Produits du bois et du papier, imprimerie, édition
20	Wood and wood products, except furniture	Bois et produits du bois, sauf meubles
21/22	Paper and products, printing and publishing	Papier et produits du papier, imprimerie, édition
23/25	All chemical products	Produits chimiques, total
23	Refined petroleum and coal products	Raffineries de pétrole et dérivés du charbon
24/25	Chemicals, rubber and plastics products	Produits chimiques, caoutchouc et plastiques
24	Chemical products	Produits chimiques
2423	Pharmaceuticals	Produits pharmaceutiques
25	Rubber and plastics products	Caoutchouc et plastiques
26	Non-metallic mineral products	Produits minéraux non métalliques
27/28	Basic and fabricated metal products	Métallurgie et ouvrages en métaux
27	Basic metals	Métallurgie de base
28	Fabricated metal products	Ouvrages en métaux
29/32	Total machinery and equipment	Machines et matériels, total
29/30	Non-electrical machinery and equipment	Machines et matériels non électriques
29	Machinery and equipment n.e.c.	Machines et matériels non électriques n.c.a.
30	Office, accounting and computing machinery	Machines de bureau et ordinateurs
31/32	Electrical machinery and electronic equipment	Machines électriques et électroniques
31	Electrical machinery and apparatus n.e.c.	Machines électriques n.c.a.
32	Radio, TV and communication equipment	Appareil de radio, télévision et télécommunication
33	Medical, precision, opt. instruments, watches	Instruments médicaux, de précision, optique, horlogerie
34/35	Transport equipment	Matériel de transport
34	Motor vehicles	Véhicules automobiles
35	Other transport equipment	Autres matériels de transport
351	Shipbuilding and repairing	Construction navale
353	Aircraft and spacecraft	Construction aéronautique et spatiale
36/37	Furniture, recycling and manufacturing n.e.c.	Meubles, récupération et industries manufacturières n.c.a.
40/45	Electricity, gas and water supply, construction	Electricité, gaz et eau, construction
50/55	Trade, repair, hotels and restaurants	Commerce, réparation, hôtels, restaurants
65/74	Finance, insurance, real estate, business act.	Finance, assurances, immobilier, services aux entreprises
Other activities	Other activities	Autres activités
01/99	TOTAL	TOTAL

List of industries grouped by level of technology
(ISIC Revision 3)

Liste des industries par groupe de niveau technologique
(CITI révision 3)

Industries in ISIC revision 3	Industries en CITI révision 3
High - Medium high technology group	*Groupe des technologies Haute - Moyenne haute*

353	Aircraft and spacecraft	Construction aéronautique et spatiale
352	Railway	Construction de matériel ferroviaire
30	Office, accounting and computing machinery	Machines de bureau et ordinateurs
2423	Pharmaceuticals	Produits pharmaceutiques
24	Chemical products	Produits chimiques
29	Machinery and equipment n.e.c.	Machines et matériels non électriques n.c.a.
33	Medical, precision, opt. instruments, watches	Instruments médicaux, de précision, optique, horlogerie
31/32	Electrical machinery and electronic equipment	Machines électriques et électroniques
34	Motor vehicles	Véhicules automobiles

	Low - Medium low technology group	*Groupe des technologies Basse - Moyenne basse*

23	Refined petroleum and coal products, nuclear fuel	Raffineries de pétrole et dérivés du charbon, comb. nucléaire
25	Rubber and plastics products	Caoutchouc et plastiques
26	Non-metallic mineral products	Produits minéraux non métalliques
351	Shipbuilding and repairing	Construction navale
27/28	Basic and fabricated metal products	Métallurgie et ouvrages en métaux
36/37	Furniture, recycling and manufacturing n.e.c.	Meubles, récupération et industries manufacturières n.c.a.
20/22	Wood and paper products, publishing, printing	Produits du bois et du papier, imprimerie, édition
15/16	Food, beverages and tobacco	Alimentation, boissons, tabac
17/19	Textiles, wearing apparel, leather, footwear	Textiles, habillement, cuir, chaussures

OECD PUBLICATIONS, 2, rue André-Pascal, 75775 PARIS CEDEX 16
PRINTED IN FRANCE
(92 2002 02 3 P) ISBN 92-64-09673-6 – No. 52222 2002